Wisdom, Intelligence, and Creativity Synthesized

Intelligence, a Harvard psychologist famously remarked, is whatever intelligence tests measure. The observation may have been made in jest, but its effects have been all too serious. A multibillion dollar "intelligence testing" industry largely determines which children attend the best schools and universities. And local communities, under government pressure to produce results, institute curricula that teach to the test but leave little room for "luxuries" such as music and the arts. But what if the essential nature of intelligence is grossly distorted by the testing industry? For thirty years, Robert J. Sternberg has been among the most vocal critics of narrow conceptions of intelligence. In his most recent book, *Wisdom, Intelligence, and Creativity Synthesized*, Professor Sternberg critically reviews and summarizes the best research available on human intelligence. He argues that any serious understanding of intelligence must go beyond the standard paper and pencil tests currently in use. In addition to analytical and quantitative abilities, a theory of intelligence must take into account people's creative abilities – their ability to go beyond given information and imagine new and exciting ways of reformulating old problems. It must also take into account wisdom – people's ability to weigh options carefully and to act prudently. Understanding one's own intellectual shortcomings and learning how to overcome, Professor Sternberg argues, is just as important as developing one's strengths. As he weaves his way through decades of important research – including recent international studies – on these questions, Professor Sternberg develops a vision of human intelligence that is far more nuanced and accurate than anything offered previously. *Wisdom, Intelligence, and Creativity Synthesized* will be essential reading for psychologists, cognitive scientists, educators, and organizational researchers.

Robert J. Sternberg is IBM Professor of Psychology and Education and Director of the Center for the Psychology of Abilities, Competencies, and Expertise at Yale University. He is also 2003 President of the American Psychological Association and Editor of the *APA Review of Books: Contemporary Psychology*. Professor Sternberg is the author of roughly 950 books, book chapters, and articles in the field of psychology.

Wisdom, Intelligence, and Creativity Synthesized

ROBERT J. STERNBERG
Yale University

CAMBRIDGE
UNIVERSITY PRESS

PUBLISHED BY THE PRESS SYNDICATE OF THE UNIVERSITY OF CAMBRIDGE
The Pitt Building, Trumpington Street, Cambridge, United Kingdom

CAMBRIDGE UNIVERSITY PRESS
The Edinburgh Building, Cambridge CB2 2RU, UK
40 West 20th Street, New York, NY 10011-4211, USA
477 Williamstown Road, Port Melbourne, VIC 3207, Australia
Ruiz de Alarcón 13, 28014 Madrid, Spain
Dock House, The Waterfront, Cape Town 8001, South Africa

http://www.cambridge.org

First published 2003

Printed in the United States of America

Typeface Palatino 10/12 pt.   *System* LATEX 2$_\varepsilon$ [TB]

A catalog record for this book is available from the British Library.

Library of Congress Cataloging in Publication data

Sternberg, Robert J.
Wisdom, intelligence, and creativity synthesized / Robert J. Sternberg.
    p.   cm.
Includes bibliographical references and index.
ISBN 0-521-80238-5
1. Intellect.   2. Creative ability.   3. Creative thinking.   4. Wisdom.   I. Title.
BF431.S7385   2003
153.9–dc21   2003043751

ISBN 0 521 80238 5 hardback

This book is dedicated to Elena L. Grigorenko

Contents

Preface

Professor Wormbog had every beastie in his collection except one (Mayer, 1976). He had everything from A to Y: an askingforit, a blowfat-glowfish, a croonie, a diddly-dee, an errg, a fydolagump, and everything else up to the yalapappus. But he lacked the crucial Z, the zipperump-a-zoo. He therefore set out to find the missing zipperump-a-zoo and looked everywhere, including the most exotic places in the world. But the zipperump-a-zoo eluded him. Finally he gave up, came back home, and went to sleep, exhausted. As soon as he fell asleep, a whole tribe of zipperump-a-zoos emerged to party, right in his house. They had been there all the time, hiding. In asking in what exotic place they might be, he had neglected to ask whether they might be in the most obvious place of all, right in his own home. Because he had asked the wrong question, he emerged with the wrong answer.

This book represents, in a sense, a recounting of the tale of a search for my own zipperump-a-zoo (Sternberg, 2000b), the nature of the mind – of human intelligence, creativity, and wisdom, and how they interrelate. I have learned a crucial lesson from Professor Wormbog: You will never come up with the right answer if you ask the wrong question. I still have not figured out quite the right question, but that's fortunate because there is still hope for what's left of the second half of my career.

Because this book represents the culmination of all the work on the human mind I have done in the roughly thirty years since I started graduate school, I should like to say something about how the book came to be, to indulge myself in recounting the tale. (In the main text, I stick to theories, data, and interpretations.) I tell the tale from my own point of view, but I wish to emphasize that I have done nothing by myself. Without support from my family, my mentors, research advisors, granting agencies, and most important, my research group, now the PACE Center at Yale, there would be no story to tell. The critical lesson of the tale is that what seems to be a complete answer at one stage of a career seems, at a later stage, to be woefully incomplete.

THE PREHISTORY

The prehistory of my search began when I was a primary school student and turned in a dismal performance on the required group IQ tests. I was so test-anxious I could hardly get myself to answer the test questions. When I heard other students turn the test pages, it was all over for me. For three years, my teachers thought me stupid, and I obliged, pleasing them by confirming their self-fulfilling prophecies for me. They were happy, I was happy; everyone was pretty damn happy.

In grade 4, at age nine, I had a teacher who believed in me, and to please her, I became an "A" student. I also learned that, when authority figures set high expectations for a student, it is amazing how quickly that student can defy earlier low expectations.

By age thirteen, I was determined to understand why I was now achieving at high levels despite my low IQ, so I did a science project on mental testing. I found the Stanford-Binet Intelligence test in the adult section of my town library and thought it would be good practice to give it to some classmates. I chose poorly. The first person I selected was a girl in whom I was romantically interested, and I soon discovered that giving a potential girl friend an IQ test is a bad way to break the ice. The second person I chose tattled on me, and I ended up in serious trouble with the school authorities when they learned I was giving IQ tests to my classmates. After they threatened to burn the book if I ever brought it to school again, I went underground, only to re-emerge some years later.

I also thought it would be a good idea to create a group test comprising not just eight or nine subtests, but two dozen. My idea was to improve IQ testing by giving a wider range of subtests. So I created the Sternberg Test of Mental Abilities (STOMA), no copies of which I have been able to locate in my adulthood. I had asked the wrong question – whether adding more of essentially the same kinds of subtests to create a super-duper-extra-long test would substantially improve reliability or validity. The answer was no. I quickly stumbled into the general (g) factor, which represents the individual-differences variation common to virtually all conventional psychometric tests of intellectual abilities. I was a bit too late. Charles Spearman (1904) had already speculated on the g factor at the turn of the twentieth century, as have many others since. Spearman believed the g factor represents "mental energy." Other psychologists have had other ideas about it, but the question of what it represents remains unresolved even today.

As a youth, I discovered that mental testing has many peculiarities. Over the summer after grade 10, when I was sixteen, I did a project on the effect of distractions on mental ability test scores. I discovered that of four distractions – a car headlamp shining in the eyes, a slowly ticking metronome, a rapidly ticking metronome, and the Beatles singing "She has the Devil in Her Heart" – only one had an effect relative to a control condition in which there were no distractions. Students performed better on both verbal and math ability tests when listening to the Beatles!

The next year, at seventeen, I created a Physics Aptitude Test as a physics project to save my flagging physics grade, and the test was successful, predicting physics grades with a correlation in the mid .60s. The test actually was used by my high school for several years after I created it to help screen for honors physics.

At age twenty, as a junior in college, I thought I really had the solution: The answer to the problem of understanding intelligence was not more tests, but more refined scoring of the items already in tests. So I devised partial systems of scoring psychometric test items, and discovered, as had many of my colleagues at the Educational Testing Service (where I worked for the summer), that partial scoring adds very little reliable or valid variation in test scores. Wrong question again: The answer was not to be found in cosmetic manipulations such as adding more of essentially the same kinds of items or in seeking to extract partial information from such items. And so ended my largely futile prehistory as an apprentice.

THE HISTORY

Stage 1: Componential Analyses of Analytical Abilities

As a first-year graduate student I despaired of having any good ideas for studying intelligence. One day, I saw Betty, my wife at the time, using People Pieces in her work – a math-manipulative material for young children consisting of small square tiles that vary with respect to four binary features – color, height, weight, and sex. I visualized creating analogies from them, and so began my efforts at what I came to call componential analyses of human abilities.

The basic idea of componential analysis is that underlying intelligence is a series of information-processing components. The questions intelligence researchers should be asking are not merely what psychometric factors underlie these tests, but also (a) what information-processing components underlie the tests, (b) on what forms of mental representation these components act, (c) how the components combine into coherent strategies for solving problems, (d) how long each component consumes in real time, and (e) how liable each component is to errors in implementation. I started by describing componential analysis in detail and showing its implementation with various kinds of analogies (such as People Pieces, verbal, and figural ones – Sternberg, 1977).

Componential analyses served many useful purposes. They told psychologists how people were processing IQ-test-like problems in real time. The models accounted for large proportions of both stimulus and person variation in reaction-time data. Interesting specific findings also emerged. For example, I discovered that early real-time information processing in the solution of a given analogy is exhaustive and then later becomes self-terminating. I also found that being smart is not just a matter of being fast: Better reasoners tend to spend relatively more time encoding the terms of analogy problems but relatively less time operating on those encodings (Sternberg & Rifkin, 1979). They want to make sure they have understood what they are doing before they go ahead and do it.

The methodology also enabled me to discover why people may be doing poorly on a given type of test item. For example, is a low verbal-analogies score due to problems understanding the vocabulary required to solve the analogies or is it due to faulty reasoning operating on known vocabulary (Sternberg, 1977)?

Stage 1 of my research was actually divided into two substages. In Substage 1a, I merely posited the existence of information-processing components (Sternberg, 1977). In Substage 1b, I distinguished metacomponents – higher order executive processes that decide what to do, how to do it, and how well it was done; performance components – lower order processes that execute the instructions of the metacomponents; and knowledge-acquisition components, which figure out how to do things in the first place (Sternberg, 1980b). Using this framework, I was able to discover that better reasoners tend, for example, to spend relatively more time on the metacomponent of global planning, but less time on the metacomponent of local planning, than do poorer reasoners (Sternberg, 1981). In other words, the better reasoners realize that they need to plan in advance to conserve time and effort when they later begin getting into the details of the problem. We were also able to isolate the knowledge-acquisition components used in the acquisition of vocabulary from context (Sternberg & Powell, 1983), such as selective encoding of relevant cues in distinction from irrelevant cues for figuring out a word's meaning.

But the wrong questions had once again led to the wrong answers, or, to be more precise, *incomplete* answers. Puzzles were emerging. Why was the regression constant (i.e., the a in the equation $a + bx$) instead of the regression coefficient (i.e., the b in the equation) for the mathematical models we were constructing the best predictor of scores on psychometric tests? Were we just rediscovering g again, but this time as an information-processing construct? Why, when we assessed people's implicit (folk) theories of intelligence, were analytical abilities only a small aspect of what people broadly consider intelligence to be (Okagaki & Sternberg, 1993; Sternberg, 1985b; Sternberg, Conway, Ketron, & Bernstein, 1981; see also Yang & Sternberg,

1997b)? The main factor leading to my puzzlement, however, was really not a research finding, but an observation.

Stage 2: The Triarchic Theory of Human Intelligence

I have always been one to get most of my ideas not from reading academic materials or listening to academic lectures, but from my daily experience. And my experience was not fitting my theory. I was teaching three graduate students who provided a curious contrast. (The names given below are fictitious, although they represent real people.)

One, who I call Alice, was brilliant academically and at the kinds of memory and analytical skills conventional psychometric tests of intelligence emphasize. She started off our graduate program in psychology as one of the top students in the program but ended up as one of the bottom students. The reason was transparent: Alice was brilliant analytically but showed only the most minimal creative skills. I was not convinced that Alice was born creatively retarded. It seemed more likely that Alice had been so over-reinforced for her school smarts during her life that she had never had any incentive to develop or even to find whatever creative skills may have lain latent within her.

Another student, Barbara, was marvelously creative, if we were to believe her portfolio of research work and the recommendations of her undergraduate professors, but her scores on the largely analytical Graduate Record Examination (GRE) were weak. Other professors were reluctant to admit her because of these GRE scores, and Barbara was rejected from our program, with mine the only vote in her favor. I hired her as a research associate, which gave her a chance to show her creative brilliance. Barbara was admitted as the top pick to our graduate program a couple of years later. Some years later, we did a study on twelve years of graduate students in psychology at Yale. The study showed that, although the GRE was a good predictor of first-year grades, it was a satisfactory predictor of little else, such as students' analytical, creative, practical, research, or teaching abilities, or the quality of their dissertations (Sternberg & Williams, 1997). Concerning these other criteria, for men the analytical section (since discontinued) had some predictive power; for women none of the sections had significant predictive power.

The third student, Celia, was admitted not because she was spectacular but because she appeared to be good (but not great) in both analytical and creative skills, and every program needs students who are good in several things, if not great in any of them. But Celia surprised us when she was besieged with job offers. She was the kind of person who could go into a job interview, figure out what her potential employers wanted to hear, and give it to them. In contrast, Paul, a student who was analytically and creatively brilliant, received many job interviews but only one very weak job offer. In some respects the opposite of Celia, he managed to insult his interviewers at every turn. He was as low as Celia was high in practical intelligence.

I now realize that once again I had been asking the wrong question. By asking what information-processing components underlie performance on conventional mental tests, I had been able to identify how people solve such conventional problems. But I had assumed that these tests measured the universe of skills relevant to intelligence, and my assumption was false. By asking the wrong question, I ended up with an incomplete answer.

These observations led to the development of the triarchic theory of human intelligence (Sternberg, 1984, 1985a, 1988c). This theory has three subtheories. A componential subtheory specifies the information-processing components of human intelligence, such as recognizing, defining, and representing problems. An experiential subtheory specifies the regions of experience at which these components are most relevant to the demonstration and assessment of intelligence. These regions are relative novelty and automatization. The former region refers to the solving of problems that are rather different in kind from what one is used to, but not wholly different. A problem that is too novel (e.g., calculus problems for five-year-olds) does not provide a good measure of intelligence. The second region refers to rendering unconscious and automatic a process that starts off as conscious and controlled, such as reading (see Sternberg, 1985a). A contextual subtheory specifies the real-world contextual functions of intelligence: adaptation to existing environments; shaping of existing environments into new and, it is hoped, better environments; and selection of different environments (usually when adaptation and shaping fail).

Analytical abilities are engaged when information-processing components are applied to relatively familiar problems that are largely academic because they are abstracted from the substance of everyday life. Creative abilities are engaged when the components are applied to relatively novel problems. Finally, practical abilities are engaged when the components are applied to adaptation to, shaping of, and selection of everyday environments.

My group expanded its research into the creative and practical domains, with some interesting results, we thought.

In Stage 2a, we focused on creative abilities, which seemed complementary to analytical ones. Some of this research used convergent measures. For example, we might introduce participants to relatively novel concepts, such as Goodman's (1955) concepts of *grue* – say, of the color green until the year 3000 and blue thereafter – and *bleen* – say, of the color blue until the year 3000 and green thereafter. We pointed out that one could not say whether an emerald was green or grue because one would not know until the year 3000 (actually, 2000 in the research, which was done in the 1980s: Sternberg, 1982; Tetewsky & Sternberg, 1986). Or we might introduce participants to the planet Kyron, where there are four kinds of people – *plins,* who are born young and die young; *kwefs,* who are born old and die old; *balts,* who are born young and die old; and *prosses,* who are born old and die young. Participants had to solve reasoning problems that involved these novel concepts. We found that the information-processing component that distinguished the more from the less creative reasoners was the component that measured the ability to transit back and forth between conventional (*green–blue*) and unconventional (*grue–bleen*) thinking. The more creative individuals found it easier to switch back and forth.

In Stage 2b, which largely overlapped with Stage 2a, we focused on practical abilities. The basic idea motivating this research is that practical intelligence derives largely from the acquisition and utilization of *tacit knowledge* – the procedural knowledge not explicitly taught and often not even verbalized that one needs to know to succeed in an environment. For an academic psychologist, for example, tacit knowledge would include knowing how to win acceptance of articles submitted to journals and knowing how to get resources from the Chair of one's department. We represent this knowledge in the form of production systems, which are ordered series of conditional ("if–then") statements. Thus, one keeps asking which piece of tacit knowledge to apply (the "if" antecedent) and executes the tacit knowledge (the "then" consequent) when the right piece of tacit knowledge is found.

We have developed (Sternberg, Wagner, Williams, & Horvath, 1995; Wagner & Sternberg, 1985) and continue to develop (Sternberg et al., 2000) instruments to assess the acquisition and utilization of tacit knowledge. We have now tested thousands of people in more than two dozen occupations, including that of academic psychologist.

The tests are all based on the same notion. Participants are presented with scenarios from the everyday life of people going about their business (as students, as employees, or whatever). The participants then either state a solution to the problem posed in the scenario (in one format), or evaluate the quality of alternative solutions proposed to them (in another format).

The results have been fairly consistent across studies: Tacit knowledge typically does not correlate with IQ-based measures but predicts school and job performance as well as or better than IQ-based measures. The correlations are not always zero. At the lower (but not higher) ranks of military officers, we obtained weak but significant positive correlations. Among children in rural Kenya, we obtained significant negative correlations: The anthropological members of our team – Wenzel Geissler and Ruth Prince – recognized a fundamental fact about family values. The children saw that their path to success was not through obtaining high grades in formal schooling but rather through acquiring the tacit knowledge that led to adaptation to the demands of village life.

In other words, our measures supplement, although obviously do not replace, the IQ-based measures. They are not replacements because we are focusing here on practical abilities, whereas IQ-based measures focus on analytical abilities.

But I eventually came to the conclusion that I was once again asking the wrong question. I was emphasizing analytical, creative, and practical abilities and thinking loosely in terms of some additive combination rule. Observation of effective people in a variety of occupations convinced me that there was no single combination rule, however. For example, my two mentors and greatest role models – Endel Tulving and Gordon Bower – are both wonderfully successful psychologists, but they have gotten to where they are in very different ways. There seems to be an infinite number of combination rules.

Stage 3: The Theory of Successful Intelligence

The theory of successful intelligence (Sternberg, 1997b, 1999d) is in many respects an expansion of the triarchic theory. It states that people are successfully intelligent to the extent that they have the abilities needed to succeed in life, according to their own definition of success within their sociocultural context. They succeed by adapting to, shaping, and selecting environments, which they do by recognizing and then capitalizing on their strengths, and by recognizing and then compensating for or correcting their weaknesses. Thus, there is no one path to success in life. Each person must chart his or her own way, and the job of the teacher is to help students in this endeavor. Teaching in just one way can never work.

Many societies, especially developed ones, tend to focus a spotlight on just one group of students – those with high levels of memory and analytical abilities. But in doing so, they create self-fulfilling prophecies, developing assessments of ability, instruction, and assessments of achievement that identify as intelligent this one group of students. They can create whatever kinds of self-fulfilling prophecies they wish. If they bestow benefits primarily or exclusively on children of certain religions, castes, skin colors, or accents of speech, they quickly find that only those children succeed. They then convince themselves, as did Herrnstein and Murray (1994), that the success of these individuals represents an "invisible hand of nature" rather than a system created by the society.

Our research has shown that analytical, creative, and practical abilities are largely independent. When students' abilities and achievements are assessed not just for memory and analytical abilities, but also for creative and practical abilities, students formerly considered as not very bright can succeed in school at higher levels (Sternberg, Grigorenko, Ferrari, &

Clinkenbeard, 1999). Moreover, students taught for successful intelligence do better across grade levels and subject matter areas, regardless of how their performance is assessed, and even if it is assessed merely for memory learning (Sternberg, Torff, & Grigorenko, 1998a). The students learn better because they can use their abilities more effectively and because the greater interest of the material better motivates them to learn.

Stage 4: The Investment Theory of Creativity and the Propulsion Theory of Creative Contributions

After studying intelligence for a number of years, it became clear to me that there is more to creativity than creative intelligence. There are people who appear to have creative intelligence but are unable to use it effectively in their lives because they have various kinds of blocks. More and more, I came to believe that creativity is a decision.

Eventually, Todd Lubart and I (Sternberg & Lubart, 1991, 1995) proposed an investment theory of creativity, according to which more creative thinkers are those who buy low and sell high in the world of ideas (Sternberg & Lubart, 1995). In other words, they are people who generate ideas that are relatively unpopular (buy low); convince others of the worth of these ideas (sell high); and then move on to the next unpopular idea. We had people write stories with diverse titles such as *The Octopus's Sneakers*; or do art work for topics such as *Earth from an Insect's Point of View*; or produce advertisements for boring products such as a new brand of bow tie; or solve quasi-scientific problems such as how we could tell whether there are extraterrestrial aliens among us seeking to escape detection. Products were evaluated for their novelty and quality.

Two major findings emerged. First, creativity tends to be fairly but not completely domain-specific. Second, it tends to be rather but not totally distinct from psychometrically measured intelligence.

Today, I believe the investment theory was a bit of an oversimplification. Whereas the investment theory holds that creative ideas tend to be unappreciated and devalued, I now believe, according to a new propulsion theory of creative contributions (Sternberg, 1999c; Sternberg, Kaufman, & Pretz, 2002), that whether creative ideas are valued or not depends on which of seven kinds of creative ideas they are. Ideas that are consistent with ongoing paradigms tend to be welcome. Forward incrementations, for example, which move existing paradigms forward, tend to be valued. Redirections, which move existing paradigms in new directions, or re-initiations, which reject current paradigms and start at a different point of departure, tend not to be recognized as creative because they are often too novel for people to appreciate their value. Of course, novelty is no guarantee of quality.

Stage 5: The Balance Theory of Wisdom

My latest work has taken a somewhat different direction. I have come to realize that some of the world's cruelest despots and greediest business tycoons are successfully intelligent. They have played within the socio-cultural rules, which they have largely set. Thus, they have been enormously successful, often at the expense of countless countrymen who are left to their own devices, and often to death. It is for this reason that I have now turned my attention to wisdom (Sternberg, 1998b, 2001a). In my balance theory, I view wisdom as the value-laden application of tacit knowledge not only for one's own benefit (as can be the case with successful intelligence) but also for the benefit of others, in order to attain a common good. The wise person realizes that what matters is not just knowledge, or the intellectual skills one applies to this knowledge, but how the knowledge is used.

IQs have been rising over the past several generations (Flynn, 1987; Neisser, 1998). The perpetuation of ever worse massacres and genocides suggests that wisdom has not been rising concomitantly. If there is anything the world needs, it is wisdom. Without it, I exaggerate not at all in saying that very soon, there may be no world, or at least none with humans populating it. Perhaps the only ones left will be zipperump-a-zoos.

Preparation of this book was supported by Contract DAS W01-00-K-0014 from the U.S. Army Research Institute; by Grant REC-9979843 from the National Science Foundation; by a government grant under the Javits Act Program (Grant No. R206R000001) as administered by the Institute of Educational Sciences, formerly the Office of Educational Research and Improvement, U.S. Department of Education; by a grant from the W. T. Grant Foundation; and by a grant from the College Board. Grantees undertaking such projects are encouraged to express freely their professional judgment. This work, therefore, does not necessarily represent the positions or the policies of any of the funding agencies.

Robert J. Sternberg
March 2003

PART I

INTELLIGENCE

1

Background Work on Intelligence

In the year 2000, Al Gore ran against George W. Bush for the presidency of the United States. Both candidates had highly successful political careers, Gore as a U.S. senator from the state of Tennessee and as vice-president of the United States, Bush as governor of the state of Texas, certainly one of the most complex states in the United States. Their success in politics was not preceded by success in school (Simon, 2000). Both men were mediocre students in college. In four years at Yale University, Bush never received an A, and Gore's grades at Harvard were even lower than Bush's at Yale. During his sophomore year, Gore received one B, two Cs, and a D (on a scale where A is high and D is the lowest passing grade). Their college admission test scores were also undistinguished. Gore received a 625 on the verbal SAT (on a scale where 200 is low, 500 average, and 800 high, and where the standard deviation is 100 points). Bush received a score of 566. Bill Bradley, a former U.S. senator and a Democratic presidential primary candidate, received an even less impressive score of 485.

Are these famous politicians unintelligent, intelligent in some way not measured by conventional tests, or what? What does it mean to be intelligent, anyway, and how does our understanding of the nature of intelligence help us understand concrete cases such as Bradley, Bush, and Gore?

CONCEPTIONS OF THE NATURE OF INTELLIGENCE

Anyone who has seriously studied the history of the United States or of any other country knows that there is not one history of a country but many histories. The history of the United States as told by some American Indians, for example, would look quite different from the history as told by some of the later settlers, and even within these groups, the stories would differ. Similarly, there is no one history of the field of intelligence, but rather, many histories, depending on who is doing the telling. For example, the largely laudatory histories recounted by Carroll (1982, 1993), Herrnstein and Murray (1994), and Jensen (1998, 2002) read very differently from the largely skeptical histories recounted by Gardner (1983, 1999), Gould (1981) or Sacks (1999). And there are differences within these groups of authors.

These differences need mentioning because, although all fields of psychology are perceived through ideological lenses, few fields seem to have lenses with so many colors and, some might argue, with so many different distorting imperfections as do the lenses through which are seen the field of intelligence. The different views come not only from ideological biases affecting what is said, but also from affecting what is included. For example, there is virtually no overlap in the historical data used by Carroll (1993) and those used by Gardner (1983) to support their respective theories of intelligence.

Although no account can be truly value-free, I try in this chapter to clarify values in three ways. First, I attempt to represent the views of the investigators and their times in presenting the history of the field. Second, I critique this past work, but make my own personal opinions clear by labeling evaluative sections "Evaluation." Third, I try to represent multiple points of view in a dialectical fashion (Hegel, 1807/1931; see Sternberg, 1999a), pointing out both the positive and negative sides of various contributions. This representation recognizes that all points of view taken in the past can be viewed, with "20/20 hindsight," as skewed, in much the same way that present points of view will be viewed as skewed in the future. A dialectical form of examination will serve as the basis for the entire chapter. The basic idea is that important ideas, good or bad, eventually serve as the springboard for other new ideas that grow out of unions of past ideas that may once have seemed incompatible.

The emphasis in this chapter is on the background history of the field of intelligence, particularly with reference to theories of intelligence. Readers interested primarily in measurement issues might consult relevant chapters in Sternberg (1982, 1994b, 2000b).

Perhaps the most fundamental dialectic in the field of intelligence arises from the question of how we should conceive of intelligence. Several different positions have been staked out (Sternberg, 1990a). Many of the differences in ideology that arise in accounts of the history of the field of intelligence arise from differences in the model of intelligence to which an investigator adheres. To understand the history of the field of intelligence, one must understand the alternative epistemological models that can give rise to the concept of intelligence. But before addressing these models, consider simply the question of how psychologists in the field of intelligence have defined the construct on which they base their models.

Expert Opinions on the Nature of Intelligence

Historically, one of the most important approaches to figuring out what intelligence is has relied on the opinions of experts. Such opinions are sometimes referred to as *implicit theories*, to distinguish them from the more formal *explicit theories* that serve as the bases for scientific hypotheses and subsequent data collections.

Implicit theories (which can be those of laypersons as well as experts) are important to the history of a field for at least three reasons (Sternberg, Conway, Ketron, & Bernstein, 1981). First, experts' implicit theories are typically what give rise to their explicit theories. Second, much of the history of intelligence research and practice is much more closely based on implicit theories than it is on formal theories. Most of the intelligence tests that have been used, for example, are based more on the opinions of their creators as to what intelligence is than on formal theories. Third, people's everyday judgments of each other's intelligence always have been and continue to be much more strongly guided by their implicit theories of intelligence than by any explicit theories.

Intelligence Operationally Defined. E. G. Boring (1923), in an article in the *New Republic*, proposed that intelligence is what the tests of intelligence test. Boring did not believe that this operational definition was the end of the line for understanding intelligence. On the contrary, he saw it as a "narrow definition, but a point of departure for a rigorous discussion . . . until further scientific discussion allows us to extend [it]" (p. 35). Nevertheless, many psychologists and especially testers and interpreters of tests of intelligence have adopted this definition or something similar to it.

From a scientific point of view, the definition is problematic. First, the definition is circular: It defines intelligence in terms of what intelligence tests test, but what the tests test can only be determined by one's definition of intelligence. Second, the definition legitimates rather than calling into scientific question whatever operations are in use at a given time to measure intelligence. To the extent that the goal of science is to disconfirm existing scientific views (Popper, 1959), such a definition will not be useful. Third, the definition assumes that what intelligence tests test is uniform. But this is not the case. Although tests of intelligence tend to correlate positively with each other (the so-called *positive manifold* first noted by Spearman, 1904), such correlations are far from perfect, even controlling for unreliability. Thus, what intelligence tests test is not just one uniform thing. Moreover, even the most ardent proponents of a general factor of intelligence (a single element common to all of these tests) acknowledge there is more to intelligence than just the general factor.

The 1921 Symposium. Probably the best-known study of experts' definitions of intelligence was one done by the editors of the *Journal of Educational*

Psychology ("Intelligence and its measurement," 1921). Contributors to the symposium were asked to address two issues: (a) what they conceived intelligence to be and how it best could be measured by group tests, and (b) what the most crucial next steps would be in research. Fourteen experts gave their views on the nature of intelligence, with such definitions as the following:

1. the power of good responses from the point of view of truth or facts (E. L. Thorndike)
2. the ability to carry on abstract thinking (L. M. Terman)
3. sensory capacity, capacity for perceptual recognition, quickness, range or flexibility of association, facility and imagination, span of attention, quickness or alertness in response (F. N. Freeman)
4. having learned or ability to learn to adjust oneself to the environment (S. S. Colvin)
5. ability to adapt oneself adequately to relatively new situations in life (R. Pintner)
6. the capacity for knowledge and knowledge possessed (B. A. C. Henmon)
7. a biological mechanism by which the effects of a complexity of stimuli are brought together and given a somewhat unified effect in behavior (J. Peterson)
8. the capacity to inhibit an instinctive adjustment, the capacity to redefine the inhibited instinctive adjustment in the light of imaginally experienced trial and error, and the capacity to realize the modified instinctive adjustment in overt behavior to the advantage of the individual as a social animal (L. L. Thurstone)
9. the capacity to acquire capacity (H. Woodrow)
10. the capacity to learn or to profit by experience (W. F. Dearborn)
11. sensation, perception, association, memory, imagination, discrimination, judgment, and reasoning (N. E. Haggerty)

Others of the contributors to the symposium did not provide clear definitions of intelligence but rather concentrated on how to test it. B. Ruml refused to present a definition of intelligence, arguing that not enough was known about the concept. S. L. Pressey described himself as uninterested in the question, although he became well known for his tests of intelligence.

There have been many definitions of intelligence since those presented in the *Journal* symposium, and an essay has been written on the nature of definitions of intelligence (Miles, 1957). One well-known set of definitions was published in 1986 as an explicit follow-up to the 1921 symposium (Sternberg & Detterman, 1986).

Sternberg and Berg (1986) attempted a comparison of the views of experts (P. Baltes, J. Baron, J. Berry, A. Brown & J. Campione, E. Butterfield, J. Carroll, J. P. Das, D. Detterman, W. Estes, H. Eysenck, H. Gardner,

R. Glaser, J. Goodnow, J. Horn, L. Humphreys, E. Hunt, A. Jensen, J. Pellegrino, R. Schank, R. Snow, R. Sternberg, E. Zigler) with those of the experts in 1921. They reached three general conclusions.

First, there was at least some general agreement across the two symposia regarding the nature of intelligence. When attributes were listed for frequency of mention in the two symposia, the correlation was .50, indicating moderate overlap. Attributes such as adaptation to the environment, basic mental processes, higher order thinking (e.g., reasoning, problem solving, and decision making) were prominent in both symposia.

Second, central themes occurred in both symposia. One theme was the one versus the many: Is intelligence one thing or is it multiple things? How broadly should intelligence be defined? What should be the respective roles of biological versus behavioral attributes in seeking an understanding of intelligence?

Third, despite the similarities in views over the sixty-five years, some salient differences could also be found. Metacognition – conceived of as both knowledge about and control of cognition – played a prominent role in the 1986 symposium but virtually no role at all in 1921. The later symposium also placed a greater emphasis on the role of knowledge and the interaction of mental processes with this knowledge.

Lay Conceptions of Intelligence

In some cases, Western notions about intelligence are not shared by other cultures. For example, the Western emphasis on speed of mental processing (Sternberg, Conway, Ketron, & Bernstein, 1981) is not shared by many cultures. Other cultures may even be suspicious of the quality of work that is done very quickly. They emphasize depth rather than speed of processing. They are not alone: Some prominent Western theorists have pointed out the importance of depth of processing for full command of material (e.g., Craik & Lockhart, 1972).

Yang and Sternberg (1997a) have reviewed Chinese philosophical conceptions of intelligence. The Confucian perspective emphasizes the characteristic of benevolence and of doing what is right. As in the Western notion, the intelligent person spends a great deal of effort in learning, enjoys learning, and persists in lifelong learning with a great deal of enthusiasm. The Taoist tradition, in contrast, emphasizes the importance of humility, freedom from conventional standards of judgment, and full knowledge of oneself as well as of external conditions.

The differences between Eastern and Western conceptions of intelligence have extended beyond ancient times and persist even in the present day. Yang and Sternberg (1997b) studied contemporary Taiwanese Chinese conceptions of intelligence, and found five factors underlying these conceptions: (a) a general cognitive factor, much like the *g* factor in conventional

Western tests; (b) interpersonal intelligence; (c) intrapersonal intelligence; (d) intellectual self-assertion; and (d) intellectual self-effacement. In a related study but with different results, Chen (1994) found three factors underlying Chinese conceptualizations of intelligence: nonverbal reasoning ability, verbal reasoning ability, and rote memory. The difference may be due to different subpopulations of Chinese, to differences in methodology, or to differences in when the studies were done.

The factors uncovered in both studies differ substantially from those identified in U.S. people's conceptions of intelligence by Sternberg, Conway, Ketron, and Bernstein (1981) – (a) practical problem solving, (b) verbal ability, and (c) social competence – although in both cases, people's implicit theories of intelligence seem to go quite far beyond what conventional psychometric intelligence tests measure. Comparing the Chen (1994) study to the Sternberg and colleagues (1981) study simultaneously naturally must take into account both language and culture.

Chen and Chen (1988) considered only language. They explicitly compared the concepts of intelligence of Chinese graduates from Chinese-language versus English-language schools in Hong Kong. They found that both groups considered nonverbal reasoning skills as the most relevant skill for measuring intelligence. Verbal reasoning and social skills came next, and then numerical skill. Memory was seen as least important. The Chinese-language-schooled group, however, tended to rate verbal skills as less important than did the English-language-schooled group. Moreover, in an earlier study, Chen, Braithwaite, and Huang (1982) found that Chinese students viewed memory for facts as important for intelligence, whereas Australian students viewed these skills as of only trivial importance.

Das (1994), reviewing Eastern notions of intelligence, has suggested that in Buddhist and Hindu philosophies, intelligence involves waking up, noticing, recognizing, understanding, and comprehending, but also includes such things as determination, mental effort, and even feelings and opinions in addition to more intellectual elements.

Differences between cultures in conceptions of intelligence have been recognized for some time. Gill and Keats (1980) noted that Australian university students value academic skills and the ability to adapt to new events as critical to intelligence, whereas Malay students value practical skills, as well as speed (which is more typical of the West than of the East) and creativity. Dasen (1984) found Malay students to emphasize both social and cognitive attributes in their conceptions of intelligence.

The differences between East and West may be due to differences in the kinds of skills valued by the two kinds of cultures (Srivastava & Misra, 1996). Western cultures and their schools emphasize what might be called "technological intelligence" (Mundy-Castle, 1974), and so things like artificial intelligence and so-called smart bombs are viewed, in some sense, as intelligent.

Western schooling also emphasizes other factors (Srivastava & Misra, 1996), such as generalization, or going beyond the information given (Connolly & Bruner, 1974; Goodnow, 1976), speed (Sternberg, 1985a), minimal moves to a solution (Newell & Simon, 1972), and creative thinking (Goodnow, 1976). Moreover, silence is interpreted as a lack of knowledge (Irvine, 1978). In contrast, the Wolof tribe in Africa views people of higher social class and distinction as speaking less (Irvine, 1978). This difference between the Wolof and Western notions suggests the usefulness of looking at African notions of intelligence as a possible contrast to those of the United States.

Studies in Africa in fact provide yet another window on the substantial differences. Ruzgis and Grigorenko (1994) have argued that, in Africa, conceptions of intelligence revolve largely around skills that help to facilitate and maintain harmonious and stable intergroup relations; intragroup relations are probably equally important and at times more so. For example, Serpell (1974, 1982, 1996) found that Chewa adults in Zambia emphasize social responsibilities, cooperativeness, and obedience as important to intelligence; intelligent children are expected to be respectful of adults. Kenyan parents also emphasize responsible participation in family and social life as important aspects of intelligence (Super & Harkness, 1982, 1986, 1993). In Zimbabwe, the word for intelligence, *ngware*, actually means to be prudent and cautious, particularly in social relationships. Among the Baoule, service to the family and community and politeness toward and respect for elders are seen as key to intelligence (Dasen, 1984).

Similar emphasis on social aspects of intelligence has been found as well among two other African groups – the Songhay of Mali and the Samia of Kenya (Putnam & Kilbride, 1980). The Yoruba, another African tribe, emphasize the importance of depth – of listening rather than just talking – to intelligence, and of being able to see all aspects of an issue and to place the issue in its proper overall context (Durojaiye, 1993).

The emphasis on the social aspects of intelligence is not limited to African cultures. Notions of intelligence in many Asian cultures also emphasize the social aspect more than does the conventional Western or IQ-based view (Azuma & Kashiwagi, 1987; Lutz, 1985; Poole, 1985; White, 1985).

It should be noted that neither Africans nor Asians emphasize exclusively social notions of intelligence. Although their conceptions much more emphasize social skills than do the conventional U.S. ideas, at the same time they recognize the importance of cognitive aspects of intelligence. In a study of Kenyan conceptions of intelligence (Grigorenko et al., 2001), it was found that there are four distinct terms constituting conceptions of intelligence among rural Kenyans, *rieko* (knowledge and skills), *luoro* (respect), *winjo* (comprehension of how to handle real-life problems), and *paro* (initiative), with only the first directly referring to knowledge-based skills (including but not limited to the academic).

It is important to recognize that there is no one overall U.S. conception of intelligence. Indeed, Okagaki and Sternberg (1993) found that different ethnic groups in San Jose, California, had rather different conceptions of what it means to be intelligent. Latino parents of schoolchildren tended to emphasize the importance of social-competence skills in their conceptions, whereas Asian parents tended rather heavily to emphasize the importance of cognitive skills. Anglo parents also emphasized cognitive skills. Teachers, representing the dominant culture, more emphasized cognitive than social-competence skills. The rank order of performance among children of various groups (including subgroups within the Latino and Asian groups) could be perfectly predicted by the extent to which their parents shared the teachers' conceptions of intelligence. Teachers tended to reward those children who were socialized into a view of intelligence that happened to correspond to their own. Yet, as we shall argue later, social aspects of intelligence, broadly defined, may be as important as, or even more important than, cognitive aspects of intelligence in later life. Some, however, prefer to study intelligence not in its social aspect, but in its cognitive one.

Definitions of any kind can provide a basis for explicit scientific theory and research, but they do not provide a substitute for them. Thus it was necessary for researchers to move beyond definitions, which they indeed did. Many of them moved to models based on individual differences.

Intelligence as Arising from Individual Differences: The Differential Model

McNemar (1964) was one of the most explicit in speculating on why we even have a concept of intelligence and in linking the rationale for the concept to individual differences. He queried whether identical twins stranded on a desert island and growing up together would ever generate the notion of intelligence if they never encountered individual differences in their mental abilities.

Perhaps without individual differences, societies would never generate the notion of intelligence and languages would contain no corresponding term. Actually, some languages, such as Mandarin Chinese, have no concept that corresponds precisely to the Western notion of intelligence (Yang & Sternberg, 1997a, 1997b), although they have related concepts that are closer, say, to the Western notion of wisdom or other constructs. Whatever may be the case, much of the history of the field of intelligence is based on an epistemological model deriving from the existence of one or more kinds of individual differences.

THE SEMINAL VIEWS OF GALTON AND BINET

If current thinking about the nature of intelligence owes a debt to any scholars it is to Sir Francis Galton and Alfred Binet. These two investigators –
Galton at the end of the nineteenth century and Binet at the beginning of
the twentieth century – have had a profound impact on thinking about
intelligence, an impact felt to this day. Many present conflicting views regarding the nature of intelligence can be traced to a dialectical conflict
between Galton and Binet.

Intelligence is Simple: Galton's Theory of Psychophysical Processes

Intelligence as Energy and Sensitivity. The publication of Darwin's
(1859) *Origin of Species* had a profound impact on many lines of scientific
endeavor. One of these lines of endeavor was the investigation of human
intelligence. The book suggested that the capabilities of humans were in
some sense continuous with those of lower animals, and hence could be
understood through scientific investigation.

Galton (1883) followed up on these notions to propose a theory of the
"human faculty and its development." Because Galton also proposed techniques for measuring the "human faculty," his theory could be applied
directly to human behavior.

Galton proposed two general qualities that he believed distinguish the
more from the less intellectually able. His epistemological rooting, therefore, was in the individual-differences approach. The first quality was
energy, or the capacity for labor. Galton believed that intellectually gifted
individuals in a variety of fields are characterized by remarkable levels of
energy. The second general quality was *sensitivity*. Galton observed that
the only information that can reach us concerning external events passes
through the senses and that the more perceptive the senses are of differences in luminescence, pitch, odor, or whatever, the larger would be the
range of information on which intelligence could act. Galton's manner of
expression was direct:

The discriminative facility of idiots is curiously low; they hardly distinguish between heat and cold, and their sense of pain is so obtuse that some of the more
idiotic seem hardly to know what it is. In their dull lives, such pain as can be
excited in them may literally be accepted with a welcome surprise. (p. 28)

For seven years (1884–1890), Galton maintained an anthropometric laboratory at the South Kensington Museum in London where, for a small fee,
visitors could have themselves measured on a variety of psychophysical
tests. What, exactly, were these tests?

One was for weight discrimination. The apparatus consisted of cases
of shot, wool, and wadding. The cases were identical in appearance and

differed only in their weight. Participants were tested by a sequencing task. They were given three cases and, with their eyes closed, had to arrange them in proper order of weight. The weights formed a geometric series of heaviness, and the examiner recorded the finest interval that an examinee could discriminate. Galton suggested that similar geometric sequences could be used for testing other senses, such as touch and taste. With touch, Galton proposed the use of wirework of various degrees of fineness, whereas for taste he proposed the use of stock bottles of solutions of salt of various strengths. For olfaction, he suggested the use of bottles of attar of rose mixed in various degrees of dilution.

Galton also contrived a whistle for ascertaining the highest pitch that different individuals could perceive. Tests with the whistle enabled him to discover that people's ability to hear high notes declines considerably as age advances. He also discovered that people are inferior to cats in their ability to perceive tones of high pitch.

It is ironic, perhaps, that a theory that took off from Darwin's theory of evolution ended up in what some might perceive as a predicament, at least for those who believe that evolutionary advance is, in part, a matter of complexity (Kauffman, 1995). In most respects, humans are evolutionarily more complex than cats. Galton's theory, however, would place cats, who are able to hear notes of higher pitch than humans, at a superior level to humans at least with respect to this particular aspect of what Galton alleged to be intelligence.

Cattell's Operationalization of Galton's Theory.   James McKeen Cattell brought many of Galton's ideas across the ocean to the United States. As head of the psychological laboratory at Columbia University, Cattell was in a good position to publicize the psychophysical approach to the theory and measurement of intelligence. J. M. Cattell (1890) proposed a series of fifty psychophysical tests. Four examples were

1. *Dynamometer pressure.* The dynamometer-pressure test measures the pressure resulting from the greatest possible squeeze of one's hand.
2. *Sensation areas.* This test measures the distance on the skin by which two points must be separated in order for them to be felt as separate points. Cattell suggested that the back of the closed right hand between the first and second fingers be used as the basis for measurement.
3. *Least noticeable difference in weight.* This test measures the least noticeable differences in weights by having participants judge weights of small wooden boxes. Participants were handed two such boxes and asked to indicate which was heavier.
4. *Bisection of a 50-cm line.* In this test, participants were required to divide a strip of wood into two equal parts by means of a movable line.

Wissler Blows the Whistle. A student of Cattell's, Clark Wissler (1901), decided to validate Cattell's tests. Using twenty-one of the tests, he investigated among Columbia University undergraduates the correlations of the tests with each other and with college grades. The results were devastating: Test scores neither intercorrelated much among themselves nor did they correlate significantly with undergraduate grades. The lack of correlation could not have been due entirely to unreliability of the grades or to restriction of range, because the grades did correlate among themselves. A new approach seemed to be needed.

Evaluation. Even those later theorists who were to build on Galton's work (e.g., Hunt, Frost, & Lunneborg, 1973) recognized that Galton was overly simplistic in his conception and measurement of intelligence. Galton was also pejorative toward groups whom he believed to be of inferior intelligence. Yet one could argue that Galton set at least three important precedents.

A first precedent was the desirability of precise quantitative measurement. Much of psychological measurement, particularly in the clinical areas, has been more qualitative, or based on dubious rules about translations of qualitative responses to quantitative measurements. Galton's psychometric precision set a different course for research and practice in the field of intelligence. His combination of theory and measurement techniques set a precedent: Many future investigators would tie their theories, strong or weak, to operations that would enable them to measure the intelligence of a variety of human populations.

A second precedent was the interface between theory and application. Galton's Kensington Museum enterprise set a certain kind of tone for the intelligence measurement of the future. No field of psychology, perhaps, has been more market-oriented than has been the measurement of intelligence. Testing of intelligence has been highly influenced by market demands, more so, say, than testing of memory abilities or social skills. It is difficult to study the history of the field of intelligence without considering both theory and practice.

A third precedent was a tendency to conflate scores on tests of intelligence with some kind of personal value. Galton made no attempt to hide his admiration for hereditary geniuses (Galton, 1869) nor to hide his contempt for those at the lower end of the intelligence scale as he perceived it (Galton, 1883). He believed those at the high end of the scale had much more to contribute than those at the low end. The same kinds of judgments do not pervade the literatures of, say, sensation or memory. This tendency to conflate intelligence with some kind of economic or social value to society and perhaps beyond society has continued to the present day (for example, Herrnstein & Murray, 1994; Schmidt & Hunter, 1998).

Intelligence is Complex: Binet's Theory of Judgment

In 1904, the Minister of Public Instruction in Paris established a commission charged with studying or creating tests that would insure that mentally defective children (as they then were called) would receive an adequate education. The commission decided that no child suspected of retardation should be placed in a special class for children with mental retardation without first being given an examination, "from which it could be certified that because of the state of his intelligence, he was unable to profit, in an average measure, from the instruction given in the ordinary schools" (Binet & Simon, 1916a, p. 9).

Binet and Simon devised a test based on a conception of intelligence very different from Galton's and Cattell's. They viewed judgment as central to intelligence. At the same time, they viewed Galton's tests as ridiculous. They cited Helen Keller as an example of someone who was very intelligent but who would have performed terribly on Galton's tests.

Binet and Simon's (1916b) theory of intelligent thinking in many ways foreshadowed later research on the development of metacognition (for example, Brown & DeLoache, 1978; Flavell & Wellman, 1977; Nelson, 1999). According to Binet and Simon (1916a), intelligent thought comprises three distinct elements: direction, adaptation, and control.

Direction consists in knowing what has to be done and how it is to be accomplished. When we are required to add three numbers, for example, we give ourselves a series of instructions on how to proceed, and these instructions form the direction of thought.

Adaptation refers to one's selection and monitoring of one's strategy during task performance. For example, in adding two numbers, one first needs to decide on a strategy to add the numbers. As we add, we need to check (monitor) that we are not repeating the addition of any of the digits we already have added.

Control is the ability to criticize one's own thoughts and actions. This ability often occurs beneath the conscious level. If one notices that the sum one attains is smaller than either number (if the numbers are positive), one recognizes there is a mistake in one's addition and one must add the numbers again.

Binet and Simon (1916a) distinguished between two types of intelligence, ideational intelligence and instinctive intelligence. *Ideational intelligence* operates by means of words and ideas. It uses logical analysis and verbal reasoning. *Instinctive intelligence* operates by means of feeling. It refers not to the instincts attributed to animals and to simple forms of human behavior, but to lack of logical thinking. This two-process kind of model adumbrates many contemporary models of thinking (for example, Epstein, 1985; Evans, 1989; Sloman, 1996), which make similar distinctions.

What are some examples of the kinds of problems found on a Binet-based test (for example, Terman & Merrill, 1937, 1973; Thorndike, Hagen, & Sattler, 1986)? In one version (Terman & Merrill, 1973), two-year-olds are given a three-hold form board, into which they are required to place in the appropriate indentations circular, square, and triangular pieces. Another test requires children to identify body parts on a paper doll. Six years later, by age eight, the character of the test items changes considerably. By age eight, the tests include vocabulary, which requires children to define words; verbal absurdities, which require recognition of why each of a set of statements is foolish; similarities and differences, which require children to say how each of two objects is the same as and different from each other; and comprehension, which requires children to solve practical problems of the sort encountered in everyday life. At age fourteen, there is some overlap with the age eight tests as well as some different kinds. For example, in induction, the experimenter makes a notch in an edge of some folded paper and asks participants how many holes the paper will have when it is unfolded. On a reasoning test, participants need to solve arithmetic word problems. Ingenuity requires individuals to indicate the series of steps that could be used to pour a given amount of water from one container to another.

The early Binet and Simon tests (preceding the finalized ones), like those of Cattell, were soon put to a test, in this case by Sharp (1899). Although her results were not entirely supportive, she generally accepted the view of judgment, rather than psychophysical processes, as underlying intelligence. Most subsequent researchers have accepted this notion as well.

Evaluation. Binet's work was to have far more influence than Galton's. First, the kinds of test items used by Binet are, for the most part, similar to those used today. From the standpoint of modern test constructors, Binet "largely got it right." Indeed, a current test, the Stanford-Binet Intelligence Scale (4th ed.) (Thorndike, Hagen, & Sattler, 1986) is a direct descendant of the Binet test. The Wechsler tests (Wechsler, 1991), although somewhat different in their conceptualization, owe a great deal to Binet.

Second, Binet grounded his tests in competencies that are central to schooling and perhaps less central to the world of adult work. Such grounding made sense, given the school-based mission with which Binet was entrusted. Although intelligence test scores correlate both with school grades and with work performance, their correlation with school grades is substantially higher, and they correlate better with job training performance than with work performance (see reviews in Mackintosh, 1998; Wagner, 2000).

Third, intelligence tests continue today, as in Binet's time, to be touted as serving a protective function. The goal of Binet's test was to protect children from being improperly classified in school. Today, test users point out how test scores can give opportunities to children who otherwise would not get them. For example, children from lower-level or even middle-level socioeconomic backgrounds, who would not be able to pay for certain kinds of schooling, may receive admission or scholarships on the basis of test scores. At the same time, there is a dialectic in action here, whereby opponents of testing, or at least of certain kinds of testing, would argue that the conventional tests do more damage than good (Gardner, 1983; Sacks, 1999), taking away opportunities rather than providing them to many children.

An important aspect of Binet's theory has been lost to many. This was Binet's belief that intelligence is malleable and could be improved by "mental orthopedics." To this day, many investigators are interested in raising levels of mental functioning (see review by Grotzer & Perkins, 2000). But many other investigators, even those who use Binet-based tests, question whether intelligence is malleable in any major degree (e.g., Jensen, 1969, 1998).

MODELS OF THE NATURE OF INTELLIGENCE

A number of different types of models have been proposed to characterize intelligence (Sternberg, 1990a). What are the principal models, and how are they similar to and different from one another?

Psychometric Models

The early efforts of intelligence theorists largely built on the Binetian school of thought rather than the Galtonian school of thought. The most influential theorist, historically and perhaps even into the present, was also among the first, a British psychologist named Charles Spearman.

Spearman's Two-Factor Theory. Spearman (1904, 1927) proposed a two-factor theory of intelligence, a theory still very much alive and well today (for example, Brand, 1996; Jensen, 1998, 2002). The theory posits a general factor (g) common to all tasks requiring intelligence and one specific factor (s) unique to each different type of task. Thus, there are two types of factors, rather than, strictly speaking, two factors.

Spearman (1904) got this idea as a result of looking at data processed by a statistical technique of his own invention, *factor analysis*, which attempts to identify latent sources of individual (or other) differences that underlie observed sources of variation in test performance. Spearman observed that when he analyzed a correlation matrix, the two kinds of factors appeared – the general factor common to all the tests, and the specific factors unique to each particular test.

Spearman (1927) admitted he was not sure of what the psychological basis of g is, but suggested that it might be mental energy (a term he never defined very clearly). Whatever it was, it was a unitary and primary source of individual differences in intelligence test performance.

The Theories of Bonds and of Connections

Theory of Bonds. Spearman's theory was soon challenged, and continues to be challenged today (for example, Gardner, 1983; Sternberg, 1999d). One of Spearman's chief critics was British psychologist Sir Godfrey Thomson, who accepted Spearman's statistics but not his interpretation. Thomson (1939) argued that it is possible to have a general psychometric factor in the absence of any kind of general ability. In particular, he argued that *g* is a statistical reality but a psychological artifact. He suggested that the general factor might result from the working of an extremely large number of what he called *bonds*, all of which are sampled simultaneously in intellectual tasks. Imagine, for example, that each of the intellectual tasks found in the test batteries of Spearman and others requires certain mental skills. If each test samples all these mental skills, then their appearance will be perfectly correlated with each other because they always co-occur. Thus, they will give the appearance of a single general factor, when in fact they are multiple.

Although Thomson did not attempt to specify exactly what the bonds might be, it is not hard to speculate on what some of these common elements are. For example, they might include understanding the problems and responding to them.

Theory of Connections. Thorndike, Bregman, Cobb, and Woodyard (1926) proposed a quite similar theory, based on Thorndike's theory of learning. They suggested that

in their deeper nature the higher forms of intellectual operations are identical with mere association or connection forming, depending on the same sort of physiological connections but requiring *many more of them*. By the same argument the person whose intellect is greater or higher or better than that of another person differs from him in the last analysis in having, not a new sort of physiological process, but simply a larger number of connections of the ordinary sort. (p. 415)

According to this theory, then, learned connections, similar to Thomson's bonds, are what underlie individual differences in intelligence.

Thurstone's Theory of Primary Mental Abilities

Louis L. Thurstone, like Spearman, was an ardent advocate of factor analysis as a method of revealing latent psychological structures underlying observable test performances. Thurstone (1938, 1947) believed, however, that it was a mistake to leave the axes of factorial solutions unrotated. He believed that the solution thus obtained was psychologically arbitrary. Instead, he suggested rotation to what he referred to as *simple structure*, which is designed to clean up the columns of a factor pattern matrix so that the factors display either relatively high or low loadings of tests on given factors, rather than large numbers of moderate ones. Using simple-structure rotation, Thurstone and Thurstone (1941) argued for the existence of seven primary mental abilities.

1. *Verbal comprehension:* the ability to understand verbal material. This ability is measured by tests such as vocabulary and reading comprehension.
2. *Verbal fluency:* the ability involved in rapidly producing words, sentences, and other verbal material. This ability is measured by tests such as one that requires the examinee to produce as many words as possible beginning with a certain letter in a short amount of time.
3. *Number:* the ability to compute rapidly. This ability is measured by tests requiring solution of numerical arithmetic problems and simple arithmetic word problems.
4. *Memory:* the ability to remember strings of words, letters, numbers, or other symbols or items. This ability is measured by serial- or free-recall tests.
5. *Perceptual speed:* the ability to recognize letters, numbers, or other symbols rapidly. This ability is measured by proofreading tests, or by tests that require individuals to cross out a given letter (such as *A*) in a string of letters.
6. *Inductive reasoning:* the ability to reason from the specific to the general. This ability is measured by tests such as letter series ("What letter comes next in the following series? b, d, g, k, ...") and number series ("What number comes next in the following series? 4, 12, 10, 30, 28, 84, . . .").
7. *Spatial visualization:* the ability involved in visualizing shapes, rotations of objects, and how pieces of a puzzle would fit together. This ability is measured by tests that require mental rotations or other manipulations of geometric objects.

The argument between Spearman and Thurstone could not be resolved on mathematical grounds, simply because in exploratory factor analysis, any of an infinite number of rotations of axes is acceptable. As an analogy, consider axes used to understand world geography (Vernon, 1971). One can use lines of longitude and latitude, but really, any axes at all could be used, orthogonal or oblique, or even axes that serve different functions, such as in polar coordinates. The locations of points, and the distances between them, do not change in Euclidean space as a result of how the axes are placed.

Because Thurstone's primary mental abilities are intercorrelated, Spearman and others have argued that they are nothing more than varied manifestations of g: Factor analyze these factors, and a general factor will emerge as a second-order factor. Thurstone argued that the primary mental abilities were more basic. Such arguments became largely polemical because there neither was nor is any way of resolving the debate in the terms in which it was presented. Some synthesis was needed for the opposing thesis of g versus the antithesis of primary mental abilities.

Hierarchical Theories

The main synthesis to be proposed was to be hierarchical theories – theories that assume that abilities can be ordered in terms of levels of generality. Rather than arguing which abilities are more fundamental, hierarchical theorists have argued that all the abilities have a place in a hierarchy of abilities from the general to the specific.

Holzinger's Bifactor Theory. Holzinger (1938) proposed a bifactor theory of intelligence, which retained both the general and specific factors of Spearman, but also permitted group factors such as those found in Thurstone's theory. Such factors are common to more than one test, but not to all tests. This theory helped form the basis for other hierarchical theories that replaced it.

Burt's Theory. Sir Cyril Burt (1949), known primarily for his widely questioned work on the heritability of intelligence, suggested that a five-level hierarchy would capture the nature of intelligence. At the top of Burt's hierarchy was "the human mind." At the second level, the "relations level," are g and a practical factor. At the third level are associations, at the fourth level, perception, and at the fifth level, sensation. This model has proved not to be durable and is relatively infrequently cited today.

Vernon's Theory of Verbal : Educational and Spatial : Mechanical Abilities. A more widely adopted model has been that of Vernon (1971), which proposes the general factor, g, at the top of the hierarchy. Below this factor are two group factors, $v{:}ed$ and $k{:}m$. The former refers to verbal-educational abilities of the kinds measured by conventional tests of scholastic abilities. The latter refers to spatial-mechanical abilities (with k perhaps inappropriately referring to the nonequivalent term *kinesthetic*).

Cattell's Theory of Fluid and Crystallized Abilities. More widely accepted than any of the above theories is that of Raymond Cattell (1971), which is somewhat similar to Vernon's theory. Cattell's theory proposes general ability at the top of the hierarchy and two abilities immediately beneath it, fluid ability, or g_f, and crystallized ability, or g_c. Fluid ability is the ability to think flexibly and to reason abstractly. It is measured by tests such as number series and figural analogies. Crystallized ability is the accumulated knowledge base one has developed over the course of one's life as the result of the application of fluid ability. It is measured by tests such as vocabulary and general information.

More recent work has suggested that fluid ability is extremely difficult to distinguish statistically from general ability (Gustafsson, 1984, 1988). The tests used to measure fluid ability are often identical to the tests used to measure what is supposed to be pure g. An example of such a test would be the Raven Progressive Matrices (Raven, 1986), which measures people's ability to fill in a missing part of a matrix comprising abstract figural drawings.

Horn (1994) has greatly expanded on the hierarchical theory as originally proposed by Cattell. Most notably, he has suggested that g can be split into three more factors nested under fluid and crystallized abilities. These three other factors are visual thinking (g_v), auditory thinking (g_a), and speed (g_s). The visual thinking factor is probably closer to Vernon's *k:m* factor than it is to the fluid ability factor.

Carroll's Three-Stratum Theory. Perhaps the most widely accepted hierarchical model today is that proposed by Carroll (1993), which is based on the reanalysis of (more than 450) data sets from the past. At the top of the hierarchy is general ability; in the middle of the hierarchy are various broad abilities, including fluid and crystallized intelligence, learning and memory processes, visual and auditory perception, facile production, and speed. At the bottom of the hierarchy are fairly specific abilities.

Guilford's Structure-of-Intellect Model. Although many differential theorists followed the option of proposing a hierarchical model, not all did. J. P. Guilford (1967, 1982; Guilford & Hoepfner, 1971) proposed a model with 120 distinct abilities (increased to 150 in 1982 and to 180 in later manifestations). The basic theory organizes abilities along three dimensions: operations, products, and contents. In the best known version of the model, there are five operations, six products, and four contents. The five operations are cognition, memory, divergent production, convergent production, and evaluation. The six products are units, classes, relations, systems, transformations, and implications. The four contents are figural, symbolic, semantic, and behavioral. Because these dimensions are completely crossed with each other, they yield a total of $5 \times 6 \times 4$ or 120 different abilities. For example, inferring a relation in a verbal analogy (such as the relation between BLACK and WHITE in BLACK : WHITE :: HIGH : LOW) would involve cognition of semantic relations.

Guilford's model has not fared well psychometrically. Horn and Knapp (1973) showed that random theories could generate support equal to that obtained by Guilford's model when the same type of rotation was used that Guilford used – so-called "Procrustean rotation." Horn (1967) showed that equal support could be obtained with Guilford's theory, but with data generated randomly rather than with real data. These demonstrations do not prove the model wrong: They show only that the psychometric support that Guilford claimed for his model was not justified by the methods he used.

Guttman's Radex Model.   The last psychometric model to be mentioned is one proposed by Louis Guttman (1954). The model is what Guttman referred to as a radex, or radial representation of complexity.

The radex consists of two parts. The first part Guttman calls a simplex. If one imagines a circle, then the simplex refers to the distance of a given point (ability) from the center of the circle. The closer a given ability is to the center of the circle, the more central that ability is to human intelligence. Thus, g could be viewed as being at the center of the circle, whereas the more peripheral abilities such as perceptual speed would be nearer to the periphery of the circle. Abilities nearer to the periphery of the circle are viewed as being constituents of abilities nearer the center of the circle, so the theory has a hierarchical element.

The second part of the radex is called the circumplex. It refers to the angular orientation of a given ability with respect to the circle. Thus, abilities are viewed as being arranged around the circle with abilities that are more highly related (correlated) nearer to each other in the circle. Thus, the radex functions through a system of polar coordinates. Snow, Kyllonen, and Marshalek (1984) used nonmetric multidimensional scaling on a Thurstonian type of test to demonstrate that the Thurstonian primary mental abilities actually could be mapped into a radex.

Evaluation

Psychometric theories of intelligence have been enormously influential, particularly in North America and in the United Kingdom. In many respects, they have served the field well. First, they have provided a Zeitgeist for three generations of researchers. Second, they have provided a systematic means for studying individual differences. Arguably, no other paradigm has provided a means nearly as systematic or successful in so many respects. Third, the theories cross well between theory and application. Few theories have proved to have as many and as diverse practical applications. Finally, they have provided a model for how theory and measurement can evolve in synchrony.

At the same time, there have been problems with the differential approach. First, although factor analysis, as a method, is neither good nor bad, it has frequently been subject to misuse (Horn & Knapp, 1974; Humphreys, 1962; McNemar, 1951). Second, factor analyses have sometimes been not so much misinterpreted as overinterpreted. What one gets out of a factor analysis is simply a psychometric transformation of what one puts in. It is possible to support many different theories by choosing one's tests with a certain goal in mind. The resulting factors simply reflect the choice of tests and their interrelationships. Third, in exploratory factor analysis, the rotation issue has proven to be a thorny one. Any rotation is mathematically correct and equivalent in Euclidean space. Arguments over which theory is correct often have boiled down to little more than arguments over which rotation is psychologically more justified. But no adequate basis has been found for supporting one rotation as psychologically preferred over all others. Fifth and finally, the whole issue of deriving a theory of intelligence from patterns of individual differences has never received fully adequate examination by differential psychologists. Evolutionary theorists (e.g., Pinker, 1997; see Sternberg & Kaufman, 2001) would argue that intelligence needs to be understood in terms of commonalities, not differences. Experimental psychologists have made the same claim for many decades, preferring to view individual differences as noise in their data. Perhaps the best solution is some kind of synthesis, as recommended by Cronbach (1957). Jean Piaget, disheartened with his observations from work in Binet's laboratory, provided a synthesis of sorts. He combined measurement with a more cognitive framework for understanding intelligence.

INTELLIGENCE AS ARISING FROM COGNITIVE STRUCTURES AND PROCESSES

Cognitive Structures

Piaget (1952, 1972), among others, has staked out an alternative position to the differential one. Piaget, who was never very interested in individual differences, viewed intelligence as arising from cognitive schemas, or structures that mature as a function of the interaction of the organism with the environment.

Equilibration.   Piaget (1926, 1928, 1952, 1972), like many other theorists of intelligence, recognized the importance of adaptation to intelligence. Indeed, he believed adaptation to be its most important principle. In adaptation, individuals learn from the environment and learn to address the changes in the environment. Adjustment consists of two complementary processes: assimilation and accommodation. *Assimilation* is the process of absorbing new information and fitting it into an already existing cognitive structure about what the world is like. The complementary process, *accommodation*, involves forming a new cognitive structure in order to understand information. In other words, if no existing cognitive structure seems adequate to understand new information, a new cognitive structure must be formed through the accommodation process.

The complementary processes of assimilation and accommodation, taken together in an interaction, constitute what Piaget referred to as equilibration. *Equilibration* is the balancing of the two and it is through this balance that people either add to old schemas or form new ones. A *schema*, for Piaget, is a mental image or action pattern. It is essentially a way of organizing sensory information. For example, we have schemas for going to the bank, riding a bicycle, eating a meal, visiting a doctor's office, and the like.

Stages of Intellectual Development. Piaget (1972) suggested that the intelligence of children matures through four discrete stages, or periods of development. Each of these periods builds on the preceding one, so that development is essentially cumulative.

The first period is the *sensorimotor period*, which occupies birth through roughly two years of age. By the end of the sensorimotor period, the infant has started to acquire object permanence, or the realization that objects can exist apart from him or herself. In early infancy, the infant does not ascribe a separate reality to objects. Thus, if a toy is hidden under a pillow or behind a barrier, the infant will not search for the toy because as far as he or she is concerned, it no longer exists when it goes out of sight. By the end of the period, the infant knows that a search will lead to finding the object.

The second period is the *preoperational period*, which emerges roughly between ages two and seven. The child is now beginning to represent the world through symbols and images, but the symbols and images are directly dependent on the immediate perception of the child. The child is still essentially egocentric: He or she sees objects and people only from his or her own point of view. Thus, to the extent that thinking takes place, it is egocentric thinking.

The third period is the *concrete–operational period*, which occupies roughly ages seven through eleven. In this period, the child is able to perform concrete mental operations. Thus, the child now can think through sequences of actions or events that previously had to be enacted physically. The hallmark of concrete-operational thought is reversibility. It is now possible for the child to reverse the direction of thought. He or she comes to understand, for example, that subtraction is the reverse of addition and division is the reverse of multiplication. The child can go to the store and back home again or trace out a route on a map and see the way back.

The period is labeled as one of "concrete" operations because operations are performed for objects that are physically present. A major acquisition of the period is conservation, which involves a child's recognition that objects or quantities can remain the same, despite changes in their physical appearance. Suppose, for example, a child is shown two glasses, one short and fat and the other tall and thin. If a preoperational child watches water poured from the short, fat glass to the tall, thin one, he or she will say that the tall, thin glass has more water than the short, fat one had. But the concrete–operational child will recognize that the quantity of water is the same in the new glass as in the old glass, despite the change in physical appearance.

The period of *formal operations* begins to evolve at around eleven years of age and usually will be fairly fully developed by sixteen years of age, although some adults never completely develop formal operations. In the period of formal operations, the child acquires the ability to think abstractly and hypothetically, not just concretely. The individual can view a problem from multiple points of view and think much more systematically than in the past. For example, if asked to provide all possible permutations of the numbers 1, 2, 3, and 4, the child can now implement a systematic strategy for listing all these permutations. In contrast, the concrete–operational child will have essentially listed permutations at random, without a systematic strategy. The child can now think scientifically and use the hypotheticodeductive method to generate and test hypotheses.

Vygotsky and Feuerstein's Theories.   Whereas Piaget has emphasized primarily biological maturation in the development of intelligence, other theorists interested in structures, such as Vygotsky (1978) and Feuerstein (1979), have more emphasized the role of interactions of individuals with the environment. Vygotsky suggested that basic to intelligence is *internalization*, which is the internal reconstruction of an external operation. The basic notion is that we observe those in the social environment around us acting in certain ways and we internalize their actions so that they become a part of us.

Vygotsky (1978) gave an example of internalization in the development of pointing. He suggested that, initially, pointing is nothing more than an unsuccessful attempt to grasp something. The child attempts to grasp an object beyond his reach and fails. When the mother sees the child attempting to grasp the object, she comes to his aid and is likely to point to it. He thereby learns to do the same. Thus, the child's unsuccessful attempt engenders a reaction from the mother or some other individual, which leads to his being able to perform that action. Note that it is the social mediation, rather than the object itself, which provides the basis for the child's learning to point.

Vygotsky also proposed the important notion of a *zone of proximal development*, which refers to functions that have not yet matured but are in the process of maturation. The basic idea is to look not only at developed abilities, but also at abilities that are developing. This zone is often measured as the difference between performance before and after instruction. Thus, instruction is given at the time of testing to measure the individual's ability to learn in the testing environment (Brown & French, 1979; Feuerstein, 1980; Grigorenko & Sternberg, 1998). The research suggests that tests of the zone of proximal development tap abilities not measured by conventional tests.

Related ideas have been proposed by Feuerstein (1979, 1980). Feuerstein has suggested that much of intellectual development derives from the mediation of the environment by the mother or other adults. From Feuerstein's point of view, parents serve an important role in development not only for the experiences with which they provide children, but also for the way they help children understand these experiences. For example, what would be important would be not so much encouraging children to watch educational television or taking children to museums, but rather, helping them interpret what they see on television or in museums.

Evaluation

By any standard, Piaget's contribution to the study of intelligence was profound. First, his theory stands alone in terms of its comprehensiveness in accounting for intellectual development. There is no competition in this respect. Second, even the many individuals who have critiqued Piaget's work have honored it by deeming it worthy of criticism. To the extent that a theory's value is heuristic, in its giving way to subsequent theories, Piaget's work is almost without par. Much research today, especially in Europe, continues in the tradition of Piaget. Neo-Piagetians, although they have changed many of the details, still build on many Piagetian theoretical ideas and tasks for studying development. Third, even the most ardent critics of Piaget would concede that many of his ideas, such as of centration, conservation, and equilibration, were correct and remain alive today in a wide variety of forms. Fourth, Piaget provided an enormous database for developmental psychologists to deal with today. Replications generally have proven to be successful (Siegler, 1998).

Yet the theory of Piaget has not stood the test of time without many scars. Consider some of the main ones.

First, Piaget's interpretations of data have proven to be problematical in many different respects. The list of such critiques is very long. For example, there is evidence that infants achieve object permanence much earlier than Piaget had thought (for example, Baillargeon, 1987; Cornell, 1978). There is also evidence that conservation begins earlier than Piaget suspected (Au, Sidle, & Rollins, 1993). As another example, difficulties that Piaget attributed to reasoning appear in some instances actually to have been due to memory (e.g., Bryant & Trabasso, 1971).

Second, it now appears that children often failed Piagetian tasks not because they were unable to do them, but because they did not understand the task in the way the experimenter intended. Piaget's research points out how important it is to make sure one understands a problem not only from one's own point of view as experimenter, but also from the child's point of view as participant. For example, being asked whether a collection of marbles contains more blue marbles or more marbles can be confusing, even to an adult.

Third, many investigators today question the whole notion of stages of development (for example, Brainerd, 1978; Flavell, 1971). Piaget fudged a bit with the concept of *horizontal décalage*, or nonsimultaneous development of skills within a given stage across domains; many investigators believe that development is simply much more domain-specific than Piaget was willing to admit (e.g., Carey, 1985; Keil, 1989). As another example, children master different kinds of conservation problems at different ages, with the differences appearing in a systematic fashion (Elkind, 1961; Katz & Beilin, 1976; Miller, 1976), with conservation of number appearing before conservation of solid quantity, and conservation of solid quantity before weight.

Fourth, many investigators have found Piaget's theory to better characterize children's competencies than their performance (for example, Green, Ford, & Flamer, 1971). Indeed, Piaget (1972) characterized his model as a competency model. For this reason, it may not be optimally useful in characterizing what children are able to do on a day-to-day basis.

Fifth, although Piaget believed that cognitive development could not be meaningfully accelerated, the evidence suggests the contrary (Beilin, 1980; Field, 1987). Piaget probably took too strong a position in this regard.

Finally, some have questioned the emphasis Piaget placed on logical and scientific thinking (for example, Sternberg, 1990c). People often seem less rational and more oriented toward heuristics than Piaget believed (Gigerenzer, Todd, & the ABC Research Group, 1999).

Vygotsky's theory is, at the turn of the century, more in vogue than Piaget's. It better recognizes the important role of the social-cultural environment in intellectual development. And it also suggests how conventional tests may fail to unearth developing intellectual functions that give children added potential to succeed intellectually. Vygotsky's theory is rather vague, however, and much of the recent development has gone considerably beyond anything Vygotsky proposed. Perhaps if he had not died tragically at an early age (thirty-eight years), he would have extensively amplified on his theory.

Cognitive Processes

A related position is that of cognitive theorists (e.g., Anderson, 1983; Miller, Galanter, & Pribram, 1960; Newell & Simon, 1972), who seek to understand intelligence in terms of the processes of human thought and the architecture that holds these processes together. These theorists may use the software of a computer as a model of the human mind, or in more recent theorizing, the massively parallel operating systems of neural circuitry (for example, Rumelhart, McClelland, & the PDP Research Group, 1986). Much of the history of this field is relatively recent, simply because much of the "early" development of the field has occurred in recent times. The field today, for example, has advanced quite far beyond where it was thirty years ago. At the same time, the origins of the field go back to early in the twentieth century and even beyond, depending on how broad one is in labeling work as related to this approach.

The Origins of the Process-Based Approach in Spearman's Principles of Cognition

Although some psychologists in the nineteenth century were interested in information processing (e.g., Donders, 1868/1969), the connection between information processing and intelligence seems to have been explicitly drawn first by Charles Spearman (1923), also known for initiating serious psychometric theorizing about intelligence.

Spearman (1923) proposed what he believed to be three fundamental qualitative principles of cognition. The first, *apprehension of experience*, is what today might be called the encoding of stimuli (see Sternberg, 1977). It involves perceiving the stimuli and their properties. The second principle, *eduction of relations*, is what today might be labeled inference. It is the inferring of a relation between two or more concepts. The third principle, *eduction of correlates*, is what today might be called application. It is the application of an inferred rule to a new situation. For example, in the analogy, WHITE : BLACK :: GOOD : ?, apprehension of experience would involve reading each of the terms. Eduction of relations would involve inferring the relation between WHITE and BLACK. And eduction of correlates would involve applying the inferred relation to complete the analogy with BAD. Tests that measure these attributes without contamination from many other sources, such as the Raven Progressive Matrices tests, generally provide very good measures of psychometric g.

The Cognitive-Correlates Approach

Lee Cronbach (1957) tried to revive interest in the cognitive approach with an article on "the two disciplines of scientific psychology," and there were some fits and starts during the 1960s in an effort to revive this approach. But serious revival can probably be credited in large part to the work of Earl Hunt. Hunt (1980; Hunt, Frost, & Lunneborg, 1973; Hunt, Lunneborg, & Lewis, 1975) was the originator of what has come to be called the *cognitive-correlates approach* to integrating the study of cognitive processing with the study of intelligence (Pellegrino & Glaser, 1979).

The proximal goal of this research is to estimate parameters representing the durations of performance for information-processing components constituting experimental tasks commonly used in the laboratories of cognitive psychologists. These parameters are then used to investigate the extent to which cognitive components correlate with each other across participants and with scores on psychometric measures commonly believed to measure intelligence, such as the Raven Progressive Matrices tests. Consider an example.

In one task – the Posner and Mitchell (1967) letter-matching task – participants are shown pairs of letters such as "A A" or "A a." After each pair, they are asked to respond as rapidly as possible to one of two questions: "Are the letters a physical match?" or "Are the letters a name match?" Note that the first pair of letters provides an affirmative answer to both questions, whereas the second pair of letters provides an affirmative answer only to the second of the two questions. That is, the first pair provides both a physical and a name match, whereas the second pair provides a name match only.

The goal of such a task is to estimate the amount of time a given participant takes to access lexical information – letter names – in memory. The physical-match condition is included to subtract out (control for) sheer time to perceive the letters and respond to questions. The difference between name and physical match time thus provides the parameter estimate of interest for the task. Hunt and his colleagues found that this parameter and similar parameters in other experimental tasks typically correlate about −.3 with scores on psychometric tests of verbal ability.

The precise tasks used in such research have varied. The letter-matching task has been a particularly popular one, as has been the short-term memory scanning task originally proposed by S. Sternberg (1969). Other researchers have preferred simple and choice reaction time tasks (for example, Jensen, 1979, 1982). Most such studies have been conducted with adults, but some have been conducted developmentally with children of various ages (e.g., Keating & Bobbitt, 1978).

The Cognitive-Components Approach

An alternative approach has come to be called the *cognitive-components approach* (Pellegrino & Glaser, 1979). In this approach, participants are tested in their ability to perform tasks of the kinds actually found on standard psychometric tests of mental abilities – for example, analogies, series completions, mental rotations, and syllogisms. Participants typically are timed and response time is the principal dependent variable, with error rate and pattern-of-response choices serving as further dependent variables. This approach was suggested by Sternberg (1977; see also Royer, 1971).

The proximal goal in this research is, first, to formulate a model of information processing in performance on the types of tasks found in conventional psychometric tests of intelligence. Second, it is to test the model at the same time as parameters for the model are estimated. Finally, it is to investigate the extent to which these components correlate across participants with each other and with scores on standard psychometric tests. Because the tasks that are analyzed are usually taken directly from psychometric tests of intelligence or are very similar to such tasks, the major issue in this kind of research is not whether there is any correlation at all between cognitive tasks and psychometric test scores. Rather, the issue is one of isolating the locus or loci of the correlations that are obtained. One seeks to discover what components of information processing are the critical ones from the standpoint of the theory of intelligence (Carroll, 1981; Pellegrino & Glaser, 1979, 1980, 1982; Royer, 1971; Sternberg, 1977, 1980b, 1983; Sternberg & Gardner, 1983).

Consider the analogies task mentioned above. The participant might be presented with an analogy such as WHITE : BLACK :: GOOD : (A) BAD, (B) BETTER. The task is to choose the better of the two response options as quickly as possible. Cognitive-components analysis might extract a number of components from the task, using an expanded version of Spearman's theory (Sternberg, 1977). These components might include (a) the time to *encode* the stimulus terms, (b) the time to *infer* the relation between WHITE and BLACK, (c) the time to *map* the relation from the first half of the analogy to the second, (d) the time to *apply* the inferred relation from GOOD to each of the answer options, (e) the time to *compare* the two response options, (f) the time to *justify* BAD as the preferable option, and (g) the time to *respond* with (A).

The Cognitive-Training Approach

The goal of the *cognitive-training approach* is to infer the components of information processing from how individuals perform when they are trained. According to Campione, Brown, and Ferrara (1982), one starts with a theoretical analysis of a task and a hypothesis about a source of individual differences within that task. It might be assumed, for example, that components A, B, and C are required to carry out Task X and that less able children do poorly because of a weakness in component A. To test this assertion, one might train less able participants in the use of A and then retest them on X. If performance improves, the task analysis is supported. If performance does not improve, then either A was not an important component of the task or participants were originally efficient with regard to A and did not need training, or the training was ineffective (see also Belmont &

Butterfield, 1971; Belmont, Butterfield, & Ferretti, 1982; Borkowski & Wanschura, 1974).

The Cognitive-Contents Approach

In the *cognitive-contents approach*, one seeks to compare the performances of experts and novices in complex tasks such as physics problems (for example, Chi, Feltovich, & Glaser, 1981; Chi, Glaser, & Rees, 1982; Larkin, McDermott, Simon, & Simon, 1980), the selection of moves and strategies in chess and other games (Chase & Simon, 1973; DeGroot, 1965; Reitman, 1976), and the acquisition of domain-related information by groups of people at different levels of expertise (Chiesi, Spilich, & Voss, 1979). The notion underlying such research can be seen as abilities being forms of developing expertise (Sternberg, 1998a). In other words, the experts have developed high levels of intellectual ability in particular domains as results of the development of their expertise. Research on expert–novice differences in a variety of task domains suggests the importance of the amount and form of information storage in long-term memory as key to expert–novice differences.

Evaluation

The information-processing approach to understanding intelligence has been very productive in helping to elucidate the nature of the construct. First, it has been uniquely successful in identifying processes of intelligent thinking. Second, it has not been bound to individual differences as a source of determining the bases of human intelligence. It can detect processes, whether they are shared across individuals or not. Third, it is the approach that seems most conducive to the use of conventional experimental methods of analysis, so it is possible to gain more control in experimentation by the use of these methods than by the use of alternative methods.

The approach also has its weaknesses, though. First, in many cases, information-processing psychologists have not been terribly sensitive to individual differences. Second, information-processing psychologists have often been even less sensitive to contextual variables (see Neisser, 1976; Sternberg, 1997b). Third, although information-processing analyses are not subject to the rotation dilemma, it is possible to have two quite different models that nevertheless account for comparable proportions of variation in the response-time or error-rate data, thereby making the models indistinguishable. In other words, difficulties in distinguishing among models can plague this approach every bit as much as they can plague psychometric models (Anderson, 1983). Finally, the approach simply never produced much in the way of useful tests. More than a quarter of a century after its initiation, the approach has little to show for itself by way of useful or at least marketable products. Perhaps this is because it never worked quite the way it was supposed to. For example, Sternberg (1977) and Sternberg and Gardner (1983) found the individual parameter representing a regression constant showed higher correlations with psychometric tests of abilities than did parameters representing well-defined information-processing components.

BIOLOGICAL BASES OF INTELLIGENCE

Some theorists have argued that notions of intelligence should be based on biological notions, and usually, on scientific knowledge about the brain. The idea here is that the base of intelligence is in the brain and that behavior is interesting in large part as it elucidates the functioning of the brain.

Classical Approaches

One of the earlier theories of brain function was proposed by Halstead (1951). Halstead suggested four biologically based abilities: (a) the integrative field factor (C), (b) the abstraction factor (A), (c) the power factor (P), and (d) the directional factor (D). Halstead attributed all four of these abilities primarily to the cortex of the frontal lobes. Halstead's theory became the basis for a test of cognitive functioning, including intellectual aspects (the Halstead-Reitan Neuropsychological Test Battery).

A more influential theory, perhaps, has been that of Donald Hebb (1949). Hebb suggested the necessity of distinguishing among different intelligences. *Intelligence A* is innate potential. It is biologically determined and represents the capacity for development. Hebb described it as "the possession of a good brain and a good neural metabolism" (p. 294). *Intelligence B* is the functioning of the brain in which development has occurred. It represents an average level of performance by a person who is partially grown. Although some inference is necessary in determining either intelligence, Hebb suggested that inferences about intelligence A are far less direct than inferences about intelligence B. A further distinction could be made with regard to *Intelligence C*, which is the score one obtains on an intelligence test. This intelligence is Boring's intelligence as the tests test it.

A theory with an even greater impact on the field of intelligence research is that of the Russian psychologist, Alexander Luria (1973, 1980). Luria believed that the brain is a highly differentiated system whose parts are responsible for different aspects of a unified whole. In other words, separate cortical regions act together to produce thoughts and actions of various kinds. Luria (1980) suggested that the brain comprises three main units. The first, a unit of arousal, includes the brain stem and midbrain structures. Included within this first unit are the medulla, reticular activating system, pons, thalamus, and hypothalamus. The second unit of the brain is a sensory-input unit, which includes the temporal, parietal, and occipital lobes. The third unit includes the frontal cortex, which is involved in organization and planning. It comprises cortical structures anterior to the central sulcus.

The most active research program based on Luria's theory has been that of J. P. Das and his colleagues (for example, Das, Kirby, & Jarman, 1979; Das, Naglieri, & Kirby, 1994; Naglieri & Das, 1990, 1997). The theory as they conceive it is the PASS theory, referring to *planning, attention, simultaneous processing,* and *successive processing.* The idea is that intelligence requires the ability to plan and to pay attention. It also requires the ability to attend to many aspects of a stimulus, such as a picture, simultaneously, or, in some cases, to process stimuli sequentially, as when one memorizes a string of digits to remember a telephone number. Other research and tests also have been based on Luria's theory (e.g., Kaufman & Kaufman, 1983).

An entirely different approach to understanding intellectual abilities has emphasized the analysis of hemispheric specialization in the brain. This work goes back to a finding of an obscure country doctor in France, Marc Dax, who in 1836 presented a little-noticed paper to a medical society meeting in Montpelier. Dax had treated a number of patients suffering from loss of speech as a result of brain damage. The condition, known today as aphasia, had been reported even in ancient Greece. Dax noticed that in all of more than forty patients with aphasia, there had been damage to the left hemisphere of the brain but not to the right. His results suggested that speech and perhaps verbal intellectual functioning originated in the left hemisphere of the brain.

Perhaps the best known figure in the study of hemispheric specialization is Paul Broca. At a meeting of the French Society of Anthropology, Broca claimed that a patient of his who was suffering a loss of speech was shown post mortem to have a lesion in the left frontal lobe of the brain. At the time no one paid much attention. But Broca soon became involved in a hot controversy over whether functions, in particular speech, are indeed localized in the brain. The area that Broca identified as involved in speech is today referred to as Broca's area. By 1864, Broca was convinced that the left hemisphere is critical for speech. Carl Wernike, a German neurologist of the late nineteenth century, identified language-deficient patients who could speak, but whose speech made no sense. He also traced language ability to the left hemisphere, though to a different precise location, which is now known as Wernicke's area.

Nobel-Prize-winning physiologist and psychologist Roger Sperry (1961) later suggested that the two hemispheres behave in many respects like separate brains, with the left hemisphere more localized for analytical and verbal processing and the right hemisphere more localized for holistic and imaginal processing. Today it is known that this view was an oversimplification, and that the two hemispheres of the brain largely work together (Gazzaniga, Ivry, & Mangun, 1998).

Contemporary Approaches. More recent theories have dealt with more specific aspects of brain or neural functioning. One contemporary biological theory is based on speed of neuronal conduction. For example, one theory has suggested that individual differences in nerve-conduction velocity are basis for individual differences in intelligence (for example, Reed & Jensen, 1992; Vernon & Mori, 1992). Two procedures have been used to measure conduction velocity, either centrally (in the brain) or peripherally (e.g., in the arm).

Reed and Jensen (1992) tested brain nerve conduction velocities via two medium-latency potentials, N70 and P100, which were evoked by pattern-reversal stimulation. Subjects saw a black and white checkerboard pattern in which the black squares would change to white and the white squares to black. Over many trials, responses to these changes were analyzed via electrodes attached to the scalp in four places. Correlations of derived latency measures with IQ were small (generally in the .1 to .2 range of absolute value), but were significant in some cases, suggesting at least a modest relation between the two kinds of measures.

Vernon and Mori (1992) reported on two studies investigating the relation between nerve-conduction velocity in the arm and IQ. In both studies, nerve-conduction velocity was measured in the median nerve of the arm by attaching electrodes to the arm. In the second study, conduction velocity from the wrist to the tip of the finger was also measured. Vernon and Mori found significant correlations with IQ in the .4 range, as well as somewhat smaller correlations (around −.2) with response-time measures. They interpreted their results as supporting the hypothesis of a relation between speed of information transmission in the peripheral nerves and intelligence. These results must be interpreted cautiously, however, as Wickett and Vernon (1994) later tried unsuccessfully to replicate these earlier results.

Other work has emphasized P300 as a measure of intelligence. Higher amplitudes of P300 are suggestive of higher levels of extraction of information from stimuli (Johnson, 1986, 1988) and also more rapid adjustment to novelty in stimuli (Donchin, Ritter, & McCallum, 1978). However, attempts to relate P300 and other measures of amplitudes of evoked potentials to scores on tests of intelligence have led to inconclusive results (Vernon, Wickett, Bazana, & Stelmack, 2000). The field has gotten a mixed reputation because so many successful attempts have later been met with failure to replicate.

There could be a number of reasons for these failures. One is almost certainly that there are just so many possible sites, potentials to measure, and ways of quantifying the data that the huge number of possible correlations creates a greater likelihood of Type 1 errors than would be the case for more typical cases of test-related measurements. Investigators using such methods therefore must take special care to guard against Type 1 errors.

Another approach has been to study *glucose metabolism*. The underlying theory is that when a person processes information, there is more activity in a certain part of the brain. The better the person is at the behavioral activity, the less is the effort required by the brain. Some of the most interesting recent studies of glucose metabolism have been done by Richard Haier and his colleagues. For example, Haier and colleagues (1988) showed that cortical glucose metabolic rates as revealed by positron emission tomography (PET) scan analysis of subjects solving Raven Matrix problems were lower for more intelligent than for less intelligent subjects. These results suggest that the more intelligent participants needed to expend less effort than the less intelligent ones in order to solve the reasoning problems. A later study (Haier, Siegel, Tang, Abel, & Buschsbaum, 1992) showed a similar result for more versus less practiced performers playing the computer game of Tetris. In other words, smart people or intellectually expert people do not have to work so hard as less smart or intellectually expert people at a given problem.

What remains to be shown, however, is the causal direction of this finding. One could sensibly argue that the smart people expend less glucose (as a proxy for effort) because they are smart, rather than that people are smart because they expend less glucose. Or both high IQ and low glucose metabolism may be related to a third causal variable. In other words, we cannot always assume that the biological event is a cause (in the reductionistic sense). It may be, instead, an effect.

Another approach considers *brain size*. The theory is simply that larger brains are able to hold more neurons and, more important, more and more complex intersynaptic connections between neurons. Willerman, Schultz, Rutledge, and Bigler (1991) correlated brain size with Wechsler Adult Intelligence Scale (WAIS-R) IQs, controlling for body size. They found that IQ correlated .65 in men and .35 in women, with a correlation of .51 for both sexes combined. A follow-up analysis of the same forty subjects suggested that, in men, a relatively larger left hemisphere better predicted WAIS-R verbal than it predicted nonverbal ability, whereas in women a larger left hemisphere predicted nonverbal ability better than it predicted verbal ability (Willerman, Schultz, Rutledge, & Bigler, 1992). These brain-size correlations are suggestive, but it is difficult to say what they mean at this point.

Yet another approach that is at least partially biologically based is that of behavior genetics. A fairly complete review of this extensive literature is found in Sternberg and Grigorenko (1997). The basic idea is that it should be possible to disentangle genetic from environmental sources of variation in intelligence. Ultimately, one would hope to locate the genes responsible for intelligence (Plomin, McClearn, & Smith, 1994, 1995; Plomin & Neiderhiser, 1992; Plomin & Petrill, 1997). The literature is complex, but it appears that about half the total variance in IQ scores is accounted for by genetic factors (Loehlin, 1989; Plomin, 1997). This figure may be an underestimate, because the variance includes error variance and because most studies of heritability have been with children, but we know that heritability of IQ is higher for adults than for children (Plomin, 1997). Also, some studies, such as the Texas Adoption Project (Loehlin, Horn, & Willerman, 1997), suggest higher estimates: .78 in the Texas Adoption Project, .75 in the Minnesota Study of Twins Reared Apart (Bouchard, 1997; Bouchard, Lykken, McGue, Segal, & Tellegen, 1990), and .78 in the Swedish Adoption Study of Aging (Pedersen, Plomin, Nesselroade, & McClearn, 1992).

At the same time, some researchers argue that effects of heredity and environment cannot be clearly and validly separated (Bronfenbrenner & Ceci, 1994; Wahlsten & Gottlieb, 1997). Perhaps the direction for future research should be to figure out how heredity and environment work together to produce phenotypic intelligence (Scarr, 1997), concentrating especially on within-family environmental variations, which appear to be more important than between-family variations (Jensen, 1997). Such research requires, at the very least, very carefully prepared tests of intelligence, perhaps some of the newer tests described in the next section.

Evaluation

The biological approach has provided unique insights into the nature of intelligence. Its greatest advantage is its recognition that, at some level, the brain is the seat of intelligence. In modern times, and to a lesser extent in earlier times, it has been possible to pinpoint areas of the brain responsible for various functions. The approach is now probably among the most productive in terms of the sheer amount of research being generated.

The greatest weakness of the approach is not so much a problem of the approach as in its interpretation. Reductionists would like to reduce all understanding of intelligence to understanding of brain function, but it just will not work. If we want to understand how to improve the school learning of a normal child through better teaching, we are not going to find an answer, in the foreseeable future, through the study of the brain. Culture certainly affects what kinds of behavior are viewed as more or less intelligent within a given setting, and again, the biology of the brain will not settle the question of what behavior is considered intelligent within a given culture, or why it is considered to be so.

Another weakness of the approach, or at least of its use, has been invalid inferences. Suppose one finds that a certain evoked potential is correlated with a certain cognitive response. All one knows is that there is a correlation. The potential could cause the response, the response could cause the potential, or both could be based on some higher order factor. Yet, reports based on the biological approach often seem to suggest that the biological response is somehow causal (e.g., Hendrickson & Hendrickson, 1980). Useful though the biological approach may be, it will always need to be supplemented by other approaches.

CULTURE AND SOCIETY

A rather different position has been taken by more anthropologically oriented investigators. Modern investigators trace their work back at the very least to Kroeber and Kluckhohn (1952), who studied culture as patterns of behavior acquired and transmitted by symbols. Much of the work in this approach, like that in the cognitive approach, is relatively recent.

The most extreme position is one of radical cultural relativism, proposed by Berry (1974), which rejects assumed psychological universals across cultural systems and requires the generation from within each cultural system of any behavioral concepts to be applied to it (the so-called emic approach). According to this viewpoint, therefore, intelligence can be understood only from within a culture, not in terms of views imposed from outside that culture (the so-called etic approach). Even in present times, psychologists have argued that the imposition of Western theories or tests on non-Western cultures can result in seriously erroneous conclusions about the capabilities of individuals within those cultures (Greenfield, 1997; Sternberg et al., 2000).

Other theorists have taken a less extreme view. For example, Michael Cole and his colleagues in the Laboratory of Comparative Human Cognition (1982) argued that the radical position does not take into account the fact that cultures interact. Cole and his colleagues believe that a kind of conditional comparativism is important, so long as one is careful in setting the conditions of the comparison.

Cole and his colleagues gave as an example a study done by Super (1976). Super found evidence that African infants sit and walk earlier than do their counterparts in the United States and Europe. But does such a finding mean that African infants are better walkers, in much the same way that North American psychologists have concluded that American children are better thinkers than African children (for example, Herrnstein & Murray, 1994)? On the contrary, Super found that mothers in the culture he studied made a self-conscious effort to teach babies to sit and walk as early as possible. He concluded that the African infants are more advanced because they are specifically taught to sit and walk earlier and are encouraged through the provision of opportunities to practice these behaviors. Other motor behaviors were not more advanced. For example, infants who sat and walked early were actually found to crawl later than did infants in the United States.

Evaluation

The greatest strength of cultural approaches is their recognition that intelligence cannot be understood fully outside its cultural context. However common may be the thought processes that underlie intelligent thinking, the behaviors that are labeled as intelligent by a given culture certainly vary from one place to another, as well as from one epoch to another.

The greatest weakness of cultural approaches is their vagueness. They tend to say more about the context of intelligent behavior than they do about the causes of such behavior. Intelligence probably always will have to be understood at many different levels, and any one level in itself will be inadequate. It is for this reason, presumably, that systems models have become particularly popular in recent years. These models attempt to provide an understanding of intelligence at multiple levels.

SYSTEMS MODELS

The Nature of Systems Models

In recent times, systems models have been proposed as useful bases for understanding intelligence. These models seek to understand the complexity of intelligence from multiple points of view, and generally combine at least two and often more of the models described above.

The Theory of Multiple Intelligences. Gardner (1983, 1993, 1999) has proposed a theory of multiple intelligences, according to which intelligence is not just one thing, but multiple things. According to this theory, there are eight or possibly even ten intelligences – linguistic, logical–mathematical, spatial, musical, bodily–kinesthetic, interpersonal, intrapersonal, naturalist, and possibly existential and spiritual.

True Intelligence. Perkins (1995) has proposed a theory of what he refers to as *true intelligence*, which he believes synthesizes classic views as well as new ones. According to Perkins, there are three basic aspects to intelligence: neural, experiential, and reflective.

Neural intelligence concerns what Perkins believes to be the fact that some people's neurological systems function better than those of others, running faster and with more precision. He mentions "more finely tuned voltages" and "more exquisitely adapted chemical catalysts" as well as a "better pattern of connecticity in the labyrinth of neurons" (Perkins, 1995, p. 97), although it is not entirely clear what any of these terms means. Perkins believes this aspect of intelligence to be largely genetically determined and unlearnable. It seems to be somewhat similar to Cattell's (1971) idea of fluid intelligence.

The experiential aspect of intelligence is what has been learned from experience. It is the extent and organization of the knowledge base, and thus is similar to Cattell's (1971) notion of crystallized intelligence.

The reflective aspect of intelligence refers to the role of strategies in memory and problem solving, and appears to be similar to the construct of metacognition or cognitive monitoring (Brown & DeLoache, 1978; Flavell, 1981).

There have been no published empirical tests of the theory of true intelligence, so it is difficult to evaluate the theory at this time. Like Gardner's (1983) theory, Perkins's theory is based on literature review, and as noted above, such literature reviews often tend to be selective and interpreted so as to maximize the fit of the theory to the available data.

The Bioecological Model of Intelligence.   Ceci (1996) has proposed a bioecological model of intelligence, according to which multiple cognitive potentials, context, and knowledge are all essential bases of individual differences in performance. Each of the multiple cognitive potentials enables relationships to be discovered, thoughts to be monitored, and knowledge to be acquired within a given domain. Although these potentials are biologically based, their development is closely linked to environmental context, and hence it is difficult if not impossible cleanly to separate biological from environmental contributions to intelligence. Moreover, abilities may express themselves very differently in different contexts. For example, children given essentially the same task in the context of a video game and in the context of a laboratory cognitive task performed much better when the task was presented in the video game.

The bioecological model appears in many ways to be more a framework than a theory. At some level, the theory must be right. Certainly, both biological and ecological factors contribute to the development and manifestation of intelligence. Perhaps what the theory needs most at this time are specific and clearly falsifiable predictions that would set it apart from other theories.

Emotional Intelligence.   Emotional intelligence is the ability to perceive accurately, appraise, and express emotion; the ability to access and/or generate feelings when they facilitate thought; the ability to understand emotion and emotional knowledge; and the ability to regulate emotions to promote emotional and intellectual growth (Mayer, Salovey, & Caruso 2000a, 2000b). The concept was introduced by Salovey and Mayer (Mayer & Salovey, 1993; Salovey & Mayer, 1990), and popularized and expanded upon by Goleman (1995).

There is some, although still tentative, evidence for the existence of emotional intelligence. For example, Mayer and Gehr (1996) found that emotional perception of characters in a variety of situations correlates with

SAT scores, with empathy, and with emotional openness. Full convergent-discriminant validation of the construct, however, appears to be needed. The results to date are mixed, with some studies supportive (Mayer, Salovey, & Caruso, 2000a; 2000b) and others not (Davies, Stankov, & Roberts, 1998).

The Theory of Successful Intelligence. Sternberg (1985a, 1988c, 1997b, 1999d) has proposed a theory of successful intelligence, according to which intelligence can be seen in terms of various kinds of information-processing components combining in different ways to generate analytical, creative, and practical abilities. This theory is the subject of the next chapter.

Evaluation

The complexity of systems models is both a blessing and a curse. It is a blessing because it enables such models to recognize the multiple complex levels of intelligence. It is a curse because the models become more difficult to test. One of the most popular models, that of Gardner (1983), was proposed some time ago, but as of this writing, there has not been even one empirical test of the model as a whole, scarcely a commendable record for a scientific theory. This record compares with thousands of predictive empirical tests of psychometric or Piagetian models, and probably hundreds of tests of information-processing models. Sternberg's (1997b) triarchic theory of successful intelligence has been predictively empirically tested numerous times (see, e.g., Sternberg et al., 2000), but because most of these tests have been by members of Sternberg's research group, the results cannot be considered definitive at this time.

CONCLUSION: RELATIONS AMONG THE VARIOUS MODELS OF THE NATURE OF INTELLIGENCE

There are different ways of resolving the conflicts among alternative models of the nature of intelligence.

Different Names

One way of resolving the conflicts is to use different names for different constructs. For example, some researchers stake their claim on a certain number of intelligences or intellectual abilities. Is intelligence, fundamentally, one important thing (Spearman, 1904), or seven things (Gardner, 1983), or maybe ten things (Gardner, 1999), or perhaps 120 things (Guilford, 1967) or even 150 or more things (Guilford, 1982)? Some might say that those who are splitters are actually talking of "talents" rather than intelligence, or that they are merely slicing the same "pie" everyone else is eating, but very thinly.

Sometimes different names are used to reflect the same construct. For example, what was once the Scholastic Aptitude Test became the Scholastic Assessment Test and still later became simply the SAT, an acronym perhaps belatedly asserted to stand for nothing in particular. This illustrates how, over time and place, similar or even identical constructs can be given names in order to reflect temporally or spatially local sensibilities in what constitutes desirable or even acceptable terminology. Many similar efforts, such as referring to what usually is called *intelligence* as *cognitive development* (Thorndike, Hagen, & Sattler, 1986), point out the extent to which the history of intelligence is in part a battle over names.

In a sense, the history of the field of intelligence bifurcates. Some investigators, perhaps starting with Boring (1923), have suggested we define intelligence as what intelligence tests measure and get on with testing it, and other investigators, such as Spearman (1904, 1927) and Thurstone (1938) have viewed the battle over what intelligence is as determining what should be tested.

Fighting for "Truth"

A second response to the differences among theories has been for researchers to stake their ground and then "slug it out" in a perceived fight for the truth. Some of these battles, to be described later, became rather bitter. Underlying them is the notion that only one model or theory embedded under a model could be correct, and the goal of research should be to figure out which one that is.

Dialectical Synthesis

A third response has been to seek some kind of dialectical synthesis among alternative models or theories embedded under these models. There have been different kinds of syntheses.

Approach or Methodology Subject to Improvement. Some investigators have argued that their approach is the best the field can do at the time, but eventually should be replaced. For example, Louis L. Thurstone suggested that factor analysis is useful in the early stages of investigation followed by laboratory research. In other words, the differential approach could be replaced by a more cognitively based one. Thurstone (1947), who was largely a psychometric theorist, argued that

The exploratory nature of factor analysis is often not understood. Factor analysis has its principal usefulness at the borderline of intelligence. It is naturally superseded by rational formulations in terms of the science involved. Factor analysis is useful, especially in those domains where basic and fruitful concepts are essentially lacking and where crucial experiments have been difficult to conceive.... But if we have scientific intuition and sufficient ingenuity, the rough factorial map of a new domain will enable us to proceed beyond the exploratory factorial stage to the more direct forms of psychological experimentation in the laboratory. (p. 56)

Coexistence. Other investigators have argued for coexistence. Charles Spearman, for example, had both a differential theory of intelligence (Spearman, 1927) and a cognitively based one (Spearman, 1923) (both of which will be described later). Cronbach (1957) argued for the merger of the fields of differential and experimental psychology.

Synthetic Integration. Perhaps the best way to achieve a certain coherence in the field is to recognize that there is no one right "model" or "approach" and that different ones elucidate different aspects of a very complex phenomenon. Models such as the systems models are useful in attempting integrations, but they fall short in integrating all that we know about intelligence. The time may come when such large-scale integrations can be achieved in ways that are theoretically meritorious and empirically sound. In the meantime, it is likely that many different conceptions of intelligence will compete for the attention of the scientific world as well as of the lay public.

2

The Theory of Successful Intelligence

The theory of successful intelligence views intelligence as broader than do most theories. In general, the conception fits best with the systems theories discussed in Chapter 1.

The Definition of Successful Intelligence

1. *Intelligence is defined in terms of the ability to achieve success in life in terms of one's personal standards, within one's sociocultural context.* The field of intelligence has at times tended to put "the cart before the horse," defining the construct conceptually on the basis of how it is operationalized rather than vice versa. This practice has resulted in tests that stress the academic aspect of intelligence, as one might expect, given the origins of modern intelligence testing in the work of Binet and Simon (1916b) in designing an instrument to distinguish children who would succeed from those who would fail in school. But the construct of intelligence needs to serve a broader purpose, accounting for the bases of success in all one's life.

The use of societal criteria of success (e.g., school grades, personal income) can obscure the fact that these operationalizations often do not capture people's personal notions of success. Some people choose to concentrate on extracurricular activities such as athletics or music and pay less attention to grades in school; others may choose occupations that are personally meaningful to them but that will never yield the income they might gain doing other work. Although scientific analysis of some kinds requires nomothetic operationalizations, the definition of success for an individual is idiographic. In the theory of successful intelligence, however, the conceptualization of intelligence is always within a sociocultural context. Although the processes of intelligence may be common across such contexts, what constitutes success is not. Being a successful member of the clergy of a particular religion may be highly rewarded in one society and viewed as a worthless pursuit in another.

2. *One's ability to achieve success depends on capitalizing on one's strengths and correcting or compensating for one's weaknesses.* Theories of intelligence typically specify some relatively fixed set of abilities, whether one general factor and a number of specific factors (Spearman, 1904), seven multiple factors (Thurstone, 1938), eight multiple intelligences (Gardner, 1983, 1999), or 150 separate intellectual abilities (Guilford, 1982). Such a nomothetic specification is useful in establishing a common set of skills to be tested. But people achieve success, even within a given occupation, in many different ways. For example, successful teachers and researchers achieve success through many different blendings of skills rather than through any single formula that works for all of them.

3. *Balancing abilities is achieved in order to adapt to, shape, and select environments.* Definitions of intelligence traditionally have emphasized the role of adaptation to the environment (Intelligence and its measurement, 1921; Sternberg & Detterman, 1986). But intelligence involves not only modifying oneself to suit the environment (adaptation), but also modifying the environment to suit oneself (shaping), and sometimes, finding a new environment that is a better match to one's skills, values, or desires (selection).

Not all people have equal opportunities to adapt to, shape, and select environments. In general, people of higher socioeconomic standing tend to have more opportunities and people of lower socioeconomic standing have fewer. The economy or political situation of the society can also be factors. Other variables that may affect such opportunities are education and especially literacy, political party, race, religion, and so forth. For example, someone with a college education typically has many more possible career options than does someone who has dropped out of high school. Thus, how and how well an individual adapts to, shapes, and selects environments must always be viewed in terms of the opportunities the individual has.

4. *Success is attained through a balance of analytical, creative, and practical abilities.* Analytical abilities are the abilities primarily measured by traditional tests of abilities. But success in life requires one not only to analyze one's own ideas as well as the ideas of others, but also to generate ideas and to persuade other people of their value. This necessity occurs in the world of work, as when a subordinate tries to convince a superior of the value of his or her plan; in the world of personal relationships, as when a child attempts to convince a parent to do what he or she wants or when a spouse tries to convince the other spouse to do things his or her preferred way; and in the world of school, as when a student writes an essay arguing for a point of view.

Information-Processing Components Underlying
Successful Intelligence

According to the proposed theory of human intelligence and its development (Sternberg, 1980b, 1984, 1985a, 1990a, 1997b, 1999d), a common set of processes underlies all aspects of intelligence. These processes are hypothesized to be universal. For example, although the solutions to problems that are considered intelligent in one culture may be different from the solutions considered to be intelligent in another culture, the need to define problems and translate strategies to solve these problems exists in any culture.

Metacomponents, or executive processes, plan what to do, monitor the plans as they are being carried out, and evaluate them after they are done. Examples of metacomponents are recognizing the existence of a problem, defining the nature of the problem, deciding on a strategy for solving the problem, monitoring the solution of the problem, and evaluating the solution after the problem is solved.

Performance components execute the instructions of the metacomponents. For example, inference is used to decide how two stimuli are related and application is used to apply what one has inferred (Sternberg, 1977). Other examples of performance components are comparison of stimuli, justification of a given response as adequate although not ideal, and actually making the response.

Knowledge-acquisition components are used to learn how to solve problems or simply to acquire declarative knowledge in the first place (Sternberg, 1985a). Selective encoding is used to decide what information is relevant in the context of one's learning. Selective comparison is used to bring old information to bear on new problems. And selective combination is used to put together the selectively encoded and compared information into a single and sometimes insightful solution to a problem.

Although the same processes are used for all three aspects of intelligence universally, these processes are applied to different kinds of tasks and situations depending on whether a given problem requires analytical thinking, creative thinking, practical thinking, or a combination of these kinds of thinking. In particular, analytical thinking is invoked when components are applied to fairly familiar kinds of problems abstracted from everyday life. Creative thinking is invoked when the components are applied to relatively novel kinds of tasks or situations. Practical thinking is invoked when the components are applied to experience to adapt to, shape, and select environments.

Figure 2.1 shows the interrelationships among the elements of the theory: metacomponents and active performance and knowledge-acquisition components, which in turn provide feedback to the metacomponents. When these components are applied to relatively abstract but familiar

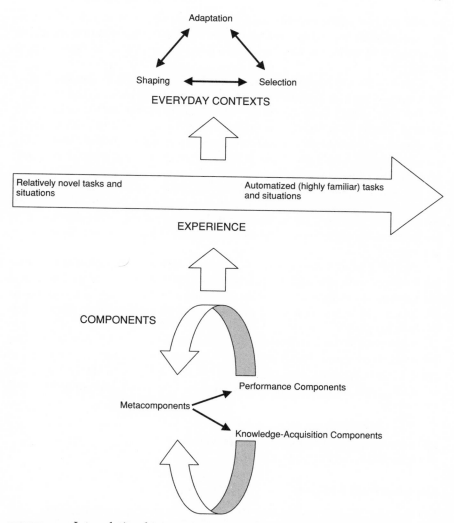

FIGURE 2.1. Interrelationships among metacomponents and performance and knowledge-acquisition components of theory of human intelligence.

problems, the problems call upon analytical abilities. When the components are applied to novel tasks or situations, they call upon creative abilities. And when they are applied to adapt to, shape, or select environments, they call upon practical abilities.

More details regarding the theory can be found in Sternberg (1985a, 1997b). Because the theory of successful intelligence comprises three subtheories – a componential subtheory dealing with the components of intelligence, an experiential subtheory dealing with the importance of coping with relative novelty and of automatization of information processing, and a contextual subtheory dealing with processes of adaptation, shaping, and selection, the theory has been referred to from time to time as *triarchic*.

People who are high in conventional intelligence but low in successful intelligence are susceptible to committing four fallacies in their thinking.

The first, which I call the *stable-trait fallacy*, is the belief that once smart, always smart. They think that because of their high test scores or grades in school, they can pretty much count on being smart forever. As a result, some of them do not actively engage in life-long learning, with unfortunate results. They lose their edge.

The second fallacy is the *general-ability fallacy*, or the belief that if you are smart in one thing, you are smart in everything. People who do well on tests and in school often think that their high levels of performance in these domains mean they will be expert in any domain. Typically, they are wrong.

The third fallacy, the *life-success fallacy*, is based on the belief that if they succeed on tests, the rest is guaranteed. Some of them never learn that conventional intelligence at some level may be necessary for success in life, but is far from sufficient. People cannot succeed in their lives on the basis of IQ alone.

The fourth fallacy is the *moral-equivalence fallacy*, the belief that to be smart is to be good. Herrnstein and Murray (1994) seem to come quite close in their book to committing this fallacy, at times equating the smart with the good. There are many people who are smart, but not good, and vice versa.

INTERNAL VALIDATION OF THE THEORY OF SUCCESSFUL INTELLIGENCE

Componential Analyses

Componential analyses involve studying the information-processing components underlying performance on cognitive tasks. These kinds of analyses have been used to study both analytical and creative thinking abilities.

Analytical Intelligence. Analytical intelligence is involved when the components of intelligence (which are specified by the componential subtheory of the triarchic theory) are applied to analyze, evaluate, judge, or compare and contrast. It typically is involved when components are applied to relatively familiar kinds of problems where the judgments to be made are of a fairly abstract nature.

In some early work, it was shown how analytical kinds of problems, such as analogies or syllogisms, can be analyzed componentially

(Guyote & Sternberg, 1981; Sternberg, 1977, 1980b, 1983; Sternberg & Gardner, 1983; Sternberg & Turner, 1981), with response times or error rates decomposed to yield their underlying information-processing components. The goal of this research was to understand the information-processing origins of individual differences in (the analytical aspect of) human intelligence. With componential analysis, one could specify sources of individual differences underlying a factor score such as that for "inductive reasoning." For example, response times on analogies (Sternberg, 1977) and linear syllogisms (Sternberg, 1980a) were decomposed into their elementary performance components. The general strategy of such research is to (a) specify an information-processing model of task performance; (b) propose a parameterization of this model, so that each information-processing component is assigned a mathematical parameter corresponding to its latency (and another corresponding to its error rate); and (c) construct cognitive tasks administered in such a way that it is possible through mathematical modeling to isolate the parameters of the mathematical model. It is thus possible to specify, in the solving of various kinds of problems, several sources of important individual or developmental differences (Sternberg, 1977, 1983):

1. What performance components are used?
2. How long does it takes to execute each component?
3. How susceptible is each component to error?
4. How are the components combined into strategies?
5. What are the mental representations on which the components act?

For example, using componential analysis, it was possible to decompose inductive-reasoning performance into a set of underlying information-processing components. The analogy $A : B : C : D_1, D_2, D_3, D_4$ will be used as an example to illustrate the components. These components are (a) *encoding*, the amount of time needed to register each stimulus ($A, B, C, D_1, D_2, D_3, D_4$); (b) *inference*, the amount of time needed to discern the basic relation between given stimuli (A to B); (c) *mapping*, the amount of time needed to transfer the relation from one set of stimuli to another (needed in analogical reasoning) (A to C); (d) *application*, the amount of time needed to apply the relation as inferred (and sometimes as mapped) to a new set of stimuli (A to B to C to $?$); (e) *comparison*, the amount of time needed to compare the validity of the response options (D_1, D_2, D_3, D_4); (f) *justification*, the amount of time needed to justify one answer as the best of the bunch (e.g., D_1); and (g) *preparation response*, the amount of time needed to prepare for problem solution and to respond.

Studies of reasoning need not use artificial formats. In a more recent study, Sternberg and a colleague looked at predictions for everyday kinds of situations, such as when milk will spoil (Sternberg & Kalmar, 1997). In this study, the investigators looked at both predictions and postdictions (hypotheses about the past where information about the past is unknown) and found that postdictions took longer to make than did predictions.

Research on the components of human intelligence yielded some interesting results. Consider some examples. First, execution of early components (e.g., inference and mapping) tends exhaustively to consider the attributes of the stimuli, whereas execution of later components (e.g., application) tends to consider the attributes of the stimuli in self-terminating fashion, with only those attributes processed that are essential for reaching a solution (Sternberg, 1977). Second, in a study of the development of figural analogical reasoning, it was found that although children generally became quicker in information processing with age, not all components were executed more rapidly with age (Sternberg & Rifkin, 1979). The encoding component first showed a decrease in component time with age and then an increase. Apparently, older children realized that their best strategy was to spend more time in encoding the terms of a problem so that later they would be able to spend less time in operating on these encodings. A related, third finding was that better reasoners tend to spend relatively more time than do poorer reasoners in global, up-front metacomponential planning, when they solve difficult reasoning problems. Poorer reasoners, on the other hand, tend to spend relatively more time in local planning (Sternberg, 1981). Presumably, the better reasoners recognize that it is better to invest more time up front so as to be able to process a problem more efficiently later on. Fourth, it was also found in a study of the development of verbal analogical reasoning that, as children grew older, their strategies shifted. They relied on word association less and abstract relations more (Sternberg & Nigro, 1980).

Some of the componential studies concentrated on knowledge-acquisition components rather than performance components or meta-components. For example, in one set of studies, the investigators were interested in sources of individual differences in vocabulary (Sternberg & Powell, 1983; Sternberg, Powell, & Kaye, 1983; see also Sternberg, 1987b). The researchers were not content just to view these as individual differences in declarative knowledge. They wanted to understand why it was that some people acquired this declarative knowledge and others did not. What they found is that there are multiple sources of individual and developmental differences. The three main sources are in knowledge-acquisition components, use of context clues, and use of mediating variables. For example, in the sentence, "The blen rises in the east and sets in the west," the knowledge-acquisition component of selective comparison is used to relate prior knowledge about a known concept, the sun, to the unknown word (neologism) in the sentence, "blen." Several context cues appear in the sentence, such as the fact that a blen rises, the fact that it sets, and the information about where it rises and sets. A mediating variable is that the information can occur after the presentation of the unknown word.

Sternberg and his colleagues did research such as that described above because they believed that conventional psychometric research sometimes incorrectly attributed individual and developmental differences. For example, a verbal analogies test that might appear on its surface to measure verbal reasoning might in fact measure primarily vocabulary and general information (Sternberg, 1977). In some populations, reasoning might hardly be a source of individual or developmental differences at all. And if researchers then look at the sources of the individual differences in vocabulary, they would need to understand that the differences in knowledge do not come from nowhere: Some children have much more frequent and better opportunities to learn word meanings than others.

Creative Intelligence. Intelligence tests contain a range of problems, some of them more novel than others. In some of the componential work Sternberg and his colleagues have shown that when one goes beyond the range of unconventionality in the kinds of items that appear on tests of intelligence, one starts to tap sources of individual differences measured little or not at all by the tests. According to the theory of successful intelligence, (creative) intelligence is particularly well measured by problems assessing how well an individual can cope with relative novelty. Thus it is important to include in a battery of tests problems that are relatively novel in nature. These problems can be either convergent or divergent in nature.

In work with convergent problems, Sternberg and his colleagues presented eighty individuals with novel reasoning problems that had a single best answer. For example, they might be told that some objects are green and others blue; but still other objects might be grue, meaning green until the year 2000 and blue thereafter, or bleen, meaning blue until the year 2000 and green thereafter. Or they might be told of four kinds of people on the planet—Kyron, blens, who are born young and die young; kwefs, who are born old and die old; balts, who are born young and die old; and prosses, who are born old and die young (Sternberg, 1982; Tetewsky & Sternberg, 1986). Their task was to predict future states from past states, given incomplete information. In another set of studies, sixty people were given more conventional kinds of inductive reasoning problems, such as analogies, series completions, and classifications and were told to solve them. But the problems had premises preceding them that were either conventional (dancers wear shoes) or novel (dancers eat shoes). The participants had to solve the problems as though the counterfactuals were true (Sternberg & Gastel, 1989a, 1989b).

In these studies, Sternberg and his colleagues found that correlations with conventional kinds of tests depended on how novel or nonentrenched the conventional tests were. The more novel the items, the higher the correlations of the tests with scores on successively more novel conventional tests. Thus, the components isolated for relatively novel items would tend to correlate more highly with more unusual tests of fluid abilities (for example, that of Cattell & Cattell, 1973) than with tests of crystallized abilities. Sternberg and his colleagues also found that when response times on the relatively novel problems were componentially analyzed, some components better measured the creative aspect of intelligence than did others. For example, in the "grue–bleen" task mentioned above, the information-processing component requiring people to switch from conventional green–blue thinking to grue–bleen thinking and then back to green–blue thinking again was a particularly good measure of the ability to cope with novelty.

Componential analyses provide one means of internal validation of the triarchic theory. But their emphasis is on testing specific models of task performance for particular components of information processing. Is it possible internally to validate the triarchic theory as a whole?

Factor Analyses

Internal Validity.   Four separate factor-analytic studies support the internal validity of the theory of successful intelligence.

In one study (Sternberg, Grigorenko, Ferrari, & Clinkenbeard, 1999), Sternberg and his colleagues used the so-called Sternberg Triarchic Abilities Test (STAT – Sternberg, 1993) to investigate the internal validity of the theory. Three hundred twenty-six high school students from diverse parts of the United States took the test, which comprised twelve subtests in all. There were four subtests measuring analytical, creative, and practical abilities. For each type of ability, there were three multiple-choice tests and one essay test. The multiple-choice tests, in turn, involved, verbal, quantitative, and figural content. Consider the content of each test:

1. Analytical–Verbal: Figuring out meanings of neologisms (artificial words) from natural contexts. Students see a novel word embedded in a paragraph, and have to infer its meaning from the context.

2. Analytical–Quantitative: Number series. Students have to say what number should come next in a series of numbers.

3. Analytical–Figural: Matrices. Students see a figural matrix with the lower right entry missing. They have to say which of the options fits into the missing space.

4. Practical–Verbal: Everyday reasoning. Students are presented with a set of everyday problems in the life of an adolescent and have to select the option that best solves each problem.

5. Practical–Quantitative: Everyday math. Students are presented with scenarios requiring the use of math in everyday life (e.g., buying tickets for a ball game), and have to solve math problems based on the scenarios.

6. Practical–Figural: Route planning. Students are presented with a map of an area (e.g., an entertainment park) and have to answer questions about navigating effectively through the area depicted by the map.

7. Creative–Verbal: Novel analogies. Students are presented with verbal analogies preceded by counterfactual premises (e.g., money falls off trees). They have to solve the analogies as though the counterfactual premises were true.

8. Creative–Quantitative: Novel number operations. Students are presented with rules for novel number operations, for example, "flix," which involves numerical manipulations that differ as a function of whether the first of two operands is greater than, equal to, or less than the second. Participants have to use the novel number operations to solve presented math problems.

9. Creative–Figural: In each item, participants are first presented with a figural series that involves one or more transformations; they then have to apply the rule of the series to a new figure with a different appearance, and complete the new series.

10. Analytical Essay: This essay requires students to analyze the use of security guards in high schools: What are the advantages and disadvantages and how can these be weighed to make a recommendation?

11. Practical Essay: Give three practical solutions to a problem you are currently having in your life.

12. Creative Essay: Describe the ideal school.

Confirmatory factor analysis on the data was supportive of the triarchic theory of human intelligence, yielding separate and uncorrelated analytical, creative, and practical factors. The lack of correlation was due to the inclusion of essay as well as multiple-choice subtests. Although multiple-choice tests tended to correlate substantially with other multiple-choice tests, their correlations with essay tests were much weaker. The multiple-choice analytical subtest loaded most highly on the analytical factor, but the creative and practical essay subtests loaded most highly on their respective factors. Thus, measurement of creative and practical abilities probably ideally should be accomplished with other kinds of testing instruments that complement multiple-choice instruments.

In a second study, the investigators developed a revised version of the STAT, which, in a preliminary study of fifty-three college students, showed outstanding internal and external validation properties (Grigorenko, Gil, Jarvin, & Sternberg, 2000). This test supplements the creative and practical measures described above with performance-based measures. For example, creative abilities are additionally measured by having people write and tell short stories, by having them do captions for cartoons, and by having them use computer software to design a variety of products, such as greeting cards and a company logo. Practical skills are measured additionally by solving everyday problems presented by means of films, and by an office-based situational-judgment inventory and a college-student situational-judgment inventory. These tests require individuals to make decisions about everyday problems faced in office situations and in school.

Grigorenko and her colleagues found that the creativity tests are moderately correlated with each other and the practical tests are highly correlated with each other. The two kinds of tests are distinct from one another, however. It is interesting that exploratory factor analysis reveals the performance-based assessments tend to cluster separately from multiple-choice assessments measuring the same skills (similar to our earlier findings of essay measures tending to be distinctive from multiple-choice measures). These results further suggest the need for measuring not only a variety of abilities, but also for measuring these abilities through various modalities of testing.

In a third study, conducted with 3,252 students in the United States, Finland, and Spain, Sternberg and his colleagues used the multiple-choice section of the STAT to compare five alternative models of intelligence, again via confirmatory factor analysis. A model featuring a general factor of intelligence fit the data relatively poorly. The triarchic model, allowing for intercorrelation among the analytic, creative, and practical factors, provided the best fit to the data (Sternberg, Castejón, Prieto, Hautamäki, & Grigorenko, 2001).

In a fourth study, Grigorenko and Sternberg (2001) tested 511 Russian school children (ranging in age from eight to seventeen years) as well as 490 mothers and 328 fathers of these children. They used entirely distinct measures of analytical, creative, and practical intelligence. Consider, for example, the tests used for adults. (Similar tests were used for children.)

In these tests, fluid analytical intelligence was measured by two subtests of a test of nonverbal intelligence. The *Test of g: Culture Fair, Level II* (Cattell & Cattell, 1973) is a test of fluid intelligence designed to reduce, as much as possible, the influence of verbal comprehension, culture, and educational level, although no test eliminates such influences. In the first subtest, *Series*, individuals were presented with an incomplete, progressive series of figures. The participants' task was to select, from among the choices provided, the answer that best continued the series. In the *Matrices* subtest, the task was to complete the matrix presented at the left of each row.

The test of crystallized intelligence was adapted from existing traditional tests of analogies and synonyms/antonyms used in Russia. Grigorenko and Sternberg used adaptations of Russian rather than American tests because the vocabulary used in Russia differs from that used in the United States. The first part of the test included twenty verbal analogies (KR20 = 0.83). An example is *circle − ball = square − ? (a) quadrangular, (b) figure, (c) rectangular, (d) solid, (e) cube.* The second part included thirty pairs of words. The participants' task was to specify whether the words in the pair were synonyms or antonyms (KR20 = 0.74). Examples are *latent – hidden*, and *systematic – chaotic*.

The measure of creative intelligence also comprised two parts. The first part asked the participants to describe the world through the eyes of insects. The second part asked participants to describe who might live and what might happen on a planet called "Priumliava." No additional information on the nature of the planet was specified. Each part of the test was scored in three different ways to yield three different scores. The first score was for originality (novelty); the second was for the amount of development in the plot (quality); and the third was for creative use of prior knowledge in these relatively novel kinds of tasks (sophistication). The mean inter-story reliabilities were .69, .75, and .75 for the three respective scores, all of which were statistically significant at the $p < .001$ level.

The measure of practical intelligence was self-report and also comprised two parts. The first part was designed as a twenty-item, self-report instrument, assessing practical skills in the social domain (e.g., effective and successful communication with other people), in the family domain (e.g., how to fix household items, how to run the family budget), and in the domain of effective resolution of sudden problems (e.g., organizing something that has become chaotic). For the subscales, internal-consistency estimates varied from 0.50 to 0.77. In this study, only the total practical intelligence self-report scale was used (Cronbach's alpha = .71). The second part had four vignettes, based on themes that appeared in popular Russian magazines in the context of discussion of adaptive skills in the current society. The four themes were how to maintain the value of one's savings, what to do when one purchases an item and discovers that it is broken, how to locate medical assistance in a time of need, and how to manage a salary bonus one has received for outstanding work. Each vignette was accompanied by five choices and participants had to select the best one. Obviously, there is no one "right" answer in this type of situation. Hence Grigorenko and Sternberg used the most frequently chosen response as the keyed answer. To the extent that this response was suboptimal, this suboptimality would work against the researchers in subsequent analyses relating scores on this test to other predictor and criterion measures.

In this study, exploratory principal-component analysis for both children and adults yielded very similar factor structures. Both varimax and oblimin rotations yielded clear-cut analytical, creative, and practical factors for the tests. Thus, a sample of a different nationality (Russian), a different set of tests, and a different method of analysis (exploratory rather than confirmatory analysis) again supported the theory of successful intelligence.

In a recent collaborative study involving fifteen different high schools, colleges, and universities, we investigated the construct validity of the theory of successful intelligence in the context of predicting college success

(Sternberg & The Rainbow Project Collaborators, in press). The study, involving just over a thousand students, utilized an expanded battery of analytical, creative, and practical assessments to predict first-year college GPA. Our goals in the study were threefold: (a) to construct validate the theory of successful intelligence, (b) to improve prediction of first-year college GPA over and above the prediction obtained through high school grade-point average and SAT, and (c) to increase potential diversity by showing reduced ethnic-group differences on our test.

The test incorporated the Sternberg Triarchic Abilities Test, as described earlier, plus some new tests. The new tests were of creative and practical skills.

For creativity, there were three additional measures. One provided students with unusual titles for short stories. The students were asked to use two of the titles as a basis for writing two very short stories. A second provided pictorial collages. Students were asked to pick two of them, and orally tell a short story based on these collages. A third measure required students to caption cartoons.

There were also three additional practical tests. One required students to indicate how they would solve everyday problems encountered in school. The second required students to indicate how they would solve typical problems encountered in the workplace. The third presented problems students encounter in movies. The movies would stop, and then students would have to indicate how they would solve the problems.

The results were very promising. The Rainbow measures clustered into three factors. One was a strong practical factor. The second was a weaker creative factor. And the third – the analytical factor – was represented by the paper-and-pencil tests. The Rainbow measures significantly and substantially increased prediction of first-year college GPA. The creative measures provided more incremental validity than the practical ones. Oral stories was especially effective as an incremental predictor. And the Rainbow measures showed much less effect of ethnic group than did the SAT. The measures thus appear to provide further construct validation of the theory of successful intelligence.

EXTERNAL VALIDATION OF THE THEORY OF
SUCCESSFUL INTELLIGENCE

The external validity of the triarchic theory of successful intelligence has been tested via two methods: correlational studies and instructional studies.

Correlational Studies

Analytical Intelligence. In the componential-analysis work described above, correlations were computed between component scores of individuals and scores on tests of different kinds of psychometric abilities. First, in the studies of inductive reasoning (Sternberg, 1977; Sternberg & Gardner, 1982, 1983), it was found that although inference, mapping, application, comparison, and justification tended to correlate with such tests, the highest correlation typically was with the preparation-response component. This result was puzzling at first, because this component was estimated as the regression constant in the predictive regression equation. This result ended up giving birth to the concept of the metacomponents: higher order processes used to plan, monitor, and evaluate task performance. It was also found, second, that the correlations obtained for all the components showed convergent-discriminant validation: They tended to be significant with psychometric tests of reasoning but not with psychometric tests of perceptual speed (Sternberg, 1977; Sternberg & Gardner, 1983). Moreover, third, significant correlations with vocabulary tended to be obtained only for encoding of verbal stimuli (Sternberg, 1977, Sternberg & Gardner, 1983). Fourth, it was found in studies of linear-syllogistic reasoning (e.g., *John is taller than Mary; Mary is taller than Susan; who is tallest?*) that components of the proposed (mixed linguistic-spatial) model that were supposed to correlate with verbal ability did so and did not correlate with spatial ability; components that were supposed to correlate with spatial ability did so and did not correlate with verbal ability. In other words, it was possible successfully to validate the proposed model of linear-syllogistic reasoning not only in terms of the fit of response time or error data to the predictions of the alternative models, but also in terms of the correlations of component scores with psychometric tests of verbal and spatial abilities (Sternberg, 1980a). Fifth and finally, it was found that there were individual differences in strategies in solving linear syllogisms, whereby some people used a largely linguistic model, others a largely spatial model, and most the proposed linguistic-spatial mixed model. Thus, sometimes, a less than perfect fit of a proposed model to group data may reflect individual differences in strategies among participants.

Creative Intelligence. In our work on external correlates, we found that the best predictor of creative aspects of thinking seemed to be the efficiency with which an individual is able to transition between conventional and unconventional ways of thinking. In particular, in the grue–bleen conceptual-projection task described above, we found that those individuals who were able to transition effectively from "green–blue" to "grue–bleen" thinking and back again tended to be best able to think in creative ways (Sternberg, 1982).

Practical Intelligence. Practical intelligence involves individuals applying their abilities to the kinds of problems that confront them in daily life, on the job or in the home. Practical intelligence involves applying the components of intelligence to experience to (a) adapt to, (b) shape, and (c) select environments. Adaptation is involved when one changes oneself to suit the environment. Shaping is involved when one changes the environment to suit oneself. And selection is involved when one decides to seek out another environment that is a better match to one's needs, abilities, and desires. People differ in their balance of adaptation, shaping, and selection, and in the competence with which they balance among the three possible courses of action.

Much of the work of Sternberg and his colleagues on practical intelligence has centered on the concept of tacit knowledge. They have defined this construct as what one needs to know in order to work effectively in an environment that one is not explicitly taught and that often is not even verbalized (Sternberg et al., 2000; Sternberg & Wagner, 1993; Sternberg, Wagner, & Okagaki, 1993; Sternberg, Wagner, Williams, & Horvath, 1995; Wagner, 1987; Wagner & Sternberg, 1986). Sternberg and his colleagues represent tacit knowledge in the form of production systems, or sequences of "if–then" statements that describe procedures one follows in various kinds of everyday situations.

Sternberg and colleagues typically have measured tacit knowledge using work-related problems that one might encounter on the job. They have measured tacit knowledge for both children and adults, and among adults, for people in over two dozen occupations, such as management, sales, academia, teaching, school administration, secretarial work, and the military. In a typical tacit-knowledge problem, people are asked to read a story about a problem someone faces and to rate, for each statement in a set of statements, how adequate a solution the statement represents. For example, in a paper-and-pencil measure of tacit knowledge for sales, one of the problems deals with sales of photocopy machines. A relatively inexpensive machine is not moving out of the showroom and has become overstocked. The examinee is asked to rate the quality of various solutions for moving the particular model out of the showroom. In a performance-based measure for salespeople, the test taker makes a phone call to a supposed customer, who is actually the examiner. The test taker tries to sell advertising space over the phone. The examiner raises various objections to buying the advertising space. The test taker is evaluated for the quality, rapidity, and fluency of his or her responses.

In the tacit-knowledge studies, Sternberg and his colleagues have found, first, that practical intelligence as embodied in tacit knowledge increases with experience, but it is profiting from experience, rather than experience per se, that results in increases in scores. Some people can be in a job for years and still acquire relatively little tacit knowledge. Second, they also have found that subscores on tests of tacit knowledge – such as for managing oneself, managing others, and managing tasks – correlate significantly with each other. Third, scores on various tests of tacit knowledge, such as for academics and managers, are also correlated fairly substantially (at about the .5 level) with each other. Thus, fourth, tests of tacit knowledge may yield a general factor across these tests. However, fifth, scores on tacit-knowledge tests do not correlate with scores on conventional tests of intelligence, whether the measures used are single-score measures of multiple-ability batteries. Thus, any general factor from the tacit-knowledge tests is not the same as any general factor from tests of academic abilities (suggesting that neither kind of g factor is truly general, but rather, general only across a limited range of measuring instruments). Sixth, despite the lack of correlation of practical-intellectual with conventional measures, the scores on tacit-knowledge tests predict performance on the job as well as or better than do conventional psychometric intelligence tests. In one study done at the Center for Creative Leadership, they further found, seventh, that scores on our tests of tacit knowledge for management were the best single predictor of performance on a managerial simulation. In a hierarchical regression, scores on conventional tests of intelligence, personality, styles, and interpersonal orientation were entered first and scores on the test of tacit knowledge were entered last. Scores on the test of tacit knowledge were the single best predictor of managerial simulation scores. Moreover, these scores also contributed significantly to the prediction even after everything else was entered first into the equation. In recent work on military leadership (Hedlund et al., 1998; Sternberg et al., 2000), it was found, eighth, that scores of 562 participants on tests of tacit knowledge for military leadership predicted ratings of leadership effectiveness, whereas scores on a conventional test of intelligence and on a tacit-knowledge test for managers did not significantly predict the ratings of effectiveness.

One might expect performance on such tests to be hopelessly culture-specific. In other words, it might be expected that what is adaptive in the workplace of one culture may have little to do with what is adaptive in the workplace of another culture. This appears not to be the case, however. In one study, Grigorenko and her colleagues gave a tacit-knowledge test for entry-level employees to workers in a wide variety of jobs in the United States and in Spain. They then correlated preferred responses in the two countries. The correlation was .91, comparable to the reliability of the test (Grigorenko, Gil, Jarvin, & Sternberg, 2000)!

Sternberg and his colleagues have also done studies of social intelligence, which is viewed in the theory of successful intelligence as a part of practical intelligence. In these studies, forty individuals were presented with photos and asked to make judgments about them. In one kind of photo, they were asked to evaluate whether a male–female couple was a genuine couple (i.e., really involved in a romantic relationship) or a phony couple posed by the experimenters. In another kind of photo, they were asked to indicate which of two individuals was the other's supervisor (Barnes & Sternberg, 1989; Sternberg & Smith, 1985). Sternberg and his colleagues found females to be superior to males on these tasks. Scores on the two tasks did not correlate with scores on conventional ability tests, nor did they correlate with each other, suggesting a substantial degree of domain-specificity in the task.

In a study in Usenge, Kenya, near the town of Kisumu, Sternberg and his colleagues were interested in school-age children's ability to adapt to their indigenous environment. They devised a test of practical intelligence for adaptation to the environment (see Sternberg & Grigorenko, 1997; Sternberg, Nokes, et al., 2001). The test of practical intelligence measured children's informal tacit knowledge of natural herbal medicines that the villagers believe can be used to fight various types of infections. At least some of these medicines appear to be effective (Dr. Frederick Okatcha, personal communication) and most villagers certainly believe in their efficacy, as shown by the fact that children in the villages use their knowledge of these medicines an average of once a week in medicating themselves and others. Thus, tests of how to use these medicines constitute effective measures of one aspect of practical intelligence as defined by the villagers as well as their life circumstances in their environmental contexts. Middle-class Westerners might find it quite a challenge to thrive or even survive in these contexts, or, for that matter, in the contexts of urban ghettos often not distant from their comfortable homes.

The researchers measured the Kenyan children's ability to identify the medicines, where they come from, what they are used for, and how they are dosed. Based on work the researchers had done elsewhere, they expected that scores on this test would not correlate with scores on conventional tests of intelligence. In order to test this hypothesis, they also administered to the eighty-five children the Raven Coloured Progressive Matrices Test, which is a measure of fluid or abstract-reasoning-based abilities, as well as the Mill Hill Vocabulary Scale, which is a measure of crystallized or formal-knowledge-based abilities. In addition, they gave the children a comparable test of vocabulary in their own Dholuo language. The Dholuo language is spoken in the home, English in the schools.

The researchers did indeed find no correlation between the test of indigenous tacit knowledge and scores on the fluid-ability tests. But to their surprise, they found statistically significant correlations of the tacit-knowledge tests with the tests of crystallized abilities. The correlations, however, were *negative*. In other words, the higher the children scored on the test of tacit knowledge, the lower they scored, on average, on the tests of crystallized abilities. This surprising result can be interpreted in various ways, but based on the ethnographic observations of the anthropologists on the team, Geissler and Prince, the researchers concluded that a plausible scenario takes into account the expectations of families for their children.

Many children drop out of school before graduation, for financial or other reasons, and many families in the village do not particularly value formal Western schooling. There is no reason they should, as the children of many families will for the most part spend their lives farming or engaged in other occupations that make little or no use of Western schooling. These families emphasize teaching their children the indigenous informal knowledge that will lead to successful adaptation in the environments in which they will really live. Children who spend their time learning the indigenous practical knowledge of the community generally do not invest themselves heavily in doing well in school, whereas children who do well in school generally do not invest themselves so heavily in learning the indigenous knowledge – hence the negative correlations.

The Kenya study suggests that the identification of a general factor of human intelligence may tell us more about how abilities interact with patterns of schooling and especially Western patterns of schooling than it does about the structure of human abilities. In Western schooling, children typically study a variety of subject matters from an early age and thus develop skills in a variety of skill areas. This kind of schooling prepares the children to take a test of intelligence, which typically measures skills in a variety of areas. Often intelligence tests measure skills that children were expected to acquire a few years before taking the intelligence test. But as Rogoff (1990) and others have noted, this pattern of schooling is not universal and has not even been common for much of the history of humankind. Throughout history and in many places still, schooling, especially for boys, takes the form of apprenticeships in which children learn a craft from an early age. They learn what they will need to know to succeed in a trade, but not a lot more. They are not simultaneously engaged in tasks that require the development of the particular blend of skills measured by conventional intelligence tests. Hence it is less likely that one would observe a general factor in their scores, much as the investigators discovered in Kenya. Some years back, Vernon (1971) pointed out that the axes of a factor analysis do not necessarily reveal a latent structure of the mind but rather represent a convenient way of characterizing the organization of mental abilities. Vernon believed that there was no one "right" orientation of axes, and indeed, mathematically, an infinite number of orientations of axes can be fit to any solution in an exploratory factor analysis. Vernon's point seems perhaps to have been forgotten or at least ignored by later theorists.

The test of practical intelligence developed for use in Kenya, as well as some of the other practicality-based tests described in this book, may seem more like tests of achievement or of developing expertise (see Ericsson, 1996; Howe, Davidson, & Sloboda, 1998) than of intelligence. But it can be argued that intelligence is itself a form of developing expertise – that there is no clearcut distinction between the two constructs (Sternberg, 1998b, 1999d). Indeed, one might argue that all measures of intelligence measure a form of developing expertise.

An example of how tests of intelligence measure developing expertise emanates from work Sternberg, Grigorenko, and their colleagues have done in Tanzania. A study done in Tanzania (see Sternberg & Grigorenko,

1997; Sternberg, Grigorenko, et al., 2002) points out the risks of giving tests, scoring them, and interpreting the results as measures of some latent intellectual ability or abilities. The investigators administered to 358 schoolchildren between the ages of eleven and thirteen years near Bagamoyo, Tanzania, tests including a form-board classification test, a linear syllogisms test, and a Twenty Questions Test, which measure the kinds of skills required on conventional tests of intelligence. The investigators obtained scores that they could analyze and evaluate, ranking the children in terms of their supposed general or other abilities. However, they administered the tests dynamically rather than statically (Brown & Ferrara, 1985; Budoff, 1968; Day, Engelhardt, Maxwell, & Bolig, 1997; Feuerstein, 1979; Grigorenko & Sternberg, 1998; Guthke, 1993; Haywood & Tzuriel, 1992; Lidz, 1987, 1991; Tzuriel, 1995; Vygotsky, 1978). Dynamic testing is like conventional static testing in that individuals are tested and inferences about their abilities made. But dynamic tests differ in that children are given some kind of feedback to help them improve their scores. Vygotsky (1978) suggested that the children's ability to profit from the guided instruction they received during the testing session could serve as a measure of their zone of proximal development (ZPD), or the difference between their developed abilities and their latent capacities. In other words, testing and instruction are treated as being of one piece rather than as being distinct processes. This integration makes sense in terms of traditional definitions of intelligence as the ability to learn ("Intelligence and its measurement," 1921; Sternberg & Detterman, 1986). What a dynamic test does is directly measure processes of learning in the context of testing rather than measuring these processes indirectly as the product of past learning. Such measurement is especially important when not all children have had equal opportunities to learn in the past.

In our assessments, children were first given the ability tests. Then they were given a brief period of instruction in which they were able to learn skills that would potentially enable them to improve their scores. Then they were tested again. Because the instruction for each test lasted only about five or ten minutes, one would not expect dramatic gains. Yet, on average, the gains were statistically significant. More important, scores on the pretest showed only weak although significant correlations with scores on the post-test. These correlations, at about the .3 level, suggested that when tests are administered statically to children in developing countries, they may be rather unstable and easily subject to influences of training. The reason could be that the children are not accustomed to taking Western-style tests, and so profit quickly from even small amounts of instruction as to what is expected from them. Of course, the more important question is not whether the scores changed or even correlated with each other, but rather how they correlated with other cognitive measures. In other words, which test was a better predictor of transfer to other cognitive performances, the pretest score or the post-test score? The investigators found the post-test score to be the better predictor.

In interpreting results, whether from developed or developing cultures, it is always important to take into account the physical health of the participants one is testing. In a study we did in Jamaica (Sternberg, Powell, McGrane, & McGregor, 1997), we found that Jamaican schoolchildren who suffered from parasitic illnesses (for the most part, whipworm or Ascaris) did more poorly on higher-level cognitive tests (such as of working memory and reasoning) than did children who did not suffer from these illnesses, even after controlling for socioeconomic status. Why might such a physical illness cause a deficit in higher-level cognitive skills?

Ceci (1996) has shown that increased levels of schooling are associated with higher IQ. Why would there be such a relation? Presumably, in part, because schooling helps children develop the kinds of skills measured by IQ tests, and that are important for survival in school. Children with whipworm-induced and related illnesses are less able to profit from school than are other children. Every day they go to school, they are likely to experience symptoms such as listlessness, stomachache, and difficulties in concentrating, which reduce the extent to which they are able to profit from instruction and thus their ultimate performance on higher-level cognitive tests.

Crystallized-ability tests, such as tests of vocabulary and general information, certainly measure the developing and developed knowledge base. Available data suggest that fluid-ability tests, such as tests of abstract reasoning, measure developing and developed expertise even more strongly than do crystallized-ability tests. Probably the best evidence for this claim is that fluid-ability tests have shown much greater increases in scores over the last several generations than have crystallized-ability tests (Flynn, 1984, 1987, 1998; Neisser, 1998). The relatively brief period of time during which these increases have occurred (about nine points of IQ per generation) suggests an environmental rather than a genetic cause of the increases. And the substantially greater increase for fluid than for crystallized tests suggests that fluid tests, like all other tests, actually measure an expertise acquired through interaction with the environment. This is not to say that genes do not influence intelligence: Almost certainly they do (Bouchard, 1997; Plomin, 1997; Scarr, 1997). The point is that the environment always mediates their influence and tests of intelligence measure gene–environment interaction effects. The measurement of intelligence is by assessment of various forms of developing expertise.

The forms of developing expertise that are viewed as practically or otherwise intelligent may differ from one society to another or from one sector of a given society to another. For example, procedural knowledge about natural herbal medicines, on the one hand, or Western medicines, on the other, may be critical to survival in one society, and irrelevant to survival in another (where one or the other type of medicine is not available). Whereas what constitutes components of intelligence is universal, the content that constitutes the application of these components to adaptation to, shaping, and selection of environments is culturally and even subculturally variable.

In another study – the Grigorenko–Sternberg (2001) study in Russia described above – the analytical, creative, and practical tests the investigators employed were used to predict mental and physical health among the Russian adults. Mental health was measured by widely used paper-and-pencil tests of depression and anxiety and physical health was measured by self-report. The best predictor of mental and physical health was the practical-intelligence measure. Analytical intelligence came second and creative intelligence came third. All three contributed to prediction, however. Thus, the researchers again concluded that a theory of intelligence encompassing all three elements provides a better prediction of success in life than does a theory comprising just the analytical element.

Instructional Studies

Improving School Achievement.   In a first set of studies, researchers explored the question of whether conventional education in school systematically discriminates against children with creative and practical strengths (Sternberg & Clinkenbeard, 1995; Sternberg, Ferrari, Clinkenbeard, & Grigorenko, 1996; Sternberg, Grigorenko, Ferrari, & Clinkenbeard, 1999). Motivating this work was the belief that the systems in most schools strongly tend to favor children with strengths in memory and analytical abilities. However, schools can be unbalanced in other directions as well. One school Sternberg and Grigorenko visited in Russia in 2000 placed a heavy emphasis on the development of creative abilities – much more so than on the development of analytical and practical abilities. While on this trip, they were told of yet another school – catering to the children of Russian businessmen – that strongly emphasized practical abilities, and in which children who were not practically oriented were told that, eventually, they would be working for their classmates who were practically oriented.

In the United States and some other countries, the Sternberg Triarchic Abilities Test, as described earlier in the chapter, was administered to 326 children who were identified by their schools as gifted by any standard whatsoever. Children were selected for a summer program at Yale University in (college-level) psychology if they fell into one of five ability groupings: high analytical, high creative, high practical, high balanced (high in all three abilities), or low balanced (low in all three abilities). The students were divided into four instructional groups. Students in all four groups used the same introductory psychology textbook (a preliminary version of Sternberg [1995]) and listened to the same psychology lectures. What differed among them was the type of afternoon discussion section to which they were assigned, emphasizing either memory, analytical, creative, or practical instruction. For example, in the memory condition, they might be asked to describe the main tenets of a major theory of depression. In the analytical condition, they might be asked to compare and contrast two theories of depression. In the creative condition, they might be asked to formulate their own theory of depression. In the practical condition, they might be asked how they could use what they had learned about depression to help a friend who was depressed.

Students in all four instructional conditions were evaluated in terms of their performance on homework, a midterm exam, a final exam, and an independent project. Each type of work was evaluated for memory, analytical, creative, and practical quality. Thus, all students were evaluated in exactly the same way.

Our results suggested the utility of the theory of successful intelligence. This utility showed itself in several ways.

First, the investigators observed when the students arrived at Yale that those in the high creative and high practical groups were much more diverse in terms of racial, ethnic, socioeconomic, and educational backgrounds than were the students in the high analytical group, suggesting that correlations of measured intelligence with status variables such as these may be reduced by using a broader conception of intelligence. Thus, the kinds of students identified as strong differed in terms of populations from which they were drawn in comparison with students identified as strong solely by analytical measures. More important, just by expanding the range of abilities measured, the investigators discovered intellectual strengths that might not have been apparent through a conventional test.

Second, the investigators found that all three ability tests – analytical, creative, and practical – significantly predicted course performance. When multiple-regression analysis was used, at least two of these ability measures contributed significantly to the prediction of each of the measures of achievement. Perhaps as a reflection of the difficulty of deemphasizing the analytical way of teaching, one of the significant predictors was always the analytical score. (However, in a replication of our study with low-income African-American students from New York, Deborah Coates of the City University of New York found a different pattern of results. Her data indicated that the practical tests were better predictors of course performance than were the analytical measures, suggesting that which ability test predicts which criterion depends on population as well as mode of teaching.)

Third and most important, there was an aptitude-treatment interaction whereby students who were placed in instructional conditions that better matched their pattern of abilities outperformed students who were mismatched. In other words, when students are taught in a way that fits how they think, they do better in school. Children with creative and practical abilities, who are almost never taught or assessed in a way that matches their pattern of abilities, may be at a disadvantage in course after course, year after year.

A follow-up study (Sternberg, Torff, & Grigorenko, 1998a, 1998b) examined learning of social studies and science by third graders and eighth graders. The 225 third graders were students in a very low-income neighborhood in Raleigh, North Carolina. The 142 eighth graders were students who were largely middle- to upper-middle class studying in Baltimore, Maryland, and Fresno, California. In this study, students were assigned to one of three instructional conditions. In the first condition, they were taught the course that basically they would have learned had there been no intervention. The emphasis in the course was on memory. In a second condition, students were taught in a way that emphasized critical (analytical) thinking. In the third condition, they were taught in a way that emphasized analytical, creative, and practical thinking. All students' performances were assessed for memory learning (through multiple-choice assessments) as well as for analytical, creative, and practical learning (through performance assessments).

As expected, students in the successful intelligence (analytical, creative, practical) condition outperformed the other students in terms of the performance assessments. One could argue that this result merely reflected the way they were taught. Nevertheless, the result suggested that teaching for these kinds of thinking succeeded. More important, however, was the result that children in the successful intelligence condition outperformed the other children even on the multiple-choice memory tests. In other words, to the extent that one's goal is just to maximize children's memory for information, teaching for successful intelligence is still superior. It enables children to capitalize on their strengths and to correct or compensate for their weaknesses, and it allows children to encode material in a variety of interesting ways.

Grigorenko and her colleagues have now extended these results to reading curricula at the middle school and the high school level. In a study of 871 middle school students and 432 high school students, researchers taught reading either triarchically or through the regular curriculum. At the middle school level, reading was taught explicitly. At the high school level, reading was infused into instruction in mathematics, physical sciences, social sciences, English, history, foreign languages, and the arts. In all settings, students who were taught triarchially substantially outperformed students who were taught in standard ways (Grigorenko, Sternberg, & Jarvin, 2002).

Thus the results of three sets of studies suggest that the theory of successful intelligence is valid as a whole. Moreover, the results suggest that the theory can make a difference not only in laboratory tests, but in school classrooms and in the everyday life of adults as well.

Improving Abilities. The kinds of analytical, creative, and practical abilities discussed in this book are not fixed, but rather, modifiable.

Analytical skills can be taught. For example, in one study, Sternberg (1987a) tested whether it is possible to teach people better to decontextualize meanings of unknown words presented in context. In one study, Sternberg gave eighty-one participants in five conditions a pretest on their ability to decontextualize word meanings. Then the participants were divided into five conditions, two of which were control conditions that lacked formal instruction. In one condition, participants were not given any instructional treatment. They were merely asked later to take a post-test. In a second condition, they were given practice as an instructional condition, but there was no formal instruction, per se. In a third condition, they were taught knowledge-acquisition component processes that could be used to decontextualize word meanings. In a fourth condition, they were taught to use context cues. In a fifth condition, they were taught to use mediating variables. Participants in all three of the theory-based formal-instructional conditions outperformed participants in the two control conditions, whose performance did not differ. In other words, theory-based instruction was better than no instruction at all or just practice without formal instruction.

Creative-thinking skills can also be taught and a program has been devised for teaching them (Sternberg & Williams, 1996; see also Sternberg & Grigorenko, 2000). In some relevant work, the investigators divided eighty-six gifted and nongifted fourth grade children into experimental and control groups. All children took pretests on insightful thinking. Then some of the children received their regular school instruction whereas others received instruction on insight skills. After the instruction of whichever kind, all children took a post-test on insight skills. The investigators found that children taught how to solve the insight problems using knowledge-acquisition components gained more from pretest to post-test than did students who were not so taught (Davidson & Sternberg, 1984).

Practical-intelligence skills can also be taught. Williams and her colleagues have developed a program for teaching practical–intellectual skills, aimed at middle school students, that explicitly teaches students "practical intelligence for school" in the contexts of doing homework, taking tests, reading, and writing (Williams et al., 1996). Sternberg and his colleagues have evaluated the program in a variety of settings (Gardner, Krechevsky, Sternberg, & Okagaki, 1994; Sternberg, Okagaki, & Jackson, 1990) and found that students taught via the program outperform students in control groups that did not receive the instruction.

Individuals' use of practical intelligence can be to their own gain in addition to or instead of the gain of others. People can be practically intelligent for themselves at the expense of others. It is for this reason that wisdom needs to be studied in its own right in addition to practical or even successful intelligence (Baltes & Staudinger, 2000; Sternberg, 1998b).

In sum, practical intelligence, like analytical intelligence, is an important antecedent of life success. Because measures of practical intelligence predict everyday behavior at about the same level as do measures of analytical intelligence (and sometimes even better), the sophisticated use of such tests could roughly double the explained variance in various kinds of criteria of success. Using measures of creative intelligence as well might improve prediction still more. Thus, tests based on the construct of successful intelligence might take us to new and higher levels of prediction. At the same time, expansion of conventional tests that stay within the conventional framework of analytical tests based on standard psychometric models do not seem likely to expand greatly our predictive capabilities (Schmidt & Hunter, 1998). But how did psychologists get to where they are, with respect to both levels of prediction and the kinds of standard psychometric tests used to attain these levels of prediction?

THE SOCIETAL DILEMMA OF INTELLIGENCE

The Societal System Created by Tests

Tests of intelligence-related skills predict success in many cultures. People with higher test scores seem to be more successful in a variety of ways and those with lower test scores seem to be less successful (Herrnstein & Murray, 1994; Hunt, 1995). Why are scores on intelligence-related tests closely related to societal success? Consider two points of view.

According to Herrnstein and Murray (1994), Wigdor and Garner (1982), and others, conventional tests of intelligence account for about 10 to 15 percent of the variation, on average, in various kinds of real-world outcomes. This figure increases if one makes various corrections to it (for example, for attenuation in measures or for restriction of range in particular samples). Although this percentage is not particularly large, it is not trivial either. It is difficult to find any other kind of predictor that fares as well. Clearly, the tests have some value (Hunt, 1995; Schmidt & Hunter, 1981, 1998). They predict success in many jobs, and predict success even better in schooling for jobs. Rankings of jobs by prestige usually show higher prestige jobs associated with higher levels of intelligence-related skills. Theorists of intelligence differ as to why the tests have some success in prediction of job level and competency.

The Discovery of an "Invisible Hand of Nature"?   Some theorists believe that the role of intelligence in society is along the lines of some kind of natural law. In their book, Herrnstein and Murray (1994) refer to an "invisible hand of nature" guiding events such that people with high IQs tend to rise toward the top socioeconomic strata of a society and people with low IQs tend to fall toward the bottom strata. Jensen (1969, 1998) has made related arguments, as have many others (see, for example, [largely unfavorable] reviews by Gould, 1981; Lemann, 1999; Sacks, 1999; Zenderland, 1998). Herrnstein and Murray present data to support their argument, although many aspects of their data and their interpretations of these data are arguable (Fraser, 1995; Gould, 1995; Jacoby & Glauberman, 1995; Sternberg, 1995).

This point of view has a certain level of plausibility to it. First, more complex jobs almost certainly do require higher levels of intelligence-related skills. Presumably, lawyers need to do more complex mental tasks than do street cleaners. Second, reaching the complex jobs via the educational system almost certainly requires a higher level of mental performance than does reaching less complex jobs. Finally, there is at least some heritable component of intelligence (Plomin, DeFries, McClearn, & Rutter, 1997), so that nature must play some role in who gets what mental skills. Despite this plausibility, there is an alternative point of view.

A Societal Invention? An alternative point of view is that the sorting influence of intelligence in society is more a societal invention than a discovery of an invisible hand of nature (Sternberg, 1997b). The United States and some other countries have created societies in which test scores matter profoundly. High test scores may be needed for placement in higher tracks in elementary and secondary school. They may be needed for admission to selective undergraduate programs. They may be needed again for admission to selective graduate and professional programs. Highest scores help individuals gain the access routes to many of the highest paying and most prestigious jobs. Low GRE scores, in contrast, may exclude one not only from one selective graduate program, but from many others as well. To the extent that there is error of measurement, it will have comparable effects in many schools.

According to this point of view, there are many able people who may be disenfranchised because the kinds of abilities they have, although important for job performance, are not important for test performance. For example, the kinds of creative and practical skills that matter to success on the job typically are not measured on the tests used for admission to educational programs. At the same time, society may be overvaluing those who have a fairly narrow range of skills, and a range of skills that may not serve them particularly well on the job, even if they do lead to success in school and on the tests.

On this view, it is scarcely surprising that ability tests predict school grades, because the tests originally were explicitly designed for this purpose (Binet & Simon, 1916b). In effect, the United States and other societies have created closed systems: Certain abilities are valued in instruction, for example, memory and analytical abilities. Ability tests are then created that measure these abilities and thus predict school performance. Then assessments of achievement are designed that also assess for these abilities. Little wonder that ability tests are more predictive in school than in the workplace: Within the closed system of the school, a narrow range of abilities leads to success on ability tests, in instruction, and on achievement tests. But these same abilities are less important later on in life.

According to the societal-invention view, closed systems can be and have been constructed to value almost any set of attributes. In some societies, caste is used. Members of certain castes are allowed to rise to the top; members of other castes have no chance. The members of the successful castes believe they are getting their due, much as did the nobility in the Middle Ages who were born at the top and, without thought, subjugated their serfs. Even in the United States, if one were born a slave before 1863, one's IQ would make little difference: One would die a slave. Slave owners and others rationalized the system, as social Darwinists always have, by believing that the fittest were in the roles they rightfully belonged in.

The general conclusion is that societies can and do choose a variety of criteria to sort people. Some societies have used or continue to use caste systems. Others use or have used race, religion, or wealth of parents as bases for sorting people. Many societies use a combination of criteria. Once a system is in place, those who gain access to the power structure, whether through elite education or otherwise, are likely to look for others like themselves to enter into positions of power. The reason, quite simply, is that there probably is no more powerful basis of interpersonal attraction than similarity, so that people in a power structure look for others similar to themselves. The result is a potentially endlessly looping closed system that keeps replicating itself.

INTERIM SUMMARY

The time has come to move beyond conventional theories of intelligence. In this discussion we have provided data suggesting that conventional theories and tests of intelligence are incomplete. The general factor is an artifact of limitations in populations of individuals tested, types of materials with which they are tested, and types of methods used in testing. Our studies show that even when one wants to predict school performance, the conventional tests are somewhat limited in their predictive validity (Sternberg & Williams, 1997). Sternberg has proposed a theory of successful intelligence and its development that fares well in construct validations, whether one tests in the laboratory, in schools, or in the workplace. The greatest obstacle to moving on is in vested interests, both in academia and in the world of tests. Psychologists now have ways to move beyond conventional notions of intelligence; they need only the will.

The time perhaps has come to expand our notion and everyone's notion of what it means to be intelligent. Exactly what kind of expansion should take place? An expansion of the conventional conception of intelligence to include not just memory and analytical abilities, but creative and practical abilities as well has been suggested here. Other expansions are also possible. For example, research is ongoing with regard to emotional intelligence (Mayer, Salovey, & Caruso, 2000a; 2000b; Davies, Stankov, & Roberts, 1998), with promising although as yet mixed results. It is hoped that predictive empirical research will also be forthcoming regarding the theory of multiple intelligences (Gardner, 1983, 1999). Ultimately, the answer to the question of how to expand psychological conceptions of intelligence will depend in part on the imagination of theorists, but more important, on the data showing construct validity, and in particular, incremental internal and external validity over the conventional notions that have dominated theory and research on intelligence to date. The memory and analytical abilities measured by these tests have been and likely will continue to matter for many forms of success in life. They never have been, and are unlikely ever to be, the only intellectual abilities that matter for success. It is for this reason that psychologists have needed and will continue to need theories such as the theory of successful intelligence.

INTELLIGENCE AS DEVELOPING EXPERTISE

The conventional view of intelligence is that it is some relatively stable attribute of individuals that develops as an interaction between heredity and environment. Factor analysis and related techniques can be used on tests of intelligence to determine the structure of intellectual abilities, as illustrated by the massive analysis of Carroll (1993).

The argument of this chapter, following on the theory of successful intelligence and advancing that of Sternberg (1997b), is that this view of what intelligence is and of what intelligence tests measure may be incorrect. An alternative view is that of intelligence as developing expertise and intelligence tests as measuring an aspect – typically a limited aspect – of developing expertise. Developing expertise is defined here as the ongoing process of the acquisition and consolidation of a set of skills needed for a high level of mastery in one or more domains of life performance. Good performance on intelligence tests requires a certain kind of expertise, and to the extent that this expertise overlaps with the expertise required by schooling or by the workplace, there will be a correlation between the tests and performance in school or in the workplace. But such correlations represent no intrinsic relation between intelligence and other kinds of performances, but rather overlaps in the kinds of expertise needed to perform well under different kinds of circumstances. The goal here is to carry the argument made by Sternberg (1998a) a step further by showing that a conjunction of research results that would seem puzzling and contradictory when taken together make sense as a whole when considered from the standpoint of ability tests as measuring developing expertise (Sternberg, 2001b).

There is nothing privileged about intelligence tests. One could as easily use, say, academic achievement to predict intelligence-related scores. For example, it is as simple to use the SAT-II (a measure of achievement) to predict the SAT-I (a measure formerly called the Scholastic Assessment Test and before that the Scholastic Aptitude Test) as vice versa, and the levels of prediction will be the same. Both tests measure achievement, although the kinds of achievements they measure are different.

According to this view, although ability tests may have temporal priority relative to various criteria in their administration (that is, ability tests are administered first, and later, criterion indices of performance, such as grades or achievement test scores, are collected), they have no psychological priority. All the various kinds of assessments are of the same kind psychologically. What distinguishes ability tests from other kinds of assessments is how the ability tests are used (usually predictively) rather than what they measure. There is no qualitative distinction among the various kinds of assessments. All tests measure various kinds of developing expertise.

Conventional tests of intelligence and related abilities measure achievement that individuals should have accomplished several years back (see also Anastasi & Urbina, 1997). Tests such as vocabulary, reading comprehension, verbal analogies, arithmetic problem solving, and the like are all, in part, tests of achievement. Even abstract-reasoning tests measure achievement in dealing with geometric symbols, skills taught in Western schools (Laboratory of Comparative Human Cognition, 1982). One might as well use academic performance to predict ability test scores. The problem regarding the traditional model is not in its statement of a correlation between ability tests and other forms of achievement but in its proposal of a causal relation whereby the tests reflect a construct that is somehow causal of, rather than merely temporally antecedent to, later success. The developing-expertise view in no way rules out the contribution of genetic factors as a source of individual differences in who will be able to develop a given amount of expertise. Many human attributes, including intelligence, reflect the covariation and interaction of genetic and environmental factors. But the contribution of genes to an individual's intelligence cannot be directly measured or even directly estimated. Rather, what is measured is a portion of what is expressed, namely, manifestations of developing expertise, the kind of expertise that potentially leads to reflective practitioners in a variety of fields (Schon, 1983). This approach to measurement is used explicitly by Royer, Carlo, Durfresne, and Mestre (1996), who have shown that it is possible to develop measurements of reading skill reflecting varying levels of developing expertise. In such assessments, outcome measures reflect not simply quantitative assessments of skill, but qualitative differences in the types of developing expertise that have emerged (for example, ability to understand technical text material, ability to draw inferences from this material, or ability to conceive "big ideas" from technical text).

According to this view, measures of intelligence *should* be correlated with later success, because both measures of intelligence and various measures of success require developing expertise of related types. For example, both typically require what I have referred to as *metacomponents* of thinking: recognition of problems, definition of problems, formulation of strategies to solve problems, representation of information, allocation of resources, and monitoring and evaluation of problem solutions. These skills develop as results of gene–environment covariation and interaction. If we wish to call them *intelligence*, that is certainly fine, so long as we recognize that what we are calling intelligence is a form of developing expertise.

A major goal of work under the point of view presented here is to integrate the study of intelligence and related abilities (see reviews in Sternberg, 1990c, 1994a, 2000b) with the study of expertise (Chi, Glaser, & Farr, 1988; Ericsson, 1996; Ericsson & Smith, 1991; Hoffman, 1992). These literatures, typically viewed as distinct, are here viewed as ultimately involved with the same psychological mechanisms.

The Specifics of the Developing-Expertise Model

The specifics of the developing-expertise model are shown in Figure 2.2. The model shows the relation of intelligence to other relevant constructs. At the heart of the model is the notion of *developing expertise* – that individuals are constantly in a process of developing expertise when they work within a given domain. They may and do, differ in rate and asymptote of development. The main constraint in achieving expertise is not some fixed prior level of capacity, but purposeful engagement involving direct instruction, active participation, role modeling, and reward.

Elements of the Model

The model of developing expertise has five key elements (although certainly they do not constitute an exhaustive list of elements in the development of expertise): metacognitive skills, learning skills, thinking skills, knowledge, and motivation. Although it is convenient to separate these five elements, they are fully interactive, as shown in the figure. They influence each other, both directly and indirectly. For example, learning leads to knowledge, but knowledge facilitates further learning.

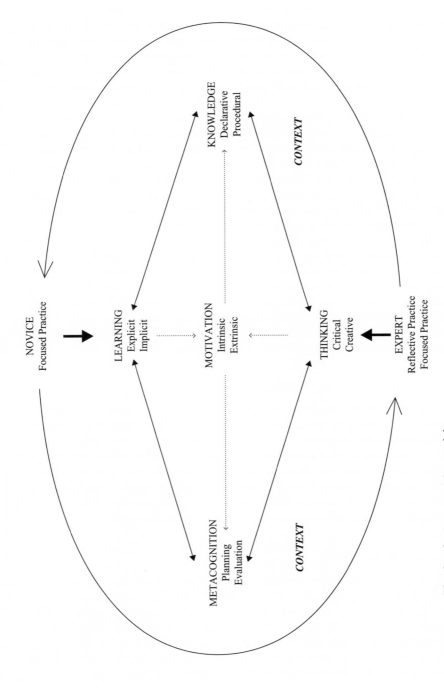

FIGURE 2.2. The developing-expertise model.

These elements are, to a large extent, domain-specific. The development of expertise in one area does not necessarily lead to the development of expertise in another area, although there may be some transfer, depending on the relationship of the areas, a point that has been made with regard to intelligence by others as well (for example, Gardner, 1983).

In the theory of successful intelligence (Sternberg, 1985a, 1997b), intelligence is viewed as having three aspects: analytical, creative, and practical. Our research suggests that the development of expertise in one creative domain (Sternberg & Lubart, 1995) or in one practical domain (Sternberg, Wagner, Williams, & Horvath, 1995) shows modest correlations with the development of expertise in other such domains. Psychometric research suggests more domain-generality for the analytical domain (Jensen, 1998). Moreover, people can show analytical, creative, or practical expertise in one domain without showing all three of these kinds of expertise, or even two of the three.

1. Metacognitive Skills. Metacognitive skills (or metacomponents – Sternberg, 1985a) refer to people's understanding and control of their own cognition. For example, such skills would encompass what an individual knows about writing papers or solving arithmetic word problems, both with regard to the steps that are involved and to how these steps can be executed effectively. Seven metacognitive skills are particularly important, as discussed earlier: problem recognition, problem definition, problem representation, strategy formulation, resource allocation, monitoring of problem solving, and evaluation of problem solving (Sternberg, 1985a, 1986). All these skills are modifiable (Sternberg, 1986, 1988c; Sternberg & Spear-Swerling, 1996).

2. Learning Skills. Learning skills (knowledge-acquisition components) are essential to the model (Sternberg, 1985a, 1986), although they are certainly not the only learning skills that individuals use. Learning skills are sometimes divided into explicit and implicit ones. Explicit learning is what occurs when we make an effort to learn; implicit learning is what occurs when we pick up information incidentally, without any systematic effort. Examples of learning skills are selective encoding, which involves distinguishing relevant from irrelevant information; selective combination, which involves putting together the relevant information; and selective comparison, which involves relating new information to information already stored in memory (Sternberg, 1985a).

3. Thinking Skills. There are three main kinds of thinking skills (or performance components) that individuals need to master (Sternberg, 1985a, 1986, 1994b). It is important to note that these are sets of, rather than individual, thinking skills. Critical (analytical) thinking skills include analyzing, critiquing, judging, evaluating, comparing and contrasting, and assessing. Creative thinking skills include creating, discovering, inventing, imagining, supposing, and hypothesizing. Practical thinking skills include applying, using, utilizing, and practicing (Sternberg, 1997b). They are the first step in the translation of thought into real-world action.

4. Knowledge.   There are two main kinds of knowledge that are relevant in academic situations. Declarative knowledge is of facts, concepts, principles, laws, and the like. It is "knowing that." Procedural knowledge is of procedures and strategies. It is "knowing how." Of particular importance is procedural tacit knowledge, which involves knowing how the system in which one is operating functions (Sternberg, Wagner, Williams, & Horvath, 1995).

5. Motivation.   One can distinguish among several different kinds of motivation. A first kind of motivation is achievement motivation (McClelland, 1985; McClelland, Atkinson, Clark, & Lowell, 1976). People who are high in achievement motivation seek moderate challenges and risks. They are attracted to tasks that are neither very easy nor very hard. They are strivers – constantly trying to better themselves and their accomplishments. A second kind of motivation is competence (self-efficacy) motivation, which refers to persons' beliefs in their own ability to solve the problem at hand (Bandura, 1977, 1996). Experts need to develop a sense of their own efficacy to solve difficult tasks in their domain of expertise. This kind of self-efficacy can result from both intrinsic and extrinsic rewards (Amabile, 1996; Sternberg & Lubart, 1996). Other kinds of motivation are important, too. Motivation is perhaps the indispensable element needed for school success. Without it, the student never even tries to learn.

6. Context.   All the elements discussed above are characteristics of the learner. Returning to the issues raised at the beginning of this chapter, a problem with conventional tests is that they assume that individuals operate in a more or less decontextualized environment. A test score is interpreted largely in terms of the individual's internal attributes. But a test measures much more, and the assumption of a fixed or uniform context across test takers is not realistic. Contextual factors that can affect test performance include native language, emphasis of test on speedy performance, importance to the test taker of success on the test, and familiarity with the kinds of material on the test.

Interactions of Elements

The novice works toward expertise through deliberate practice. But this practice requires an interaction of all five of the key elements. At the center, driving the elements, is motivation. Without it, the elements remain inert. Eventually, one reaches a kind of expertise, at which one becomes a reflective practitioner of a certain set of skills. But expertise occurs at many levels. The expert first-year graduate or law student, for example, is still a far cry from the expert professional. People thus proceed through many cycles on the way to successively higher levels of expertise. They do so through the elements in the figure.

Motivation drives metacognitive skills, which in turn activate learning and thinking skills, which then provide feedback to the metacognitive skills, enabling one's level of expertise to increase (see also Sternberg, 1985a). The declarative and procedural knowledge acquired through the extension of the thinking and learning skills also results in these skills being used more effectively in the future.

All these processes are affected by, and can in turn affect, the context in which they operate. For example, if a learning experience is in English but the learner has only limited English proficiency, his or her learning will be inferior to that of someone with more advanced English-language skills. Or if material is presented orally to someone who is a better visual learner, the quality of that individual's performance will be reduced.

How does this model of developing expertise relate to the construct of intelligence?

The g Factor and the Structure of Abilities

Some intelligence theorists point to the stability of the alleged general factor of human intelligence as evidence for the existence of some kind of stable and overriding structure of human intelligence. But the existence of a g factor may reflect little more than an interaction between whatever latent (and not directly measurable) abilities individuals have and the kinds of expertise that are developed in school. With different forms of schooling, g could be made either stronger or weaker. In effect, Western forms and related forms of schooling may, in part, create the g phenomenon by providing a kind of schooling that teaches in conjunction the various kinds of skills measured by tests of intellectual abilities.

Suppose, for example, that children were selected from an early age to be schooled for a certain trade. Throughout most of human history, this is in fact the way most children were schooled. Boys, at least, were apprenticed at an early age to a master who would teach them a trade. There was no point in their learning skills that would be irrelevant to their lives.

To bring the example into the present, imagine that we decided that certain students from an early age would study English (or some other native language) to develop language expertise; other students would study mathematics to develop their mathematical expertise. Still other students might specialize in developing spatial expertise to be used in flying airplanes or doing shop work or whatever. Instead of specialization beginning at the university level, it would begin from the age of first schooling.

This point of view is related to, but different from, that typically associated with the theory of crystallized and fluid intelligence (Cattell, 1971; Horn, 1994). In that theory, fluid ability is viewed as an ability to acquire and reason with information whereas crystallized ability is viewed as the information so acquired. According to this view, schooling primarily develops crystallized ability, based in part on the fluid ability the individual brings to bear on school-like tasks. In the theory proposed here, however, both fluid and crystallized ability are roughly equally susceptible to development through schooling or other means societies create for developing expertise. One could argue that the greater validity of the position presented here is shown by the near-ubiquitous Flynn effect (mentioned earlier – Flynn, 1987; Neisser, 1998), which documents massive gains in IQ around the world throughout most of the twentieth century. The effect must be due to environment, because large genetic changes worldwide in such a short time frame are virtually impossible. It is interesting that the gains are substantially larger in fluid abilities than in crystallized abilities, suggesting that fluid abilities are likely to be as susceptible as or probably more susceptible than crystalloid abilities to environmental influences. Clearly, the notion of fluid abilities as some basic genetic potential one brings into the world, whose development is expressed in crystallized abilities, does not work.

In sum, intelligence in the theory of successful intelligence is viewed not as fixed, but as flexible and modifiable. How can it be modified?

DEVELOPING SUCCESSFUL INTELLIGENCE

Our goal is to raise the achievement of all students by teaching them in a way that matches the way they learn. The question is, how to do it? We think we have a way. Of course, it is not the only way. But so far, it seems to work for a wide variety of students of varied ages and in diverse subject-matter areas.

The Problem: Schools that Work for Some Students but Not for Others

The problem is that some children seem to benefit just fine from the schooling they get, but others do not. Teachers try very hard to reach all students, but rather frequently find that there are some students who just seem hard to reach. There can be many reasons for this – disabilities, disorders, motivational problems, health problems, and so forth. One reason, though, can be the mismatch between a pattern of strengths and weaknesses on the part of the student and the particular range of methods a teacher is using.

"Teaching for successful intelligence" provides a series of techniques for reaching as many students as possible (Sternberg & Grigorenko, 2000; Sternberg & Spear-Swerling, 1996; Sternberg & Williams, 1996).

The theory of successful intelligence holds that some students who do not do well in conventional courses may, in fact, have the ability to succeed if they are taught in a way that better fits their patterns of abilities. For example, when I took my introductory psychology course, I was very motivated to become a psychologist. I received a grade of "C" in the course. The grade was extremely discouraging to me, as was my instructor's comment that "There is a famous Sternberg in psychology, and judging from this grade, there won't be another one." I decided that I did not have the ability to major in psychology, so I switched to mathematics. This was a fortunate decision for me, because on the midterm in advanced mathematics, I got a grade of "F." Now, the "C" was looking pretty good, so I switched back to psychology. I received higher grades in subsequent courses, and today, I am a psychologist and was just recently elected president of the American Psychological Association, a national organization of about 155,000 psychologists. Incidentally, Phil Zimbardo, past president of the Association, also received a grade of "C" in his introductory psychology course.

The problem is that many children who might like to study a given subject area – whether language arts, mathematics, history, science, foreign language, or whatever – may give up because they think they cannot succeed in studying it. They may either stop taking courses in the subject area, or just give up in the courses they are taking. Teaching for successful intelligence can give these students the chance to succeed that they might not otherwise have.

What is Teaching for Successful Intelligence?

Teaching for successful intelligence involves a way of looking at the teaching–learning process that broadens the kinds of activities and assessments teachers traditionally employ. Many good teachers "teach for successful intelligence" spontaneously. But, for one reason or another, most do not. Teaching for successful intelligence involves, at minimum, using a set of prompts that encourages students to engage in memory learning as well as analytical, creative, and practical learning.[1]

The key strategies are these:

Strategy 1: Teaching for Memory Learning
Most conventional teaching is teaching for memory learning. Teaching for successful intelligence does not ask teachers to stop what they are already doing. Rather, it asks them to build on it. Teaching for memory is the

---

[1] Because of space limitations, it is not possible to describe each of the kinds of teaching in detail. More details are contained in Sternberg and Grigorenko (2000).

foundation for all other teaching, because students cannot think critically (or any other way) about what they know if they do not know anything. Teaching for memory basically involves assisting or assessing students' memory of the *who* (for example, "Who did something?"), *what* (for example, "What did they do?"), *where* ("Where did they do it?"), *when* ("When did they do it?"), *why* ("Why did they do it?"), and *how* ("How did they do it?") of learning.

Here are some examples of teaching and assessing for memory learning:

- *Recall* a fact they have learned, such as the name of the king of England during the American Revolution, or the product of 7×8, or the chemical formula for sodium.
- *Recognize* a fact they have learned, such as which of the following countries is in Central America: Bolivia, Ecuador, Guatemala, or Brazil; or whether the product of 7×8 is 54, 56, 48, or 60; or whether the chemical formula for sodium is So, Na, Sd, or Nd.
- *Match* one set of items of one kind with another set of items of another kind, such as the list of the elements hydrogen, sodium, oxygen, and potassium with the list of abbreviations H, K, Na, and O.
- *Verify* statements, such as whether the statement "Vladimir Putin is currently the president of Russia," or "The atomic number for uranium is 100," is true or false.
- *Repeat* what you have learned, such as a poem, an article of the Constitution, a scientific formula, or a mathematical formula.

Research suggests that there are certain things teachers can do to help students maximize their memory-based learning (see Williams & Sternberg, 2002). These things include encouraging students (a) to space their learning over time and study sessions rather than massing it into a small number of study sessions, (b) to avoid studying materials that are similar (for example, French and Spanish) in close temporal proximity, to avoid confusion (or, in technical terms, proactive [forward] and retroactive [backward] interference), and to study the most important information near the beginning and the end of a session (the so-called serial-position effect, which gives a benefit to things studied near the beginning or ending of a session).

Strategy 2: Teaching for Analytical Learning
Teachers who teach for successful intelligence do not teach only for memory, because some students are not particularly adept as memory learners. I, myself, was not, as I mentioned above, and am not to this day. Many students have the ability to learn, but fail miserably when they sit down and try to memorize a set of isolated facts, or even when they are asked merely to recall a set of isolated facts.

Here are examples of teaching and assessing for analytical learning and thinking:

- *Analyze* an issue, such as why genocides continue to occur even today, or why certain elements are radioactive, or why children still find *Tom Sawyer* entertaining, or how to solve a particular algebraic factoring problem.
- *Evaluate* an issue, such as why unlimited political contributions can lead to corruption in a political system, how the Internet is vulnerable to catastrophic sabotage, what part of speech a certain word is, or how best to make a cake.
- *Explain* how the British Parliamentary system works, or why a wool blanket produces static electricity, or how to solve an arithmetic word problem, or why a character in a short story acted the way she did.
- *Compare and contrast* two or more items, such as the systems of government in China and England, or igneous and sedimentary rocks, or two different ways of proving a geometric theorem, or two novels.
- *Judge* the value of the characteristics of something, such as a law, or a scientific experiment, or a poem, or the metric system of measurement.

We have found it useful, in teaching for analytical thinking, to teach students how to use a problem-solving cycle in their thinking. The steps of the problem-solving cycle are what we refer to as metacomponents, or higher-order executive processes that are used to plan, monitor, and evaluate problem solving (Sternberg, 1985a). First, students need to recognize the existence of a problem (for example, the need to write a term paper). Second, they need to define exactly what the problem is (for example, what the topic of the term paper will be). Third, they need to allocate resources for the problem (for example, how much time to spend on the term paper). Fourth, they need to represent information about the problem (for example, using note cards, outlines, etc.). Fifth, they need to formulate a strategy for solving the problem (getting the paper done). Sixth, they need to monitor their progress as they solve the problem (is the paper getting done, or has one gotten stuck on some aspect of it?). Finally, they need to evaluate their work after it is done (proofread the paper and see how it reads).

Strategy 3: Teaching for Creative Learning

Teaching for successful intelligence also involves encouraging students to use and develop their creative-thinking skills. Such skills involve production of ideas that are novel, high in quality, and appropriate to the task at hand (Sternberg & Lubart, 1995). Teachers who teach for successful intelligence recognize that some students learn best when they are allowed to find their own way to learning material, and when they are left free to explore ideas that go beyond those in books or lectures.

Here are some examples of teaching and assessing for creative learning and thinking:

- *Create* a game for learning the names of the states, or a poem, or a haiku or a new numerical operation, or a scientific experiment.
- *Invent* a toy, or a new way of solving a difficult mathematics problem, or a new system of government that builds on old systems.
- *Explore* new ways of solving a mathematics problem beyond those taught by the teacher, or how to achieve a certain chemical reaction, or different ways of reading so as to improve your reading comprehension, or the nature of volcanoes.
- *Imagine* what it would be like to live in another country, or what will happen if temperatures on the Earth keep rising, or what Picasso might have been thinking when he painted *Guernica*, or what might happen if the government of England made it a crime to speak ill of the government.
- *Suppose* that people were paid to inform on their neighbors to the political party in power – what would happen?, or that all lakes instantly dried up – what would happen?, or that schools stopped teaching mathematics – what would happen, or that Germany had won World War II – what would have happened?
- *Synthesize* your knowledge of the Gulf War and the recent war in Afghanistan to propose a set of battle techniques likely to work in many unfamiliar terrains.

I believe that, to a large extent, creative thinking represents a decision to do thinking certain ways and to do certain things. To teach students to think creatively, they need to learn to make these decisions (Sternberg, 2000a). These decisions include, among other things, (a) redefining problems rather than merely accepting the way problems are presented, (b) being willing to take intellectual risks, (c) being willing to surmount obstacles when people criticize one's attempts at being creative, (d) being willing to work to persuade people of the value of one's creative ideas, and (e) believing that one truly has the potential to produce creative ideas in the first place.

Strategy 4: Teaching for Practical Learning
Some students are primarily practical learners. They do not catch on unless they see some kind of practical use for what they are learning. That is, they learn best if the material facilitates their adaptation to, shaping of, and selection of environments (Sternberg et al., 2000).

Here are some examples of teaching and assessing for practical learning and thinking:

- *Put into practice* what you have learned about measurement in baking a cake; your foreign-language instruction in speaking with a foreigner;

your knowledge of soils to determine whether a particular plant can grow adequately in a given soil.

- *Use* your knowledge of percentages or decimals in computing discounts; a lesson learned by a character in a novel in your own life; your knowledge of the effects of particulate matter in the atmosphere on vision to figure out whether a car driving behind you in the fog is substantially closer than it appears to be.
- *Utilize* a physical formula to figure out the speed at which a falling object will actually hit the ground; your understanding of cultural customs to figure out why someone from another culture behaves in a way you consider to be strange; the lesson you learned from a fable or a proverb to change your behavior with other people.
- *Implement* a plan for holding a classroom election; a strategy for conserving energy in your home; what you have learned in a driver education class in your actual driving; a psychological strategy for persuading people to contribute to charity.
- *Apply* your knowledge of political campaigns in history to run for class president; your knowledge of the principles of mixture problems to mixing paints to achieve a certain color; your understanding of the principles of good speaking to give a persuasive talk.

Part of teaching for practical thinking is teaching students to adopt certain attitudes in their intellectual work (Sternberg, 1986). These attitudes include ones such as (a) combating the tendency to procrastinate, (b) organizing oneself to get one's work done, (c) figuring out how one learns best, (d) avoiding the tendency to use self-pity as an excuse for working hard, and (e) avoiding blaming others for one's own failings.

Some General Principles

In teaching for successful intelligence, one is helping all students make the most of their skills by addressing all students at least some of the time. It is important to realize that teaching for successful intelligence does not mean teaching everything three times. Rather, one balances one's teaching strategies, so that one is teaching in each of the ways part of the time. An advantage of this procedure is that one does not have to know each student's exact strengths and weaknesses. By teaching in all of the ways, one is addressing some students' strengths at the same time one is addressing other students' weaknesses. Balancing teaching strategies guarantees that one will be addressing each student's strength at least some of the time. But one does not want to teach only to strengths, as students also need to learn how to compensate for and correct weaknesses.

It is also important to ensure that one's assessment practices match one's teaching practices. Sometimes, teachers teach in one way but assess in another way. For example, they may encourage critical thinking in class, but then give tests that merely measure recall. Students quickly learn that the real game of getting good marks is not the apparent game. The students then respond to the way they are assessed, not to the way they are taught. So it is crucial that the teacher value the same things in his or her assessment as in his or her teaching.

Comparison to Other Pedagogical Theories

No psychological theory or set of teaching techniques is completely new. Rather, theories and the teaching techniques that derive from them build on each other. It is thus useful to point out similarities and differences between teaching for successful intelligence and other ways of teaching, based on different theories.

One well-known theory is that of Bloom (1976; Bloom, Engelhart, Frost, Hill, & Krathwohl, 1956), known as Bloom's taxonomy. Bloom proposes a six-level taxonomy: knowledge, comprehension, application, analysis, synthesis, and evaluation. Teaching for memory is related to teaching for knowledge and comprehension; teaching for analytical thinking, to teaching for analysis and evaluation; teaching for creative thinking, to teaching for synthesis; and teaching for practical thinking, to teaching for application.

There are a few differences between the current theory and Bloom's. Here are four main ones.

First, the theory of successful intelligence does not view the three kinds of abilities as "hierarchically related." For example, one does not need to think for application (practically – lower in Bloom's hierarchy) in order to think for synthesis (creatively – higher in Bloom's hierarchy). On the contrary, much creative thinking is not necessarily practical at all (for example, most academic scholarship), and much practical thinking is not necessarily creative (for example, the thinking involved in filling out bureaucratic forms).

Second, the theory of successful intelligence parses skills differently. Analysis and evaluation are separated by synthesis in Bloom's theory, but in the theory of successful intelligence, they are seen as more related to each other than either is to synthetic thinking.

Third, the concepts of analytical, creative, and practical thinking are each somewhat broader than the terms of Bloom's taxonomy. As shown above, each of the three kinds of teaching includes, but is not limited to, the terms in Bloom's taxonomy. For example, synthesis is part of teaching for creative thinking, but only a small part of it.

Fourth, the techniques involved in teaching for successful intelligence derive from a theory of intelligence that has been tested in many different ways. Bloom's theory is not and was not intended to be a theory of intelligence.

Another related theory is that of Gardner (1983, 1993, 1999). Gardner's theory of multiple intelligences, like the theory of successful intelligence, attempts to extend our thinking about the nature of intelligence. Again, though, there are some key differences.

First, Gardner's theory deals with domains, positing linguistic intelligence, logical/mathematical intelligence, spatial intelligence, musical intelligence, naturalistic intelligence, bodily-kinesthetic intelligence, interpersonal intelligence, intrapersonal intelligence, and possibly existential intelligence. The theory of successful intelligence specifies classes of processes. Thus, at one level, the theories are largely complementary. One can teach analytically, creatively, or practically, for example, in the linguistic domain (analytical – analyze a poem, creative – write a short story, practical – write a persuasive essay), or in any other domain.

Second, Gardner includes as intelligences sets of skills that perhaps would not be viewed as intelligences in the theory of successful intelligence. For example, to survive in the world, everyone has to have at least some ability to think analytically, creatively, and practically. But it is not clear that, to survive in the world, everyone has to think musically.

Third, the theory of successful intelligence has been extensively validated predictively, and these predictions have been largely upheld. For example, in a series of studies, we have shown that the exploratory and confirmatory factor structures of sets of tests designed to measure triarchic abilities do indeed provide distinct factors corresponding to analytical, creative, and practical abilities, and that the model proposing these three separate factors is superior to alternative factorial models (Sternberg, Castejón, Prieto, Hautamäki, & Grigorenko, 2001; Sternberg, Grigorenko, Ferrari, & Clinkenbeard, 1999). In other studies, we have shown that the theory holds up cross culturally, for example, that the analytical and practical aspects of intelligence can be distinguished as well in countries outside the United States as they can in the United States (for example, Grigorenko & Sternberg, 2001; Sternberg et al., 2001). I am unaware of any predictive tests of the theory of multiple intelligences. Although such tests may seem like an abstract detail to many teachers, validation of a theory helps ensure that it does, indeed, characterize how people really think, rather than merely the investigators' or others' opinions of how they really think.

Generally, then, there are similarities and differences between the theory of successful intelligence, on the one hand, and two others theories – those of Bloom and Gardner – on the other. Effective teachers will probably not totally "buy into" any one theory. Rather they will select techniques from each theory that work most effectively for them.

The truth is that most educational programs are based on *no* theory. They are simply programs that their proponents believe to be successful, often without any data to back their efficacy. Why base an educational program on a theory in the first place? There are at least four reasons.

First, a theory potentially suggests what should be taught, how it should be taught, when it should be taught, to whom it should be taught, and why it should be taught. Atheoretical programs do not have this kind of motivation. Second, in a theory-based program, it is possible to state what the essential aspects of the program are (that is, those based on the theory) and what the nonessential aspects are. With an atheoretical program, it is hard to distinguish what is necessary from what is not. Third, a theory-based program suggests what forms assessments should take to match instruction. Atheoretical programs do not suggest assessment options. Finally, use of a theory-based program can advance scientific knowledge by testing the theory. If the theory is good, the program should work. If the program does not work, either the theory is wrong or the operationalization of the theory is inadequate. Atheoretical programs do not advance science in this way.

Why Teaching for Successful Intelligence is Successful

Earlier, we presented data regarding the success of teaching for successful intelligence. Why does teaching for successful intelligence work? There are at least six reasons:

- *Helping students capitalize on strengths.* Teaching for successful intelligence helps students learn in ways that work for them, rather than forcing them to learn in ways that do not work.
- *Helping students correct or compensate for weaknesses.* Teaching for successful intelligence helps students correct deficient skills, or at least to develop methods of compensation for these skills.
- *Multiple encodings.* This form of teaching encourages students to encode material not just in one way, but in three or four different ways (memory, analytical, creative, practical), so the students are more likely to retrieve the material when they need it.
- *Deeper encodings.* Teaching in this way also helps students encode material more deeply because the presentation of the material is more meaningful and more closely related to what they already know.
- *Motivation.* Teaching for successful intelligence is more interesting to most students, and hence motivates them more.
- *Job relevance.* Much of what students learn, and the way they learn it, bears little resemblance to what they will need to succeed on the job. For example, a typical introductory psychology course may require the

memorization of a great amount of material, but psychologists do not spend much of their time memorizing books or retrieving facts from books. Teaching for successful intelligence better helps students prepare for what they later will need to do on the job.

Objections

When any new system for teaching and assessment is introduced, teachers and administrators sometimes have objections. What kinds of objections have we encountered with the system of teaching for successful intelligence, and what are our replies? Here are five typical objections.

- *It is only for gifted students.* Some teachers believe that their students have enough of a problem learning the conventional way. Why introduce other ways that will just confuse them, especially teaching for creative thinking, which these teachers may see as high-falutin'? But these teachers have things backwards. The problem is that many students simply do not learn well in conventional ways. Teaching in other ways, rather than confusing them, enlightens them. Unless they are taught in other ways, they will just not learn much. And teaching for creative thinking is not high-falutin'. In these times of rapid change, all students need to learn to think in a way that maximizes their flexibility.
- *It is only for weak students.* Then there are teachers who say that teaching for successful intelligence is only for weak students. Their regular students learn just fine with the current system. But do they really learn so well? And is it ever the case that their learning cannot be improved? We believe that teaching always can be improved, and that teaching for successful intelligence is one way of doing it. Moreover, many good students are "good" in the sense of having developed adequate memory and analytical skills. But later in life, they will need creative and practical skills too. Schools should help students develop these skills.
- *It takes too much time to teach everything three ways.* This objection is based on a misunderstanding of what teaching for successful intelligence requires. It does not require everything be taught three times in three ways. Rather, the idea is for teachers to alternate, so that some material is being taught one way, other material, another way.
- *It is too hard to do.* Good teachers naturally teach for successful intelligence. They need only the bare minimum of instruction. Other teachers need more time to catch on. But once one catches on – which usually does not take an inordinate amount of time – it becomes like second nature. It is no harder, and perhaps even easier, than teaching in the regular way, because one begins to see alternative natural ways of teaching the same material.

- *My supervisor (principal, director, etc.) will not allow it.* This might be true in some instances. But our experience has been that school administrators are open to almost any form of teaching that is ethical so long as it improves student achievement and motivation.

CONCLUSION

Successful intelligence involves teaching students for memory, as well as analytically, creatively, and practically. It does not mean teaching everything in three ways. Rather, it means alternating teaching strategies so that teaching reaches (almost) every student at least some of the time. Teaching for successful intelligence also means helping students to capitalize on their strengths and to correct or compensate for their weaknesses. We believe we have good evidence to support teaching for successful intelligence. It improves learning outcomes, even if the only outcome measure is straightforward memory learning. We therefore encourage teachers seriously to consider use of this teaching method in their classrooms – at all grade levels and for all subject matter.

At this time, we have active research sites testing the efficacy of innovative aspects of our programs in many parts of the United States and abroad. We also have developed a software system, "CORE," which enables teachers to communicate with us and with each other if they encounter any problems while using our materials. In this way, they can get immediate feedback to help them solve problems, rather than waiting until someone can help them, perhaps much later.

Teaching for successful intelligence potentially provides benefits at multiple levels. It helps students to achieve at a level commensurate with their skills, rather than letting valuable skills, which could be used in facilitating learning, go to waste. It helps schools reach higher levels of achievement as a whole. And in these days of school accountability, reaching higher average scores is a goal virtually every school wants to reach. Finally, it helps society make better use of its human resources. There is no reason for a society to waste its most precious resource – its human talent. Teaching for successful intelligence helps ensure that talent will not go to waste.

PART II

CREATIVITY

3

Background Work on Creativity

Creativity is the ability to produce work that is novel (that is, original, unexpected), high in quality, and appropriate (that is, useful, meets task constraints) (Lubart, 1994; Ochse, 1990; Sternberg, 1988b, 1999b; Sternberg & Lubart, 1995, 1996). Creativity is a topic of wide scope, important at both the individual and societal levels for a wide range of task domains. At an individual level, creativity is relevant, for example, when solving problems on the job and in daily life. At a societal level, creativity can lead to new scientific findings, new movements in art, new inventions, and new social programs. The economic importance of creativity is clear because new products or services create jobs. Furthermore, individuals, organizations, and societies must adapt existing resources to changing task demands to remain competitive.

CREATIVITY AS A NEGLECTED RESEARCH TOPIC

As the first half of the twentieth century gave way to the second half, J. P. Guilford (1950), in his APA presidential address, challenged psychologists to address what he found to be a neglected but extremely important attribute: creativity. Guilford reported that less than two-tenths of one percent of the entries in *Psychological Abstracts* up to 1950 focused on creativity.

Interest in creativity research began to grow somewhat in the 1950s and a few research institutes concerned with creativity were founded. However, several indicators of work on creativity show that it remained a relatively marginal topic in psychology, at least until recently. Robert Sternberg and Todd Lubart (1996) analyzed the number of creativity references in *Psychological Abstracts* from 1975 to 1994. To conduct this analysis, they searched the computerized PsychLit database of journal articles using the database keywords of "creativity," "divergent thinking," and "creativity

This chapter was written in part in collaboration with Todd I. Lubart.

measurement." These terms are assigned by the database to articles whose content concerns primarily the subject of creativity. They also identified additional entries that contained the word stem "creativ-" somewhere in the title or abstract of the article but were not indexed by one of the keywords for creativity. They examined a random subset of these additional entries and found that they did not concern creativity to any notable extent and should be excluded from the set of articles on the subject. This analysis showed that approximately one-half of one percent of the articles indexed in *Psychological Abstracts* from 1975 to 1994 concerned creativity. For comparative purposes, articles on reading accounted for approximately one and one-half percent of the entries in *Psychological Abstracts* during the same twenty-year period, three times greater than for creativity.

If we look at introductory psychology textbooks as another index, we find that creativity is barely covered. Whereas intelligence, for example, gets a chapter or a major part of one, creativity gets a few paragraphs, if that (for example, Gleitman, 1986). Major psychology departments rarely give courses on creativity, although such courses are sometimes offered in educational psychology programs.

If creativity is so important to society, why has it traditionally been one of psychology's orphans? We believe that, historically, the study of creativity has had several strikes against it. We attempt to elicit what these strikes might be by reviewing briefly some of the history of the study of creativity (see Albert & Runco, 1999, for more details). During our analysis, we consider several of the main approaches to studying creativity, including mystical, pragmatic, psychoanalytic, psychometric, cognitive, and social–personality approaches. We then consider what we believe to be the most promising approach for future work on creativity, the confluence approach.

MYSTICAL APPROACHES TO THE STUDY OF CREATIVITY

The study of creativity has always been tinged – some might say tainted – with associations to mystical beliefs. Perhaps the earliest accounts of creativity were based on divine intervention. The creative person was seen as an empty vessel that a divine being filled with inspiration. The individual poured out the inspired ideas, forming an otherworldly product.

In this vein, Plato argued that a poet is able to create only that which the Muse dictates, and even today, people sometimes refer to their own muse as a source of inspiration. In Plato's view, one person might be inspired to create choral songs, another, epic poems (Rothenberg & Hausman, 1976). Mystical sources have often been suggested in creators' introspective reports (Ghiselin, 1985). For example, Rudyard Kipling referred to the "Daemon" that lives in the writer's pen: "My Daemon was with me in the Jungle Books, Kim, and both Puck books, and good care I took to walk delicately, lest he should withdraw.... When your Daemon is in charge, do not think consciously. Drift, wait, and obey" (Kipling, 1937/1985, p. 162).

The mystical approaches to the study of creativity have probably made it harder for scientists to be heard. Many people seem to believe, as they believe for love (see Sternberg, 1988a, 1988b), that creativity is something that just doesn't lend itself to scientific study, because it is a more spiritual process. We believe that it has been hard for scientific work to shake the deep-seated view of some that scientists are treading where they should not.

PRAGMATIC APPROACHES

Equally damaging for the scientific study of creativity, in our view, has been the takeover of the field, in the popular mind, by those who follow what might be referred to as a pragmatic approach. Those taking this approach have been concerned primarily with developing creativity, secondarily with understanding it, but almost not at all with testing the validity of their ideas about it.

Perhaps the foremost proponent of this approach is Edward De Bono, whose work on *lateral thinking* – seeing things broadly and from varied viewpoints – as well as other aspects of creativity has had what appears to be considerable commercial success (De Bono, 1971, 1985, 1992). De Bono's concern is not with theory, but with practice. Thus, for example, he suggests using a tool such as PMI to focus on the aspects of an idea that are pluses, minuses, and interesting. Or he suggests using the word *po*, derived from hypothesis, suppose, possible, and poetry, to provoke rather than judge ideas. Another tool, that of "thinking hats," has individuals metaphorically wear different hats, such as a white hat for data-based thinking, a red hat for intuitive thinking, a black hat for critical thinking, and a green hat for generative thinking, to stimulate seeing things from different points of view.

De Bono is not alone in this enterprise. Osborn (1953), based on his experiences in advertising agencies, developed the technique of brainstorming to encourage people to solve problems creatively by seeking many possible solutions in an atmosphere constructive rather than critical and inhibitory. Gordon (1961) developed a method called synectics, which involves primarily seeing analogies but also stimulating creative thinking.

More recently, authors such as Adams (1974) and von Oech (1983) have suggested that people often construct a series of false beliefs that interfere with creative functioning. For example, some people believe that there is only one "right" answer and that ambiguity must be avoided whenever possible. People can become creative by identifying and removing these mental blocks. Von Oech (1986) has also suggested that we need to adopt the roles of explorer, artist, judge, and warrior in order to foster our creative productivity.

These approaches have had considerable public visibility, in much the way that Leo Buscaglia gave visibility to the study of love. And they may well be useful. From our point of view as psychologists, however, the approaches lack any basis in serious psychological theory nor have there been serious empirical attempts to validate them. Techniques can work in the absence of psychological theory or validation, but the effect of such approaches is often to leave people associating a phenomenon with commercialization, and to see it as less than a serious endeavor for psychological study.

THE PSYCHODYNAMIC APPROACH

The psychodynamic approach can be considered the first of the major twentieth-century theoretical approaches to the study of creativity. Based on the idea that creativity arises from the tension between conscious reality and unconscious drives, Freud (1908/1959) proposed that writers and artists produce creative work as a way to express their unconscious wishes in a publicly acceptable fashion. These unconscious wishes may concern power, riches, fame, honor, or love (Vernon, 1970). Case studies of eminent creators, such as Leonardo da Vinci (Freud, 1910/1964), were used to support these ideas.

Later, the psychoanalytic approach introduced the concepts of adaptive regression and elaboration for creativity (Kris, 1952). *Adaptive regression*, the primary process, refers to the intrusion of unmodulated thoughts in consciousness. Unmodulated thoughts can occur during active problem solving, but often occur during sleep, intoxication from drugs, fantasies or daydreams, or psychoses. *Elaboration*, the secondary process, refers to the reworking and transformation of primary-process material through reality-oriented, ego-controlled thinking. Other theorists (for example, Kubie, 1958) emphasized that the preconscious, which falls between conscious reality and the encrypted unconscious, is the true source of creativity because thoughts are loose and vague but interpretable. In contrast to Freud, Kubie claimed that unconscious conflicts actually have a negative effect on creativity because they lead to fixated, repetitive thoughts. Recent work has recognized the importance of both the primary and secondary processes (Noy, 1969; Rothenberg, 1979; Suler, 1980; Werner & Kaplan, 1963).

Although the psychodynamic approach may offer some insights into creativity, psychodynamic theory was not at the center of the emerging scientific psychology. The early twentieth-century schools of psychology, such as structuralism, functionalism, and behaviorism, devoted practically no resources at all to the study of creativity. The Gestaltists studied a portion of creativity – insight – but their study never went much beyond labeling, as opposed to characterizing the nature of insight.

Further isolating creativity research, the psychodynamic approach and other early work on creativity relied on case studies of eminent creators. This methodology has been criticized historically because of the difficulty of measuring proposed theoretical constructs (such as primary process thought), and the amount of selection and interpretation that can occur in a case study (Weisberg, 1993). Although there is nothing a priori wrong with case study methods, the emerging scientific psychology valued controlled, experimental methods. Thus both theoretical and methodological issues served to isolate the study of creativity from mainstream psychology.

PSYCHOMETRIC APPROACHES

When we think of creativity, eminent artists or scientists such as Michelangelo or Einstein immediately come to mind. These highly creative people are rare, however, and difficult to study in the psychological laboratory. In his APA address, Guilford (1950) noted that the difficulty of studying highly creative people in the laboratory had limited research on creativity. He proposed that creativity could be studied in everyday subjects using paper-and-pencil tasks. One of these was the Unusual Uses Test, in which an examinee thinks of as many uses for a common object (such as a brick) as possible. Many researchers adopted Guilford's suggestion and "divergent thinking" tasks quickly became the main instruments for measuring creative thinking. The tests were a convenient way of comparing people on a standard "creativity" scale.

Building on Guilford's work, Torrance (1974) developed the *Torrance Tests of Creative Thinking*. These tests consist of several relatively simple verbal and figural tasks that involve divergent thinking plus other problem-solving skills. The tests can be scored for fluency (total number of relevant responses), flexibility (number of different categories of relevant responses), originality (the statistical rarity of the responses), and elaboration (amount of detail in the responses). Some of the subtests from the Torrance battery include:

1. Asking questions: The examinee writes out all the questions he or she can think of, based on a drawing of a scene.
2. Product improvement: The examinee lists ways to change a toy monkey so that children will have more fun playing with it.
3. Unusual uses: The examinee lists interesting and unusual uses for a cardboard box.
4. Circles: The examinee expands empty circles into different drawings and titles them.

Catherine Cox (1926), working with Lewis Terman, believed that exceptionally creative people are also exceptionally intelligent. She published

IQ estimates for 301 of the most eminent persons who lived between 1450 and 1850. They selected their names from a list of one thousand prepared by James McKeen Cattell, who determined eminence by the amount of space allotted in biographical dictionaries. From Cattell's list, they deleted hereditary aristocracy and nobility unless those individuals distinguished themselves beyond the status due to their birth, those born before 1450, those with a rank of over No. 510 on the original list, and eleven names for whom no adequate records of creative contributors were available. These deletions left 282 persons whose IQs were summarized as Group A. In addition, they discussed a Group B, which consisted of 19 miscellaneous cases from those over No. 510 on the original list, bringing the grand total to 301.

To estimate IQ, Cox, Terman, and Maud Merrill (Cox, 1926) examined biographies, letters, and other writings and records for evidence of the earliest period of instruction; the nature of the earliest learning; the earliest productions; age of first reading and of first mathematical performance; typical precocious activities; unusually intelligent applications of knowledge; the recognition of similarities or differences; the amount and character of the reading; the range of interests; school standing and progress; early maturity of attitude or judgment; the tendency to discriminate, to generalize, or to theorize; and family standing. Their IQ estimates are necessarily subjective. In a sense, though, the estimates have an ecological validity with regard to real-life intelligence that is not seen in standard IQ tests. The final estimated IQs were averaged from the individual estimates of the three expert raters mentioned above, Cox, Terman, and Merrill. Interrater reliability was .90 for the childhood estimate and .89 for the young adulthood estimate (calculated from intercorrelations in Cox, 1926, pp. 67–68).

An example of some of the factors that contributed to their estimates can be seen in a description of Francis Galton, whose IQ Terman estimated to be 200. "Francis knew his capital letters by twelve months and both his alphabets by eighteen months; . . . he could read a little book, *Cobwebs to Catch Flies*, when $2\frac{1}{2}$ years old, and could sign his name before 3 years" (Cox, 1926, pp. 41–42). By four years of age, he could say all the Latin substantives, adjectives, and active verbs; could add and multiply; read a little French; and knew the clock. At five, he was quoting from Walter Scott. By six, he was familiar with the *Iliad* and the *Odyssey*. At seven, he was reading Shakespeare for fun and could memorize a page by reading it twice. Clearly, Galton's record is one of an exceptional child.

Cox concluded that the average IQ of the group, 135 for childhood and 145 for young adulthood, was probably too low because of instructions to regress toward the mean of 100 for unselected populations (whereas this group's means were 135 and 145) whenever data were unavailable. Also, unreliability of the data may have caused regression to the mean. One of the problems Cox noted in the data was a strong correlation, .77, between IQ and the reliability of the available data: The more reliable the data, the higher the IQ, and the higher the IQ, the more reliable the data on which it was based. She concluded that if more reliable data had been available, all the IQs would have been estimated as higher. She therefore corrected the original estimates, bringing the group average up to 155 for childhood and 165 for young adulthood.

As Cox was careful to point out, the IQs are not estimates of the actual person's IQ, but rather, estimates of the record of that person. "The IQ of Newton or of Lincoln recorded in these pages is the IQ of the Newton or of the Lincoln of whom we have record. But the records are admittedly incomplete" (Cox, 1926, p. 8).

Cox found the correlation between IQ and rank order of eminence to be .16, plus or minus .039 (Cox, 1926, p. 55), after correcting for unreliability of the data. Dean Simonton (1976) reexamined the Cox data using multiple regression techniques. He showed that the correlation between intelligence and ranked eminence that Cox found was an artifact of unreliability of data and, especially, of a time-wise sampling bias – those more recently born had both lower estimated IQs and lower ranks of estimated eminence. In Simonton's analysis, the relationship between intelligence and ranked eminence was zero if birth year was controlled for (Simonton, 1976, pp. 223–224). In any case, Cox recognized the role of factors other than IQ in eminence and concluded that "high but not the highest intelligence, combined with the greatest degree of persistence, will achieve greater eminence than the highest degree of intelligence with somewhat less persistence" (Cox, 1926, p. 187).

Three basic findings concerning conventional conceptions of intelligence as measured by IQ and creativity are generally agreed on (see, for example, Barron & Harrington, 1981; Lubart, 1994). First, creative people tend to show above average IQs, often above 120 (see Renzulli, 1986). This figure is not a cutoff, but rather an expression of the fact that people with low or even average IQs do not seem to be well represented among the ranks of highly creative individuals. Cox's (1926) geniuses had an estimated average IQ of 165. Barron estimated the mean IQ of his creative writers to be 140 or higher, based on their scores on the Terman Concept Mastery Test (Barron, 1963, p. 242). The other groups in the IPAR studies, that is, mathematicians and research scientists, were also above average in intelligence. Anne Roe (1952, 1972), who did similarly thorough assessments of eminent scientists before the IPAR group was set up, estimated IQs for her participants that ranged between 121 and 194, with medians between 137 and 166, depending on whether the IQ test was verbal, spatial, or mathematical.

Second, above an IQ of 120, IQ does not seem to matter as much to creativity as it does below 120. In other words, creativity may be more highly correlated with IQ below an IQ of 120, but only weakly or not at all correlated with it above an IQ of 120. (This relationship is often called the threshold theory. See the contrast with Hayes's [1989] certification theory discussed below). In the architects study, in which the average IQ was 130 (significantly above average), the correlation between intelligence and creativity was −.08, not significantly different from zero (Barron, 1969, p. 42). But in the military officer study, in which participants were of average intelligence, the correlation was .33 (Barron, 1963, p. 219). These results suggest that extremely highly creative people often have high IQs, but not necessarily that people with high IQs tend to be extremely creative.

Some investigators (for example, Simonton, 1994; Sternberg, 1996) have suggested that very high IQ may actually interfere with creativity. Those who have very high IQs may be so highly rewarded for their IQ-like (analytical) skills that they fail to develop their creative potential. In a reexamination of the Cox (1926) data, Simonton (1976) found that the eminent leaders showed a significant negative correlation, −.29, between their IQs and eminence. Simonton explained that

> leaders must be understood by a large mass of people before they can achieve eminence, unlike the creators, who need only appeal to an intellectual elite. . . . Scientific, philosophical, literary, artistic, and musical creators do not have to achieve eminence in their own lifetime to earn posterity's recognition, whereas military, political, or religious leaders must have contemporary followers to attain eminence. (Simonton, 1976, pp. 220–222)

Third, the correlation between IQ and creativity is variable, usually ranging from weak to moderate (Flescher, 1963; Getzels & Jackson, 1962; Guilford, 1967; Herr, Moore, & Hasen, 1965; Torrance, 1962; Wallach & Kogan, 1965; Yamamoto, 1964). The correlation depends in part on what aspects of creativity and intelligence are being measured, and how they are being measured as well as in what field the creativity is manifested. The role of intelligence is different in art and music, for instance, than it is in mathematics and science (McNemar, 1964).

An obvious drawback to the tests used and assessments done by Roe and Guilford is the time and expense involved in administering them as well as the subjective scoring. In contrast, Mednick (1962) produced a thirty-item, objectively scored, forty-minute test of creative ability called the Remote Associates Test (RAT). The test is based on his theory that the creative thinking process is the "forming of associative elements into new combinations which either meet specified requirements or are in some way useful. The more mutually remote the elements of the new combination, the more creative the process or solution" (Mednick, 1962). Because the ability to make these combinations and arrive at a creative solution necessarily depends on the existence of the stuff of the combinations, that is, the associative elements, in a person's knowledge base and because the probability and speed of attainment of a creative solution are influenced by the organization of the person's associations, Mednick's theory suggests that creativity and intelligence are very related; they are overlapping sets.

In the RAT the test-taker supplies a fourth word that is remotely associated with three given words. Samples (not actual test items) of given words are:

1) rat   blue   cottage

2) surprise   line   birthday

3) out   dog   cat

(Answers are 1. *cheese;* 2. *party;* 3. *house.*)

Moderate correlations of .55, .43, and .41 have been shown between the RAT and the WISC (Wechsler Intelligence Scale for Children), the SAT verbal, and the Lorge-Thorndike Verbal intelligence measures, respectively (Mednick & Andrews, 1967). Correlations with quantitative intelligence measures were lower ($r = .20$–$.34$). Correlations with other measures of creative performance have been more variable (Andrews, 1975).

This psychometric revolution for measuring creativity had both positive and negative effects on the field. On the positive side, the tests facilitated research by providing a brief, easy to administer, objectively scorable assessment device. Furthermore, research was now possible with "everyday" people (that is, noneminent samples). However, there were some negative effects as well. First, some researchers criticized brief paper-and-pencil tests as trivial, inadequate measures of creativity; larger productions such as actual drawings or writing samples should be used instead. Second, other critics suggested that neither fluency, flexibility, originality, nor elaboration scores captured the concept of creativity. In fact, the definition and criteria for creativity are a matter of ongoing debate and relying on the objectively defined statistical rarity of a response with regard to all the responses of a subject population is only one of many options. Other possibilities include using the social consensus of judges. Third, some researchers rejected the assumption that noneminent samples could shed light on eminent levels of creativity, which was the ultimate goal for many studies of creativity. Thus a certain malaise developed toward, and continues to accompany, the paper-and-pencil assessment of creativity. Some psychologists, at least, avoided this measurement quagmire in favor of less problematic research topics.

COGNITIVE APPROACHES

The cognitive approach to creativity seeks to understand the mental representations and processes underlying creative thought. By studying, say, perception, or memory, one would already be studying the bases of creativity; thus, the study of creativity would merely represent an extension, and perhaps not a very large one, of work already being done under another guise. For example, in the cognitive area, creativity was often subsumed under the study of intelligence. We do not argue with the idea that creativity and intelligence are related to each other. However, the subsumption has often been so powerful that researchers such as Wallach and Kogan (1965), among others, had to write at length on why creativity and intelligence should be viewed as distinct entities. In more recent cognitive work, Weisberg (1986, 1988, 1993, 1999) has proposed that creativity involves essentially ordinary cognitive processes yielding extraordinary products. Weisberg attempted to show that the insights depend on subjects using conventional cognitive processes (such as analogical transfer) applied to knowledge already stored in memory. He did so through the use of case studies of eminent creators and laboratory research, such as studies with Duncker's (1945) candle problem. This problem requires participants to attach a candle to a wall using only objects available in a picture (candle, box of tacks, and book of matches). Langley and colleagues (1987) made a similar claim about the ordinary nature of creative thinking.

As a concrete example of this approach, Weisberg and Alba (1981) had people solve the notorious nine-dot problem. In this problem, people are asked to connect all the dots, which are arranged in the shape of a square with three rows of three dots each, using no more than four straight lines, never arriving at a given dot twice, and never lifting their pencil from the page. The problem can be solved only if people allow their line segments to go outside the periphery of the dots. Typically, the solution of this task had been viewed as hinging on the insight that one had to go "outside the box." Weisberg and Alba showed that even when people were given the insight, they still had difficulty in solving the problem. In other words, whatever is required to solve the nine-dot problem, it is not just some kind of extraordinary insight.

There have been studies with both human subjects and computer simulations of creative thought. Approaches based on the study of human subjects are perhaps prototypically exemplified by the work of Finke, Ward, and Smith (1992) (see also contributions to Smith, Ward, & Finke, 1995; Sternberg & Davidson, 1994; Ward, Smith, & Finke, 1999). Finke and his colleagues have proposed what they call the *Geneplore model*, according to which there are two main processing phases in creative thought: a generative phase and an exploratory phase. In the generative phase, an individual constructs mental representations referred to as preinventive structures, which have properties promoting creative discoveries. In the exploratory phase, these properties are used to come up with creative ideas. A number of mental processes may enter into these phases of creative invention, such as retrieval, association, synthesis, transformation, analogical transfer, and categorical reduction (that is, mentally reducing objects or elements to more primitive categorical descriptions). In a typical experimental test based on the model (see, for example, Finke, 1990), participants will be shown parts of objects, such as a circle, a cube, a parallelogram, and a cylinder. On a given trial, three parts will be named, and participants will be asked to imagine combining the parts to produce a practical object or device. For example, participants might imagine a tool, a weapon, or a piece of furniture. The objects thus produced are then rated by judges for their practicality and originality.

Computer-simulation approaches, reviewed by Boden (1992, 1999), have as their goal the production of creative thought by a computer in a manner that simulates what people do. Langley, Simon, Bradshaw, and Zytgow (1987), for example, developed a set of programs that rediscover basic scientific laws. These computational models rely on heuristics – problem-solving guidelines – for searching a data set or conceptual space and finding hidden relationships between input variables. The initial program, called BACON, uses heuristics such as "if the value of two numerical terms increases together, consider their ratio" to search data for patterns. One of BACON's accomplishments has been to examine observational data on the orbits of planets available to Kepler and to rediscover Kepler's third law of planetary motion. This program is unlike creative functioning, however, in that the problems are given to it in structured form, whereas creative functioning is largely about figuring out what the problems are. Further programs have extended the search heuristics, the ability to transform data sets, and the ability to reason with qualitative data and scientific concepts. There are also models concerning an artistic domain. For example, Johnson-Laird (1988) developed a jazz improvisation program in which novel deviations from the basic jazz chord sequences are guided by harmonic constraints (or tacit principles of jazz) and random choice when several allowable directions for the improvisation exist.

SOCIAL-PERSONALITY APPROACHES

Developing in parallel with the cognitive approach, work in the social–personality approach has focused on personality variables, motivational variables, and the sociocultural environment as sources of creativity. Researchers such as Amabile (1983), Barron (1968, 1969), Eysenck (1993), Gough (1979), MacKinnon (1965) and others have noted that certain personality traits often characterize creative people. Through correlational studies and research contrasting high- and low-creative samples (at both eminent and everyday levels), a large set of potentially relevant traits has been identified (Barron & Harrington, 1981). These traits include independence of judgment, self-confidence, attraction to complexity, aesthetic orientation, and risk taking.

Proposals regarding self-actualization and creativity can also be considered within the personality tradition. According to Maslow (1968), boldness, courage, freedom, spontaneity, self-acceptance, and other traits lead a person to realize his or her full potential. Rogers (1954) described the tendency toward self-actualization as having motivational force and being promoted by a supportive, evaluation-free environment.

Focusing on motivation for creativity, a number of theorists have hypothesized the relevance of intrinsic motivation (Amabile, 1983; Crutchfield, 1962; Golann, 1962), need for order (Barron, 1963), need for achievement (McClelland, Atkinson, Clark, & Lowell, 1953), and other motives. Amabile (1983; Hennessey & Amabile, 1988) and her colleagues have conducted seminal research on intrinsic and extrinsic motivation. Studies using motivational training and other techniques have manipulated these motivations and observed effects on creative performance tasks, such as writing poems and making collages.

Finally, the relevance of the social environment to creativity has also been an active area of research. At the societal level, Simonton (1984, 1988, 1994, 1999) has conducted numerous studies in which eminent levels of creativity over large spans of time in diverse cultures have been statistically linked to environmental variables. These variables include, among others, cultural diversity, war, availability of role models, availability of resources (such as financial support), and number of competitors in a domain. Cross-cultural comparisons (for example, Lubart, 1990) and anthropological case studies (for example, Maduro, 1976; Silver, 1981) have demonstrated cultural variability in the expression of creativity. Moreover, they have shown that cultures differ simply in how much they value the creative enterprise.

The cognitive and social–personality approaches have each provided valuable insights into creativity. If you look for research that investigates both cognitive and social-personality variables at the same time, however, you would find only a handful of studies. The cognitive work on creativity has tended to ignore the personality and social system, and the social–personality approaches have tended to have little or nothing to say about the mental representations and processes underlying creativity.

Looking beyond the field of psychology, Wehner, Csikszentmihalyi, and Magyari-Beck (1991) examined 100 recent doctoral dissertations on creativity. They found a "parochial isolation" of the various studies concerning creativity. There were relevant dissertations from psychology, education, business, history, history of science, and other fields, such as sociology and political science. The different fields tended to use different terms, however, and focus on different aspects of what seemed to be the same basic phenomenon. For example, business dissertations used the term "innovation" and tended to look at the organizational level whereas psychology dissertations used the term "creativity" and looked at the level of the individual. Wehner, Csikszentmihalyi, and Magyari-Beck (1991) describe the situation with creativity research in terms of the fable of the blind men and the elephant. "We touch different parts of the same beast and derive distorted pictures of the whole from what we know: 'The elephant is like a snake,' says the one who only holds its tail; 'The elephant is like a wall,' says the one who touches its flanks" (p. 270).

EVOLUTIONARY APPROACHES TO CREATIVITY

The evolutionary approach to creativity was instigated by Donald Campbell (1960), who suggested that the same mechanisms that have been applied to the study of the evolution of organisms could be applied to the evolution of ideas. This idea has been enthusiastically picked up by a number of investigators (Perkins, 1995; Simonton, 1995, 1998, 1999).

The idea underlying this approach is that there are two basic steps in the generation and propagation of creative ideas. The first is *blind variation*, by which the creator generates an idea without any real idea of whether the idea would be successful (selected for) in the world of ideas. Indeed, Dean Simonton (1996) argues that creators do not have the slightest idea which of their ideas will succeed. As a result, their best bet for producing lasting ideas is to go for a large quantity of ideas. The reason is that their hit rate remains relatively constant through their professional life span. In other words, they have a fixed proportion of ideas that will succeed. The more ideas they have in all, the more ideas they have that will achieve success.

The second step is *selective retention*. In this step, the field in which the creator works either retains the idea for the future or lets it die out. Those ideas that are selectively retained are the ones that are judged to be novel and of value, that is, creative. This process as well as blind generation are described further by Cziko (1998).

Does an evolutionary model really adequately describe creativity? Robert Sternberg (1997b) argues that it does not, and David Perkins (1998) also has doubts. Sternberg argues that it seems utterly implausible that great creators such as Mozart, Einstein, or Picasso were using nothing more than blind variation to come up with their ideas. Good creators, like experts of any kind, may or may not have more ideas than other people have, but they have better ideas, ones that are more likely to be selectively retained. And the reason they are more likely to be selectively retained is that they were not produced in a blind fashion. This debate is by no means resolved, however, and is likely to continue into the future for some time to come.

Were it the case that an understanding of creativity required a multidisciplinary approach, the result of a unidisciplinary approach might be that we would view a part of the whole as the whole. At the same time, though, we would have an incomplete explanation of the phenomenon we are seeking to explain, leaving dissatisfied those who do not subscribe to

the particular discipline doing the explaining. We believe that traditionally this has been the case for creativity. Recently, theorists have begun to
develop confluence approaches to creativity, which we now discuss.

CONFLUENCE APPROACHES TO THE STUDY OF CREATIVITY

Many recent works on creativity hypothesize that multiple components
must converge for creativity to occur (Amabile, 1983; Csikszentmihalyi,
1988; Gardner, 1993; Gruber, 1989; Gruber & Wallace, 1999; Lubart, 1994;
Mumford & Gustafson, 1988; Perkins, 1981; Simonton, 1988; Sternberg,
1985a; Sternberg & Lubart, 1991, 1995; Weisberg, 1993; Woodman &
Schoenfeldt, 1989). Sternberg (1985b), for example, examined laypersons'
and experts' conceptions of the creative person. People's implicit theories contain a combination of cognitive and personality elements, such
as "connects ideas," "sees similarities and differences," "has flexibility,"
"has aesthetic taste," "is unorthodox," "is motivated," "is inquisitive," and
"questions societal norms."

At the level of explicit theories, Amabile (1983, 1996; Collins &
Amabile, 1999) describes creativity as the confluence of intrinsic motivation, domain-relevant knowledge and abilities, and creativity-relevant
skills. The creativity-relevant skills include (a) a cognitive style that involves coping with complexities and breaking one's mental set during
problem solving, (b) knowledge of heuristics for generating novel ideas,
such as trying a counterintuitive approach, and (c) a work style characterized by concentrated effort, an ability to set aside problems, and high
energy.

Gruber and his colleagues (Gruber, 1981, 1989; Gruber & Davis, 1988)
have proposed a developmental *evolving-systems model* for understanding creativity. A person's knowledge, purpose, and affect grow over time,
amplify deviations that an individual encounters, and lead to creative products. Developmental changes in the knowledge system have been documented in cases such as Charles Darwin on evolution. Purpose refers to
a set of interrelated goals, which also develop and guide an individual's
behavior. Finally, the affect or mood system notes the influence of joy or
frustration on the projects undertaken.

Csikszentmihalyi (1988, 1996) has taken a different "systems" approach
and highlights the interaction of the individual, domain, and field. An individual draws on information in a domain and transforms or extends
it via cognitive processes, personality traits, and motivation. The field,
consisting of people who control or influence a domain (for example, art
critics and gallery owners), evaluates and selects new ideas. The domain, a
culturally defined symbol system, preserves and transmits creative products to other individuals and future generations. Gardner (1993; see also
Policastro & Gardner, 1999) has conducted case studies that suggest that

the development of creative projects may stem from an anomaly within a system (for example, tension between competing critics in a field) or moderate asynchronies between the individual, domain, and field (for example, unusual individual talent for a domain). In particular, Gardner (1993) has analyzed the lives of seven individuals who made highly creative contributions in the twentieth century, each specializing in one of the multiple intelligences (Gardner, 1983): Sigmund Freud (intrapersonal), Albert Einstein (logical–mathematical), Pablo Picasso (spatial), Igor Stravinsky (musical), T. S. Eliot (linguistic), Martha Graham (bodily–kinesthetic), and Mohandas Gandhi (interpersonal). Charles Darwin would be an example of someone with extremely high naturalist intelligence. Gardner points out, however, that most of these individuals actually had strengths in more than one intelligence, and that they had notable weaknesses in others (for example, Freud's weaknesses may have been in spatial and musical intelligences).

Although creativity can be understood in terms of uses of the multiple intelligences to generate new and even revolutionary ideas, Gardner's (1993) analysis goes well beyond the intellectual. For example, Gardner pointed out two major themes in the behavior of these creative giants. First, they tended to have a matrix of support at the time of their creative breakthroughs. Second, they tended to drive a "Faustian bargain" whereby they gave up many of the pleasures people typically enjoy in life in order to attain extraordinary success in their careers. It is not clear that these attributes are intrinsic to creativity, per se, however: Rather, they seem to be associated with those who have been driven to exploit their creative gifts in a way that leads them to attain eminence.

Gardner further followed Csikszentmihalyi (1988, 1996) in distinguishing between the importance of the domain (the body of knowledge about a particular subject area) and the field (the context in which this body of knowledge is studied and elaborated on, including the persons working with the domain, such as critics, publishers, and other "gate keepers"). Both are important to the development, and ultimately, the recognition of creativity.

A final confluence theory considered here is Sternberg and Lubart's (1991, 1995) *investment theory of creativity*. This theory is discussed in the next chapter.

In general, confluence theories of creativity offer the possibility of accounting for diverse aspects of creativity (Lubart, 1994). For example, analyses of scientific and artistic achievements suggest that the median creativity of work in a domain tends to fall toward the lower end of the distribution and the upper – high creativity – tail extends quite far. This pattern can be explained through the need for multiple components of creativity to co-occur in order for the highest levels of creativity to be achieved. As another example, the partial domain-specificity of creativity that is often observed can be explained through the mixture of some relatively domain-specific components for creativity such as knowledge and other more domain-general components such as, perhaps, the personality trait of perseverance. Creativity, then, is largely something that people show in a particular domain.

TYPES OF CREATIVE CONTRIBUTIONS

Generally, we think of creative contributions as being of a single kind. A number of researchers on creativity have questioned this assumption, however. There are a number of ways of distinguishing among types of creative contributions. It is important to remember, though, that creative contributions can be viewed in different ways at different times. At a given time, the field can never be sure whose work will withstand the judgments of the field over time (such as that of Mozart) and whose work will not (such as that of Salieri) (Therivel, 1999).

Theorists of creativity and related topics have recognized that there are different types of creative contributions (see reviews in Ochse, 1990; Sternberg, 1988b; Weisberg, 1993). For example, Kuhn (1970) distinguished between normal and revolutionary science. Normal science expands on or otherwise elaborates on an already existing paradigm of scientific research, whereas revolutionary science proposes a new paradigm. The same kind of distinction can be applied to the arts and letters.

Gardner (1993, 1994) has also described different types of creative contributions individuals can make. They include (a) solving a well-defined problem, (b) devising an encompassing theory, (c) creating a "frozen work," (d) performing a ritualized work, and (e) rendering a "high-stakes" performance.

Other bases for distinguishing among types of creative contributions also exist. For example, psychoeconomic models such as those of Rubenson and Runco (1992) and Sternberg and Lubart (1991, 1995, 1996) can distinguish different types of contributions in terms of the parameters of the models. In the Sternberg-Lubart model, contributions might differ in the extent to which they "defy the crowd" or in the extent to which they redefine how a field perceives a set of problems.

Simonton's (1997) model of creativity also proposes parameters of creativity, and that contributions might be seen as differing in terms of the extent to which they vary from other contributions and in the extent to which they are selected for recognition by a field of endeavor (see also Campbell, 1960; Perkins, 1995; Simonton, 1997). But in no case were these models intended explicitly to distinguish among types of creative contributions.

Maslow (1967) distinguished more generally between two types of creativity, which he referred to as primary and secondary. Primary creativity is the kind a person uses to become self-actualized – to find fulfillment in him- or herself and in his or her life. Secondary creativity is the kind with which scholars in the field are more familiar – the kind that leads to creative achievements typically recognized by a field.

Ward, Smith, and Finke (1999) have noted that there is evidence to favor the roles of both focusing (Bowers et al., 1990; Kaplan & Simon, 1990) and exploratory thinking (Bransford & Stein, 1984; Getzels & Csikszentmiyalyi, 1976) in creative thinking. In focusing, one concentrates on pursuing a single problem-solving approach, whereas in exploratory thinking one considers many such approaches. A second distinction made by Ward and his colleagues is between domain-specific (Clement, 1989; Langley, Simon, Bradshaw, & Zytkow, 1987; Perkins, 1981; Weisberg, 1986) and universal (Finke, 1990, 1995; Guilford, 1968; Koestler, 1964) creativity skills. Finally, Ward and his colleagues distinguish between unstructured (Bateson, 1979; Findlay & Lumsden, 1988; Johnson-Laird, 1988) and structured or systematic (Perkins, 1981; Ward, 1994; Weisberg, 1986) creativity.

SUMMARY

Creativity is the ability to produce novel, high-quality, task-appropriate products. Creativity has been a relatively neglected topic in psychology. Among those who have studied creativity, a number of different approaches have been used. Mystical approaches have suggested that creativity has ineffable properties that are impervious to scientific investigation. Pragmatic approaches generally focus on the use of creativity and how to increase creativity. Psychodynamic approaches focus on the unconscious processes underlying creativity. Psychometric approaches concentrate on how creativity can be measured. Cognitive approaches deal with the information processing and mental representations underlying creativity. Social–personality approaches deal with the roles of other people and of personality traits as well as motivation. Evolutionary approaches view creativity as an adaptation that enhances an individual's chances of survival and hence of reproduction. And confluence approaches integrate these various other approaches.

4

The Investment Theory of Creativity as a Decision

What is creativity and how does it develop? Underlying this chapter is a single central notion – that, to a large extent, creativity is a decision. The chapter is divided into three parts: the decision to be creative, the decision of how to be creative, and implementation of these decisions.

Our investment theory (Sternberg & Lubart, 1991, 1995) concerns the *decision to be creative*. Called the investment theory, it is based on the notion that creative people *decide* to buy low and sell high in the world of ideas – that is, they generate ideas that tend to "defy the crowd" (buy low), and then, when they have persuaded many people, they sell high, meaning they move on to the next unpopular idea (see also Rubenson & Runco, 1992). I first describe the proposed theory. Then I describe empirical work supporting at least some aspects of the theory.

I consider creativity in both a minor ("little c") and a major ("big C") sense. The difference between the two often is whether a contribution is creative only with respect to myself or with respect to a field as well. Psychologically, however, the processes may be quite similar or the same. From the point of view of the field the contributions are quite different.

Research within the investment framework has yielded support for this model (Lubart & Sternberg, 1995). This research has used tasks such as (a) writing short stories using unusual titles (for example, "The Octopus' Sneakers"), (b) drawing pictures with unusual themes (for example, the earth from an insect's point of view), (c) devising creative advertisements for boring products (for example, cufflinks), and (d) solving unusual scientific problems (for example, how we could tell if someone had been on the moon within the past month). This research showed creative performance to be moderately domain specific, and to be predicted by a combination of certain resources, as described next.

Work on the nature and testing of the investment theory was done in collaboration with Todd I. Lubart. Work on developing creative thinking has been done in collaboration with Wendy Williams and Elena L. Grigorenko.

According to the investment theory, creativity requires a confluence of six distinct but interrelated resources: intellectual abilities, knowledge, styles of thinking, personality, motivation, and environment. Although levels of these resources are sources of individual differences, often the decision to use a resource is a more important source of individual differences. Below I discuss the resources and the role of decision making in each.

Intellectual skills. Three intellectual skills are particularly important (Sternberg, 1985a): (a) the creative skill to see problems in new ways and to escape the bounds of conventional thinking; (b) the analytic skill to recognize which of one's ideas are worth pursuing and which are not; and (c) the practical–contextual skill to know how to persuade others of the value of one's ideas. The confluence of these three skills is important. Using analytic skills in the absence of the other two results in powerful critical, but not creative, thinking. Using creative skill in the absence of the other two results in new ideas that are not subjected to the scrutiny required to improve them and make them work. And using practical–contextual skill alone may result in societal acceptance of ideas not because the ideas are good, but because they have been well and powerfully presented.

To be creative, one must first *decide* to generate new ideas, analyze these ideas, and sell the ideas to others. In other words, a person may have synthetic, analytical, or practical skills, but not apply them to problems that potentially involve creativity. For example, one may decide to follow other people's ideas rather than synthesize one's own; or not to subject one's ideas to a careful evaluation; or to expect other people to listen to one's ideas and therefore decide not to try to persuade other people of their value. The skill is not enough: One first needs to make the decision to use the skill. Our studies on the role of intelligence in creativity are discussed in Chapter 2. They emphasize the ability to switch between conventional and unconventional modes of thinking.

One aspect of switching between conventional and unconventional thinking is the decision that one is willing and able to think in unconventional ways, that one is willing to accept thinking in terms different from those to which one is accustomed and with which one feels comfortable. People show reliable individual differences in the willingness to do so (Dweck, 1999). Some people (what Dweck calls "entity theorists") prefer to operate primarily or even exclusively in domains relatively familiar to them. Other people (what Dweck calls "incremental theorists") seek out new challenges and new conceptual domains within which to work.

Knowledge. Concerning knowledge, on the one hand, one needs to know enough about a field to move it forward. One cannot move beyond where a field is if one doesn't know where it is. On the other hand, knowledge about a field can result in a closed and entrenched perspective, confining a person to the way in which he or she has seen problems in the past

(Frensch & Sternberg, 1989). Thus, one needs to decide to use one's past knowledge, but also *decide* not to let the knowledge become a hindrance rather than a help. Everyone has a knowledge base. How they choose to use it is a decision they must make.

Thinking styles. Thinking styles are preferred ways of using one's skills. In essence, they are *decisions* about how to deploy the skills available to one. With regard to thinking styles, a legislative style is particularly important for creativity (Sternberg, 1988b, 1997b), that is, a preference for thinking and a decision to think in new ways. This preference needs to be distinguished from the ability to think creatively: Someone may like to think along new lines, but not think well, or vice versa. It also helps to become a major creative thinker if one is able to think globally as well as locally, distinguishing the forest from the trees and thereby recognizing which questions are important and which ones are not.

Personality. Numerous research investigations (summarized in Lubart, 1994, and Sternberg & Lubart, 1991, 1995) have supported the importance of certain personality attributes for creative functioning. These attributes include, but are not limited to, willingness to overcome obstacles, willingness to take sensible risks, willingness to tolerate ambiguity, and self-efficacy. In particular, buying low and selling high typically means defying the crowd, so one has to be willing to stand up to conventions if one wants to think and act in creative ways. Often, creative people seek opposition, in that they decide to think in ways that countervail how others think. Note that none of the attributes of creative thinking is fixed. One can *decide* to overcome obstacles, take sensible risks, and so forth.

Motivation. Intrinsic, task-focused motivation is also essential to creativity. The research of Amabile (1983) and others has shown the importance of such motivation for creative work, and has suggested that people rarely do truly creative work in an area unless they really love what they are doing and focus on the work rather than the potential rewards. Motivation is not something inherent in a person: One *decides* to be motivated by one thing or another. Often, people who need to work in a certain area that does not particularly interest them will decide that, given the need to work in that area, they had better find a way to make it interest them. They will then look for some angle on the work they need to do that makes this work appeal to rather than bore them.

Environment. Finally, one needs an environment that is supportive and rewarding of creative ideas. One could have all of the internal resources needed in order to think creatively, but without some environmental support (such as a forum for proposing those ideas), the creativity that a person has within him or her might never be displayed.

Environments typically are not fully supportive of the use of one's creativity. The obstacles in a given environment may be minor, as when an individual receives negative feedback on his or her creative thinking, or major, as when one's well-being or even life are threatened if one thinks in a manner that defies convention. The individual therefore must *decide* how to respond in the face of the pretty close to omnipresent environmental challenges that exist. Some people let unfavorable forces in the environment block their creative output; others do not.

Confluence. Concerning the confluence of these six components, creativity is hypothesized to involve more than a simple sum of a person's level on each component. First, there may be thresholds for some components (for example, knowledge) below which creativity is not possible regardless of the levels on other components. Second, partial compensation may occur in which a strength on one component (for example, motivation) counteracts a weakness on another component (for example, environment). Third, interactions may also occur between components, such as intelligence and motivation, in which high levels on both components could multiplicatively enhance creativity.

Creative ideas are both novel and valuable. But they are often rejected when the creative innovator stands up to vested interests and defies the crowd (cf. Csikszentmihalyi, 1988). The crowd does not maliciously or willfully reject creative notions. Rather, it does not realize, and often does not want to realize, that the proposed idea represents a valid and advanced way of thinking. Society often perceives opposition to the status quo as annoying, offensive, and reason enough to ignore innovative ideas.

Evidence abounds that creative ideas are often rejected (Sternberg & Lubart, 1995). Initial reviews of major works of literature and art are often negative. Toni Morrison's *Tar Baby* received negative reviews when it was first published, as did Sylvia Plath's *The Bell Jar*. The first exhibition in Munich of the work of Norwegian painter Edvard Munch opened and closed the same day because of the strong negative response from the critics. Some of the greatest scientific papers have been rejected not just by one, but by several journals before being published. For example, John Garcia, a distinguished biopsychologist, was immediately denounced when he first proposed that a form of learning called classical conditioning could be produced in a single trial of learning (Garcia & Koelling, 1966).

From the investment view, then, the creative person buys low by presenting an idea that initially is not valued and then attempting to convince others of its value. After convincing others that the idea is valuable, which increases the perceived value of the investment, the creative person sells high by leaving the idea to others and moving on to another idea. People typically want others to love their ideas, but immediate universal applause for an idea often indicates that it is not particularly creative.

Creativity is as much a decision about and an attitude toward life as it is a matter of ability. Creativity is often obvious in young children, but it may be harder to find in older children and adults because their creative potential has been suppressed by a society that encourages intellectual conformity.

DEVELOPING CREATIVITY AS A DECISION

Creativity, according to the investment theory, is in large part a decision. The view of creativity as a decision suggests that creativity can be developed. I have proposed twenty-one ways to develop creativity as a decision (Sternberg, 2001c). Here they are.

The Strategies

Redefine Problems.   Redefining a problem means taking a problem and turning it on its head. Many times in life individuals have a problem and they just don't see how to solve it. They are stuck in a box. Redefining a problem essentially means extricating oneself from the box. It is an aspect of problem finding, as opposed merely to problem solving. This process is the divergent part of creative thinking.

A good example of redefining a problem is summed up in the story of an executive at one of the biggest automobile companies in the Detroit area. The executive held a high-level position, and he loved his job and the money he made on the job. He despised the person he worked for, however, and because of this, he decided to find a new job. He went to a headhunter, who assured him that a new job could be easily arranged. After this meeting the executive went home and talked to his wife, who was teaching a unit on redefining problems as part of a course she was teaching on Intelligence Applied (Sternberg, 1986). The executive realized that he could apply what his wife was teaching to his own problem. He returned to the headhunter and gave the headhunter his boss's name. The headhunter found a new job for the executive's boss, which the boss – having no idea of what was going on – accepted. The executive then got his boss's job. He had decided for creativity by redefining a problem.

There are many ways teachers and parents can encourage children to define and redefine problems for themselves, rather than – as is so often the case – doing it for them. Teachers and parents can promote creative performance by encouraging their children to define and redefine *their own* problems and projects. Adults can encourage creative thinking by having children choose their own topics for papers or presentations, choose their own ways of solving problems, and sometimes by having them choose again if they discover that their selection was a mistake.

Adults cannot always offer children choices, but giving choices is the only way for children to learn how to choose. A real choice is not deciding between drawing a cat or a dog, nor is it picking one state in the United States to present at a project fair. It is deciding what to draw or what topic on which to do a project. Giving children latitude in making choices helps them to develop taste and good judgment, both of which are essential elements of creativity.

At some point everyone makes a mistake in choosing a project or in the method he or she selects to complete it. Teachers and parents should remember that an important part of creativity is the analytic part – learning to recognize a mistake – and give children the chance and the opportunity to redefine their choices.

Question and Analyze Assumptions.   Everyone has assumptions. Often one does not know he or she has these assumptions because they are widely shared. Creative people question assumptions and eventually lead others to do the same. Questioning assumptions is part of the analytical thinking involved in creativity. When Copernicus suggested that Earth revolves around the sun, the suggestion was viewed as preposterous because everyone could see that the sun revolves around Earth. Galileo's ideas, including the relative rates of falling objects, caused him to be denounced as a heretic. When an employee questions the way his boss manages the business, the boss does not smile. The employee is questioning assumptions that the boss and others simply accept – assumptions that they do not wish to open up to questions.

Sometimes it is not until many years later that society realizes the limitations or errors of their assumptions and the value of the creative person's thoughts. Those who question assumptions promote cultural, technological, and other forms of advancement.

Teachers and parents can be role models for questioning assumptions by showing children that what they assume they know, they really do not know. Children shouldn't question every assumption. There are times to question and try to reshape the environment, and there are times to adapt to it. Some creative people question so many things so often that others stop taking them seriously. Everyone must learn which assumptions are worth questioning and which battles are worth fighting. Sometimes it's better for individuals to leave the inconsequential assumptions alone so that they have an audience when they find something worth the effort.

Teachers and parents can help children develop this talent by making questioning a part of the daily exchange. It is more important for children to learn what questions to ask – and how to ask them – than to learn the answers. Adults can help children evaluate their questions by discouraging the idea that the adults ask questions and children simply answer them. Adults need to avoid perpetuating the belief that their role is to teach children the facts, and instead help them understand that what matters is the ability to use facts. This can help children learn how to formulate good questions and how to answer questions.

Society tends to make a pedagogical mistake by emphasizing the answering and not the asking of questions. The good student is perceived as the one who rapidly furnishes the right answers. The expert in a field thus becomes the extension of the expert student – the one who knows and can recite a lot of information. As John Dewey (1933) recognized, how one thinks is often more important than what one thinks. Schools need to teach children how to ask the right questions (questions that are good, thought-provoking, and interesting) and lessen the emphasis on rote learning.

Do Not Assume That Creative Ideas Sell Themselves: Sell Them.   As Galileo, Edvard Munch, Toni Morrison, Sylvia Plath, and millions of others have discovered, creative ideas do not sell themselves. On the contrary, creative ideas are usually viewed with suspicion and distrust. Moreover, those who propose such ideas may be viewed with suspicion and distrust as well. Because people are comfortable with the ways they already think, and because they probably have a vested interest in it, it can be extremely difficult to dislodge them from that current way.

Thus, children need to learn how to persuade other people of the value of their ideas as part of the practical aspect of creative thinking. If children do a science project, it is a good idea for them to present it and demonstrate why it makes an important contribution. If they create a piece of artwork, they should be prepared to describe why they think it has value. If they develop a plan for a new form of government, they should explain why it is better than the existing form. At times, teachers may find themselves having to justify their ideas about teaching to their principal. They should prepare their children for the same kind of experience.

Encourage Idea Generation.   As mentioned earlier, creative people demonstrate a "legislative" style of thinking: They like to generate ideas (Sternberg, 1997a). The environment for generating ideas can be constructively critical, but it must not be harshly or destructively critical. Children need to acknowledge that some ideas are better than others. Adults and children should collaborate to identify and encourage any creative aspects of ideas that are presented. When suggested ideas don't seem to have much value, teachers should not just criticize. They should suggest new approaches, preferably ones that incorporate at least some aspects of the previous ideas that seemed in themselves not to have much value. Children should be praised for generating ideas, regardless of whether some are silly or unrelated, while being encouraged to identify and develop their best ideas into high-quality projects.

Recognize That Knowledge Is a Double-Edged Sword and Act Accordingly.   Some years ago, I was visiting a very famous psychologist who lives abroad. As part of the tour he had planned for me, he invited me to visit the local zoo. We went past the cages of the primates, who were at the time engaged in what euphemistically could be called "strange and unnatural sexual behavior." I averted my eyes, but my host did not. After observing the primates for a short amount of time, he astonished me by analyzing their sexual behavior in terms of his theory of intelligence. I realized then, as I have many times since, how knowledge and expertise can be a double-edged sword.

On the one hand, one cannot be creative without knowledge. Quite simply, one cannot go beyond the existing state of knowledge if one does not know what that state is. Many children have ideas that are creative with respect to themselves, but not with respect to the field because others have had the same ideas before. Those with a greater knowledge base can be creative in ways that those who are still learning about the basics of the field cannot be.

At the same time, those who have an expert level of knowledge can experience tunnel vision, narrow thinking, and entrenchment. Experts can become so stuck in a way of thinking that they become unable to extricate themselves from it. In a study of expert and novice bridge players, for example (Frensch & Sternberg, 1989), we found that experts outperformed novices under regular circumstances. When a superficial change was made in the surface structure of the game, the experts and novices were both hurt slightly in their playing, but quickly recovered. When a profound, deep-structural change was made in the game, the experts initially were hurt more than the novices, although they later recovered. The reason, presumably, is that experts make more and deeper use of the existing structure, and hence have to reformulate their thinking more than do novices when there is a deep-structural change in the rules of the game.

Encourage Children to Identify and Surmount Obstacles.   Buying low and selling high means defying the crowd. And people who defy the crowd – people who think creatively – almost inevitably encounter resistance. The question is not whether one will encounter obstacles; one will. When one buys low, one defies the crowd, and generally engenders in others a reaction of, at best, puzzlement, and, at worst, hostility. The question is whether the creative thinker has the fortitude to persevere. I have often wondered why so many people start off their careers doing creative work and then vanish from the radar screen. I think I know at least one reason why: Sooner or later, they decide that being creative is not worth the resistance and punishment. The truly creative thinkers pay the short-term price because they recognize that they can make a difference in the long term, although it is often a long while before the value of creative ideas is recognized and appreciated.

Parents and teachers can prepare children for these types of experiences by describing obstacles that they, their friends, and well-known figures in society have faced while trying to be creative; otherwise, children may think they are the only ones confronted by obstacles. Teachers should include stories about people who weren't supportive, about bad grades for unwelcome ideas, and about frosty receptions to what they may have thought were their best ideas. To help children deal with obstacles, parents and teachers can remind them of the many creative people whose ideas were initially shunned and help them to develop an inner sense of awe of the creative act. Suggesting that children reduce their concern over what others think is also valuable. However, it is often difficult for children to lessen their dependence on the opinions of their peers.

When children attempt to surmount an obstacle, they should be praised for the effort, whether or not they were entirely successful. Teachers and parents can point out aspects of the effort that were successful and why, and suggest other ways to confront the obstacles. Having the class brainstorm about ways to confront a given obstacle can get the class thinking about the many strategies people can use to confront problems. Some obstacles are within oneself, such as performance anxiety. Other obstacles are external, such as the bad opinions of others. Whether internal or external, obstacles must be overcome.

Encourage Sensible Risk-Taking.   I took a risk as an assistant professor when I decided to study intelligence. The field of intelligence has low prestige within academic psychology. When I was being considered for tenure, it came to my attention that my university was receiving letters that questioned why it would want to give tenure to someone in such a marginal and unprestigious field. I sought advice from a senior professor, Wendell Garner, telling him that perhaps I had made a mistake in labeling my work as being about intelligence. I could have done essentially the same work but labeled it as "thinking" or "problem solving" – fields with more prestige. He reminded me that I had come to Yale wanting to make a difference in the field of intelligence. I had made a difference, but now I was afraid it might cost me my job. I was right: I had taken a risk. But he maintained that there was only one thing I could do – exactly what I was doing. If this field meant so much to me, then I needed to pursue it, even if it meant losing my job. I am still at the university, but other risks I have taken have not turned out so well. When taking risks, one must realize that some of them just will not work, and that is the cost of doing creative work.

When creative people defy the crowd by buying low and selling high, they take risks in much the same way as do people who invest. Some such investments simply may not pan out. The person may generate an idea that is unpopular and stays unpopular over the long term. Defying the crowd means risking the crowd's disdain for "buying" into the wrong idea, or even its wrath. But there are levels of sensibility to keep in mind

when defying the crowd. Creative people may take sensible risks and produce ideas that others ultimately admire and respect as trend-setting. But
sometimes they make mistakes, fail, and fall flat on their faces.

I emphasize the importance of sensible risk-taking because I am not
talking about risking life and limb for creativity. To help children learn to
take sensible risks, adults can encourage them to take some intellectual
risks with courses, with activities, and with what they say to adults – to
develop a sense of how to assess risks.

Nearly every major discovery or invention entailed some risk. When
a movie theater was the only place to see a movie, someone created the
idea of the home video machine. Skeptics questioned if anyone would
want to see movies on a small screen. Another initially risky idea was the
home computer. Many wondered if anyone would have enough use for a
home computer to justify the cost. These ideas were once risks but are now
ingrained in our society.

Few children are willing to take risks in school, because they learn that
taking risks can be costly. Perfect test scores and papers receive praise and
open up future possibilities. Failure to attain a certain academic standard
is perceived as deriving from a lack of ability and motivation and may
lead to scorn and lessened opportunities. Why risk taking hard courses
or saying things that teachers may not like when that may lead to low
grades or even failure? Teachers may inadvertently advocate that children
"play it safe" when they give assignments without choices and allow only
particular answers to questions. Thus, teachers need not only encourage
sensible risk-taking, but also reward it.

Encourage Tolerance of Ambiguity.   People often like things to be in black
and white. They like to think a country is good or bad (ally or enemy) or
that a given idea in education works or does not work. The problem is
that there are a lot of grays in creative work, just as there are when one
invests in a stock whose value may or may not go up. Many stocks are
low-valued. The ambiguities arise as to which will go up, when they will
go up, and, even, for some individuals, what they can do to make them go
up. Artists working on new paintings and writers working on new books
often report feeling scattered and unsure in their thoughts. They need to
figure out whether they are even on the right track. Scientists often are
not sure whether the theory they have developed is exactly correct. These
creative thinkers need to tolerate the ambiguity and uncertainty until they
get the idea just right.

A creative idea tends to come in bits and pieces and develops over time.
The period in which the idea is developing tends to be uncomfortable,
however. Without time or the ability to tolerate ambiguity, many may jump
to a less than optimal solution. When a student has almost the right topic
for a paper or almost the right science project, it's tempting for teachers

to accept the near miss. To help children become creative, teachers need to encourage the children to accept and extend the period in which their ideas do not quite converge. Children need to be taught that uncertainty and discomfort are a part of living a creative life. Ultimately, they will benefit from their tolerance of ambiguity by coming up with better ideas.

Help Children Build Self-Efficacy.   Many people eventually reach a point where they feel as if no one believes in them. I reach this point frequently, feeling that no one values what I am doing. Because creative work often doesn't get a warm reception, it is extremely important that creative people believe in the value of what they are doing. This is not to say that individuals should believe that every idea they have is a good idea. Rather, individuals need to believe that, ultimately, they have the ability to make a difference.

The main limitation on what children can do is what they think they can do. All children have the capacity to be creators and to experience the joy associated with making something new, but first they must be given a strong base for creativity. Sometimes teachers and parents unintentionally limit what children can do by sending messages that express or imply limits on children's potential accomplishments. Instead, these adults need to help children believe in their own ability to be creative.

I have found that probably the best predictor of success among my children is not their ability, but their belief in their ability to succeed. If children are encouraged to succeed and to believe in their own ability to succeed, they very likely will find the success that otherwise would elude them.

Help Children Find What They Love to Do.   Teachers must help children find what excites them to unleash their best creative performances. In the investment metaphor, one needs to find an area in which to invest about which one feels some excitement, so that one will do what one can to maximize the value of one's investments. Teachers need to remember that what they happen to teach may not be what really excites the children they are teaching. People who truly excel creatively in a pursuit, whether vocational or avocational, almost always genuinely love what they do. Certainly, the most creative people are intrinsically motivated in their work (Amabile, 1996). Less creative people often pick a career for the money or prestige and are bored with or loathe their careers. Most often, these people do not do work that makes a difference in their field.

I often meet students who are pursuing a certain career interest not because it is what they want to do, but because it is what their parents or other authority figures expect them to do. I always feel sorry for such students, because I know that although they may do good work in that field, they almost certainly will not do great work. It is hard for people to do great work in a field that simply does not interest them.

Encouraging the child's interests rather than one's own is easier said than done. When my son was young, I was heartened that he wanted to play the piano. I play the piano, and was glad that he wanted to play the piano, too. But then he stopped practicing and ultimately quit, and I felt badly. A short time thereafter he informed me that he wanted to play the trumpet. I reacted very negatively, pointing out to him that he had already quit the piano and probably would quit the trumpet, too.

I then found myself wondering why I had been so harsh. How could I have said such a thing? But then I quickly understood it. If someone else's child wanted to play the trumpet, that was fine. But I couldn't imagine any Sternberg child playing the trumpet. It did not fit my ideal image of a Sternberg child. I realized I was being narrow-minded and doing exactly the opposite of what I had told everyone else to do. It's one thing to talk the talk, another to walk the walk. I backpedaled, and Seth started playing the trumpet.

Eventually, he did, in fact, quit the trumpet. Finding the right thing is frustrating work! Seth eventually did find the right thing. Today he is a college student and already has started two businesses. I don't like businesses at all. But businesses and my son are the right thing – absolutely. He is doing what is right for him. Whether it is right for me doesn't matter.

Helping children find what they really love to do is often hard and frustrating work. Yet, sharing the frustration with them now is better than leaving them to face it alone later. To help children uncover their true interests, teachers can ask them to demonstrate a special talent or ability for the class, and explain that it doesn't matter what they do (within reason), only that they love the activity.

Teach Children the Importance of Delaying Gratification. Part of being creative means being able to work on a project or task for a long time without immediate or interim rewards, just as in investing one often must wait quite a while for the value of a stock to rise. Children must learn that rewards are not always immediate and that there are benefits to delaying gratification. In the short term, people are often ignored when they do creative work or even punished for doing it.

Many people believe that they should reward children immediately for a good performance, and that children should expect rewards. This style of teaching and parenting emphasizes the here and now and often comes at the expense of what is best in the long term.

An important lesson in life – and one that is intimately related to developing the discipline to do creative work – is to learn to wait for rewards. The greatest rewards are often those that are delayed. Teachers can give their children examples of delayed gratification in their lives and in the lives of creative individuals and help them apply these examples to their own lives.

Hard work often does not bring immediate rewards. Children do not immediately become expert baseball players, dancers, musicians, or sculptors. And the reward of becoming an expert can seem very far away. Children often succumb to the temptations of the moment, such as watching television or playing video games. The people who make the most of their abilities are those who wait for a reward and recognize that few serious challenges can be met in a moment. Ninth-grade children may not see the benefits of hard work, but the advantages of solid academic performance will be obvious when they apply to college.

The short-term focus of most school assignments does little to teach children the value of delaying gratification. Projects are clearly superior in meeting this goal, but it is difficult for teachers to assign home projects if they are not confident of parental involvement and support. By working on a task for many weeks or months, children learn the value of making incremental efforts for long-term gains.

I can relate to the concept of delayed gratification. Some years ago I contracted with a publisher to develop a test of intelligence based on my theory of intelligence (Sternberg, 1985a). Things were going well until the president of the company left and a new president took over. Shortly after that, my project was canceled. The company's perception was that there was not enough of a potential market for a test of intelligence based on my theory of analytical, creative, and practical abilities. My perception was that the company and some of its market were stuck in the past, endlessly replicating the construction and use of the kinds of tests that have been constructed and used since the turn of the century.

Whoever may have been right, a colleague and I ultimately decided that if we wanted to make this test work, we would have to look elsewhere. Years later, the College Board provided funding for the testing project, and it is now evolving again. But I had to wait many years to see progress resume.

Role-Model Creativity. There are many ways teachers and parents can provide an environment that fosters creativity (Sternberg & Williams, 1996). The most powerful way for teachers to develop creativity in children is to *role model creativity*. Children develop creativity not when they are told to, but when they are shown how.

The teachers most people probably remember from their school days are not those who crammed the most content into their lectures. The teachers most people remember are those whose thoughts and actions served as a role model. Most likely they balanced teaching content with teaching children how to think with and about that content. The Nobel laureates, before they received their prizes, made excellent role models in large part because they were outstanding examples of creativity in action that students could emulate (Zuckerman, 1977, 1983).

Cross-Fertilize Ideas. Teachers can also stimulate creativity by helping children *to cross-fertilize in their thinking*, to think across subjects and disciplines. The traditional school environment often has separate classrooms and classmates for different subjects and seems to influence children into thinking that learning occurs in discrete boxes – the math box, the social studies box, and the science box. Creative ideas and insights often result, however, from integrating material across subject areas, not from memorizing and reciting material.

Teaching children to cross-fertilize draws on their skills, interests, and abilities, regardless of the subject. If children are having trouble understanding math, teachers might ask them to draft test questions related to their special interests. For example, they might ask the baseball fan to devise geometry problems based on a game. The context may spur creative ideas because the student finds the topic (baseball) enjoyable and it may counteract some of the anxiety caused by geometry. Cross-fertilization motivates children who aren't interested in subjects taught in the abstract.

One way teachers can promote cross-fertilization in the classroom is to ask children to identify their best and worst academic areas. Children can then be asked to come up with project ideas in their weak area based on ideas borrowed from one of their strongest areas. For example, teachers can explain to children that they can apply their interest in science to social studies by analyzing the scientific aspects of trends in national politics.

Allow Time for Creative Thinking. Teachers also need *to allow children the time to think creatively*. Often, creativity requires time for incubation (Wallas, 1926). Many societies today are societies in a hurry. People eat fast food, rush from one place to another, and value quickness. One way to say someone is smart is to say that the person is *quick* (Sternberg 1985a), a clear indication of an emphasis on time. This is also indicated by the format of many of the standardized tests used – lots of multiple-choice problems squeezed into a brief time slot.

Most creative insights do not happen in a rush (Gruber & Davis, 1988). People need time to understand a problem and to toss it around. If children are asked to think creatively, they need time to do it well. If teachers stuff questions into their tests or give their children more homework than they can complete, they are not allowing them time to think creatively.

Instruct and Assess for Creativity. Teachers also should *instruct and assess for creativity*. If teachers give only multiple-choice tests, children quickly learn the type of thinking that teachers value, no matter what they say. If teachers want to encourage creativity, they need to include at least some opportunities for creative thought in assignments and tests. Questions that require factual recall, analytic thinking, *and* creative thinking should be asked. For example, children might be asked to learn about a law, analyze the law, and then think about how the law might be improved.

Reward Creativity. Teachers also need *to reward creativity.* They may choose differentially to reward the different kinds of creative contributions, depending on the circumstances and the students. For example, if teachers ask students to be bold in their thinking, the teachers may choose to reward conceptual replications less than bolder redirections (at levels of innovation characteristic of students, of course). Thus, teachers may choose not to limit their rewards to "crowd-defying creativity," but may choose to allocate rewards, depending on circumstances and expectations for particular students. It is not enough to talk about the value of creativity. Children are used to authority figures who say one thing and do another. They are exquisitely sensitive to what teachers value when it comes to the bottom line – the grade or evaluation.

Creative efforts should be rewarded. For example, teachers can assign a project and remind children that they are looking for them to demonstrate their knowledge, analytical and writing skills, and creativity. They should let children know that creativity does not depend on the teacher's agreement with what children write, but rather with ideas they express that represent a synthesis between existing ideas and their own thoughts. Teachers need to care only that the ideas are creative from the student's perspective, not necessarily creative with regard to the state-of-the-art findings in the field. Children may generate an idea that someone else has already had, but if the idea is an original to the student, the student has been creative.

Some teachers complain that they cannot apply as much objectivity to grading creative responses as they can to multiple-choice or short-answer responses. They are correct in that there is some sacrifice of objectivity. However, research shows that evaluators are remarkably consistent in their assessments of creativity (Amabile, 1996; Sternberg & Lubart, 1995). If the goal of assessment is to instruct children, then it is better to ask for creative work and evaluate it with somewhat less objectivity than to evaluate children exclusively on uncreative work. Teachers should let children know that there is no completely objective way to evaluate creativity.

Allow Mistakes. Teachers also need *to allow mistakes.* Buying low and selling high carries a risk. Many ideas are unpopular simply because they are not good. People often think a certain way because that way works better than other ways. But once in a while, a great thinker comes along – a Freud, a Piaget, a Chomsky, or an Einstein – and shows us a new way to think. These thinkers made contributions because they allowed themselves and their collaborators to take risks and make mistakes.

Many of Freud's and Piaget's ideas turned out to be wrong. Freud confused Victorian issues regarding sexuality with universal conflicts and

Piaget misjudged the ages at which children could perform certain cognitive feats. Their ideas were great not because they lasted forever, but because they became the basis for other ideas. Freud's and Piaget's mistakes allowed others to profit from their ideas.

Although being successful often involves making mistakes along the way, schools are often unforgiving of mistakes. Errors on schoolwork are often marked with a large and pronounced X. When a student responds to a question with an incorrect answer, some teachers pounce on the student for not having read or understood the material, as classmates snicker. In hundreds of ways and in thousands of instances over the course of a school career, children learn that it is not alright to make mistakes. The result is that they become afraid to risk the independent and the sometimes-flawed thinking that leads to creativity.

When children make mistakes, teachers should ask them to analyze and discuss the mistakes. Often, mistakes or weak ideas contain the germ of correct answers or good ideas. In Japan, teachers spend entire class periods asking children to analyze the mistakes in their mathematical thinking. For the teacher who wants to make a difference, exploring mistakes can be an opportunity for learning and growing.

Take Responsibility for Both Successes and Failures. Another aspect of teaching children to be creative is teaching them *to take responsibility for both successes and failures*. Teaching children how to take responsibility means teaching children to (1) understand their creative process, (2) criticize themselves, and (3) take pride in their best creative work. Unfortunately, many teachers and parents look for – or allow children to look for – an outside enemy responsible for failures.

It sounds trite to say that teachers should teach children to take responsibility for themselves, but sometimes there is a gap between what people know and how they translate thought into action. In practice, people differ widely in the extent to which they take responsibility for the causes and consequences of their actions. Creative people need to take responsibility for themselves and for their ideas.

Encourage Creative Collaboration. Teachers can also work *to encourage creative collaboration* (Chadwick & Courtivron, 1996; John-Steiner, 2000). Creative performance is often viewed as a solitary occupation. We may picture the writer writing alone in a studio, the artist painting in a solitary loft, or the musician practicing endlessly in a small music room. In reality, people often work in groups. Collaboration can spur creativity. Teachers can encourage children to learn by example by collaborating with creative people.

Imagine Things from Others' Points of View.   Children also need to learn how *to imagine things from other viewpoints*. An essential aspect of working with other people and getting the most out of collaborative creative activity is to imagine oneself in other people's shoes. Individuals can broaden their perspective by learning to see the world from different points of view. Teachers and parents should encourage their children to see the importance of understanding, respecting, and responding to other people's points of view. This is important, as many bright and potentially creative children never achieve success because they do not develop practical intelligence (Sternberg, 1985a, 1997b). They may do well in school and on tests, but they may never learn how to get along with others or to see things and themselves as others see them.

Maximize Person–Environment Fit.   Teachers also need to help children recognize person–environment fit. What is judged as creative is an interaction between a person and the environment (Csikszentmihalyi, 1988, 1996; Gardner, 1993; Sternberg & Lubart, 1995). The very same product that is rewarded as creative in one time or place may be scorned in another.

In the movie *The Dead Poets Society*, a teacher the audience might well judge to be creative is viewed as incompetent by the school's administration. Similar experiences occur many times a day in many settings. There is no absolute standard for what constitutes creative work. The same product or idea may be valued or devalued in different environments. The lesson is that individuals need to find a setting in which their creative talents and unique contributions are rewarded, or they need to modify their environment.

I once had a student to whom I gave consummately bad advice concerning environment. She had two job offers. One was from an institution that was very prestigious, but not a good fit to the kind of work she valued. The other institution was a bit less prestigious, but was a much better fit to her values. I advised her to take the job in the more prestigious institution, telling her that if she did not accept the job there, she would always wonder what would have happened if she had. Bad advice: She went there and never fit in well. Eventually she left, and now she is at an institution that values the kind of work she does. Now I always advise people to go for the best fit.

By building a constant appreciation of the importance of person-environment fit, teachers prepare their children for choosing environments that are conducive to their creative success. Encourage children to examine environments to help them select and match environments with their skills. And while encouraging the children to do it, do it yourself!

People who are uncreative, and perhaps especially people who are smart in a traditional sense but uncreative, are particularly susceptible to four fallacies.

The first, the *should-be fallacy*, is the belief that what is, should be. The second, the *must-be fallacy*, is the belief that what is, must be. In Leibnizian philosophy, it is the principle of sufficient reason – that whatever exists can exist only if there is a sufficient reason for it to exist. The third fallacy is the *always-will-be fallacy*, the belief that the way things are now is the way they always will be. And the fourth fallacy is the *safety fallacy*, which is the belief that regardless of what should be or must be, doing what others are doing is the safe way to live.

5

The Propulsion Theory of Creative Contributions

There are tens of thousands of artists, musicians, writers, scientists, and inventors today. What makes some of them stand out from the rest? Why will some of them become distinguished contributors in the annals of their field and others be forgotten? Although many variables may contribute to who stands out from the crowd, certainly creativity is one of them. The standouts are often those who are doing particularly creative work in their line of professional pursuit. Are these highly creative individuals simply doing more highly creative work than their less visible counterparts, or does the creativity of their work also differ in quality? One possibility is that creative contributors make different *decisions* regarding *how* to express their creativity. This section describes a propulsion theory of creative contributions (Sternberg, 1999c; Sternberg, Kaufman, & Pretz, 2002) that addresses this issue of how people decide to invest their creative resources. The basic idea is that creativity can be of different kinds, depending on how it propels existing ideas forward. When developing creativity in children, we can develop different kinds of creativity, ranging from minor replications to major redirections in their thinking.

Creative contributions differ not only in their amounts but also in the types of creativity they represent. For example, both Sigmund Freud and Anna Freud were highly creative psychologists, but the nature of their contributions seems in some way or ways to have been different. Sigmund Freud proposed a radically new theory of human thought and motivation and Anna Freud largely elaborated on and modified Sigmund Freud's theory. How do creative contributions differ in quality and not just in quantity?

The type of creativity exhibited in a creator's works can have at least as much of an effect on judgments about that person and his or her work as does the amount of creativity exhibited. In many instances, it may have more of an effect. For example, a contemporary artist might have thought

Portions of this chapter are based on collaborative work with James Kaufman and Jean Pretz.

processes, personality, motivation, and even background variables similar to those of Monet, but that artist, painting today in the style of Monet, probably would not be judged to be creative in the way Monet was. He or she was born too late. Artists, including Monet, have experimented with impressionism, and unless the contemporary artist introduced some new twist, he or she might be viewed as imitative rather than creative.

The importance of context is illustrated by the difference, in general, between creative discovery and rediscovery. For example, BACON and related programs of Langley, Simon, Bradshaw, and Zytgow (1987) rediscover important scientific theorems that were judged to be creative discoveries in their time. The processes by which these discoveries are made via computer simulation are presumably not identical to those by which the original discoverers worked. One difference derives from the fact that contemporary programmers can provide, in their programming of information into computer simulations, representations and particular organizations of data that may not have been available to the original creators. Moreover, the programs solve problems, but do not define them. But putting aside the question of whether the processes are the same, a rediscovery might be judged to be creative with respect to the rediscoverer, but would not be judged to be creative with respect to its field at the time the rediscovery is made.

Given the importance of purpose, creative contributions must always be defined in some context. If the creativity of an individual is always judged in a context, then it will help to understand how the context interacts with how people are judged. In particular, what are the types of creative contributions a person can make within a given context? Most theories of creativity concentrate on attributes of the individual (see Sternberg, 1999b). But to the extent that creativity is in the interaction of person with context, we would need to concentrate as well on the attributes of the individual and the individual's work relative to the environmental context.

A taxonomy of creative contributions needs to deal with the question not just of in what domain a contribution is creative, but of what the type of creative contribution is. What makes one work in biology more creative or creative in a different way from another work in biology, or what makes its creative contribution different from that of a work in art? Thus, a taxonomy of domains of work is insufficient to elucidate the nature of creative contributions. A field needs a basis for scaling how creative contributions differ quantitatively and, possibly, qualitatively.

Creativity as Propulsion.   A creative contribution represents an attempt to propel a field from wherever it is to wherever the creator believes the field should go. Thus, creativity is by its nature *propulsion*. It moves a field from some point to another. It also always represents a decision to exercise leadership. The creator tries to bring others to a particular point in the multidimensional creative space. The attempt may or may not succeed. There are different kinds of creative leadership that the creator may attempt to exercise, depending on how he or she decides to be creative.

Eight Types of Creative Contributions. The propulsion model suggests eight types of contributions that can be made to a field of endeavor at a given time. Although the eight types of contributions may differ in the extent of creative contribution they make, the scale of eight types presented here is intended as closer to a nominal one than to an ordinal one. There is no fixed a priori way of evaluating *amount* of creativity on the basis of the *type* of creativity. Certain types of creative contributions probably tend, on average, to be greater in amounts of novelty than are others. But creativity also involves quality of work, and the type of creativity does not make any predictions regarding quality of work.

The panels of Figure 5.1 summarize the eight types of contributions and are referred to in the following discussion. To foreshadow the following discussion, the eight types of creative contributions are divided into three major categories, contributions that accept current paradigms, contributions that reject current paradigms, and paradigms that attempt to integrate multiple current paradigms. There are also subcategories within each of these two categories: paradigm-preserving contributions that leave the field where it is (Types 1 and 2), paradigm-preserving contributions that move the field forward in the direction it already is going (Types 3 and 4), paradigm-rejecting contributions that move the field in a new direction from an existing or pre-existing starting point (Types 5 and 6), paradigm-rejecting contributions that move the field in a new direction from a new starting point (Type 7), and paradigm-integrating contributions that combine approaches (Type 8).

Thus, Type 1, the limiting case, is not crowd-defying at all (unless the results come out the wrong way!). Type 2 may or may not be crowd-defying, if the redefinition goes against the field. Type 3 typically leads the crowd. Type 4 goes beyond where the crowd is ready to go, so may well be crowd-defying. And Types 5 to 8 typically are crowd-defying in at least some degree. Obviously, there is often no "crowd" out there just waiting to attack. Rather, there is a field representing people with shared views regarding what is and is not acceptable, and if those views are shaken, the people may not react well.

Types of Creativity that Accept Current Paradigms and Attempt to Extend Them

1. REPLICATION. The contribution is an attempt to show that the field is in the right place. The propulsion keeps the field where it is rather than moving it. This type of creativity is represented by stationary motion, as of a wheel that is moving but staying in place.

2. REDEFINITION. The contribution is an attempt to redefine where the field is. The current status of the field thus is seen from different points of view. The propulsion leads to circular motion, such that the creative work leads back to where the field is, but viewed in a different way.

3. FORWARD INCREMENTATION. The contribution is an attempt to move the field forward in the direction it already is going. The propulsion leads to forward motion.

4. ADVANCE FORWARD INCREMENTATION. The contribution is an attempt to move the field forward in the direction it is already going, but beyond where others are ready for it to go. The propulsion leads to forward motion that is accelerated beyond the expected rate of forward progression.

Types of Creativity that Reject Current Paradigms and Attempt to Replace Them

5. REDIRECTION. The contribution is an attempt to redirect the field from where it is toward a different direction. The propulsion thus leads to motion in a direction that diverges from the way the field is currently moving.

6. RECONSTRUCTION / REDIRECTION. The contribution is an attempt to move the field back to where it once was (a reconstruction of the past) so that it may move onward from that point, but in a direction different from the one it took before. The propulsion thus leads to motion that is backward and then redirective.

7. REINITIATION. The contribution is an attempt to move the field to a different as yet unreached starting point and then to move from that point. The propulsion is thus from a new starting point in a direction that is different from the one the field previously pursued.

A Type of Creativity That Merges Disparate Current Paradigms

8. INTEGRATION. The contribution is an attempt to integrate two formerly diverse ways of thinking about phenomena into a single way of thinking about a phenomenon. The propulsion thus is a combination of two different approaches that are linked together.

The eight types of creative contributions described above are largely qualitatively distinct. Within each type there can be quantitative differences. For example, a forward incrementation can represent a fairly small step forward or a substantial leap. A reinitiation can restart a subfield (for example, the work of Leon Festinger on cognitive dissonance) or an entire field (for example, the work of Einstein on relativity theory). Thus, the theory distinguishes contributions both qualitatively and quantitatively.

In the discussion below, I demonstrate each type of creative contribution with exemplars from a variety of fields, including especially one of my own fields of research, the field of intelligence. The examples below are from Sternberg (1999c) and from Sternberg, Kaufman, and Pretz (2002).

Replication
(Stationary Motion)

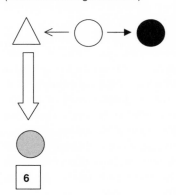

1

Redefinition
(Circular Motion)

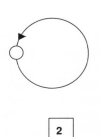

2

Forward
Incrementation
(Forward Motion)

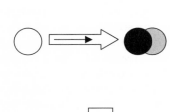

3

Advance Forward Incrementation
(Accelerated Forward Motion)

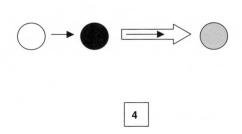

4

Redirection
(Divergent Motion)

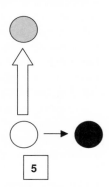

5

Reconstruction
(Backward/Divergent Motion)

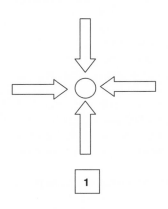

6

Reinitiation
(Reinitiated Motion)

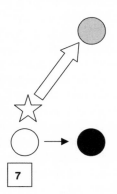

7

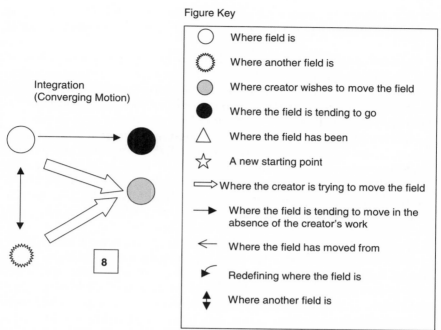

Figure Key

○	Where field is
(starburst)	Where another field is
(gray circle)	Where creator wishes to move the field
●	Where the field is tending to go
△	Where the field has been
☆	A new starting point
⟹	Where the creator is trying to move the field
→	Where the field is tending to move in the absence of the creator's work
←	Where the field has moved from
⤶	Redefining where the field is
↕	Where another field is

Integration
(Converging Motion)

8

FIGURE 5.1. Types of creativity. Type 1: Replication helps solidify the current state of a field. Type 2: Redefinition involves a change in perception as to where the field is. Type 3: Incrementation occurs when a piece of work takes the field where it is and moves it forward from that point in the space of contributions in the direction it is already going. Type 4: Advance incrementation occurs when an idea is "ahead of its time." Type 5: Redirection involves taking the field where it is at a given time but attempting to move it in a new direction. Type 6: Reconstruction/redirection involves moving the field back to a point it previously was and then moving it in a different direction. Type 7: Reinitiation occurs when a contributor suggests that a field or subfield has reached an undesirable point or has exhausted itself moving in the direction it is moving. The contributor suggests moving in a different direction from a different point in the multidimensional space of contributions. Type 8: Integration occurs when a contributor suggests putting together ideas formerly seen as distinct and unrelated or even as opposed.

Paradigm-Preserving Contributions that Leave the Field Where It Is

TYPE 1: REPLICATION.   Replication is illustrated in Panel 1 of Figure 5.1. Replications help solidify the current state of a field. The goal is not to move a field forward so much as to establish that it really is where it is supposed to be. Thus, in science, if a finding is surprising, then a replication can help establish that the finding is a serious one. If the replication fails then contributors in the field need to question whether they are where they have supposed themselves, or perhaps have hoped themselves, to be. In art or literature, replications essentially show that a style of work can be applied not just to a single artwork or literary work, but to other works as well.

Replications are limiting cases in that they in some sense seem, on their face, to offer the least that is new in terms of the types of creative contributions considered in this taxonomy of types of contributions. Yet replications are important because they can help either to establish the validity or invalidity of contributions, or the utility or lack of utility of approaches.

For example, consider the choice reaction-time paradigm and its implications. As background, Jensen (1982) and others argued that correlations between scores on choice reaction-time tests and scores on intelligence tests suggest that individual differences in human intelligence could be traced to individual differences in velocity of neural conduction. Because tests of choice reaction time in no way measure neural conduction velocity, such interpretations of results were wholly speculative.

Vernon and Mori (1992) tested and seemingly confirmed Jensen's hypothesis. They developed a paradigm whereby they could measure speed of neural conduction in the arm. They found that neural-conduction velocity did indeed predict scores on conventional tests of intelligence. This was a startling finding because it suggested that what previously had been a speculative claim that was at best very loosely tied to data was instead a serious empirically supported claim. However, Wickett and Vernon (1994) later reported a failure to replicate this result so its empirical status was cast into doubt. The Wickett and Vernon study was a replication study, and the failure to replicate arguably was as important to the field as would have been a replication. Failures to replicate can prevent a field from pursuing red herrings.

Although work designed to yield exact replications and conceptual replications (where the generality of a finding or kind of product is assessed by trying to replicate it under circumstances somewhat different from those that originally gave rise to it) is about as unglamorous as any kind of work can be, it is necessary for the development of a field. Without replications the field would be (and probably often is) very susceptible to Type 1 errors (false alarms). In science, replications help ensure the solidity of the base of empirical findings on which future researchers build.

In the arts and letters, replications help ensure that an approach is robust and can generate a number and variety of works. For example, many artists imitated Monet's impressionistic technique, and although they added nothing new, they showed the robustness of the technique. Perhaps the limiting case in the art world is the work of forgers, who attempt to reproduce exactly the work of a (usually well-known) creator. Replications are not limited to forgers, however. Many visitors to museums have encountered individuals studiously copying great works of art and proudly displaying their work for what it is.

Perhaps the crucial insight for the contributor is to know when there is a need for replication in the first place. In science, this need is associated with findings that are surprising or that seem on their face to be sufficiently dubious that either their existence or their generality needs to be demonstrated. In the arts and letters, this need is associated with techniques that may seem to be limited to a single artwork or artist, or literary work or writer, but that could be used more widely.

TYPE 2: REDEFINITION. Redefinition is illustrated in Panel 2 of Figure 5.1. Redefinition, like replication, involves little or even no change of where a field is. What redefinition involves is a change in perception as to where that is. A redefinition in a conceptual space leads people to realize that the field is not where they had thought. Work of this type is judged to be creative to the extent that the redefinition of the field is different from the earlier definition (novelty) and to the extent that the redefinition is judged to be plausible or correct (quality).

An example of a redefinition is provided by the work of Thomson (1939), who reinterpreted the work of Spearman (1904, 1927). Spearman was the English psychologist who invented factor analysis and who used this technique to argue that underlying performance on all tests of mental abilities is a general factor, which he labeled g. Spearman's analysis had a powerful effect on the field and continues to have such an effect today, with many theorists still believing in the existence and importance of the general factor (for example, Brand, 1996; Carroll, 1993; Horn, 1994; Jensen, 1998).

Spearman believed his work to show that a single mental entity was responsible for interesting and consequential individual differences in performance on mental tests. Spearman (1927) suggested that this entity was mental energy. Thomson (1939) proposed that although Spearman was correct in positing a general factor underlying performance on mental tests, he was incorrect in his interpretation of it. According to Thomson, the general factor actually represents the workings of multitudinous "bonds." These bonds are all alleged to be those mental processes common to performance on all mental tests. Thus, because all such tests require people to understand the instructions, read the terms of the problems, provide a response, and so forth, there might be many different sources of individual differences shared across these tests. They might appear via factor analysis to be a single entity, but in fact they are multifarious. Thus, Thomson proposed to change not the empirical status of work on intelligence, but how its empirical status was conceptualized. He argued that the field was not where Spearman and others thought it to be.

Similarly, Minkowski r-metrics represent a redefinition of the notion of spatial metaphors (see Kruskal, 1964a, 1964b). In computing distances in a multidimensional space, people traditionally had assumed that distance is Euclidean – to compute distances, one squares differences between coordinates and then takes the square root of the sum of the squared differences. Minkowski's generalization shows that there is nothing privileged about the r-value of 2. One can use any number at all as the basis for exponentiation. For example, an r-value of 1 yields a city-block metric, where distances are computed as they would be in a city where it is impossible to construct a hypotenuse through buildings. An r-value of infinity yields a max metric, where only the longest within-dimensional distance contributes to the total distance. Thus, the Minkowski r-metric shows that the way distances were computed was not unique but rather one of many possible cases: The r-metric redefines through a generalization the already existing distance construct.

An interesting example of redefinition in the arts is the work of the late Roy Lichtenstein. Lichtenstein took a form of art – the comic – that was viewed as debased and turned it into a serious art form. Lichtenstein's work originally met with tremendous opposition, which never really ended, at least in some quarters. Yet in his later career, his comic works of art brought large sums of money as well as the kind of serious study that showed what had been perceived as a base art form had come to be taken seriously, at least by many. Andy Warhol is a second example of an artist in this tradition, turning studies of soda bottles into pieces of art valued by many collectors.

Paradigm-Preserving Contributions that Move the Field Forward in the Direction It Already Is Going

TYPE 3: FORWARD INCREMENTATION.   This type of creative contribution is illustrated in Panel 3 of Figure 5.1. It probably represents the most common type of creative contribution. It occurs when a piece of work takes the field at the point where it is and moves it forward from that point in the space of contributions in the direction it is already going. There is no change in the trajectory of the field. Work of this type is judged to be creative to the extent that it seems to move the field forward from where it is and to the extent that the movement appears to be correct or desirable.

Hunt, Frost, and Lunneborg (1973) proposed that intelligence could be studied by investigators examining individual differences in cognitive performance on the kinds of tasks cognitive psychologists study in their laboratories. A few years later, Hunt, Lunneborg, and Lewis (1975) published an incrementation study that extended the range of tasks that could be studied using this paradigm, suggesting that certain of these tasks were particularly useful for studying individual differences in verbal ability. The second study was an incrementation study, building on a paradigm that Hunt and his colleagues had already established. The second study provided a fairly substantial increment in both increasing the range of tasks and in focusing in particular on verbal ability.

Most studies published in scientific journals can be characterized as forward incrementations. For example, after the initial groundbreaking study of Festinger and Carlsmith (1959) on cognitive dissonance, huge numbers of follow-up studies were done on phenomena of cognitive dissonance and cognitive consistency (Abelson et al., 1968). These studies helped elucidate the phenomenon and its limiting circumstances. As these forward incrementations made the limits of the cognitive-dissonance phenomenon clearer, other theories came to be proposed that provided alternative (Bem, 1967) or more refined explanations of when people exhibit cognitive dissonance and when they exhibit other kinds of reactions – such as self-perception reactions – in the face of cognitive inconsistencies (Fazio, Zanna, & Cooper, 1977).

Forward incrementations can also be found in genre fiction that pushes the envelope. The hard-boiled detective story pioneered by Dashiell Hammett and Raymond Chandler has been elaborated on by countless writers, some of them moving the genre forward in major ways, such as Ross MacDonald, who introduced identity confusions as a major theme in his work. But MacDonald's work and that of others have their roots in the paradigm introduced by Hammett and Chandler.

Jonathan Kellerman's psychological thrillers take the genre a step further by having the hero, Alex Delaware, actually be a clinical psychologist. Patricia Cornwell's suspense novels have Kay Scarpetta, a medical examiner, as the protagonist. Using these nonstandard professions instead of the usual cops and detectives adds an extra layer of authenticity to the stories, and allows for much more technical detail to be realistically added to the plots. Kellerman's plots, for example, often hinge on Delaware identifying various psychological syndromes (for example, Munchausen Syndrome by Proxy), whereas Cornwell has Scarpetta discover essential clues in her autopsies. The forward incrementations can also be found in the plots of genre fiction. Agatha Christie's classic *The Murder of Roger Ackroyd* (1926) is a fairly standard murder mystery ... until the then-startling ending of the narrator turning out to be the killer. These advances certainly move the field forward, but in a nonstartling way. Kellerman and Cornwell still work within the pre-established conventions of the field, and Christie's famed novel still obeyed most of the "rules" of a murder mystery.

TYPE 4: ADVANCE FORWARD INCREMENTATION. This type of creative contribution is illustrated in Panel 4 of Figure 5.1. Advance incrementation occurs when an idea is "ahead of its time." The field is moving in a certain direction but is not yet ready to reach a given point ahead. Someone has an idea that leads to that point. The person pursues the idea and produces a work. The value of the work is often not recognized at the time because the field has not yet reached the point where the contribution can be adequately understood. The creator accelerates beyond where others in his or her field are ready to go – often "skipping" a step that others will need to take. The value of the work may be recognized later or some other creator who has the idea at a more opportune time may end up getting credit for it.

For example, Alfred Binet is best known for his work on intelligence, but as pointed out by Siegler (1992), Binet did work on the nature of expertise in outstanding chess play and on the validity of eyewitness testimony. That work, which did not even remotely fit into existing paradigms of the time, was largely ignored. By the second half of the twentieth century, these and other topics that Binet studied had gained prominence. Binet is virtually never cited in the current work on these topics, however.

Royer (1971) published an article that was an information-processing analysis of the digit–symbol task on the Wechsler Adult Intelligence Scale (WAIS). In the article, Royer showed how information-processing analysis could be used to decompose performance on the task and understand the elementary information processes underlying the performance. Royer's work foreshadowed the later work of Hunt (Hunt, Frost, & Lunneborg, 1973; Hunt, Lunneborg, & Lewis, 1975) and especially of Sternberg (1977, 1983), but his work went largely (although not completely) unnoticed. There could be any number of reasons for this, but it is likely the field was not quite ready for Royer's contribution. The field and possibly even Royer himself did not recognize fully the value of the approach he was taking.

Advance incrementations can occur in any field. For example, the ancient Greek philosopher Democritus was way ahead of his time in proposing ideas that later gave rise to the theory of atoms. In the nineteenth century, Ignaz Semmelweis, a Hungarian obstetrician, proposed the idea of microorganisms contaminating the hands of doctors and was so scoffed at that eventually he was driven crazy. It is often only later that the value of an idea is appreciated.

An advance forward incrementation is a work whose potential typically is not realized at its premiere, yet is later recognized as a step along the historical path of a genre, and then seen as a work ahead of its time. Perhaps the most memorable premiere in music history is that of Igor Stravinsky's ballet *The Rite of Spring* in 1913. This performance so shocked its Parisian audience that the instrumentalists could not hear themselves play over the riotous crowd. At the time, French ballet music was very backward-looking and accompanied a very stylized choreography. The usual ballet patrons were bound to be overwhelmed by the enactment of barbaric rituals accented by the pulsating rhythms and dissonant harmonies featured in Stravinsky's new work.

Although *The Rite* was vehemently rejected, Stravinsky's innovation was rooted in the past and proved to be an important step in the future course of music history. The pressing and irregular rhythms of ritual in this work continued the rhythmic experimentation begun by Stravinsky's teacher, Nikolai Rimsky-Korsakov. This de-emphasis of melody and harmony became characteristic of works later in the century. Just as Stravinsky borrowed elements from folk music for this piece, many twentieth century composers also made extensive use of diverse sources in their compositions. Although *The Rite* was so poorly received at its premiere, its contribution to the field of music can be considered simply ahead of its time (Machlis, 1979).

Paradigm-Rejecting Contributions that Move the Field in a New Direction from an Existing or a Pre-Existing Starting Point

TYPE 5: REDIRECTION.　Redirection is illustrated in Panel 5 of Figure 5.1. Redirection involves accepting the field where it is at a given time but attempting to move it in a new direction. Work of this type is creative to the extent that it moves a field in a new direction (novelty) and to the extent that this direction is seen as desirable for research (quality).

The pioneering Hunt, Frost, and Lunneborg (1973) article mentioned earlier suggested that researchers of intelligence use cognitive-psychological paradigms to study intelligence. The basic idea was to correlate scores on cognitive tasks with scores on psychometric tests. Sternberg (1977) used cognitive techniques as a starting point, but suggested that research move in a direction different from that suggested by Hunt. In particular, he suggested that complex cognitive tasks (such as analogies and classifications) be used instead of simple cognitive tasks (such as lexical access) and that the goal should be to decompose information processing on these tasks into its elementary information-processing components. Sternberg argued that Hunt was right in suggesting the use of cognitive tasks, but wrong in suggesting the use of very simple ones, which he believed involved only fairly low levels of intelligent thought. Sternberg was thus suggesting a redirection in the kind of cognitive work Hunt had initiated.

Edward Tolman (1932) made an effort to redirect the field of learning, an effort that today has earned Tolman a place in virtually every serious textbook on learning or even on introductory psychology. Tolman accepted many of the conventions of the day – experiments with rats, use of mazes, and multi-trial laboratory learning experiments. But he proposed to take all these features of research in a new direction, one that would allow for purposiveness and latent learning on the part of the animals he was studying. Today, these concepts are widely accepted, although at the time Tolman proposed them, the reaction was mixed, at best.

Beethoven's work can also be viewed as a redirection from the classical style of music that had been employed so successfully by Haydn, Mozart, and others. Beethoven used many of the same classical forms as his predecessors, but he also showed that a greater level of emotionality could be introduced into the music without sacrificing those forms.

Vonnegut questioned the very fabric of what constitutes a war novel, and in doing so pointed a path for the field to take. Re-creations and straightforward stories of the horrors of war (such as Stephen Crane's *The Red Badge of Courage* or MacKinlay Kantor's *Andersonville*) are powerful, Vonnegut might argue, but to truly convey the nature of war an author must go beyond this. O'Brien picks up on Vonnegut's path and takes yet another direction: An author *cannot* convey the nature of war to someone who has not experienced it. All he or she can do is convey the feelings and thoughts one might have in these situations. O'Brien and Vonnegut are not re-initiators, as they accept the same starting point for war novels that other novelists have used. Their work is not merely a type of forward incrementation, however, because they have taken a radically different view of the way in which a war novel should be written.

TYPE 6: RECONSTRUCTION/REDIRECTION. This type of creative contribution is illustrated in Panel 6 of Figure 5.1. In using reconstruction, an individual suggests that the field should move *backward* to a previous point but from there move in a direction divergent from that it had taken. In other words, the individual suggests that at some time in the past, the field went off track. The individual suggests the point at which this occurred and how the field should have moved forward from that point. The work is judged as creative to the extent that the individual is judged as correctly recognizing that the field has gone off track and to the extent that the new direction is viewed as a useful one for the field to pursue.

In the early part of the century, intelligence tests seemed to have potential for helping society understand why certain groups rose to the top of the society and other groups fell to the bottom (see Carroll, 1982; Ceci, 1996; Gould, 1981). This often thinly disguised social Darwinism was based on the notion that those with more adaptive skills, on average, should and in fact did have more success in adapting to the demands of the social structure of the society. Those with fewer adaptive skills, on average, did and should fall to the bottom. This kind of thinking became unpopular in the latter half of the century. Environment came to be seen as much more important than it had before (Kamin, 1974; Lewontin, 1982). As a result, intelligence-test scores were no longer being looked at as a cause of group differences, but rather as an effect.

This balance was upset when Herrnstein and Murray (1994) argued that the older views were most likely correct in many respects: It is plausible, they argued, to believe that group differences in IQ are in fact due to genetic factors, and that these group differences result in social mobility. Herrnstein and Murray further suggested that what they considered a humane social policy could be constructed on the basis of these alleged facts. Many people who were more comfortable with the older views or who were ready to be persuaded of them found the Herrnstein-Murray arguments convincing. Others, especially those believing in multiple intelligences or the importance of environment, were not at all convinced.

My goal here is not to argue about the validity of the Herrnstein-Murray position, which I have discussed elsewhere (Sternberg, 1995). Rather, it is to suggest that the work of Herrnstein and Murray was serving a reconstructive function. Herrnstein and Murray were suggesting that the field had gone off course in the desire of its members to accept certain beliefs that, however charitable they might be, were incorrect. These authors suggested the field return to a point that many (although certainly not all) investigators had thought had been left behind, and advance from that point.

B. F. Skinner's (1972) analysis of creativity represents another example of reconstruction/redirection. Skinner apparently was perturbed that the analysis of creativity had moved further and further away from the kinds of behavioristic principles that he and his colleagues believed applied to *all* behavior. The 1972 paper was, in large part, an argument that the field of creativity had lost its foundations, and that it needed to return to the kinds of behavioristic analyses that Skinner believed he and others had shown could account for creative behavior.

Some literary scholars are now suggesting that literary criticism, too, has gone off track – that the kind of deconstructionism introduced by Derrida (1992) and others has produced a literary nihilism that has resulted in a degeneration of the field of literary criticism. These individuals, such as Bloom (1994), suggest that literary scholars return to their earlier tradition of finding specific meaning in literary works rather than asserting that virtually any meaning can be read into any literary work.

The musical "Take It Easy" (1996) is an exemplar of reconstruction/ redirection. Author Raymond G. Fox's musical takes place in the 1940s, and the music is a reconstruction of the "swing" sound. The characters are intentionally stereotypes, such as The Bookworm and The All-American Hero. The ultimate goal of the show is to re-create the feel of a 1940s college musical, with young, good-looking, and patriotic characters. Several other recent Broadway shows, such as "Triumph of Love" (book by James Magruder, music by Jeffrey Stock, and lyrics by Susan Birkenhead) and "Big" (book by John Weidman, music by David Shire, and lyrics by Richard Maltby, Jr.) have been "throwback" musicals that reflect the more simplistic plot, characters, and musical tone of musicals of the 1950s. Unlike more modern shows, which tend to be entirely sung and have either an operatic or rock musical style, these shows take the structure and values of more classic musicals (such as "Oklahoma!" or "My Fair Lady") and update the topics and sensibilities to the 1990s (for example, in "Big," characters refer to rap music).

Paradigm-Rejecting Contributions that Restart the Field in a New Place and Move in a New Direction from There

TYPE 7: REINITIATION.   This type of creative contribution is illustrated in Panel 7 of Figure 5.1. In reinitiation, a contributor suggests that a field or subfield has reached an undesirable point or has exhausted itself moving in the direction in which it is moving. But rather than suggesting that the field or subfield move in a different direction from where it is (as in redirection), the contributor suggests moving in a different direction from a different point in the multidimensional space of contributions. In effect, the contributor is suggesting people question their assumptions and "start over" from a point that most likely makes different assumptions. This form of creative contribution represents a major paradigm shift.

Two notable examples of this type of creativity can be found in the contributions to the field of intelligence made by Spearman (1904) and by Binet and Simon (1916a). Spearman reinvented the field of intelligence theory and research by his invention of factor analysis and by proposing his two-factor theory (general ability and specific abilities), based on his factor-analytic results. Spearman's contribution was to put theorizing about intelligence on a firm quantitative footing, a contribution that lives on today, whether or not one agrees with either Spearman's theory or his methodology. Binet and Simon (1916a) reinvented the field of intelligence measurement. Whereas Galton (1883) had proposed that intelligence should be understood in terms of simple psychophysical processes, Binet and Simon proposed that intelligence should be understood in terms of higher-order processes of judgment. For the most part, the measurements of intelligence today are still based on this notion of Binet and Simon.

Spearman's (1904, 1927) reinitiating emphasis on general ability was not shared by all investigators. For example, Thurstone (1938), Guilford (1967), and many other theorists have suggested that intelligence comprises multiple abilities and that any general factor obtained in factor analyses was likely to be at best, unimportant, and at worst, epiphenomenal. In all cases, however, intelligence was accepted as a unitary construct. What differed were investigators' views on how, if at all, the unitary construct should be divided up.

Festinger and Carlsmith's (1959) initial paper on cognitive dissonance, mentioned earlier, represents a reinitiation, an attempt to make a new start in the field of social psychology. A more recent example of a reinitiation is Bem's (1996) theory of homosexuality, according to which what initially is exotic for an individual later in life becomes erotic. Bem's is a theory arguing for environmental causes of homosexuality at a time when biological theories have largely gained acceptance.

Revolutionary works tend to be major reinitiations. In the field of linguistics, Chomsky's (1957) transformational grammar changed the way many linguists looked at language. Linguists following Chomsky began analyzing deep syntactic structures, not just surface structures. And of course Einstein revolutionized physics, showing that Newtonian physics represented only a limiting case of physics, in general, and further showing the relativity of notions about space and time. Reinitiations can apply to entire fields, as in the case of Einstein, or to smaller subfields. In each case, however, the creators are arguing for a fresh approach to creative work.

Reinitiative contributions are often bold and daring gestures. One prime example can be found in sculpture, with Marcel Duchamp's 1917 *Fountain*. Duchamp's Dada piece is simply a urinal turned on its back. The very act of entering such a piece in an art show is a statement about art – Duchamp's sculpture made art-making focus on the definition of exactly what art is and what art can be. Duchamp's urinal became a piece of art, and he and his fellow Dada creators set the stage for other modern art that challenges our ideas of what "art" encompasses (Hartt, 1993).

Another radical reinitiator is one of Duchamp's friends, the composer John Cage. He often employed unconventional sound materials and for a period his compositional process (and often performance) was determined entirely by chance. The philosophy that led Cage to compose in this unorthodox manner can be considered essentially a rejection of some basic tenets of the Western musical tradition, including the definition of music itself. Cage declared music to be all sound, including the whispers and heartbeats we perceive while silent. His affinity for Eastern philosophy caused him to focus on the importance of awareness in the human experience, and he used his music to foster awareness in his listeners.

An illustration of this point is his piece *4' 33"*. The performance of this piece consists of four minutes and thirty-three seconds of "silence," or rather, in Cage's terminology, "unintentional sound." In performance, the instrumentalist approaches her instrument, prepares to play, and proceeds to sit, without sound, for four minutes and thirty-three seconds. The only pauses are those indicated by Cage which signal the change of movement. The music, therefore, is that sound that exists in the environment. Cage's statement is that there is music being played around us all the time; we must reject the notion of music as organized melody, harmony, and rhythm to include all sound, even the rush of traffic beyond the door and the buzzing of the fluorescent lights above our heads (Cage, 1961; Hamm, 1980).

TYPE 8: INTEGRATION. In this type of creative contribution, illustrated in Panel 8 of Figure 5.1, the creator puts together two types of ideas previously seen as unrelated or even as opposed. Formerly viewed as distinct ideas, they now are viewed as related and capable of being unified. Integration is a key means by which progress is attained in the sciences.

One example of an integration is *Fatherland* (Harris, 1992), Robert Harris's best-selling novel of historical speculation. In the genre of historical speculation the author imagines a world different from the one we live in because of a fundamental change in history, perhaps a world in which a famous event in the past did not occur (for example, if John F. Kennedy had not been assassinated). Or a world in which an event that did not occur had, in fact, happened (if Adolf Hitler had been assassinated). In *Fatherland*, Harris conceptualizes a world in which Germany defeated the Allies in World War II. But rather than devoting most of the book to setting up the world and describing the "new" history, Harris plunges right in and begins a suspense thriller. Harris took the two genres – historical speculation and suspense thriller – and fused them together into a well-received novel.

Another example of integration is the innovative artwork of Rob Silvers. Silvers (1997) takes Georges Seurat's pointillist technique of using many small dots to form a larger work and combines it with the field of photography. Silvers uses thousands of tiny photographs and puts them together to form a larger image. His type of work, called photo mosaics, has become well known; Silvers designed the movie poster for *The Truman Show* and has done portraits of such disparate individuals as Princess Diana, Abraham Lincoln, and Darth Vader.

General Issues.   In considering the eight types of creative contributions, one must realize that certain types of creative contributions may be, in practice, more highly creative than others, but that there can be no claim, in principle, that contributions of one type are more creative than others (with the possible exception of replications). Contributions can vary in novelty and quality. Consider as an example a reinitiation versus a forward incrementation. A reinitiation is, on average, more defiant of existing paradigms than is a forward incrementation. But a reinitiation is not necessarily more creative than a forward incrementation. The reinitiation may differ only trivially from existing paradigms or it may differ in a way that moves the field in a fruitless direction. The forward incrementation, on the other hand, may be one that has eluded all or almost all other investigators and thus is highly novel; moreover, it may be a contribution that makes just the step that makes a great difference to a field, such as the step that yields a vaccine against a serious illness. Thus, types of creative contributions do not immediately translate into levels of creative contributions. The relative levels of creativity of two contributions have to be determined on other grounds.

Nevertheless, individual investigators or institutions may have preferences for one type of creative contribution over another. The management of one institution may feel threatened by redefinitions or reinitiations whereas the management of another institution welcomes them. One graduate advisor may encourage his or her students to strike out on their own in crowd-defying directions whereas another graduate advisor insists that students work only within existing paradigms or perhaps even only the advisor's own paradigm. Undoubtedly, graduate training plays an important role not only in socializing students with respect to doing worthwhile research but also with respect to the kinds of research considered to be worthwhile. As always, what is viewed as creative will depend on the match between what an individual has to offer and what the context is willing to value. We also need to keep in mind that contributions are judged on the basis of many attributes, not just their creativity. A contribution that is creative may be valued or devalued in a society for any number of reasons, for example, its "political correctness" or the gender, ethnic group, or status of its creator.

Understanding Creativity-Related Phenomena via the Propulsion Model. The propulsion model may help explain several creativity-related phenomena, although it does not provide a unique explanation.

First, the propulsion model may help reconcile the fact that creativity tends to generate negative reactions with the fact that most people seem to believe that they support creativity (Sternberg & Lubart, 1995). The present model suggests that positive or negative reactions to a given contribution are likely to vary with the type of creativity evinced in a given creative contribution. For example, the kind of paradigm-rejecting, crowd-defying creativity dealt with by the investment theory of creativity (Sternberg & Lubart, 1995) is probably largely of the later three types: redirection (type 5), reconstruction/redirection (type 6), and especially reinitiation (type 7). Paradigm-accepting creativity is more likely to generate a favorable response, at least initially. Forward incrementations, for example, are creative but occur within existing paradigms and hence are more likely to engender favorable reactions, whether from journal editors, grant reviewers, or critics of music and art. In the short run, artists, scientists, and others who provide forward incrementations may have the easiest time getting their work accepted; in the long run, however, their contributions may not be the longest lasting or the most important.

Second, the propulsion model helps psychologists better understand the nature of the relation between creativity and leadership (see, for example, Gardner, 1993, 1995). Leadership, like creativity, is propulsion. Hence, creativity always represents at least a weak attempt to lead. In the case of replication, the attempt is rather trivial. In the case of redirection, reconstruction/redirection, or reinitiation, it may be quite dramatic. In each of these cases, the creative individual is trying to lead the field in a direction different from the one in which it is going. Even advance incrementation represents an impressive form of leadership, in that it attempts to lead a field rather far away from where it is in the multidimensional space, albeit in the same direction as the field already is going.

Examples of the application of the propulsion model to creative leadership can be inferred from an analysis of university presidents by Levine (1998). Levine provides examples of two failed presidents – Francis

Wayland of Brown (president from 1827 to 1855) and Henry Tappan of the University of Michigan (1852 to 1863) – both of whom failed because their ideas were ahead of their time. Their ideas would succeed in other institutions, but later. Both presidents exemplified forward advance incrementations in the attempts at creative leadership of their institutions. Robert Hutchins, president of the University of Chicago from 1929 to 1951, was removed from his presidency because his ideas were behind the times. Hutchins wished to set off in a new direction from a set of ideas that had become passé in the minds of his constituents. He illustrated reconstruction/redirection. Clark Kerr, president of the University of California, Berkeley, from 1959 to 1967, ultimately failed because he became the wrong person at the wrong time when Ronald Reagan became governor of California. In essence, Reagan moved the multidimensional space to a new point, one that left Kerr outside the realm viewed as acceptable. The mantle of creative leadership thus was taken on by a governor, leaving the university president out of a job.

Third, the propulsion model helps address the question of whether programs based on artificial intelligence are creative (see discussions in Boden, 1992, 1999; Csikszentmihalyi, 1988; Dreyfus, 1992). To the extent that computer programs *replicate* past discoveries, no matter how creative those discoveries were, they are nevertheless replications, which is creativity (type 1), although perhaps of a more modest type. To the extent that computers actually are able to move a field forward or in a new direction, they may be creative in other senses. My reading of the present literature is that these programs are certainly creative in the sense of replication and that they also probably have been creative in the sense of forward incrementations. It is not clear that they have shown the more crowd-defying forms of creativity (types 5–7: redirection, reconstruction/redirection, reinitation).

Fourth, the propulsion model may be relevant to the long-standing issue (raised above) of the extent to which creativity is domain-specific or domain-general. I would speculate that the ability to do reasonably successful forward incrementations may be largely domain-general and may even be highly correlated with scores on tests of conventional (analytical) abilities. A forward incrementation seems to require, for the most part, a high level of understanding of an extant knowledge base and an analysis of the trajectory of that field. The ability to acquire, understand, and analyze a knowledge base is largely what is measured by conventional standardized tests (Sternberg, 1997b). But the ability to perform a reinitiation may be quite a bit more domain-specific, requiring a sense or even feeling for a field that goes well beyond the kinds of more generalized analytical abilities measured by conventional tests. People who engage in creativity of types 5 (redirection), 6 (reconstruction/redirection), and 7 (reinitiation) may be less susceptible than others to the entrenchment that can accompany expertise (Frensch & Sternberg, 1989; Sternberg & Lubart, 1995).

The propulsion model certainly has weaknesses and ambiguities. First, it is new and has yet to be quantitatively tested. Such tests are planned, based on classifications of creative contributions and analyses of various measures of their impact. Second, contributions cannot be unequivocally classified into the different types. Bach, for example, was viewed in his time as, at best, making small forward incremental contributions or even as being a replicator. Today he is perceived by many as having helped to redefine Baroque music. Moreover, because we are always making judgments from whatever perspective we may hold, it is impossible to ensure "objective" judgments of the type of creative contribution a particular work makes or has made. Third, the model proposed here is probably not exhaustive with respect to the types of creative contributions that can be made. There may well be others and the ones proposed here almost certainly could be subdivided. Fourth, a given contribution may have elements of more than one type of contribution. Finally, the spatial metaphor used as a basis for the theory obviously is an oversimplification. There is no one point in a multidimensional space that can adequately represent a field or a subfield, nor is all research in the field or subfield moving in a single direction.

Ultimately, it is unlikely that there is any one "right" model of types of creative contributions. Rather, models such as this one can help people expand their thinking about the types of creative contributions that can be made in a field. And to the extent this model accomplishes that goal, it is accomplishing what it should. Creative contributions differ not only in amounts but also in types, and the eight types represented here are ones that presumably occur in all fields at all times. We should be aware of them when they occur. We also may wish to steer our children and ourselves toward certain types of creative contributions, ideally the types that are most compatible with what these children or we wish to offer. Do we wish our children to be replicators, to be forward incrementers, to be redirectors, to know when to be which? These are the decisions we must make in socializing our children. Ultimately, the children will need to decide for themselves, as they grow older, how they wish to unlock and express their creative potential. But the thing that is certain is that they will decide, because creativity is a decision. How can one encourage people to decide for creativity? According to the view of creativity as a decision, fomenting creativity is largely a matter of fomenting a certain attitude toward problem solving and even toward life. Creativity researchers may have a great deal of academic knowledge about creativity, but they do not necessarily interact with students in a way that maximizes the chances that students will decide for creativity.

PART III

WISDOM

6

Background Work on Wisdom

Many societies today are preoccupied with the development of cognitive skills in schoolchildren. In U.S. society, cognitive skills have become practically equated with intellectual skills – the mental bases of intelligence.[1] This equation is a mistake.

Given that IQs have been rising (Flynn, 1998), what does our world have to show for it? Judging by the seriousness and sheer scale of global conflict, perhaps not much. There is no reason to believe that increasing IQs have improved people's or nations' relations with each other.

The memory and analytical skills so central to intelligence are certainly important for school and life success, but perhaps they are not sufficient. Arguably, wisdom-related skills are at least as important or even more important.

Wisdom can be defined as the "power of judging rightly and following the soundest course of action, based on knowledge, experience, understanding, etc." (*Webster's New World College Dictionary*, 1997, p. 1533). Such a power would seem to be of vast importance in a world that at times seems bent on destroying itself.

MAJOR APPROACHES TO UNDERSTANDING WISDOM

A number of psychologists have attempted to understand wisdom in different ways. The approaches underlying some of these attempts are summarized in Sternberg (1990b). A more detailed review of some of the major

---

[1] By *intellectual skills*, I refer to those skills that are relevant to a given theory of intelligence. For example, Spearman (1927) included among such skills apprehension of experience (encoding), eduction of relations (inference), and eduction of correlates (application). Binet and Simon (1916b) included judgment skills, Galton (1883), psychophysical skills. Such skills are a subset of cognitive skills, which include skills that both are and are not relevant to intelligence within a given theoretical framework. Which cognitive skills would count as intellectual skills will vary with the theory of intelligence.

approaches to wisdom can be found in Baltes and Staudinger (2000) or in Sternberg (1990b, 1998b, 2000c). The main approaches might be classified as philosophical approaches, implicit-theoretical approaches, and explicit-theoretical approaches.

Philosophical Approaches

Philosophical approaches have been reviewed by Robinson (1990; see also Robinson, 1989, with regard to the Aristotelian approach in particular, and Labouvie-Vief, 1990, for a further review). Robinson notes that the study of wisdom has a history that long antedates psychological study, with the Platonic dialogues offering the first intensive analysis of the concept of wisdom. Robinson points out that, in these dialogues, there are three different senses of wisdom: wisdom as (a) *sophia*, which is found in those who seek a contemplative life in search of truth; (b) *phronesis*, which is the kind of practical wisdom shown by statesmen and legislators; and (c) *episteme*, which is found in those who understand things from a scientific point of view.

Implicit-theoretical Approaches

Implicit-theoretical approaches to wisdom have in common the search for an understanding of people's folk conceptions of what wisdom is. Thus, the goal is not to provide a "psychologically true" account of wisdom, but rather an account that is true with respect to people's beliefs, whether these beliefs are right or wrong. Some of the earliest work of this kind was done by Clayton (1975, 1976; Clayton & Birren, 1980), who multidimensionally scaled ratings of pairs of words potentially related to wisdom for three samples of adults differing in age (younger, middle-aged, older). In her earliest study (Clayton, 1975), the terms scaled were such as *experienced, pragmatic, understanding,* and *knowledgeable.*

Holliday and Chandler (1986) also used an implicit-theories approach to understanding wisdom. Approximately five hundred participants were studied across a series of experiments. The investigators were interested in determining whether the concept of wisdom could be understood as a prototype (Rosch, 1975), or central concept. Principal-components analysis of one of their studies revealed five underlying factors: exceptional understanding, judgment and communication skills, general competence, interpersonal skills, and social unobtrusiveness.

Sternberg (1985b, 1990a) has reported a series of studies investigating implicit theories of wisdom. In one study, two hundred professors each of art, business, philosophy, and physics were asked to rate the characteristic-ness of each of the behaviors obtained in a prestudy from the corresponding population with respect to the professors' conception of an ideally wise, intelligent, or creative individual in their occupation. Laypersons were also asked to provide these ratings but for a hypothetical ideal individual without regard to occupation. Correlations were computed across the three ratings. In each group except philosophy, the highest correlation was between wisdom and intelligence; in philosophy, the highest correlation was between intelligence and creativity. The correlations between wisdom and intelligence ratings ranged from .42 to .78 with a median of .68. For all groups, the lowest correlation was between wisdom and creativity (which ranged from −.24 to .48 with a median of .27).

In a second study, forty college students were asked to sort three sets of forty behaviors each into as many or as few piles as they wished. The forty behaviors in each set were the top-rated wisdom, intelligence, and creativity behaviors from the previous study. The sortings were subjected to nonmetric multidimensional scaling. For wisdom, six components emerged: *reasoning ability, sagacity, learning from ideas and environment, judgment, expeditious use of information*, and *perspicacity*. These components can be compared with those that emerged from a similar scaling of people's implicit theories of intelligence, which were *practical problem-solving ability, verbal ability, intellectual balance and integration, goal orientation and attainment, contextual intelligence*, and *fluid thought*. In both cases, cognitive abilities and their use are important. In wisdom, however, some kind of balance appears to emerge as important that does not emerge as important in intelligence, in general.

In a third study, fifty adults were asked to rate descriptions of hypothetical individuals for wisdom, intelligence, and creativity. Correlations were computed between pairs of ratings of the hypothetical individuals' levels of the three traits. Correlations between the ratings were .94 for wisdom and intelligence, .62 for wisdom and creativity, and .69 for intelligence and creativity, again suggesting that wisdom and intelligence are highly correlated in people's implicit theories, at least in the United States.

Explicit-Theoretical Approaches

Explicit-theoretical approaches have in common a formal theory of wisdom that is proposed to account for wisdom. The most extensive program of research has been that conducted by Baltes and his colleagues. This program of research is related to Baltes's long-standing program of research on intellectual abilities and aging. For example, Baltes and Smith (1987, 1990) gave adult participants life-management problems, such as "A fourteen-year-old girl is pregnant. What should she, what should one, consider and do?" and "A fifteen-year-old girl wants to marry soon. What should she, what should one, consider and do?" This same problem might be used to measure the pragmatics of intelligence, about which Baltes has written at length. Baltes and Smith tested a five-component model of wisdom on participants' protocols in answering these and other questions, based on a notion of wisdom as expert knowledge about fundamental life matters (Smith & Baltes, 1990) or of wisdom as good judgment and advice in important but uncertain matters of life (Baltes & Staudinger, 1993).

Three kinds of factors – general person factors, expertise-specific factors, and facilitative experiential contexts – were proposed to facilitate wise judgments. These factors are used in life planning, life management, and life review. Wisdom is in turn reflected in five components: (a) rich factual knowledge (general and specific knowledge about the conditions of life and its variations), (b) rich procedural knowledge (general and specific knowledge about strategies of judgment and advice concerning matters of life), (c) life span contextualism (knowledge about the contexts of life and their temporal [developmental] relationships), (d) relativism (knowledge about differences in values, goals, and priorities), and (e) uncertainty (knowledge about the relative indeterminacy and unpredictability of life and ways to manage). An expert answer should reflect more of these components, whereas a novice answer should reflect fewer. The data collected to date generally have been supportive of the model. These factors seem to reflect the pragmatic aspect of intelligence but go beyond it, for example, in the inclusion of factors of relativism and uncertainty.

Over time, Baltes and his colleagues (for example, Baltes, Smith, & Staudinger, 1992; Baltes & Staudinger, 1993) have collected a wide range of data showing the empirical utility of the proposed theoretical and measurement approaches to wisdom. For example, Staudinger, Lopez and Baltes (1997) found that measures of intelligence (as well as personality) overlap with, but are nonidentical to, measures of wisdom in terms of constructs measured and Staudinger, Smith, and Baltes (1992) showed that human-services professionals outperformed a control group on wisdom-related tasks. They also showed that older adults performed as well on such tasks as did younger adults, and that older adults did better on such tasks if there was a match between their age and the age of the fictitious characters about whom they made judgments. Baltes, Staudinger, Maercker, and Smith (1995) found that older individuals nominated for their wisdom performed as well as did clinical psychologists on wisdom-related tasks. They also showed that up to the age of eighty, older adults performed as well on such tasks as did younger adults. In a further set of studies, Staudinger and Baltes (1996) found that performance settings that were ecologically relevant to the lives of their participants and that provided for actual or "virtual" interaction of minds increased wisdom-related performance substantially.

Some theorists have viewed wisdom in terms of postformal–operational thinking, thereby viewing wisdom as extending beyond the Piagetian stages of intelligence (Piaget, 1972). Wisdom thus might be a stage of thought beyond Piagetian formal operations. For example, some authors have argued that wise individuals are those who can think reflectively or dialectically, in the latter case with the individuals realizing that truth is not always absolute but rather evolves in an historical context of theses, antitheses, and syntheses (for example, Basseches, 1984; Kitchener, 1983, 1986; Kitchener & Brenner, 1990; Kitchener & Kitchener, 1981; Labouvie-Vief, 1980, 1982, 1990; Pascual-Leone, 1990; Riegel, 1973). Other theorists have viewed wisdom in terms of finding important problems to solve (Arlin, 1990).

Although most developmental approaches to wisdom are ontogenetic, Csikszentmihalyi and Rathunde (1990) have taken a philogenetic or evolutionary approach, arguing that constructs such as wisdom must have been selected for over time, at least in a cultural sense. They have defined wisdom as having three basic dimensions of meaning: (a) that of a cognitive process or a particular way of obtaining and processing information; (b) that of a virtue or socially valued pattern of behavior; and (c) that of a good or a personally desirable state or condition.

Several of the theories described above emphasize the importance of various kinds of integrations or balances in wisdom. At least three major kinds of balances have been proposed: among various kinds of thinking (for example, Labouvie-Vief, 1990), among various self-systems, such as the cognitive, conative, and affective (for example, Kramer, 1990), and among various points of view (for example, Kitchener & Brenner, 1990). Baltes has also argued for the importance of balance (Baltes, 1993, 1994; Baltes & Staudinger, 2000; Staudinger, Lopez, & Baltes, 1997). The view presented here expands on but also differs from these kinds of notions in also providing for particular kinds of balance in wisdom.

7

The Balance Theory of Wisdom

The current theory views successful intelligence and creativity as the bases for wisdom. Successful intelligence and creativity are necessary, but not sufficient, conditions for wisdom. Particularly important is tacit knowledge, which is critical to practical intelligence.

THE BALANCE THEORY

Wisdom as Successful Intelligence and Creativity Balancing Interests

Wisdom is defined as the application of successful intelligence and creativity as mediated by values toward the achievement of a common good through a balance among (a) intrapersonal, (b) interpersonal, and (c) extrapersonal interests, over (a) short and (b) long terms, in order to achieve a balance among (a) adaptation to existing environments, (b) shaping of existing environments, and (c) selection of new environments, as shown in Figure 7.1.

Thus, wisdom is not just about maximizing one's own or someone else's self-interest, but about balancing various self-interests (intrapersonal) with the interests of others (interpersonal) and of other aspects of the context in which one lives (extrapersonal), such as one's city or country or environment or even God. Wisdom also involves creativity, in that the wise solution to a problem may be far from obvious.

An implication of this view is that when one applies successful intelligence and creativity, one may deliberately seek outcomes that are good for oneself and bad for others. In wisdom, one certainly may seek good ends for oneself, but one also seeks common good outcomes for others. If one's motivations are to maximize certain people's interests and minimize other people's, wisdom is not involved. In wisdom, one seeks a common good, realizing that this common good may be better for some than for others. A

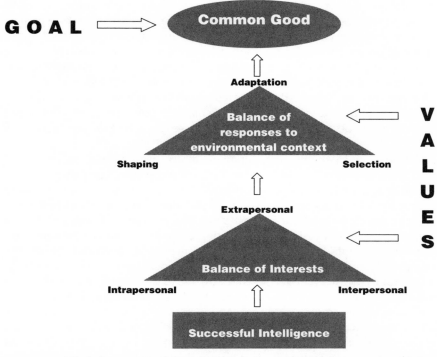

FIGURE 7.1. Wisdom as successful intelligence balancing goals, responses, and inter- ests. The individual applies successful intelligence in order to seek a common good. Such application involves balancing of intrapersonal, interpersonal, and extraper- sonal interests to adapt to, shape, and select environments. Judgments regarding how to achieve a common good inevitably involve the infusion of values.

terrorist may be academically intelligent; he may be practically intelligent; he cannot be wise.

Problems requiring wisdom always involve at least some element of each of intrapersonal, interpersonal, and extrapersonal interests. For ex- ample, one might decide that it is wise to take a particular teaching posi- tion, a decision that seemingly involves only one person. But many people are typically affected by an individual's decision to take a job – significant others, children, perhaps parents and friends. And the decision always has to be made in the context of what the whole range of available options is. Thus, people have to know what the options are and what they mean. To be wise, one must know what one knows, know what one does not know, know what can be known, and know what cannot be known at a given time or place.

What kinds of considerations might be included under each of the three kinds of interests? Intrapersonal interests might include the desire to enhance one's popularity or prestige, to make more money, to learn more, to increase one's spiritual well-being, to increase one's power, and so forth. Interpersonal interests might be quite similar, except as they apply to other people rather than oneself. Extrapersonal interests might include contributing to the welfare of one's school, helping one's community, contributing to the well-being of one's country, or serving God, and so forth. Different people balance these interests in different ways. At one extreme, a malevolent dictator might emphasize his or her own personal power and wealth; at the other extreme, a saint might emphasize only serving others and God.

Failures in balancing intrapersonal, interpersonal, and extrapersonal interests can have devastating effects. Consider some examples.

Although both Richard Nixon and Bill Clinton, as presidents, were rather self-absorbed, neither was wise. Wisdom involves a balancing not only of the three kinds of interests, but also of three possible courses of action in response to this balancing: adaptation of oneself or others to existing environments; shaping of environments in order to render them more compatible with oneself or others; and selection of new environments. In adaptation, the individual tries to find ways to conform to the existing environment that forms his or her context. Sometimes adaptation is the best course of action under a given set of circumstances. But typically one seeks a balance between adaptation and shaping, realizing that fit to an environment requires not only changing oneself, but changing the environment as well. When an individual finds it impossible or at least implausible to attain such a fit, he or she may decide to select a new environment altogether, leaving, for example, a job, a community, a marriage, or whatever.

Wisdom manifests itself as a series of processes, which are typically cyclical and can occur in a variety of orders. These processes are the metacomponents of thought, including (a) recognizing the existence of a problem, (b) defining the nature of the problem, (c) representing information about the problem, (d) formulating a strategy for solving the problem, (e) allocating resources to the solution of a problem, (f) monitoring one's solution of the problem, and (g) evaluating feedback regarding that solution. In deciding about a teaching job, for example, one first has to see both taking the position and not taking it as viable options (problem recognition); then figure out exactly what taking or not taking the position would mean for oneself (defining the problem); then consider the costs and benefits to oneself and others (representing information about the problem); and so forth.

Wisdom is typically acquired by what I have referred to earlier as knowledge-acquisition components (Sternberg, 1985a). Its acquisition depends on (a) selectively encoding new information that is relevant for one's purposes in learning about that context; (b) selectively comparing this information to old information to see how the new fits with the old; and

(c) selectively combining pieces of information to make them fit together into an orderly whole (Sternberg, Wagner, & Okagaki, 1993).

This treatment of wisdom, which emphasizes the role of tacit knowledge, should not be interpreted to mean that formal knowledge is not or cannot be relevant to wise judgments and decision making. Quite the contrary: Obviously formal knowledge can be and often is extremely relevant to wise judgments and decision making. For example, consider the story of Solomon's judgment regarding the two women claiming to be the mother of the same infant. Stories of wise leadership are often learned in formal settings. But these aspects of knowledge, although relevant to wise judgments, need to be connected to such judgments via tacit knowledge. For example, consider the decision of Nelson Mandela in school to unify his country. But when to apply this knowledge, where to apply it, how to apply it, to whom to apply it, even why to apply it – these are the stuff of tacit knowledge. They are not and cannot be directly taught in school lessons. They are the lessons learned from experience. They can be learned in school, but they are not directly taught out of textbooks or lectures.

SOURCES OF DEVELOPMENTAL AND INDIVIDUAL DIFFERENCES IN WISDOM

The balance theory suggests a number of sources of developmental and individual differences in wisdom. In particular, there are two kinds of sources, those directly affecting the balance processes and those that are antecedent.

Individual and Developmental Differences Directly Affecting the Balance Processes

There are seven sources of differences directly affecting the balance processes. Consider, as an example, a teacher who has been instructed by a principal to spend almost all of his time teaching in a way to maximize students' scores on a statewide assessment test, but who believes that the principal is essentially forcing him to abandon truly educating his students.

1. Goals. People may differ in terms of the extent to which they seek a common good, and thus in the extent to which they aim for the essential goal of wisdom. They also may differ in terms of what they view as the common good. The teacher may believe it is not in the children's best interest to engage in what he views as mindless drills for a test. The principal, however, may have a different view. The teacher is thus left with the responsibility of deciding what is in the best interests of all concerned.

2. Balancing Responses to Environmental Contexts.   People may differ in their balance of responses to environmental contexts. Responses always reflect in the interaction of the individual making the judgment and the environment, and people can interact with contexts in myriad ways. The teacher may adapt to the environment and do exactly what the principal has told him to do, or shape the environment and do exactly what he believes he should do, or try to find some balance between adaptation and shaping that largely meets the principal's goals but also largely meets his own. Or the teacher may decide that the environment of the school is sufficiently aversive to his philosophy of teaching that he would prefer to teach elsewhere.

3. Balancing of Interests.   People may balance interests in different ways. The teacher must decide how to balance his own interests in good teaching and also in staying on good terms with the principal; the children's interests in learning but also doing well on the statewide tests; the parents' interests in having well-educated children; and so on.

4. Balancing of Short and Long Terms.   People may differ in their emphases. The teacher may believe that, in the long run, a proper education involves much more than preparing for statewide tests, but at the same time realize that, in the short run, the children's scores on the tests will affect their future as well as his future and possibly those of his principal and school.

5. Acquisition of Tacit Knowledge.   People differ in the extent to which they acquire tacit knowledge. The teacher may bring relatively sophisticated tacit knowledge to solving this problem of how to teach the children, or may bring virtually no tacit knowledge and may have no clear option other than to do what the principal says.

6. Utilization of Tacit Knowledge.   People differ in how well and how fully they utilize the tacit knowledge they have acquired. The teacher may decide to teach in a way that represents a compromise between his own views and those of the principal, but the way in which this decision is implemented will depend on his knowledge of how to balance the various interests involved in the decision.

7. Values.   People have different values mediating their utilization of intelligence and creativity in the balancing of interests and responses. Values may vary somewhat across space and time, as well as among individuals within a given cultural context. The teacher's values may require him to diverge at least somewhat from the instructions of the principal. Another teacher's values might lead him to do what the principal says, regardless of how he personally feels. Nevertheless, there seem to be certain core values that are common to the world's great ethical systems and religions. They include values such as honesty, sincerity, reciprocity, compassion, and courage.

These sources of differences produce variations in how wise people are and in how well they can apply their wisdom in different kinds of situations. To the extent that wisdom is typically associated with greater intellectual and even physical maturity, it is presumably because the development of tacit knowledge and of values is something that unfolds over the course of the life span, not in childhood or in the early years of adulthood.

The above sources of individual differences pertain to the balancing processes. Other sources are antecedent to these processes.

Relations of Wisdom to Other Skills

Wisdom is related to other psychological constructs but not identical to any of them. In particular, it is related to knowledge, as well as to analytical, creative, and practical aspects of intelligence, and other aspects of intelligence.

First, wisdom requires knowledge, but the heart of wisdom is tacit, informal knowledge of the kind learned in the school of life, not the kind of explicit formal knowledge taught in schools. One could be a "walking encyclopedia" and show little or no wisdom because the knowledge one needs to be wise is not found in encyclopedias or even, generally, in the type of teaching found in most schools (with the possible exception of those that teach Socratically).

Second, wisdom requires analytical thinking, but it is not the kind of analytical thinking typically emphasized in schools or measured on tests of academic abilities and achievements (discussed in Sternberg, 1980b). Rather it is the analysis of real-world dilemmas where clean and neat abstractions often give way to messy and disorderly concrete interests. The kind of abstract analytical thinking that may lead to outstanding performance on a test such as the Raven Matrices, which present figural reasoning items, will be of some but not much use in complex real-world dilemmas such as how to defuse the conflict between India and Pakistan.

An important part of analytical thinking is metacognition. Wisdom seems related to metacognition because the metacomponents involved in wisdom are similar or identical to those that follow from other accounts of metacognition (for example, Campione, Brown, & Ferrara, 1982; Nelson, 1999). Thus, in wisdom, as in other types of thinking, one needs to define problems, formulate strategies to solve problems, allocate resources to the solution of these problems, and so forth. These processes are used in wisdom, as they are in other types of thinking, but in wisdom they are used to balance different types of interests in order to seek a common good.

Third, wise solutions are often creative ones, as King Solomon demonstrated in cleverly determining which of two women was truly the mother of a child. But the kind of crowd-defying, buy-low, sell-high attitude that leads to creative contributions does not in itself lead to wisdom. Creative people often tend toward extremes, although their later contributions may be more integrative (Gardner, 1993). Creative thinking is often brash whereas wise thinking is balanced. This is not to say that the same people cannot be both creative and wise. It is to say, however, that the kinds of thinking required to be creative and wise are different and thus will not necessarily be found in the same person. Moreover, teaching people to think creatively (see, for example, Sternberg & Williams, 1996) will not teach them to think wisely.

Wisdom is also related to creatively insightful thinking. According to Sternberg and Davidson (1982), the three knowledge-acquisition components correspond to three kinds of insights, and these three components of knowledge acquisition are also used in the acquisition of wisdom and other kinds of thinking. Selective comparison insights, for example, are used in analogical problem solving when one solves a current problem by applying information obtained in the past in solving a related kind of problem. For example, deciding whether a military campaign will prove to be another "Vietnam" involves selective comparison: Is the new campaign going to be enough like the Vietnam campaign to lead to a similar disaster?

It is important to note that although wise thinking must be, to some extent, creative, creative thinking (as discussed above) need not be wise. Wise thinking must be creative to some extent because it generates a novel and problem-relevant high-quality solution involving balancing of interests, and novelty and appropriate quality are the two hallmarks of creativity (see essays in Sternberg, 1999b). But a solution can be creative – as in solving a mathematical proof – but have no particular characteristics of wisdom. The proof involves no balancing of interests and no search for a common good. It is simply an intellectual problem involving creative thinking.

Fourth, practical thinking is closer to wisdom than are analytical and creative thinking, but again, it is not the same. Wisdom is a particular kind of practical thinking. It (a) balances competing intrapersonal, interpersonal, and extrapersonal interests, over short and (b) long terms, (c) balances adaptation to, shaping of, and selection of environments, in (d) the service of a common good. Thus, people can be good practical thinkers without being wise but they cannot be wise without being good practical thinkers. Good practical thinking is necessary but not sufficient for the manifestation of wisdom.

Fifth, wisdom also seems to bear at least some relation to constructs such as social intelligence (Cantor & Kihlstrom, 1987; Kihlstrom & Cantor, 2000; Sternberg & Smith, 1985), emotional intelligence (Goleman, 1995; Mayer &

Salovey, 1993; Salovey & Mayer, 1990), and interpersonal and intrapersonal intelligences (Gardner, 1983, 1999). There are also differences, however. Social intelligence can be applied to understanding and getting along with others, to any ends, for any purposes. Wisdom seeks out a good through a balancing of interests. Thus, a salesperson who figures out how to sell a worthless product to a customer might do so through using social intelligence to understand the customer's wants, but has not applied wisdom in the process. Emotional intelligence involves understanding, judging, and regulating emotions. These skills are an important part of wisdom. But making wise judgments requires going beyond the understanding, regulation, or judgment of emotions. It requires processing the information to achieve a balance of interests and formulating a judgment that makes effective use of the information to achieve a common good. Moreover, wisdom may require a balance of interpersonal and intrapersonal intelligences, but it also requires an understanding of extrapersonal factors, and a balance of these three factors to attain a common good. Thus wisdom seems to go somewhat beyond these theoretically distinct kinds of intelligences as well. Perhaps the most salient difference among constructs is that wisdom is applied toward the achievement of ends that are perceived as yielding a common good, whereas the various kinds of intelligences may be applied deliberately toward achieving either good ends or bad ones, at least for some of the parties involved. It is interesting that the conception of wisdom proposed here is substantially closer to Chinese than to American conceptions of intelligence (Yang & Sternberg, 1997a, 1997b). One of the words used in Chinese to characterize intelligence is the same as the word used to characterize wisdom.

MEASUREMENT OF TACIT KNOWLEDGE IN WISDOM

Can wisdom be measured? We believe so. Consider problems we have used in the past to measure the tacit knowledge underlying practical intelligence, for which we have collected extensive data, and then consider problems we are using in our current research to measure wisdom.

We have devised a series of twenty-four problems to measure wisdom. The validity of these problems is currently being assessed. Here is an example of one (see below for a further example being used at a lower level of schooling).

"Felicia and Alexander have been in an intimate relationship for their entire four years of college. Felicia has now been accepted for graduate school in French by a prestigious graduate program in northern California. Alexander was not admitted to the law school in this university, nor to any other law school in the northern California area. Alexander was admitted to a good although not outstanding law school in southern California, but he was also admitted to an outstanding law school in Massachusetts. Felicia has no viable opportunities for graduate study on the East Coast, at least at this time. Alexander is trying to decide whether to attend the less prestigious law school in southern California or the more prestigious one in Massachusetts. He would like to continue the relationship, as would Felicia, and both ultimately hope to marry. A complicating factor is that the law school in Massachusetts has offered Alexander a half-scholarship, whereas the law school in southern California has not offered financial aid for the first year, although it has indicated that there is a possibility of financial aid in subsequent years. Alexander's parents have indicated that while they would be willing to pay his half-tuition for the more prestigious law school, they do not believe it is fair to ask them to pay full tuition for the less prestigious one. They also believe his going to the less prestigious law school will only hurt Alexander's career advancement. Felicia is torn and is leaving it to Alexander to decide what to do. What should Alexander do and why?"

FOOLISHNESS

Foolishness is the absence of wisdom. Smart people can be foolish and, are at times especially susceptible to foolishness. Foolish people are susceptible to four fallacies in thinking.

The *fallacy of egocentrism* occurs when an individual starts to think that the world centers around him or her. In life, it's all about that individual. Other people come to be seen merely as tools in the attainment of one's goals. Why would smart people think egocentrically, when one would expect that they would have abandoned the stage of egocentrism many years ago? The reason is, I believe, that conventionally smart people have been so highly rewarded for being smart that they lose sight of their own limitations. Wisdom requires one to know what one does know and does not know. Smart people often lose sight of what they do not know, leading to the second fallacy.

The *fallacy of omniscience* results from having available at one's disposal essentially any knowledge one might want that, is, in fact, knowable. With a phone call, a powerful leader can have almost any kind of knowledge made available to him or her. At the same time, people look up to the powerful leader as extremely knowledgeable or even close to all-knowing. The powerful leader may then come to believe that he or she really is all-knowing. So may his or her staff, as illustrated by Janis (1972) in his analysis of victims of groupthink. In case after case, brilliant government officials made the most foolish of decisions, in part because they believed they knew much more than they did.

The *fallacy of omnipotence* results from the extreme power one wields. In certain domains, one essentially can do almost whatever one wants to do. The risk is that the individual will start to overgeneralize and believe that this high level of power applies in all domains.

The *fallacy of invulnerability* comes from the illusion of complete protection, such as from a huge staff. People and especially leaders seem to have many friends ready to protect them at a moment's notice. The leaders may shield themselves from individuals who are anything less than sycophantic. Harry Truman suggested that high-powered (Washington) leaders who want friends ought to buy themselves a dog. As soon as things turn bad, many individuals who once seemed friends prove to be anything but.

In terms of the balance theory of wisdom, foolishness always involves interests going out of balance. Usually, the individual places self-interest way above other interests. But not always. Chamberlain may truly have believed he was doing the best for Great Britain. But in ignoring the interests of all the other countries being crushed under Hitler's brutal reign, Chamberlain was ignoring the common good, and, as it turned out, the long-term good of his own country.

Occasionally people sacrifice everything for another individual, only to be crushed by their own foolishness. The "classic" case is that of the prolonged war between Greece and Troy. Was Helen of Troy worth the war? Many wars have started over slights or humiliations, and the interests of the slighted or humiliated have taken precedence over the interests of the thousands who have been sacrificed to avenge the slight. There are those who believe that the war in Chechnya resulted in part from the humiliation suffered by the Russian army in the earlier war there. Certainly events in post-World War I contributed to Germany's humiliation after that war.

Wisdom involves a balancing not only of the three kinds of interests, but also of three possible courses of action in response to this balancing: adaptation of oneself or others to existing environments; shaping of environments to render them more compatible with oneself or others; and selection of new environments. Foolishness is reflected in action that represents poor use and balance of these processes. Wars are examples of shaping of the environment that often have proved to be of little avail. What, for example, did the Hundred Year War have to show for itself in the end? Or, for that matter, the more-recent Cold War? National leaders shaped environments in ways that caused great harm, suffering, and distress. In much of the world, they are continuing to do so.

Foolishness does not only derive from inappropriate shaping of the environment. One can adapt to a tyrannical environment to save one's own skin, only to find oneself paying the ultimate price. An example of this principle is shown in this quotation from Pastor Martin Niemöller:

> In Germany first they came for the communists
> and I did not speak out –
> because I was not a communist.

Then they came for the Jews
and I did not speak out –
because I was not a Jew.

Then they came for the trade unionists
and I did not speak out –
because I was not a trade unionist.

Then they came for the Catholics
and I did not speak out –
because I was a Protestant.

Then they came for me –
and there was no one left
to speak out for me.
            — Pastor Martin Niemöller

Selection also can be foolish, as when old individuals leave good or at least acceptable marriages for much younger partners whose main goal appears to be sharing the older person's financial success. Selection can be with respect to environments rather than people. An individual may love the idea of living in a place, move to the place, and then find that the reality bears little resemblance to the ideal. An American living abroad commented to me somewhat bitterly that the reasons one moved to the country in which he lived were inevitably different from the reasons for which one stayed. Those who hoped to find some satisfaction abroad inevitably returned to the United States, because they never found it.

How can we teach people to think wisely rather than foolishly?

DEVELOPING WISE THINKING

Why Should Wisdom be Included in the School Curriculum?

The development of wisdom is beneficial because the judgments it yields can improve our quality of life and conduct (Kekes, 1995). Knowledge can and indeed must accompany wisdom. People need knowledge to draw on in rendering judgments – knowledge of human nature, of life circumstances, or strategies that succeed and strategies that fail. Although knowledge is necessary for wisdom, it is not sufficient for it. Merely having knowledge does not entail its use in judging rightly, soundly, or justly. Many highly knowledgeable individuals lead lives that are unhappy. Some of them make decisions that are poor or even reprehensible. This century provides many examples of such decisions.

There are several reasons why schools should seriously consider including instruction in wisdom-related skills in the school curriculum.

First, as noted above, knowledge is insufficient for wisdom and certainly does not guarantee satisfaction or happiness. Wisdom seems a better vehicle for the attainment of these goals.

Second, wisdom provides a mindful and considered way to enter considered and deliberative values into important judgments. One cannot be wise and at the same time impulsive or mindless (Langer, 1997) in one's judgments.

Third, wisdom represents an avenue to creating a better, more harmonious world. Dictators such as Adolf Hitler and Joseph Stalin may have been knowledgeable and may even have been good critical thinkers, at least with regard to the maintenance of their own power. Given the definition of wisdom, however, it would be hard to argue they were wise.

Fourth and finally, students – who will later become parents and leaders – are always part of a greater community and hence will benefit from learning to judge rightly, soundly, or justly on behalf of their community (Ardelt, 1997; Sternberg, 1990b, 1998b, 1999d; Varela, 1999).

If the future is plagued with conflict and turmoil, this instability does not simply reside *out there somewhere*; it resides and has its origin *in ourselves*. For all these reasons, we endorse teaching students not only to recall facts and to think critically (and even creatively) about the content of the subjects they learn, but to think wisely about it, too.

Some Past Orientations and Programs Relevant to the Development of Wisdom

What would education that fostered wisdom look like? Three previous programs seem particularly related to the goals of the proposed orientation of teaching for wisdom. All have been proposed by educators with a primarily philosophical orientation. The first program, *Philosophy for Children* (Lipman, 1982; Lipman, Sharp, & Oscanyan, 1980), uses a set of novels to develop analytical-thinking skills in children. Children read the novels and learn to evaluate information in them and to make judgments about the characters in the novels and the kinds of choices they should make in their lives. The second program is Paul's (1987) program, which emphasizes dialogical thinking, or seeing problems from a variety of perspectives. The third program is that of Perkins (1986), which emphasizes understanding of "knowledge by design" – in other words, how knowledge is designed and used to solve problems in the world. Ennis (1987) has provided a taxonomy of critical-thinking skills, many of which are required for wise thinking, and Bransford and Stein (1993), Feuerstein (1980), and Halpern (1996) have all provided systematic courses that teach skills of critical thinking needed for wise thinking. Feuerstein's (1980) program has been the most widely used of this group. Other programs also touch on aspects of the proposed instruction described here (see Reigeluth's [1999] book on instructional-design theories and models for descriptions of a variety of programs).

It is impossible to speak of wisdom outside the context of a set of values, which in combination may lead one to a moral stance, or, in Kohlberg's (1969, 1983) view, stage. The same can be said of all practical intelligence: Behavior is viewed as practically intelligent as a function of what is valued in a societal/cultural context. Values mediate how one balances interests and responses, and collectively contribute even to how one defines a common good. The intersection of wisdom with the moral domain can be seen in the overlap between the notion of wisdom presented here and that of moral reasoning as it applies in the two highest stages (4 and 5) of Kohlberg's (1969) theory. Wisdom also involves caring for others as well as oneself (Gilligan, 1982). At the same time, wisdom is broader than moral reasoning. It applies to any human problem involving a balance of intrapersonal, interpersonal, and extrapersonal interests, whether or not moral issues are at stake.

Sixteen Principles of Teaching for Wisdom Derived from the Balance Theory of Wisdom

There are sixteen principles derived from the balance theory that form the core of how wisdom can be developed in the classroom:

1. Explore with students the notion that conventional abilities and achievements are not enough for a satisfying life. Many people become trapped in their lives and, despite feeling conventionally successful, feel that their lives lack fulfillment. Fulfillment is not an alternative to success, but is an aspect of it that, for most people, goes beyond money, promotions, large houses, and so forth.
2. Demonstrate how wisdom is critical for a satisfying life. In the long run, wise decisions benefit people in ways that foolish decisions never do.
3. Teach students the usefulness of interdependence – a rising tide raises all ships; a falling tide can sink them.
4. Teach role-model wisdom because what you do is more important than what you say. Wisdom is action-dependent and wise actions need to be demonstrated.
5. Have students read about wise judgments and decision making so they understand that there are such means of judging and decision making.
6. Help students to recognize their own interests, those of other people, and those of institutions.
7. Help students to balance their own interests, those of other people, and those of institutions.

8. Teach students that the "means" by which the end is obtained matters, not just the end.
9. Help students learn the roles of adaptation, shaping, and selection, and how to balance them. Wise judgments are dependent in part on selecting among these environmental responses.
10. Encourage students to form, critique, and integrate their own values in their thinking.
11. Encourage students to think dialectically, realizing that both questions and their answers evolve over time, and that the answer to an important life question can differ at different times in one's life (such as whether to go to college).
12. Show students the importance of dialogical thinking, whereby they understand interests and ideas from multiple points of view.
13. Teach students to search for and then try to reach the common good – a good where everyone wins, not only those with whom one identifies.
14. Encourage and reward wisdom.
15. Teach students to monitor events in their lives and their own thought processes about these events. One way to recognize others' interests is to begin to identify one's own.
16. Help students understand the importance of inoculating oneself against the pressures of unbalanced self-interest and small-group interest.

Procedures to Follow in Teaching for Wisdom

There are several procedures a teacher can follow in teaching for wisdom. First, students would read classic works of literature and philosophy (whether Western or otherwise) to learn and reflect on the wisdom of the sages. The rush to dump classic works in favor of modern ones makes sense only if the wisdom the modern works impart equals or exceeds that of the classic works.

Second, students would engage in class discussions, projects, and essays that encourage them to discuss the lessons they have learned from the classic works, and how they can be applied to their own lives and the lives of others. A particular emphasis would be placed on the development of dialogical and dialectical thinking. Dialogical thinking (see Principle 12) involves understanding significant problems from multiple points of view, how others can legitimately conceive of things in a way quite different from one's own. Dialectical thinking (see Principle 11) involves understanding that ideas and the paradigms under which they fall evolve and keep evolving, not only from the past to the present, but from the present to the future (Hegel, 1807/1931; see also Sternberg, 1998c).

Third, students would study not only "truth," as we know it, but values as well. They would not be force-fed a set of values, but would be encouraged to develop their own values.

Fourth, such instruction would place an increased emphasis on critical, creative, and practical thinking in the service of good ends – ends that benefit not only the individual doing the thinking but others as well. All these types of thinking would be valued, not just critical thinking.

Fifth, students would be encouraged to think about how almost everything they study might be used for better or worse ends, and to realize that the ends to which knowledge is put *do* matter.

Finally, teachers would realize that the only way they can develop wisdom in their students is to serve as role models of wisdom themselves. This would, I believe, take a much more Socratic approach to teaching than teachers customarily employ. Students often want large quantities of information spoon-fed or even force-fed to them. They attempt to memorize this material for exams, only to forget it soon thereafter. In a wisdom-based approach to teaching, students will need to take a more active role. But a wisdom-based approach is not tantamount to a constructivist approach to learning. Students have not achieved or even come close to achieving wisdom when they have merely constructed their own learning. They must be able to construct knowledge not only from their own point of view, but from the point of view of others. Constructionism from only a single point of view can lead to egocentric rather than balanced understanding.

Lessons taught to emphasize wisdom would have a rather different character from lessons as they are often taught today. Consider examples.

First, social studies and especially history lessons would look very different. High school American history books typically teach American history from only one point of view, that of the new Americans. Thus Columbus is referred to as having "discovered" America, a strange notion from the standpoint of the many occupants who already lived here when it was "discovered." The conquest of the Southwest and the fall of the Alamo are presented only from the point of view of the new settlers, not from the standpoint of, say, the Mexicans who lost roughly half their territory to the invaders. This kind of ethnocentric and frankly propagandistic teaching would have no place in a curriculum that sought to develop wisdom and an appreciation of the need to balance interests.

Second, science teaching would no longer be about facts presented as though they are the final word. Science is often presented as though it represents the end of a process of evolution of thought rather than one of many midpoints (Sternberg, 1998a). Students can scarcely realize from this kind of teaching that the paradigms of today, and thus the theories and findings that emanate from them, will eventually be superseded, as the paradigms, theories, and findings of yesterday were replaced by those of today. Students would learn that, contrary to the way many textbooks are written, the classical "scientific method" is largely a fantasy rather than a reality and that scientists are as susceptible to fads as are members of other groups.

Third, teaching literature would reflect a kind of balance often absent. Literature is often taught and characters judged in terms of the standards and context of the contemporary U.S. scene today, rather than those of the time and place in which the events took place. From the proposed standpoint, the study of literature must, to some extent, proceed in the context of the study of history. Banning books often reflects the application of certain contemporary standards of which an author from the past never could have been aware.

Fourth, foreign languages would be taught in the cultural context in which they are embedded. Perhaps American students have so much more difficulty learning foreign languages than do children in much of Europe not because they lack the ability but because they lack the motivation. They do not see the need to learn another language whereas, say, a Flemish-speaking child in Belgium does. Americans might be better off if they made more of an attempt wisely to understand other cultures rather than just expecting people from other cultures to understand them. Learning the language of a culture is a key to understanding. Americans might be less quick to impose their cultural values on others if they understood the cultural values of others. It is interesting to speculate on why Esperanto, a language designed to provide a common medium of communication across cultures, has been a notable failure. Perhaps it is because Esperanto is embedded in no culture at all. It is the language of no one.

Culture cannot be taught, in the context of foreign-language learning, in the way it now often is – as an aside divorced from the actual learning of the language. It should be taught as an integral part of the language, as a primary context in which the language is embedded. The vituperative fights we see about bilingual education and about the use of Spanish in the United States or French in Canada are not just, or even primarily, fights about language. They are fights about culture, and they are fights in need of wise resolutions.

Finally, as implied throughout these examples, the curriculum needs to be far more integrated. Literature needs to be integrated with history, science with history and social-policy studies, foreign language with culture. Even within disciplines, far more integration is needed. Different approaches to psychology, for example, are often taught as competing when in fact they are totally compatible. Thus, biological, cognitive, developmental, social, and clinical psychology provide complementary viewpoints on human beings. They do not each claim to be the "right approach." The study of the brain is important, for example, but most of the insights about learning and memory that can be applied to instruction have come from behavioral and cognitive approaches, not from the biological approach.

And some of the insights that have supposedly come from the biological approach – such as "left-brain" and "right-brain" learning – are based on ignorant or outdated caricatures of research in this area rather than on actual findings.

TESTING THE BALANCE THEORY IN THE CLASSROOM

Can these ideas be applied and tested in an educational setting? In collaboration with Elena L. Grigorenko and others at the PACE center at Yale, I am currently working on a project funded by the W. T. Grant Foundation to determine whether wisdom can be successfully taught to students at the middle-school level. It will take several years to complete this project and I show here how the theory is being tested, rather than providing concrete results. I hope the paradigm described will be of interest to others who would apply teaching for wisdom in the classroom.

We are working with roughly three dozen middle-school teachers and roughly six hundred middle-school students. This particular selection is based on several considerations.

First, students in middle school represent an age group ripe for the development of unbalanced thinking, with potentially devastating consequences. Students in middle school are close to the age when they will begin to make important life decisions involving sex, drugs, smoking tobacco, and violence. Wisdom-related skills need to be imparted and nurtured before the children start deciding their course of action on such vital life matters.

Second, students in middle school have acquired a level of cognitive development that renders them suitable to understand the different aspects of wisdom-related skills. Middle-school students can think abstractly about concepts, in which myriad possibilities are explored and weighed in the path to a solution (Piaget, 1952). Thinking abstractly is central to dialectical thinking. They have also developed metacognitive skills adequate for thinking wisely (Sternberg, 1985a, 1988c).

Third, unlike teachers of higher grades, teachers in middle schools often teach all subject-matter areas and so have direct control over the manner in which the subject matter is taught. This makes it possible to integrate a wisdom-related curriculum seamlessly into their regular teaching.

We are planning to develop an infused curriculum for teaching wisdom. We prefer an infused model of teaching rather than a separate "wisdom curriculum" for several reasons. First, most teachers seem to believe that they do not have the time in the school day to teach yet another subject. Second, infusion helps students transfer wisdom-related skills to skills they acquire in the course of their regular school learning. Third, we believe an infused program is more likely to result in knowledge that will interconnect with children's lives.

Finally, we believe that the curriculum in middle schools is in need of a richer, more penetrating program targeted not only at accumulating various academic skills, but also at adding richness, depth, and orientation to the formation of the higher-order thinking skills that the present curriculum sometimes appears to lack.

Wisdom-Related Curriculum

The following twelve major topics are covered in the wisdom-related curriculum we are developing, one per week, over a twelve-week curriculum (roughly one semester). The curriculum will be written for teachers to teach to their students:

1. What is wisdom – Part 1 (analyzing people's implicit theories)?
2. What is wisdom – Part 2 (analyzing famous definitions)?
3. Why is wisdom important to individuals, society, and the world?
4. Some big ideas about wisdom – Part 1 (the common good)
5. Some big ideas about wisdom – Part 2 (the role of values)
6. Some big ideas about wisdom – Part 3 (the role of interests)
7. Some big ideas about wisdom – Part 4 (the role of environmental responses)
8. Integration: Famous examples of wise individuals and why they were considered wise
9. Applying wisdom across the ages – Part 1 (earlier times)
10. Applying wisdom across the ages – Part 2 (present times)
11. Applying wisdom in students' daily life
12. Applying wisdom to create a better world

The design of the project involves three conditions: two experimental conditions and one control condition. Each condition includes twelve teachers and at least two hundred students. The first experimental condition incorporates the "Teaching for Wisdom" curriculum, the second experimental condition incorporates a critical-thinking skills curriculum, and the third control condition incorporates the regular curriculum. There are two reasons for including the critical-thinking condition.

First, we wish to avoid the possibility of a Hawthorne effect (Parsons, 1974). That is, if we find positive effects associated with the wisdom condition in relation to the regular-curriculum control, we want to know that the effects originated from the wisdom curriculum specifically and not from the implementation of a new curriculum generally.

Second, including a critical-thinking condition can inform us whether any new curriculum involving critical thinking, whether it focuses explicitly on wisdom or not, potentially can increase wisdom-related skills. We believe that critical thinking is not sufficient for wise thinking, but this remains to be shown.

Teachers in the wisdom condition are to implement the twelve-week course for teaching for wisdom. We are developing a curriculum handbook for teachers to use in their preparation and teaching. We are constructing this curriculum handbook along the same lines as the handbook for helping teachers develop students' Practical Intelligence For School ("PIFS"; Williams, Blythe, White, Li, Sternberg, & Gardner, 1996). In the wisdom handbook, as in the PIFS handbook, each chapter is dedicated to implementing a part of the curriculum. For example, one chapter introduces the notion of wisdom and why it is important. Other chapters instruct teachers how to incorporate wisdom-related skills in daily lesson plans in language arts, social science, and natural science following the sixteen principles mentioned above. Some topics might include wisdom and foolishness in literature, analysis of historical decisions using wisdom-related skills as criteria, and the costs of pollution to the world. The handbook can also help teachers coordinate the activities required for developing wisdom-related skills, such as generating dialectical thinking, group discussions, and ideas for modeling.

In addition, before they start teaching the curriculum, teachers are to attend twenty hours of professional development in-service meetings, where they will have an opportunity to orient themselves to, discuss, and use the information presented in the handbook. An additional ten hours of in-service are scheduled while the curriculum is running to give feedback to the teachers and the investigators.

We are implementing a twelve-week course for teaching critical-thinking skills. As in the wisdom condition, we are developing a curriculum handbook for teachers to use in their preparation and teaching along the same lines as the handbook for teaching for wisdom. The teaching of critical-thinking skills to middle-school students has been implemented before in past studies of Sternberg's triarchic theory of intelligence (see Sternberg, Torff, & Grigorenko, 1998b). Teaching these skills involves explaining to students the uses of analytical reasoning along with the strategies that foster and actualize critical thinking. For example, teachers might have students analyze flaws in an historical figure's political strategy, in a science experiment, or in a commentary devoted to a piece of literature.

The conventional instructional condition does not involve any specific course, per se. However, we provide the same level of in-service to teachers. The in-services are on effective assessment, including both conventional and performance assessments. We are preparing a handbook comparable to those in the other conditions.

The same evaluations are used in all conditions. The main dependent variables in this study are measures of students' levels of wisdom-related skills. These will be measured in three phases. We are also evaluating how closely teachers in the two experimental conditions followed their corresponding curricula, as well as the overall impressions of the curricula of teachers and students.

The first evaluation will be administered prior to the beginning of the twelve-week period (pre-test); a second evaluation will be administered during the curriculum delivery period (intervention stage); a third evaluation will be administered at the end of the twelve-week period (post-test); and a fourth evaluation will take place after an interval of two to three months following the twelve-week period (durability test). The first evaluation is designed to measure students' baseline levels of wisdom-related skills by condition. The second is designed to monitor the change during the curriculum delivery. The third is conceived to measure the effectiveness of each curriculum condition on students' wisdom-related skills immediately following the twelve-week curriculum. The fourth is designed to measure the durability of the effect of each curriculum condition on students' wisdom-related skills.

The materials with which we will assess students' level of wisdom-related skills include conflict-resolution scenarios (Sternberg & Dobson, 1987; Sternberg & Soriano, 1984) and unanticipated but highly plausible dilemmas, including dilemmas prepared by us and by others (for example, Staudinger, 1996; Staudinger & Baltes, 1996). This latter method of evaluating wisdom-related judgment has been successfully used in past research (for example, Staudinger & Baltes, 1996).

Conflict-resolution scenarios involve problematic situations with multiple interests that can be considered in finding a resolution to the problem. One such scenario for middle-school students is presented below:

Mary is fighting with her parents over a sleepover she wants to go to at her friend Lisa's house. Her parents have told her that they are worried about the lack of supervision at the sleepover and are worried about whether the children's behavior may get out of hand. Mary has had a number of problems with her classmates in the past year and sees this sleepover as an opportunity to strengthen friendships she has made or would like to make. What should Mary do?

The unanticipated but highly plausible dilemmas also require students to respond to open-ended scenarios. Students' responses will then be evaluated by trained raters according to a pre-specified set of criteria derived from the balance theory of wisdom. Ultimately, each response will be associated with a set of ratings corresponding to the set of criteria as well as an overall rating. There will be at least two raters per response to be rated.

The particular ratings (on a seven-point Likert scale) will consider

1. demonstration of attempt to reach a common good;
2. balancing of intrapersonal, interpersonal, and extrapersonal interests;

3. taking into account both short- and long-term factors;
4. justification for adaptation to, shaping of, and selection of environments;
5. mindful use of values;
6. overall quality (wisdom) of process of solution;
7. overall quality (wisdom) of the solution itself.

We will also collect other, more qualitative measures of students' wisdom-related skills. These other measures include evaluations of students' assignments completed during the twelve-week curriculum. For example, we will collect weekly journals, homework assignments, and reports that the students complete in each of the conditions. These measures will be rated according to the above criteria from the balance theory of wisdom.

Evaluating students' wisdom-related skills is only one part of a complete evaluation of the teaching for wisdom initiative. A second part is evaluating how closely and how well the wisdom and critical-thinking curricula were observed by teachers. Evaluating how closely the curricula were followed is essential to evaluation of the students' wisdom-related skills. For example, only if the wisdom curriculum is properly implemented can we expect students' wisdom-related skills to increase. Only if the critical-thinking curriculum is properly implemented can we expect to compare it against the effect of the wisdom curriculum. We plan to monitor the implementation of both curricula in four ways.

First, we are providing in-service professional training for teachers and helping them instantiate the curriculum as described in the curriculum handbook and we will assess their performance in the in-services. Second, we plan periodically to visit participating school classrooms and sit in on lectures and view lesson plans. Third, we intend to look at students' daily journals to check the content of the actual lesson plans they received. Fourth, we intend to survey the participating teachers for their thoughts on the curricula and on how well it was realized. Finally, we need to survey participating children for their evaluation of the curricula.

In addition to the above evaluations, we will ask students to complete two related measures: The Cornell Critical Thinking Test (CCTT; Ennis, 1987) and the Sternberg Triarchic Abilities Test, Level 1 (STAT; Sternberg, 1993). The Cornell Critical Thinking Test is a seventy-one-item, paper-and-pencil measure used to assess a student's ability to decide whether a set of premises supports a given conclusion, to judge the reliability of information, and whether specific statements follow from others. The STAT contains thirty-six multiple-choice and three essay items measuring analytical, creative, and practical thinking in the verbal, quantitative, and figural domains. Both these measures are designed to assess quality of thinking in middle-school students. They are included to assess whether effects from the wisdom and critical-thinking curricula are positively or negatively related to critical thinking and related skills.

We will also ask teachers to rate student achievements of various kinds in each condition before and after the twelve-week period to assess any possible transfer of the curricula to school performance.

CONCLUSIONS

The road to this new approach of teaching for wisdom is bound to be a rocky one. First, entrenched structures, whatever they may be, are difficult to change, and wisdom is neither taught in schools nor even discussed. Second, many people will not see the value of teaching something that shows no promise of raising conventional test scores. These scores, which formerly were predictors of more interesting criteria, have now become criteria, or ends in themselves. The society has lost track of why they ever mattered in the first place and they have engendered the same kind of mindless competition we see in people who relentlessly compare their economic achievements with those of others. Third, wisdom is much more difficult to develop than is the kind of achievement that can be developed and readily tested via multiple-choice tests. Finally, people who have gained influence and power in a society via one means are unlikely to want either to give up that power or to see a new criterion established on which they might not rank so favorably. Thus, there is no easy path to wisdom. There never was, and probably never will be.

Wisdom might bring us a world that would seek to better itself and the conditions of all the people in it. At some level, we as a society have a choice. What do we wish to maximize through our schooling? Is it just knowledge? Is it just intelligence? Or is it also wisdom? If it is wisdom, then we need to put our students on a much different course. We need to value not only how they use their outstanding individual abilities to maximize their attainments but also how they use their individual abilities to maximize the attainments of others. We need, in short, to value wisdom.

PART IV

SYNTHESIS

8

WICS: The Relations among Intelligence, Creativity, and Wisdom

The goal of this book is not only to discuss intelligence, creativity, and wisdom, but also to explore the interrelationships among them. These interrelationships can be assessed at two levels, at least based on the research we have done. The first level is that of implicit theories, the second, that of explicit theories.

IMPLICIT THEORIES

Sternberg (1985b), as mentioned earlier, assessed people's implicit theories of intelligence, creativity, and wisdom, as well as the implicit theories among these constructs. The study was done among experts and laypersons in the United States, and hence does not necessarily apply beyond this country.

Nonmetric multidimensional scaling was used to assess the dimensions for each construct. Table 8.1 shows the results of these scalings. Table 8.2 shows the intercorrelations of ratings of behaviors on a master list for different occupations of individuals. Note that there are differences in the correlations, and that, in business, creativity and wisdom show a negative correlation!

The data show that people's conceptions of intelligence overlap with, but go beyond, the skills measured by conventional intelligence tests. Thus, the problem-solving (fluid ability) and verbal-comprehension (crystallized ability) skills measured by intelligence tests appear most prominently in the dimensions of the derived implicit theory of intelligence. Thus, the intelligent individual is perceived as solving problems well, reasoning clearly, thinking logically, displaying a good vocabulary, and drawing on a large store of information – just the kinds of things conventional intelligence tests measure. But also embedded within people's conceptions of intelligence are ability to balance information, to be goal-oriented and aim for achievement of one's goals, and to show intelligence in worldly, as opposed to

TABLE 8.1. *Nonmetric multidimensional scaling solutions for behaviors*[a]

Intelligence	Creativity	Wisdom
I. Practical problem-solving ability	*I. Nonentrenchment*	*I. Reasoning ability*
Tends to see attainable goals and accomplish them	Makes up rules as he or she goes along	Has the unique ability to look at a problem or situation and solve it
Is good at distinguishing between correct and incorrect answers	Is impulsive	Has good problem-solving ability
Has good problem-solving ability	Takes chances	Has a logical mind
Has ability to change directions and use another procedure	Tends not to know own limitations and tries to do what others think is impossible	Is good at distinguishing between correct and incorrect answers
Has rationality: ability to reason clearly	Is emotional	Is able to apply knowledge to particular problems
Is able to apply knowledge to particular problems	Has a free spirit	Is able to put old information, theories, and so forth, together in a new way
Has the unique ability to look at a problem or situation and solve it	Builds castles in the sky	Has a huge store of information
Has a logical mind	Is a nonconformist	Has the ability to recognize similarities and differences
II. Verbal ability	Is unorthodox	Has rationality: ability to reason clearly
Can converse on almost any topic	*II. Integration and intellectuality*	Makes connections and distinctions between ideas and things
Attaches importance to ideas	Makes connections and distinctions between ideas and things	*II. Sagacity*
Is inquisitive	Has the ability to understand and interpret his or her environment	Displays concern for others
Studies and reads quite a lot	Has the ability to recognize similarities and differences	Considers advice
Has demonstrated a good vocabulary	Is able to grasp abstract ideas and focus his or her attention on those ideas	Understands people through dealing with a variety of people
Expresses broad concepts concisely	Is productive	Feels he or she can always learn from other people
Has a good command of language	Has a high IQ level	Knows self best
Has a huge store of information	Attaches importance to ideas	Is thoughtful
Attaches importance to well-presented ideas	Possesses ability for high achievement	Is fair
III. Intellectual balance and integration	Is always thinking	Is a good listener
Has the ability to recognize similarities and differences	Is able to put old information, theories, and so forth together in a new way	Is not afraid to admit making a mistake, will correct the mistake, learn, and go on
Makes connections and distinctions between ideas and things	*III. Aesthetic taste and imagination*	Listens to all sides of an issue
Listens to all sides of an issue	Has an appreciation of art, music, and so forth	*III. Learning from ideas and environment*
Is able to grasp abstract ideas and focus his or her attention on those ideas		Attaches importance to ideas

Is perceptive
Has the ability to integrate information
Has the ability to grasp complex situations

IV. *Goal orientation and attainment*
Tends to obtain and use information for specific purposes
Possesses ability for high achievement
Seeks out information, especially details
Is motivated by goals
Is inquisitive at an early age
Sees opportunities and knows when to take them

V. *Contextual intelligence*
Learns and remembers and gains information from past mistakes or successes
Has the ability to understand and interpret his or her environment
Knows what's going on in the world

VI. *Fluid throught*
Has a thorough grasp of mathematics, or good spatial ability, or both
Has a high IQ level
Thinks quickly

Likes to be alone when creating something new
Can write, draw, compose music
Has good taste
Uses the materials around him or her and makes something unique out of them
Is in harmony with the materials or processes of expression
Is imaginative

IV. *Decisional skill and flexibility*
Follows his or her gut feelings in making decisions after weighing the pros and cons
Has ability to change direction and use another procedure

V. *Perspicacity*
Questions societal norms, truisms, assumptions
Is perceptive
Is willing to take a stand

VI. *Drive for accomplishment and recognition*
Is motivated by goals
Likes to be complimented on his or her work
Is energetic
Has a sense of humor

VII. *Inquisitiveness*
Is inquisitive at an early age
Is inquisitive

VIII. *Intuition*
Has intuition

Is perceptive
Learns from other people's mistakes

IV. *Judgment*
Acts within own physical and intellectual limitations
Is sensible
Has good judgment at all times
Thinks before acting or making decisions
Is able to take the long view (as opposed to considering only short-term outcomes)
Thinks before speaking
Is a clear thinker

V. *Expeditious use of information*
Is experienced
Seeks out information, especially details
Has age, maturity, or longexperience
Learns and remembers and gains information from past mistakes or successes
Changes mind on basis of experience

VI. *Perspicacity*
Has intuition
Can offer solutions that are on the side of right and truth
Is able to see through things – read between the lines
Has the ability to understand and interpret his or her environment

---

[a] After Sternberg (1985b, pp. 614–616). Behaviors are listed in order of decreasing weights within dimension.
Note: Stress (formula 1) = .14. R^2 = .87.

strictly academic, contexts. People thus seem to be more concerned with the practical and worldly side of intelligence than are intelligence testers.

Conceptions of creativity overlap with those of intelligence, but there is much less emphasis in implicit theories of creativity on analytical abilities, whether they be directed toward abstract problems or toward verbal materials. For example, the very first dimension shows a greater emphasis on nonentrenchment, or the ability and willingness to go beyond ordinary limitations of self and environment and to think and act in unconventional and even dreamlike ways. The creative individual has a certain freedom of spirit and an unwillingness to be bound by the unwritten canons of society, characteristics not necessarily found in the highly intelligent individual. Implicit theories of creativity encompass a dimension of aesthetic taste and imagination absent in implicit theories of intelligence, and also encompass aspects of inquisitiveness and intuitiveness that do not seem to enter into the implicit theories of intelligence. Implicit theories of creativity go far beyond conventional psychometric creativity tests. A person's ability to think of unusual uses for a brick, or to form a picture based on a geometric outline, scarcely does justice to the kind of freedom of spirit and intellect captured in implicit theories of creativity.

Finally, the wise individual is perceived as having much the same analytical reasoning ability as the intelligent individual. But the wise person has a certain sagacity not necessarily found in the intelligent person: He or she listens to others, knows how to weigh advice, and knows how to deal with a variety of different kinds of people. In seeking as much information as possible for decision making, the wise individual reads between the lines as well as making use of the obviously available information. The wise individual is especially able to make clear, sensible, and fair judgments, and in doing so, takes a long-term as well as a short-term view of the consequences of the judgments made. The wise individual is perceived as profiting from the experience of others, and learning from others' mistakes, as well as from his or her own mistakes. This individual is not afraid to change his or her mind as experience dictates, and the solutions offered to complex problems tend to be the right ones. It is not surprising that the correlations between creativity and wisdom are the lowest of the three possible pairs (intelligence–creativity, intelligence–wisdom, creativity–wisdom) and in one case, the correlation is even negative: Whereas the wise person is perceived to be a conserver of worldly experience, the creative person is perceived to be a defier of such experience.

EXPLICIT THEORIES

The WICS (Wisdom, Intelligence, and Creativity Synthesized) theory views intelligence, creativity, and wisdom as different, but as involving fundamental similarities.

TABLE 8.2. *Intercorrelations of ratings of behaviors on master list for each occupation providing ratings*[a]

Measures	Intelligence	Creativity	Wisdom
Art			
Intelligence	1.00	.55	.78
Creativity		1.00	.48
Business			
Intelligence	1.00	.29	.51
Creativity		1.00	−.24
Philosophy			
Intelligence	1.00	.56	.42
Creativity		1.00	.37
Physics			
Intelligence	1.00	.64	.68
Creativity		1.00	.14
Laypersons			
Intelligence	1.00	.33	.75
Creativity		1.00	.27

[a] Based on Sternberg (1985b, Table 2, p. 612).

The Basic Relationships

The basic relationship between intelligence, creativity, and wisdom is shown in Figure 8.1. The basis for "intelligence" narrowly defined, as it is measured by successful intelligence, is the analytical aspect of successful intelligence. The basis for creativity is the creative aspect of successful intelligence. And the basis for wisdom is the practical aspect of successful intelligence, and in particular, tacit knowledge. Thus, successful intelligence lies at the basis of conventional intelligence, creativity, and wisdom. But there is more to each of these constructs than just successful intelligence. What is that something more?

The Role of Components

Metacomponents.   Metacomponents play a key role in intelligence, creativity, and wisdom. They form the central executive functions without which none of these three attributes could operate. To think intelligently, creatively, or wisely, one needs to be able to recognize the existence of problems, define the problems, formulate strategies to solve the problems, and so forth. The difference in their application lies in the kinds of problems to which they are applied.

In intelligence they are applied to several kinds of problems. First, when they are applied to relatively familiar kinds of problems that are somewhat

Conventional Intelligence   Creativity   Wisdom

Analytical Aspect   Creative Aspect   Practical Aspect

SUCCESSFUL INTELLIGENCE

FIGURE 8.1. The basic relation between successful intelligence, conventional intelligence, creativity, and wisdom.

abstracted from the world of everyday experience, they are applied to problems requiring analytical intelligence. Second, when they are applied to relatively novel kinds of problems that are relatively nonentrenched in nature, then they are applied to problems requiring creative intelligence. Third, when they are applied to relatively practical problems that are highly contextualized in nature, then they are applied to problems requiring practical intelligence.

All problems requiring creativity require creative intelligence, but not all problems requiring creative intelligence require creativity. Creativity – at least according to the investment theory – requires more than just creative intelligence. It also requires knowledge, certain thinking styles, certain personality attributes, and certain motivational attributes. Thus people can be creatively intelligent but not creative. They may think in novel ways, but perhaps lack the persistence, or the propensity toward risk-taking, or the willingness to grow that one needs to be fully creative. Problems requiring full creativity thus tend to be more complex than problems requiring just creative intelligence. For example, a conceptual-projection problem (about grue and bleen), as described earlier, requires creative intelligence. But it does not require creativity in the same sense that writing an important novel does. The novel involves far more components of creativity than does the conceptual-projection problem. Thus, coping with novelty is only one aspect of creativity.

Metacomponents are especially important to define and redefine creative problems. As Getzels and Csikszentmihalyi (1976) have pointed out, finding and then clearly defining good problems is an essential element of creativity. Metacomponents are also important for monitoring and evaluating one's products. No one, no matter how creative, hits the creative heights every time. A creative individual needs to devise a system to separate his or her own wheat from the chaff.

Metacomponents also apply in the solution of problems requiring wisdom. Much of the difficulty of a wisdom-related problem is in figuring out exactly what the problem is, whose interests are involved, and what their interests are. One then needs to formulate a strategy to deal with the problem and a way of monitoring whether the strategy is working.

Performance Components.   Performance components also are involved in solving each of the three kinds of problems. For example, one almost inevitably needs to make inferences in solving each kind of problem, whether it is in inferring relations in test-like analogy problems, inferring analogical relations in order to propose a new model of a phenomenon based on a model of a phenomenon (such as Freud's applying the hydraulic model to the psyche), or inferring what a participant in a negotiation really is looking for so that one can offer a wise solution that balances interests.

Knowledge-Acquisition Components.   Finally, knowledge-acquisition components are involved in all three kinds of problems as well.

In learning the meanings of new words embedded in context, the reader has to separate helpful and relevant information in context from extraneous material that is irrelevant to, or may actually get in the way of, learning the meaning of the words. Moreover, the reader must combine the selected information into a meaningful whole, using past information about the nature of words as a guide. Deciding what things would be useful for defining a new word and deciding what to do with these useful things once they are isolated are processes that are guided by the use of old information. The reader constantly seeks to connect the context of the unknown word to something with which he or she is familiar. Thus, we see that processing the available information requires three distinct operations: (a) locating relevant information in context, (b) combining this information into a meaningful whole, and (c) interrelating this information to what the reader already knows. These processes will be referred to from now on as selective encoding, selective combination, and selective comparison, respectively.

Selective encoding involves sifting out relevant from irrelevant information. When you encounter an unfamiliar word in context, cues relevant to deciphering its meaning are embedded within large amounts of unhelpful or possibly even misleading information. You must separate the wheat from the chaff by sifting out the relevant cues. Most readers selectively encode information without being aware that they are doing it. By becoming more aware of this process, you are in a better position to improve your use of it.

When you encounter an unfamiliar word, imagine the word to be the center of a network of information. Seek out cues concerning its meaning in the sentence where the unknown word occurs. Then expand your systematic search, checking the sentences surrounding it.

Consider the brief passage below. Even in this rather obvious example, there is much information to weed out. For instance, in order to figure out the meaning of the word *macropodida*, we need not know that the man in the passage was on a business trip, that he was tired, or that he squinted in the bright sunlight. Although such information may be quite relevant to the story as a whole, it is entirely irrelevant to our purpose of figuring out the meaning of the unknown word.

He first saw a *macropodida* during a trip to Australia. He had just arrived from a business trip to India, and he was exhausted. Looking out at the plain, he saw a *macropodida* hop across it. It was a typical marsupial. While he watched, the animal pranced to and fro, intermittently stopping to chew on the surrounding plants. Squinting because of the bright sunlight, he noticed a young *macropodida* securely fastened in an opening in front of the mother.

In the first sentence, there are two important cues: (1) the man saw a macropodida, so macropodidae must be visually perceptible, and (2) the man saw the macropodida in Australia, so macropodidae must be found in that continent. As we have seen, the second sentence does not contain any information relevant to the unknown word. The next sentence informs us that macropodidae hop and can be found on plains. In the fourth sentence, we learn that a macropodida is a marsupial, and in the fifth sentence, we find out something about what macropodidae eat. Finally, the last sentence informs us that mother macropodidae carry their young in openings on their front sides.

Normally, readers would not selectively encode all the available information before proceeding to combine and compare the relevant facts. Usually, readers will shift from one process to another as they proceed through the paragraph. Listing relevant data is merely an attempt to show you the kinds of information that can be selectively encoded.

Selective combination involves combining selectively encoded information in such a way as to form an integrated, plausible definition of the previously unknown word. Simply sifting out the relevant cues is not enough to arrive at a tentative definition of a word: We must know how to combine these cues into an integrated representation of the word. When we encounter an unfamiliar word, we must selectively encode information about the meaning of the word before we can do anything else, but we usually do not selectively encode all the relevant information before moving on to the selective combination of this information. The process of selective combination can begin just as soon as the second piece of information has been selectively encoded.

Typically, the available information can be combined in many ways, and inevitably, different persons will produce slightly different combinations. Usually, however, there is one optimal combination of information that exceeds in usefulness any other possibilities. You can imagine an analogy to the job detectives do. First, they have to decide what the relevant clues are in figuring out who committed the crime (selective encoding). Once they have figured out some relevant clues, they begin to combine them selectively in such a way as to build a plausible case against the suspect. Combining the clues in an improper way can result in a false lead, and ultimately, the apprehension of the wrong suspect. Just as the detective has to track down the individual who actually perpetrated the crime, you have to track down the meaning of the word that is appropriate in the given instance or instances.

Consider how the process of selective combination can be applied to the *macropodida* above. From the first sentence, we selectively encode the fact that macropodidae are something we can see, and that they are found in Australia. Thus, we know that they are something that we can see when we go to Australia. The third sentence provides us with the knowledge that macropodidae can be found on plains and that they hop. We thus now know that macropodidae are something that we can see hopping on the plains of Australia. We learn that they are marsupials, that they eat plants, and that they carry their young in front openings. In sum, we now know that macropodidae are plant-eating marsupials that can be seen hopping on the plains of Australia, and that may be carrying their young in openings in front of them.

We now have a fairly extensive network of information about the word macropodida. Putting all the information together in a systematic manner yields a definition: A macropodida is a kangaroo.

Selective comparison involves relating newly acquired information to information acquired in the past. As readers decide what information to encode and how to combine this information, what they already know about the topic can be quite useful as a guide. Any given bit of relevant information will probably be nearly useless if it cannot somehow be related to past knowledge. Without previous knowledge, the helpful hints that would normally lead readers to the definition of an unknown term will be meaningless, and the readers will probably not even recognize the hints as relevant information. New information can be related to old information, and vice versa, by the use of similes, metaphors, analogies, and models, but the goal is always the same: to give the new information meaning by connecting it to old information that is already known.

Look again at the passage above to analyze how selective comparison operates. In selective comparison, we try to establish how the new word is similar to and different from old words that we already have stored in memory. We may end up deciding either that the new word is a synonym for an old word that we already know, or that a new concept has to be constructed that expands on our old concepts. In the case of the macropodida, the more information we have, the more restricted is the range of things that it might be. Initially, it might be anything that we might see in Australia – a very long list. We are able to reduce our list as we learn that a macropodida is something seen on a plain and something that hops. We

can restrict our list of possibilities further when we learn that it is a herbi-
vorous marsupial. If our original list of things indigenous to or particularly
characteristic of Australia included such items as Aborigines, kangaroos,
sheep, and eucalyptus trees, our developing list can no longer include all
these things. By the time we are done with the passage, the only item on
the list that the passage could describe is the kangaroo. Thus, the process
of selective comparison includes a whittling-down process whereby large
numbers of possibilities are successively further reduced. Eventually, if
only one possibility remains, that possibility is a likely synonym for the
unknown word. If no possibilities remain, then we probably have to form a
new concept that is related to, but different from, all old concepts we have
stored in memory.

The knowledge-acquisition processes apply in creative thinking to insightful problem solving. The view of insight that we prefer (Davidson &
Sternberg, 1984; Sternberg & Davidson, 1982) is that insight consists of not
one, but three separate but related psychological processes.

Significant problems generally present us with large amounts of information, only some of which is relevant and worthy of selective encoding
for problem solution. For example, the facts of a legal case are usually both
numerous and confusing: An insightful lawyer must figure out which of
the myriad facts are relevant to principles of law. Similarly, a doctor or
a psychotherapist must sift out those facts that are relevant for diagnosis
or treatment. Perhaps the occupation that most directly must employ selective encoding is that of the detective: In trying to figure out who has
perpetrated a crime, the detective must figure out what the relevant facts
are. Failure to do so may result in following up on false leads, or in having
no leads to follow up on at all.

Selective combination involves combining what might originally seem
to be isolated pieces of information into a unified whole that may or may not
resemble its parts. For example, the lawyer must know how the relevant
facts of a case fit together to make (or break) the case. A doctor or psychotherapist must be able to figure out how to combine information about
various isolated symptoms to identify a given medical (or psychological)
syndrome. A detective, having collected the facts that seem relevant to
the case, must determine how they fit together to point at the guilty party
rather than at anyone else.

Problem solving by analogy, for example, is an instance of selective
comparison: The solver realizes that new information is similar to old information in certain ways (and dissimilar from it in other ways) and uses
this information better to understand the new information. For example, an
insightful lawyer will relate a current case to past legal precedents; choosing the right precedent is absolutely essential. A doctor or psychotherapist
relates the current set of symptoms to previous case histories. Again, choosing the right precedent is essential. A detective may have been involved

in or know about a similar case where the same modus operandi was used to commit a crime. Drawing an analogy to the past case may be helpful to the detective both in understanding the nature of the crime and in figuring out who did it.

It should be evident that the processes of insight that are being proposed here are the same as the processes of knowledge acquisition proposed earlier. Is insight, then, really nothing at all special, but merely a mundane extension of knowledge-acquisition skills? We do not believe this to be the case. What seems to separate insightful use of selective encoding, selective combination, and selective comparison from ordinary use of these processes is the nonobviousness of how they are applied, or the nonobviousness of the appropriateness of their application. By contrast, the nature of the problem in learning vocabulary from context is very clear: The task is to define the unknown word. Moreover, the kinds of clues that are useful in defining an unknown word are circumscribed in scope. Thus, with practice, the finding and use of these clues can become fairly routine. In insightful selective encoding, selective combination, and selective comparison, it is not obvious how to apply these processes, and often it is not even obvious that they are appropriate in the first place.

The processes of insight are the same as ordinary cognitive processes, but the circumstances of their application are different. It is much more difficult to apply selective encoding, selective combination, and selective comparison in an insightful way than it is to apply them in a routine way.

Coping with Novelty Skills

Coping with novelty is relevant in conventional intelligence, creativity, and wisdom. In conventional intelligence, coping with novelty is involved in fluid abilities (see Carroll, 1993; Cattell, 1971). It is the essential ingredient of creative thinking. And most wisdom problems are at least somewhat novel; in other words, they present new aspects that old problems have not presented. When problems are more routine, they may be referred to as requiring common sense, but they are not likely to be referred to as requiring wisdom.

Practical Skills

Practical skills are involved in all three sets of skills as well. They are probably least involved in conventional intelligence. Here they are most likely to apply to knowing what kinds of strategies and solutions are expected in taking tests and in school (Williams et al., 1996, 2002). They are required in creativity to employ ideas so they can be implemented and one can convince others of their worth. And they are required in wisdom to solve the problems. Tacit knowledge is a basis for wise thinking.

IN SUM

In sum, the components of intelligence are at the base of successful intelligence, creativity, and wisdom. They are applied in intelligence, broadly defined, to experience in order to adapt to, shape, and select environments. When the components are involved in fairly abstract but familiar kinds of tasks, they are used analytically. When they are involved in relatively novel tasks and situations, they are used creatively. When they are involved in adaptation to, shaping of, and selection of environments, they are used practically.

Creative intelligence is a part of, but not the entirety of, human creativity. Creativity also involves aspects of knowledge, styles of thinking, personality, and motivation, as well as these psychological components in interaction with the environment. An individual with the intellectual skills for creativity but without the other personal attributes is unlikely to do creative work.

Wisdom results from the application of successful intelligence and creativity toward the common good through a balancing of intrapersonal, interpersonal, and extrapersonal interests over the short and long terms. Wisdom is not just a way of thinking about things; it is a way of doing things. If people wish to be wise, they have to act wisely, not just think wisely. We all can do this. Whether we do is our choice.

References

Abelson, R. P., Aronson, E., McGuire, W. J., Newcomb, T. M., Rosenberg, M. J., & Tannenbaum, P. H. (Eds.). (1968). *Theories of cognitive consistency: A sourcebook.* Chicago: Rand McNally.

Adams, J. L. (1974). *Conceptual blockbusting: A guide to better ideas.* San Francisco: Freeman.

Albert, R. S., & Runco, M. A. (1999). A history of research on creativity. In R. J. Sternberg (Ed.), *Handbook of creativity* (pp. 16–31). New York: Cambridge University Press.

Amabile, T. M. (1983). *The social psychology of creativity.* New York: Springer.

Amabile, T. M. (1996). *Creativity in context.* Boulder, CO: Westview.

Anastasi, A., & Urbina, S. (1997). *Psychological testing* (7th ed.). Upper Saddle River, NJ: Prentice-Hall.

Anderson, J. R. (1983). *The architecture of cognition.* Cambridge, MA: Harvard University Press.

Andrews, F. M. (1975). Social and psychological factors which influence the creative process. In I. A. Taylor & J. W. Getzels (Eds.), *Perspectives in creativity* (pp. 117–145). Chicago: Aldine.

Ardelt, M. (1997). Wisdom and life satisfaction in old age. *Journals of Gerontology Series B-Psychological Sciences & Social Sciences, 52B,* 15–27.

Arlin, P. K. (1990). Wisdom: the art of problem finding. In R. J. Sternberg (Ed.), *Wisdom: Its nature, origins, and development* (pp. 230–243). New York: Cambridge University Press.

Au, T. K., Sidle, A. L., Rollins, K. B. (1993). Developing an intuitive understanding of conservation and contamination: Invisible particles as a plausible mechanism. *Developmental Psychology, 29,* 286–299.

Azuma, H., & Kashiwagi, K. (1987). Descriptions for an intelligent person: A Japanese study. *Japanese Psychological Research, 29,* 17–26.

Baillargeon, R. L. (1987). Young infants' reasoning about the physical and spatial properties of a hidden object. *Cognitive Development 2(3),* 179–200.

Baltes, P. B. (1993). The aging mind: Potential and limits. *The Gerontologist, 33,* 580–594.

Baltes, P. B. (1994). *Wisdom*. Unpublished manuscript, Max-Planck-Institut für Bildungsforschung, Berlin.

Baltes, P. B., & Smith, J. (1987, August). *Toward a psychology of wisdom and its ontogenesis*. Paper presented at the Ninety-Fifth Annual Convention of the American Psychological Association, New York.

Baltes, P. B., & Smith, J. (1990). Toward a psychology of wisdom and its ontogenesis. In R. J. Sternberg (Ed.), *Wisdom: Its nature, origins, and development* (pp. 87–120). New York: Cambridge University Press.

Baltes, P. B., Smith, J., & Staudinger, U. (1992). Wisdom and successful aging. In T. B. Sonderegger (Ed.), *Psychology and aging* (pp. 123–167). Lincoln, NE: University of Nebraska Press.

Baltes, P. B., & Staudinger, U. (1993). The search for psychology of wisdom. *Current Directions in Psychological Science, 2,* 75–80.

Baltes, P. B., & Staudinger, U. M (2000). Wisdom: A metaheuristic (pragmatic) to orchestrate mind and virtue toward excellence. *American Psychologist, 55,* 122–135.

Baltes, P. B., Staudinger, U. M., Maercker, A., & Smith, J. (1995). People nominated as wise: A comparative study of wisdom-related knowledge. *Psychology and Aging, 10,* 155–166.

Bandura, A. (1977). Self-efficacy: Toward a unifying theory of behavioral change. *Psychological Review, 84,* 181–215.

Bandura, A. (1996). *Self-efficacy: The exercise of control*. New York: Freeman.

Barnes, M. L., & Sternberg, R. J. (1989). Social intelligence and decoding of nonverbal cues. *Intelligence, 13,* 263–287.

Barron, F. (1963). *Creativity and psychological health*. Princeton, NJ: Van Nostrand.

Barron, F. (1968). *Creativity and personal freedom*. New York: Van Nostrand.

Barron, F. (1969). *Creative person and creative process*. New York: Holt, Rinehart & Winston.

Barron, F., & Harrington, D. M. (1981). Creativity, intelligence, and personality. *Annual Review of Psychology, 32,* 439–476.

Basseches, J. (1984). *Dialectical thinking and adult development*. Norwood, NJ: Ablex.

Bateson, G. (1979). *Mind and nature*. London: Wildwood House.

Beilin, H. (1980). Piaget's theory: Refinement, revision, or rejection? In R. H. Kluwee & H. Spada (Eds.), *Developmental models of thinking* (pp. 245–261). New York: Academic Press.

Belmont, J. M., & Butterfield, E. C. (1971). What the development of short-term memory is. *Human Development, 14,* 236–248.

Belmont, J. M., Butterfield, E. C., & Ferretti, R. P. (1982). To secure transfer of training instruct self-management skills. In D. K. Detterman & R. J. Sternberg (Eds.), *How and how much can intelligence be increased*. Norwood, NJ: Ablex Publishing Company.

Bem, D. J. (1967). Self-perception: An alternative interpretation of cognitive dissonance phenomena. *Psychological Review, 74,* 183–200.

Bem, D. J. (1996). Exotic becomes erotic: A developmental theory of sexual orientation. *Psychological Review, 81,* 320–335.

Berry, J. W. (1974). Radical cultural relativism and the concept of intelligence. In J. W. Berry & P. R. Dasen (Eds.), *Culture and cognition: Readings in cross-cultural psychology* (pp. 225–229). London: Methuen.

Binet, A., & Simon, T. (1916a). *The development of intelligence in children*. Baltimore: Williams & Wilkins (originally published in 1905).

Binet, A., & Simon, T. (1916b). *The intelligence of the feeble-minded* (E. S. Kite, Trans.). Baltimore: Williams & Wilkins.

Bloom, B. S. (1976). *Human characteristics and school learning*. New York: McGraw-Hill.

Bloom, B. S., Engelhart, M. D., Frost, E. J., Hill, W. H., & Krathwohl, D. R. (1956). *Taxonomy of educational objectives. Handbook I: Cognitive domain*. New York: David McKay.

Bloom, H. (1994). *The Western canon: The books and school of the ages*. New York: Harcourt Brace.

Boden, M. A. (1992). *The creative mind: Myths and mechanisms*. New York: Basic Books.

Boden, M. A. (1999). Computer models of creativity. In R. J. Sternberg (Ed.), *Handbook of creativity* (pp. 351–372). New York: Cambridge University Press.

Boring, E. G. (1923, June 6). Intelligence as the tests test it. *New Republic*, 35–37.

Borkowski, J., & Wanschura, P. (1974). Mediational processes in the retarded. In N. Ellis (Ed.), *International review of research in mental retardation, Vol. 7*. New York: Academic Press.

Bouchard, T. J., Jr. (1997). IQ similarity in twins reared apart: Findings and responses to critics. In R. J. Sternberg & E. L. Grigorenko (Eds.), *Intelligence, heredity, and environment* (pp. 126–160). New York: Cambridge University Press.

Bouchard, T. J., Jr., Lykken, D. T., McGue, M., Segal, N. L., & Tellegen, A. (1990). Sources of human psychological differences: The Minnesota study of twins reared apart. *Science, 250*, 223–228.

Bowers, K. S., Regehr, G., Balthazard, C., & Parker, K. (1990). Intuition in the context of discovery. *Cognitive Psychology, 22*, 72–109.

Brainerd, C. J. (1978). The stage question in cognitive-developmental theory. *Behavioral and Brain Sciences, 1*, 173–182.

Brand, C. (1996). *The g factor: General intelligence and its implications*. Chichester, England: Wiley.

Bransford, J. D., & Stein, B. (1984). *The IDEAL problem solver*. New York: Freeman.

Bransford, J. D., & Stein, B. S. (1993). *The IDEAL problem solver: A guide for improving thinking, learning, and creativity* (2nd ed). New York: Freeman.

Bronfenbrenner, U., & Ceci, S. J. (1994). Nature-nurture reconceptualized in developmental perspective: A bioecological model. *Psychological Review, 101*, 568–586.

Brown, A. L., Bransford, J. D., Ferrara, R. A., & Campione, J. C. (1983). Learning, remembering, and understanding. In J. H. Flavell & E. M. Markman (Eds.), *Handbook of child psychology, Vol. III*. New York: Wiley.

Brown, A. L., & DeLoache, J. S. (1978). Skills, plans, and self-regulation. In R. Siegler (Ed.), *Children's thinking: What develops?* Hillsdale, NJ: Erlbaum.

Brown, A. L., & Ferrara, R. A. (1985). Diagnosing zones of proximal development. In J. V. Wertsch (Ed.), *Culture, communication, and cognition: Vygotskian perspectives* (pp. 273–305). New York: Cambridge University Press.

Brown, A. L., & French, A. L. (1979). The zone of potential development: Implications for intelligence testing in the year 2000. In R. J. Sternberg & D. K. Detterman (Eds.), *Human intelligence: Perspectives on its theory and measurement* (pp. 217–235). Norwood, NJ: Ablex.

Bryant, P. E., & Trabasso, T. (1971). Transitive inferences and memory in young children. *Nature, 232*(5311), 456–458.

Budoff, M. (1968). Learning potential as a supplementary assessment procedure. In J. Hellmuth (Ed.), *Learning disorders* (Vol. 3, pp. 295–343). Seattle, WA: Special Child.

Burt, C. (1949). Alternative methods of factor analysis and their relations to Pearson's method of "principal axis." *British Journal of Psychology, Statistical Section, 2,* 98–121.

Cage, J. (1961). *Silence.* Middletown, CT: Wesleyan University Press.

Campbell, D. T. (1960). Blind variation and selective retention in creative thought and other knowledge processes. *Psychological Review, 67,* 380–400.

Campione, J. C., Brown, A. L., & Ferrara, R. (1982). Mental retardation and intelligence. In R. J. Sternberg (Ed.), *Handbook of human intelligence* (pp. 392–490). New York: Cambridge University Press.

Cantor, N., & Kihlstrom, J. F. (1987). *Personality and social intelligence.* Englewood Cliffs, NJ: Prentice-Hall.

Carey, S. (1985). *Conceptual change in childhood.* Cambridge, MA: MIT Press.

Carroll, J. B. (1981). Ability and task difficulty in cognitive psychology. *Educational Researcher, 10,* 11–21.

Carroll, J. B. (1982). The measurement of intelligence. In R. J. Sternberg (Ed.), *Handbook of human intelligence* (pp. 29–120). New York: Cambridge University Press.

Carroll, J. B. (1993). *Human cognitive abilities: A survey of factor-analytic studies.* New York: Cambridge University Press.

Cattell, J. M. (1890). Mental tests and measurements. *Mind, 15,* 373–380.

Cattell, R. B. (1971). *Abilities: Their structure, growth and action.* Boston: Houghton Mifflin.

Cattell, R. B., & Cattell, H. E. P. (1973). *Measuring intelligence with the Culture Fair Tests.* Champaign, IL: Institute for Personality and Ability Testing.

Ceci, S. J. (1996). *On intelligence* (expanded ed.). Cambridge, MA: Harvard University Press.

Chadwick, W., & Courtivron, I. (Eds.). (1996). *Significant others: Creativity & intimate partnership.* New York: Thames & Hudson.

Chase, W. G., & Simon, H. A. (1973). The mind's eye in chess. In W. G. Chase (Ed.), *Visual information processing* (pp. 215–281). New York: Academic Press.

Chen, M. J. (1994). Chinese and Australian concepts of intelligence. *Psychology and Developing Societies, 6,* 101–117.

Chen, M. J., Braithwaite, V., & Huang, J. T. (1982). Attributes of intelligent behaviour: Perceived relevance and difficulty by Australian and Chinese students. *Journal of Cross-Cultural Psychology, 13,* 139–156.

Chen, M. J., & Chen, H. C. (1988). Concepts of intelligence: A comparison of Chinese graduates from Chinese and English schools in Hong Kong. *International Journal of Psychology, 223,* 471–487.

Chi, M. T. H., Feltovich, P. J., & Glaser, R. (1981). Categorization and representation of physics problems by experts and novices. *Cognitive Science, 5*, 121–152.

Chi, M. T. H., Glaser, R., & Farr, M. J. (Eds.). (1988). *The nature of expertise.* Hillsdale, NJ: Erlbaum.

Chi, M. T. H., Glaser, R., & Rees, E. (1982). Expertise in problem solving. In R. J. Sternberg (Ed.), *Advances in the psychology of human intelligence* (Vol. 1, pp. 7–75). Hillsdale, NJ: Erlbaum.

Chiesi, H. L., Spilich, G. J., & Voss, J. F. (1979). Acquisition of domain-related information in relation to high and low domain knowledge. *Journal of Verbal Learning and Verbal Behavior, 18*, 257–274.

Chomsky, N. (1957). *Syntactic structures.* The Hague, Netherlands: Mouton.

Clayton, V. (1975). Erickson's theory of human development as it applies to the aged: Wisdom as contradictory cognition. *Human Development, 18*, 119–128.

Clayton, V. (1976). *A multidimensional scaling analysis of the concept of wisdom.* Unpublished doctoral dissertation, University of Southern California.

Clayton, V., & Birren, J. E. (1980). The development of wisdom across the life-span: A reexamination of an ancient topic. In P. B. Baltes & O. G. Brim (Eds.), *Life-span development and behavior* (Vol. 3, pp. 103–135). New York: Academic Press.

Clement, J. (1989). Learning via model construction and criticism: Protocol evidence on sources of creativity in science. In G. Glover, R. Ronning, & C. Reynolds (Eds.), *Handbook of creativity* (pp. 341–381). New York: Plenum.

Collins, M. A., & Amabile, T. M. (1999). Motivation and creativity. In R. J. Sternberg (Ed.), *Handbook of creativity* (pp. 297–312). New York: Cambridge University Press.

Connolly, H., & Bruner, J. (1974). Competence: Its nature and nurture. In K. Connolly & J. Bruner (Eds.), *The growth of competence.* New York: Academic Press.

Cornell, E. H. (1978). Learning to find things: A reinterpretation of object permanence studies. In L. S. Siegel & C. J. Brainerd (Eds.), *Alternatives to Piaget: Critical essays on the theory* (pp. 11–27). New York: Academic Press.

Cox, C. M. (1926). *The early mental traits of three hundred geniuses.* Stanford, CA: Stanford University Press.

Craik, F. I. M., & Lockhart, R. S. (1972). Levels of processing: A framework for memory research. *Journal of Verbal Learning and Verbal Behavior, 11*, 671–684.

Cronbach, L. J. (1957). The two disciplines of scientific psychology. *American Psychologist, 12*, 671–684.

Crutchfield, R. (1962). Conformity and creative thinking. In H. Gruber, G. Terrell, & M. Wertheimer (Eds.), *Contemporary approaches to creative thinking* (pp. 120–140). New York: Atherton Press.

Csikszentmihalyi, M. (1988). Society, culture, and person: A systems view of creativity. In R. J. Sternberg (Ed.), *The nature of creativity* (pp. 325–339). New York: Cambridge University Press.

Csikszentmihalyi, M. (1996). *Creativity: Flow and the psychology of discovery and invention.* New York: HarperCollins.

Csikszentmihalyi, M., & Rathunde, K. (1990). The psychology of wisdom: An evolutionary interpretation. In R. J. Sternberg (Ed.), *Wisdom: Its nature, origins, and development* (pp. 25–51). New York: Cambridge University Press.

Cziko, Gary A. (1998). From blind to creative: In defense of Donald Campbell's selectionist theory of human creativity. *Journal of Creative Behavior, 32*, 192–208.

Darwin, C. (1859). *The origin of species.* London: Murray.

Das, J. P. (1994). Eastern views of intelligence. In R. J. Sternberg (Ed.), *Encyclopedia of human intelligence* (Vol. 1, pp. 387–391). New York: Macmillan.

Das, J. P., Kirby, J. R., & Jarman, R. F. (1979). *Simultaneous and successive cognitive processes.* New York: Academic Press.

Das, J. P., Naglieri, J. A., & Kirby, J. R. (1994). *Assessment of cognitive processes: The PASS theory of intelligence.* Needham Heights, MA: Allyn & Bacon.

Dasen, P. (1984). The cross-cultural study of intelligence: Piaget and the Baoule. *International Journal of Psychology, 19,* 407–434.

Davidson, J. E., & Sternberg, R. J. (1984). The role of insight in intellectual giftedness. *Gifted Child Quarterly, 28,* 58–64.

Davies, M., Stankov, L., & Roberts, R. D. (1998). Emotional intelligence: In search of an elusive construct. *Journal of Personality & Social Psychology, 75,* 989–1015.

Day, J. D., Engelhardt, J. L., Maxwell, S. E., & Bolig, E. E. (1997). Comparison of static and dynamic assessment procedures and their relation to independent performance. *Journal of Educational Psychology, 89*(2), 358–368.

De Bono, E. (1971). *Lateral thinking for management.* New York: McGraw-Hill.

De Bono, E. (1985). *Six thinking hats.* Boston: Little, Brown.

De Bono, E. (1992). *Serious creativity: Using the power of lateral thinking to create new ideas.* New York: HarperCollins.

DeGroot, A. D. (1965). *Thought and choice in chess.* The Hague: Mouton.

Derrida, J. (1992). *Acts of literature.* (D. Attridge, Ed.). New York: Routledge.

Dewey, J. (1933). *How we think.* Boston: Heath.

Donchin E., Ritter, W., & McCallum, W. C. (1978). Cognitive psychophysiology: The endogenous components of the ERP. In P. Tueting & S. H. Koslow (Eds.), *Event-related brain potentials in man* (pp. 349–441). New York: Academic Press.

Donders, F. C. (1868/1969). Over de snelheid van psychische processen. Onderzoekingen gedaan in het Physiologisch Laboratorium der Utrechtsche Hoogeschool. *Tweede reeks, II,* 92–120.

Dreyfus, H. L. (1992). *What computers still can't do.* Cambridge, MA: MIT Press.

Duncker, K. (1945). On problem solving. *Psychological Monographs, 68*(5), 270.

Durojaiye, M. O. A. (1993). Indigenous psychology in Africa. In U. Kim & J. W. Berry (Eds.), *Indigenous psychologies: Research and experience in cultural context* (pp. 211–220). Newbury Park, CA: Sage.

Dweck, C. S. (1999). *Self-theories: Their role in motivation, personality, and development.* Philadelphia: Psychology Press/Taylor & Francis.

Elkind, D. (1976). *Child development and education: a Piagetian perspective.* New York: Oxford University Press.

Ennis, R. H. (1987). A taxonomy of crticial thinking dispositions and abilities. In J. B. Baron & R. J. Sternberg (Eds.), *Teaching thinking skills: Theory and practice* (pp. 9–26). New York: Freeman.

Epstein, S. (1985). The implications of cognitive-experiential self-theory for research in social psychology and personality. *Journal for the Theory of Social Behaviour, 15,* 283–310.

Ericsson, K. A. (Ed.). (1996). *The road to excellence.* Mahwah, NJ: Lawrence Erlbaum Associates.

Ericsson, K. A., & Smith, J. (1991). Prospects and limits in the empirical study of expertise: An introduction. In K. A. Ericsson & J. Smith (Eds.), *Toward a general theory of expertise: Prospects and limits* (pp. 19–38). Cambridge, U.K.: Cambridge University Press.

Evans, J. (1989). Problem solving, reasoning and decision making. In A. D. Baddeley & N. O. Bernsen (Eds.), *Cognitive psychology: Research directions in cognitive science: European perspective* (Vol. 1, pp. 85–102). Hove, U.K.: Lawrence Erlbaum Associates.

Eysenck, H. J. (1993). Creativity and personality: A theoretical perspective. *Psychological Inquiry, 4,* 147–178.

Fazio, R. H., Zanna, M. P., & Cooper, J. (1977). Dissonance and self-perception: An integrative view of each theory's proper domain of application. *Journal of Experimental Social Psychology, 13,* 464–479.

Festinger, L., & Carlsmith, J. M. (1959). Cognitive consequences of forced compliance. *Journal of Abnormal and Social Psychology, 58,* 203–210.

Feuerstein, R. (1979). *The dynamic assessment of retarded performers: The learning potential assessment device theory, instruments, and techniques.* Baltimore, MD: University Park Press.

Feuerstein, R. (1980). *Instrumental enrichment: An intervention program for cognitive modifiability.* Baltimore, MD: University Park Press.

Field, D. (1987). A review of preschool conservation training: An analysis of analyses. *Developmental Review, 7*(3), 210–251.

Findlay, C. S., & Lumsden, C. J. (1988). The creative mind: Toward an evolutionary theory of discovery and invention. *Journal of Social and Biological Structures, 11,* 3–55.

Finke, R. (1990). *Creative imagery: Discoveries and inventions in visualization.* Hillsdale, NJ: Lawrence Erlbaum Associates.

Finke, R. A. (1995). Creative insight and preinventive forms. In R. J. Sternberg & J. E. Davidson (Eds.), *The nature of insight* (pp. 255–280). Cambridge, MA: MIT Press.

Finke, R. A., Ward, T. B., & Smith, S. M. (1992). *Creative cognition: Theory, research, and applications.* Cambridge, MA: MIT Press.

Flavell, J. H. (1971). Stage-related properties of cognitive development. *Cognitive Psychology, 2*(4), 421–453.

Flavell, J. H. (1981). Cognitive monitoring. In W. P. Dickson (Ed.), *Children's oral communication skills* (pp. 35–60). New York: Academic Press.

Flavell, J. H., & Wellman, H. M. (1977). Metamemory. In R. V. Kail, Jr. & J. W. Hagen (Eds.), *Perspectives on the development of memory and cognition.* Hillsdale, NJ: Lawrence Erlbaum Associates.

Flescher, I. (1963). Anxiety and achievement of intellectually gifted and creatively gifted children. *Journal of Psychology, 56,* 251–268.

Flynn, J. R. (1984). The mean IQ of Americans: Massive gains 1932 to 1978. *Psychological Bulletin, 95,* 29–51.

Flynn, J. R. (1987). Massive IQ gains in 14 nations. *Psychological Bulletin, 101,* 171–191.

Flynn, J. R. (1998). WAIS-III and WISC-III gains in the United States from 1972 to 1995: How to compensate for obsolete norms. *Perceptual & Motor Skills, 86,* 1231–1239.

Fraser, S. (Ed.). (1995). *The bell curve wars: Race, intelligence and the future of America*. New York: Basic Books.

Frensch, P. A., & Sternberg, R. J. (1989). Expertise and intelligent thinking: When is it worse to know better? In R. J. Sternberg (Ed.), *Advances in the psychology of human intelligence* (Vol. 5, pp. 157–158). Hillsdale, NJ: Lawrence Erlbaum Associates.

Freud, S. (1908/1959). The relation of the poet to day-dreaming. In *Collected papers* (Vol. 4, pp. 173–183). London: Hogarth Press.

Freud, S. (1910/1964). *Leonardo da Vinci and a memory of his childhood*. New York: Norton (original work published in 1910).

Galton, F. (1869). *Hereditary genius: An inquiry into its laws and consequences*. London: Macmillan.

Galton, F. (1883). *Inquiry into human faculty and its development*. London: Macmillan.

Garcia, J., & Koelling, R. A. (1966). The relation of cue to consequence in avoidance learning. *Psychonomic Science, 4*, 123–124.

Gardner, H. (1983). *Frames of mind: The theory of multiple intelligences*. New York: Basic Books.

Gardner, H. (1993). *Multiple intelligences: The theory in practice*. New York: Basic Books.

Gardner, H. (1994). The stories of the right hemisphere. In W. D. Spaulding, et al. (Eds.), *Integrative views of motivation, cognition, and emotion. Nebraska symposium on motivation* (Vol. 41, pp. 57–69). Lincoln, NE: University of Nebraska Press.

Gardner, H. (1995). *Leading minds*. New York: Basic Books.

Gardner, H. (1999). *Intelligence reframed: Multiple intelligences for the 21st century*. New York: Basic Books.

Gardner, H., Krechevsky, M., Sternberg, R. J., & Okagaki, L. (1994). Intelligence in context: Enhancing students' practical intelligence for school. In K. McGilly (Ed.), *Classroom lessons: Integrating cognitive theory and classroom practice* (pp. 105–127). Cambridge, MA: MIT Press.

Gazzaniga, M. S., Ivry, R. B., Mangun, G. (1998). *Cognitive neuroscience: The biology of the mind*. New York: W.W. Norton & Co.

Getzels, J., & Csikszentmihalyi, M. (1976). *The creative vision: A longitudinal study of problem finding in art*. New York: Wiley–Interscience.

Getzels, J. W., & Jackson, P. W. (1962). *Creativity and intelligence: Explorations with gifted students*. New York: John Wiley & Sons.

Ghiselin, B. (Ed.). (1985). *The creative process: A symposium*. Berkeley, CA: University of California Press.

Gigerenzer, G., Todd, P. M., & The ABC Research Group. (1999). *Simple heuristics that make us smart*. New York: Oxford University Press.

Gill, R., & Keats, D. M. (1980). Elements of intellectual competence: Judgments by Australian and Malay university students. *Journal of Cross-Cultural Psychology, 11*, 233–243.

Gilligan, C. (1982). *In a different voice: Psychological theory and women's development*. Cambridge, MA: Harvard University Press.

Gleitman, H. (1986). *Psychology* (2nd Ed.). New York: W. W. Norton & Co.

Golann, S. E. (1962). The creativity motive. *Journal of Personality, 30*, 588–600.

Goleman, D. (1995). *Emotional intelligence*. New York: Bantam Books.

Goodman, N. (1955). *Fact, fiction, and forecast.* Cambridge, MA: Harvard University Press.

Goodnow, J. J. (1976). The nature of intelligent behavior: Questions raised by cross-cultural studies. In L. Resnick (Ed.), *The nature of intelligence* (pp. 169–188). Hillsdale, NJ: Lawrence Erlbaum Associates.

Gordon, W. J. J. (1961). *Synectics: The development of creative capacity.* New York: Harper & Row.

Gough, H. G. (1979). A creativity scale for the Adjective Check List. *Journal of Personality and Social Psychology, 37,* 1398–1405.

Gould, S. J. (1981). *The mismeasure of man.* New York: W. W. Norton & Co.

Gould, S. J. (1995). Curveball. In S. Fraser (Ed.), *The bell curve wars* (pp. 11–22). New York: Basic Books.

Green, D. R., Ford, M. P., & Flamer, G. B. (1971). *Measurement and Piaget.* New York: McGraw-Hill.

Greenfield, P. M. (1997). You can't take it with you: Why abilities assessments don't cross cultures. *American Psychologist, 52*(10), 1115–1124.

Grigorenko, E. L., Geissler, P. W., Prince, R., Okatcha, F., Nokes, C., Kenny, D. A., Bundy, D. A., & Sternberg, R. J. (2001). The organisation of Luo conceptions of intelligence: A study of implicit theories in a Kenyan village. *International Journal of Behavioral Development, 25*(4), 367–378.

Grigorenko, E. L., Gil, G., Jarvin, L., & Sternberg, R. J. (2000). Toward a validation of aspects of the theory of successful intelligence. Unpublished manuscript.

Grigorenko, E. L., Jarvin, L., & Sternberg, R. J. (2002). School-based tests of the triarchic theory of intelligence: Three settings, three samples, three syllabi. *Contemporary Educational Psychology, 27,* 167–208.

Grigorenko, E. L., & Sternberg, R. J. (1998). Dynamic testing. *Psychological Bulletin, 124,* 75–111.

Grigorenko, E. L., & Sternberg, R. J. (2001). Analytical, creative, and practical intelligence as predictors of self-reported adaptive functioning: A case study in Russia. *Intelligence, 29,* 57–73.

Grotzer, T. A., & Perkins, D. A. (2000). Teaching of intelligence: A performance conception. In R. J. Sternberg (Ed.), *Handbook of intelligence* (pp. 492–515). New York: Cambridge University Press.

Gruber, H. E. (1981). *Darwin on man: A psychological study of scientific creativity* (2nd ed.). Chicago: University of Chicago Press. (Original work published 1974.)

Gruber, H. E. (1989). The evolving systems approach to creative work. In D. B. Wallace & H. E. Gruber (Eds.), *Creative people at work: Twelve cognitive case studies* (pp. 3–24). New York: Oxford University Press.

Gruber, H. E., & Davis, S. N. (1988). Inching our way up Mount Olympus: The evolving-systems approach to creative thinking. In R. J. Sternberg (Ed.), *The nature of creativity* (pp. 243–270). New York: Cambridge University Press.

Gruber, H. E., & Wallace, D. B. (1999). The case study method and evolving systems approach for understanding unique creative people at work. In R. J. Sternberg (Ed.), *Handbook of creativity* (pp. 93–115). New York: Cambridge University Press.

Guilford, J. P. (1950). Creativity. *American Psychologist, 5,* 444–454.

Guilford, J. P. (1967). *The nature of human intelligence.* New York: McGraw-Hill.

Guilford, J. P. (1968). Intelligence has three facets. *Science, 160*(3828), 615–620.

Guilford, J. P. (1982). Cognitive psychology's ambiguities: Some suggested reme-
dies. *Psychological Review, 89*, 48–59.

Guilford, J. P., & Hoepfner, R. (1971). *The analysis of intelligence*. New York:
McGraw-Hill.

Gustafsson, J. E. (1984). A unifying model for the structure of intellectual abilities.
Intelligence, 8, 179–203.

Gustafsson, J. E. (1988). Hierarchical models of the structure of cognitive abilities.
In R. J. Sternberg (Ed.), *Advances in the psychology of human intelligence* (Vol. 4,
pp. 35–71). Hillsdale, NJ: Lawrence Erlbaum Associates.

Guthke, J. (1993). Current trends in theories and assessment of intelligence. In
J. H. M. Hamers, K. Sijtsma, & A. J. J. M. Ruijssenaars (Eds.), *Learning potential
assessment* (pp. 13–20). Amsterdam: Swets & Zeitlinger.

Guttman, L. (1954). A new approach to factor analysis: The radix. In P. F. Lazarsfeld
(Ed.), *Mathematical thinking in the social sciences* (pp. 258–348). New York: Free
Press.

Guyote, M. J., & Sternberg, R. J. (1981). A transitive-chain theory of syllogistic
reasoning. *Cognitive Psychology, 13*, 461–525.

Haier, R. J., Nuechterlein, K. H., Hazlett, E., Wu, J. C., Pack, J., Browning, H. L., &
Buchsbaum, M. S. (1988). Cortical glucose metabolic rate correlates of abstract
reasoning and attention studied with positron emission tomography. *Intelligence,
12*, 199–217.

Haier, R. J., Siegel, B., Tang, C., Abel, L., & Buchsbaum, M. S. (1992). Intelligence and changes in regional cerebral glucose metabolic rate following learning.
Intelligence, 16, 415–426.

Halpern, D. F. (1996). *Thought and knowledge: An introduction to critical thinking*
(2nd ed.). Mahwah, NJ: Lawrence Erlbaum Associates.

Halstead, W. C. (1951). Biological intelligence. *Journal of Personality, 20*,
118–130.

Hamm, C. (1980). John Cage. In *The new Grove dictionary of music and musicians*
(Vol. 3, pp. 597–603). London: Macmillan.

Harris, Robert. (1992). *Fatherland*. New York: Random House.

Hartt, F. (1993). *Art: A history of painting, sculpture, architecture* (4th Ed.). Englewood
Cliffs, NJ: Prentice Hall.

Hayes, J. R. (1989). Cognitive processes in creativity. In J. A. Glover, R. R.
Ronning, & C. R. Reynolds (Eds.), *Handbook of creativity* (pp. 135–145). New York:
Plenum.

Haywood, H. C., & Tzuriel, D. (Eds.). (1992). *Interactive assessment*. New York:
Springer-Verlag.

Hebb, D. O. (1949). *The organization of behavior: A neuropsychological theory*. New
York: Wiley.

Hedlund, J., Horvath, J. A., Forsythe, G. B., Snook, S., Williams, W. M., Bullis,
R. C., Dennis, M., & Sternberg, R. J. (1998). *Tacit Knowledge in Military Leadership:
Evidence of Construct Validity* (Technical Report 1080). Alexandria, VA: U.S. Army
Research Institute for the Behavioral and Social Sciences.

Hegel, G. W. F. (1931). *The phenomenology of the mind* (2nd ed.; J. D. Baillie, Trans).
London: Allen & Unwin (original work published 1807).

Hendrickson A. E., & Hendrickson, D. E. (1980). The biological basis for individual
differences in intelligence. *Personality and Individual Differences, 1*, 3–33.

Hennessey, B. A., & Amabile, T. M. (1988). The conditions of creativity. In R. J. Sternberg (Ed.), *The nature of creativity* (pp. 11–38). New York: Cambridge University Press.

Herr, E. L., Moore, G. D., & Hasen, J. S. (1965). Creativity, intelligence, and values: A study of relationships. *Exceptional Children, 32*, 114–115.

Herrnstein, R. J., & Murray, C. (1994). *The bell curve.* New York: Free Press.

Hoffman, R. R. (Ed.). (1992). *The psychology of expertise: Cognitive research and empirical AI.* New York: Springer-Verlag.

Holliday, S. G., & Chandler, M. J. (1986). *Wisdom: explorations in adult competence.* Basel, Switzerland: Karger.

Holzinger, K. J. (1938). Relationships between three multiple orthogonal factors and four bifactors. *Journal of Educational Psychology, 29*, 513–519.

Horn, J. L. (1967). On subjectivity in factor analysis. *Educational and Psychological Measurement, 27*, 811–820.

Horn, J. L. (1994). Theory of fluid and crystallized intelligence. In R. J. Sternberg (Ed.), *The encyclopedia of human intelligence* (Vol. 1, pp. 443–451). New York: Macmillan.

Horn, J. L., & Knapp, J. R. (1973). On the subjective character of the empirical base of Guilford's structure-of-intellect model. *Psychological Bulletin, 80*, 33–43.

Horn, J. L., & Knapp, J. R. (1974). Thirty wrongs do not make a right: Reply to Guilford. *Psychological Bulletin, 81*(8), 502–504.

Howe, M. J., Davidson, J. W., & Sloboda, J. A. (1998). Innate talents: Reality or myth? *Behavioral & Brain Sciences, 21*, 399–442.

Humphreys, L. (1962). The organization of human abilities. *American Psychologist, 17*, 475–483.

Hunt, E. B. (1980). Intelligence as an information-processing concept. *British Journal of Psychology, 71*, 449–474.

Hunt, E. B. (1995). *Will we be smart enough? A cognitive analysis of the coming workforce.* New York: Russell Sage Foundation.

Hunt, E., Frost, N., & Lunneborg, C. (1973). Individual differences in cognition: A new approach to intelligence. In G. Bower (Ed.), *The psychology of learning and motivation* (Vol. 7, pp. 87–122). New York: Academic Press.

Hunt, E. B., Lunneborg, C., & Lewis, J. (1975). What does it mean to be high verbal? *Cognitive Psychology, 7*, 194–227.

Intelligence and its measurement: A symposium (1921). *Journal of Educational Psychology, 12*, 123–147, 195–216, 271–275.

Irvine, J. T. (1978). "Wolof magical thinking": Culture and conservation revisited. *Journal of Cross-Cultural Psychology, 9*, 300–310.

Jacoby, R. & Glauberman, N. (Eds.). (1995). *The bell curve debate.* New York: Times Books.

Janis, I. L. (1972). *Victims of groupthink.* Boston: Houghton-Mifflin.

Jensen, A. R. (1969). Intelligence, learning ability and socioeconomic status. *Journal of Special Education, 3*, 23–35.

Jensen, A. R. (1979). *g*: Outmoded theory or unconquered frontier? *Creative Science and Technology, 2*, 16–29.

Jensen, A. R. (1982). Reaction time and psychometric g. In H. J. Eysenck (Ed.), *A model for intelligence.* Heidelberg: Springer-Verlag.

Jensen, A. R. (1997). The puzzle of nongenetic variance. In R. J. Sternberg & E. L. Grigorenko (Eds.), *Intelligence, heredity, and environment* (pp. 42–88). New York: Cambridge University Press.

Jensen, A. R. (1998). *The g factor: The science of mental ability.* Westport, CT: Praeger/Greenwoood.

Jensen, A. R. (2002). Psychometric g: Definition and substantiation. In R. J. Sternberg & E. L. Grigorenko (Eds.), *The general factor of intelligence: How general is it?* (pp. 39–53). Mahwah, NJ: Lawrence Erlbaum Associates.

Johnson, R., Jr. (1986). A triarchic model of P300 amplitude. *Psychophysiology, 23,* 367–384.

Johnson, R., Jr. (1988). The amplitude of the P300 component of the vent-related potential: Review and synthesis. In P. K. Ackles, J. R. Jennings, & M. G. H. Coles (Eds.), *Advances in psychophysiology: A research manual* (Vol. 3, pp. 69–138). Greenwich, CT: CAI Press.

Johnson-Laird, P. N. (1988). Freedom and constraint in creativity. In R. J. Sternberg (Ed.), *The nature of creativity* (pp. 202–219). New York: Cambridge University Press.

John-Steiner, V. (2000). *Creative collaboration.* New York: Oxford University Press.

Kamin, L. (1974). *The science and politics of IQ.* Hillsdale, NJ: Lawrence Erlbaum Associates.

Kaplan, C. A., & Simon, H. A. (1990). In search of insight. *Cognitive Psychology, 22,* 374–419.

Katz, H., & Beilin, H. (1976). A test of Bryant's claims concerning the young child's understanding of quantitative invariance. *Child Development, 47,* 877–880.

Kauffman, S. (1995). *At home in the universe: The search for laws of self-organization and complexity.* New York: Oxford University Press.

Kaufman, A. S., & Kaufman, N. L. (1983). *Kaufman assessment battery for children: Interpretive manual.* Circle Pines, MN: American Guidance Service.

Keating, D. P., & Bobbit, B. (1978). Individual and developmental differences in cognitive processing components of mental ability. *Child Development, 49,* 155–169.

Keil, F. C. (1989). *Concepts, kinds, and cognitive development.* Cambridge, MA: MIT Press.

Kekes, J. (1995). *Moral wisdom and good lives.* Ithaca, NY: Cornell University Press.

Kihlstrom, J. F., & Cantor, N. (2000). Social intelligence. In R. J. Sternberg (Ed.), *Handbook of intelligence* (2nd ed.) (pp. 359–379). Cambridge, U.K.: Cambridge University Press.

Kipling, R. (1985). Working-tools. In B. Ghiselin (Ed.), *The creative process: A symposium* (pp. 161–163). Berkeley, CA: University of California Press (original article published 1937).

Kitchener, K. S. (1983). Cognition, metacognition, and epistemic cognition: A three-level model of cognitive processing. *Human Development, 4,* 222–232.

Kitchener, K. S. (1986). Formal reasoning in adults: A review and critique. In R. A. Mines & K. S. Kitchener (Eds.), *Adult cognitive development.* New York: Praeger.

Kitchener, K. S., & Brenner, H. G. (1990). Wisdom and reflective judgment: Knowing in the face of uncertainty. In R. J. Sternberg (Ed.), *Wisdom: Its nature, origins, and development* (pp. 212–229). New York: Cambridge University Press.

Kitchener, K. S., & Kitchener, R. F. (1981). The development of natural rationality: Can formal operations account for it? In J. Meacham & N. R. Santilli (Eds.), *Social development in youth: Structure and content*. Basel, Switzerland: Karger.

Koestler, A. (1964). *The act of creation*. New York: Dell.

Kohlberg, L. (1969). Stage and sequence: The cognitive-developmental approach to socialization. In G. A. Goslin (Ed.), *Handbook of socialization theory and research* (pp.347–380). Chicago: Rand McNally.

Kohlberg, L. (1983). *The psychology of moral development*. New York: Harper & Row.

Kramer, D. A. (1990). Conceptualizing wisdom: The primacy of affect-cognition relations. In R. J. Sternberg (Ed.), *Wisdom: Its nature, origins, and development* (pp. 279–313). New York: Cambridge University Press.

Kris, E. (1952). *Psychoanalytic exploration in art*. New York: International Universities Press.

Kroeber, A. L., & Kluckhohn, C. (1952). Culture: A critical review of concepts and definitions. *Papers. Peabody Museum of Archaeology & Ethnology, Harvard University, 47*, viii, 223.

Kruskal, J. B. (1964a). Multidimensional scaling by optimizing goodness of fit to a nonmetric hypothesis. *Psychometrika, 20*, 1–27.

Kruskal, J. B. (1964b). Nonmetric multidimensional scaling: A numerical method. *Psychometrika, 20*, 115–129.

Kubie, L. S. (1958). *The neurotic distortion of the creative process*. Lawrence: University of Kansas Press.

Kuhn, T. S. (1970). *The structure of scientific revolutions* (2nd ed.). Chicago: University of Chicago Press.

Laboratory of Comparative Human Cognition (1982). Culture and intelligence. In R. J. Sternberg (Ed.), *Handbook of human intelligence* (pp. 642–719). New York: Cambridge University Press.

Labouvie-Vief, G. (1980). Beyond formal operations: Uses and limits of pure logic in life span development. *Human Development, 23*, 141–161.

Labouvie-Vief, G. (1982). Dynamic development and mature autonomy. *Human Development, 25*, 161–191.

Labouvie-Vief, G. (1990). Wisdom as integrated thought: Historical and developmental perspectives. In R. J. Sternberg (Ed.), *Wisdom: Its nature, origins, and development* (pp. 52–83). New York: Cambridge University Press.

Langer, E. J. (1997). *The power of mindful learning*. Reading, MA: Addison-Wesley Publishing Co, Inc.

Langley, P., Simon, H.A., Bradshaw, G.L., & Zytkow, J.M. (1987). *Scientific discovery: Computational explorations of the creative processes*. Cambridge, MA: MIT Press.

Larkin, J. H., McDermott, J., Simon, D. P., & Simon, H. A. (1980). Expert and novice performance in solving physics problems. *Science, 208*, 1335–1342.

Lemann, N. (1999). *The big test: The secret history of the American meritocracy*. New York: Farrar, Straus & Giroux.

Levine, A. (1998). Succeeding as a leader; failing as a president. *Change*, January/February, 43–45.

Lewontin, R. (1982). *Human diversity*. New York: Freeman.

Lidz, C. S. (Ed.). (1987). *Dynamic assessment*. New York: Guilford Press.

Lidz, C. S. (1991). *Practitioner's guide to dynamic assessment*. New York: Guilford Press.

Lipman, M. (1982). *Harry Stottlemeier's discovery.* Upper Montclair, NJ: First Mountain Foundation.

Lipman, M., Sharp, A. M., & Oscanyan, F. S. (1980). *Philosophy in the classroom.* Philadelphia, PA: Temple University Press.

Loehlin, J. C. (1989). Group differences in intelligence. In R. J. Sternberg (Ed.), *Handbook of intelligence* (pp. 176–193). New York: Cambridge University Press.

Loehlin, J. C., Horn, J. M., & Willerman, L. (1997). Heredity, environment, and IQ in the Texas adoption project. In R. J. Sternberg & E. L. Grigorenko (Eds.), *Intelligence, heredity, and environment* (pp. 105–125). New York: Cambridge University Press.

Lubart, T. I. (1990). Creativity and cross-cultural variation. *International Journal of Psychology, 25,* 39–59.

Lubart, T. I. (1994). Creativity. In R. J. Sternberg (Ed.), *Thinking and problem solving* (pp. 290–332). San Diego: Academic Press.

Lubart, T. I., & Sternberg, R. J. (1995). An investment approach to creativity: Theory and data. In S. M. Smith, T. B. Ward, & R. A. Finke (Eds.), *The creative cognition approach.* Cambridge, MA: MIT Press.

Luria, A. R. (1973). *The working brain.* New York: Basic Books.

Luria, A. R. (1980). *Higher cortical functions in man* (2nd ed., rev & expanded). New York: Basic Books.

Lutz, C. (1985). Ethnopsychology compared to what? Explaining behaviour and consciousness among the Ifaluk. In G. M. White & J. Kirkpatrick (Eds.), *Person, self, and experience: Exploring Pacific ethnopsychologies* (pp. 35–79). Berkeley: University of California Press.

Machlis, J. (1979). *Introduction to contemporary music* (2nd ed.). New York: W. W. Norton & Co.

MacKinnon, D. W. (1965). Personality and the realization of creative potential. *American Psychologist, 20,* 273–281.

Mackintosh, N. J. (1998). *IQ and human intelligence.* Oxford: Oxford University Press.

Maduro, R. (1976). *Artistic creativity in a Brahmin painter community.* Research monograph 14, Berkeley, CA: Center for South and Southeast Asia Studies, University of California.

Maslow, A. (1967). The creative attitude. In R. L. Mooney & T. A. Rasik (Eds.), *Explorations in creativity* (pp. 43–57). New York: Harper & Row.

Maslow, A. (1968). *Toward a psychology of being.* New York: Van Nostrand.

Mayer, J. D., & Gehr, G. (1996). Emotional intelligence and the identification of emotion. *Intelligence, 22,* 89–114.

Mayer, J. D., & Salovey, P. (1993). The intelligence of emotional intelligence. *Intelligence, 17,* 433–442.

Mayer, J. D., Salovey, P., Caruso, D. (2000a). Emotional intelligence. In R. J. Sternberg (Ed.), *Handbook of intelligence* (pp. 396–421). New York: Cambridge University Press.

Mayer, J. D., Salovey, P., Caruso, D. (2000b). Emotional intelligence meets traditional standards for an intelligence. *Intelligence, 27,* 267–298.

Mayer, M. (1976). *Professor Wormbog in search of the Zipperump-a-zoo.* New York: Golden Press.

McClelland, D. C. (1985). *Human motivation.* New York: Scott Foresman.

McClelland, D. C., Atkinson, J. W., Clark, R. A., & Lowell, E. L. (1953). *The achievement motive.* New York: Appleton-Century-Crofts, Inc.

McClelland, D. C., Atkinson, J. W., Clark, R. A., & Lowell, E. L. (1976). *The achievement motive*. New York: Irvington.

McNemar, Q. (1951). The factors in factoring behavior. *Psychometrika, 16,* 353–359.

McNemar, Q. (1964). Lost: Our intelligence? Why? *American Psychologist, 19,* 871–882.

Mednick, M. T., & Andrews, F. M. (1967). Creative thinking and level of intelligence. *Journal of Creative Behavior, 1,* 428–431.

Mednick, S. A. (1962). The associative basis of the creative process. *Psychological Review, 69,* 220–232.

Miles, T. R. (1957). On defining intelligence. *British Journal of Educational Psychology, 27,* 153–165.

Miller, G. A., Galanter, E. H., & Pribram, K. H. (1960). *Plans and the structure of behavior*. New York: Holt, Rinehart & Winston.

Miller, S. A. (1976). Nonverbal assessment of Piagetian concepts. *Psychological Bulletin, 83,* 405–430.

Mumford, M. D., & Gustafson, S. B. (1988). Creativity syndrome: Integration, application, and innovation. *Psychological Bulletin, 103,* 27–43.

Mundy-Castle, A. C. (1974). Social and technological intelligence in Western or Nonwestern cultures. *Universitas, 4,* 46–52.

Naglieri, J. A., & Das, J. P. (1990). Planning, attention, simultaneous, and successive cognitive processes as a model for intelligence. *Journal of Psychoeducational Assessment, 8,* 303–337.

Naglieri, J. A., & Das, J. P. (1997). *Cognitive assessment system*. Itasca, IL: Riverside Publishing Company.

Neisser, U. (1976). *Cognition and reality: Principles and implications of cognitive psychology*. San Francisco: Freeman.

Neisser, U. (Ed.). (1998). *The rising curve*. Washington, D.C.: American Psychological Association.

Nelson, T. O. (1999). Cognition versus metacognition. In R. J. Sternberg (Ed.), *The nature of cognition* (pp. 625–641). Cambridge, MA: The MIT Press.

Newell, A., & Simon, H. A. (1972). *Human problem solving*. Englewood Cliffs, NJ: Prentice-Hall.

Noy, P. (1969). A revision of the psychoanalytic theory of the primary process. *International Journal of Psychoanalysis, 50,* 155–178.

Ochse, R. (1990). *Before the gates of excellence*. New York: Cambridge University Press.

Okagaki, L., & Sternberg, R. J. (1993). Parental beliefs and children's school performance. *Child Development, 64*(1), 36–56.

Osborn, A. F. (1953). *Applied imagination*. New York: Scribner.

Parsons, H. M. (1974). What happened at Hawthorne? *Science, 183,* 922–932.

Pascual-Leone, J. (1990). An essay on wisdom: Toward organismic processes that make it possible. In R. J. Sternberg (Ed.), *Wisdom: Its nature, origins, and development* (pp. 244–278). New York: Cambridge University Press.

Paul, R. W. (1987). Dialogical thinking: Critical thought essential to the acquisition of rational knowledge and passions. In J. B. Baron & R. J Sternberg (Eds.), *Teaching thinking skills: Theory and practice* (pp. 127–148). New York: Freeman.

Pedersen, N. L., Plomin, R., Nesselroade, J. R., & McClearn, G. E. (1992). A quantitative genetic analysis of cognitive abilities during the second half of the life span. *Psychological Science. Vol. 3*, 346–353.

Pellegrino, J. W., & Glaser, R. (1979). Cognitive correlates and components in the analysis of individual differences. In R. J. Sternberg & D. K. Detterman (Eds.), *Human intelligence: Perspectives on its theory and measurement* (pp. 61–88). Norwood, NJ: Ablex.

Pellegrino, J. W., & Glaser, R. (1980). Components of inductive reasoning. In R. E. Snow, P.-A. Federico, & W. E. Montague (Eds.), *Aptitude, learning, and instruction: Cognitive process analyses of aptitude* (Vol. 1, pp. 177–217). Hillsdale, NJ: Lawrence Erlbaum Associates.

Pellegrino, J. W., & Glaser, R. (1982). Analyzing aptitudes for learning: Inductive reasoning. In R. Glaser (Ed.), *Advances in instructional psychology* (Vol.2). Hillsdale, NJ: Lawrence Erlbaum Associates.

Perkins, D. N. (1981). *The mind's best work*. Cambridge, MA: Harvard University Press.

Perkins, D. N. (1986). *Knowledge as design*. Hillsdale, NJ: Lawrence Erlbaum Associates.

Perkins, D. N. (1995). *Outsmarting IQ: The emerging science of learnable intelligence*. New York: Free Press.

Perkins, D. N. (1998). In the country of the blind: An appreciation of Donald Campbell's vision of creative thought. *Journal of Creative Behavior. Vol. 32(3)*, 177–191.

Piaget, J. (1926). *Ideas of the world in children. A sequel to preceding studies on the thought of the child*. Paris: Alcan.

Piaget, J. (1928). *Judgement and reasoning in the child*. London: Routledge & Kegan Paul.

Piaget, J. (1952). *The origins of intelligence in children*. New York: International Universities Press.

Piaget, J. (1972). *The psychology of intelligence*. Totowa, NJ: Littlefield Adams.

Pinker, S. (1997). *How the mind works*. New York: W. W. Norton & Co.

Plomin, R. (1997). Identifying genes for cognitive abilities and disabilities. In R. J. Sternberg & E. L. Grigorenko (Eds.), *Intelligence, heredity, and environment* (pp. 89–104). New York: Cambridge University Press.

Plomin, R., DeFries, J. C., McClearn, G. E., & Rutter, M. (1997). *Behavioral genetics* (3rd ed.). New York: Freeman.

Plomin, R., McClearn, D. L., & Smith, D. L. (1994). DNA markers associated with high versus low IQ: The IQ QTL Project. *Behavior Genetics, 24*, 107–118.

Plomin, R., McClearn, D. L., & Smith, D. L. (1995). Allelic associations between 100 DNA markers and high versus low IQ. *Intelligence, 21*, 31–48.

Plomin, R., & Neiderhiser, J. M. (1992). Quantitative genetics, molecular genetics, and intelligence. *Intelligence, 15*, 369–387.

Plomin, R., & Petrill, S. A. (1997). Genetics and intelligence: What is new? *Intelligence, 24*, 53–78.

Polanyi, M. (1976). Tacit knowledge. In M. Marx & F. Goodson (Eds.), *Theories in contemporary psychology* (pp. 330–344). New York: Macmillan.

Policastro, E., & Gardner, H. (1999). From case studies to robust generalizations: An approach to the study of creativity. In R. J. Sternberg (Ed.), *Handbook of creativity* (pp. 213–225). New York: Cambridge University Press.

Poole, F. J. P. (1985). Coming into social being: Cultural images of infants in Bimin-Kuskusmin folk psychology. In G. M. White & J. Kirkpatrick (Eds.), *Person, self, and experience: Exploring Pacific ethnopsychologies* (pp. 183–244). Berkeley: University of California Press.

Popper, K. R. (1959). *The logic of scientific discovery*. London: Hutchinson.

Posner, M. I., & Mitchell, R. F. (1967). Chronometric analysis of classification. *Psychological Review, 74*, 392–409.

Putnam, D. B., & Kilbride, P. L. (1980). *A relativistic understanding of social intelligence among the Songhay of Mali and Smaia of Kenya*. Paper presented at the meeting of the Society for Cross-Cultural Research, Philadelphia, PA.

Raven, J. (1986). *Manual for Raven Progressive Matrices and Vocabulary Scales*. London: Lewis.

Reed, T. E., & Jensen, A. R. (1992). Conduction velocity in a brain nerve pathway of normal adults correlates with intelligence level. *Intelligence, 16*, 259–272.

Reigeluth, C. M. (Ed.) et al. (1999). *Instructional-design theories and models: A new paradigm of instructional theory, Vol. II*. Mahwah, NJ: Lawrence Erlbaum Associates.

Reitman, J. (1976). Skilled perception in GO: Deducing memory structures from interresponse times. *Cognitive Psychology, 8*, 336–356.

Renzulli, J. S. (1986). The three-ring conception of giftedness: A developmental model for creative productivity. In R. J. Sternberg & J. E. Davidson (Eds.), *Conceptions of giftedness* (pp. 53–92). New York: Cambridge University Press.

Riegel, K. F. (1973). Dialectical operations: The final period of cognitive development. *Human Development, 16*, 346–370.

Robinson, D. N. (1989). *Aristotle's psychology*. New York: Columbia University Press.

Robinson, D. N. (1990). Wisdom through the ages. In R. J. Sternberg (Ed.), *Wisdom: Its nature, origins, and development* (pp. 13–24). New York: Cambridge University Press.

Roe, A. (1952). *The making of a scientist*. New York: Dodd, Mead.

Roe, A. (1972). Patterns of productivity of scientists. *Science, 176*, 940–941.

Rogers, C. R. (1954). Toward a theory of creativity. *ETC: A Review of General Semantics, 11*, 249–260.

Rogoff, B. (1990). *Apprenticeship in thinking. Cognitive development in social context*. New York: Oxford University Press.

Rosch, E. (1975). Cognitive representations of semantic categories. *Journal of Experimental Psychology: General, 104*, 192–233.

Rothenberg, A. (1979). *The emerging goddess*. Chicago: University of Chicago Press.

Rothenberg, A., & Hausman, C. R. (Eds.). (1976). *The creativity question*. Durham, NC: Duke University Press.

Royer, F. L. (1971). Information processing of visual figures in the digit symbol substitution task. *Journal of Experimental Psychology, 87*, 335–342.

Royer, J. M., Carlo, M. S., Dufresne, R., & Mestre, J. (1996). The assessment of levels of domain expertise while reading. *Cognition & Instruction, 14*(3), 373–408.

Rubenson, D. L., & Runco, M. A. (1992). The psychoeconomic approach to creativity. *New Ideas in Psychology, 10,* 131–147.

Rumelhart, D. E., McClelland, J. L., & the PDP Research Group. (1986). *Parallel distributed processing. Explorations in the microstructure of cognition: Vol. 1. Foundations.* Cambridge, MA: MIT Press.

Ruzgis, P. M., & Grigorenko, E. L. (1994). Cultural meaning systems, intelligence and personality. In R. J. Sternberg and P. Ruzgis (Eds.), *Personality and intelligence* (pp. 248–270). New York: Cambridge University Press.

Ryle, G. (1949). *The concept of mind.* London: Hutchinson.

Sacks, P. (1999). *Standardized minds: The high price of America's testing culture and what we can do to change it.* Cambridge, MA: Perseus Books.

Salovey, P., & Mayer, J. D. (1990). Emotional intelligence. *Imagination, Cognition, and Personality, 9,* 185–211.

Scarr, S. (1997). Behavior-genetic and socialization theories of intelligence: Truce and reconciliation. In R. J. Sternberg & E. L. Grigorenko (Eds.), *Intelligence, heredity and environment* (pp. 3–41). New York: Cambridge University Press.

Schmidt, F. L., & Hunter, J. E. (1981). Employment testing: Old theories and new research findings. *American Psychologist, 36,* 1128–1137.

Schmidt, F. L., & Hunter, J. E. (1998). The validity and utility of selection methods in personnel psychology: Practical and theoretical implications of 85 years of research findings. *Psychological Bulletin, 124,* 262–274.

Schon, D. A. (1983). *The reflective practitioner.* New York: Basic Books.

Serpell, R. (1974). Aspects of intelligence in a developing country. *African Social Research,* No. 17, 576–596.

Serpell, R. (1982). Measures of perception, skills, and intelligence. In W. W. Hartup (Ed.), *Review of child development research* (Vol. 6, pp. 392–440). Chicago: University of Chicago Press.

Serpell, R. (1996). Cultural models of childhood in indigenous socialization and formal schooling in Zambia. In C. P. Hwang & M. E. Lamb (Eds.), *Images of childhood.* (pp. 129–142). Mahwah, NJ: Lawrence Erlbaum Associates.

Sharp, S. E. (1899). Individual psychology: A study in psychological method. *American Journal of Psychology, 10,* 329–391.

Siegler, R. S. (1988). Individual differences in strategy choices: Good students, not-so-good students, and perfectionists. *Child Development, 59*(4), 833–851.

Siegler, R. S. (1992). The Other Alfred Binet. *Developmental Psychology, 28*(2), 179–190.

Siegler, R. S. (1998). *Children's thinking* (3rd ed.). Upper Saddle River, NJ: Prentice-Hall.

Silver, H. R. (1981). Calculating risks: The socioeconomic foundations of aesthetic innovation in an Ashanti carving community. *Ethnology, 20*(2), 101–114.

Silvers, R. (1997). *Photomosaics.* Henry Holt.

Simon, R. (2000). Who's the dimmest dim bulb? *U.S. News and World Report,* April 3, 20.

Simonton, D. K. (1976). Biographical determinants of achieved eminence: A multivariate approach to the Cox data. *Journal of Personality and Social Psychology, 33,* 218–226.

Simonton, D. K. (1984). *Genius, creativity, and leadership.* Cambridge, MA: Harvard University Press.

Simonton, D. K. (1988). Age and outstanding achievement: What do we know after a century of research? *Psychological Bulletin, 104,* 251–267.

Simonton, D. K. (1994). *Greatness: Who makes history and why?* New York: Guilford.

Simonton, D. K. (1995). Foresight in insight: A Darwinian answer. In R. J. Sternberg & J. E. Davidson (Eds.), *The nature of insight* (pp. 495–534). Cambridge, MA: MIT Press.

Simonton, D. K. (1996). Creative expertise: A life-span developmental perspective. In K. A. Ericsson (Ed.), *The road to excellence* (pp. 227–253). Lawrence Erlbaum Associates.

Simonton, D. K. (1997). Creative productivity: A predictive and explanatory model for career trajectories and landmarks. *Psychological Review, 104,* 66–89.

Simonton, D. K. (1998). Donald Campbell's model of the creative process: Creativity as blind variation and selective retention. *The Journal of Creative Behavior, 32,* 153–158.

Simonton, D. K. (1999). Talent and its development: An emergenic and epigenetic mode. *Psychological Review, 106,* 435–457.

Skinner, B. F. (1972). A behavioral model of creation. In B. F. Skinner (Ed.), *Cumulative record: A selection of papers* (pp. 345, 350–355). Englewood Cliffs, NJ: Prentice-Hall.

Sloman, S. A. (1996). The empirical case for two systems of reasoning. *Psychological Bulletin, 119,* 3–22.

Smith, J., & Baltes, P. B. (1990). Wisdom-related knowledge: Age/cohort differences in response to life-planning problems. *Developmental Psychology, 26,* 494–505.

Smith, S. M., Ward, T. B., & Finke, R. A. (Eds.). (1995). *The creative cognition approach.* Cambridge, MA: MIT Press.

Snow, R. E., Kyllonen, P. C., & Marshalek, B. (1984). The topography of ability and learning correlations. In R. J. Sternberg (Ed.), *Advances in the psychology of human intelligence* (Vol. 2, pp. 47–103). Hillsdale, NJ: Lawrence Erlbaum Associates.

Spearman, C. (1904). 'General intelligence,' objectively determined and measured. *American Journal of Psychology. Vol 15(2),* 201–293.

Spearman, C. (1923). Further note on the "theory of two factors." *British Journal of Psychology, 13,* 266–270.

Spearman, C. (1927). *The abilities of man.* London: Macmillan.

Sperry, R. W. (1961). Cerebral organization and behavior. *Science, 133,* 1749–1757.

Srivastava, A. K., & Misra, G. (1996). Changing perspectives on understanding intelligence: An appraisal. *Indian Psychological Abstracts and Review, 3,* 1–34.

Staudinger, U. M. (1996). Wisdom and the social-interactive foundation of the mind. In P. B. Baltes & U. M. Staudinger (Eds.), *Interactive minds* (pp. 276–315). New York: Cambridge University Press.

Staudinger, U. M., & Baltes, P. B. (1996). Interactive minds: A facilitative setting for wisdom-related performance? *Journal of Personality and Social Psychology, 71,* 746–762.

Staudinger, U. M., Lopez, D. F., & Baltes, P. B. (1997). The psychometric location of wisdom-related performance: Intelligence, personality, and more? *Personality & Social Psychology Bulletin, 23,* 1200–1214.

Staudinger, U. M., Smith, J., & Baltes, P. B. (1992). Wisdom-related knowledge in life review task: Age differences and the role of professional specialization. *Psychology and Aging, 7,* 271–281.

Sternberg, R. J. (1977). Intelligence, information processing, and analogical reasoning: The componential analysis of human abilities. Hillsdale, NJ: Lawrence Erlbaum Associates.

Sternberg, R. J. (1980a). The development of linear syllogistic reasoning. *Journal of Experimental Child Psychology, 29,* 340–356.

Sternberg, R. J. (1980b). Sketch of a componential subtheory of human intelligence. *Behavioral and Brain Sciences, 3,* 573–584.

Sternberg, R. J. (1981). Intelligence and nonentrenchment. *Journal of Educational Psychology, 73,* 1–16.

Sternberg, R. J. (1982). Nonentrenchment in the assessment of intellectual giftedness. *Gifted Child Quarterly, 26,* 63–67.

Sternberg, R. J. (1983). Components of human intelligence. *Cognition, 15,* 1–48.

Sternberg, R. J. (1984). Toward a triarchic theory of human intelligence. *Behavioral and Brain Sciences, 7,* 269–287.

Sternberg, R. J. (1985a). *Beyond IQ: A triarchic theory of human intelligence.* New York: Cambridge University Press.

Sternberg, R. J. (1985b). Implicit theories of intelligence, creativity, and wisdom. *Journal of Personality and Social Psychology, 49*(3), 607–627.

Sternberg, R. J. (1986). *Intelligence applied: Understanding and increasing your intellectual skills.* San Diego: Harcourt Brace Jovanovich.

Sternberg, R. J. (1987a). Most vocabulary is learned from context. In M. G. McKeown & M. E. Curtis (Eds.), *The nature of vocabulary acquisition* (pp. 89–105). Hillsdale, NJ: Lawrence Erlbaum Associates.

Sternberg, R. J. (1987b). The psychology of verbal comprehension. In R. Glaser (Ed.), *Advances in instructional psychology* (Vol. 3, pp. 97–151). Hillsdale, NJ: Lawrence Erlbaum Associates.

Sternberg, R. J. (1988a). Counting the ways: The scientific measurement of love. In J. Brockman (Ed.), *The reality club I* (pp. 151–173). New York: LYNX.

Sternberg, R. J. (Ed.). (1988b). *The nature of creativity: Contemporary psychological perspectives.* New York: Cambridge University Press.

Sternberg, R. J. (1988c). *The triarchic mind: A new theory of human intelligence.* New York: Viking.

Sternberg, R. J. (1990a). *Metaphors of mind: Conceptions of the nature of intelligence.* New York: Cambridge University Press.

Sternberg, R. J. (Ed.). (1990b). *Wisdom: Its nature, origins, and development.* New York: Cambridge University Press.

Sternberg, R. J. (1990c). Wisdom and its relations to intelligence and creativity. In R. J. Sternberg (Ed.), *Wisdom: Its nature, origins, and development* (pp. 142–159). New York: Cambridge University Press.

Sternberg, R. J. (1993). *Sternberg Triarchic Abilities Test.* Unpublished test.

Sternberg, R. J. (Ed.). (1994a). *Encyclopedia of human intelligence.* New York: Macmillan.

Sternberg, R. J. (1994b). The triarchic theory of human intelligence. In R. J. Sternberg (Ed.), *Encyclopedia of human intelligence* (pp. 1087–1091). New York: Macmillan.

Sternberg, R. J. (1995). For whom the bell curve tolls: A review of *The bell curve*. *Psychological Science, 6*, 257–261.

Sternberg, R. J. (1996). IQ counts, but what really counts is successful intelligence. *NASSP Bulletin, 80*, 18–23.

Sternberg, R. J. (1997a). Styles of thinking and learning. *Canadian Journal of School Psychology, 13(2)*, 15–40.

Sternberg, R. J. (1997b). *Successful intelligence*. New York: Plume.

Sternberg, R. J. (1998a). Abilities are forms of developing expertise. *Educational Researcher, 27*, 11–20.

Sternberg, R. J. (1998b). A balance theory of wisdom. *Review of General Psychology, 2*, 347–365.

Sternberg, R. J. (1998c). The dialectic as a tool for teaching psychology. *Teaching of Psychology, 25*, 177–180.

Sternberg, R. J. (1999a). A dialectical basis for understanding the study of cognition. In R. J. Sternberg (Ed.), *The nature of cognition* (pp. 51–78). Cambridge, MA: MIT Press.

Sternberg, R. J. (Ed.). (1999b). *Handbook of creativity*. New York: Cambridge University Press.

Sternberg, R. J. (1999c). A propulsion model of types of creative contributions. *Review of General Psychology, 3*, 83–100.

Sternberg, R. J. (1999d). The theory of successful intelligence. *Review of General Psychology, 3*, 292–316.

Sternberg, R. J. (2000a). Creativity is a decision. In A. L. Costa (Ed.), *Teaching for intelligence II* (pp. 85–106). Arlington Heights, IL: Skylight Training and Publishing Inc.

Sternberg, R. J. (Ed.). (2000b). *Handbook of intelligence*. New York: Cambridge University Press.

Sternberg, R. J. (2000c). Intelligence and wisdom. In R. J. Sternberg (Ed.), *Handbook of intelligence* (pp. 629–647). New York: Cambridge University Press.

Sternberg, R. J. (2001a). How wise is it to teach for wisdom? A reply to five critiques. *Educational Psychologist, 36(4)*, 269–272.

Sternberg, R. J. (2001b). Intelligence tests as measures of developing expertise. In C. Chiu, F. Salili, & Y. Hong (Eds.), *Multiple competencies and self-regulated learning: Implications for multicultural education* (pp. 17–27). Greenwich, CT: Information Age Publishing.

Sternberg, R. J. (2001c). Teaching psychology students that creativity is a decision. *The General Psychologist, 36(1)*, 8–11.

Sternberg, R. J., & Berg, C. A. (1986). Quantitative integration: Definitions of intelligence: A comparison of the 1921 and 1986 symposia. In R. J. Sternberg & D. K. Detterman (Eds.), *What is intelligence: Contemporary viewpoints on its nature and definition* (pp. 155–162). Norwood, NJ: Ablex.

Sternberg, R. J., Castejón, J. L., Prieto, M. D., Hautamäki, J., & Grigorenko, E. L. (2001). Confirmatory factor analysis of the Sternberg triarchic abilities test in three international samples: An empirical test of the triarchic theory of intelligence. *European Journal of Psychological Assessment, 17(1)*, 1–16.

Sternberg, R. J., & Clinkenbeard, P. R. (1995). A triarchic model of identifying, teaching, and assessing gifted children. *Roeper Review, 17 (4)*, 255–260.

Sternberg, R. J., Conway, B. E., Ketron, J. L., & Bernstein M. (1981). People's conceptions of intelligence. *Journal of Personality and Social Psychology, 41*, 37–55.

Sternberg, R. J., & Davidson, J. E. (1982, June). The mind of the puzzler. *Psychology Today, 16*, 37–44.

Sternberg, R. J., & Davidson, J. E. (Eds.). (1994). *The nature of insight*. Cambridge, MA: MIT Press.

Sternberg, R. J., & Detterman, D. K. (1986). *What is intelligence?* Norwood, N.J.: Ablex.

Sternberg, R. J., & Dobson, D. M. (1987). Resolving interpersonal conflicts: An analysis of stylistic consistency. *Journal of Personality and Social Psychology, 52*, 794–812.

Sternberg, R. J., Ferrari, M., Clinkenbeard, P. R., & Grigorenko, E. L. (1996). Identification, instruction, and assessment of gifted children: A construct validation of a triarchic model. *Gifted Child Quarterly, 40*, 129–137.

Sternberg, R. J., Forsythe, G. B., Hedlund, J., Horvath, J., Snook, S., Williams, W. M., Wagner, R. K., & Grigorenko, E. L. (2000). *Practical intelligence in everyday life*. New York: Cambridge University Press.

Sternberg, R. J., & Gardner, M. K. (1982). A componential interpretation of the general factor in human intelligence. In H. J. Eysenck (Ed.), *A model for intelligence* (pp. 231–254). Berlin: Springer-Verlag.

Sternberg, R. J., & Gardner, M. K. (1983). Unities in inductive reasoning. *Journal of Experimental Psychology: General, 112*, 80–116.

Sternberg, R. J., & Gastel, J. (1989a). Coping with novelty in human intelligence: An empirical investigation. *Intelligence, 13*, 187–197.

Sternberg, R. J., & Gastel, J. (1989b). If dancers ate their shoes: Inductive reasoning with factual and counterfactual premises. *Memory and Cognition, 17*, 1–10.

Sternberg, R. J., & Grigorenko, E. L. (1997). The cognitive costs of physical and mental ill health: Applying the psychology of the developed world to the problems of the developing world. *Eye on Psi Chi, 2(1)*, 20–27.

Sternberg, R. J., & Grigorenko, E. L. (2000). *Teaching for successful intelligence*. Arlington Heights, IL: Skylight Training and Publishing Inc.

Sternberg, R. J., Grigorenko, E. L., Ferrari, M., & Clinkenbeard, P. (1999). A triarchic analysis of an aptitude-treatment interaction. *European Journal of Psychological Assessment, 15*, 1–11.

Sternberg, R. J., Grigorenko, E. L., Ngrosho, D., Tantufuye, E., Mbise, A., Nokes, C., Jukes, M., & Bundy, D. A. (2002). Assessing intellectual potential in rural Tanzanian school children. *Intelligence, 30*, 141–162.

Sternberg, R. J., & Kalmar D. A. (1997). When will the milk spoil? Everyday induction in human intelligence. *Intelligence, 25(3)*, 185–203.

Sternberg, R. J., & Kaufman, J. C. (Eds.). (2001). *The evolution of intelligence*. Mahwah, NJ: Lawrence Erlbaum Associates.

Sternberg, R. J., Kaufman, J. C., & Pretz, J. E. (2002). *The creativity conundrum: A propulsion model of kinds of creative contributions*. New York: Psychology Press.

Sternberg, R. J., & Lubart, T. I. (1991). Creating creative minds. *Phi Delta Kappan, 8*, 608–614.

Sternberg, R. J., & Lubart, T. I. (1995). *Defying the crowd: Cultivating creativity in a culture of conformity*. New York: Free Press.

Sternberg, R. J., & Lubart, T. I. (1996). Investing in creativity. *American Psychologist*, *51*(7), 677–688.

Sternberg, R. J., & Nigro, G. (1980). Developmental patterns in the solution of verbal analogies. *Child Development*, *51*, 27–38.

Sternberg, R. J., Nokes, K., Geissler, P. W., Prince, R., Okatcha, F., Bundy, D. A., & Grigorenko, E. L. (2001). The relationship between academic and practical intelligence: A case study in Kenya. *Intelligence*, *29*, 401–418.

Sternberg, R. J., Okagaki, L., & Jackson, A. (1990). Practical intelligence for success in school. *Educational Leadership*, *48*, 35–39.

Sternberg, R. J., Powell, C., McGrane, P. A., & McGregor, S. (1997). Effects of a parasitic infection on cognitive functioning. *Journal of Experimental Psychology: Applied*, *3*, 67–76.

Sternberg, R. J., & Powell, J. S. (1983). The development of intelligence. In P. H. Mussen (Series Ed.), J. Flavell, & E. Markman (Volume Eds.), *Handbook of child psychology* (Vol. 3, 3rd ed., pp. 341–419). New York: Wiley.

Sternberg, R. J., Powell, J. S., & Kaye, D. B. (1983). Teaching vocabulary-building skills: A contextual approach. In A. C. Wilkinson (Ed.), *Classroom computers and cognitive science* (pp. 121–143). New York: Academic Press.

Sternberg, R. J., & The Rainbow Project Collaborators (in press). The Rainbow Project: Enhancing the SAT through assessments of analytical, practical, and creative skills. College Board Technical Report. New York: The College Board.

Sternberg, R. J., & Rifkin, B. (1979). The development of analogical reasoning processes. *Journal of Experimental Child Psychology*, *27*, 195–232.

Sternberg, R. J., & Smith, C. (1985). Social intelligence and decoding skills in nonverbal communication. *Social Cognition*, *2*, 168–192.

Sternberg, R. J., & Soriano, L. J. (1984). Styles of conflict resolution. *Journal of Personality and Social Psychology*, *47*, 115–126.

Sternberg, R. J., & Spear-Swerling, L. (1996). *Teaching for thinking*. Washington, D.C.: American Psychological Association.

Sternberg, R. J., Torff, B., & Grigorenko, E. L. (1998a). Teaching for successful intelligence raises school achievement. *Phi Delta Kappan*, *79*(9), 667–669.

Sternberg, R. J., Torff, B., & Grigorenko, E. L. (1998b). Teaching triarchically improves school achievement. *Journal of Educational Psychology*, *90*(3), 1–11.

Sternberg, R. J., & Turner, M. E. (1981). Components of syllogistic reasoning. *Acta Psychologica*, *47*, 245–265.

Sternberg, R. J., & Wagner, R. K. (1993). The g-ocentric view of intelligence and job performance is wrong. *Current Directions in Psychological Science*, *2*, 1–4.

Sternberg, R. J., Wagner, R. K., & Okagaki, L. (1993). Practical intelligence: The nature and role of tacit knowledge in work and at school. In H. Reese & J. Puckett (Eds.), *Advances in lifespan development* (pp. 205–227). Hillsdale, NJ: Lawrence Erlbaum Associates.

Sternberg, R. J., Wagner, R. K., Williams, W. M., & Horvath, J. A. (1995). Testing common sense. *American Psychologist*, *50*, 912–927.

Sternberg, R. J., & Williams, W. M. (1996). *How to develop student creativity*. Alexandria, VA: Association for Supervision and Curriculum Development.

Sternberg, R. J., & Williams, W. M. (1997). Does the *Graduate Record Examination* predict meaningful success in the graduate training of psychologists? A case study. *American Psychologist*, *52*, 630–641.

Sternberg, S. (1969). Memory-scanning: Mental processes revealed by reaction-time experiments. *American Scientist, 4,* 421–457.

Suler, J. R. (1980). Primary process thinking and creativity. *Psychological Bulletin, 88,* 555–578.

Super, C. M. (1976). Environmental effects on motor development: The case of African infant precocity. *Developmental Medicine and Child Neurology, 18,* 561–567.

Super, C. M., & Harkness, S. (1982). The development of affect in infancy and early childhood. In D. Wagner & H. Stevenson (Eds.), *Cultural perspectives on child development* (pp. 1–19). San Francisco: W. H. Freeman.

Super, C. M., & Harkness, S. (1986). The developmental niche: A conceptualization at the interface of child and culture. *International Journal of Behavioral Development, 9,* 545–569.

Super, C. M., & Harkness, S. (1993). The developmental niche: A conceptualization at the interface of child and culture. In R. A. Pierce & M. A. Black (Eds.), *Life-span development: A diversity reader* (pp. 61–77). Dubuque, IA: Kendall/Hunt Publishing Co.

Terman, L. M., & Merrill, M. A. (1937). *Measuring intelligence.* Boston: Houghton Mifflin.

Terman, L. M., & Merrill, M. A. (1973). *Stanford–Binet Intelligence Scale: Manual for the third revision.* Boston: Houghton Mifflin.

Tetewsky, S. J., & Sternberg, R. J. (1986). Conceptual and lexical determinants of nonentrenched thinking. *Journal of Memory and Language, 25,* 202–225.

Therivel, W. A. (1999). Why Mozart and not Salieri? *Creativity Research Journal, 12,* 67–76.

Thomson, G. H. (1939). *The factorial analysis of human ability.* London: University of London Press.

Thorndike, E. L., Bregman, E. D., Cobb, M. V., & Woodyard, E. I. (1926). *The measurement of intelligence.* New York: Teachers College.

Thorndike, R. L., Hagen, E. P., & Sattler, J. M. (1986). *Technical manual for the Stanford-Binet Intelligence Scale.* (4th edition). Chicago: Riverside.

Thurstone, L. L. (1938). *Primary mental abilities.* Chicago: University of Chicago Press.

Thurstone, L. L. (1947). *Multiple factor analysis.* Chicago: University of Chicago Press.

Thurstone, L. L., & Thurstone, T. C. (1941). *Factorial studies of intelligence.* Chicago: University of Chicago Press.

Tolman, E. C. (1932). *Purposive behavior in animals and men.* New York: Appleton-Century-Crofts.

Torrance, E. P. (1962). *Guiding creative talent.* Englewood Cliffs, NJ: Prentice-Hall.

Torrance, E. P. (1974). *Torrance tests of creative thinking.* Lexington, MA: Personnel Press.

Tzuriel, D. (1995). *Dynamic-interactive assessment: The legacy of L. S. Vygotsky and current developments.* Unpublished manuscript.

Varela, F. J. (1999). *Ethical know-how: Action, wisdom, and cognition.* Stanford, CA: Stanford University Press.

Vernon, P. A., & Mori, M. (1992). Intelligence, reaction times, and peripheral nerve conduction velocity. *Intelligence, 8,* 273–288.

Vernon, P. A., Wickett, J. C., Bazana, P. G., & Stelmack, R. M. (2000). The neuropsychology and psycholophysiology of human intelligence. In R. J. Sternberg (Ed.), *Handbook of intelligence* (pp. 245–264). New York: Cambridge University Press.

Vernon, P. E. (Ed.). (1970). *Creativity: Selected readings* (pp. 126–136). Baltimore, MD: Penguin Books.

Vernon, P. E. (1971). *The structure of human abilities*. London: Methuen.

von Oech, R. (1983). *A whack on the side of the head*. New York: Warner.

von Oech, R. (1986). *A kick in the seat of the pants*. New York: Harper & Row.

Vygotsky, L. S. (1978). *Mind in society: The development of higher psychological processes*. Cambridge, MA: Harvard University Press.

Wagner, R. K. (1987). Tacit knowledge in everyday intelligent behavior. *Journal of Personality and Social Psychology, 52*, 1236–1247.

Wagner, R. K. (2000). Practical intelligence. In R. J. Sternberg (Ed.), *Handbook of human intelligence* (pp. 380–395). New York: Cambridge University Press.

Wagner, R. K., & Sternberg, R. J. (1985). Practical intelligence in real-world pursuits: The role of tacit knowledge. *Journal of Personality and Social Psychology, 49*, 436–458.

Wagner, R. K., & Sternberg, R. J. (1986). Tacit knowledge and intelligence in the everyday world. In R. J. Sternberg & R. K. Wagner (Eds.), *Practical intelligence: Nature and origins of competence in the everyday world* (pp. 51–83). New York: Cambridge University Press.

Wahlsten, D., & Gottlieb, G. (1997). The invalid separation of effects of nature and nurture: Lessons from animal experimentation. In R. J. Sternberg & E. L. Grigorenko (Eds.), *Intelligence, heredity, and environment* (pp. 163–192). New York: Cambridge University Press.

Wallach, M., & Kogan, N. (1965). *Modes of thinking in young children*. New York: Holt, Rinehart, & Winston.

Wallas, G. (1926). *The art of thought*. New York: Harcourt, Brace.

Wanschura, P. B., & Borkowski, J. G. (1974). Development and transfer of mediational strategies by retarded children in paired-associate learning. *American Journal of Mental Deficiency, 78*(5), 631–639.

Ward, T. B. (1994). Structured imagination: The role of conceptual structure in exemplar generation. *Cognitive Psychology, 27*, 1–40.

Ward, T. B., Smith, S. M., & Finke, R. A. (1999). Creative cognition. In R. J. Sternberg (Ed.), *Handbook of creativity* (pp. 189–212). New York: Cambridge University Press.

Wechsler, D. (1991). *Manual for the Wechsler Intelligence Scales for Children* (3rd ed.), (WISC_III). San Antonio, TX: Psychological Corporation.

Wehner, L., Csikszentmihalyi, M., & Magyari-Beck, I. (1991). Current approaches used in studying creativity: An exploratory investigation. *Creativity Research Journal, 4*(3), 261–271.

Weisberg, R. W. (1986). *Creativity, genius and other myths*. New York: Freeman.

Weisberg, R. W. (1988). Problem solving and creativity. In R. J. Sternberg (Ed.), *The nature of creativity* (pp. 148–176). New York: Cambridge University Press.

Weisberg, R. W. (1993). *Creativity: Beyond the myth of genius*. New York: Freeman.

Weisberg, R. W. (1999). Creativity and knowledge: A challenge to theories. In R. J. Sternberg (Ed.), *Handbook of creativity* (pp. 226–250). New York: Cambridge University Press.

Weisberg, R. W., & Alba, J. W. (1981). An examination of the alleged role of "fixation" in the solution of several "insight" problems. *Journal of Experimental Psychology: General, 110,* 169–192.

Werner, H., & Kaplan, B. (1963). *Symbol formation.* Hillsdale, NJ: Lawrence Erlbaum Associates.

White, G. M. (1985). Premises and purposes in a Solomon Islands ethnopsychology. In G. M. White & J. Kirkpatrick (Eds.), *Person, self, and experience: Exploring Pacific ethnopsychologies* (pp. 328–366). Berkeley: University of California Press.

Wickett, J. C., & Vernon, P. A. (1994). Peripheral nerve conduction velocity, reaction time, and intelligence: An attempt to replicate Vernon and Mori. *Intelligence, 18,* 127–132.

Wigdor, A. K., & Garner, W. R. (Eds.). (1982). *Ability testing: Uses, consequences, and controversies.* Washington, D.C.: National Academy Press.

Willerman, L., Schultz, R., Rutledge, J. N., & Bigler, E. D. (1991). In vivo brain size and intelligence. *Intelligence, 15,* 223–228.

Willerman, L., Schultz, R., Rutledge, J. N., & Bigler, E. D. (1992). Hemisphere size asymmetry predicts relative verbal and nonverbal intelligence differently in the sexes: An MRI study of structure function relations. *Intelligence, 16,* 315–328.

Williams, W. M., Blythe, T.,White, N., Li, J., Gardner, H., & Sternberg, R. J. (2002). Practical intelligence for school: Developing metacognitive sources of achievement in adolescence. *Developmental Review 22*(2), 162–210.

Williams, W. M., Blythe, T., White, N., Li, J., Sternberg, R. J., & Gardner, H. I. (1996). *Practical intelligence for school: A handbook for teachers of grades 5–8.* New York: HarperCollins.

Williams, W. M., & Sternberg, R. J. (2002). How parents can maximize children's cognitive abilities. In M. Borstein (Ed.), *Handbook of parenting (Vol. 5: Practical Issues in Parenting).* Mahwah, NJ: Lawrence Erlbaum Associates.

Wissler, C. (1901). The correlation of mental and physical tests. *Psychological Review, Monograph Supplement 3*(6).

Woodman, R. W., & Schoenfeldt, L. F. (1989). Individual differences in creativity: An interactionist perspective. In J. A. Glover, R. R. Ronning & C. R. Reynolds (Eds.), *Handbook of creativity.* New York: Plenum.

Yamamoto, K. (1964). Creativity and sociometric choice among adolescents. *Journal of Social Psychology, 64,* 249–261.

Yang, S., & Sternberg, R. J. (1997a). Conceptions of intelligence in ancient Chinese philosophy. *Journal of Theoretical and Philosophical Psychology, 17*(2), 101–119.

Yang, S., & Sternberg, R. J. (1997b). Taiwanese Chinese people's conceptions of intelligence. *Intelligence, 25*(1), 21–36.

Zenderland, L. (1998). *Measuring minds: Henry Goddard and the origins of American intelligence testing.* New York: Cambridge University Press.

Zuckerman, H. (1977). *Scientific elite: Nobel laureates in the United States.* New York: Free Press.

Zuckerman, H. (1983). The scientific elite: Nobel laureates' mutual influences. In R. S. Albert (Ed.), *Genius and eminence* (pp. 241–252). Oxford, U.K.: Pergamon.

Index

DATE DUE

Robert Browning and His World

Books by Maisie Ward

The Wilfrid Wards and the Transition
Insurrection versus Resurrection
Gilbert Keith Chesterton
Young Mr. Newman
Return to Chesterton
Saints Who Made History
Caryll Houselander: Divine Eccentric
Unfinished Business (An Autobiography)

Robert Browning

October 1855

and His World:

The Private Face [*1812–1861*]

BY MAISIE WARD

Holt, Rinehart and Winston
New York   Chicago
San Francisco

Robert Browning, 1855
From a painting by
D. G. Rossetti

Designer: Ernst Reichl
8655805
Printed in the United States of America

For two Franks—

my husband and my grandson

Acknowledgments

I am grateful for permission to use quotations from the following published works: from *New Letters of Robert Browning* to Kenneth Leslie Knickerbocker and Yale University Press; from *Letters of the Brownings to George Barrett,* to Paul Landis and University of Illinois Press; from *Dearest Isa,* to Edward C. McAleer and University of Texas Press; from *Learned Lady,* to Edward C. McAleer and Harvard University Press.

I am also grateful to John Murray for the general permission to quote from the following collections of letters on which he owns the copyright: *Letters of Elizabeth Barrett Browning to her Sister,* edited by Leonard Huxley; *Robert Browning and Julia Wedgwood,* edited by Richard Curle; and *Robert Browning: A Portrait* by Betty Miller. For permission to quote from *Poetry of Experience* by Robert Langbaum my thanks to the author and Random House; from *Religious Trends in English Poetry Vol. IV* by Hoxie Neale Fairchild, to the author and Columbia University Press. Further, for permission to quote from *Essays in London and Elsewhere* by Henry James, to Harper and Row; from *The Middle Years* by Henry James, to Charles Scribner's Sons. Lines from *Little Boxes,* words and music by Malvina Reynolds copyright 1962 by Schroder Music Company, Berkeley, California, used by permission.

For permission to quote from *Letters to Robert and Elizabeth Browning from Owen Meredith,* edited by Aurelia B. Harlan and J. Harlan Junior, I thank Baylor University—to which I also owe a deep debt of gratitude for access to much valuable unpublished material, especially *The Poet Robert Browning and His Kinsfolk* by his cousin, Cyrus Mason, from which I was allowed to quote freely; to the Henry W. and Albert A. Berg Collection of the New York Public Library; to the Astor, Lenox, and Tilden Foundations for quotations from Elizabeth Barrett Browning's childhood letters and her letters to her sister, Arabel, and to Sophia Eckley; to the University of Texas for access to the drawings and notebooks of Robert Browning's father and permission to use two unpublished letters of the poet to Sarah Flower; to

Wellesley College for access to much interesting correspondence—and an examination of the Love Letters still in the box where Browning placed them a century ago; to the Pierpont Morgan Library for permission to quote from Mrs. Jameson's letters to Lady Noel Byron; to the Victoria and Albert Museum for a photostat of, and permission to quote, Mill's discussion of *Pauline* with Browning's annotations; and to the Trustees of the British Museum for permission to quote from the Kenyon typescript containing passages and complete letters omitted from the printed volume of *The Letters of Elizabeth Barrett Browning*.

In all these libraries I have received most courteous attention. I would like to thank especially Hannah French, Research Librarian at Wellesley; Dr. John Gordan and Mrs. Szladits at the Berg Collection and Professor Herring at Baylor. To Mrs. Veva Wood of the Armstrong Library, Baylor University, I find it hard to express my gratitude adequately, for her unremitting help and co-operation during my two visits to Baylor and in subsequent correspondence.

I am most grateful to Professor Edward C. McAleer, who has long been helping me by advice and the loan of books, and who has read this first volume in manuscript and made valuable suggestions; and to Professors Park Honan and Robert Langbaum for rapidly reading and commenting on the proofs, in the middle of a busy semester. Also, to the helpful staff of the Public Library of Newark, New Jersey for their help over many months of reading and research.

Contents

Introduction

I guess I'm half a quack,
For whom ten lines of Browning whack
The whole of the Zodiac.

D. G. ROSSETTI

POETS' CORNER

"Do you object to all this adulation?" Browning was asked when surrounded by admiring undergraduates.

"Object to it! No; I have waited forty years for it, and now—I like it."

The chief regret felt by Henry James, present in Westminster Abbey for the funeral at which England paid "her greatest honour to one of her greatest poets," was that Browning could not write about it: "His own analytic spirit would have rejoiced . . . the pictorial sense would have intertwined itself with the metaphysical. . . . Passion and ingenuity, irony and solemnity, the impressive and unexpected, would each have forced their way through . . . even perhaps to the dim corners where humour and the whimsical lurk."

Looking around him, James seemed to see in the dark chapels and crowded transepts a "company in possession," gazing with cold eyes on this newcomer with his "bewildering modernness." Yet the very fact of his "lying there among the classified and protected makes even Robert Browning lose a portion of the bristling surface of his actuality." Among the great writers, among the oddities gathered in the Abbey, "none of

the odd ones have been so great and none of the great ones so odd . . .
there is no poetic head of equal power—crowned and recrowned by
almost importunate hands—from which so many people would with-
hold the distinctive wreath."

Browning is today labeled a Victorian, with every implication of the
stuffiness attached to the word, but James found his distinguishing mark
to be his difference: "a tremendous and incomparable modern," with
"boldnesses and overgrowths, rich roughnesses and humours . . . what
he takes into the Abbey is an immense expression of life—of life
rendered with large liberty and free experiment, with an unprejudiced
intellectual eagerness to put himself in other people's place, to participate in complications and consequences; a restlessness of psychological research that might well alarm any pale company for their formal
orthodoxies."

Browning would have enjoyed "prefiguring and playing with the
mystifications, the reservations, even perhaps the slight buzz of scandal
in the Poets' Corner to which his own obsequies might give rise! . . . we
leave our sophisticated modern conscience, and perhaps even our hetero-
geneous modern vocabulary, in his charge among the illustrious."[1]

When Browning said he had "waited forty years" for appreciation,
he forgot one brief interlude. Criticism had gone far toward establishing him by warm praise of *Paracelsus;* but after the "incomprehensible"
Sordello, it turned against him and so remained for another thirty years.
From then onward the "importunate hands" that were crowning him
went on to heap the wreaths perhaps too incessantly, too indiscrimi-
nately. Nor was it only the poetry. The "immortal lovers" were called
so once too often. The Brownings, like Aristides, are suffering today for
being painted by their admirers as too good to be true and too admirable
to be endurable.

WHAT THEN DOES
MR. BROWNING MEAN?

When Kingsley asked the question: "What then does Mr. Newman mean?" it was a double-edged one calling for a twofold answer. As a challenge to Newman's thought the *University Sermons* already contained the answer, though expressed too subtly and too profoundly for Kingsley. As a challenge to his integrity it called forth the *Apologia*. At Baylor University I saw Browning's high desk from the Casa Guidi, and I wondered: Did the poet really stand to write or was a tall stool the answer? Then imagination displaced the poet for the priest. Newman did, we know, stand far into the night penning, with the tears his generation so freely shed, the answer that was the history of his mind. Yet who shall say that after the *Apologia* had been written John Henry Newman had really made plain what Henri Bremond much later could still call "The Mystery of Newman"?

There is quite as certainly a Mystery of Browning, possibly insoluble, but certainly not to be penetrated on the intellectual level by those who, as he himself complained, read poetry as a substitute for a cigar or a game of dominoes. As Swinburne pointed out, the best hours of the day, the clearest state of the mind, are called for. Those inured to modern poetry will find Browning's less formidable than did their grandparents; the thing they will not find is that he ever improved matters by talking in prose. Browning knew very well, when he resolutely refused to talk about his own poetry, that he would only make it more difficult by trying to "explain." It was poured out (the best of it) in hours of high exaltation: How could he say anything but "What I have written I have written"?

Browning, says Robert Langbaum, "was actually telling his age that they were asking the wrong questions of the universe; he was himself reaching for the right questions for which the proper vocabulary has been supplied only in our time through the philosophies of existential-

ism and symbolic form." And he dissents from the attempt made by so
many to discuss as separate propositions Browning the poet and Browning the thinker. "Are we to conclude," he asks (in *Victorian Poetry*,
Spring, 1965), "that while Browning may have a future as a poet, he
can have none as a thinker? We cannot if we believe that poetry is a
form of thought."

While we stammer, the poet can find full utterance; while we build,
as Browning himself told Ruskin, the tidy rows of houses erected "so
cleverly" in many a suburb, his is a Stonehenge of rough half-hewn
rocks, or a cathedral perhaps only half finished.

Langbaum is pointing toward a new understanding of Browning's
poetry as belonging to our age more than to the nineteenth century.
But of late much other writing has been done about Browning which
asks what he means in the second sense in which Kingsley challenged
Newman. A tendency is rife to treat him as a psychological patient
with the critic as his analyst. He was noisy and healthy—a sure sign of
his insecurity and fundamental ill health. He married a woman six years
older than himself—"a fact which even those with the least possible
touch of Freudianism may find relevant." He was self-assertive, yet he
would gossip about everything but "never about Robert Browning." His
apparent masculinity was really "over compensation." This and much
more does Richard Altick assert, with a confidence few psychologists
would feel in analyzing a man they had never seen, never questioned; a
man nearly eighty years dead.

Two things might help if such an analysis is to be attempted: first
the testimony of wife, friends, enemies, and casual contemporary gossip;
but all this gives much the picture Browning's critics are bent on
destroying.

Second, and even more important, is his poetry; and it is astonishing
how little awareness of this is shown in much contemporary writing.
"Browning," we read, "had no real interest in anything that went on in
the world except as it touched Robert Browning." There are less extreme
cases than this, but certainly many critics appear not to have read *as
poetry* the poems which have excited other poets from Rossetti through

Swinburne to Ezra Pound and Robert Lowell. They approach Browning as a man might approach the Venus de Milo, observing with cool
realist's eye that the arms are broken, but observing almost nothing else!

Too bad Browning did not simplify the critics' task by being a
womanizer, a homosexual, drunkard, or drug addict.[2] All that remained
was to discover some sort of intellectual weakness plus an unhealthy
relation with his mother. Professor Altick in *The Browning Critics* and
Mrs. Miller in *Robert Browning: A Portrait* find this in his marriage to
an older woman: she was a mother figure. Jeannette Marks in *The
Family of the Barrett* discovered even more convincingly that Elizabeth
Barrett underwent a "transference" when her father and her doctor
disappointed her—and found a father figure in Browning. A sort of
double incest?

All this is a bit confusing perhaps, but not really as startling as a
recent remark assuming that Browning was haunted through life by
a teen-age betrayal of Shelley. Dying at the age of seventy-seven, did
Browning, a reviewer wonders, "hear the cock crow for the third time"?

He would have rubbed his eyes to see himself thus cast as Peter to
Shelley's Christ. There is no slightest trace at any time in his life of
this sense of guilt. In his teens he came close to idolatry of Shelley and
continued, though to a modified degree, to admire the poet all his life,
blenching only over Shelley the man when finally realizing his conduct
toward his wife Harriet.

The theory of Browning's betrayal derives almost certainly from
Mrs. Miller's book in which Browning, cast as the anti-hero, is portrayed
as failing in all the great relations of his life: his integrity to his ideals;
his behavior as son, husband, father. Wonderfully ingenious and brilliantly written, the book received the reviews usually accorded a best-
selling novel, which indeed it notably resembles.

My first feeling was that I must begin my own book by answering
hers, for it was the first full-length treatment to appear for more than
half a century, and the last before this one. But discussion detail by
detail can mean nothing prior to an over-all view. I may fail as an artist
in giving that view, but the answers to misrepresentations fit inevitably
into this book. Mrs. Orr's biography, Griffin and Minchin's are both

excellent; William Sharp's, though a little overenthusiastic, contains valuable elements. I owe something to them all, and still more to such learned writers as De Vane; and to the insights of men like Dowden, Herford, Raymond, Edwin Muir, and Langbaum. Despite many errors of detail, Chesterton casts a brilliant light on the poet; both Robert Lowell and Robert Langbaum have told me they think his the best book in the vast Browning literature. An enormous amount of fresh material has become available, scattered over the world, laid up in libraries, or buried in obscure periodicals.

The books and articles actually being published seem endless— letters especially, and really valuable criticism; but I was surprised at the rich vein of unpublished material not fully explored.

There are in the British Museum the four large volumes of the Kenyon typescript (considerably expurgated in the published edition); the letters to Browning's son, Pen, at Balliol College; the correspondence with Mr. Furnivall, founder of the Browning Society, in the Huntingdon Library. Add to these the letters at the University of Texas—to Pen's tutor, Gillespie, and his art teacher, Heyermans; to the Mr. Natrop with whom Pen shared a studio and who introduced him to Rodin; the letters to Millais at the Pierpont Morgan Library and to Kenyon at Wellesley College. From these we get a change of proportion as compared with the letters to women, continually pouring in later years from Browning's pen. Ladies with abundant time for writing certainly got in return the lion's share, but Browning also had many men friends. Much of this material belongs in my second volume; but for this one I gained light from Baylor University's *The Poet Robert Browning and His Kinsfolk*, written by his cousin, Cyrus Mason; the three hundred unpublished letters in the New York Public Library's Berg Collection from Elizabeth to Arabel Barrett and to Mrs. Eckley— besides her own childhood letters and youthful self-portraiture.

Ideas have changed as to the function of the biographer—at once narrowing and widening it. The duty of a full mastery of the material and as rich and balanced a presentation of it as possible is today often played down in favor of an attempt to do the impossible in penetration of motives and thoughts hidden in the subconscious. An exaggeration of good has swung into a greater exaggeration of evil—colored usually by an imperfect apprehension of the psychiatry of the moment. Even if I agreed with that of fifteen years ago (when Mrs. Miller was writing), I should feel it illegitimate to use it, not as a literary critic but as a biographer. Only a novelist has the right to create a character; when faced with "dry, puzzling, authentic fact," one sometimes envies him. Above all some problems must be left as the problems that they are. The biographer is not a judge. His task is different from that of the painter. He has not just to deal with given features—item two gray eyes and the rest. From an immense mass of material he must try to make so fair a selection that the reader can use it to form his own picture. Just as acquaintances quarrel over a man's character, so should readers.

I do not for a moment disclaim that warm sympathy with my subject once considered desirable in a biographer. Without sympathy, empathy is impossible. Yet it remains a dubious compliment when everybody agrees that the picture given is "convincing," when no loophole is left for another view.

Robert Browning's poetry, his personality, his family and friends were primarily his world, but much else is needed to understand a man living in an era so different from ours, one who inside his own period lived in three immensely various worlds. There was the middle-class dissenting English society of his boyhood; the Italy, so ancient and so new, of his younger manhood; the aristocratic English world of his fifties into his old age—each as different from the others as any of them are from the English, or American, world of today.

I have been tempted to some such titles as *Triumphant Failure* and *Success* instead of the two that have emerged. For Browning's greatest work was undoubtedly done when nobody wanted it, and his noblest period was that when he was proud to be, as Elizabeth called him, lover, husband, and nurse; or as others less kindly said, *"le mari de Madame."* Apart from an occasional crank, it is only after her death that he is depicted as bad-tempered, snobbish in society, prolix in the poetry now in such demand. Even then this is a minor note in a general chorus of admiration, though a note that must be listened to. The earlier Browning does not pose the riddle offered by the later, and especially emphasized by his younger contemporary, Henry James, in his theory of the two Brownings, poet and socialite. Yet in this sharp-cut distinction the subtle critic was perhaps for once oversimplifying.

I have tried to study the backgrounds of all Browning's worlds, to grow intimate with some of the leading characters who were his friends or critics—Fox, "Weaver Boy" and minister; Mill and Macready, Rossetti, Tennyson, Disraeli, and Gladstone; Mrs. Jameson and Lady Ashburton; Thackeray's daughter and many others, besides a multitude of diarists from England and the United States—to see through their eyes as well as through Browning's poetry the man as he appeared and as he was.

After traveling, reading, meditating, not only on the facts but on many interpretations new and old, I believe that there is still a lot to be said for the old Browning tradition. But the note of inquiry should be struck again and again, should even be held down firmly on dubious points. No canonization can proceed until the devil's advocate has been allowed, indeed urged, to bring out every dark spot in the alleged saint's life. Well, I do not propose to canonize Browning; the extremists on both sides shall speak—and nearly everyone who knew him was an extremist.

One cannot meditate on a man for years without forming views or at least surmises about his character. But these too belong to my second volume. They can make sense to the reader only if tested, as they have been formed, after the study of a completed life. I do not believe it possible to reach a total understanding of anything, let alone any person, in this strange, terrible, beautiful, mysterious world. Dealing with genius, especially, analysis is often baffled. Mystery need not be a fog; it may be a piercing clarity to which our fogbound sight must be adjusted. Genius can co-exist wth weakness, weakness with strength. Juvenal's *maxima reverentia* is due not to the young alone but to every human soul—reverence and pity.

As you read a poet, you see that he, who is deeper in the mystery of life than we, sees more mystery there; that the tension between the greatness of what he sees and the limits of language and of his own personality bring struggle, physical and mental exhaustion, perhaps neurosis.

> All I could never be
> All, men ignored in me,
> This I was worth to God . . .

P.S. BY WAY OF APOLOGIA

I have been writing this book for more than four years and in this period have flown round the world twice and had a major operation in Sydney, Australia. With my earlier biographies—of my parents, Chesterton, the young Newman—all the material was at hand. But I have written this book in Australia, England, France, Italy, and the United States. The impossibility of carrying a library by air, of ever having all my authorities in one place, the increasing weight of notes sent across two oceans and not always reaching their destination, plus the use of nine or ten different stenographers—all this has made the job of checking peculiarly onerous. I hope the learned scholars, of whom I stand in awe, will be lenient as to "commas and dots to i's."

On the other hand I have never believed in a multitude of references; they mean nothing to the general reader and are not particularly useful to students. When the source of a quotation is shown in the text, or when its matter is uncontroversial I have added no note. All the letters quoted to Arabel and to Mrs. Eckley are in the Berg Collection. In general the notes are directed towards helping students with guidance on further reading.

I could not have completed my work without the generous help of librarians, some of whom have passed into the second category of personal friends, to all of whom acknowledgment is made on pp. iii and iv. My gratitude is truly heartfelt.

Robert Browning and His World

1 The Browning Family

> This curse of class difference confronts you like a
> wall of stone. Or rather it is not so much like a stone
> wall as the plate-glass pane of an aquarium; it is so
> easy to pretend that it isn't there, and so impossible
> to get through it.
>
> GEORGE ORWELL

SELDOM can anyone have been subjected to an odder series of con-
jectures as to his ancestry than was Robert Browning. The story of the
family's descent, on which were based tales of chivalry told by an uncle
to himself and his sister, had been current, Browning said, in his father's
family. Mrs. Orr declares that *he* neither accepted nor repudiated it.
He did, however, in later years, use on some of his letter paper the
coat of arms which his son flaunted at the Palazzo Rezzonico. The
painter Rudolf Lehmann noted in Browning a surprising "punctilious-
ness on the subject of his and his family's pedigrees." Cyrus Mason, son
of Mr. Browning's sister, presents in his biography such evidence as
there is of their family descent—and it is weak indeed.

It is unquestioned that their common grandfather, another Robert
Browning, came from Dorset to London in the eighteenth century, and
that *his* father had died at Pentridge, having occupied a house which was
afterward a coaching inn. This is confirmed by Sir Vincent Baddeley
K.C.B., a more distant cousin, in an interesting article in *The Genealogists' Magazine* (March, 1938). But Cyrus Mason is not content with
leaving his great-grandfather as the first known ancestor. Seizing on
the name Browning, the county Dorset, and the Christian names John,

Robert, and William, he links his own and the poet's great-grandfather with another family, possessors of various manors granted by Edward III in another part of Dorset. One of them was Sheriff of Dorset and Somerset under Edward IV. These were "fighting men from Poole," whose name began as Bruning, then became Brownyng, and finally Browning. None of this does Sir Vincent Baddeley regard as proved.

Mason is on surer ground when showing that his grandfather was an educated man, describing the books eighteenth-century Robert[1] and his brother brought with them to London, and the ease with which Robert, the elder, got a post at the Bank of England, rising to a position of heavy responsibility and turning into a "somewhat pompous" city man. "A substantial resident of Peckham," he became "a staunch supporter of the Church of England," regarding it as "the soundest buttress of the British constitution."

To this man's younger brother, Reuben, Browning's father owed the cultivation of literary and artistic tastes, his own father regarding "students of literature, art or music as little better than vagabonds." Reuben remained a Nonconformist, though his brother considered this faith "only suitable to the spiritual wants of petty tradesmen or the religious guidance of people struggling against poverty, certainly not for well-placed gentlefolk."

Rushing to the opposite extreme from Cyrus Mason, Furnivall, the founder of the Browning Society, did something so incredible that, were not Sir Vincent Baddeley an actual eyewitness, one would refuse to believe it. Building on the fact that their former home was now an inn, Furnivall declared that Browning's great-grandfather was the innkeeper, *his* father having been first page at Corfe Castle, then footman and butler there. He was made to withdraw the footman story, but subsequently, says Sir Vincent, he erected a tombstone with an inscription devised by himself:

Robert Browning of Woodyates in this Parish died Nov. 25, 1746.
He is the first known forefather of Robert Browning poet.
He was formerly footman and butler in the Bankes family.

"ALL SERVICE RANKS THE SAME WITH GOD."
BROWNING

Sir Vincent called on the churchwardens and Council of the Parish, had the tomb altered, and the quotation deleted! It was not so easy to delete men's memories of what they had read or heard—this, or Furnivall's other stories of Jewish descent, of colored ancestry, of anything or everything of speculative interest.

Of Jewish ancestry the poet would have been proud; his admiration for that great race was frequently expressed. By colored blood—called at that date "a touch of the tar brush"—he would inevitably have been embarrassed. Furnivall was, however, more convinced of this than of the possible Jewish element; and Jeannette Marks, after careful research in Jamaica and St. Kitts, believes it to be a possibility. For John Tittle, Browning's maternal great-grandfather, was, she says, "ignored" in the strangest manner by his mother, Lucy Tittle. He had a difficult character, "ambitious, imprudent, impulsive," and had embroiled himself with his brother to whom father and mother were clearly devoted and to whom most of their property was bequeathed. But Mrs. Marks feels we must look to some deeper reason for their attitude, and at that date especially the color question could be that reason.

Could—but need not. For John became a clergyman with "an indifferent or tollerable (sic) good parish" in St. Kitts, also sharing a plantation with a man who had "vile principles" and did not pay him his dues; he sent by every ship complaints about everybody to the Bishop of London—accompanied by gifts. He married Margaret Strachan. His daughter, Margaret Tittle, was Browning's grandmother and through her Dr. Furnivall suggested a possible way for the element of color to have come. But surely her portrait is almost aggressively Aryan.

Browning might have laughed at this; yet he might also have squirmed, for he was a man of his age. And in that age Disraeli's picture in *Sybil* does not at all exaggerate the pedigrees constructed by the Heralds' College for the *noveaux riches,* or the enormous importance attached to descent. The poet preserved, Mrs. Orr tells us, "the old framed coat of arms handed down to him from his grandfather"; and wore a signet ring engraved from it, the "gift of an uncle." And she adds that the older members of the family accepted as a certainty this very problematical pedigree.

There was certainly some excuse in the fact that, if the thing mattered at all, the reality was seldom the same as the appearance. In how many English villages even today do the ancient owners' descendants live in a cottage while the rich—and now titled—manufacturer owns their ancestral home! Browning's great-grandfather *may* have kept an inn, and may too have had the right to bear arms centuries old. The inn, at whatever date it became one, was a chief ground of Moulton Barrett's objection to Browning as a son-in-law. But if, as was later alleged, Browning's own son wanted to marry an innkeeper's daughter at Dinant, the poet (though with other good reasons for objecting) may well have been haunted by the proverb: "Three generations from shirt sleeves to shirt sleeves."

To return to what we know: Margaret Tittle's son (father of the poet) married Sarah Anna Weidemann, a Scot from Dundee, descended from a German, spoken of by Mrs. Orr as a shipowner, and hailing from Hamburg. Mrs. Miller could not find his name in any list of Dundee shipowners. She discovered in the *Register of Sasines* a William Wiedemann, Mariner. A friend, checking for me at Hamburg, could not find the name on any list still existing.

Browning's father was an interesting and rather eccentric character. "Lovable beyond description," said D. G. Rossetti, "a complete oddity." His nephew describes his exaggerated interest in anatomy, declaring that on his wedding day he disappeared and was found dissecting a dead duck; that for the same purpose he once kept a rat "too long" in his desk at the bank. He had "a taste for the horrible," but also a taste so strong for poetry that the family suspected him as the author of some of his son's verses. Actually it was a painter's career he had longed for, and much remains to suggest that there was truth in the view of others besides his half brother, Reuben, and his nephew, Cyrus, that he might have brought fame to the family a generation earlier than his son. As it was, Cyrus, obviously disliking his cousin, perhaps envying his good luck, declares that this uncle of his *planned* to educate his son to be a poet. It was apparently a family decision, for Cyrus had never heard his own mother, another aunt (perhaps Mrs. Silverthorne), or

Browning's parents suggest any other future for "young Robert." Cyrus clearly believes that it was by no power born in him but sheerly by parental teaching and family fostering that this particular poet was made.

Not knowing their relative ages, one cannot tell whether all this means that by the time Cyrus was old enough to begin observing, the die had been cast for a poetic career. Certainly the impression is strong that during Robert's early childhood Mr. Browning would have liked to see his son become the successful painter that he himself might have been. He was always drawing: groups in the street, clients calling at the bank, individual heads. They often carry a caption which makes one feel he might have become an Osbert Lancaster, commenting cynically on the world of politics, high finance, and law. There are quite a number of these captioned drawings at Baylor University and Wellesley College.

Rossetti greatly admired Mr. Browning's sketches, saying that he had "a real genius for drawing," though "caring for nothing except Dutch boors." He and all his friends agreed that he *could* not draw a pretty face. There is indeed at Wellesley what I can only hope was a caricature of his daughter Sarianna. How could she have borne to see it or he to keep it? Reuben Browning put the effect of these drawings rather quaintly by saying that they always awakened "the admiration and risible qualites of the company."

Good as they are, these collections do not compare with the richness and variety of the drawings at the University of Texas; these were made for Alice Corkran and are described by her in *Chapters from the Story of My Girlhood* and also in an article in *The Bookman* of April, 1896.

In his old age Mr. Browning became intimate wth the family of an English journalist in Paris with two daughters, Henriette and Alice, to whom he meant more than many a grandfather. The two small girls would sit on each side of Mr. Browning at a large littered table while he drew and painted. One quite lovely thing is a map of *Pilgrim's Progress*, depicting Vanity Fair, The City of Destruction, The Wilderness, the Slough of Despond, The Valley of the Shadow of Death, The

Delectable Mountains. All delicately colored, they are explained in tiny exquisitely written notes.

Seen by *The Bookman* as having an "eye for faces not less keen than his son's," Mr. Browning relates *The Ghost Story* as going on "amid a series of interruptions and cross questions, each new personage interpolating a remark which prevents the last speaker from proceeding ... believers and unbelievers ... hit off with delicious fun ... London of the thirties comes alive." And already spiritualism is rife—"a very small party ... nobody danced but a hat and a table."

Notebooks crammed with reading lists, chiefly historical, and notes of English, Scotch, French history, complicated genealogies, odd bits of verse, complete this collection:

> I write the wonders for the News
> I criticize for the reviews.

Thackeray's daughter gives a rather horrific account of her childish fright the sketches Mr. Browning poured out of the ill-treated slaves on his mother's plantation; but of the dozens of drawings I have seen, only one could be called even faintly frightening. Neither Alice nor Henriette Corkran, who knew him so intimately, seem to have seen any. "Often," says Henriette, "he would stop in front of cabarets and draw groups of workmen, drinking, smoking, gesticulating. ... His sketches were admirable, they were so full of life. ... The grotesque appealed strongly to Mr. Browning."

It would be surprising, however, if he had not at times drawn those men and scenes which had made so deep an impression on him in boyhood—and it may have been some of these sketches that impressed Cyrus as horrible. Browning told Elizabeth Barrett that his father shivered and turned pale at the recollection of the cruelties he had witnessed and even at the sight of blood. For the poet's grandfather, the "pompous" one of Peckham, having lost his first wife and married again, had sent his eldest son out to work in the West Indies. When he refused to have a part or lot in the horrible institution of slavery, this singular parent not only disinherited him of the estate which should have come to him from his mother, but also sent him a bill for his education. It was, by this time, too late to follow his artistic bent, and to serve in the Bank of England was at least better than to rule a slave compound. But Cyrus Mason believed it was the lack of culture not the slavery that caused his uncle to leave Jamaica.

The only prose work I have read of Mr. Browning's is dull enough —the story being at once wildly improbable and pedestrian in its telling. But his drawings and comic verse are a very different matter, and the son may well have caught the trick of absurd double and even treble rhyming from his father.

More than once they chose the same subject to write about. With the "Pied Piper" we know that the story was in Wanley's *Wonders of the Little World* and in other books in Mr. Browning's library, and his cartoons show how he came to write and illustrate a poem on a spiritualist medium. When Browning began on the Piper, the admiring father abandoned his own version unfinished. But a few lines of it are worth quoting:

> There is at a moderate distance from Hanover—
> A town on the Weser of singular fame:
> A place which the French and the rats often ran over—
> But though my tale varies
> Yet sage antiquaries
> Are all in one story concerning its name—
> 'Tis Hammelin (but you had better perhaps
> Turn over your atlas and look at the maps)
> Which, without flattery
> Seemed one vast rattery . . .

As a boy, Mr. Browning had shared with John Kenyon—also of Jamaican origin—the organizing of mock combats among their schoolfellows "exciting themselves to battle by insulting speeches derived from the Homeric text." He told Henriette Corkran that in boyhood he had known by heart the first book of the *Iliad* and the Odes of Horace, and it seemed to her that he also knew by heart "the Bible and history generally." When his son was a baby, he would send him to sleep by humming odes of Anacreon, and he taught him grammar by setting in grotesque rhymes the words to be remembered.

Mr. Browning was in fact a born educator. He looked, Henriette thought, much more like a poet than his son and had, even in his seventies, "great vivacity and freshness of mind." A picture emerges as we watch this older Robert Browning—at once guiding and yielding, probably both with a good deal of wisdom. Most of our knowledge of him comes through the poet, but something also from his half brother, Reuben, who describes him as a walking encyclopedia. He could find his way in the dark to the right bookcase in his huge library, and to the right book, and bring it back into the light for any needed reference, which he also turned up with miraculous speed. At Baylor are some of the volumes he had bound with added pages for his own notes. He knew rare books so well that he could tell which bookseller had the Codex or Elzevir in question and what price it was likely to fetch.

Mr. Browning's work at the bank appears to have been as much of practical everyday life as he cared to be bothered with. We learn that he changed the restaurant at which he lunched because they insisted on his choosing what he would eat. Cyrus Mason says he was shaved daily by his wife and that both wife and daughter disliked his absorption in verses, drawing, and learned books. Probably day-to-day "practical" matters were left to the two able-bodied women, at home all day with servants to wait on them, while husband and father earned the income he allowed them to spend—except for what went on his treasured library. But a bibliophile with tastes for drawing, verse-making, and conversation has not done too badly if, in addition to all this, he has earned the family living and done more than his share in the production and education of a poet.

How seriously to take Cyrus I am not sure, yet as the poet's cousin and near neighbor he was in a position to observe, and if we allow for a certain bias, his observations are worth noting. The Browning household was, he says, "maintained in some style with my uncle's salary." He himself found it "genteely dreary" and the family enveloped in "a misty pride."

Another aunt, Mrs. Silverthorne, and her three sons were very fond of "young Robert," but no one who knew the Brownings ever seems to have mentioned the Masons.

Cyrus and his mother noted with displeasure that Robert's sister, Sarianna, would walk to the chapel she attended followed by a maid carrying her books. He felt that "each of the occupants" of the house was "constantly self-absorbed," Uncle Robert studying a learned book or making grotesque drawings, Aunt Robert with her roses "or some household punctilio," Sarianna full of her own importance and her chapel, and (apparently dating the observations and explaining the sting), "the poet so preoccupied with his love affair that he found no opportunity to show any attention to kinsfolk."[2]

One suspects that the Brownings were bored to death by the Masons, and it might be refreshing to hear the Silverthorne opinion of both families and their mutual relationship! But one thing emerges—a clear picture of parents nurturing in a son, on whom all their hopes were set, the genius in which they so fully believed. "Young Robert," Cyrus says (whether from his own observation or that of his mother), "was developed by his father into an acknowledged genius."

Of Browning's mother—Sarah Anna, elided for her daughter into Sarianna—we know so little that speculation is as easy as it is futile. Carlyle described her as "the fine type of a Scottish gentlewoman." Mr. Kenyon declared that she would not need to go to heaven as she made heaven around her. Her religious views were narrow, and Mrs. Orr says that "in all her goodness and sweetness she seems to have been somewhat matter-of-fact," with nothing of the artistic qualities of her son and husband save her musical talent. Both Sarianna and her brother loved their mother with a deep affection, and Alfred Domett describes the family as most happy and united. Browning himself spoke of his mother as "a divine woman." He and she, while not alike intellectually, were curiously close physically. In the famous Love Letters he often tells Elizabeth how neuralgic headaches would affect them both simultaneously, and simultaneously depart.

The family way of life was certainly comfortable. We learn casually of Browning's pony in the stable, of a large garden, of Mr. Browning's collections of prints, his library of six thousand books, many of them very valuable, including a first edition of *Paradise Lost*. He was, of course, clever at picking up these treasures, though too generous in parting with them. Browning's masters in music, Italian, fencing, and the rest must have cost money, and so must the excellent bindings in which his father reclothed the books, to which he had added blank pages.

There was a degree of ease not today associated with a salary of £250 rising to £320. Indeed these figures need very considerable translating to discover their equivalent in our present inflated money.

It was not as simple as I had expected to find enlightening books on household expenses of more than a century ago. All those offered to me at the London Library and the British Museum dealt with tons of meat, hundreds of bundles of carrots, and the like. Translating, I got the impression that meat would have retailed at between threepence and five-pence a pound, a dozen bottles of wine at less than the cost of one bottle today. (Certain imported or hothouse luxuries were, of course, much more expensive. Cyrus was impressed by his uncle having, in Jamaica, often exchanged a pineapple for a sheet of writing paper while in London pineapples cost three to five guineas.)

I found two further sources of information, Dickens and the London School of Economics, a graduate of which told me I should be well within the mark if I multiplied by ten the income figure of 1830 or thereabouts. This would give Browning's father at his top earning point over £3,200 a year in today's money, *free of income tax* before we add anything for interest from his inherited money.

As to Dickens, information is scattered through all his books: The clerks' lunch in *Bleak House* cost threepence each for meat, a penny for marrow pie; the waitress was tipped a penny. In *The Old Curiosity Shop* Kit Nubbles, earning £6 a year, takes his mother, his small brother, his fellow servant, and her mother out to a play and an oyster supper; yet Kit was no lad to spend his entire quarter's wage of thirty shillings on one evening's entertainment.

In *Our Mutual Friend* Bella Wilfer's husband had a salary of thirty shillings a week, which enabled her to keep a neat little maid in a neat little cottage. And in *A Christmas Carol* the entire Cratchit family were living on fifteen shillings a week of Scrooge's money, while the eldest boy dreamed of the splendors of a first job at five shillings. Eighteen shillings a week was the full board paid by the youngest gentleman at

Mrs. Todgers' very exclusive boardinghouse, and her efforts to avoid offending Mr. Pecksniff were censured by him as worshiping the golden calf of Baal. "Oh calf, calf," he repeated mournfully, "Oh Baal, Baal."

Yet, however comfortable a family might be on an average clerk's salary, it would not be easy to get out of it fairly large sums in ready cash —the regular payments of £16 a time which Mr. Browning produced for the printing of the son's earlier books, still less the £100 which made him a foundation member of London University, the £100 he later lent to facilitate Browning's marriage and journey to Italy. (Cyrus Mason declares, but Mrs. Orr seems to deny, that this was supplied by Uncle Reuben.)

A salary, however, was not all the money there was in the family. Although Mr. Browning was disinherited and therefore relatively poor, some money had been willed to him by his "Uncle Tittle" and "Aunt Mill." Mrs. Miller says this can have been very little, as the Tittles were cordwainers in Jamaica and made shoes for the Barrett family there. They were, and no doubt did. *But a century earlier.* For by 1739 their carriages along with the Barretts' were to be seen at the welcome to Admiral Vernon; and the head of the family was buried in 1742 under the velvet pall reserved for the most important citizens. There is indeed as we have seen some mystery about Browning's direct ancestor, but, while much less wealthy than his brother, he also owned both property and slaves. Earthquakes and the destruction of papers make the details difficult to trace, but certainly none of the family ever returned to the humble origins in which Mrs. Miller leaves them.[3]

Browning's father had renounced the property that involved slave-owning. His aunt and his uncle were making him some compensation. One wonders what is the relevance of the footnote quotation from *Andrea del Sarto* with which Mrs. Miller emphasizes her treatment of Browning's relationship to his parents:

> My father and my mother died of want,
> Well, had I riches of my own? . . .
>   Some good son
> Paint my two hundred pictures—let him try.

2 The Boy Browning

My Father, who knew better than turn straight
Learning's full flare on weak-eyed ignorance,
Or, worse yet, leave weak eyes to grow sunblind,
Content with darkness and vacuity.

"DEVELOPMENT"[1]

ONE OF Browning's earliest memories was of watching his mother holding a parasol over her head while she searched for a spotted frog in the strawberry bed. He had insisted on the frog as a condition for taking his medicine, and this very compliant parent had yielded. Swallowing the nauseous mixture the child improvised:

Good people all who wish to see
A boy take physic look at me.

Robert Browning was born May 7, 1812, at Camberwell where the family lived up to his twenty-fifth year. Today long swallowed by London, it was then surrounded by open fields. Pleasant walks led to Dulwich, to London itself or, farther afield, through woods and country lanes.

Animals were a passion with Browning and he had an extraordinary influence over them. He amassed in his private collection owls and monkeys, magpies and hedgehogs, an eagle, and two large snakes. There was also a toad, left in its own habitat but coming out to greet him as well as a toad can, and following him about the garden. A story of a lion kicked to death by an ass upset him so much that he hid the book; and both his two years younger sister and he cried so bitterly over the story of a parrot, set free but dying of hunger and cold, that their parents had to change the end of the story before reading it to them again. It is a rather remarkable case of heredity through at least three generations, inherited from his mother who could even tame butterflies, passed on to his son who could safely persuade a large snake to remain draped around his model for Dryope. Among the reasons for the break-up of his son's marriage was the menagerie of beasts and overvocal birds at the Palazzo Rezzonico.

Park Honan in *Browning's Characters* has a fascinating chapter on Imagery, tracing among other forms the use made by Browning of animal imagery. Dr. Honan found in "Caliban's" 295 lines sixty-three references to animals. And while in this instance their chief effect was "that of picturing Caliban's animality generically," similar imagery is used by Browning in illustration of individual character. In the *Ring and the Book* Guido is likened to a "wolf-in-sheepskin, scorpion, wildcat, dog and hawk," and many other beasts; Caponsacchi is "lamb-pure, lion-brave"; Pompilia "a white ermine, a fawn, a bird." And the lawyer Archangeli, only concerned with what brings himself nourishment and enjoyment ("for lambkins we must live") mentions more animals "in terms of food than in terms which relate them to the attributes of other characters."

A lion the Browning children had seen in captivity in the famous Royal Menagerie reappears in *The Glove,* with black mane and glowing eyes.

> And you saw by the flash on his forehead,
> By the hope in those eyes wide and steady,
> He was leagues in the desert already,
> Driving the flocks up the mountain.

We can imagine the little Brownings as they listened to the roar from the cages and passed through the rooms of the Menagerie "painted with exotic scenes" to add to the drama. Not that Browning needed much help in creating drama for himself. His mother recorded the first real walk on which she took him, when he poured out descriptions of houses and other property owned by him with so much topographical detail that she remarked, "Why, sir, you are quite a geographer."

Born, would one say, to be a naturalist? But when only two years and three months old he had drawn a cottage—colored with currant juice, for paint on brushes was poisonous if sucked—which his father dated and treasured. Surely Robert's works would one day be hung on the walls of the great galleries. Long before the authorized age of four-teen, Mr. Browning took his son to the Dulwich collection—the one place in their neighborhood where any art existed, and the predecessor by twenty-four years of the National Gallery, which was opened only in August, 1838. There the boy would sit in front of a single picture for a good hour at a time. Would he then be an artist? Well, perhaps; but young as he was on his first effort at painting, he may have been yet younger when he rushed down from his bedroom to listen to his mother's playing and when she stopped sobbed out "Play, play." One of his own earliest memories, before his small hand could stretch an oc-tave, was of her playing Avison's "Grand March in C."

"I was studying the grammar of music," he told a friend, "when most children are learning the multiplication table." And it was this musical bent that he was satisfying in part as he pulled himself up to the table before he could walk unaided and went round and round it improvising verses. Of the career of a musician he certainly thought in youth—but it was by no means the only thought. (One would love to know what prompted an entry in his journal at the age of seven "mar-ried two wives this morning.")

It is almost bewildering to see a boy so young dragged in so many different directions, for music and painting were not mere dilettante tastes; each was entered upon passionately. From infancy, says Mrs. Orr, he had "an unresting activity and a fiery temper. He clamoured for occupation from the moment he could speak." But later on this oc-cupation might be one of pure mind and feeling—essentially contem-plative. Besides the quiet gazing at a single picture, he could, says Wil-liam Sharp, lie "beside a hedge or deep in meadow grasses and there give himself up so absolutely to the life of the moment that even shy birds

Preface aloud to me as we took a walk together up Nunhead Hill, Surrey, when I was a boy." For the hundred pages of this preface the eager boy was keeping pace physically and mentally with an even more eager father. Entranced by pictures, friend of beasts and lover of nature, passionate addict of music—but books still came first. There was *Robinson Crusoe* in a first edition; but Quarles' *Emblems* and Wanley's *Wonders of the Little World* were his earliest favorites—rare books both, dating from the seventeenth century. It would be unthinkable to give either to a child today.

The introduction to *Emblems* in the edition of 1777 tells us that the book had been "generally known and well received for more than a century past." It is a work of intense piety with references to Augustine, Gregory, Jerome, Cyprian, Bernard, and many less-known writers of the early and medieval Christian periods. There are biblical allusions innumerable and a severe moral note throughout:

> Think ye the pageants of your hopes are able
> To stand secure when earth itself's unstable?
> Come dunghill worldlings . . .

Strange little woodcuts depict the soul as a child, Cupid and Mammon, devils with pitchforks, angels, et cetera. The devil is shown in the chariot of the world driving it fiercely, and again standing between the contestants in a game of bowls. And what, I wonder, could a child make of the lines about earth's motherhood?

> The ubrous breasts, when fully drawn, repast
> The thriving infant with their milky flood,
> But being overstrained return at last
> Unwholesome gulps composed of wine and blood.

The attraction of this book must have lain in the meter and the many new words. The rhythm varies; the vocabulary is a large one; there are Titans, spangled nymphs, Astrea, Cupid, Stygian night, and other fascinating puzzles. The classics were as familiar to Quarles (graduate of Cambridge, barrister, chronologer to the city of London) as they were quickly becoming to his young reader: "The busy mint / Of our laborious thoughts is ever going / And coining new desires."

Wanley's *Wonders of the Little World* sounds innocent enough, but it is much more astonishing for a child's reading. It shows "by many thousands of examples . . . what MAN hath been from the First Ages of the World to these Times in respect of his Body, Senses, Passions, Affections, His Virtues and Perfections, his Vices and Defects." All this and more is set out on the title page as "collected from the writings of the most approved Historians, Philosophers, Physicians, Philologists and others by Nathaniel Wanley Vicar of Trinity Parish in the City of Coventry, London 1678."

The many pages of contents are hair-raising. To summarize a few: Infants heard to cry in mother's womb . . . carried dead in womb for some years . . . petrified in womb. Persons who have made entrance to the world in a different manner from the rest of mankind.

Of giants, pygmies, dwarfs . . . Of persons who have renewed their age and grown young again. Of persons who have changed their sex.

Of the strange rigours in punishments used by several persons and nations. (This heading is implemented by stories of torture too horrible to do more than glance at.)

Of unusual diseases . . . "This world is a kind of great hospital . . ." Of unusual ways of dying . . . Of people supposed dead returning . . . Of strange ways murders are discovered.

Of force of imagination and phantasie. Of people seeing in the dark . . . Of varieties in senses: hearing, touch, taste (The story is here told of a man who ate two live mice which gnawed his vitals).

Of the Passion of Love . . . Of extreme Hatred . . . Of Fear . . . also of Panick Fears.

Had Browning read all the pages that followed one can imagine him as suffering from "panick fears." It is hard to tell; much passes over a child's consciousness which would pierce the adult's, but does it pierce later? And what did he make of the Passion of Jealousy, illustrated by a man who "caused himself to be gelded" so that he could be entirely certain, if his wife had a baby, that he was not its father? His biographers have found in Wanley the roots of a good many of Browning's poems; but till I held the huge volume in my hands I never guessed what else he was poring over in those mysterious years of childhood.

It was certainly in Wanley that he first read "The Pied Piper" and "The Cardinal and the Dog." The haunting notion in that poem—of evil in the shape of a black dog—occurred again in the story of the magician Agrippa from whom he borrowed the introduction to *Pauline*. Always keenly alive to the struggle between good and evil, alive too to the dangers of the occult, he found in Wanley the character of Paracelsus—chosen for his second great poem. The story in *The Ring and the Book* of Pope Stephen feeding to the fish the fingers of his dead predecessor, the very name of a "garden fancy" *Schnafnaburgensis* (which means simply a native of Aschafenburg), were dropped by Wanley into a memory which, as Browning himself once said, lost nothing committed to it except "names and the battle of Waterloo." And we can scarcely doubt the book's share in awakening Browning's lifelong interest in abnormal psychology.

But this library of his father's fed also tastes that with many boys would have inhibited learning—music and painting. Avison's book on musical expression set on foot a whole train of thought about shifting tastes in music. How early, I wonder, did John Relfe, "musician in ordinary to the King" become "Master of mine, learned, redoubtable"? He lived at Camberwell, and taught Browning musical theory—and this introduced yet more books. For Relfe had written a learned *Principles of Harmony* and other works through which Browning learned to write accompaniments, later destroyed by him, but above all his musical poems about music: "A Toccata of Galuppi" and "Abt Vogler."

Then there was Gerard de Lairesse, the painter, on the flyleaf of whose book *The Art of Painting in all its Branches,* Browning wrote: "I read this book more often and with greater delight when I was a child than any other: and still remember the main of it most gratefully for the good I seem to have got from the prints and the wonderful text." We owe to the Griffin-Minchin biography and to De Vane's work on Browning's *Parleyings* a realization of how important were these books, and the others there discussed, to Browning's development. This is in part the answer to a question that fascinated Chesterton: Why did he so frequently choose unimportant or forgotten people to write about? Partly perhaps from a democracy which knew that no man is unimpor-

tant; but chiefly because he had met these people at the impressionable
age of earliest encounters.

The *Biographie Universelle* in fifty volumes was also on his father's
shelves and here were garnered more facts about Paracelsus, the subject
of his proposed tragedy "Narses," ideas for *King Victor and King
Charles* and for *The Return of the Druses*. "One would almost surmise," says Griffin, "that he had read its fifty volumes through."

Miserably undated as this childhood is, we only learn that the days
of fullest absorption and happiest occupation were rudely curtailed
when Browning became, at eight or nine, a weekly boarder in a school
of which the junior part was taught by the Misses Ready and the senior
by their brother the Reverend Thomas Ready.

Alfred Domett, later one of Browning's closest friends, had two
older brothers who were his schoolfellows, and one of them remembered
"young Browning in a pinafore of brown Holland such as small boys
used to wear in those days." Six years older than Browning, he recalled
how they "used to pit him against much older and bigger boys in a chaf-
fing match to amuse themselves with the little bright-eyed fellow's readiness and acuteness of repartee."

But to Browning the weekly boarding spelt undiluted misery. On
hearing the decree, he chose, says Mrs. Orr, a leaden cistern in the
school for his "place of burial." It had on it a raised image of a face. He
imagined this face as his epitaph, passing his hands over it again and
again and chanting, "In memory of unhappy Browning." Time softened
the pain of the endless weekly exile, but not the intense dislike of the
school. At first the big boys bullied him, he later told Domett, but the
thing went much deeper than that. The teachers were kind enough,
and he remembered with shame having written verses in praise of the
headmaster which enabled him to get away with many small tricks. On
Prize Day, although he tells us he never won a prize—a difficult feat
says Mrs. Orr, so many were given—he was chosen to recite. But he
probably reserved his energies for the weekend and the holidays. It
would be characteristic if he chose deliberately not to compete—it is
likely enough that he had no equals with whom to compete: what other

boy of eight was reading Pope's *Iliad* and beginning to learn Greek? Who might be reading the *Biographie Universelle*? How many of them had a father knowing Greek, Latin, French, Spanish, Italian, and Hebrew and taking very good care to pass on his learning to his children?

And how many books did they own? How many had they read? Even an ordinary child going from an immensely cultured home to a second-rate school detests and despises it. Let the masters be as kind as they will, it does not make up for mediocrity. Browning stated his complaint to Domett quite simply, "he says they taught him nothing there." Hearing of a "heavy" sermon preached by Thomas Ready, seven years after he had left school, Browning improvised

> A *heavy* sermon—sure the error's great
> For not a word Tom utters has its weight.

Browning was in fact suffering from the change described by Chesterton when instead of learning—such joy at home—he was being taught by someone he did not know something that he did not want to know.

But at some date in his school life came a curious interlude.

In Sotheby's catalogue of the sale of Browning material in 1913, Lot 1047, is a two-volume edition of the plays of Nicholas Rowe with Elizabeth Barrett's signature in each volume, and on a flyleaf of Volume I "Robert Browning (who at school revived 'The Royal Convert' and acted Aribert therein etc.)"

Nicholas Rowe (1674–1718), a friend of Pope, who called him a delightful companion often "drinking and drolling" late into the night, wrote many plays in which the leading actors of the day appeared. "He seldom pierces the breast," said Johnson, "but he always delights the ear and often improves the understanding." *The Royal Convert* was first staged in 1707.

If the play was put on without cuts, Browning had an immense part to learn—but at twelve or fourteen the memory is at its best. Aribert is the brother of Hengist, king of Kent, son of that Hengist who first invaded Britain. He is secretly married to a British Christian, Ethelinda, and has himself become a Christian. King Hengist is be-

trothed to Rodogune, a Saxon princess. But unfortunately he has fallen
in love with Ethelinda, while Rodogune is passionately enamored of
Aribert.

Through five acts of noble sentiments, threats, and denunciations
a double theme is played: religion and love. Aribert, prepared "To
scorn / And trample on their ignominious altars" is threatened by his
brother:

> "Tis well Sir! Impious boy!
>   One to the priests."
> (*Exit a Gent*)
> "Bid 'em be swift and dress their bloody altars!"
> (*The Priests bind Aribert, and lead him to the altar, while
> the solemn musick is playing.*)

The young Christian pair exchange pages of noble sentiments about
the superiority of the heaven for which they are bound, interspersed
with occasional sighs for a little happiness on earth. It looks as though,
if Aribert would give up Ethelinda to his brother and turn to Rodogune,
their religion could be forgiven them. But Aribert asks his brother the
meaning of

> This frantick, wild demand? What should I yield,
> Give up my love, my wife, my Ethelinda
> To an incestuous brother's dire embrace?

Of course it all ends well—but the plot and the language remind
one that even the pious nonconformist world of that date was not yet
Victorianized.

Clearly this "revival" was a regular school play, possibly the finale
to Browning's five or six years in the school. We can imagine the scene
in Belloc's words:

> The upper school had combed and oiled their hair,
> And all the parents of the boys were there

to witness young Browning, to listen to stilted denunciations of pagan-
ism and passionate proclamations of a readiness for martyrdom, and an

exaltation of Britannia, with Saxon, Celt, and Roman welded into one triumphant ruler of the waves.

The endless soliloquies and speeches may well have later affected adversely Browning's own plays; his considerable acting powers probably showed themselves, but it may be that the false note struck in the noble speeches of Aribert were, with other elements in the boy's small world, preparing him for the disruptive influence two years later of his introduction to the poet Shelley.

A memory with which Browning made even his pious mother laugh reluctantly, had been that of the Misses Ready drilling the smaller boys in brushing their hair to the accompaniment of Dr. Watts' hymns; Browning would illustrate "with voice and gesture the ferocious emphasis with which the brush would swoop down in the accentuated syllables":

> Lord 'tis a pleasant thing to stand
> In gardens planted by Thy hand. . . .
> Fools never raise their thoughts so high,
> Like *brutes* they live, like BRUTES they die.

But the fact of the mother's reluctance to laugh poses another question: In all the delights of learning—to which were added as the years went on dancing lessons, fencing lessons, riding lessons—was there one supremely irksome element, to feel which irksome was to feel wicked: religion?

As a small child Browning describes himself as "passionately religious." Preaching once to his even smaller sister, he reduced her to tears, and then, turning, said to an imaginary official, "Pew opener, remove that child." He read the Bible, probably with the interest that he gave to every book. But the chapel to which Congregationalists or other Nonconformists would repair depended far too much on the abilities of the incumbent of the moment. Few men can pray with thoughts and words suited for other minds. And Browning had certainly been unfortunate in the ministers of his earlier life. Speaking of one of them, the Reverend George Clayton, another minister, Edward White, said he felt impelled as a boy to gnaw the pew top as he listened to lengthy "prayers which were newspapers, entering into every particular of births, marriages and deaths and foreign travel, of deacons and the like." Clayton was said to be of "the old school" and "to have stiffened and starched" those who sat under him. Edward White's brother relates how Browning, stationed with his parents in the front of the gallery, "did not care to conceal his something more than indifference to the ministrations to which he listened weekly, and which once brought down upon him a rebuke from the Pastor in open Church!"

No better than George Clayton and George Ready was the Reverend Mr. Irons, to whose chapel the Browning family chiefly repaired— to be "ironed" as some of their friends put it. Domett recalls in his diary going up Camberwell Grove to test how far off he could hear "Mr. Irons bawling out his sermon." From a distance he could clearly hear the words, "I am very sorry to say it, beloved brethren, but it is an undoubted fact that Roman Catholic and midnight assassin are synonymous terms."

According to "Christmas-Eve" a sermon might have ten headings, and it may have been Browning's own boyhood that evoked the picture of how, whatever their intrinsic value,

> . . . Such truths looked false to your eyes,
> With his provings and parallels twisted and twined,
> Till how could you know them, grown double their size
> In the natural fog of the good man's mind, . . .
>   The zeal was good and the aspiration;
> And yet, and yet, yet, fifty times over,
>   Pharaoh received no demonstration,
> By his Baker's dream of Baskets Three,
> Of the doctrine of the Trinity,—
> Although, as our preacher thus embellished it,
> Apparently his hearers relished it.

Religion then had begun to be weariness, as so often in adolescence, and in Browning's case with considerable reason. Like school it was a waste of the hours he longed to have—for everything.

At thirteen Browning was still at the Ready school; was, one supposes, still taken to church on Sundays to be starched or ironed, but there was possible a good deal of that absence of mind which has been defined as presence of mind on something else.

That his biographers should rejoice over the destruction of *Incondita*, written when he was twelve or thirteen, is bewildering. The poems could not be other than immature, but his was a fascinating and pregnant immaturity. How much went into these verses of flowers and birds, of music and vivid pictures—of Men and Women? Were there any of the horrors of Wanley's *Little World?* As Clayton or Irons droned on, were other verses made in his mind—to emerge later in his lyrics? Were pictures formed for "The Flight of the Duchess" as he walked past the gypsy camps in Dulwich wood? For he would, says William Sharp, his earliest biographer, "join company with any tramps, gypsies or other wayfarers."

There were fairs at Camberwell and Greenwich and at Peckham just opposite Mr. Ready's school. "For three days each summer," writes Mr. Hall Griffin, "the Walworth Road from Camberwell gate to the village green—a goodly mile—was aglow after sunset with candles beneath coloured shades on the road-side stalls." There was the canvas-covered avenue with its gingerbread booths, there was music and dancing . . . there was the ever-popular Richardson's Theatre—"appreciated, it is said, by the poet in his younger days."

In our era of mass illumination one longs sometimes for the more subdued glow of the candles throwing up the color of their shades or sparkling with the brilliants of their chandeliers—made brighter by the surrounding darkness, today totally excluded.

Much of these younger days of Browning's must have found their echo in poems so greatly admired by the boy's father that he sought a publisher for them—but in vain. *Incondita* he had called them, for his mind was still like the beginnings of creation not yet formed and ordered, but present also was the beginning of the light that would become sun, moon, and stars as the spirit of God moved over the waters.

Two sisters, Eliza and Sarah Flower, are mixed up with the story of *Incondita* and much speculation has been poured out over Browning's feelings toward them. Was he in love with either or both? And if so at what date? For while he knew them both from early childhood, they were respectively nine and seven years older than he was and from the age of sixteen to that of twenty he appears to have lost sight of them. Browning's first two biographers knew him personally—Mrs. Orr by far the better—both in later life. Sharp suggests that he had "more than one episode of the heart." Mrs. Orr is convinced that, *if* Browning was ever in love before he met Elizabeth, it was with Eliza Flower—and of course such a love in a precocious adolescent between the age of twelve and sixteen is not at all improbable. After that the break of four years seems to have been complete. We know so little. Yet so much has been written about all this, from Hovelaque's treatment of Browning's youth —dwelling especially on *Pauline, Paracelsus* and *Sordello* and opting for a Browning fascinated by both sisters, but chiefly the younger—to Mrs. Miller's skilful reconstruction of the Flower and Fox families, at the later date when Browning was a fairly frequent visitor but much wrapped up in his own poetical career.

Eliza and Sarah Flower were daughters of the then famous Benjamin Flower, editor of *The Cambridge Intelligencer*. Most shamefully had he been imprisoned and fined for breach of privilege, in a prosecution brought by the House of Lords for a comment on the political inconsistency of a bishop. A young schoolmistress Eliza Gould, given the choice between abandoning *The Cambridge Intelligencer* or her job, unhesitatingly left her pupils and repaired to Newgate where she found Flower and "bestowed her heart on the spot and her hand upon his release." She had died in 1810 and Benjamin had tried to be both father and mother to the girls, bringing them up in an atmosphere of idealism and poetry rather than of the strict attention to needlework and household management then deemed the chief essential in a girl's education. Harriet Martineau, who had emerged from her own subjection to this, who lived in the same world, political and social, is said to have painted their portraits both in *Deerbrook* and in *Five Years of Youth or Sense and Sentiment*.

"When the sisters sat in the balcony their voices would ring out clear and sweet by the hour together." To this singing Browning may have listened with renewal of the transport his mother's playing brought in babyhood: "I knew the Flowers when I was five or six years old," he wrote many years later, "earlier I do think. When I got older, perhaps at twelve or thirteen, I wrote a book of verses which Eliza read and wrote to me about." Eliza made a copy for herself and showed it to William Fox—"which verses," says Browning, "he praised not a little, which comforted me not a little." Nonetheless "in a few months . . . I saw the proper way, and put my blessed poems in the fire."[2]

Fox, who had come to know the Flowers the previous year on a tour in Scotland, was in February, 1824, opening a new Unitarian Chapel in South Place Finsbury. Brought up, as he put it, on "the sour milk of Calvinism," on a poor Norfolk farm where his father had suffered under the iniquitous game laws—being prosecuted for killing a pheasant which was devouring his grain—William Fox himself began life as a bank clerk, went on to the ministry, and became finally a publicist and politician. He never forgot his origins and what they had taught him, and during his campaign against the Corn Laws (which should, Miss Martineau said, be described more clearly in terms of the bread they were keeping from the poor) he signed himself "The Norwich Weaver Boy." But at this date Fox was primarily a minister. He had, his biographer says, "a miraculous gift of preaching," not unhelped by his piercing eyes and his melodious voice. He was regarded as a "safe man," who made no attempt to arouse in his congregation "unseemly ecstasy." (Carlyle described him as having "a tendency to pot-belly and snuffiness.") The Flower sisters were producing hymns for the Chapel— Sarah writing the verses and Eliza supplying the music. Untrained though Eliza was, her reputation became a high one, and Browning wrote twenty years later: "I put it apart from all other English music I know, and fully believe it is the music we have all waited for."

That Browning should first have striven for the publication of *Incondita* and so soon afterward destroyed it is surely not unconnected with the fact that in the year 1826 he first read a volume of Shelley's verse.

In *Browning and Shelley: A Myth and Some Facts,* Frederick Pottle tells the fascinating story of his own search for this volume, long supposed to have been a pirated edition of *Queen Mab,* but in fact containing almost all else. "It is," he writes, "a little duodecimo volume bound in light drab boards. . . . The back is missing and the covers have been carefully stitched in again with coarse linen thread—by Browning's mother? I hope so." Inside the cover is written: "This book was given to me, probably as soon as published, by my cousin J. S. The foolish markings, and still more foolish scribblings show the impression made on a boy by this first specimen of Shelley's poetry. June 2nd 1878 'O World, O Life, O Time.' "

A facsimile page shows us how Browning worked at effacing most of the "foolish scribblings" of his fourteen-year-old frenzy of admiration. His mother procured for him the poems of Keats, and the rest of Shelley —almost certainly including *Queen Mab,* which made him a vegetarian. Pottle quotes: "No longer now / He slays the lamb that looks him in the face." But it was poetry that transfigured the world of boyhood's imagination, and Keats with Shelley became embodied for Browning in two nightingales that still sang in the gardens of Camberwell.

For long it was supposed that nothing of *Incondita* remained. Both Flower sisters died of tuberculosis (or consumption as it was then called) in early middle age and Browning recovered and destroyed the copy made by Eliza. But Sarah too had been busy copying, and two poems of some length survived and can be read today in Browning's collected works: "The First-Born of Egypt" and "The Dance of Death." For a boy of his age they are almost as remarkable as Sarah thought them and, while certainly imitating Byron, show also the influence of his Bible reading, of Wanley's gloomy pages—and it may well be of some boyhood experience of his own. For although it would be many years before the Flower sisters died, hardly a family at that date went untouched by fever or consumption. Of nine children often five, four, or fewer became adults. Typhoid, cholera, famine, and rabies dispute in one poem their right to be crowned lord of death—while the last of Egypt's ten plagues pictures the horror of a night which begins with "sunset glories flooding the pale clouds / With liquid gold," and ends with the death of each family's first-born, from Pharaoh's heir to the child in "poverty's lone hut"—as

> . . . each one owned
> In silence the dread majesty—the might
> Of Israel's God, whose red hand had avenged
> His servants' cause so fearfully.

Curious topics to be chosen by the boy who in manhood would be unthinkingly dismissed as a facile optimist. Curious, too, that Browning on recovering these poems might have thrown them also into the fire—but did not. Certainly as he grew older he grew more interested in his own past, and it may be he felt on seeing them again that they were not, for a boy, such poor stuff as he had remembered.

3 *Pauline*

Amid his wild-wood sights he lived alone.
As if the poppy felt with him! Though he
Partook the poppy's red effrontery
Till Autumn spoilt their fleering quite with rain.

"SORDELLO"

BROWNING'S education from the age of fourteen was carried on at home apart from a brief attendance at the new London University during its opening term. His abrupt return thence is by Professor Saintsbury deemed the sheerest of blessings: to those two terms he chooses to attribute Browning's strange usages in Greek nomenclature . . . Alcestis would just be Alkestis . . . but, "nymph," he complained, was "numph" and "psyche" presumably "psuche."

London University was a new and bold experiment, but there can be little doubt that Browning would have gained something from any university. He was beginning to outgrow his father's tutelage and had little companionship, least of all companionship of the intellect.

There were his Silverthorne cousins, reputed as "wild lads," with one of whom, James, he shared a love of music and a passionate enthusiasm for the theater. They would walk from Camberwell to Richmond to watch Edmund Kean—one such occasion being commemorated in *Pauline*, obscurely enough to be missed by John Stuart Mill. James was the one witness present at Browning's wedding, and in his memory was written "May and Death." There was his young half-uncle, Reuben. There were the two Dowson brothers to one of whom, Christopher,

is addressed a very early letter of Browning's (1830): he married Mary
Domett, whose brother Alfred became one of the poet's closest friends.
Such scattered friendships are no real substitute for a public school or
university relationship. They did gradually coalesce, around an eccentric Captain Pritchard, into a group calling themselves The Set or The
Convivialists, but for some years Browning was altogether more lonely
than was healthy for mind and body.

A curious problem existed for folk like the Brownings in the England of that day. The aristocracy, the gentry, had a certain education
and society as of right; the Norwich Weaver Boy had won it by main
force. But a boy in the comfortable middle class who, Nonconformist
in religion, could not go to Oxford or Cambridge, had no great incentive
to struggle for entry into a world he did not know when he had out-
grown his own.

Perhaps Cerutti, Browning's Italian tutor, a political exile, introduced him in imagination to the country which he was to call later his
university. "The Italian in England" might have been written after
years of residence in Italy; surely friendship with a man who had
known was its chief inspiration. Working under Relfe on the theory,
and under his other teacher on the practice, of music, Browning wrote
accompaniments which he later destroyed.

But much was postponed in his development during these years,
much that should have flowered was half frosted. It is strange, Mrs. Orr
comments, how Shelley established himself in Browning's imagination
both as a maligned and persecuted man and as a "lofty spirit, one dwelling in the communion of higher things," but perhaps not as inconsistent
as she felt it that the influence was a subversive one. For Browning was
also reading Voltaire—and he was very ready to be subverted. Atheism
was the natural if not really the logical outcome of a course of Ready,
Clayton, and Irons. And most adolescents are ready for rebellion.

Browning's vegetarianism lasted for about two years till the weakening of his eyesight persuaded him back to normal food; but before
being cured himself, Browning had affected Sarah Flower with his religious disquiet. Feeling that she could not communicate with her
father, Sarah wrote to William Fox "a regular confession of faith, or

rather the want of it . . . the heinous sin of unbelief. . . ." She still believed in God, but "I would fain go to my Bible as I used to—but I cannot. The cloud has come over me gradually, and I did not discover the darkness in which my soul was shrouded until, in seeking to give light to others, my own gloomy state became too settled to admit of doubt. It was in answering Robert Browning that my mind refused to bring forward argument, turned recreant and sided with the enemy."

At home it was, said Browning's sister, the least amiable period of his life. Probably the two years on bread and potatoes damaged other things besides his eyesight, and the spiritual struggle—to be revealed in *Pauline*—was showing in daily life. He himself never spoke of this time except in words of strong self-condemnation. Sarah Flower, after recovering from her "gloomy state," wrote one of the best-known hymns in the English language: "Nearer, My God, to Thee."

Many years later Browning, writing to Julia Wedgwood, analyzed what he believed from his own experience to be the common attitude of the young toward the religious teaching given to them—an undoubting acceptance combined with a "practical atheism, . . . they have not a natural need for what you artificially give them . . ." Children have what to a child appear "better ways of their own for righting matters: whereas the real instinct is developed with mature years, and, then only, substitutes itself for the previous motives which are losing their virtue of impelling or repressing one—hence the new birth: while this life suffices, I don't see that another incentive to push on through its insufficiency, in the shape of a conceived possibility of a life beyond, is ever given us."

When in 1864 he speaks of "thirty-five years ago," it would seem to be not so much the child as the sixteen- or seventeen-year-old boy to whom he refers as "the wise person of my perfect remembrance and particular dislike."

Part of this self-reproach was probably over his behavior in leaving London University so abruptly. He was only sixteen when he went there. He was, according to his father, immensely keen to go, and his education at home had been strong in Latin and Greek. Had he been going to Oxford, meeting men from Eton and Winchester, it would have been very different. But I think we can be fairly certain that in London the professors, however able, would have been obliged to gear their classes to students from schools similar to the one where Browning had raged with boredom. He might well have been learning again what his father had already taught him!

Mr. Browning had entered his son only for Classics and German, and had taken lodgings for him in the college neighborhood. After one term Browning gave up both the early-morning German class and the lodgings. At the end of the second term he threw up the whole thing, his father thus incurring the loss of £100 with which he had become a foundation member of the University.

No explanation has ever been given. Browning at that date, as he later said, did only that which seemed good to him in his own eyes.[1] He was a spoiled only son with adoring parents, who watched him in bewilderment, and it probably did not console them greatly to find that he was reading and digesting the whole of Johnson's Dictionary. William Sharp casts a vivid light on how a youthful poet is supposed to act when he describes Browning in what was still the countryside, walking about, his hat in his left hand, waving his right, declaiming biblical poetry. His hair was waving in the wind and he was quite oblivious to a following of small children. Many years later Sharp heard Browning say, in reply to the remark that only in Italy did romance still remain: "Ah well, I should like to include poor old Camberwell."

This was the time when even Mrs. Orr calls him wild, and Sharp says "he would join company with any tramps, gypsies or other way-farers." The fair at Camberwell with its crowds and its music, the lights in the surrounding blackness, the sudden glimpses of wild loveliness perhaps meant more to the youth of sixteen than to the boy of twelve. Was Browning's poem more than forty years later the re-creation of earlier meetings with a more glamorous Fifine?[2]

We know almost nothing about these years of genius on the boil, of the confusions of adolescence, and the coming of manhood.

Browning was only twenty years younger than Shelley and was subjected to many of the same influences. Shelley before him had studied Paracelsus and was familiar with the literature of the occult.

Both he and Browning attended medical lectures. And Shelley's mottoes to *Queen Mab* in Latin, Greek, and French, with long notes in all three, gave Browning a pattern which he followed in *Pauline,* published in March, 1833, just before his twenty-first birthday: "an account," says William De Vane (in the *Handbook*), "of his victory over the forces of doubt, skepticism and self-centeredness, and his winning to faith, hope and love . . . thoroughly autobiographical."

Never was a poem addressed to a woman who remains as unreal as this one, despite the French note at the end in which she herself speaks. She is nothing except the patient listener to the story of a boy's wanderings, conflicts, aberrations, and aspirations. "If she *existed* and loved him," said John Stuart Mill, "he treats her most ungenerously and unfeelingly." But Mill saw Pauline as "evidently a mere phantom," a recipient of the poet's self-revelation.

It is not surprising, one critic commented, that Pauline should have advised him to destroy a poem in which she, nominally its object, bore so minute a part. But Pauline's doubts as to whether or not the poem ought to be destroyed were, of course, Browning's own—and in astonishingly fluent French this boy was writing, under Pauline's name, a criticism of his own work that went deeper than that of Mill or of any other outside commentator.

Already his intellect was what Herford would later describe as "God intoxicated," and the poem is a confession to the God to whom he is returning. E. I. Watkin in *Poets and Mystics* sees Browning in "Christmas Eve" as expressing a true mystical experience, and so perhaps is he in *Pauline:* a direct recognition of reality—of the supreme Reality—by a man's whole nature, not step by step in what he calls "reason's pedantry," but with a wide opening of the eyes of the mind, an *intense reception* of their vision.

> And what is that I hunger for but God?

> My God, my God, let me for once look on thee
> As though nought else existed, we alone!
> And as creation crumbles, my soul's spark
> Expands till I can say,—Even from myself

I need thee and I feel thee and I love thee.
I do not plead my rapture in thy works
For love of thee, nor that I feel as one
Who cannot die: but there is that in me
Which turns to thee, which loves or which should love.

The last two lines summarize what has recently come to be called the "betrayal" of Shelley. In what lay the betrayal? Not certainly in the abandonment of atheism. As Mrs. Miller notes (p. 19), "the least significant as well as the least durable result of his passionate preoccupation [with Shelley] was the adolescent atheism and vegetarianism which for a time accompanied it." What many critics agree with her in seeing is a rejection by Browning of "the fearless spiritual independence of Shelley," which the boy had recognized as measuring "the very nature of integrity itself." And Browning, it is felt, admits it with the words "I flung all honour from my soul."

But in *Pauline* these words, addressed as a confession to Shelley, have no reference whatever to a rejection of "spiritual independence." He is speaking of the wickedness into which he had fallen:

I lost myself
In deeds for which remorse were vain, as for
The wanderings of delirious dream; yet thence
Came cunning, envy, falsehood . . .

The effect of this stage of life is still with him in "sin and lust and pride." He cries out, "Why have I girt myself with this hell dress? / Why have I laboured to put out my life?"

Chesterton saw in the poem only the common experience of youth, which to every boy seems a secret horror of his own. Half imagination perhaps? A yielding to the mysterious promptings of sex? At that date especially this would have involved him in "falsehood and cunning"— to say nothing of "envy"!

Apart from the phantom Pauline, two persons are addressed in the course of the poem, God and Shelley, each with intense devotion. To God there are longer passages like the one just quoted, and sudden flashes:

Air, air, fresh life-blood, thin and searching air,
The clear, dear breath of God that loveth us . . .

And Shelley is there—*not as a past ideal betrayed, but as a present inspiration,* linked with the God to whom Browning has returned. The poem's final paragraph is addressed to him "Sun-treader, I believe in God and truth/ And love." Yet "I would lean on thee/ Thou must be ever with me." Earlier in the poem he has said "Thou art still for me as thou hast been." Clearly, whatever he felt at fourteen, he does not at twenty regard atheism as of Shelley's essence.

I have never seen a discussion of the relation between *Pauline* and the Dramatic Monologues of Browning's later writing. Before *Paracelsus,* and *Sordello,* it is a clear move toward them, as toward that "poem R. B." which he hoped one day to write. Indeed *Pauline* is "R. B. aetat. 20" (which may be one of the reasons for his profound dislike of it).

Shelley's effect on him was first the feeling of "a key to a new world":

I was vowed to liberty
Men were to be as gods and earth as heaven . . .

He did not stay in the "bliss" of this, not because (as Mrs. Miller thinks) it was in conflict with "the standard of an all-too-tenderly loved mother"—*she is one person we do not find in the poem*—but because, "looking on real life/The life all new to me," he found that men were not like that, earth not like that.

It is not always easy to follow the struggle as he tells it. One truth emerges which he learned in the course of it—that logic is not man's sole guide, or profoundest guide, to reality; there is intuition, there is love. This has been seen as a degradation of reason, with the consequence that he was deliberately "delivering falsely or imperfectly the message with which he had been entrusted." Seen thus it has been given as the reason for his "life-long obsession with the psychology of the charlatan, the quack." But thus to see it shows an unawareness of common experience at one end and of Existentialism at the other. Life *is* larger than logic. Poetry must utter the response to reality of the whole man; poet or philosopher must not stop short because bare intellect can go no further.

Twenty years later, in the period of his richest thought, Browning wrote an introduction to what proved some spurious letters of Shelley's. Men, he said, should not "confound, any more than God confounds, with genuine infidelity and an atheism of the heart, those passionate impatient struggles of a boy towards truth and love. . . . Crude convictions of boyhood, conveyed in imperfect and unapt forms of speech— for such things all boys have been pardoned. They are growing pains accompanied by temporary distortion of soul also."

How much was this an apologia for Shelley, how much for himself? Browning at twenty was again a Christian—but not a Christian of the Irons-Clayton-Ready school.

This recoil from his immediate past, this return to reality, could not work its cure in an instant. Many years must pass, shocks be experienced, a man's work done. But *Pauline* is of interest for several reasons: It looks back and forward. We see in it the boyhood out of which Browning has passed, the adolescence through which he is passing, wild confused ambitions, a sense of power and of beauty. It expresses all that the title *Incondita* claimed for his earlier verse. It should be studied by all who desire to understand Browning—more clearly than he understood himself.[3]

Against the background of chintz curtains, rose-gardens, much tenderness, much dull respectability, an incredibly varied library, and deadly sermons, the young poet was fighting the wild beasts of his imagination, oblivious of the world around, awakening suddenly when the work was done to the need of getting it known. His whole being was set on his poem and its success when he wrote the letter that introduced him once again to William Fox.

Describing himself as "an oddish sort of boy" whom Fox may perhaps remember, he recalls that he had been "at that time a sayer of verse and a doer of it, whose doing you had a little previously commended after a fashion," at a time when such commendation was "more thought of than all the gun, drum and trumpet of praise would be now" (at the age of twenty!)

This same boy, having heard of Fox as a contributor to the *West-minster*, ventures to send him "a free and easy sort of thing which he wrote some months ago 'on one leg' ... should it be found too insignificant for cutting up, I shall no less remain, dear Sir,

> Your most obedient servant
> R. B."

Browning's feeling, whatever it was, for Eliza Flower had had time to subside. And, adds Mrs. Orr with circumspect Victorianism, "her affections were probably engaged." It was certainly an unusual situation. Benjamin Flower had died in 1829 and had left Fox as trustee and guardian to the two girls, already women. This was less surprising at a period when the "gentler sex" were supposed incapable of managing their own affairs, but Fox was only forty-six, married and with children of his own. Mrs. Fox, a faded and ineffectual woman, was watching helplessly the growth of a love between her husband and Eliza. (She herself was also Eliza and so was their daughter. Fox always called Eliza Flower "Lizzie.")

By his account to his mother there had never been a great deal of affection on his side and no effort on his wife's to shoulder her share of a rather heavy burden. Florance, the eldest son, was deaf and dumb. Fox had to cope to a great extent with the children, besides preaching, much lecturing and writing. From about 1826 he had been editing the *Monthly Repository* (which in 1831 he bought) and endeavoring to transform it into an intellectual organ for the Unitarian body and beyond it.[4]

It may well have been a relief to him to throw himself into the congenial task of discovering a new poet. He had recognized Tennyson ahead of the world—and now, *Pauline*, "though evidently a hasty and imperfect sketch, has truth and life in it, which gave us the thrill, and laid hold of us with the power, the sensation of which has never yet failed us as a test of genius."

Fox recognized that much was left for the future to unveil: "Archimedes in the bath had many particulars to settle ... but he first gave a glorious leap—and shouted *Eureka!*"

Dr. Lounsbury in *The Early Literary Career of Robert Browning* has pointed out what a drug on the market poetry was at that date and how impossible it was to launch with the public a new poet however great. But he notes that Browning later always depicted his fate with the critics as worse than it was. He did now have a cordial mention in the *Athenaeum* which indicated the general literary despondency of the moment: "The day is past for either fee or fame in the service of the muse; but, to one who sings so naturally, poetry must be as easy as music to the bird, and no doubt it has a solace all its own."

Browning was intensely grateful to Fox, who added to his own tribute the good intention of getting a review from John Stuart Mill, a great friend of his, whose emotional situation with Harriet Taylor bore a strangely close resemblance to his own.

Harriet Taylor, friend also of the Flowers, had been to all appearances happily married to a rather dull, good-natured merchant, when she sought the advice of her minister, Mr. Fox, on some philosophical problems. He, strangely enough, suggested his young friend, John Stuart Mill, as a good counselor. Mill was at the moment thinking of marriage and it was said, according to his biographer, that "he thought of Eliza Flower, an elfin creature, musical and poetic." But at a first visit to the Taylor house he fell in love with Harriet, whose closest friend and confidante was Eliza.

"We dined," says Carlyle, "with Mrs. (Platonica) Taylor and the Unitarian Fox one day, and the husband." But "Mrs. Taylor herself did not yield unmixed satisfaction, I think, or receive it." She was, he said, "pale, passionate and sad looking." Jane Carlyle felt she "could really love 'Harriet' if it were safe and she were willing; but she is a dangerous woman and engrossed with a dangerous passion."

In both these relationships Mill-Harriet and Fox-Eliza the lovers proclaimed their innocence, but this was to give a special meaning to the term. One feels it strongly with Mill and his Harriet as she played cat and mouse with her husband, unwilling to relinquish him, yet determined to keep Mill. She had at first tried to hold the friendship on an intellectual level only, but felt, she soon claimed, a duty to humanity as well as to her family: Mill *needed* her affection. But the poor man surely needed either less or a great deal more, and Carlyle's description of him gives promise of a vitality later drained out of "the saint of rationalism," leaving him a somewhat dry and desiccated figure. He was, says Carlyle, "slender, rather tall and elegant . . . earnestly smiling eyes, modest, remarkably gifted with precision of utterance, enthusiastic yet lucid, calm."

Fox, settling an income on his wife, moved in 1834 into another house where he lived with Eliza Flower and two of his own children, joining forces with Sarah now married to William Adams. The third Fox child remained with his mother. Harriet Martineau and other friends were in no way placated by the protestations of innocence either of Eliza and Fox or of Mrs. Taylor and Mill. Unitarians and rationalists were at that date especially eager to show that intellectual emancipation did not mean a lower moral standard than that of Christians. Miss Martineau's anger indirectly affected Browning, for the sub-editor of Mill's periodical had met him at her house. So Mill refused later to review *Sordello*. But at this earlier date he set himself to read and review the anonymous *Pauline*.

Counted by years Mill was only six ahead of Browning, but in experience the gap would be hard to measure. Browning's father had made the learning of letters and all other beginnings within a child's scope a delightful game. But Mill, taught by a stern self-made father to read English at two, Greek at five, was next set to instruct his younger brothers and sisters. "I never was a boy," he told Caroline Fox,[5] "never played at cricket. It is better to let Nature have her own way." He was at twenty-six advanced in his profession, leader of a group of young radicals and a figure notable enough to have attracted strongly that searcher out of disciples, the prophet Carlyle. To him Mill confessed that, despite—or perhaps because of—his stern father's stern religion, he himself could not believe in God. Carlyle replied, "Patience, patience, time will do wonders for us." Patience Mill had, and although it never achieved this particuar end, it did make him do with immense thoroughness any job he undertook.

Pauline, commented Saintsbury many years later, owes much to Shelley, but is yet instinct with Browning's own genius. This Mill saw only in flashes; the copy annotated by him shows that he sought a second opinion: "The passages [he wrote] where the meaning is so imperfectly expressed as not to be easily understood will be marked 'X.'" Another hand is to be seen in the "beautiful" and "most beautiful" written here and there. But quite unmistakably in Mill's own hand are several acknowledgements of poetic power. After one regret over obscurity, he adds "the meaning if I can guess it right is really poetical." And again of the verses about the young witch: "curious idealization of self-worship, very fine though." Three descriptive pages won the commendation of being "finely painted and evidently from experience."

These were slight efforts toward the favorable review with which he had hoped to oblige Fox, and it may well be that he did his best. Browning used to speak later as though Mill's review would have changed the book's fate for the better. It did not appear, for *Pauline* had already been briefly dismissed by another reviewer as "a pure piece of bewilderment" under the heading "Other Books."

The density of thought, the multiplicity of imagery and description in the poem might have baffled even a sympathetic reviewer. The "living hedgerows," "the quick glancing serpent," "tall rushes and thick flag-knots," "the pale snake," the wild mice, the stream so noiseless till "it joins its parent-river with a shout"—one is in the woods with Browning or gazing at the clouds or sea. Nor is there absent the element which later reviewers in the full tide of Victorianism called sensuality. The trees bend over the water "as wild men watch a sleeping girl." Pauline's neck "looks like marble misted o'er / With love-breath." For, however abstract as a person, Pauline is as woman "so close by me, the roughest swell / Of wind in the tree-tops hides not the panting / Of thy soft breasts. . . ."

We do not know whether Browning actually saw the abortive review. He did see what Mill had half advised Fox not to show him—the annotated copy, beginning on the title page itself, "too much pretension in this motto"; "not I think an appropriate image"; "not even poetically dramatical"; "Query meaning?"; "more prose than poetry"; "explain better"; "self-flattery."

Browning leaves most of these comments untouched, but occasionally fights back vigorously.[6] On the lines: ". . . so much was light / Lent

back by others, yet much was my own," Mill objects to the recurrence of
" 'so,' according to the colloquial vulgarism in the sense of therefore or
accordingly, from which occasionally come great obscurity and ambiguity—as here."

"The *recurrence*," says Browning "of 'so' thus employed is as vulgar
as you please: but the usage itself of '*so* in the sense of accordingly' is
perfectly authorised—take an instance or two from Milton." And he
proceeds to take ten instances giving each reference from *Paradise Lost*.
Browning's tone in this to-and-fro is a thoroughly good-tempered one.
But Mill tends to righteous wrath, especially over the last lines of the
poem. Here the poet, from speaking to Pauline turns to Shelley, and
then to his readers, begging them to "love me and wish me well." Beneath this line is printed "Richmond October 22, 1832."

Mill writes, "This transition from speaking to Pauline to writing a
letter to the public with *place* and *date* is quite horrible."

The word Richmond is underlined in ink and marked with a cross.
Beneath it Browning writes "Kean was acting there: I saw him in
Richard III that night. . . . There is an allusion to Kean p 47. I don't
know whether I had not made up my mind to *act* as well as to make
verses, and music, and God knows what—que de Chateaux en Es-
pagne."

The lover, the musician, the painter, the actor, all experience
packed into one life—a first attempt at his undying ambition to pull the
infinite into the finite—all this was struggling in the young Browning.
And he saw himself triumphing over old age as he witnessed Kean triumphing, at a time when the world knew he was drinking himself to
death.

> I will be gifted with a wondrous mind,
> Yet sunk by error to men's sympathy,
> And in the wane of life, . . .
> And lo, I fling age, sorrow, sickness off,
> And rise triumphant, triumph through decay.

All this suggests to the irreverent James Thurber's *The Secret Life
of Walter Mitty*—or perhaps just a poet's enlargement of every boy's

dreams. Browning had in the poem passed on from himself as an instrument of God in the rescue of Andromeda ("By the dark rock, and the white wave just breaking / At her feet; quite naked and alone") to himself as the great actor he has just witnessed. We can almost see the boy that he was, walking home under the stars and seeing Robert Browning as the supreme interpreter of Shakespeare.

A year had passed and here was the first of his dreams—*the* real dream, for a poet he supremely meant to be—rudely shattered. A bale of sheets came from the publisher: *Pauline,* Browning says, did not sell a copy. But far worse was this annotated horror Fox had sent him. On the final page Mill wrote at length:

> With considerable poetic powers, the writer seems to me possessed with a more intense and morbid self-consciousness than I ever knew in any sane human being. I should think it a sincere confession, though of a most unlovable state, if the "Pauline" were not evidently a pure phantom . . . the psychological history of himself is powerful and truthful—*truth-like* certainly, all but the last stage. *That,* he evidently has not yet got into. The self-seeking and self-worshipping state is well described—beyond that, I should think the writer had made, as yet, only the next step, viz. into despising his own state. I even question whether part even of that self-disdain is not *assumed.* He is evidently *dissatisfied,* and feels part of the badness of his state; he does not write as if it were purged out of him. If he once could muster a hearty hatred of his selfishness it would *go;* as it is he feels only the *lack* of *good,* not the positive evil. He feels not remorse, but only disappointment; a mind in that state can only be regenerated by some new passion, and I know not what to wish for him but that he may meet with a *real* Pauline.
>
> Meanwhile he should not attempt to show how a person may be *recovered* from this morbid state—for *he* is hardly convalescent, and what should we speak of but that which we know?

This final condemnation is weakened by two blind spots in Mill himself: he did not understand the outpouring of a poet who cannot, like a philosopher or a scientist, weigh and measure each word; he did not understand the Christian who had seen once more his lode star "A need, a trust, a yearning after God." And who now is bewildered "that I could doubt/ Even his being—e'en the while I felt/ His presence . . ."

The poem shows a recognition of "All my sad weaknesses, this wavering will,/ This selfishness . . ."

Mill wrote his condemnation at the end of the book, but on the first page Browning added:

> The following Poem was written in pursuance of a foolish plan which occupied me mightily for a time, and which had for its object the enabling me to assume and realise I know not how many different characters:—meanwhile the world was never to guess that "Brown, Smith, Jones and Robinson" (as the spelling books have it) the respective authors of this poem, the other novel, such an opera, such a speech etc., etc., were no other than one and the same individual. The present abortion was the first work of the *Poet* of the batch, who would have been more legitimately *myself* than most of the others: but I surrounded him with all matter of (to my then notion) poetical accessories, and had planned quite a delightful life for him.
>
> Only this crab remains of the shapely Tree of Life in this Fool's paradise of mine.

This must surely have been written a little later, looking back dispassionately, not when the bale from the publishers and Mill's biting words struck simultaneously.

The blow was a doubly heavy one, for on the moral side his own conscience reinforced it. He *was* self-centered, self-conscious, selfish, already aware of what he could not later bear to recall, but also he had now revealed this ugly self of his to a world which must have appeared at that moment made up of John Stuart Mills. So *Pauline* became an abortion, to be destroyed, to be forgotten. And he seems to have convinced himself that as poetry too it was worthless. He found it almost impossible to show it to Elizabeth: "Will you and must you see it?" he asked plaintively. And he would not put it into collections of his work until menaced by the fear of a pirated edition—and even then it was heavily edited. Rossetti discovered it twenty years later, was convinced that only the author of *Paracelsus* could have written it, and copied it out by hand.

In 1896 a copy of *Pauline* was sold for $700, in 1929 another is said to have fetched $1,600. What would they command today?

4 Paracelsus

Measure your mind's height
by the shade it casts!

"PARACELSUS"

BROWNING had not, like the prodigal son, asked for the immediate gift of an inheritance that would later be his, for he never spent anything "living riotously." But he was supported at home while he worked at what he believed to be his vocation. Was he wrong? We can perhaps dismiss Mrs. Miller's special criticism of his three expensive journeys. One was made on a cargo boat, one in the Russian Consul General's carriage, and I think we may assume that the Consul paid all expenses for his "secretary" as Browning was termed. And surely a passage in the Love Letters refers to the third of these journeys—the second to Italy. Quoting Shelley on "those globes of deep red gold—/which in the woods the strawberry-tree doth bear," Browning tells Elizabeth that "when my Uncle walked into a sorb-tree . . . and I felt the fruit against my face, the little ragged bare-legged guide fairly laughed at my knowing them so well—'Niursi—sorbi!'" Browning, travelling with Uncle Reuben, was not likely to have been dipping deep into the parental exchequer.

Cyrus Mason's statement that the Browning parents had decided their son should be a poet and a poet only was probably based, in part at least, on the rejection of such jobs as would be normal for a youth of his social position at that date. Mr. Browning had refused an offer from the Bank of England which he himself had so longed to avoid. There can be little doubt that the Silverthorne uncle, father of Browning's favorite cousin, would have found a place for him in his brewery. But this would have meant no less drudgery, no better future prospects than the bank, and if Mason's view of the worldliness of the family is correct, they would certainly have aimed at something more socially acceptable.

Mrs. Orr tells us that Browning had considerable dramatic power and also that his father considered law as a possible career for him. And Cyrus Mason writes: "There were many serious discussions as to the propriety of 'young Robert' entering upon matters connected with the theatre." This may of course refer to a later date when he was writing plays, but to his mother if not to his father the acting profession would have been religiously anathema. The law had been chosen by Browning's two friends, Alfred Domett and Joseph Arnould, but their experience is so typical as to explain why, although attracted, the Brownings decided against it.

Domett had not long been called to the Bar before realizing the wearing delays during which a man's family must support a young barrister, and the slim chances of success without powerful connections. He decided for more rapid success and a wider life in New Zealand. His story may be read in *The Diary of Alfred Domett,* and in the *New Zealand Dictionary of Biography*—his mediation between the colonials and the British Government, his brief period as Prime Minister. One can only hope that Browning would have opposed his friend's deplorable support of the colonists in their grabbing of Maori land and their treatment of these highly developed people as savages. Domett combined this with writing romantic poetry about their legends and, after his return to England, Browning arranged for its publication.

Arnould's experience began later, for he was a Fellow of his College at Cambridge until he married. He was more successful than most young barristers, but only on private means could he keep a wife and family. For a long period he earned in fees only about £50 a year. His big success, too, came outside the home country, when he was invited to India and made Chief Justice of Bombay. Browning's future brother-in-law, George Barrett, would struggle (or saunter) on for years before he gave up the Bar for the farm.

It is fascinating to speculate on the effect Australia or New Zealand would have had on Browning had one of these countries instead of Italy become his "University"—whether his poetry would have gained or lost. The years saved of futile struggle to become a playwright might have been a gain, the grandeur of the physical scenes a revelation. But what of the world of men and women?

Browning himself was attracted by the diplomatic service, but had a boy in his social position the faintest chance of entering that stronghold of privilege? And if he had, could his parents possibly have paid out the large allowance often required for so long? Robert Lytton was *for eight years* an unpaid attaché at expensive embassies; and he, with immense social advantages, still felt that having been neither at Oxford or Cambridge was a crippling drawback.

But the effort was made and an ambiguous letter conveyed the impression that Browning had been accepted. In a letter to Sarah Flower (dated only Camberwell, Feb 4) he writes: "I don't go to Persia, and the Right Hon. Henry Ellis etc., etc. may go to a hotter climate for a perfect fool—(that at Bagdad in October, 127 Fahrenheit in the shade)."

This letter and another, dated "Wednesday mg" suggest high spirits despite repeated failures: ". . . on Saturday I waited on Murray, or rather Murray's son, and on presenting the kind puff of Mr. [illegible initial] I learnt that 'King Pandion he is dead: and all his peers wrapped up in lead', i.e., Lord Byron is 'no mo' and Poetry is 'no go.' Mr. Fox said much last Sunday of a Printing press at work just now in the S. Sea Isles. . . . Do you think Hokey-Pokey-Wankey-Fum would offer terms?"[1]

It was not so rare then for a man to be just a poet. There was Wordsworth, there was Tennyson, following Byron and Shelley.

Byron and Shelley were rich men by inheritance; Tennyson had his Cambridge friends to further his career. Browning's father told him that his sister, Sarianna, was taken care of and that there would be enough for him, but obviously enough would not be a feast. He was accepting, and his father for him, a narrow financial future, unless—

and probably both hoped for this with some confidence—his poetry had big sales. It seems likely that Reuben and the Silverthornes and Masons disapproved, that it was with aunts and uncles that the battles were fought to which he alludes in the Love Letters.

Mrs. Miller describes Browning's former schoolfellows working at their desks, his old friend Fox returning from a day at his office with the remark that now he felt like an honest man, and contrasts this with Browning's idleness. *"Pauline,"* she writes, "was published in March, 1833 . . . 'Beneath a flowering thicket lay Sordello.' " She adds the footnote "And there he still lay in May 1844, when *Sibrandus Schafna-burgensis* finds him reading in the garden, at ease 'under the arbute and the laurestine.' "

She quotes Browning telling Elizabeth that he was never obliged to do a given thing at a given time, but she does *not* quote Edmund Gosse, told by Browning that "freedom led to a super-abundance of production since on looking back he could see that he had often, in his unfettered leisure, been afraid to do nothing."

In success or failure, wrote Arnould to Domett, "the effect on him will be the same, viz to make him work, work, work."

Summing up the verse he actually published (to say nothing of what was written and destroyed) in the ten years which follow his twentieth birthday: *Pauline* 1,031 lines, *Paracelsus* 4,152, *Strafford* 2,200, *Sordello* 5,800, *Pippa Passes* 1,722, *King Victor and King Charles* 1,626, *The Return of the Druses* 1,780, *A Blot in the 'Scutcheon* 1,324.

Most important of all was the volume of *Dramatic Lyrics* with its sixteen poems, in which we find the first and one of the most perfect of Browning's dramatic monologues, "My Last Duchess."

All this was indeed to "work, work, work" and this creative effort of his whole being was made no easier by frequent crippling headaches. Conrad declared that he would far rather move heavy sacks all day long under a burning sun than write his novels. Chesterton claimed that a day's office work was nothing beside the exhaustion of original writing. Newman spoke of his writing as "getting rid of pain by pain."

The Russian Consul General, Chevalier George de Benkhausen, invited Browning in March, 1834, to go with him on a "special mission" to his own country. There were no trains in much of Europe and from Rotterdam they traveled night and day as fast as horses could take them through the Low Countries and eastern Prussia. At Tilsit Browning saw snowdrops in blossom, but Russia was icebound: "the huge inns with their double-windowed, stove-heated dining-rooms, festooned with ivy and other climbing plants, which grew as if in a hot-house," sheepskin-clad peasants, scattered villages wooden-gabled, the frozen Dwina, the hills and valleys of Livonia, the sandy soil and pinewoods of Esthonia— all ending in what was then St. Petersburg. Unfortunately Browning destroyed his letters home, but the memory remained with his sister "how strangely he was impressed . . . above all by the endless monotony of snow-covered pine forests, through which he and his companion rushed for days and nights at the speed of six post-horses, without seeming to move from one spot."

He saw the breakup of ice on the Neva, the long-booted, gaily shirted workmen held back by police with poleaxes as they pressed to watch the huge ice field split and crack and whirl away in broken fragments. And then the Tsar drank a goblet of water, the wooden bridges swung into place and the city feasted the coming of spring.

Russian music fascinated Browning and half a century later, meeting Prince Gagarin in Venice, he sang some of the airs he had picked up on this short visit, so that the Prince exclaimed in astonishment at such musical memory "better than my own, on which I have hitherto piqued myself not a little."[2]

Back home by the Rhine three months later. And now came the problem of deciding what was to be written next. Browning had formed another friendship with a young Frenchman, agent of the Bourbons, Count Amédée de Ripert-Monclar[3] who suggested Paracelsus for subject, and the Browning library contained several books about that strange and fascinating character. But the poet, a year earlier, in March, 1833, had begun working on *Sordello*, which he wrote and rewrote, spending seven years on it, longer than on any other poem except *The*

Ring and the Book. His Italian tutor, Cerutti, had written about Sordello and discussed his place in Dante's *Purgatorio,* and he also appeared in the ever-useful *Biographie Universelle.* De Vane has shown that Browning used in *Paracelsus* some of the ideas originally intended for *Sordello.* In both, his "stress lay on the incidents in the development of a soul: little else is worth study." This he said in the preface to *Sordello* and developed more fully when writing to Isa Blagden many years later in relation to Tennyson:

> We look at the object of art in poetry so differently! Here is an Idyll about a knight being untrue to his friend and yielding to the temptation of that friend's mistress after having engaged to assist him in his suit. I should judge the conflict in the knight's soul the proper subject to describe: Tennyson thinks he should describe the castle, and the effect of the moon on its towers, and anything *but* the soul.

Yet nobody saw better than Browning the interaction between the soul and the material creation which "wrought upon" it. Think for instance of the meeting between Karshish and Lazarus: [4]

> I crossed a ridge of short sharp broken hills
> Like an old lion's cheek teeth. Out there came
> A moon made like a face with certain spots
> Multiform, manifold and menacing:
> Then a wind rose behind me. So we met.

Browning told Julia Wedgwood [5] many years later that he wrote *Paracelsus* on recovery from a fever and sore throat. How much had intensity of creation caused the fever—with *Sordello* already slowly maturing, and the conception of *Paracelsus* to be so swiftly completed? Or perhaps Browning's fevered state actually contributed something. Later in another fever a long poem was born, of which *Artemis Prologuizes* is all that he wrote down. Again he felt impelled by fever to recite aloud the poetry of Donne. And once in a dream he rewrote a play of Shakespeare. An acquaintance tells of meeting the Brownings on their first return to England; the poet "in very lively mood" had entertained them "with quotations from a dream the previous night, in which he had rewritten *Richard the Third*. The tent scene, in particular, was one of the maddest mixtures of Shakespearean poetry and modern slang that could be imagined."

Browning always spoke of the soul as a force behind and directing the mind—conceiving the mind as that which goes step by reasoned step. Whether we speak of soul and mind or mind and brain, the one thing certain is that we know but little of their possibilities in our hours of unconsciousness—sleep, fever, or even mental aberration. "The night brings counsel" applies not only to a night spent in watching, but also to emergence from profoundest slumber. Browning was fascinated by Christopher Smart's *Song of David,* the only great poem he believed Smart ever wrote—with a door key on the walls of his asylum.

Another element in Browning's best work is easier to state. Indeed he has stated it himself. He is struggling with the limitations of ordinary human language. The poet is the seer on whom is laid the burden of becoming the sayer—he is indeed entrusted with a message. George Duckworth sees Browning as suffering whenever he approached the "white light" of complete expression, which, in a letter to Elizabeth Barrett, he contrasts with the "prismatic hues" into which he commonly broke it.[6] In his first three long poems we can surely see the struggle, and mind and body both suffered in their interaction.

In form *Paracelsus* lies between the confessional of *Pauline* and the theatrical on which Browning wasted so many years. It is the closest of his early works to the dramatic monologues of his best period. We see him feeling after this form in his Introduction to the first edition of *Paracelsus,* strangely enough subsequently withdrawn:

> I have endeavoured to write a poem not a drama: the canons of the drama are well known, and I cannot but think that, inasmuch as they have immediate regard to stage representation, the peculiar advantages they hold out are really such only so long as the purpose for which they were first instituted is kept in view. I do not very well understand what is called a Dramatic Poem, wherein all those

restrictions, only submitted to on account of compensating good in the original scheme are scrupulously retained, as though for some special fitness in themselves—and all new facilities placed at an author's disposal by the vehicle he selects, as pertinaciously rejected. It is certain, however, that a work like mine depends more immediately on the intelligence and sympathy of the reader for its success: indeed were my scenes stars, it must be his co-operating fancy which, supplying all chasms, should connect the scattered lights into one constellation—a Lyre or a Crown.

Paracelsus was the name chosen—to indicate his superiority to Celsus—by Philippus Bombastus, "a remarkable physician, who has removed with miraculous art those dire diseases, leprosy, gout, dropsy and other incurable and contagious diseases of the body, and ordered his property to be sold and distributed to the poor." So said his epitaph. He discovered laudanum and other drugs and also, a century ahead of Harvey, the circulation of the blood. He was reputed to have the secret of transmuting metals and he certainly in his youth practiced astrology and various kinds of magic. Wandering from country to country, he visited England—and, said his enemies, stole the secrets of one Roger Bacon! Despite marvelous cures and immense generosity to the poor, his arrogance and bad temper made enemies for him on a vast scale.

"You shall follow me," he proclaimed, "you Avicenna, Galen, Rhasis, Montagnana, Mesues, you gentlemen of Paris, Montpellier, Germany, Cologne, Vienna, and whomsoever the Rhine and Danube nourish; you who inhabit the isles of the sea; you likewise, Dalmatians, Athenians; thou Arab, thou Greek, thou Jew: all shall follow me, and the monarchy shall be mine."

There is in Browning himself at this point something of Paracelsus, and of Cyrano de Bergerac. But underneath the panache a struggle is engaged; conviction of his own powers is having a hard job in overcoming insecurity. Still vividly remembered is the Mill attack on *Pauline*. On April 16, 1838, writing to Fox, who had given him an introduction to two publishers, Browning describes the "dolorous" accent of the first when mentioning poetry, the "better hope" with the second, yet he is "not over sanguine."

Scared at the thought of a fresh eye

> . . . discovering blemishes of all sorts . . . obscure passages, slipshod verses, and much that worse is,—yet on the whole I am not much afraid of the issue, and I would give something to be allowed to read it some morning to you—for every rap o' the knuckles I should get a clap o' the back, I know.

This time there is to be no anonymity:

> I really shall *need* your notice, on this account; I shall affix my name and stick my arms akimbo; there are a few precious bold bits here and there, and the drift and the scope are awfully radical—I am "off" for ever with the other side, but must by all means be "on" with yours—a position once gained, worthier works shall follow— therefore a certain writer [evidently Mill] . . . must be benignant or supercilious as he shall choose, but in no case an idle spectator . . .
> Excuse all this swagger, I know you will.[7]

The typical Renaissance passion for universal knowledge and some facts of his career are used by Browning in *Paracelsus*. But the character is chiefly his own conception—largely perhaps of himself. Aprile, the poet conjectured to be drawn from Shelley, is his creation. So are Festus and Michal, a husband and wife who love Paracelsus but fear the results of his arrogance and self-confidence as he leaves them for the wider world he is determined to conquer. It is through knowledge that this conquest is to be achieved, and in his ambition Paracelsus is typical of the high Renaissance in Europe. But he has forgotten that men must love as well as know until he meets Aprile, who talks of love in im- passioned fashion until finally Paracelsus cries out:

> . . . We must never part.
> Are we not halves of one dissevered world,
> Whom this strange chance unites once more?
> Part? Never!

> Till thou, the lover, know; and I, the knower,
> Love—until both are saved. . . .

But part they must for Aprile is dying, and Paracelsus cries:

> Thy spirit, at least, Aprile! Let me love! . . .

> I have attained and now I may depart.

Attainment was not so easy and the next scene is again entitled "Paracelsus Aspires." Five years have passed and Festus, himself on his way to Wittenburg to see Luther, finds Paracelsus a professor at Basle. He pictures him breaking the shackles of an outworn science, Luther renewing religion. But Paracelsus ends the conversation by rejecting his friend's homage. He has had successes, wrought some startling cures, made some minor discoveries. But he has not succeeded in the vast aims of his youth; he is worn out before his time. For a while, he tells Festus, he had tried like Aprile to live for love alone; but found

> My nature cannot lose her first imprint;
> I still must hoard and heap and class all truths
> With one ulterior purpose: I must know!

He has sunk from a state in which the body "used to care / For its bright master's cares and quite subdue / Its proper cravings . . ." into one where the body is chiefly concerned with delights of its own. (Historically Paracelsus had become a heavy drinker, often spent the night in some tavern, and went to bed in his clothes.) Festus speaks to him of God's will, but he has not found that so easy to discover. His mood is one of misery though not quite despair: "Utter damnation is reserved for hell!" But when Festus reminds him "That there is yet another world to mend / All error and mischance . . ." it is the old Paracelsus who bursts out—the Paracelsus of the Renaissance at its best, before faith in God was lost, when a certain fresh wind of belief in this life was blowing strong:

> Another world!
> And why this world, this common world, to be
> A make-shift, a mere foil, how fair soever,
> To some fine life to come? Man must be fed

With angels' food, forsooth; and some few traces
Of a diviner nature which look out
Through his corporeal baseness, warrant him
In a supreme contempt of all provision
For his inferior tastes—some straggling marks
Which constitute his essence, just as truly
As here and there a gem would constitute
The rock, their barren bed, one diamond.
But were it so—were man all mind—he gains
A station little enviable. From God,
Down to the lowest spirit ministrant,
Intelligence exists which casts our mind
Into immeasurable shade. No, no:
Love, hope, fear, faith—these make humanity;
These are its sign and note and character,
And these I have lost! . . .

Yet Paracelsus will aspire again.

The next scene shows him, dubbed charlatan and deceiver, cast out
from his post at Basle, meeting Festus with an air of conviction that he
will build upon the ruins. But for this close friend the "horrible despondency" of their last meeting was less alarming than to ". . . hear these
incoherent words and see / This flushed cheek and intensely-sparkling
eye."

Half crazed in this fourth scene, Paracelsus is dying in the sixth. In
his delirium he speaks to the dead Aprile, to Festus, and supremely to
God:

Thou art good,
And I should be content. Yet—yet first show
I have done wrong in daring! Rather give
The supernatural consciousness of strength
which fed my youth! . . .
Lost, lost! Thus things are ordered here!
    God's creatures,
And yet he takes no pride in us!—None, none!
Truly there needs another life to come!
If this be all— . . .

> How very full
> Of wormwood 'tis, that just at altar service,
> The rapt hymn rising with the rolling smoke,
> When glory dawns and all is at the best,
> The sacred fire may flicker and glow faint
> And die for want of a wood-piler's help!

He gathers together the forces of this failing body which has of old heaped its wood on the soul's sacred flame, asks for his gown, the chain for his neck, his sword Azoth, and stands for the last time as though to deliver a lecture. His death cell becomes: "A shrine, for here God speaks to men through me."

A treasure of the Berg collection is a copy of the first edition of *Paracelsus,* corrected and altered by Browning at Pisa just after his marriage. Many lines are added, many greatly altered, and a few passages are cut out altogether. One change is fascinating. As we now have the poem, Aprile says, "God is the perfect poet / Who in his person acts his own creations." In the original version the second line reads "Who in creation acts his own conceptions." It is followed by six lines which Browning chose to delete:

> Shall man refuse to be aught less than God?
> Man's weakness is his glory—for the strength
> Which raises him to heaven and near God's self.
> Came spite of it—God's strength his glory is,
> For thence came with our weakness sympathy
> Which brought God down to earth a man like us.

These lines show already present in Browning's thinking the idea of the Incarnation, imaginatively seen in *Pauline,* later to become a key theme. Why did he decide to withdraw them from the second edition of *Paracelsus,* leaving only a hierarchy of being which culminates in a prophet through whom God speaks to man? Ten years later we find a similar hesitation: the version of "Saul" he published in 1845 consisted of the first nine stanzas only. David's vision of Christ was not included. We must wait for *Christmas Eve and Easter Day* (1850) and *Men and Women* (1855), with "Saul," now completed, for Browning's utterance of the faith, written into and then withdrawn from *Paracelsus*, that God became man. Yet even with the omission the poem is incarnational:

> So glorious is our nature, so august
> Man's inborn uninstructed impulses,
> His naked spirit so majestical! . . .
>   savage creatures seek
> Their loves in wood and plain—and God renews
> His ancient rapture. Thus he dwells in all,
> From life's minute beginnings, up at last
> To man—the consummation of this scheme
> Of being, the completion of this sphere
> Of life . . .

A passage deals with the assembling in man of all the scattered elements, hints and fragments in creation, meant by God

> To be united in some wondrous whole, . . .
> But the new glory mixes with the heaven
> And earth; man, once descried, imprints for ever
> His presence on all lifeless things: the winds
> Are henceforth voices, . . .
> The herded pines commune and have deep thoughts,
> A secret they assemble to discuss
> When the sun drops behind their trunks which glare
> Like grates of hell: the peerless cup afloat
> Of the lake-lily is an urn, some nymph
> Swims bearing high above her head: no bird
> Whistles unseen . . .

Not by Browning, certainly, but one cannot at all imagine the historical Paracelsus walking godlike through creation, seeing it all as good because beautiful, because strange; seeing "enterprise" in the moon or a shape in the forest "with small puckered mouth and mocking eyes." This is not Paracelsus but Browning. Paracelsus would have been looking for material for his cures, or trying to turn rocks into gold. Ambitious for himself and for his fellows, he saw God

> ... glorified in man,
> And to man's glory vowed I soul and limb.
> Yet constituted thus, and thus endowed,
> I failed: I gazed on power till I grew blind.

In this blindness even the love which he had been slowly learning
was ill directed. He

> ... saw no good in man,
> To overbalance all the wear and waste
> Of faculties, displayed in vain, but born
> To prosper in some better sphere: and why?
> In my own heart love had not been made wise
> To trace love's faint beginnings in mankind,
> To know even hate is but a mask of love's,
> To see a good in evil, and a hope
> In ill-success; to sympathize, be proud
> Of their half-reasons, faint aspirings, dim
> Struggles for truth ...
> Their error upward tending all though weak,
> Like plants in mines which never saw the sun,
> But dream of him, and guess where he may be,
> And do their best to climb and get to him.
> All this I knew not, and I failed. ...
> Meanwhile, I have done well, though not all well.
> As yet men cannot do without contempt;
> 'Tis for their good, and therefore fit awhile
> That they reject the weak, and scorn the false,
> Rather than praise the strong and true, in me:
> But after, they will know me. If I stoop
> Into a dark tremendous sea of cloud,
> It is but for a time; I press God's lamp
> Close to my breast; its splendour, soon or late,
> Will pierce the gloom, I shall emerge one day.

Paracelsus like *Pauline* was a financial failure, but contrary to all
that Browning said in his later life, it was in every other respect a remarkable success. The earliest notices were somewhat feeble; but none
of them justifies his statement that until the appearance of Forster's

article in the *Examiner,* the poem was laughed at and denounced. As it appeared in mid-August and Forster's review on September 6, there would have been little time for any devastating effect from earlier notices. The *Spectator,* the *Atlas* and the *Athenaeum* had been hurried and cautious. The words "dreamy" and "obscure" were used and the *Metropolitan Magazine* had called it "a poem ambitiously unpopular." But there was nothing worse.

Forster wrote three columns full of copious quotation and praise: "It is some time since we have read a work of more unequivocal power. . . . We conclude that its author is a young man . . . we may safely predict for him a brilliant career." In a later long article in *The New Monthly Magazine* he spoke yet more strongly: "Without the slightest hesitation we name Mr. Robert Browning at once with Shelley, Coleridge, Wordsworth."

As Dr. Lounsbury points out, the praise grew stronger as time went on—for time was needed that all the greatness of the poem could sink into the reader's mind, all the ideas in it be assimilated. Of all the reviewers only Fox was a friend of the still so youthful poet.

No one reading contemporary biography can doubt that this acclaim in the periodicals expressed and increased a real wave of enthusiasm in the intellectual world. Browning at twenty-three had arrived. Even those who had not read *Paracelsus* realized that they ought to, while those who had were looking forward with eagerness to its successor. But few except intellectuals care to buy books, nor have most intellectuals got money to buy them with. A system of borrowing from libraries and among friends did not go far toward paying the expenses of publication, and Browning's father was out of pocket again.

The chief immediate effects of *Paracelsus* were to make Browning a desired guest in many houses and to start him on his career as a playwright. And, whatever he may have said later, he realized enough of what the poem had done for him to put under his name on future works "By the author of *Paracelsus.*"

5 Browning and Macready

> *The medium of poetry is* WORDS, *the medium of
> drama is people moving about on a stage and using
> words.*
>
> EZRA POUND

HIS INTRODUCTION to William Macready is one of the milestones in Browning's life. The friendship led to others and also distracted him into the writing of a series of plays neither good nor successful. The inevitable quarrel with which their relations ended drove him back into poetry, but perhaps the plays prepared him for the dramatic monologue—a form which was to become distinctively his.

Macready kept a diary, written with rare frankness about himself—and (less uncommonly) about others: "My greatest enemy" he wrote "—*the stumbling block of my life*—has been *passion,* and its consequent evil, *precipitation.*" His pages are full of "this St. Vitus's dance of the mind," but also of bitter repentance, prayerful resolve, despairing self-pity: "I could curse the fate that threw me into a sphere of life with violent passions, where these passions are so *cruelly* acted on."

Macready was educated at Rugby till the age of sixteen, when the failure of his father as manager of a provincial theater threw him into a debtors' prison, and young William had to take charge of the theater and company until his release. With prospects of the university and a legal career thus destroyed, Macready appeared at Birmingham in the character of Romeo, announced only as "A young gentleman, being his first appearance on any stage." So great was his success that henceforward, under his own name, he played the leading parts in town after town for six years. He then got an engagement at Covent Garden and was, at twenty-three, recognized as "an actor of the first rank."

Convinced that he "must strain every nerve of thought or triumph is hopeless," he would study each character, trying to get the key to Macbeth, Othello, Lear, yet "*I cannot reach in execution the standard of my own conception.*"

He tells of "rising thoughts over the madness of King Lear . . . that possession of my mind which is necessary to success"; and when acting the part he wept—"Tears . . . not those of a woman or a driveller, they really stained a 'man's cheeks.' "

The performance of a character was, Macready said, his "day"; he could do nothing else. Four different plays might be acted in a week, and he had to insist on a rehearsal when the management suddenly changed the play. He firmly refused to act, at royal command, the part of Joseph Surface, being, he said, "out of the character." "The King [William IV] cares for neither the play, nor the actors, nor their act and I see no reason why I should inconvenience myself for him." For Queen Victoria he acted often, though grumbling when she (aged after all only eighteen!) chose the Pantomime or *Rob Roy* in preference to Shakespeare.

Despite hours of immense triumph ("when wearied of shouting they turned the applause to a stamping of feet, which sounded like thunder; it was grand and awful"), Macready was never reconciled to his profession. An actor stood low in the fashionable world; he could not for instance attend a levee at Court. ("My pariah profession brings lavish expression of public praise but excludes from distinctions which all my compeers enjoy.") When letters came addressed "Mr." instead of "Esq.," he returned them or put them unread into the fire. He often suspected insult ("He advanced with one finger; I met him with one finger"). He got himself a coat of arms. Above all he rendered himself desperately unpopular with his fellow players by dissociating himself from them; despising the profession to which both he and they belonged, he acted as from an imagined height above them. However absurd this was socially, it was often warranted by bad acting which affected him acutely and sometimes ruined his own effects. "My experience of the professors of my art confirms me in my opinion of their vileness, their utter unworthiness." "I wish they were all tied in a sack together! they worry my heart out." Actors were "ignorant and conceited vermin."

So it would seem were most of the human race. An Irish audience made "blackguard noises"; indeed the "Dublin ruffians" were the worst specimens of human nature. The *Times* was a "base and profligate paper," its newsmen "dirty scribblers."

"Did the fiendish host whose name was legion . . . survive their leap and transmigrate through the bodies of certain reviewers?" Scott's son-in-law, J. W. Lockhart, one of these—a "hireling defamer," "a malignant trader in circumstances pointed to stab and draw by slow droppings the life-blood of a man's heart—is of the base the basest."

Macready was a proclaimed republican. Enthusiasm for the Queen was "the worship which the base wretches of this world are transferring from their God to a girl of eighteen whom they choose to call a Queen." "The self-praised aristocracy of England" are "gold-besotted, prurient, frivolous, and heartless wretches! The cellars and garrets of Manchester, and the dens and pig-holes of Ireland are echoing the moans of agony, as the boxes of these *things* at the opera-house are shaking with their applause of—what?" "What" was the opera, for which he had a supreme disdain; but he did not dislike the presence and applause of aristocrats at his own performances.

Despite his vanity and snobbery, Macready emerges from the diaries as an attractive personality. He was utterly devoted to his wife and children, and his chief concern in gaining success was to gain with it enough money to secure their future. When, with the awful inevitableness of that "scientific" age, first one daughter and then another died young, when his eldest son was stricken with an obscure disease, his grief is touching, and his total devotion to each small sufferer: ". . . went up to look at my dear dead child . . . I could only see visions of the little bright-eyed creature, entering from her walks, sitting at the table, laughing in her wild way on the stairs. . . . My boy once a wonder of beauty and intelligence will soon be laid by the side of his sweet sister."

No one knew better than he how false were certain of his habitual assumptions: "As I sat at dinner . . . the servant in livery attending on me . . . I thought how difficult it must be, and it is, for men to draw back their *naked selves*—their ideas of man, as God made him—from the disguise of pomp and circumstance with which they have invested him. Oh God . . . teach me the duties of charity, of kind consideration, of compassionate allowance."

Macready noted in his diary on September 6, 1835, that he had been reading extracts from *Paracelsus*—"of great merit." Lady Pollock relates how, learning she had not read the poem, he exclaimed, "Oh good God" —and adjured her to "hand over the babies to the nurse, and read *Paracelsus."*

Two months later he was still reading "beautiful and touching extracts" and was "very much pleased" to meet Browning at William Fox's house. "His face is full of intelligence, my time passed most agreeably. . . . I took Mr. Browning on, and requested to be allowed to improve my acquaintance with him. He expressed himself warmly . . . wished to send me his book."

And on December 7: "Read *Paracelsus,* a work of great daring, starred with poetry of thought, feeling and diction, but occasionally obscure; the writer can scarcely fail to be a leading spirit of his time." Finishing the poem on the following day, Macready felt again the fault of obscurity but also "the profoundest and the grandest thoughts and most musically uttered. The writer is one, I think, destined for great things."

On a first visit to Macready's home at Elstree, Browning was "very popular with the whole party; his simple and enthusiastic manner engaged attention and won opinions from all present; he looks and speaks more like a youthful poet than any man I ever saw." It was New Year's Eve and "we poured out a libation as a farewell to the Old Year and a welcome to the New."

Forster was present, the future biographer of Dickens, who had, with both Browning and Macready, a lifelong friendship broken by many quarrels but always mended again. "Browning," Macready remarked, "is his present *all-in-all."*

The poet was as enthusiastic over Macready's acting as the actor was over Browning's poetry; he came often into his room after the play and "seemed much delighted." On February 15, "Forster walked to chambers and took tea with me, reading to me passages from a poem by Browning"; and on the next day they both called and began to talk over the plot of a tragedy that Browning might write. "He said that I had bit him by my performance of Othello, and I told him I hoped I should make the blood come."

Browning was more and more winning a place in Macready's affections. Despite his "enthusiastic" manner, the actor felt his presence to be more soothing than that of Forster and other friends. "My nerves and spirit," one entry runs, "were quite quelled by them all, and I rejoiced at seeing them leave me—except Browning, whose gentle manners always make his presence acceptable." And of "a note from Browning" after his acting of Ion he writes: "It was a tribute which remunerated me from the annoyances and cares of years: it was one of the very highest, may I not say the highest, honours I have through life received."

Ion, famous in its day but now forgotten, was the work of Serjeant Talfourd, at whose house a supper party was held to celebrate the success of the play. The actor proposed the health of the dramatist, who ended his speech of thanks by returning the compliment "with much of eulogy . . . it became then, a succession of personal toasts. . . . I was very happily placed between Wordsworth and Landor with Browning opposite."

Both Mrs. Orr and Dr. Hall Griffin relate how at this supper Wordsworth joined in drinking a toast proposed by Talfourd to the "Poets of England"—and associated by him with the author of *Paracelsus*. Wordsworth, Griffin adds, "leaned across the table and remarked 'I am proud to drink to your health, Mr. Browning.' "

No authority is given for this story, which had gone unquestioned until Mrs. Miller's entertaining reconstruction (in the *Twentieth Century*, 1953, CLIV, p. 53) of "This Happy Evening." Crabbe Robinson's diary, which she quotes, shows that he and Wordsworth left the party together before Macready's reply to the toast of himself—and could not therefore have been present for this later one. (Henry Crabbe Robinson traveled all over Europe with Wordsworth and was one of his closest friends. He left thirty-five volumes of diary besides notebooks innumerable.)

Mrs. Miller's account of both play and supper suggests that the event was for most of the participants very far from the "Happy Evening" proclaimed by Macready.

Miss Mitford was there and Macready spoke to her, "observing in badinage that the present occasion should stimulate her to write a play; she quickly said, 'Will you act in it?' I was silent." Another guest, felt by Macready to have inflicted on him "a deep and assassin-like wound," in *Blackwood's Magazine* said, "Aye, hold him to that"; whereat, says Macready, "I could not repress the expression of indignant contempt which found its way to my face." And as they left the house, he said to Browning, "Write a play, Browning, and keep me from going to America."

Was it this incident that awakened in Miss Mitford the implacable dislike of Browning displayed in her letters? Whether she overheard the remark or not, she was probably exasperated by the atmosphere of mutual admiration which surrounded—and excluded—her; Macready for Talfourd and Browning, Browning for Talfourd and Macready, Talfourd for them both, and Forster and Fox for all three of them. There were, too, Macready's wife and sister, and their neighbor, Euphrasia Fanny Haworth, who drove home with the Macreadys, "talking of nothing but the evening's events—this happy evening. We reached home about two and went to bed with the birds singing their morning song in our tired ears. Thank God."

This entry was made on May 30. On the twenty-eighth, Browning had written of "The admiration I have for your genius . . . you comprehend me as you comprehend Macbeth or Ion,— . . . I will give my whole heart and soul to the writing a Tragedy . . . should I be unequal to the task, the excitement and extreme effort will have been their own reward:—should I succeed, my way of life will be very certain, and my name pronounced along with yours."

At Elstree, Browning made friends with the Macready family and their friends. "The Pied Piper of Hamelin" was written for and inscribed to "W. M. the younger"—and this meant Willie Macready.

Browning wrote it for the boy to illustrate during an illness—and followed it by "The Cardinal and the Dog."

But at this moment, for Macready and Browning alike, the question was all-absorbing: What should the poet write to fit the actor's creative powers? Browning chose Strafford, Lord Deputy in Ireland under Charles I; he was beheaded by the king's enemies, the king signing the bill of attainder.

When the play arrived—not absolutely completed but the missing parts sketched in—Macready wrote: "I was greatly pleased with it . . . Browning called in some anxiety . . . was very much pleased, agreeing in my objections and promising to do everything needful." This was on November 20, and two days later "Forster called with Browning's M.S." November 23: "Began *very attentively* to read over the tragedy of Strafford, in which I find more ground for objection than I had anticipated. I had been too much carried away by the truth of character to observe the meanness of plot, and occasional obscurity." A little later Browning brought in the missing scenes, but Macready felt it "still is not up to the high-water mark."

Anyone who has been a publisher's reader will sympathize with Macready's changes of mood, and it must be even harder to picture the effect of a play that is to be acted than of a book that is to be read. And, too, how widely opinions differ. William Rossetti in 1886 witnessed a "mediocre" performance of *Strafford,* found "not a dull minute," found his "eyes dim from unshed tears," saw in Pym a "marble passion of patriotism," thought the play would become "a fine established stage piece."[1]

In between readings, Macready was acting an inferior play, after which one evening "Browning, with all his kind heart, called and sat a few minutes."

Macready was reading other manuscripts of marked inferiority: "utter trash . . . I cannot longer afford the time. Read some scenes in *Strafford,* which restore one to the world of sense and feeling once again." Yet on the following day his doubts are back. "I am by no means sanguine, I lament to say, on its success."

They put off the play for a while and Browning worked on it, bringing it back on March 29. "He looked very unwell, jaded and thought-sick."

These had been trying months for them both, but the owner of the theater, Mr. Osbaldiston, shown the play, "caught at it with avidity," made Browning a good offer in terms of the times—and made him "very happy." Forster, the indefatigable, was determined to persuade Longmans to publish it, Browning intended to dedicate it to Macready, which he did "with all affectionate admiration."

But the rehearsals went ill: ". . . it dragged its slow length along . . . *I fear it will not do.*" At one point Forster became enraged and the other two sympathetically agreed as to what a difficult temper he had (a matter in which both, but especially Macready, might claim to judge). "There was a *scene*," writes Macready—but he feels that Browning behaved well. He "assented to all the proposed alterations." But then he failed utterly to carry them out: "It was too bad to trifle in this way." After another attempt, however, Browning told his friend that he "had been oppressed and incapable of carrying his intentions into action. He *wished to withdraw it.*"

With cruel kindness Macready "counseled him against any precipitate step—warned him of the consequences and called Fox into counsel." "It was fixed to be done. Heaven speed us all."

It was Macready's first and immense mistake and within a week he was repenting it—wanting Helen Faucit, who thought her part too poor, to refuse to act; longing for "a *fair* occasion to withdraw it"; expecting "it will be damned—grievously hissed at the end"—and yet most strangely feeling that friendship obliged him to go forward to disaster. So the play went on, not running into the total disaster he had predicted, but certainly no success. Macready's and Miss Faucit's excellent acting saved it despite itself and an otherwise miserable cast. On the opening day, May 1, 1837, Longmans did publish it—the first of Browning's works to be brought out at the publisher's expense.

All this *Paracelsus* had won for him; but Browning, who was modest about his great poetry, tended to overrate all his bad plays. He was, Macready says, enraged with Forster for a review which was as favorable as his friend could honestly make it. There were five performances only and everyone seems to have emerged with frayed temper.² We begin to hear less of the soothing effect on Macready of Browning's presence. He had, said the actor, a "sickly and fretful over-estimate of his work," but the experience did not carry its true lesson to either man. Browning went on writing plays; Macready went on reading them—and eventually he produced another.

Obviously, Browning later doubted the value of *Strafford,* for he omitted it from his collected works; it has been suggested that this was because Elizabeth did not care for it; it was finally restored.

The Browning-Macready friendship still flourished. It is hardly likely that every meeting was recorded, but in January, 1838, Browning dined at Elstree and "we spent a cheerful afternoon"; in August he was in Macready's room—with Dickens, Forster and Horne—and a few weeks later was again dining. In December he was invited to listen to the reading of a play. On Christmas Eve, Browning, Forster, and Dickens arrived, rather to Macready's dismay, to watch a rehearsal of the Pantomime.

On August 24, 1839, Browning called. "His object, if he exactly knew it, was to learn from me whether, if he wrote a really good play, it would have a secure chance of acceptance. I told him certainly." On September 5, however: "Read Browning's play on Victor, King of Sardinia—it turned out to be a *great mistake.* I called Browning into my room and most explicitly told him so." But to a Macready depressed about his own acting, Browning still brought comfort. He "came into my room and said all that sympathy and friendly feeling could suggest."

No less than Browning had the actor-manager confidently expected a huge success for the promised "more popular" successor to *Paracelsus.* It would redeem the failure of *Strafford* and prepare a public for his next act-worthy play. But soon, trying desperately to read *Sordello,* Macready sadly concluded: "it is *not* readable." And when offered another play on July 31, he wrote: "Reading Browning's play, and with the deepest concern I yield to the belief that he will *never write again* —to any purpose. I fear his intellect is not quite clear. I do not know how to write to Browning."

Browning saved him a letter by calling: ". . . he talked of his play and *Sordello,* and I most honestly told him my opinion . . . most anxious as I am, that he should justify the expectations formed of him, . . . he could not do so by placing himself in opposition to the world."

Yet Macready did not merely consent to read again what he called a "mystical strange and heavy play," but actually *argued* Browning into leaving it with him. An entry on August 27 runs: "Browning came before I had finished my bath, and really *wearied* me . . . with his self-opinionated persuasions upon his *Return of the Druses.* I fear he is forever gone . . ." Yet "Browning accompanied me to the theatre, *at last consenting* [italics mine] to leave the MS with me for a second perusal."

Browning could never have been sure of avoiding Macready's bath hour, for the actor often got up late and bathed at all hours; sometimes after an afternoon walk. But extraordinarily wearing for an author was the fact that Macready could never make a firm decision. One would think that by now both men would have had enough. But no. *The Druses* had returned in September, and *A Blot in the 'Scutcheon* must have reached Macready before the end of the year, with the optimistic observation from Browning: " 'The luck of he third adventure' is proverbial. I have written a spick-and-span new Tragedy (a sort of compromise between my own notion and yours—as I understand it at least). . . . There is *action* in it, drabbing, stabbing, et autres gentillesses—who knows but the Gods may make me good even yet?"

The next mention of *A Blot* is on September 29, 1841, when Macready writes: "Forster *importuned me* after dinner to read Browning's tragedy, which I did." But the decision so vital for Browning was to be delayed more than a full year longer. Forster as well as Macready felt uncertain, and it was decided to call on Dickens for an opinion, which he supplied only in November, 1842.

Though Browning was getting impatient, his letter in April, '42, was a moderate one. He had begun the series of *Bells and Pomegranates,* had postponed publishing his play in this series, but now "I have nothing by me at all fit to be substituted for the work in your hands."

Still he had to wait. Macready had, at the end of 1841, moved from Covent Garden to Drury Lane. Lounsbury has shown that Browning's memory later confused two seasons. But Macready's folly seems to have lain in not mentioning Dickens, who still held the manuscript, and a letter of October 13 shows the unhappy author denied admission by Macready's dresser when he sent up his card after a performance. He writes with restraint and dignity, assuming a mistake, but it was on the actor's part clearly a stalling for time, which ended with a letter from Dickens:

> Browning's play has thrown me into a perfect passion of sorrow. ... It is full of genius, natural and great thoughts, profound and yet simple and beautiful in its vigour. ... Mildred's recurrence to that 'I was so young—I had no mother.' I know no love like it, no passion like it, no moulding of a splendid thing after its conception, like it. And I swear it is a tragedy that MUST be played: and must be played, moreover, by Macready. ... And if you tell Browning that I have seen it, tell him that I believe from my soul there is no man living (and not many dead) who could produce such a work.

The mind staggers on reading such a judgment after reading the play, which takes us back a century or so behind Dickens' own date, perhaps to make the feudal atmosphere a trifle more plausible. A landowner, Lord Mertoun, calls on another, Lord Tresham, to ask for his very young sister's hand in marriage. Tresham delightedly agrees. But then he hears from a faithful and ancient retainer that a stranger, wrapped in a concealing cloak, is entering at night his sister's bedroom. He confronts the intruder (cloaked as before) attacks and stabs him— and then discovers he is Mildred's acknowledged suitor, Mertoun. Mertoun dies and Mildred promptly dies also (of grief), in her brother's arms. But Tresham has already taken poison, so three corpses lie upon the scene, and no amount of Greek Chorus work from another character, or suggestions of a derivation from *Romeo and Juliet,* can reconcile one to such a tissue of absurdities.

The play went on—marked from the first for disaster, chiefly because of its own intrinsic demerits, but also because Macready had taken it without really believing in it. Badly read to the cast by the prompter, it awakened laughter instead of tears. (And although Macready cut out at least one repetition of the lament Dickens found so moving, we are reminded of Oscar Wilde: "A man would need a heart of stone to read of the death of little Nell without bursting into laughter.") Macready refused to act and gave the part to Phelps. Phelps got ill, Macready learned the part and decided at the last minute to play it. But Phelps recovered and told Macready he would play if he " 'died for it' so that my time had been lost." Going down to the theater to give writer and actor the benefit of his study especially one idea which "I thought particularly valuable . . . Browning . . . in the worst taste, manner and spirit . . . expressed himself perfectly satisfied with the manner in which Mr. Phelps executed Lord Tresham. I had no more to say. I could only think Mr. Browning a very disagreeable and offensively mannered person. Voilà tout!"

Thus far Macready—but did he in fact, as Arnould wrote to Domett, even at this eleventh hour "hint" that he would himself act the part? Arnould writes vividly:

> Macready then again appears, hints that he has studied the character, will act the first night. Upon this our Robert does not fall prone at his feet and worship him for his condescending goodness— not that at all does our Robert do, but quite other than that—with laconic brevity he positively declines taking the part from Phelps, dispenses with Macready's aid &c., and all this in face of a whole green-room. You imagine the fury and whirlwind of our managerial wrath—silent fury, a compressed whirlwind, volcano fires burning white in our pent heart. We say nothing, of course, but we do our spiteful uttermost; we give no orders—we provide paltry machinery —we issue mandates to all our dependent pen-wielders—to all tribes of men who rejoice in suppers and distinguished society. Under penalty of our managerial frown they are to be up and doing in their dirty work.[3]

It certainly seems a little surprising that a man should *desire* failure for a play he was producing. Yet there is a confirmation of it in Elizabeth Barrett's correspondence with Miss Mitford to whom she writes on February 16, 1843: "Yes, Mr. Macready from all that I can understand, behaved execrably to Mr. Browning: would and would not act his play

—and at last acted it *for damnation* . . . but, not-withstanding every possible disadvantage, the poetry triumphed . . . Mr. Kenyon, who was present, bears witness to the emotion of the full house . . . to the living tears and compelled attention."

Manager and actor were certainly at war in Macready—and what bad-tempered man is swayed only by his financial interests? In those days of very brief runs, he may have thought it best, even as manager, to let the play die, as his actor's pride demanded, and put on something of which his managerial judgment approved. It lasted only three days. Later revivals in London and Washington were more successful, but even for nineteenth-century sentiment it was too cloying, while more surprisingly Thomas Woolner reports "a shower of hisses and puritanical anathemas."

One wonders whether the discussions about " 'young Robert' entering upon affairs connected with the stage" were being at this date carried on (tactlessly perhaps) by aunts and uncles, including the Masons. For Cyrus waxes indignant at Browning for bestowing no tickets on the family. Going at his own expense, he gleefully describes the " 'Scutcheon' rope ladder grotesquely managed . . . young lover swinging and singing—one line ending 'drop' wailed in a suggestive manner" and "received with titters."

Browning's two friends, Kenyon and Domett, speak of applause and tears, but the fact was damning that the play was acted in Macready's theater yet not by him. And while many applauded and some wept, there is no doubt that some also laughed, spelling death for a tragedy.

Cyrus Mason's comment on the whole story was that toward Macready young Robert had shown a temper inherited from his grandfather.

There are a few more entries about Browning in Macready's journal. He had at a chance meeting in March, 1843, accosted Macready and then hastened away "as if he had not meant to do so." He has now become one of "these wretched insects about one." And in June, 1846, at a party Macready saw *"Browning—who did not speak to me—the puppy!"*

But life goes on, and one tends to sympathize with Browning's destructive instincts when imagining the utterance of past rage or acid criticism laid up for the future biographer.

Affectionate feeling swamped all past bitterness when, in 1852, Browning heard of the death of Macready's wife. In a letter,[4] written at a time of strain, bringing back keenly the grief of Browning's mother's death, there was no room now for other than good memories of those seven wearing years:

My dear Macready,

Pray forgive me for writing if it pains or troubles you, as it may, perhaps. How can I help telling you—tho' in but a poor word or two—that I dare think I can sympathise with you—even in my infinitely removed degree—dare think I comprehend your loss, having been taught by a loss of my own. Those were happy days when I lived in such affectionate intimacy with your family: and if some few of the idler hopes of that time came to nothing, at least all the best and dearest memories of a friendship I prized so much remain fresh in my heart as ever—else it would be too sad *now*. May God comfort you in this calamity. I will only say that I am, dear Macready,

Most affectionately yours
Robert Browning

6 Sordello into Suspense

Victorian half-wits claimed that this poem was obscure.

EZRA POUND[1]

MACREADY had left Browning a legacy from the many visits to Elstree and the years of frustration as a playwright—a friendship with Euphrasia Fanny Haworth. It was never more than a friendship, but it was Fanny he thought of when several years later, Elizabeth Barrett was told that "Mr. Browning is to be married immediately to Miss Campbell." Denying even acquaintance—"I never in my life saw, to my knowledge, a woman of that name," he went on, "it must be a simple falsehood and not gossip or distortion of fact . . . I told you of the one instance where such distortion *might* take place—(Miss Haworth to avoid mistake)."

The surviving letters to Miss Haworth give a picture of a pleasant interchange, making visits to Elstree still very much worth while. In the Pfortsheimer Library, New York, is a copy of *Strafford* gilt-edged and bound in white silk, subscribed "Miss Haworth from the author." The first letter is of 1838 and begins abruptly: "Do look at a Fuchsia in full bloom and notice the clear little honey-drop depending from every flower . . . a bee's breakfast. . . . Taste and be Titania." He had himself such a love for flowers and leaves as to "satiate myself with their scent,—bite them to bits," and every scene had its own flowers which brought it back. "Snowdrops and Tilsit in Prussia go together; cowslips and Windsor Park . . . You will see *Sordello* in a trice, if the fagging fit holds." And therein she will find herself as " 'Eyebright'—meaning a simple and sad sort of translation of 'Euphrasia.' "

Only just back from Italy, he is full of the story of a "ship floating keel uppermost," discovered when righted to be a pirate full of "tobacco and cigars, good lord such heaps of them, and then bale after bale of prints and chintz, don't you call it . . ." But also were revealed the dead bodies of the sailors, floating horribly disfigured. A sketch showed Fanny how the vessels lay when the captain, fearing plague, cut the ship adrift and she went reeling off "like a mutilated creature . . . into the most gorgeous and lavish sunset in the world." But she asks for his news—he has been to Trieste, Venice, Bassano, "delicious Asolo"—and the rest . . . "Shall you come to town, anywhere near town soon? . . . I shall be vexed if you don't write soon. . . ."

The fagging fit did indeed hold—and one wonders whether, *Sordello* being already in proof, a letter from Caroline Fox to Fanny Haworth may still have contributed to seal its fate with Browning's public. For she reported how John Sterling, Carlyle's friend and admirer, had been repelled by the "Verbosity" of *Paracelsus*. "Doth not Mr. Browning know that Wordsworth will devote a fortnight to the discovery of a single word that is the one fit for his sonnet?" It was probably sheer coincidence, but in those days a great deal could be done on proofs, and Dowden notices despairingly how in *Sordello* words insignificant but essential have been omitted, thus "jamming together" those "that gleam and sparkle. . . . The mind is at once dazzled and fatigued."

Yet William Rossetti states that Browning sent *Sordello* to a friend before it was published, "saying that this time the public should not accuse him at any rate of being unintelligible," while a letter to Fanny Haworth explains in prose far more obscure than the verse itself what he had intended to say in the lines addressed to her. He goes on to defend himself for not behaving like the translator who put in brackets ten words of explanation to five of translation. He really imagined, comments Dowden, "that his shorthand was Roman type of unusual clearness." But he was grateful to Fanny. "You say roses and lilies and lilac-bunches and lemon flowers about it while everybody else pelts cabbage stump after potato paring—nay, not everybody—for Carlyle . . . but I won't tell you what Milnes told me Carlyle told him the other day."[2]

On the surface life was going on much as before, but while Fanny Haworth was writing verse in honor of Browning's poetry, Eliza Flower was disillusioned with the boy whom she had so warmly encouraged in his early teens: ". . . he has twisted the old-young shoot off by the neck," she wrote to a friend. And in another letter: "If he had not got the habit of talking of head and heart as two independent existences, one would say he was born without a heart." Mind was developing in Browning at a faster rate than heart. It is interesting to find him wanting a "subject of the most wild and passionate love" and asking Fanny Haworth for her opinion on what a complete self-forgetting devotion may mean, and whether it would be best depicted in a man or a woman! But there is a boyish touch when, hoping soon to see her, he feels sure he will do something "snubworthy."

Browning was still a frequent visitor at the new establishment in Bayswater where Fox, having settled an annuity on his wife, was living with his daughter "Tottie," his son Florance, Sarah Flower, now Mrs. Adams, and her husband—and Eliza Flower. But the two letters quoted in the last chapter seem to show Sarah as now the closer friend. Through her he sends messages to "Mr. Fox and Miss Flower," begging her to be "profuse in compliments" to the latter. She is herself with equal formality "Mrs. Adams," but there is a jestingly familiar note as he declares how proud his father will be to show her the Bank, where he hopes she will "see somethink," and how he has been ill and, longing to see her when his strength returns, yet feels " 'tis as good men hope to get to heaven—only I really wish to go."[3]

The most vivid glimpse we get of Browning's visits to that household come from "Tottie," later known as Mrs. Bridell-Fox. She remembered with special vividness (though she got the year wrong) Browning coming in one day saying that it was his birthday and would she mind if he played the piano till the others came home. The bells of a neighboring church broke out just then in a merry peal—to greet, she fancied, the young poet. Like Macready she was impressed with his

appearance "slim and dark and very handsome."[4] Sarah Flower felt he
would look "unexceptionally poetical if Nature had not played him an
ugly trick in giving him an ugly nose."

Mrs. Bridell-Fox remembered, too, how on his return from Italy in
1839 he had graphically described and pictured the scenes—smoking
a sheet of letter paper over a candle to help dark cloud effects. All
through his life there is noticeable this eager pouring out of all the
exciting, interesting, beautiful things the world had to show, but of the
man himself one's surmises must be built chiefly on the poetry, and
even then: "my deep of life I know/ Is unavailing e'en to poorly show."

It was unfortunate that *Pippa Passes,* a comprehensible poem,
should have contained a line to do Browning more harm than anything
else he ever wrote: "God's in his heaven,/ All's right with the world."
For this utterance of the little silk spinner is a direct contradiction of
Browning's chief Christian philosophy expressed by Chesterton so as
to startle us into attention—a hope founded not only on the incompleteness of man but on the incompleteness of God. God, he is saying to us
again and again in his religious poetry, would have shown less love than
man had he not with divine jealousy become man to suffer for man.

Browning has been praised or berated for discovering hidden good
in evil men, but he knew too well how much evil can lurk beneath
good, how perilous is life for us all—and thereby how exciting:

> . . . any nose
> May ravage with impunity a rose:
> Rifle a musk-pod and 'twill ache like yours!
> I'd tell you that same pungency ensures
> An after-gust, but that were overbold.
> Who would has heard Sordello's story told.

But had he?

Tennyson remarked that he understood only two lines of *Sordello,*
the first and the last: "Who will may hear Sordello's story told," and
"Who would has heard Sordello's story told"—and that those two lines
were lies. Jane Welsh Carlyle said she had read it through without dis-

covering whether Sordello was a man, a city, or a book. Douglas Jerrold, recovering from an illness, thrust the book into his wife's hands and as he saw bewilderment growing in her face gave a deep sigh of relief; after all he had *not,* as he feared, become so mentally deranged as to be unable to read the English language. And a friend to whom Charles Gavan-Duffy lent it "sent it back with an inquiry, whether by any chance it might be the sacred book of the Irvingite Church, written in their unknown tongue."

Harriet Martineau had been kept awake for the first time in her life by *Paracelsus* and had formed unbounded expectations of *Sordello.* Browning had talked it over with her and she, too, had given him bad advice. "Denies himself preface and notes," she wrote in her journal, "he must choose between being historian or poet. . . . I advised him to let the poem tell its own tale." But when it appeared, "I was so wholly unable to understand it that I supposed myself ill."

Browning was a frequent visitor to Miss Martineau and his talk she found "absolutely clear and purpose-like. He was full of good sense and fine feeling amidst occasional irritability, full also of fun and harmless satire, with some little affectations which were as droll as anything could be."

Lowell, urged to read Browning, "shocked" Moncure Conway "by echoing the commonplaces about the poet's obscurity. 'I own' he said, 'a copy of Sordello and anybody may have it who will put his hand upon his heart and say he understands it.'"

One notes even today signs of impatience against its admirers in those who have decided that the poem is unintelligible: "It will remain," says Lounsbury, "a colossal derelict upon the sea of literature, inflicting damage upon the strongest intellects that graze it even slightly, and hopelessly wrecking the frailer mental craft that come into full collision with it."

As the stories multiplied it became the fashion to abuse *Sordello;* it is not a habit of the intelligentsia to stand out against the fashion of their own age, bold though they may be against fashions already well and truly buried. D. G. Rossetti, however, insisted on its acceptance by the pre-Raphaelite brotherhood, and himself read long extracts from it to all who would listen. And a little later Swinburne would learn the entire poem by heart.

Among Browning's own friends "Orion" Horne (so called after a successful play he had written) had a mitigating word to say. "What pure diamonds of the first water," he wrote to Fox, "are to be found in this confused setting! His genius is equal to his perversity. . . . The poem wants a second volume of unreadable notes to make it quite perfect. What a waste of genius."

Tennyson's criticism was perhaps the most just and explains a good deal of the general exasperation. Sordello's thoughts are often magnificently rendered—and quite intelligibly for anyone who cares to concentrate on thought—but the story is the unintelligible thing. It is concerned with the wars of Guelphs and Ghibellines in Italy and for the modern reader, English or American, some slight historical introduction, some few notes, would be almost indispensable. But if it were concerned with the Wars of the Roses or the American Civil War, Browning's way of handling it would still be hopelessly confusing.

Sordello was a troubadour, who left thirty-five poems in Provençal which Browning must have studied. The first version of *Sordello* was devoted to his life as poet—his childhood at Goito, "Sordello in his drowsy paradise"—his contest with other troubadours, above all "the history of a soul": Sordello's adolescence, in the court and castle where he lived, his strivings to discover what a poet means, what he stands for in the world, how to communicate.

Browning's Italian tutor, Cerutti, had edited Danielo Bartoli's *De Simboli Trasportati e Morale,* which Browning took with him to Italy in 1838 as a model of style. Bartoli draws attention to Dante's treatment of Sordello in the fifth, sixth, and seventh cantos of the *Purgatorio;* Browning rereading this in 1845 told Elizabeth Barrett that Sordello was "one of the burdened contorted souls" described there. Failing on earth, they yet see a light from heaven and pass to God, "which is just my Sordello's story." The *Biographie Universelle,* which would give enough historical background for this first version, tells us that Sordello was born at Mantua about 1189, was warrior as well as troubadour and as such made his fame, that he was probably of the Visconti family, but that his parentage was uncertain, and that he met a violent death.

For some reason Browning laid *Sordello* aside to write *Paracelsus* and only after completing this returned halfheartedly to the earlier poem. I say halfheartedly because of the innumerable distractions in the two years that followed. He wrote *Strafford* and fought his first round with Macready. He dined, danced, and otherwise diverted himself, intending to complete *Sordello* after the production of *Strafford* (on the published version of which he had advertised it). But before he could do so a rival version was announced by a Mrs. Busk, telling the same story in the same kind of verse.

Browning now made a fresh start deciding to develop the warrior more and to increase the romantic element in the poem. The real Sordello had loved and been loved by Cunizza (already five times married) of the Ezzelino family, but Browning changed her into her younger half sister, Palma. Apparently when the Busk poem actually appeared, he found that it too dwelt on the warrior Sordello, after whom a square in the city of Mantua is still named, and that her poem, too, dwelt on the love theme. There must be yet more thinking, yet another start.

And there was certainly a great deal of reading done, perhaps too much for the poem—Giambatista Verci's three volume *Storia degli Ecelini*, Antonio Muratori's collection of Italian historical documents, and so on.

The uncertainty about Sordello's parentage gave Browning an opening for making him the son of the great Ghibelline leader Salinguerra. His own visit to Italy (where in Venice he witnessed scenes of great poverty), combined with his historical researches both for this poem and for *Strafford* and the liberalism first inspired by Shelley,—to create a Sordello, aware from youth of mankind's: "petty enjoyments and huge miseries."

Sordello's love for Palma, the ambitions opened by the discovery of his parentage, which would make him successor to the rule of northern Italy, war in his soul against the belief he has formed that mankind will be served, peace will be restored, only by the triumph of the Pope's party, the Guelphs, that they are the party of the people. The story, insofar as it has been told, ends with Sordello's death, brought about by the intensity of his internal struggle. But the historical Sordello lived into old age.

The poem gives the impression that Browning did not so much rewrite at each fresh start as shove new elements in among the old. And in the third book we find the author suddenly, bewilderingly "on a ruined palace-step/ At Venice," asking, "why should I break off, nor sit/ Longer upon my step, exhaust the fit/ England gave birth to?" Only after several pages of his own reflections does Book II end with the promise, again unfulfilled, "And you *shall* hear Sordello's story told." [Italics mine.]

If you read *Sordello* for ideas and descriptions, it will exhilarate you; if you read it for the story, it will have you, like Douglas Jerrold, questioning your sanity. W. S. Landor said of Browning, "I only wish he would atticise a little. Few of the Athenians had such a quarry on their property, but they constructed better roads for the conveyance of the material." Who was there to quarry for Browning or to cart the buried treasure and display it?

Chesterton (and many others following him) have attributed Browning's obscurity to two things: his knowledge of matters where the average reader has no knowledge, and his almost insane haste to get his story told. Both these elements appear all the time in the external story of *Sordello*. Republishing the poem in 1863, he added a note: "I wrote it twenty-five years ago for only a few, counting even in these on somewhat more care about its subject than they really had." Acknowledging "many" faults of expresssion, he yet clearly felt that more industry and enthusiasm would have made better readers. Brought up in a library, he expected a knowledge of words and allusions unreasonable even with educated readers in that era of high education. In the latest edition of his complete poetical works footnotes have been added from which—to take a few instances at random—one learns that a pavis is a shield, a carroch a car of state, orpine is stone crop, a valvassor is a vassal, the Miramoline signifies *Emir al Maromenim, i.e.,* Prince of the Faithful, filamot is the color of a dead leaf, a manganel is an instrument for throwing stones, knops are buds, almug is sandalwood, a pompion is a mellon, byssus is a fine cloth, a basnet a light helmet, an angelot is a lute, a platan is a plane tree, colibri are humming birds, and so on, and so on. I suppose one ought to know that Tagliafer was a minstrel knight of William the Conqueror and Eglamor a troubadour, but I didn't. Then there is the Bible and Aeschylus and Don Quixote and various Provençal terms, to say nothing of an occasional botanical one (St. Bruno's lily, the *Authericum liliastrum*).

For the enjoyment of *Sordello* I would suggest reading it through once or twice, marking the passages that most impress you, and then rereading those passages. As you go from mark to mark, you will find, I think, that you are learning much of the poetic process in Browning's mind and of the further shaping of his own convictions.

This was what he wanted us to understand—"the development of a soul: little else is worth study." But a spiritual soul involves intellect, and Sordello's intellect, as interpreted by Browning, brings with it obscurity of another kind. When he spoke of the "incidents" in that development, his critics saw them only in the tangled story of an Italian republic, but for Browning they lay as much—perhaps more— in the scenes in which young Sordello's boyhood passed, when "Virtue took form, nor vice refused a shape; / Here heaven opened, there was hell agape."

The discovery of himself as poet was for Browning the supreme event:

> He loosed that fancy from its bonds of rhyme,
> (Like Perseus when he loosed his naked love)
> Faltering; so distinct and far above
> Himself, those fancies! . . .
>   Then how he loved that art!
> The calling, making him a man apart
> From men . . .
>   Since verse, the gift,
> Was his, and men, the whole of them, must shift
> Without it, e'en content themselves with wealth
> And pomp and power, snatching a life by stealth.

But it was not easy, and here we reach the *necessary* obscurity of this very great poem. He was discussing, untrained as he was, some of the deepest problems that the greatest philosophers have discussed, which cannot of their nature be made easy for anybody. "Out of that aching brain, a very stone, / Song must be struck." It was a song whose essence sought language fiercely but often in vain:

> He left imagining, to try the stuff
> That held the imaged thing, and, let it writhe
> Never so fiercely, scarce allowed a tithe
> To reach the light—his Language.

To Domett he wrote of "the misery I made [Sordello] feel at 'inadequate vehicles' of feeling—of which this letter-writing always seemed to me the worst and is now got down to something absolutely horrible."

Venice, the mountains, devastated Ferrara, troubadours in contest, Guelphs and Ghibellines. All this "the harness of his workmanship" made easy to depict, but

> Piece after piece that armour broke away,
> Because perceptions whole, like that he sought
> To clothe, reject so pure a work of thought
> As language: thought may take perception's place
> But hardly co-exist in any case,
> Being its mere presentment—of the whole
> By parts, the simultaneous and the sole
> By the successive and the many.

But what could not be explained syllogistically might perhaps be shown.

> They climb; life's view is not at once disclosed
> To creatures caught up, on the summit left,
> Heaven plain above them, yet of wings bereft.

The dramatic monologue was Browning's true form, not the long narrative poem. Yet he did flash upon the screen the horrors of Ferrara besieged: "howe'er the battle went / The conqueror would but have a corpse to kiss",—the misery of this internecine strife:

> "... proved alike, men weighed with men
> And deed with deed, blaze, blood, with blood and blaze, ...
> The Guelph the Ghibellin may be to curse—
> I have done nothing, but both sides do worse
> Than nothing ..."

Sordello was seeking "A cause, intact, distinct from these, ordained / For me, its true discoverer." And we find him struggling with one of the unresolved problems of Browning's youthful ambition—the desire to choose everything.

> God has conceded two sights to a man—
> One, of men's whole work, time's completed plan,
> The other, of the minute's work, man's first
> Step to the plan's completeness! ...
> Read the black writing—that collective man
> Outstrips the individual ...

Man and men, time and eternity, matter and spirit, finite and infinite, man and God, these are the concepts with which he is wrestling. He discovers that whether his ambition be to shine or to serve, he can only pray:

> Let the employer match the thing employed,
> Fit to the finite his infinity, ...
>   A sphere is but a sphere;
> Small, Great, are merely terms we bandy here;
> Since to the spirit's absoluteness all
> Are like.

Browning seems, while realizing the union of matter and spirit in man, to have thought not only of God but of spirit itself as infinite. Yet he marvelously depicts the soul's effort to get from the body more than it can give, to pour in her own endlessness, "supply the power it lacked / From her infinity . . ."

> And the result is, the poor body soon
> Sinks under what was meant a wondrous boon,
> Leaving its bright accomplice all aghast.

Browning has seen a philosophic concept totally unfamiliar to his age, which Newman was hinting at in his illative sense—that of Animus and Anima. Animus all thinkers recognize, making its choices, working out its problems; but deep beneath, deeper even than the subconscious of psychology, lies Anima where God the Creator is still continually creating the being He brought out of nothingness, and it is at this depth that the great decisions of life are made. So Sordello

> . . . cast
> Himself quite through mere secondary states
> Of his soul's essence, little loves and hates,
> Into the mid deep yearnings overlaid
> By these . . .

Sordello dies of the struggle: only a very young man could so readily see in death the solution of the problems Browning sets. This death is also an overcoming:

> A triumph lingering in the wide eyes,
> Wider than some spent swimmer's if he spies
> Help from above in his extreme despair . . .

Yet, characteristically enough, the poet then takes us through an absolutely headlong summary of the history that followed Sordello's death and casts on his hero the doubts he may well have been feeling about himself:

> All he was anxious to appear, but scarce
> Solicitous to be. A sorry farce
> Such life is after all!

Was there nothing more to be said for Sordello, did he not live "for some one better thing? this way." Turning back to "sparkling Asolo," Browning sees a child "barefoot and rosy" climbing the hill.

> Up and up goes he, singing all the while
> Some unintelligible words to beat
> The lark, God's poet, swooning at his feet . . .

This boy, this lark, were the true picture of

> ... the complete Sordello, Man and Bard,
> John's cloud-girt angel, this foot on the land,
> That on the sea, with, open in his hand,
> A bitter-sweetling of a book.

But you must read *Sordello*. No brief quotation can convey the greatness of a poem which because of its great faults, fell like a stone into a sea of scorn.

"A great fuss," said a leading barrister of the hour to Holman Hunt, "had been made about one Browning, but it had all ended in smoke."

Almost fifty years later Gosse relates how Browning talked "with complete frankness" of "the long-drawn desolateness of his early and middle life as a literary man," of how "a blight had fallen upon his very admirers."

No wonder the reception of *Sordello* became a sore spot, though it was slowly that he realized the almost irreparable damage done to his reputation. Lounsbury does not exaggerate in attributing to it the determination not even to read him that began with this poem and lasted for more than a quarter century. Had *Pippa Passes* only preceded it, the fame won by *Paracelsus* might have been strengthened enough to be proof against the really immense disillusion that set in. None would review a book they believed impossible to understand.

Elizabeth Barrett had it in her heart, she said, to covet the authorship of *Pippa Passes* above all Browning's other poems. It is the story of the one day's holiday of a little silk spinner of "delicious Asolo," whose passing by influences for good people unaware of her existence. Originally the scenes were entitled Morning, Noon, Evening, and Night. The idea had occurred to Browning earlier, yet the poem stems from *Sordello,* both in its descriptions of what he had seen in Asolo and in Pippa's likeness to and contrast with the Provençal poet himself. Sordello is struggling self-consciously to help mankind; Pippa does it far more deeply in her total unconsciousness. Both are depicted as poor, and both are discovered in the end to be the children of wealthy parents. But this, which seems to fit perfectly in *Sordello,* is surely, as Chesterton notes, an artistic blemish in *Pippa Passes*. Her anonymity is of the poem's essence. Her songs and her disembodied voice are all that is known of her to those whose lives she changes.

Like Micawber prospering in Australia or Tennyson's Enoch Arden posthumously comforted by a costly funeral, Pippa's social elevation belongs to the period, as does Elizabeth's coveting of the authorship. But even the people helped by Pippa to face the evil in themselves would not have sung as she did: "God's in his heaven, / All's right with the world!"

It was after *Sordello* that the publisher suggested bringing out the next poem in a small cheap edition as the first of a series. This series Browning entitled *Bells and Pomegranates*—and into it went *Pippa Passes*.

More than forty years later, forwarding to Professor Norton the letter he received from Carlyle after having sent him *Sordello* and *Pippa*, Browning wrote: "The goodness and sympathy which began so long ago continued unabated to the end of the writer's life. I returned them with just as enduring affectionate gratitude. It was not I who ventured to make the acquaintance nor ask the correspondence of Carlyle: his love was altogether a free gift, and how much it has enriched my life, I shall hardly attempt to say . . ."

Carlyle wrote, in care of Browning's publisher:

Chelsea, June 21, 1841.

My dear Sir—Many months ago you were kind enough to send me your *Sordello*; and now this day I have been looking into your *Pippa Passes*, for which also I am your debtor. If I have made no answer hitherto, it was surely not for want of interest in you, for want of estimation of you: both Pieces have given rise to many reflexions in me, not without friendly hopes and anxieties in due measure. Alas, it is so seldom that any word one can speak is not worse than a word still unspoken;—seldom that one man, by his speaking or his silence, can, in great vital interests, help another at all!—

Unless I very greatly mistake, judging from these two works, you seem to possess a rare spiritual gift, poetical, pictorial, intellectual, by whatever name we may prefer calling it; to unfold which into articulate clearness is naturally the problem of all problems for you. This noble endowment, it seems to me farther, you are *not* at present on the best way for unfolding;—and if the world had loudly called itself content with these two Poems, my surmise is, the world could have rendered you no fataller disservice than that same! Believe me I speak with sincerity; and if I had not loved you well, I would not have spoken at all.

A long battle, I could guess, lies before you, full of toil and pain, and all sorts of real *fighting*: a man attains to nothing here below without that. Is it not verily the highest prize you fight for? Fight on; that is to say, follow truly, with steadfast singleness of purpose, with valiant humbleness and openness of heart, what best light *you* can attain to; following truly so, better and ever better light will rise on you. The light we ourselves gain, by our very errors if not otherwise, is the only precious light. Victory, what I call victory, if well fought for, is sure to you.

But spoken to a poet the suggestion that followed must have been dismaying:

If your own choice happened to point that way, I for one should hail it as a good omen that your next work were written in prose! Not that I deny you poetic faculty; far, very far from that. But unless poetic faculty mean a higher-power of common understanding, I know not what it means. One must first make a *true* intellectual representation of a thing, before any poetic interest that is true will supervene. All *cartoons* are geometrical withal; and cannot be made till we have fully learnt to make mere *diagrams* well. It is this that I mean by prose;—which hint of mine, most probably inapplicable at present, may perhaps at some future day come usefully to mind.

But enough of this: why have I written all this? Because I esteem yours no common case; and think such a man is not to be treated in the common way.

And so persist in God's name, as you best see and can; and understand always that my true prayer for you is, Good Speed in the name of God!

I would have called for you last year when I had a horse, and some twice rode thro' your suburb; but stupidly I had forgotten your address;—and you, you never came again hither!

Believe me, Yours most truly,

T. CARLYLE

Discussing *Sordello* a few years later with Gavan Duffy, Carlyle asked, "Was there any good reason why the problems of poetry should be made more abstruse and perplexing than the problems of mathematics?"

But the friendship prospered. Carlyle wrote from Scotland July 29, 1841, to

. . . apprise you straightway that your loyalminded welcome little note finds me . . . here—on the Scotch shore of the Solway Firth; . . .

I have fled hither for a few weeks of utter solitude, donothingism and sea-bathing; such as promised to prove salutary for me in the mood I was getting into. London in the long-run would surely drive one mad, if it did not kill one first. Yearly it becomes more apparent to me that, as man "was not made to be alone," so he was made to be occasionally altogether alone,—or else a foolish sounding-board of a man, no *voice* in him, but only distracted and distracting multiplicities of echoes and hearsays; a very miserable and very foolish kind of object! . . .

The spirit you profess is of the best and truest: perhaps one man only, yourself only, could do much more for you than I who can do nothing, but only say with all my heart, Good Speed! Doubt it not at all, you will prosper exactly according to your *true* quantity of effort, —and I take it you already understand that among the "*true* quantities of effort" there are many, very many which the "public," reading or other, can simply know nothing of whatever, and must consider as falsities and idlenesses, if it did. But the everlasting Heart of Nature does know them, as I say; and will truly respond to them, if not today or to-morrow, then some day after to-morrow and for many and all coming days. Courage!

A first view of Browning in "a green coat" had displeased Carlyle. We know that his early tastes were a little flamboyant: this, he has explained, was a riding coat—and he could and did ride over to Chelsea. Carlyle writes, on December 1, 1841:

> The sight of your card instead of yourself, the other day when I came down stairs, was a real vexation to me. The orders here are rigorous. "Hermetically sealed till 2 o'clock!" But had you chanced to ask for my Wife, she would have guessed that you formed an exception, and would have brought me down. We must try it another way. For example: The evenings at present, when not rainy, are bright with moonlight. We are to be at home on Friday night, and alone: could you not be induced to come and join us? Tea is at six or half-past six.—If you say nothing, let us take silence for yes, and expect you!
>
> Or if another night than Friday will suit you better, propose another; and from me in like manner, let no answer mean yes and welcome. At any rate contrive to see me.

Very soon Carlyle's inveterate habit of making his friends work for him asserted itself, and Browning was commissioned to seek out a "Mr. X," descendant of Oliver Cromwell and "some kind of a fool," in an endeavor to get some material. Later in Florence far more arduous tasks would be set him and this one was sweetened by a further invitation; he had been "absent without leave" and was to call on the Carlyle's forthwith.

Carlyle said years later to Moncure Daniel Conway:

> I remember Browning as a fine young man . . . I liked him better than any young man about here. He had simple speech and manners and ideas of his own. A good talk I recall with him, when I walked with him to the top of a hill which had a fine prospect. When he published "Paracelsus" I did not make much out of it: it

seemed to me to have something "sensational" as they say about it; but that and his other works proved a strong man.[5]

These were the years when Mill and Carlyle were intimate, and Mill told Caroline Fox that he thought the Carlyles a very happy pair, although she would in conversation invent stories about him and you could see him "panting for the opportunity to stuff in a negation." Browning, Mill, Macready, and the rest all attended Carlyle's lectures; but Mrs. Carlyle told her he was unhappy as he delivered them, wondering all the time whether people felt they were getting their guinea's worth. "It is so difficult for him," she complained, "to try to unite the characters of the prophet and the mountebank"—which sounded several degrees worse than his own comparison—prophet and actor! "Carlyle is lecturing with éclat—", wrote Browning, "the Macreadys go, and the Bishop of Salisbury, and the three Miss Styles that began German last week."

Jane must have been an awkward wife to her exceedingly difficult husband—and awkward to some of his friends. But at that time she, too, accepted the young poet. "I dined with dear Carlyle and his wife," writes Browning to Fanny Haworth "(catch me calling people dear in a hurry except in letter beginnings!) yesterday. I don't know any people like them."

Browning was a useful and agreeable guest even for those who had given him up as a poet (Kenyon admired his "inexhaustible knowledge and general reasonableness," but thought his poetry "muddy and metaphysical"). The breakfast party was for men the great opportunity for good talk, and to breakfast with Mr. Kenyon he often walked with that swift step with which, a later friend declared, he passed not between but through the vehicles in his path.

Cyrus Mason viewed his cousin's habitual headlong pace as an element in his arrogance. "Are you mad?" he cried out once, almost run down by Browning rushing by on horseback. And " 'young Robert' recognised me for he dropped his whip, without deigning to speak, wheeled the horse again towards the city and galloped away." Cyrus could never, he said, read of the good news brought to Aix without picturing that furious gallop.

At the breakfast parties, over coffee and tea and substantial viands, old friendships were strengthened and many new ones made. And the Browning family was on the move—an affair far more serious than it would be deemed today.

Browning writes in an undated letter to Laman Blanchard of having "just got up from a very sick bed, indeed, where a fortnight's brain-and-liver fever has reduced me to the shade of a shade." The family were now at Hatcham and the letter is conjecturally dated late 1841. Browning begs his friend to "conquer the interminable Kent Road," pass the turnpike at New Cross, and finally " 'descry a house resembling a goose pie'; only a crooked, hasty and rash goose-pie. We have a garden and trees, and little green hills of a sort to go out on." At present he can hardly crawl—but in a week or two "Will you come?" It seems to be especially after this illness that Browning's head so often troubled him. He speaks of it to Domett, and to Christopher Dowson he writes in '44: "I have a head that aches oftener than of old to take care of."

But not long after the brain fever he writes to Fanny Haworth in the best of spirits: "Thank you, dear friend of mine—if I can I'll call at this week's end." He is drawing again and enjoying it. Had he ever told her he was in childhood "a young wonder (as are eleven out of the dozen of us) at drawing?" He had called on Forster who "pressed me into committing verse on the instant, not the minute." And on the instant, for a Venetian scene by the painter Maclise, he poured out for a catalogue what would later go into "In a Gondola"

> I send my heart up to thee, all my heart
>   In this my singing.
> For the stars help me, and the sea bears part;
>   The very night is clinging
> Closer to Venice' streets to leave one space
>   Above me, whence thy face
> May light my joyous heart to thee its dwelling place.

"Singing and stars and night and Venice streets in depths of shade and space are 'properties' do you please to see . . ."

"In marked contrast," writes Mrs. Miller, "to the life—'so pure, so energetic, so simple, so laborious, so loftily enthusiastic'—that the young man led under his parent's roof at Camberwell or at New Cross, is the manner of his existence in London during those years in which, night after night, in the wake of Macready, he was to be found haunting the stage-doors and dressing-rooms of Covent Garden, the Haymarket, or Drury Lane."

As with Dowden, talking of *Pauline,* I can only cry "instance, instance!" For the struggle to understand an actor, write plays, and produce them is a very different thing from hanging around stage doors.

Actually the phrase quoted "so pure, so energetic . . ." is from Arnould, written to Domett, and does not, as Mrs. Miller thinks, belong to past years but to *this very period* with which she contrasts it. The two men were constantly together, the young barrister attending the rehearsals and the performance of his friend's play.

Arnould and Domett talked often of Browning in their letters: ". . . he is a fine friend," says Arnould; "he has an energy of kindness about him which never slumbers." Through him Arnould had "obtained an entrance into Periodical Literature" long promised by less zealous acquaintance. So, not at rehearsals only but at friends' houses, Arnould might meet men like Fox, Forster, Talfourd, Horne, and Landor. His letters to Domett in New Zealand usefully complement those with which Browning kept Domett informed of his own doings and feelings from 1842 until his marriage. Domett it was who inspired "Waring" and was recalled in "The Guardian Angel."

A long letter in May, 1842, seems to show Browning half doubting whether he, too, should not leave the country where he felt at times so stifled. It was probably a mood; he was still enjoying breakfast parties at Mr. Kenyon's, his arguments—perhaps even his rows—with Forster, and above all the opportunity, when it came, of sitting at the feet of Carlyle. But he was uneasy, often unhappy. A poet must crave an audience—to say nothing of the money question. The decision he had made was not irrevocable. Perhaps that magic word "Colonies" attracted him, and he felt that Domett had something he was missing.

> I shall never read over what I send you—reflect on it, care about it, or fear that you will not burn it when I ask you. So do with me. And tell me all about yourself, . . . how you are, where you are, what you do and mean to do—and to do in our way, for live properly you cannot without writing . . . the little I, or anybody, can do as it is, comes of them *going to New Zealand*—partial retirement and stopping the ears against the noise outside; but all is next to useless—for there is a creeping, magnetic, assimilating influence nothing can block out. When I block it out I shall do something. Don't you feel already older (in the wise sense of the word) and farther off, as one "having a purchase" against us? . . . At present, I don't know if I stand on head or heels; what men require I don't know—and of what they are in possession know nearly as little.

Letters came and went with a slowness we can today hardly imagine:

> You do not [writes Browning on October 9, '43]—that is, did not six months ago—write to me; . . . People read my works a little more, they say, and I have some real works here, in hand; but now that I could find it in my heart to labour earnestly, I doubt if I shall ever find it in my *head*, which sings and whirls and stops me even now at this minute—an *evening* minute by the way.

Sadly enough, between these two letters had appeared—and had sunk without a ripple in the world of contemporary literature—Browning's *Dramatic Lyrics*. In this volume he showed both the immense range of his genius—from "The Pied Piper of Hamelin" to "Soliloquy of the Spanish Cloister," and his musical power in lyric poetry—"Rudel to the Lady of Tripoli," "In a Gondola." But one poem alone should at least have stirred a rare excitement, a first dramatic monologue, never I think surpassed: "My Last Duchess."

None of this did the critics discover. John Forster praised the volume (in *The Examiner*), and it is hardly surprising that to the remark "Mr.

Browning is a genuine poet," he should have added, "and only needs to have less misgivings on the subject himself."

These must indeed have been dark years—a sense of "toiling in immeasurable sand," as play after play failed or was rejected—and now his lyrics too had fallen flat. To Domett, Browning had written that May:

> Carlyle came here a few weeks ago—walked about the place, and talked very wisely and beautifully. . . .
>
> So glides this foolish life away week by week! I have a desk full of scrawls at which I look and work a little. I want to publish a few more numbers of my "Bells"—and must also make up my mind to finish a play I wrote lately for Charles Kean, if he will have it. They take to criticizing me a little more in the reviews—and God send I be not too proud of their abuse . . . the proper old drivelling virulence with which God's Elect have in all ages been regaled.[6]

Shouting, surely to keep his spirits up. Browning was at the crossroads with no clear view of what to do next. He had made a considerable circle of friends, but the Macready row had cooled off some of them and he seemed to be cast for the part of the very promising young man who has failed to keep his promises. Depressed he might be, but he fought back at fortune, and we soon hear of a fresh attempt, in the letters of an admirer he had unknowingly won.

"I must tell you," wrote Elizabeth Barrett to Miss Mitford, "that Mr. Browning is said to have written two plays—one for Charles Kean and the public, the other for himself and *Bells and Pomegranates*. I am sorry." She was, alas, undemocratic enough to grudge him to "the Great Unwashed who can't read aright. . . . Yet after all, he is a true, soul piercing poet."

Her informant was probably Kenyon who had got as near the truth as reports commonly go. Browning had criticized Kean fiercely enough when working for his great rival, but nothing could cure him of writing plays, so *Colombe's Birthday* was finished and read to Kean and his wife who agreed to play it—but not for a year or more. Unlike Macready, Kean was a "slow study" and when he had finished his existing engagements, would need at least two months to learn the part. Meanwhile, he said, the play must *not* be published.

Another instalment was due for *Bells and Pomegranates,* and Browning surprisingly told Christopher Dowson that he felt he would lose his hold on his existing group of hearers (whom at other times one finds him treating as inexistent; his feelings seem to have gone up and down according to letters received or lacking, friends just met and suchlike impalpables). Anyhow he decided after taking advice that "for the sake of two or three hundred pounds" it was not worth waiting; into *Bells and Pomegranates* the play should go. "I sent it to press yesterday and merely put the right of *the acting* at his disposal." All this seems plain midsummer madness (though the letter was written on March 10) until one remembers the past history with Macready. "After Easter next year . . ." How long after? What fresh postponements might be hidden in the word "after"? Could an actor really, Browning asked, need two months to learn a part? He might perhaps force Kean into quick production by invoking his publishers, as he had earlier saved a play from mutilation by Macready.

If such was his train of thought, it proved erroneous. *Colombe's Birthday* went unacted until many years later. But "the good fortune" which Browning had told Dowson "seems slowly but not mistakeably settling in upon me just now" failed, as ever, to materialize. Even Forster, the one admirer of *Dramatic Lyrics,* ended his review of *Colombe's Birthday* in *The Examiner:* "As far as he has gone we abominate his taste as much as we admire his genius."

It is not surprising that estrangement should follow such blunt speech from a friend. During an earlier row we find Forster begging in a letter to Fox for Eliza Flower's opinion on his own behavior: "Her 'Roman-nosed grandeur' is the only thing that mars my self-approving recollections of the foolish quarrel." Wanting to be "quite clear in conscience," he still felt Browning should make the first move, but it would be worse to lose "a friendship on which I place no indifferent value."[7]

Eliza, laughing at Forster, may still have felt the irritation Browning provoked in her while he was Paracelsus. He seems throughout to have

enjoyed his frequent visits to her and to Fox, whom he described to
Fanny Haworth as his "literary father." But much of this pleasure, too,
was ending, for Eliza's health was causing intense anxiety. Browning
in his last letter to her—dated only "Monday," but placed by Mrs. Orr
in 1845—writes:

> Of your health I shall not trust myself to speak: you must know
> what is unspoken. I should have been most happy to see you if but
> for a minute—and if next Wednesday, I might take your hand for
> a moment—
> But you would concede that, if it were right, remembering what
> is now a very old friendship.

It was in Pisa in 1846 that he heard of Eliza's death and wrote to
Hengist Horne of "her strange, beautiful memory."

The friendship with Forster continued despite many a quarrel, but
Browning was passing through a stage of immense difficulty as poet and
as a man. Everything seemed crumbling except a social life about which
his feelings were fascinatingly ambivalent. He had not yet—did he
ever?—seized the clue to a mystery that would affect him for good or
for evil all his life through. Just now he was bewildered; lonely yet
spoiled by his family, surrounded by friends and acquaintances, a socialite (if the word had then been known) who would dance from ten
to six and come home in broad daylight, a dilettante who had written
two unsuccessful plays and done odd jobs for other writers, a spoiled
poet about whom a great fuss had once been made. But that had been
almost a decade ago.

7 Elizabeth Barrett

I have a sad heart and a merry mind.
ELIZABETH BARRETT BROWNING

ELIZABETH BARRETT BARRETT was the eldest of the eleven children (one died in infancy) of Edward Barrett Moulton Barrett. Only in England could such names be borne, in both senses of the word, but the Barretts were colonial English having large estates in Jamaica, owning many slaves until emancipation. Edward Barrett had settled in England, leaving a younger brother Sam to manage the plantation. He had bought an estate of four hundred acres in Herefordshire. There he built a "Turkish house" described by Elizabeth as "crowded with minarets and domes," and "crowned with metal spires and crescents." In *Aurora Leigh* she writes of the "sweet familiar nature" surrounding her, of trees and flowers and sun and moon, but says nothing of the large family that we meet in her early letters, undated notes mostly, and in a handwriting gradually forming.

"My dear old gentleman," she writes to her father, "say inexorable monarch of Hope End, can no entreaties mortal or immortal prevail upon you to command the crested chariot to be linked to the four high mettled steeds to bear us to Kinnersley?" But to her mother, addressed as "Dear old Lady" goes a note "Do you not think dearest Mama it would be a good way to write a nice funny letter to him, he is in a very good humour?"[1]

Edward Moulton Barrett was in those years a benevolent tyrant, and letters written to Uncle Sam in Jamaica tell of his encouragement of the family games and works. The children opened a soup kitchen for the poor, selling the soup at a penny a quart, and Elizabeth writes, "Papa has made us a handsome present of a quarter of an ox." They had put their own pocket money into the scheme, but I have found no record of how it prospered or how long it lasted.

Life was richly full. There were compositions to be written and judged by her mother—"a note by John to the schoolroom" is begged for that she may know the verdict at once. There was an immensity of reading—Corneille's *Telemaque*, Racine, the poet Southey whom she loved "contrary to all the others" excepting "Bum" (their aunt). One note to Mama asks that she may omit her music to "alter my poetry, get flowers, write my verses."

The flowers may well have been a useful excuse, for in such a household it was probably the only thing asked of a girl that could possibly be called a domestic task. No beds had to be made, no dusting done, still less sweeping. Commonly a housekeeper would even take over from the mistress of the house the onerous tasks of overseeing the cook and her provisioning, the maids and their work. "Henrietta always 'managed' everything in the house," Elizabeth would later tell Browning, "even before I was ill because she liked it and I didn't, and I waived my right to the sceptre of dinner ordering."

It was her poetry that mattered to Elizabeth. At the age of six she had been dubbed by her father Poet Laureate of Hope End, and every birthday, every "occasion," called for its appropriate verses. Then, too, she had organized a family theater. "Madame," she writes, "We have the honour to announce to you the representation of a new tragedy this evening."

In an appendix to *Letters of the Brownings to George Barrett* is one from Elizabeth to her grandmother written at the age of ten (dated July 27, 1816), describing the delights of Hope End. "Nature here displays all her art." The grapes that are ripening, the ivy that this same Nature "fastens up to some majestic tree without the aid of nails or the active gardener. . . . We have played at a new game lately, we have each been Queen or King of some country or island, for example I and Arabella are the empresses of the Hyères, Bro [her name for Edward, the oldest of her brothers] and Henrietta are the emperor and empress of Italy, Storm is the Prince of Rome, and Sam is Emperor of Oberon. . . . we sometimes have Battles, the other day Henrietta and I fought. I conquered, took her prisoner and tied her to the leg of the table."

An undated letter from Mrs. Moulton reads like a reply to this one —except for the fact that George is referred to as perhaps running about—which means that it must have been written at least a year later. Mock battles can turn into serious ones, and the grandmother feels that Elizabeth is getting "too BIG to attempt fighting with Bro. He might give you an *unlucky* Blow on your Neck which might be serious to you. He is strong and powerful."

All brothers and sisters fight when they are little; most grow out of it quickly, and Elizabeth early became too busy to do much fighting. Soup kitchens and dramas alike demanded organizing; every year there was a new brother or sister to be guided and brought on. Eldest sisters do become a little tyrannical, being encouraged in this by harassed parents or nurses who leave them in charge of "the little ones."

Elizabeth, in an Autobiography written by her at the age of fourteen, has either really forgotten or consciously pushed away the memory of early quarrels. She frankly proclaims her determination to be the undisputed ruler with "no UPSTART to usurp my authority," but goes on to state that "my dearest Bro' though my constant companion and beloved participator in all my pleasures never allowed the rage for power to injure the endearing sweetness of his temper."

Describing the Autobiography as "glimpses into my own life and literary character," she declares that "no human eye" may ever see this writing, prompted "by no excessive vanity, but perhaps SELF LOVE.

"At four I first mounted Pegasus. . . . At eleven I wished to be considered an authoress. . . . At twelve I enjoyed a literary life in all its pleasures. Metaphysics were my delight."

She does not mention here the first event that must have shaken her, as any ambitious girl of that period would be shaken: the discovery that a higher education was offered to her brother and not to herself. But she won her point when allowed to share Bro's tutor and learn Greek with him. Was an early message in Latin part of an exercise?

"Puero eruditissimo et elegantissimo Bro a manu stultissimo Sam de puella impudentissima." By her thirteenth birthday, she had, she boasts, learned "to throw away ambition," and great self-command now conceals "a turmoil of conflicting passions."

Were these passions, this turmoil, aroused when the time came for Bro to leave home for a public school? She does not record it, and we may as readily imagine either intense concealed bitterness, or long loving talks with her mother and the realization that she still reigned at home. There were other compensations: judging by the letters she wrote in French, she had good teaching in that language and it was she, not her brother, who traveled with her parents to France. Only the year before she had written her longest and most ambitious poem *The Battle of Marathon*—and now at the age of fourteen she saw herself in print. For her father, full of pride and delight, had fifty copies of the poem printed and bound.

Elizabeth prays for Bro's happiness and safety, his protection from temptation. "If I ever loved a human being I love this dear Brother—the partner of my pleasures, of my literary toils. If to save him from anxiety, from mental vexation, any effort of mine could suffice, Heaven knows my heart that I would unhesitatingly buy his happiness with my own misery."

Exclamation marks liberally bespatter this record of the "tragic comedy" of a life "chequered by my own feelings, not by external causes, and like Rosalind I have 'laughed and wept in the same breath. . . .' My destiny lies in the hands of God."

As partner of her "literary toils" Bro was presently replaced by an older man Hugh Boyd, a neighbor and classical scholar. They were mutually dependent, for Boyd was blind and Elizabeth read aloud to him by the hour, while he guided her reading of the classics and introduced her to the Greek poets of Christianity.

One element in Elizabeth's childhood reading goes unmentioned in her Autobiography. There was at Hope End a large library and Elizabeth's father had indicated one side where the books were all hers, the other where she must not read them. Obediently she avoided *Tom*

Jones, but devoured Tom Paine and Voltaire. As a very little girl she had filled her pinafore with sticks and gone out to burn a sacrificial fire to Minerva. But growing doubtful of her goddesses she fell "into a vague sort of general scepticism" and would follow the childhood's prayers she still recited with one she had found in an old book: "Oh, God, if there be a God, save my soul if I have a soul." In adult life Elizabeth became intensely religious; her poems show an awareness of God's presence; heaven was a reality to her; she could bear her narrow life, showing cheerfulness always to her family. She would not ever be guilty "Of taking vainly in a plaintive mood/The holy name of Grief— holy herein/That by the grief of One came all our good."

An intense personal devotion to Our Lord is present throughout her verse. Like Browning she was brought up a Nonconformist; she hated ritualism with a greater violence than he, loved and read the Bible and apparently even enjoyed the extempore prayers uttered by the strange father almost better known to the world in general than she is.

Between her childhood and her letters to Browning had come events that changed the precocious, gay child into the famous "poetess," recluse, and invalid.

The story of an injury when saddling her pony is today, probably correctly, dismissed as apocryphal, although one undated letter seems to confirm it. "Dr. Baron comes to examine my back accurately and with particular care. . . . I trust in God it will prove not to be the spine the restraint attending such a disease would indeed be irksome." But the accident she does not mention, then or ever. There are at the University of Illinois three letters from doctors about her illness, all published in *Letters of the Brownings to George Barrett.* These were expounded to the editor, Paul Landis, by the late Dr. D. J. Davis (Dean Emeritus of the University's Medical School) as a diagnosis of "general tuberculosis from girlhood."

The letters depict first a severe pain in the head, then in the side and back ("The suffering is agony," says Dr. Coker), paroxysms, and night frights. She was treated by bleeding, and "Opium at one time re- lieved the spasms." Having another patient with similar symptoms, who proved to be suffering from spinal trouble, Dr. Coker suggested treating

Elizabeth for this, although "the positive proofs are wanting of the existence of a diseased spine."

The doctors were in fact baffled, as so often in that century, by *the* disease of the era, tuberculosis. Blood-spitting and high fever followed, as we see from her letters to George. All three Barrett sisters probably had some slight beginnings of the disease, but with Arabel and Henrietta it had apparently cleared up. If Dr. Davis' view is correct, it would seem that in Elizabeth the disease had only been arrested and was in middle age the cause of her death.

The commonly held idea that in going to bed, and thus escaping social and family obligations, Elizabeth was almost magnificently malingering may have been started by her brother George: ". . . it isn't altogether as agreeable," she wrote to him from Torquay, "to be here half in the dark as you might possibly fancy." But the theory was strengthened and became common coin as a result of a vicious attack on Elizabeth made by Arabella Moulton Barrett (daughter of her brother "Stormie") as late as 1938. Infuriated by the play *The Barretts of Wimpole Street,* she defended her grandfather by savaging her aunt.

Jeannette Marks in *The Family of the Barrett* tells us of her discovery that opium in some form was at that date used as a common "household remedy" in Jamaica. One cannot tell whether the children's nurse was a Jamaican and had begun to give it to Elizabeth in childhood. But, as we have seen, doctors had prescribed it when she was only fifteen. Certainly she was using it at Torquay, for, in a letter to George she writes of longing for solitude "in a forest of chestnuts and cedars, in an hourly succession of poetical paragraphs and morphine draughts. . . . Not that I do such a thing." And he is to be very careful "not to say a word of the morphine when you write."

Does this mean that her father did not know about the drug? Yet he might have disapproved, even had it been given by doctor's orders.

By the time she was corresponding with Browning she could not, her physicians told her, manage without a minimum of sixty drops of laudanum a day. Morphine was another form used. Little or nothing has been said of this by most of her biographers, from what Miss Marks calls "an unthinking alliance to shield her 'reputation' . . . from some of the cruel untruths spoken of opium dependents." During her lifetime she was protected by her social position, "belonging," as Miss Mitford rather quaintly put it, to "that best class in the whole world . . . the affluent and cultivated gentry of England." A foolish "protection," Miss Marks feels, and she notes how striking in Elizabeth is the development, against odds, of "mental power, strength of character and fearless plain speaking."

Poets are half drugged by their awakening powers. Is it fancy to see also some more literal drug in Elizabeth's early verse: the storm on the Malvern Hills later described so vividly in prose to Robert Browning, the gaze "Into the deep Eleusis of my heart/To learn its secret things"? The great thunderstorm had brought deaths with it, and in her dream Elizabeth sees in the lightning's flash "a white and corpse-like heap . . . The man was my familiar."

The "familiar" is, say the dictionaries, "a supernatural spirit often embodied in an animal" and again "a demon or evil spirit supposed to attend at call." It would almost seem that Socrates' daimon had been transformed into a demon: "I knew that face," cries Elizabeth. "His who did hate me—his whom I did hate."

But there is something more deeply personal in it, closer than the demonic familiar. The poem might have depicted a struggle between that dark supernatural spirit and some bright angel—but no—the struggle was in "mine heart. For there had battled in her solitudes,/Contrary spirits." Sometimes the dark seems the real "I," sometimes the bright—either might long to do the other to death, yet shudder if in a dream he found the corpse at his feet.

Elizabeth would ask Browning, "Did you ever feel afraid of your own soul. . . ?" She saw the double personality reconciled only when "Cymon bears/dares to look at Psyche *by the force of woe.*" And in a vision of the "Divine Agony" of Christ comes reconciliation.

None of it was very clear during that night of storm, but there remained with Elizabeth a terror of thunder and lightning which her father deemed disgraceful for anyone who could read or write. And whenever it began there was, too, the opium.

Elizabeth's mother had died in 1828, the family fortunes had declined with the abolition of slavery in Jamaica, Hope End had been sold, a greatly altered father had moved them all, first to a smaller house in Devonshire, then to London. Her beloved Uncle Sam had died, also one of her brothers, another Sam. The doctors had decreed that London was no place for her to live.

She tells the story in a letter to Browning of how, sent back to an aunt at Torquay, she had been accompanied by Bro, "whom I loved best in the world beyond comparison and rivalship." The tears she shed at the thought of losing him moved her aunt to write and ask if he might stay. And the father giving permission, said "that he considered it to be *very wrong in me to exact such a thing.*" These words were "burnt into me as with fire." For Bro stayed—and then one day he went out sailing and did not return.

"For three days we waited. . . . And the sun shone as it shines today, and there was no more wind than now . . . and other boats came back one by one. Remember how you wrote in your "Gismond"

> What says the body when they spring
> Some monstrous torture-engine's whole
> Strength on it? No more says the soul,

and you never wrote anything which *lived* with me more than that. It is such a dreadful truth. But you knew it for truth, I hope, by your genius, and not by such proof as mine—I who could not speak or shed a tear, but lay for weeks and months, half unconscious, with a wandering mind, and too near to God under the crushing of His hand, to pray at all. I expiated all my weak tears before, by not being able to shed then one tear—and yet they were forbearing—and no voice said 'You have done this . . .' I do not reproach myself with such acrid thoughts as I had once—I *know* that I would have died ten times over for *him*."[2]

With immense courage she insisted after this blow on returning to London to spare her father further separations. The journey was made in a huge carriage fitted with a water bed.

All the surrounding circumstances show that despite the loss of their slaves the family was still a wealthy one and that the interests which called Mr. Barrett daily into the city were important.

But Elizabeth, although extravagant, seems to have been indifferent to wealth; its loss would have meant little to her. What had shattered her was the loss of a much-loved mother; a happy home; the two Sams, uncle and brother; and now the dearest "in all the world." Whatever the origin of her illness, she had been heavily shaken psychologically. Nor was other medical treatment of that date helpful: the doctor who took her inkstand out of the room, deeming poetry a kind of disease; the medicines used "when my pulse was above a hundred and forty with fever . . . digitalis to make me weak—and, when I could not move without fainting (with weakness) quinine to make me feverish again. Yet, and they could tell from the stethoscope, how very little was really wrong in me . . . if it were not on a vital organ—and how I should certainly live . . . if I didn't die sooner."

That was down in Devonshire, but the treatment after her return to London, with its probable effect on both body and mind, is equally inconceivable: an airless room, ivy with some difficulty trained against the windows, flowers dying in the atmosphere, dust rising from the carpet. The room was thoroughly cleaned only once a year when the family migrated to the country. One hardly finds this credible, but Elizabeth describes the dust, the swift death of the flowers, the exclusion of all air through the winter, the painting of her window and the effort to keep alive the ivy—designed like the painting to recall the nature she could no longer live with.

Into this room between eleven and twelve each night came Edward Moulton Barrett to pray over his afflicted daughter, whose reliance on him was surely a chief reason for his love: she at least, the "purest woman" he knew—and the most dependent—would never even threaten him with a love affair, as two of his children already had. For that brilliant play *The Barretts of Wimpole Street* does not give a true picture of this abnormal man. Of the special unhealthiness depicted in the play there is no historical trace: not incest but tyranny, and a strange fear of sex, set up a barrier against marriage, not for Elizabeth only but for the whole family. Two sisters and one brother married in the father's lifetime—and no one of them was forgiven. Before Bro died he had wanted to marry, and Elizabeth had tried in vain to help by making over her small fortune to him. It mattered not whether parental permission was asked or not. Henrietta asked and was refused, Elizabeth did not. Both had to escape from the house and marry secretly; both were women arrived at or nearing the age of forty.

It was a daily tyranny under which they lived. None could invite his own friends to dinner. All except Elizabeth, inheriting a little from her uncle, were wholly dependent on their father. It was some relief from the tension of his presence that he was out at business from morning to late afternoon, not near enough to Wimpole Street to get home before six or seven. But Elizabeth describes the heavy silence while he held forth on the rights of parents, the duties of children, and related topics. She tells how, when Henrietta was first discovered to be in love, "her knees were made to ring upon the floor" and she was carried out of the room "in strong hysterics," while Elizabeth herself fainted away from horror at the scene.

That had been many years ago, and as the letters go on we see poor Henrietta plucking up heart to fall in love once more. We see the three sisters in closest possible intimacy; the brothers visiting Elizabeth singly or in a body; Stormie carrying her up and down stairs as she grew stronger and able to leave her room; all of them full of gaiety when, the parental pressure lifted a little, they gathered every Sunday in Elizabeth's room. It was a tyranny limited by a large degree of self-regarding occupation, and an eye consequently blind for long periods but hideously keen once his attention was drawn. "I have," Elizabeth wrote, "a great deal of liberty, to have so many chains; we all have in this house: and though the liberty has melancholy motives, it saves some daily torment, and I do not complain of it for one."

Elizabeth lived in one large room, shared at night by her sister Arabel. Whether or not her pet dog slept there, he was always with her in the daytime. Her family visited her there; meals were brought up;

and Wilson, her personal maid, waited on her, brushed and arranged the glorious dark hair, helped her to dress and even, when she was well enough to go out, put on her boots (probably high, and buttoned with the assistance of a long silver button hook such as I once possessed—a relic, I believe, of my grandmother).

Alone for many hours Elizabeth read incessantly, following politics, but absorbed above all in current literature. She loved novels, having a special passion for George Sand (who like herself had in childhood worshiped the gods of Greece). But besides reading she wrote—both poetry and letters.

The Seraphim and other Poems had appeared in 1838, she had become a contributor to *Blackwood's Magazine* and *The Athenaeum,* and was already a more popular poet than Browning when, in 1844, she published two volumes of poems which had a vast success in the literary and sub-literary worlds of both England and America.

Receiving an immense mail, she answered nearly all of it, and her regular correspondents increased. She wrote, of course, to her brother George when he was on circuit; to Mrs. Jameson, author of *Sacred and Legendary Art,* who was also among her visitors; to old friends, Mrs. Martin and Hugh Boyd; and to a number of notable people she had never seen (and most of whom she was quite determined not to see). There was Miss Martineau, there was Haydon the painter, there was Chorley a now-forgotten writer whom Miss Mitford energetically and unsuccessfully urged her to admit.

And there was Richard Hengist ("Orion") Horne who in the autumn of 1843 asked two poets, both known to him but not to each other, Elizabeth Barrett and Robert Browning, to help him in supplying mottoes descriptive of the writers dealt with in his forthcoming book, *The New Spirit of the Age.* For Elizabeth Browning chose Shelley's lines:

> I'll sail on the flood of the tempest dark,
> With the calm within and the light around!
> —And then when the gloom is deep and stark,
> Look from thy dull earth, slumber-bound,—
> My moon-like flight thou may'st mark

The linking is fascinating between the poet so enthroned in Browning's heart and imagination and that other whom he would later call "my moon of poets." And she, already joined with him in public estimation for her obscurity, is at once attracted and alarmed. "The sin of sphinxine literature I admit," she wrote to a Mr. Westwood in April, 1845. "Do you know that I have been told that *I* have written things harder to interpret than Browning himself? Only I cannot, cannot believe it—he is so very hard. . . . Tell me honestly. . . . He cuts his language into bits—and one has to join them together, as young children do their dissected maps. . . . The depth and power of the significance (when it is apprehended) glorifies the puzzle."

Browning's circle is therefore small, "very strait and narrow. He will not die because the principle of life is in him—but he will not live the warm summer life which is permitted to many of very inferior faculty, because he does not come out into the sun."

We can watch an encounter beginning to dawn, very remotely, unseen and unguessed in its first distant prospect, through reading more of Elizabeth Barrett's letters—above all those to Miss Mitford. The author of *Our Village* was described by Jane Austen as having been the silliest, prettiest most husband-hunting of young ladies and having turned in maturity into a very stiff and proper specimen of single-blessedness. She took care of a selfish old father to whom she sacrificed all her time and money, lived away from London for his sake, but had a fair amount of social life and carried on a voluminous correspondence with many friends, including Elizabeth Barrett. There was much kindness in this: the beloved little dog Flush was her gift, named after her own dog; she sent books and periodicals and, whenever she came to London, paid long visits, first to Devonshire Place, later to Wimpole Street.

Elizabeth Barrett and Miss Mitford had long been exchanging literary and other gossip when Elizabeth wrote of *Paracelsus:* "I am a little discontented even *there* and would wish for more harmony and rather more clearness"; yet "There is a palpable power—a height and depth of thought—and suddenly repressed gushings of tenderness which suggest to us a depth beyond . . . the author is a Poet in the holy sense."

But hearing of *Strafford*, she could not "even guess how he will be quite wide awake enough, from the peculiar mystic dreaminess, to write a historical tragedy."

Elizabeth's cousin, "dear Mr. Kenyon," is in and out of these letters: he sends her a copy of *Pippa Passes* ahead of Miss Mitford; they fear for his health (Wordsworth spoke of him as of "too full a habit"). They comment on his overwhelming social engagements ("he lives in such an unnatural whirlwind or whirlpool or both"); they even scheme, not perhaps very seriously, at finding him—already twice widowed—another wife.

Elizabeth had read *Pippa Passes* three times when she wrote to Miss Mitford of the "noble and beautiful things everywhere to be broken up and looked at," of the "great tragic scene . . . which pants again with its own power." Browning, she feels, is at once affected by Landor and immensely original, but she misses music in his writing "and that struck me with a hard hand, while I was in my admiration over his *Paracelsus*."

The letters get more and more preoccupied with this new poet whose reception by the critics displeased her greatly—"that light, half jocose, pitifully jocose, downward accent of critical rallying. I would not dare speak so of Mr. Browning in a whisper."

This was written in January, 1842, and Browning was by then deep in the tunnel of critical opinion that was to remain so dark and stretch so far. And, whether it was from personal feelings, or merely because Miss Mitford was receptive to atmosphere, she had begun to lend her voice to attacks by some of those who had warmly welcomed him when *Paracelsus* had made him fashionable. Elizabeth writes on April 1, 1842: "Poor Mr. Browning! Was that extreme irritability of nerves supposed to be occasioned by the disappointment, or the exercise of an overwrought faculty?" Miss Mitford wished him to turn to some less exciting occupation: "In the first place *could* he so turn? . . . dare we ask silence from such a poet?" Like a prophet "he has a word to speak from Nature and God and he must speak it."

She still believes her friend to share her admiration for the poet, but by October she has begun to doubt: ". . . you speak more severely of Mr.

Browning than I can say 'Amen' to. Amen would stick in my throat even supposing it to rise so high." Browning is great in "my eyes, not blinded by friendship." But does Miss Mitford know that "Mr. Browning is a great favorite (I mean as a man) of Mr. Kenyon's," who speaks "warmly of his high cultivation and attainments, and singular humility of bearing. I should like to hear you praise him a little more indeed." But more criticisms follow, and the point is reached when Elizabeth, after praising Browning's "concentrated passion . . . burning through the metallic fissures of language," and promising to send her friend his latest works, goes on, "And yet you half frighten me from sending you Mr. Browning's poetry. Promise not to say again that it was a pity he missed being . . . an attorney . . . an engineer . . . a merchant's clerk . . . what trade was it?"

Nevertheless she does admit his failure as a playwright. "He appears to me capable of most dramatic effluences and passionate insights"; but still, as Miss Mitford would say, "acting a play of Mr. Browning's is like reading a riddle-book right through without stopping to guess the answers! Something like . . . perhaps, yet after all, he is a true soul-piercing poet."[3]

Mr. Kenyon was hoping and planning to bring about a meeting between them, but in January, 1845, a poem of Elizabeth's and a letter of Browning's made his intervention unnecessary.

8 Robert and Elizabeth

She was the smallest lady alive,
Made in a piece of nature's madness . . .

"THE FLIGHT OF THE DUCHESS"

"EMOTION recollected in tranquility" was Wordsworth's definition of poetry. With this Santayana agrees. Love in what he calls the
"contemplative" poets, "ceased to be a passion" and was transmuted
into reflection. But Browning's, he declares indignantly, is "the poetry
of barbarism." He writes not about, but passionately within, experience
—more especially the experience of love. His love is "lava hot from the
crater, in no way moulded, melted or refined." And again: ". . . we are
in the presence of a barbaric genius . . . of a volcanic eruption." But the
best criticism of today is beginning to say with Robert Langbaum that
when Santayana deprecates the " 'fierce paroxysm' which for Browning
is heaven . . . one has only to be a romanticist to reply 'You are quite
right about Browning, and that is why I admire him.' "

Edwin Muir had already noted that Browning "wrote unlike the
romantic poets, as a practised lover, and his subject was neither happy
nor unhappy love, but love as an experience."

Paolo and Francesca, Abelard and Heloise, Petrarch and Laura—
and Robert and Elizabeth: this last and most improbable of love stories
has long been linked with the others, but to talk of it today is felt to be
plunging into a "bath of inspirational treacle"—a phrase used by Hoxie
Fairchild (with occasional justice) of nineteenth-century enthusiasm
for Browning.[1] This reference is specifically to praise of his religious

poetry, but Dr. Fairchild appears to have an unbounded contempt for the man himself, centered especially on the unreality of his love poetry. We are told of his "cold sluggishness of temper" and "factitious ardour. . . . His robustious poetry contrasts embarrassingly with his sedentary, unadventurous, nineteenth-century bourgeois life. . . . Mrs. Miller has made out a strong case for the thesis that what he always sought in Elizabeth and in other women before and after her, was not a mate but a mother. . . . What recent studies have taught us about this man's life and character renders the aggressive virility of his love-gospel a little embarrassing."

"A most amusing essay," says a Michael Innes character, "might be written on the quite peculiar sense of evidence that the professional English scholars have developed," and surely this is an outstanding example. For speculation is not evidence and speculation is the only new element that has been produced in support of what Dr. Fairchild correctly calls a "thesis"—but treats as proven. "There is," as Hilaire Belloc says, "great psychological value in a strong affirmation."

That Browning has been idealized is true; but in trying to understand him no such shock awaits one as I, at least, felt when I met the real Abelard. Getting closer to Petrarch, if Gilson's *Choir of Muses* is reliable, also destroys a certain amount of glamour, for even the best poets are human. Browning, far nearer to us in time, has had the spotlight turned upon him in full measure; and whatever his other weaknesses, it has shown none in a relationship which began even before the writing of the first letter of his two years' correspondence with Elizabeth Barrett.

At Wellesley College, in the box in which he placed them, these letters lie, and on them he has noted each day the hours and minutes spent with her. Only one is missing—his first vehement expression of a love which swept aside apparently insuperable obstacles, above all Elizabeth's own fears and scruples—her age, her ill health, her physical dependence, the sacrifice he would be making of a possible brilliant future. Men do not take for a mother-figure the risks that Browning took when he repudiated the mere continuation of a friendship and insisted on the consummation of his love.

The letters of two years, the poetry of a lifetime expressed this love —to say nothing of four miscarriages and a baby! The evidence of scores of visitors to the Casa Guidi and the correspondence of both poets with their friends and relatives, add, if it be needed, a great weight of uncontradicted testimony—not to the absurd and unattractive idea of two people in perpetual peaceful agreement, but of two personalities each with strengths and weaknesses, each giving and each receiving in a union at once physical, intellectual, spiritual.

Both had their difficult hours, and Elizabeth writes to Mrs. Jameson (in a letter lost in the sinking of the *Titanic* of which only the catalogue quotation has survived): "You must learn Robert—he is made of moods—chequered like a chess-board; and the colour goes for too much —till you learn to treat it as a game. He was very tired that evening."

There were vast problems for Browning in the health, the nerves, the drug addiction of the woman he so loved. There are elements in him one would wish changed especially in later years, expressed in his own feeling that he must "wash his hands clean" to be fit to rejoin his love. But the story of that love is fact and, as so often, it is the cynical and destructive view which is fancy.

But how to tell with any freshness a story told so often . . .

Two green-covered volumes lay on Browning's table "at arm's length," to be reached for "when my head aches or wanders or strikes work . . . and round I turn, and . . . read read read."

To their author he wrote, on January 10, 1845, "I love your verses with all my heart, dear Miss Barrett, . . . into me has it gone, and part of me has it become, this great living poetry of yours . . . the fresh strange music, the affluent language, the exquisite pathos and true new brave thought. . . . I do, as I say, love these books with all my heart—and I love you too."

Once he had come near to seeing her, brought by Mr. Kenyon, but there was some "bar to admission, and the half-opened door shut, and I went home my thousands of miles, and the sight was never to be?"

Elizabeth answers the half-question: ". . . what I lost by one chance

I may recover by some future one. Winters shut me up as they do dormouse's eyes; in the spring, *we shall see . . ."*

Meanwhile there could be letters. And Browning marveled at the way he went "on and on to you"—he, who feels letter writing the worst of burdens and commonly comes down " 'flop' upon the sweet haven of page one, line last. . . . You will never more, I hope, talk of 'the honour of my acquaintance,' but I will joyfully wait for the delight of your friendship, and the spring . . ."

It must have been hard to fuse in one picture the poet and mystic Elizabeth had discovered in *Paracelsus* and the smart young man of London society. Browning, while often decrying the social world, dined out frequently, went on to balls and parties, dancing the polka and the "Cellarius" until six in the morning. This cannot at all have helped his exceedingly troublesome head and it all seemed to Elizabeth "a strange husk of a world!"

She was six years older than he, a fact of which she was continuously aware, as also of her ignorance of a world of which both he and she a little exaggerated his experience. He had, of course, traveled—to Russia and to Italy, through Europe—and had met many people of whom Elizabeth had only heard, whose works she had devoured, in whose personalities she took an immense interest.

In the intellectual field they were almost uncannily well matched, quoting to each other Greek, Latin, Italian, French, the English classics and the literature of their own time. Both were keen observers of nature, but while Browning wrote as spring approached of what he saw in his mother's garden, the flowers he brought her were all that Elizabeth could now observe. She had for many years, moved only from bed to sofa: ". . . the brightest place in the house," she felt, "is the leaning out of the window." And he replied: "And pray you not to 'lean out of the window' when my own foot is only on the stair; do wait a little for

Yours *ever*
R.B.

To her old friend, Hugh Boyd, Elizabeth was writing: "I am getting deeper and deeper into correspondence with Robert Browning, poet and mystic; and we are growing to be the truest of friends."[2]

They were united, she told Browning, in a popular report "that we love the darkness and use a sphinxine idiom in our talk." But if they were to collaborate, "I should not like it a bit the less for the grand supply of jests it would administer to the critical Board of Trade, about visible darkness, multiplied by two, mounting into palpable obscure." She had once planned a play in collaboration with "Orion" Horne about "a man haunted by his own soul; . . . (making her a separate personal Psyche, a dreadful, beautiful Psyche)—the man being haunted and terrified through all the turns of life by her. Did you ever feel afraid of your own soul, as I have done?"

Browning perhaps could have shared this theme with her, but certainly not Horne. Poor man! He was perpetually praying for admission to the shrine, threatening to bring his guitar and play to her sisters, leaving the door open that she too might hear and her heart be softened toward him. One wonders what would have happened had he encountered Mr. Barrett on the doorstep—no man certainly to share the vision of a haunting Psyche.

For Browning the physical and mental strain of writing was heavy; for Elizabeth writing represented all that she was missing in her lonely room: "I seem to live while I write—it is life for me. Why what is to live? Not to eat and drink and breathe—but to feel the life in you down all the fibres of being, passionately and joyfully."

On May 3 Browning writes: "If you do not continue to improve in health . . . I shall not see you—not—not—not—what 'knots' to untie. Surely the wind that sets my chestnut-tree dancing, all its baby-cone-blossoms, green now, rocking like fairy castles on a hill in an earthquake —that is South West surely! God bless you, and me in that."

Elizabeth grows as concerned about Browning's headaches as he about her health, but intimate as they are becoming, her fears continue as to that face-to-face meeting for which he so longs. It is mid-May before she is willing to agree that spring has come. And even then she warns: "There is nothing to see in me; nor to hear in me. . . . If my poetry is worth anything to any eye, it is the flower of me . . . it has all my colours; the rest of me is nothing but a root, fit for the ground and the dark."

How deep that "I love you too" went in Browning's first letter we cannot be sure; possibly he had fallen in love through reading Elizabeth's poetry, almost certainly he had before, on May 21, he called for the first time. He was thirty-three, she thirty-nine. The gap in age was probably painfully perceptible. At thirty, says Miss Mitford, Elizabeth would have passed for a mere child; she had masses of dark brown hair and beautiful eyes. She was so tiny that her brothers could easily carry her up and down stairs. But illness and grief had greatly changed her; her eyes remained beautiful, but in the careworn face of a middle-aged woman.

The lady of the poems and the letters had been as remote as she of Tripoli for Rudel the troubadour. Browning had felt "thousands and thousands of miles away," while she often wondered later at the chance (so it seemed) whereby she had chosen among the many strangers who asked—indeed vociferously demanded—to be admitted into that lonely room, just this one. "When I wrote that letter to let you come the first time, do you know, the tears ran down my cheeks . . . I could not tell why: partly it might be mere nervousness. And then, I was vexed with you for wishing to come as other people did, and vexed with myself for not being able to refuse you as I did them."

Nine years after Browning's death his son told the world how the only letters that had passed between Robert and Elizabeth (for after marriage they were never again separated) were kept "in a certain inlaid box . . . letter by letter, each in its consecutive order and numbered on the envelope by his own hand."

"There they are," Pen reported him as saying, "do with them as you please when I am dead and gone."[3]

Controversy raged: Were these letters too sacred for publication, or was Leslie Stephen right when he found his scruples "vanquished by the remarkable revelation of beautiful character. . . . These letters demonstrate to the dullest that the intensity of passion which makes the poet was equally present in the man."[4]

Few correspondences exist yielding more sheer delight to the addict, at a second, third, tenth reading. Yet whether it was wise to publish them in their entirety is another question. The Sphinxine element can be irritating—and misleading. Elizabeth herself asks for an explanation of some of Browning's "Sordelloisms," and if these were unclear to her what do they become to us? It is a peculiarly—perhaps uniquely—tantalizing correspondence: letters written daily between meetings lasting two or three hours twice a week, which go unrecorded except in an occasional cryptic allusion.

Two plain enough letters follow the first encounter. Browning hopes he may come again, that he did not stay too long, that he did not talk too loud. "I am proud and happy in your friendship." And she: "Indeed there was nothing wrong—how could there be. And there was everything right—as how should there not be?" Each feels the other's friendship to be "honour" as well as "happiness," and Elizabeth says: ". . . it is hard for you to understand with all your psychology . . . what my mental position is after the peculiar experience I have suffered." While he feels wholly at her feet, she sees him from "the height of your brilliant happy sphere" entering her dim world.

With every deep love each feels the superiority of the other, each desires to kneel—and these two were already in love, however little Elizabeth realized her own state. Browning knew his better. He received her letter on Thursday and wrote the same day a declaration of his devotion.

"I myself am supremely passionate," he told Elizabeth months later. No doubt she knew it from this letter, which badly frightened her. Whatever stirrings there were in the depths, she certainly wanted the surface of her life unruffled by passion, and she was keenly aware of her physical state: bed to sofa, sofa to bed. She begs him to let the "intemperate things" he has said "die out *between you and me alone,* like a misprint between you and the printer." His friendship she values, but should he repeat this outburst, "*I must not . . . I will not see you again*—and you will justify me later in your heart. So for my sake you will not say it—I think you will not—and spare me the sadness of having to break through an intercourse just as it is promising pleasure to me; to me who have so many sadnesses and so few pleasures." She cannot, owing to relatives arriving, see him as planned this week, but will he come the following Tuesday?

I wish we had this alarming letter of Browning's. He, too, was badly frightened, and for all his famed psychology, he acted with such incredible stupidity that only Elizabeth's heart, already more than half his, saved them from catastrophe. For he now declared that he had meant nothing by his declaration—and we can guess at the vehemence of the lost letter from the simile with which he explains it away: ". . . for every poor speck of a Vesuvius or a Stromboli in my microcosm there are huge layers of ice and pits of black cold water—and I make the most of my two or three fire-eyes, because I know, by experience, alas, how these tend to extinction—and the ice grows and grows." He speaks dramatically in his poetry, so no wonder if he "*bungle* notably" in private life, but he hopes she will not think him "very brutal if I tell you I could almost smile at your misapprehension of what I meant to write."

In a long and involved explanation which explains nothing, he goes on: "I am but a very poor creature compared to you and entitled by my wants to look up to you." Perhaps his "over-boisterous gratitude" for the pleasure of seeing her has wrought this mischief, but he will be "too much punished" if she will not let him come again. May he have back the erring letter "if you have not inflicted proper and summary justice on it?"

Elizabeth's answer shows a woman, bewildered and hurt certainly ("I assure you I never made such a mistake. . . . No, never in my life before"), but willing to take refuge in the general attitude toward Browning's poetry and carry it over into this curious prose of his: "I have observed before in my own mind, that a good deal of what is called obscurity in you, arises from a habit of very subtle association . . . till the reader grows confused as I did . . . I was certainly innocent of the knowledge of the 'ice and cold water' you introduce me to, and am only just shaking my head, as Flush would, after a first wholesome plunge." She has had the almost supernatural strength of mind not to have reread what he had written: "however (to speak of the letter critically, and as the dramatic composition it is) it is to be admitted to be very beautiful, and well worthy of the rest of its kin in the portfolio . . . 'Lays of the Poets' or otherwise . . . I venture to advise you to burn it at once. . . . And we will shuffle the cards and take patience, and begin the game again if you please—and I shall bear in mind that you are a dramatic poet . . ."

Any woman, or I at least, cannot but delight in the contrast between the appalling clumsiness of the "man of the world" and the exquisite riposte from the cloistered recluse who had esteemed his worldly knowledge so highly. But poor Browning had really thought that the postponing of his visit for a week was but the beginning, that he was to lose altogether what already he valued above all else. It was perhaps when another meeting was secure that he wrote "The Lost Mistress:"

> Tomorrow we meet the same then, dearest?
> May I take your hand in mine?
> Mere friends are we,—well, friends the merest
> Keep much that I resign . . .
>
> Yet I will but say what mere friends say,
> Or only a thought stronger;
> I will hold your hand but as long as all may,
> Or so very little longer!

Shuffle the cards as they might, they were not quite at ease. "And now," he wrote, " 'exit, prompt side, nearest door, Luria'—and enter R.B.—next Wednesday—as boldly as he suspects most people do just after they have been soundly frightened"; and she: ". . . we have both been a little unlucky, there's no denying, in overcoming the embarrassments of a first acquaintance." Each has to say several *"quite quite"* last words, and Elizabeth begs him in one letter to "make out these readings of me as a *dixit Casaubonus;* and don't throw me down as a corrupt text" . . . and again: ". . . determine to read me no more backwards with your Hebrew, putting in your own vowel points without my leave! Shall it be so?"

Their heads came to the assistance of their hearts. Soon he was helping her over her translation of *Prometheus,* and she was suggesting alterations in his new poems. Browning took criticism gladly from anyone willing and fit to give it, and most surprisingly underrated the lyrics which revealed his greatest powers. "Now I will write you the verses," he says, "some easy ones out of a paper-full meant to go between poem and poem in my next number, and break the shock of collision."

And again: "You may like some of my smaller things, which stop interstices, better than what you have seen; I shall wonder to know."

Dramatic Romances and Lyrics was to be the next in the *Bells and Pomegranates* series and the correspondence about this title is a perfect example of a problem Elizabeth took very seriously: how to make the general public read his poetry. "Do tell me," she writes on October 17, 1845, "what you mean precisely by your 'Bells and Pomegranates' title." "The Rabbis," he answered, "make Bells and Pomegranates symbolical of Pleasure and Profit, the gay and the grave, the Poetry and the Prose, Singing and Sermonizing—such a mixture of effects as in the original hour (that is quarter of an hour) of confidence and creation, I meant the whole should prove at last."

He promised a note with the next volume, but in the following March Elizabeth is again urging him: "I persist in thinking that you ought not to be too disdainful to explain your meaning. . . . Mr. Kenyon and I may fairly represent the average intelligence of your readers . . . why should you be too proud to teach such persons as only desire to be taught?"

His lyrics, too, she has to defend against their author! "Am I not to thank you for all the pleasure and pride in these poems? While you stand by and try to talk them down perhaps." But could he not indicate that "Saul" is a fragment? ". . . people can't be expected to understand the difference between incompleteness and defect unless you make a sign."

Then, too, he would throw shorter poems onto the page without any heading except a number. "Your spring-song is full of beauty as you know very well—and 'that's the wise thrush' so characteristic of you (and of the thrush too). Would it not be well if you were to stoop to the vulgarism of prefixing some word of introduction as others do, you know . . . a title . . . a name? . . . Some of the very most beautiful of your lyrics have suffered just from your disdain of the usual tactics of writers in this one respect."

Was there already growing in Browning a mustard seed of resentment against misunderstanding, which blocked him from trying to remove it in a quiet and reasonable fashion and would thirty years later burst out in *Pacchiarotto?*

It has been conjectured that by "The Flight of the Duchess" he hoped to forward more subtly the courtship his rash letter had so deeply compromised: ". . . love is the only good in the world. / Henceforth be loved as heart can love, / Or brain devise," and "If any two creatures grew into one, / They would do more than the world has done: / Though each apart were never so weak." If the poem was a love letter, he may have been disappointed to receive from Elizabeth, seventy-three suggested emendations, even though they were softened by the remark: "You are not to think that I have not a proper respect and admiration for all these new live rhymes." He accepted all but four of the changes.[5]

Emerson has said: "The greatest genius is the most indebted man" and, in relation to Elizabeth, Browning positively clamored to be indebted: ". . . when I try to build a great building, I shall want you to come with me and judge it and counsel me before the scaffolding is taken down, and while you have to make your way over hods and mortar and heaps of lime, and trembling tubs of size, and those thin broad whitewashing brushes I always had a desire to take up and bespatter with."

He seems not to have recognized that he was moving just then into his two great forms, the lyric and the dramatic monologue, but he reiterates a conviction that his best work is in the future, and that he is making a fresh start. Also we can perhaps trace the origin of certain poems. In a letter of June 30, Elizabeth says: "Miss Martineau is practising mesmerism and miracles on all sides she says, and counts on Archbishop Whately as a new adherent." And the next day Browning says of an old friend: "His poor brains are whirling with mesmerism in which he believes, as in all other unbelief." And Elizabeth: "But belief in mesmerism is not the same thing as general unbelief—to do it justice —now is it? It may be super-belief as well." But to Boyd she had written that she shrank "from these temptations as from Lord Bacon's stew of infant children for the purposes of witchcraft." She would as time went on fall to the temptation, but Browning's view is the same in his poem "Mesmerism" as in "Mr. Sludge, The Medium," written so long after it. He hates more than he disbelieves.

Another question arising in the Letters concerned the still-accepted custom of dueling, fiercely attacked by Elizabeth, defended by Browning. And I think we can see in "Before" and "After" the line the musings took, which brought him over to her view. For "Before" is a defense of the duel, with the absolute assumption that the innocent man will be a martyr, the guilty will be punished enough by living on:

> Better sin the whole sin, sure that God observes;
> Then go live his life out! Life will try his nerves,
> When the sky, which noticed all, makes no disclosure,
> And the earth keeps up her terrible composure.

As for the other:

> Ah "forgive" you bid him? While God's champion lives,
> Wrong shall be resisted: dead, why, he forgives.

How great is the drama of "After" when the "hero" has in fact killed the "villain," the "saint" destroyed the "sinner":

> Take the cloak from his face, and at first
>   Let the corpse do its worst!
>
> How he lies in his rights of a man!
>   Death has done all death can.
> And, absorbed in the new life he leads,
>   He recks not, he heeds
> Nor his wrong nor my vengeance; both strike
>   On his senses alike,
> And are lost in the solemn and strange
>   Surprise of the change.
>
> Ha! what avails death to erase
>   His offence, my disgrace?

> I would we were boys as of old
> In the field, by the fold:
> His outrage, God's patience, man's scorn
> Were so easily borne!
>
> I stand here now, he lies in his place:
> Cover the face!

They gossip in their letters as well as arguing and making love. Wordsworth had been to court in a bag wig and a borrowed court suit; bowing low he had fallen on his knees; but Elizabeth cannot agree he was wrong to become Poet Laureate; he does honor to the office, which will be the fitter for Browning to hold later. An American admirer has sent her a letter addressed Elizabeth Barrett, Poetess, London, which the Post Office has miraculously delivered. A "stray gentleman from Philadelphia" is "to perform a pilgrimage to visit the Holy Land" and herself.... And Edgar Allan Poe has dedicated a book to her. Browning is to realize, if he hears Mr. Chorley has been at Wimpole Street, that this is Miss Mitford's doing. Elizabeth has said she will not see him, that Miss Mitford must entertain him in the drawing room if he comes.

It was a tremendous problem: half literary London and all literary visiting Americans wanted to see the "poetess" of the age, as she was so generally considered and so barbarously described. Miss Mitford showed the mistaken kindness of staying five hours with a hostess who had no polite way of cutting the visit short. Almost the only other regular visitor, besides the family—of which one letter mentions forty visiting London at one time and bearing down on Wimpole Street—was Mrs. Jameson, whose books had a great influence in opening the eyes of a blind English world to the meaning and value of medieval art. Elizabeth believed women by and large were inferior to men intellectually, though by no means morally. Women's minds are "of quicker movement, but less power and depth," but Browning is never to tell Miss Martineau or Mrs. Jameson that she has said so. One exception she makes—George Sand, "a colossal nature in every way ... magnanimous and loving the truth." But he did not admire George Sand:

Consuelo "wearies me—oh, wearies," he complains. But he confesses that, unlike his "dear Romance lover," he does not enjoy romances.

Browning had begun to work steadily at raising Elizabeth from her deathbed of seven years. She must move about, leave her room, go out into the noisy house and the noisier street. In a letter postmarked June 10 she writes: "I went downstairs—or rather was carried—and am not the worse." And on the fourteenth she is "better altogether." The same day he answers: "I thank God you are better: do pray make fresh endeavours to profit by this partial respite of the weather!"

By July 8: "I have really been out; and am really alive after it—which is more surprising still—alive enough I mean to write even *so* to-night."

Browning is "happy and thankful." Indeed, she is to be sure to go out again, even if it means he shall miss his visit; he will be "as glad as if I saw you or more—*reasoned* gladness, you know." Yet already he was noting down each half hour spent in her company and once, when the question arose between Friday and Saturday, he had replied, "Friday is the best day because nearest, but Saturday is next best—it is next year, you know."

The word friend was worked hard. There is no question of first names, but they were only briefly "Mr. Browning" and "Miss Barrett." And soon "friend" alone is not enough: she is "My own dear friend," "dearest friend," "my dear first and last friend; my friend." He is "the most grateful of your friends." But he is annoyed at *her* gratitude. "I *do not* seek your friendship to do you good—any good—only to do myself good—though I would, God knows, do that too."

One chief good besides the undeniable improvement in health was the opening of her heart as never before since her brother's death. At first, "so used to discern the correcting and ministering angels by the same footsteps," she had hesitated: "Have I not been ground down to browns and blacks . . . if some natures have to be refined by the sun and some by the furnace . . . both means are to be recognised as good . . . though furnace fire leaves scorched streaks upon the fruit. . . ."

"I am like Marianna in the moated grange and sit listening too often to the mouse in the wainscot."

It came as a shock to Browning when Elizabeth told him some weeks before his first visit that sleep came to her only "in a red hood of poppies." She had called him "Paracelsus" and in his studies for that poem he had probably learned far more than she ever knew about the dangers of the drug. He began at once to combat its use—at the least to implore a cutting down. And in November she emphasizes doctor's orders as though in defense against a criticism, spoken or unspoken. She took it, not for her " 'spirits,' in the usual sense, you must not think such a thing." Her doctor one day, arriving early, had while she was "talking quite cheerfully" ordered it before the right hour "just for the need he observed in the pulse." It was designed "to give the right composure and balance to the nervous system."

The doctors had, it seems, combined with West Indian tradition to turn her into an addict—the word was probably not used at that date—and she had one quality, curiously incompatible with drug addiction—an obstinate truthfulness. Browning's eyes were wide open when his love leaped a barrier which his optimism determined to sweep away. Miss Marks believes that Elizabeth's strong feeling of unworthiness, of the harm she would do him by marrying him, was partly based on an obscure realization of an incurable addiction. The subject recurs in the Letters, and in February, 1846, Browning writes: "All the kind explaining about the opium makes me happier. 'Slowly and gradually' what may *not* be done? Then see the bright weather while I write—lilacs, hawthorn, plum-trees all in bud; elders in leaf, rose-bushes with great red shoots; thrushes, whitethroats, hedge sparrows in full song—there can, let us hope, be nothing worse in store than a sharp wind, a week of it perhaps—and then come what shall come."

This "week," thinks Miss Marks, suggests a reference to the so-called withdrawal agony, but more important perhaps was the picture of a spring that "bursting out all over" carried its message of hope into the stuffy prison of an airless room.

Half afraid to confess what in England at that date was little more respectable than to confess to Catholicism—Elizabeth tells Browning that she is a Nonconformist, and people send her " 'New Testaments' to learn from, with very kind intentions." But she hates "all that rending of the garment of Christ, which Christians are so apt to make the daily week-day of this Christianity so called" and thinks "there is only one Church in heaven and earth, with one divine High Priest to it." Despite the woeful narrowness among dissenters, she has found in a Congregational Chapel a simplicity she likes. They stand, she feels, "on a higher ground" than "those do who call themselves 'Churchmen.' "

Browning is amused. "Can it be you, my own you past putting away, *you* are a schismatic and frequenter of Independent Dissenting Chapels? And you confess this to *me*—whose father and mother went this morning to the very Independent Chapel where they took me, all those years back, to be baptised." Will she be encouraged to bring up any other points of difference "for so sure as you begin proving that there is a gulf fixed between us, so sure shall I end by proving that . . . Anne Radcliffe avert it! . . . That you are just my sister: not that I am much frightened, but there are such surprises in novels!"

Bodily exercise tired Elizabeth far more than mental, of which she was capable of a great deal. But doctors could be "tryingly stupid," telling one "not to think or feel, just as they tell one not to walk out in the dew. . . ." Her present adviser Dr. Chambers was, however, taking more seriously her physical condition and her present improvement— and talking less than former pundits about her nervous system and its "excitability," which one of them had pronounced almost unique in his experience.

Up to now Moulton Barrett had been justified by medical opinion in treating Elizabeth as a total invalid, unable to leave her room, far less to walk, drive, travel. But now Dr. Chambers pronounced that another English winter was the worst possible hazard to her health, that this year she positively must go to a warmer climate. To Miss Mitford she wrote of the medical opinion that, had she gone years ago, "I should be well now, that one lung is very slightly affected but the nervous system *absolutely shattered*."[6] In July, Malta—or Alexandria—was talked of, she heard, between her father and aunt, but, says Elizabeth,

"I suppose *I* should not be much consulted." "Sometimes," she told Browning, "I have haste to be done with it all," feeling "weary unto death with the uses of this life."

"Alexandria!" says Browning. "Well, and may I not as easily ask leave to come 'tomorrow at the Muezzin' as next Wednesday at three?"

Alexandria, Malta, Pisa. He would meet her anywhere, but would she be allowed to go? August had come and still there was silence.

Browning could bear no more. Not vehemently this time, but ardently, he wrote: "When you bade me, that time, be silent . . . dare I say you did not know . . . the power I had over myself, that I could sit and speak and listen as I have done since. Let me say now—*this only once*—that I loved you from my soul and gave you my life, so much of it as you would take,—and all that is *done,* not to be altered . . . you would not need that I tell you—(*tell* you!)—what would be supreme happiness to me in the event—however distant."

"Your life!" she answered, "if you gave it to me and I put my whole heart into it: what should I put but anxiety, and more sadness than you were born to? What could I give you that it would not be ungenerous to give?"

The doctor came again and said, "All the good" of her health "he *used* not to say." So "the Pisa case is strengthened all round by his opinion."

The "Pisa case" rested on that city's repute early in the century as a resort for English consumptives. But Elizabeth's doctor and other friends appear not to have known that it had been the presence of Dr. Vacca of the University of Pisa, not the climate, which had drawn them thither, and that with his death the special reason for going there had disappeared.

George declared there would be anger if she went, but anger also if she did not, and it would all settle down later. But there was the "dead silence of Papa," and then, when she spoke to him herself, he would not answer.

Her eyes, she told Browning, were "swelled with annotations and reflections." She could not travel alone. "I doubt about Arabel and Stormie . . . and it seems I *ought* not to mix them up in a business of

this kind." George—so often away on circuit and anyhow privileged
—need not fear what the "disobedient" Stormie and Arabel would have
to face on their return. She asks Browning's advice and some of what
he had been feeling so long bursts out:

> You have said to me more than once that you wished I might
> never know certain feelings you had been forced to endure . . . and
> I truly wish *you* may never feel what I have to bear in looking on,
> quite powerless, and silent, while you are subjected to this treatment
> which I refuse to characterize—so blind is it *for* blindness. . . . I
> wholly sympathize, however it go against me, with the highest,
> wariest, pride and love for you, and the proper jealousy and vigilance
> they entail—but now, and here, the jewel is not being over guarded,
> but ruined, cast away . . . all common sense interferes—all rationality
> against absolute no-reason at all. And you ask whether you ought
> to obey this no-reason? I will tell you: all passive obedience and
> implicit submission of will and intellect is by far too easy, if well con-
> sidered, to be the course prescribed by God to Man in this life of
> probation—for they *evade* probation altogether, though foolish
> people think otherwise. Chop off your legs, you will never go astray;
> stifle your reason altogether and you will find it is difficult to reason
> ill. . . . The partial indulgence, the proper exercise of one's faculties,
> there is the difficulty and problem for solution, set by that Providence
> which might have made the laws of Religion as indubitable as those
> of vitality, and revealed the articles of belief as certainly as that
> condition, for instance, by which we breathe so many times in a
> minute to support life. But there is no reward proposed for the feat
> of breathing, and a great one for that of believing . . . all our life is
> some form of religion, and all our action some belief, and there is
> but one law, however modified, for the greater and the less.
>
> . . . you are in what I should wonder at as the veriest slavery—
> and I who *could* free you from it, I am here scarcely daring to write
> . . . what *shall not* be again written or spoken, if you so will. . . . Now
> while I *dream*, let me once dream! I would marry you now and
> thus—I would come when you let me, and go when you bade me—I

would be no more than one of your brothers—'*no more*'—that is, instead of getting tomorrow for Saturday, I should get Saturday as well—two hours for one—when your head ached I should be *here*. I deliberately choose the realization of that dream (—of sitting simply by you for an hour every day) rather than any other, excluding you, I am able to form for this world, or any world I know. . . .

Elizabeth replied:

. . . to receive such a proof of attachment from *you,* not only overpowers every present evil, but seems to me a full and abundant amends for the merely personal sufferings of my whole life. When I had read that letter last night I *did* think so. I looked round and round for the small bitternesses which for several days had been bitter to me, and I could not find one of them. The tear-marks went away in the moisture of new, happy tears.

. . . Henceforward I am yours for everything but to do you harm . . . it rests with God and with you—only in the meanwhile you are most absolutely free . . . "unentangled" (as they call it) by the breadth of a thread—and if I did not know that you considered yourself so, I would not see you any more, let the effort cost me what it might. You force me to feel . . . but you cannot force me to *think* contrary to my first thought . . . that it were better for you to forget me at once in one relation.

And Browning:

. . . *My own,* now! For there it is—oh, do not fear I am "entangled"—my crown is loose on my head, not nailed there—my pearl lies in my hand—I may return it to the sea, if I will!

9 One Winter and Then . . .

"If we love in the other world as we do in this I shall love thee to eternity."

CERUTTI'S ITALIAN GRAMMAR

"Tell me I am not wrong," Elizabeth wrote, after a final pronouncement by her father, "in taking up my chain again. . . . The bitterest 'fact' of all is that I had believed Papa to have loved me more . . . but . . . I never would *un*know anything . . . even were it the taste of the apples by the Dead Sea . . ."

Browning, too, was feeling the strain. His headaches became more frequent and more intense: sometimes bad pain, sometimes what he calls "bewildering." He had nightmares—he who commonly never dreamed—and they were invariably "of one sort. I stand by (powerless to interpose by a word even) and see the infliction of tyranny on the unresisting man or beast—and I wake just in time not to die. . . ." But he wrote, "Be sure my own dearest love, that this is for the best . . . and you will, I know, knowing you—*will* be well this one winter if you can, and then . . ."

And she: "I *will not* be beaten down if the will can do anything. . . . My cage is not worse but better since you brought the green groundsell to it—and to dash oneself against the wires of it will not open the door. We shall see . . . and God will oversee. . . And let us both be busy and cheerful."

In that golden autumn which occasionally follows an English summer, Browning must have the news that Elizabeth is "well and walking, and working for my sake towards *the time*."

And a few days later: "Try, try dearest, every method, take every measure. . . . Why, we shall see Italy together."

His whole mind was now set on this great "consummation" to her sad life and to his own life "of wonders—absolute wonders, with God's hand over all. . . . And this last and best of all would not have begun so, and gone on so, to break off abruptly even here, in this world for the little time. . . . There is life before us."

But he must beat down Elizabeth's self-doubting, her depression, her recurrent conviction that she could only damage this other life. "I who sat here alone but yesterday, so weary of my own being that to take an interest in my very poems I had to lift them up by an effort and separate them from myself." Grateful even to Flush for staying near her, grateful to her family for not making her feel a burden, she was a burden to herself, "shut up too long face to face with my own spirit." Evil seemed to her so "dreadfully natural"; she was a Cassandra, was born under the star of Wormwood.

"My best, dear, dear one," he writes, "may you be better, less *depressed*. . . . Now, *walk*, move . . . *anima mia dolce*. Shall I not know one day how far your mouth will be from mine as we walk?"

Why will she persist, he asks, almost despairingly, in thinking of him simply as full of "fidelity to a given word and noble constancy. . . . I love you because I love you. . . . Let me have my way, live my life, love my love." And in another letter: "You say, 'I am a man and may change' —I answer yes—but, while I hold my senses, only change for the *presumable* better . . . not for the *experienced worst*." After seeing her, he can say about marriage as Voltaire did about God—if it did not exist "I should infallibly *invent* it." Her friendship, once so important, now seems nothing. "I am wedded to you now. . . . So take me and make me what you can and will. . . ."

In the first month of 1846 Elizabeth could tell him she had "walked down-stairs into the drawing-room —walked, mind. Before, I was carried by one of my brothers." This was real "glory," and her sleep too was improving, owing probably to the increase of movement and the fresh air breathed in through summer and autumn. She was as she had promised, cutting down the morphine with increasing success.

And after all he did "confidently expect *the* end." He had told Elizabeth that he always got what he wanted. They were busy and fundamentally they were happy that winter. She continued to read and criticize, growing more and more enthusiastic over " 'St. Praxed,' 'Pictor Ignotus,' 'Night and Morning'—and the 'Earth's Immortalities.' "

Earlier she had written: "The *Duchess* appears to me more than ever a new-minted golden coin—the rhythm of it answering to your own description, 'Speech half asleep or song half awake?' You have right of trove to these novel effects of rhythm. Now if people do not cry out about these poems what are we to think of the world?"

The world, alas, remained blind and deaf. Browning's poetry was newer, more startlingly original to the nineteenth century than T. S. Eliot's to the twentieth. But the twentieth is readier to welcome the new, the startling. There were one or two good reviews, but the only real enthusiasm came from Landor in a poem he sent from Italy, four lines of which especially were to become more and more appropriate:

> Since Chaucer was alive and hale,
> No man has walkt along our road with step
> So active, so inquiring eye, or tongue,
> So varied in discourse.

"Those noble verses," Browning said happily in a letter to Mr. Kenyon, who had with equal delight sent a copy to Elizabeth. It meant more than a court decoration: "I may be allowed to wear my 'order' at my button hole on gala days, therefore, and where should I go when dressed like the man whom the King delighteth to honour, if not to Miss Barrett? I sent her a copy directly; but am none the less grateful to you for your good office."[1]

As for Elizabeth, she found herself beginning to take pleasure only in those visitors who talked with appreciation of Browning. Mrs. Jameson startled her into the secret delight of realizing that *she* was thought generous and magnanimous for admiring the work of a rival poet. Miss

Mitford disliked him, and Elizabeth confesses to shame in wearying utterly of so kind a friend. Mr. Kenyon, however, did admire fittingly, so his visits would have been a pleasure but for the eyes which looked piercingly at her with the often repeated question, "Has Browning been here lately?"

These visitors, like her relatives, were accustomed to thinking of visiting Elizabeth as a pure kindness and would often leave it uncertain on which day they were to be expected. As Browning's visits grew to twice a week, the unobtrusive arranging of them became more and more difficult. "Take away the doubt about Miss Mitford," one letter runs, "and Mr. Kenyon remains—and take away Mr. Kenyon and there is Mrs. Hedley," (an aunt). Inside the house only her sisters were in the secret; of the rest—brothers, servants—she could say that there were many suspectors, but no informers. But when Mr. Kenyon asked her abruptly if there was anything between Henrietta and Captain Surtees Cook, she knew what he really meant, and only reminded him that such feelings were not allowed in this house. She rejoiced when his spectacles were broken and the gaze which made her blush idiotically became less piercing: "Those detestable spectacles—like the Greek burning glasses, turned full on my face."

Browning grew restive over these fears and precautions. He would have liked openly to approach Mr. Barrett; it was hard for any man in a century as civilized as the nineteenth to believe in what Elizabeth told him the result would be. Her letters would be intercepted and she herself guarded so closely as to make further intercourse impossible. Browning must allow, too, for a physical state which made it impossible for her to stand up to the violent scenes that would ensue. Mentally, spiritually, she would not fail; but physically she easily might; they must leave the house secretly when the day came—none must know lest they suffer for the knowledge; a servant would be summarily dismissed and the heaviest displeasure would strike sister or brother.

A defense of Moulton Barrett was put up to Jeannette Marks by his grandson. It is embodied by her in her interesting book, *The Family of the Barrett*. He was, we are told, a most affectionate father and a man of kindest heart. He treated the slaves on his plantation generously.

None of them had revolted in the big insurrection and when they were turned into apprentices, he was among the few ex-owners who remained humane and just, not like many others managing to make their last state worse than their first.

His opposition to the marriages of Henrietta and Alfred (said Alfred's son) was entirely reasonable. There had been far too much intermarrying in the Barrett family already, and these marriages were both with second cousins. This, Miss Marks objected, did not apply to Elizabeth's marriage—but here the grandson agreed with his grandfather even more thoroughly: Browning's grandfather had kept a public house!

In the terribly snobbish England of those days, the father (however cultured) a bank clerk, certainly supplied another plausible excuse. But the opposition to marriage had not begun with either of these problems. Henrietta's previous attachment, Bro's desire to marry, had been frustrated with the same brutal finality. Surtees Cook was not far out when he enquired meekly of his future father-in-law whether children were to be regarded as slaves. In spirit the ex-slaveowner, the descendant of generations of slaveowners, remained just that. Kind he could be, affectionate he could be, but he must always be supreme. No affection, no tenderness could subsist where he had been defied.

At least, Browning urged, could they not confide in Mr. Kenyon who was, he fancied, pretty well aware of the situation already? He hated to keep so warm a friend in the dark. But no, said Elizabeth, above all Mr. Kenyon must not be told: "I beseech you to avoid by every legitimate means the doing *that* . . . oh DO NOT *ever speak* THAT *to him*." Had Browning never heard Kenyon speak of his "organ of caution? . . . We should involve him in ever so many fears for us, and force him to have his share of the odium at last."

Elizabeth must have known that not only her health but the lack of finances would frighten their cautious old friend. She does comment: "A marriage without lawyers would be an abomination in his eyes. Moreover, to discover ourselves to him, and *not submit to his counsels*, would be a real offence." But he might forgive two poets if they "poetically rush into a foolishness."

They felt this problem of secrecy from different angles: she wanting to say a word to Mrs. Jameson, who kept urging her to accept her escort to Italy; he feeling treacherous to Kenyon. Then he fancied she did not want him to tell his parents; and when that was cleared up, he was distressed at her feeling that *he* should not bring his sister to see her and that *she* ought not to drive to Hatcham to see his father and mother. Each perceived so vividly one set of dangers which seemed to the other not so dangerous after all that only a profound love could have carried them through these months.

Would her health build up enough for the journey to be made before winter was upon them? Could they keep the secret as they made their plans, did such packing as was minimally necessary, and worked out traveling difficulties greater than a trip to Australia would offer today.

Flush was a minor problem; he had become jealous of Browning. He bit him twice, was smacked by the maid, Wilson, reproached by Elizabeth and told he would never be loved again. Whereupon he looked at her "with an expression of quite despair on his face." He must go with them; he *must* not bark when leaving the house. Wilson taken into confidence agreed to go with them. Elizabeth had hesitated: She was "an expensive servant—she has £16 a year!" He would, Browning answered, be "simply, exactly INSANE to move a step" without "Wilson or someone in her capacity." It was the sort of hesitation that awakened in him a half-comic, half-serious despair. "Yet you write of this to me *so*, my Ba!"

This is the first time I have written the name by which her family, and now her lover, called her—instead of the really beautiful Elizabeth. It signified, Mr. Kenyon said, that she was only half a ba-by—but it seems, alas, to have been pronounced as in Baa-lamb. Given to her by her brother in infancy, the name had stuck, as pet names will. So Browning did not, like Jane Austen's Darcy, call her, when he proposed, "Dearest, loveliest Elizabeth." He seems to have liked Ba, for Ba she remained to the end of the story.

One side event of this intense summer illustrated the problems of a secret engagement. Elizabeth had corresponded with the painter Haydon, a curious character who had gone up and come down like a rocket. He had a real talent for a likeness and has left sketches of Keats often reproduced; but he had ambitions of a more grandiose sort and was for a while paid big sums for vast historical cartoons. Success went to his head, he developed a delight in insulting other artists, and had made so many enemies that it was hard to tell how much his eclipse owed to this, how much to the fact that his pretentious canvasses had been greatly overrated.

He had married in the days of his prosperity and when his cartoons were rejected in a contest for the decoration of the new Houses of Parliament, his wife exclaimed, "Then we shall starve." Already several times imprisoned for debt, and overwhelmed with despair, he committed suicide.

Haydon, though he had never seen Elizabeth, had begged her to store for him some pictures and several trunks of papers, and now in his will came the request that she should edit them for publication. She had unwittingly brought it on herself by agreeing three years earlier to read part of his memoirs. Browning and Mr. Kenyon agreed that Haydon had hoped her ignorance of the world would result in the publication of his most treasured indiscretions! With skillful editing she felt a fascinating book was possible, but much of the manuscript was "fervid and coarse at once, with personal references blood-dyed at every page...."

"And," commented Browning, "how horrible are all these posthumous revelations,—these passions of the now passionless, errors of the at length better instructed." It was indeed a "*dispiriting* bequest." But *how* dispiriting he realized only after a dinner at the house of Sergeant Talfourd, Haydon's executor. For that busy gossip, Miss Mitford, had forwarded to Talfourd some extracts from Elizabeth's letters when first the books and pictures had been dumped on her. Landseer, Forster, Babbage and others were present, and "the words, 'H.' it seems, has been in the habit of using Miss B's house etc.' (or to that effect) had so offensive an implication,—that I felt obliged to say simply, you had never seen Haydon and were altogether amazed and distressed." Browning said only enough, he wrote, "to remove the impression from the minds of the people present that you must have 'known' Haydon, as they call 'knowing.' " But in conversation, as we learn from a letter of Elizabeth's to her brother George, he told her that "somebody said that her house appeared the receptacle for his goods against his creditors"; others wondered how Miss Barrett should have come to know a man of his type. "Poor Haydon," comments Elizabeth, "did not lead the most prudent of lives it appears. See what a scrape I am in." As to Miss Mitford "none of the ridicule of what appears to have been a most ridiculous letter fell to the ground"—least of all her grandiloquent conclusion *"And so speaks our great poetess."*

It all sounds quite bad enough, but Elizabeth adds: "Worse things were said or implied I do not doubt, than what [Mr. Browning] told me, he was *so* angry."

That evening, however, Browning managed to get Talfourd alone and he agreed to take over all responsibility; he knew George Barrett and promised to "arrange everything" with him "when I meet him on circuit."

They could breathe again, yet the letter to George is full of injunctions of caution—toward Talfourd, toward Papa, toward all the world. As to Haydon's papers, a brilliant three volumes was drawn from them seven years later, and called by Miss Mitford "the most melancholly, painful, fascinating book that I ever took up."[2]

But Elizabeth was left sad. Her help could not have filled the great abyss of Haydon's debts, yet she wished she had offered it. He was so nearly, she felt, a great man, but "Think what an agony life was to him, so constituted!—his own genius a clinging curse! the fire and the clay in him seething and quenching one another!—the man seeing maniacally in all men the assassins of his fame! . . . struggling, stifling, breaking the hearts of the creatures dearest to him, in the conflict for which there was no victory."

This tragedy crossing the path of their love has an interesting relation to Browning's own life and character. "You have the opinion," he would write in 1867 in reply to a request for criticism, "of the most unpopular poet that ever was, and so will be sure not to mind too much the sour sayings of the likes of him."

Perhaps it is easier to bear failure before than after wealth and fame.

Browning may never have been tempted to extravagant living or to envy of his fellow craftsmen. But now and throughout his married life he showed a strength the greater for its possible appearance of a weakness. His letters are at first full of suggestions as to how he could earn enough money for the cheap living offered by Italy. He had finished for Forster a life of Strafford; he had once compiled a French primer to help his teacher, and the very papers which abused *Paracelsus* had praised it highly. He could, he believed, write a novel. Or again, he could perhaps get government employment. "How do you not know," objected Elizabeth, "that you may not be sent to Russia or somewhere impossible?"

He could write for a periodical, and this she thought more feasible, but "it is not a necessity, there is no sort of need of it in fact—and why should you be tormented 'in the multitude of the thoughts within you' utterly in vain?"

The decision to live on her small fortune in the simple way both liked may have been unwise, but was certainly courageous. Is it better for the poet to be free from the toils of earning that living which poetry seldom if ever brings? For Browning it probably was. Added to his headaches, to the intense concentration on his writing, the keen and constant observation that fed it, he was now in large part taking on himself the task of nurse and doctor. He had not known when he fell in love with Elizabeth that she had money of her own, but relief must have mingled with his natural feeling that a man ought not to be dependent on his wife. She was steady in her determination that he should remain solely and totally a poet. As for what the world would say, had he, she remarked, with justice, wanted money, he would have gone for thousands and not for her poor little hundreds. He could (she claimed with less plausibility) have married the millionairess Miss Burdett Coutts, or indeed any other woman in the world.

Then, too, they always went on hoping his poems would begin to sell. Fifteen hundred of Tennyson's latest volume had sold in a year, he heard, which in those days meant a very fair sum for the author. As to work "Did not Shakespeare do more than Cromwell?" she asked.

One day when all their problems pressed, Browning felt attracted to the *sortes Virgilianae.* Reaching blindly for a book, he came up with the unhelpful Italian Grammar of his old teacher Cerutti: "What could it prove but some assurance that you were in the Dative Case, or I, not in the ablative absolute?" He would have been thankful only to find such a word as "conjunction" or "possessive pronoun." But after all it *was* an Italian Grammar and a phrase stood out from the "Promiscuous Exercises" for translation at which he opened. "*If we love in the other world as we do in this, I shall love thee to eternity.*"

"Do my eyes see double," says Elizabeth, "dazzled by the light of it? 'I shall love thee to eternity'—I *shall*."

It is often pointed out that Browning's own experiences were basis and inspiration for many of his poems, and he was now going through the greatest. While he told of triumph in "The Flight of the Duchess" and *The Ring and the Book,* he showed in "The Statue and the Bust" how close failure lay. This poem starts with love at first sight—the woman being already married. Compare the picture with that given of Elizabeth in "By the Fireside":

> Hair in heaps lay heavily
> Over a pale brow spirit-pure. . . .
> And vainly sought to dissemble her eyes
> Of the blackest black our eyes endure

Each night the man determines, each day she vows, that on the morrow they will break away:

> But next day passed, and next day yet,
> With still fresh cause to wait one day more
> Ere each leaped over the parapet. . . .
> So weeks grew months, years; gleam by gleam
> The glory dropped from their youth and love,
> And both perceived they had dreamed a dream;
>
> Which hovered as dreams do still above:
> But who can take a dream for a truth?

And again in "Youth and Art," young people too poor to marry:

> Each life unfulfilled, you see;
>   It hangs still, patchy and scrappy:

> We have not sighed deep, laughed free,
> Starved, feasted, despaired,—been happy

It would have been so terribly easy to fail. In January, 1846, Browning had written: "I claim your promise's fulfillment—say at the summer's end . . . you will think of the main fact as *ordained,* granted by God, will you not, dearest?—So, not to be put in doubt *ever again*— then we can go on quietly thinking of after matters." But this hardly seemed possible for them; quiet was not the distinctive adjective for either. A small boy once pointed to the sun's path across a room and said, "Look, that's the sun's shadow." And so Elizabeth: "You have fallen like a great luminous blot on the whole leaf of the world . . . of life and time . . . and I can see nothing beyond you, nor wish to see it."

Yet each felt uncertain in turn as they tried to complete their plans in the best possible way. Various places in Italy were thought of, and discovered to be unfit because of bad water, malaria, or the prevalence of English tourists. Various ways of travel were discussed—boat or train had each its disadvantages. The hour of her departure must be precisely one in which her family would be all safely out—or at dinner. Nothing must be done that could involve her sisters or brothers in the parental wrath. Elizabeth was immensely concerned about this, was distressed at the thought that the word "elopement" might be used of their action, kept recurring to her fear of ruining Browning's life. And, inevitable though it was, she still suffered at the thought of deceiving and distressing her father.

Browning's problem was a far greater one than the Duke's, the young artists' or even Elizabeth's own. The Duke could snap his fingers at society's judgments; the young artists had youth and strength on their side, and no watching world to condemn. Chesterton was the first to note that the best shadowing of Browning himself lies in his picture of Caponsacchi in *The Ring and the Book.* Half Rome would condemn Pompilia and Caponsacchi alike, but the main problem for him was: should he leave Pompilia to die in Arezzo at the hands of her husband, or should he risk the pursuit which might, and indeed did, equally end in death.

For this mysterious illness of Elizabeth's might have killed her on the journey. And Browning may well have been asking himself in the words of his own "Clive" "How should I have borne me, please."[3] Only one doctor had recommended an earlier journey which had everything to make it easy—sister and brother with her and plenty of money for the best hotels and the easiest traveling. And now she was going under conditions which made important the difference between tickets costing £5 or so more or less, under an intense emotional strain, into a life of comparative poverty. To all this Browning with his vivid imagination was intensely alive. Yet he had already raised her from her bed; he trusted God for the rest.

That was a tremendous element in the decision. Deeper still was the plain fact that they were so much married already. When Browning (in November '45) added up the hours they had spent together and brought them out at two days, Elizabeth said, "So little! so dreadfully little! What shallow earth for a deep root."

But there was surely also strong passion, at any rate on Browning's side. When, thinking she might be too ill for fullness of marriage, he offered to marry her and be only as one of her brothers, one realizes (and I think she did) the magnitude of the offer. And when he writes that if she rises to receive him, he will be utterly overcome; when both feel that to meet in the presence of others will be an intolerable strain; when he writes: "I that stammer and answer haphazard with you— Have you not discovered by this time that I go on talking with my thoughts away?"—they do not allude merely to the keeping of a secret. Victorian prudery brooded even over the poetry, but human passion was there.

10 Married in Italy

In the great right of an excessive wrong . . .
THE RING AND THE BOOK

BOTH WERE strained to breaking point. Browning got one of his customary disabling headaches; Elizabeth forgot her own health in anxiety for his. And then Flush was stolen by a gang which specialized in collecting ransom from distracted owners of stolen pets. Mr. Barrett forbade the brother, deputed by Elizabeth, to pay the ransom. The dog's death was threatened and Elizabeth, in desperation, herself went down to the dog stealers' haunts and interviewed the wife of the "intermediary" to whom the ransom was to be paid. For once Browning agreed in principle with his future father-in-law and wrote of the sin of encouraging this evil; but after all Flush was Flush ("a sort of dog," said Elizabeth, "to whom you couldn't reasonably refuse the franchise") and Browning would never (he said) have written thus but for the belief that Elizabeth had already got him back!

Flush was home, thin, thirsty and still terrified, on Sunday, September 7, 1846, but Browning was now in the doctor's hands and forbidden to go out until Wednesday—and on Wednesday came the parental decree that a house in the country was to be found and the Barrett family transferred to it without delay while Wimpole St. was cleaned, painted, renovated.

That day he had again been with Elizabeth and again pressing for instant action. "I will not add one word to those spoken yesterday [runs Thursday's letter] about the extreme perilousness of delay,"—and after receiving this fresh news: "I will go for a licence today and we can be married on Saturday. . . . We can leave from Dover &c., *after* that,—but otherwise impossible!"

With Wilson, on Saturday morning September 12, Elizabeth slipped out of the house and Robert and she were married at Marylebone Church at eleven. Elizabeth went on to Mr. Boyd, a visit to whom had been the cover used with her family. She sent Wilson home and lay down on the sofa to recover, her host being "happily engaged with a medical counsellor." And then came Cyprus wine and a light wedding breakfast of bread and butter, after which her sisters arrived. "And so, to complete the bravery, I went on with them in the carriage to Hampstead . . . as far as the heath,—and talked and looked."

The next day Mr. Kenyon "came with his spectacles, looking as if his eyes reached to their rim all the way round . . .'*When did you see Browning?*' . . . 'He was here on Friday' . . . Dearest he saw something but not all."

Chesterton has said and others have repeated that Browning would not come to Wimpole Street after the wedding because he scrupled to ask for his wife as Miss Barrett, but the Letters do not bear this out. On Sunday he writes "I confide in your judgment. . . . I will not ask to see you for instance—though of course a word brings me as usual to you." And on Monday she says, "It is best, I continue to think, that you should not come here. . . . I don't know how to put my feeling into words, but I do seem to feel that it would be better, and less offensive to those whom we offend." The decision to avoid another meeting before their departure was certainly hers.

Now they must write the letters and notices to be sent to their friends, and again she is terrified of his being too precipitate, especially concerning Mr. Kenyon. "Do let no letter or intimation be given till the very last. Remember that I shall be *killed*—it will be so infinitely worse than you can have an idea."

Both write to Mr. Kenyon and to Mrs. Jameson; they compose a notice of the wedding for the *Times*; Robert looks up departures of boats, gets them wrong, follows one letter with another and yet another to correct himself, fusses over the need to keep down the weight of their luggage (they might almost have been traveling by air), and she questions his impression that every pound will be charged for. Then, too, Elizabeth cannot take boxes or bags openly out of the house. Wilson contrives somehow to get the baggage sent ahead to Vauxhall station. The entire servants' hall must, of course, have been in the secret and enjoying it heartily. The postscript of the last letter Elizabeth ever wrote to Browning runs: "The boxes are *safely sent*. Wilson has been perfect to me. And *I* . . . calling her timid."

Finally Elizabeth must write the farewell to her family, and she chose her brother George as the channel of communication. This letter has survived—and very moving it is. A letter to her father is enclosed, but she begs George first to break the news to him gently—and himself to understand her letter. "Oh, love me George, while you are reading it. Love me—that I may find pardon in your heart for me after it is read." If she were to give up this prospect of life and happiness "there would be a victim without an expiation & a sacrifice without an object. My spirits would have festered on in this enforced prison & none of you all would have been the happier. . . . Also I should have wronged *another*. . . .

"If you have any affection for me George, dearest George, let me have word at Orleans."

And Browning's family? Father, mother and sister were all in the secret, bound up, as Cyrus Mason saw them, in an exclusive little enclave within the larger family; but, to that larger family, Mason witnessed a curious farewell. In the cottage at Hatch End their grandmother was sitting one afternoon, looking very pretty and well dressed, when

> . . . the door was suddenly opened and "young Robert" bounded into the room, his face ablaze with excitement. For a moment he stood admiring grandmother Browning; she sitting too astounded to speak; then for an instant the Poet regarded her approvingly, advanced, seized one of the old lady's hands in both of his and said cheerily, but not without a sort of catch in his voice:

'A monstrous mistake! According to the Book of Common Prayer a man is forbidden to marry his grandmother! The pity of it.'

He then stooped and reverently and impressively kissed the surprised and flattered old lady. I was astounded, for with him kissing was an unusual form of salutation.

Browning's entrance and exit struck Cyrus as "hysterical." Looking back, he saw it as the climax of preparation for the momentous flight, a farewell to the family conveyed by an impressive kiss to its oldest member.

Mrs. Jameson was astonished at seeing the Brownings in Paris, perhaps even before she had received their letters; she suggested that they should complete the journey to Pisa with her. She was taking her niece to Italy and she knew all there was to know of travel by diligence and rail, and of inexpensive yet adequate hotels.

" 'You wild dear creature,' " she cried as she embraced Elizabeth. " 'You dear abominable poets . . . ought to have a little prose. But he is a wise man and you are a wise woman, let the world say as it pleases. I shall dance for joy both in earth and in heaven my dear friends.' All this in interrupted interjections," writes Elizabeth to Arabel.

Mrs. Jameson, writing to her friend Lady Noel Byron, describes the arrival of "my poet" and "my poetess. . . . She is nervous, frightened, ashamed, agitated, happy, miserable." "The charming fugitive pair are a great interest and a great care . . . the deportment of both is perfect. . . . Both are *so* good."

At Orleans they would find letters from home and Elizabeth had written on the back of hers from Paris, "Do you think Arabel, dearest Papa will forgive me at last—answer."

"Love me," she had entreated her brother; and for her father's love her yearning was greater yet. But this great faculty, so strong in her and her sisters, seemed left out of the surviving men of her family. Her father, she had known, would not forgive: the only thing recorded of his letter is the accusation that Elizabeth had sold her soul (by which he probably meant her social position) for genius! But from her brothers she had expected some measure of affectionate understanding. "I thought it hard, I confess, that he [George] should have written to me so with a sword." Only her sisters sympathized—and that with all their hearts. To them she wrote of the "death warrant" she had more than half expected while she held the letters in her hand "not able to open one, and growing paler and colder every moment."

Only the kind letters would she show to Browning, whom she had sent away while she read. And there was comfort in the affectionate understanding of dear Mr. Kenyon. Never again would she fear those spectacles. "I know no two persons so worthy of each other. . . . It is a pleasant vision to me to think that, if I live, I may hereafter enjoy your joint society and affection . . . if the thing had been asked of me I should have advised it, albeit glad that I was not asked. . . ."

After all she could not but be happy, and Mrs. Jameson watched with delight "you and Mr. Browning together. If two persons were to be chosen from the ends of the earth for perfect union and fitness, there could not be a greater congruity."

To her also were shown only the kind letters, and she reports to Lady Noel that Elizabeth "is much comforted and certainly gaining strength in spite of the exertion and fatigue. As yet there is not a trace of animal spirits, though evidently a sense of deep happiness, gratitude and love. As to *him* his joy and delight, and his poetical fancies and antics, with every now and then the profoundest seriousness interrupting the brilliant current of his imagination make him altogether a most charming companion."

A little nervous as to the effect on her young niece of such an unconventional marriage, she reports once more that: "The deportment of both is in the best taste and Gerardine can only gain by what she sees and hears." But at Avignon, Elizabeth had to be lifted, fainting, from the carriage, bruised all over by the movement; the rest of the journey must be made by sea so that she could lie down. Still their guardian angel abounds in enthusiasm for the unselfish devotion of each and for a "mutual deportment . . . marked by a most graceful propriety without any appearance of gêne. Gerardine has profited every way."

At Vaucluse they honored the memory of Petrarch, and Browning enthroned Elizabeth on a high rock above the stream, in that glorious green shade shot through with sunlight, Flush barking furiously the while at the fate of his mistress.

The sea passage to Genoa took twenty-six hours, and it was even rougher on the boat to which they changed for Leghorn. The journey was completed by train and, at Pisa, Mrs. Jameson left them:

> With all the abundance of love and high principles, I have had now and then a tremor at my heart about their future. *He* is full of spirits and good humour and his turn for making the best of everything and his bright intelligence and his rare acquirements of every kind rendered him the very prince of travelling companions. *But* (always *buts!!*) he is in all the common things of this life the most impractical of men, the most uncalculating, rash, in short the worst *manager* I ever met with. She, in her present state, and from her long seclusion almost helpless. Now only conceive the menage that is likely to ensue and without FAULT on either side. For the present our first care is to get her into some comfortable lodgings.[1]

The "lodgings" were in the Collegio Ferdinando, a "huge pile" in the front of which they could count forty-seven windows and doors. It was a bitter winter in England, and Elizabeth wondered as the months passed whether this might shake the assurance of those who blamed her. In Pisa it was usually warm, but when it was not, Elizabeth kept "by the fire feeling very contented and very well." Not quite so well one day, she saw a doctor who discovered her to be over five months' pregnant. She writes to her sisters, furious at her own stupidity; all would have been well the doctor said, had he known in time. As it was, the miscarriage was quickly got over and she was able to write to Mrs. Martin: "I am wonderfully well and far better and stronger than before what you call the Pisan 'crisis.'"

On February 24, 1847, Browning was writing to his publisher Edward Moxon of a new edition of *Paracelsus, Pippa* and some "others," which would improve them not "by cutting them up and reconstructing them but by affording just the proper revision they ought to have had before they were printed at all." The Berg collection copy of

Paracelsus on which Browning worked, inscribed *To Frederick Locker from R. B. April 13, 1869,* contains a good deal of new material and many corrections, mostly augmenting the music of the verse. But the omissions are sometimes unfortunate, especially that of the Preface, where, without using the word, he made a plea for the technique of the dramatic monologue as contrasted with that of the drama. The letter to Moxon ends: "I say nothing of my wife's poems and their sale. She is, there and in all else, as high above me as I would have her."

They went on to Florence where they entertained Mrs. Jameson for a week. She arrived on Shakespeare's birthday, with a bottle of wine from Arezzo "to do it the due honours in company with 'two poets.' "[2]

In their first year in Florence they moved five times. But in April '48 they established themselves in an apartment and later an entire floor of the Casa Guidi. Robert at siesta time would settle Elizabeth in the deepest shadow to be found, "pours eau de cologne into my hands and on my forehead and fans me till my eyes shut of themselves." He persuades her in the evening to walk down the stairs into "a bath of cool air at the bottom of the house"—"last night we . . . got as far as the Baptistery where we sat down in the half-dark and talked of Dante." But by July the heat was overwhelming; they must go somewhere, Elizabeth finally setting her heart on Vallombrosa: "forty miles through the mountains of wild, roadless rock and forest." But only a monastery to receive them—and would women be received at all? To some sort of guesthouse, Elizabeth and Wilson were allowed to come, but after five days, were turned out by "that little holy abbot with the red face" who, she had feared on sight, would be "jealous of his sanctity and the approach of women." But the scenery had been glorious and Elizabeth had shown an almost incredible strength, dragged by oxen in a laundry basket along rough paths up the mountain. Returning to a slight respite in the weather, they decided to remain in Florence.

Looking across the sea from Italy to the room in Wimpole Street, Elizabeth felt that on the one side was life—on the other death. "I was buried," she wrote to Mrs. Martin, "and that was the whole. . . . A thoroughly morbid and desolate state it was, which I look back now to with a sort of horror with which one would look to one's graveclothes, if one had been clothed in them by mistake during a trance."

Mr. Kenyon had written: "I considered that you had *perilled your life* upon this undertaking, and reflecting upon your last position, I thought that *you had done well*."

"You are not improved," Mrs. Jameson said, "you are transformed." And Elizabeth had to tell Robert that he really must not boast so much of how she had walked here or walked there, as if a wife with two legs was a marvelous phenomenon in nature.

Of those nearest to her "tomb," Elizabeth wrote, "my family had become so accustomed to the idea of my living on and on in that room, that while my heart was eating itself, their love for me was consoled, and at last the evil grew scarcely perceptible. It was no want of love in them, and quite natural in itself: we all get used to the thought of a tomb."

Love would surely have welcomed the throwing off of the grave clothes, the rising from the sepulcher, but Elizabeth's father and brothers were complaining bitterly that Browning was living on his wife's money; George was asserting that no one should marry with an income of less than £2,000 a year. The disproportion is almost too great, and perhaps an underlying consciousness of their own failure was stoking the flames of their wrath. After some years Elizabeth's brothers forgave her for choosing life over death; her father never did.

Miss Marks sees in Edward Moulton Barrett's original opposition to his daughter's going abroad a fear he did not choose to voice of the absence of her doctor and the craving for her drug. His sense of personal responsibility for his children was abnormal, and it had, as she points out, gone unchallenged all their lives. There had been occasional "hysterical scenes but never year after year any persistent, courageous, and independent development of their own lives." The daughter with feeble body and shattered nerves had now found the courage to break away, and in doing so set an example. True she had what the others had not, a little money of her own, but surely their health and strength would have outweighed this. It may have been sense of his own failure that sharpened the "sword" with which George wrote to his sister.

It was not he, but Henrietta, who had broken the news to Papa. He was standing on the staircase, a heavy book in hand, which he dropped—or threw. Henrietta, dodging the book, slipped and fell. One version has it that he knocked her down; but this is improbable. As Miss Marks says, "It is one thing to throw down a book. It is another to throw down your daughter." (But Occy [Octavius, brother number eight], remarked, "My old Dad was hasty, very hasty.") And "the records suggest," Miss Marks says, "that several scenes of hurricane violence followed one another," until he lapsed into the silence which buried henceforward any mention of Elizabeth's existence. Her letters were unopened, her name unspoken. The family seems to feel that he became not quite sane on the matter. "A monomania," said Mr. Kenyon.

And Miss Marks, visiting Jamaica, studied on the spot the story of a family, generous and liberal with the slaves they had owned for three hundred years, but bringing up each eldest son with a mentality that turned his own children into replicas of well-treated slaves. "Then a member of that group," she concludes, "handicapped nervously and physically, shattered the history of three hundred years and in flight broke through and surmounted Barrett backgrounds."

But Mr. Barrett, once a Jamaican slaveowner, remained "an English gentleman" and a trader, going to the city daily to arrange about cargoes of sugar and rum from Jamaica and to hear the news of his ships *Statira* and *David Lyon*. The Barretts were living in the world of what Dickens called Podsnappery. Mr. Barrett, like Mr. Podsnap, "got up at eight, shaved close at a quarter past, breakfasted at nine, went to the city at ten" and found in this world of convention a substitute for life.

An American song takes up the Dickens theme, picturing a similar though less grim world than that of nineteenth-century England. In this modern world there are "boxes on the hillside," of one color and another color, but

> They're all made out of ticky-tacky
> And they all look just the same.

In them men and women live: "lawyers and doctors and business executives," and they marry and have children

> And they're all made out of ticky-tacky
> And they all look just the same.

The children too grow up and marry, and we leave without regret
a society where

> They're all made out of ticky-tacky
> And they all look just the same.

I have heard Browning's poetry depreciated on the ground that the later nineteenth century with its closed social life, its ingrown conformity, the blindness of the successful to human suffering, *could not* produce a major poet. I wonder whether the world of Podsnappery, of boxes made of ticky-tacky, ever can in any century. Browning had been living wholly outside that world when he wrote *Pauline* and *Paracelsus*, had never been fully immersed in it, when he escaped to Italy and entered on the period of his greatest poetry, *Christmas-Eve and Easter-Day, Men and Women*, and much of *Dramatis Personae*. Only *The Ring and the Book* belongs at once to the time when he had returned to England and to the highest peak of his genius—and, indeed, it was only after it was published that English Society really caught and held him.

To Fanny Haworth, he wrote on June 29, 1847:

> I should not altogether wonder if I do something notable one of these days, all through a desperate virtue which determines out of gratitude—(not to man or the reading public, by any means!)—to do what I *do not* please: I could, with an unutterably easy heart, never write another line while I have my being—which would surely be very wrong considering how the lines fall to poets in the places of this world generally. So I mean to do my best whatever comes of it—

They were busy now just being happy, but with all the happiness Browning was facing a huge responsibility. Perhaps as unpractical as Mrs. Jameson thinks, he had to become, and he did become, very practical in organizing their lives and caring for a physically sick and mentally overstrung wife. They continued to cut down the morphine, but could she ever entirely dispense with it? The facts must be faced that she could *never* spend a winter in England, that she could never handle for herself the affairs of daily life. There must always be a Wilson. Soon there would be a baby if the doctors (whose bills had also to be met) were successful in bringing her through her second pregnancy.

The changes of abode in Florence had come about partly through Elizabeth's precipitate choice of rooms that proved uninhabitable. To her sisters she wrote with amazed gratitude of Browning's patience, but she thought less well of his determination to pay every bill the minute it became due. Incapable with money herself, Elizabeth had always been in debt, and she considered it, she said, "morbid and unpoetical" to fuss about one's bills. Browning replied that *he* was thinking of the butcher and the baker. Mr. Barrett had refused to have anything more to do with his daughter's affairs, but Mr. Kenyon faced his wrath and took over for her such business as could only be handled on the spot.

We have to imagine a world in which were no airmails, no telephones, no automobiles, and only very incomplete rail connections. The postal arrangements in Italy were startling. Browning would call at the post office for his letters, be handed the whole bundle and allowed to select his own. Many letters were lost; all came with incredible slowness. English newspapers they almost never received; a news sheet was available at Galignani's Club (for men only). "I say," Elizabeth wrote to Henrietta, " 'Bring me back news of a revolution' and generally he brings me back news of two." In a sense we can hardly realize today, it was an exile in which their lives were lived, with ups and downs like other lives, but always with a fundamental happiness.

There are letters to Arabel and Henrietta from Robert as well as from Elizabeth; it would be hard to say which of the pair expresses the greater adoration of the other. But Robert's letters are far less interesting; devotion almost wholly fills them, while she adds a lot in the way of daily news. From her we learn how Robert bought incredibly cheap antique furniture for the Casa Guidi, his only mistake being a superfluity of chests of drawers and not enough chairs. A dinner for three sent in from the trattoria with enough left over for supper cost less than two shillings; wine was a few pence the bottle; fruit cost almost nothing, and it was delightful to see the Florentine populace enjoying it. Indeed, unlike England, the poor had the same pleasures as the rich—food and displays and music. In dress the classes were indistinguishable. There was much merriment but little crime, almost no drunkenness. The love for Italy, which became almost a passion had seized her; and, for both her and Robert, Italy was not a mere museum, picture gallery, or panorama; it was a living nation.

Elizabeth's letters are full of delight over walks and talks and music, much of it made by Browning on a hired piano. With a "spring" sofa and chair, "I resume my habits of lolling with extraordinary pleasure." Carlyle had written of their marriage as a "union indicated by the finger of Heaven itself. . . . Courage, therefore; follow piously the Heavenly Omens, and fear not . . . unless I altogether mistake, here is a life partnership which, in all kinds of weather, has in it a capacity of being blessed . . . if joy be even absent for a season, may nobleness never!" Joy was certainly present now and Elizabeth wrote: "No human being ever comprehended human love so divinely."

Carlyle's at least was an exception to a general opinion expressed in Wordsworth's comment on the marriage. "Well, I hope they may understand each other—nobody else could." Barely established in Florence, Browning wrote, entreating Carlyle to come and visit them, ". . . let us have the happiness—the entire happiness of remembering that we got ready the Prophet's-Chamber in the wall, with bed and candlestick, according to Scripture precedent." Telling him, too, of the easy journeying in Italy, the cheapness of horses, carriages, lodgings, he goes on "if ever you are disposed to pass a winter here, we will go to any part you decide for, and be ready for you at any time." His feeling was "something beyond affection and far better than pride—that you have been and are what you are to me."

He had longed to tell Carlyle of all that had led up to the marriage. "My wife, in all probability, will become quite well and strong . . . from the accounts from England, and from the nature of the place in the country to which she was to have been removed . . . this winter would have ended the seven years' confinement without my intervention." They had found in her love and reverence for Carlyle "a common point of sympathy. . . . So that there was one way left for me to love her the more."

One day in the street Browning had run into an old acquaintance, "Father Prout," and several letters home are filled with exasperation at the Irish Jesuit, turned journalist and quite a lion in London, whose pen name this was. "A Roman Catholic Priest," Jane Brookfield described him, "who only officiates as a boon companion." His was, I suspect, an influence increasing in both Brownings a jaundiced view of the Catholic Church. They were half amused, half exasperated as, long past their normal bedtime, he sat and smoked and spat into the spittoon they had provided, and called Elizabeth "Ba" without invitation. Yet "the utmost kindness and warmheartedness" had characterized him, and he had earned Elizabeth's gratitude by mixing for a weak and feverish Robert "a potion of egg and port wine," calming his pulse in a fever and sending him to sleep.

They met a few old friends and made a few new. They kept their first anniversary on a great fiesta in Florence in honor of the granting by the Grand Duke of a constitution and a national guard, rejoicing with the people. Elizabeth commented: "Our poor English want educating into gladness . . . our religious teachers in England do not sanctify the relaxations of the people." The Florentines had gone first to the cathedral to sing *Te Deum* and then been happy in the streets.

"Italy was my university," Browning said later, and it had been so, long before he and she were established there. Perhaps it was the country "seen only in his soul" as Cerutti talked to him and he read Dante, Petrarch, and this and that old chronicle. It became an intense reality on his two visits—stirring in him "No simple and self-evident delights, / But mixed desires of unimagined range, / Contrasts or combinations new and strange."

In *Sordello* we see castles, minstrels, warriors, devastated battle scenes and sunsets, intensified color, light and darkness. "O'er the far forests, like a torch-flame turned / By the wind back upon its bearer's hand / In one long flare of crimson; as a brand, / The woods beneath lay black. . . ." Breathlessness is one element in that "incomprehensible" poem, and it is there still in *Pippa Passes*. As with his love poetry, all Browning's writing is poetry of experience, "recollected" not "in tranquility," but with passion.

Sordello, Pippa Passes, King Victor and King Charles, "My Last Duchess," "The Italian in England," "The Englishman in Italy," "St. Praxed's Church," *Return of the Druses*—all these are situated in Italy, all were written in England. And Browning's special outlook and bent of mind become clearer and clearer as we read them. He said once that he loved nature, but cared more for men. And he could not think fruitfully of men as "mankind." The characters (as Macready complained) were always more important than the plot—or than the multitude. This, which would be a weakness for a social reformer, was an immense strength for a phychologically minded poet. He could not take "Italian" freedom with the same simplicity as his wife. He was too conscious of the medieval cities at war with one another (*e.g.,* Florence and Pisa in *The Druses*); of the wars of Guelphs and Ghibellines, with their incessant permutations and combinations; of complexity far greater than she saw in the relations between Pope and Emperor.

In Elizabeth's poetry mankind and causes are more alive than any individual; in *Aurora Leigh* not one of the characters lives; while Browning could write more vividly of the man caught in the political or social machine than of the masses oppressed by it. Luigi, hesitating whether or not to assassinate a tyrant, is seen as the boy, almost child, he is; Sebald, Ottima, are people; and so is the Italian in England looking back at Italy. But who cares for the "causes" in *Sordello*? And I cannot help fancying that it was chiefly through his wife's fervor that Browning became enthusiastic about the Risorgimento.

In these early years above all he was chiefly watching people, and although written a little later, "Up at a Villa—Down in the City" belongs to any year in which he was looking out of the window in any Italian city. From the Casa Guidi windows Elizabeth listened to a child singing *"O bella Liberta, O bella"* and went on to dream of the future. But the fascinating present was more intensely vivid to Browning, looking and listening, as he conceives an "Italian person of quality" would, to the sights and sounds beneath, or walking the lanes of the Tuscan countryside.

There are exquisite touches in the Villa stanzas, but the dominant note of the poem is the riotous high spirits of Mrs. Jameson's "prince of travelling companions."

Ere you open your eyes in the city, the blessed church-bells begin:
No sooner the bells leave off than the diligence rattles in:
You get the pick of the news, and it costs you never a pin.
By-and-by there's the travelling doctor gives pills, lets blood, draws teeth;
Or the Punchinello-trumpet breaks up the market beneath.
At the post-office such a scene-picture—the new play, piping hot!
And a notice how, only this morning, three liberal thieves were shot.
Above it, behold the Archbishop's most fatherly of rebukes,
And beneath, with his crown and his lion, some little new law of the
    Duke's! . . .
Noon strikes,—here sweeps the procession! our Lady borne smiling and
    smart
With a pink gauze gown all spangles, and seven swords stuck in her heart!
Bang-whang-whang goes the drum, *tootle-te-tootle* the fife;
No keeping one's haunches still: it's the greatest pleasure in life.

11 Italian Background

. . . Pure hands, stretched simply to release
A bond slave, will not need a sword to draw
To be held dreadful . . .

CASA GUIDI WINDOWS

ITALY, so long Browning's inspiration, had now become the world he lived in. Both he and Elizabeth were profoundly interested in the new nation struggling to emerge as their own *vita nuova* was growing into its fulness.

When Browning first went there, in 1838, the very name of Italy was rare except on the lips of patriots, poets, and antiquarians. "Since the fall of the Roman Empire," wrote one nineteenth-century historian, "(if even before it) there never has been a time when Italy could be called a nation any more than a stack of timber can be called a ship." Venice and Genoa, Milan and Florence, Pisa and above all Rome played their parts on the stage of medieval history, but by the eighteenth century the multitude of states had become insignificant petty princedoms. They were ruled over by Bourbon or Hapsburg princes, excepting Rome itself and the States of the Church, and Piedmont where the Dukes of Savoy straddled the Alps and had become also Kings of Sardinia.

The Napoleonic conquest had pulled the country together. Bonaparte was hardly the deliverer he proclaimed himself, but he reduced the country's political divisions from fifteen to five, crushed brigandage, made law and justice uniform and effective. In the eyes of Mazzini, despite war and political despotism, the Napoleonic domination had "elevated our souls." With it had arisen, as a picture in the distance, "the oneness of Italy, the object of all our efforts." After Napoleon's fall the diplomats restored former conditions as far as possible, but the atmosphere had changed.

It is to the Mazzini period and the Mazzini spirit that Browning's "Italian in England" belongs, the vivid picture of the man hidden in the aqueduct: "That second time they hunted me/From hill to plain, from shore to sea/The Austrian bloodhounds"; the girl accepting his message; the priest in the confessional to whom she courageously passes it. And then the exile in which the patriot, grown old, dreams of seeing Italy once again, and discovering perhaps on some small farm among his children the girl who with him had dangerously served "that dear, lost land,/Over the sea, the thousand miles."

Not improbably this exile would still be primarily a Florentine, bitterly hating the Austrians, a Neapolitan resenting the Bourbon tyranny—or even a Sicilian hating the Neapolitans through whom that tyranny extended to Sicily—for after Napoleon's fall former conditions had been restored. But the desire for a United Italy was growing, felt by men who later became bitterly opposed to one another's way of seeking it.

Pius IX had imbibed the ideas of an exiled patriot, Gioberti, who wanted a federated Italy of which the Pope would be the natural leader. Mazzini, another exile, was a republican, desiring an Italy totally unified, with no Pope and no kings. His religion was God and the People. His country he said had been murdered, and he wore black always as a sign of his grief. Still he accepted for a while the idea of papal leadership, and Garibaldi, the soldier of fortune who later conquered Sicily and Naples with an army of one thousand in a period of weeks, now offered the Pope his sword.

At this time Pius wanted no swords; this white-robed, humorous and emotional churchman fancied he could adapt the principles of liberalism to a situation infinitely more complex than he realized. "A Liberal Pope," said Metternich aghast, "is an impossibility." Austria was not going to relax her hold; the Bourbons had learned nothing; the

King of a united Sardinia and Piedmont was dreaming the dream—to be made reality for his son by Cavour—of becoming himself the ruler of a united Italy. And in France, Napoleon III was prepared to help whatever side would mean advantages to his own country.

The Pope's initial reaction against Austria, when Metternich increased the Austrian garrison inside the States of the Church, encouraged the revolutionaries to believe he was wholly on their side. He became almost insanely popular. But they *would* not, he constantly repeated learn to distinguish between the Pope, father of Christendom, and the Italian devoted to his own country. He appealed to Austria to think of Italy as a sister land in the Christian world. "Both are our daughters and very dear to us."

The first round in the fight for which all were preparing went to Austria, challenged by the united kingdom of Piedmont and Sardinia.

The Pope believed himself obliged to maintain the States of the Church; they made him independent of earthly rulers and were at that time secured by a vast multitude of Catholics in all the countries of Europe. They were in the Pope's eyes "the seamless robe of Christ," which he must keep untorn even as had the Roman soldiers on Calvary. With these views he allowed his own tiny army to march with the forces of Piedmont, stipulating that they should fight in defense of the Papal States only if these were invaded. But their commander gave a very different impression, casting the Pope in the rôle of Peter the Hermit in a crusade for the freedom of Italy.

Piedmont had been far too confident. They were up against greater forces far more ably led, and the Austrians twice inflicted heavy defeats on them, after which King Charles Albert resigned his throne into the hands of his son Victor Emmanuel.

Pope and King were identified—and discredited—in this defeat; the revolutionaries now took matters into their own hands. Pius had given the Romans a constitution; their Prime Minister, De Rossi, was not only a layman but an unbeliever, an able man working hard both for peace and the unification of Italy. But he was assassinated, a bishop shot at an open window, the Pope's guard disarmed. The Pope fled to

Gaeta and Garibaldi's army marched in. A triumvirate, of which Mazzini was one, took over the government of the city.

The rulers of the world had small sympathy with this situation. It was in "the year of revolutions" (1848) that it began, when none of them felt very secure. Even Queen Victoria, vigorous Protestant though she was, sent the Pope a message of sympathy; and *The Times* thought him a "splendid fellow" because he had modeled his newly given constitution on that of Britain. Napoleon discovered that the Pope's cause was popular with French Catholics of the left as well as of the right, and he finally decided that his best policy was to support him. So French bayonets brought Pius back, and drove Garibaldi into exile.

He was prepared to defy France, Austria, and Spain, but his small army was overwhelmed and he had to fly. His sick wife was with him and died in his arms. After years of wandering Garibaldi bought the north end of the island of Caprera whence he could look and dream and prepare, if Italy should again call him. "I am terrified," he said, "of the likely prospect of never again wielding sword or musket for Italy." But, visiting England, it was he who had the wisdom to advise Mazzini henceforward to work with Victor Emmanuel. Italy was not yet ripe for a united republic, and Piedmont-Sardinia was the only state strong enough to be their leader when the struggle was resumed.

Casa Guidi Windows (Part I written in 1848, part II in 1851) is written from the viewpoint of one side in the crusade, first with an immense optimism, later with a profound disappointment. Elizabeth Barrett Browning's prejudices against any sort of ecclesiastical ruler ran deep; those against the head of the Catholic Church were almost insurmountable, but she briefly hoped in Pius: ". . . this country saving is a glorious thing," well done if by a common man, excellent by a rich one, by a king sublime, improbable by a priest:

> A pope? Ah there we stop, and cannot bring
> Our faith up to the leap, with history's bell
> So heavy round the neck of it—albeit
> We fain would grant the possibility
> For *thy* sake Pio Nono!

One feels it must have been almost a relief to her when the bright hopes of the revolutionaries were disappointed and the Pope lost his place in the cast of this tremendous drama. But the real disappointment came over Florence and its people. She had taken the singing of a child beneath her window, *"O bella Liberta, O bella,"* as a symbol, but now she demanded of the nation itself:

> Didst thou, too, only sing of liberty
> As little children take up a high strain
> With unintentioned voices, and break off
> To sleep upon their mothers' knees again?
> Couldst thou not watch one hour. . . .

Outside Piedmont recruitment had been poor for the armies of liberation: ". . . to leave our piazzas, shops and farms/For the simple sake of fighting was not good/. . . . Desire was absent that provides great deeds."

Her much-loved Florentines did not understand "The serious sacred meaning and full use/Of freedom for a nation."

Elizabeth was not as deeply implicated in the cause of Italy at this date as she became later. She felt, looking back in 1858 upon the rebellions of 1848, that they had been only a preparation—a "dress rehearsal." Yet even at this time it is interesting to note the sustained intensity of her poem. It has been said that we owe to her the most dramatic lines in Browning's "Italian in England": "I would grasp Metternich until/I felt his red wet throat distil/In blood thro' these two hands." Not that Browning could not himself be intensely dramatic, but he is far more skilled at painting a picture that includes an intensity made greater by the fact that beauty, details of daily life, and the whole surrounding atmosphere are in it. Elizabeth's letters, but Browning's poems, transport us to the Italy of their affections:

> What I love best in all the world
> Is a castle, precipice-encurled,
> In a gash of the wind-grieved Apennine . . .
> . . . a sea-side house to the further South

Where the baked cicala dies of drouth, . . .
                    For, what expands
Before the house, but the great opaque
Blue breadth of sea without a break? . . .
A girl bare-footed brings, and tumbles
Down on the pavement green-flesh melons,
And says there's news today—the king
Was shot at, touched in the liver wing,
Goes with his Bourbon arm in a sling:
—She hopes they have not caught the felons.
Italy, my Italy!

Even at this earlier stage Elizabeth found it hard to abandon the tragic note, but she still saw the sorrows of Italy—much more than she did later—as implicated in the sorrows of a suffering world. She scorned the more fortunate part of humanity which was in 1850 "a Fair-going world." The splendors of distant lands were pouring into "the gorgeous Crystal Palace," while she was looking at "the poor who sit in darkness," at the England of brothels and of child labor, at the America of slavery, and at the slavery of nations:

Annihilated Poland, stifled Rome,
Dazed Naples, Hungary fainting 'neath the thong,
    And Austria wearing a smooth olive leaf
On her brute forehead.

12 *Life, Death, and Danger*

Robert neither eats nor sleeps when he is anxious.
ELIZABETH BARRETT BROWNING

ELIZABETH'S age and her health were both against her, but despite all fears their first and only child was born in March, 1849. "Our blessed Ba," wrote Browning to her sisters, "gave birth to a fine strong boy." The doctor assured him "without flattery, the little creature is the very model of a beautiful boy. . . . Was it not dear of Ba to refuse to look at the babe till I could show it her? . . . the little hands and fingers are wonder- fully strong"—and all the usual rest of it.

The baby was christened Robert Wiedemann Barrett "without god- fathers and godmothers," wrote Elizabeth to Mrs. Jameson, "in the simplicities of the French Lutheran Church." But when he began to speak he (naturally?) resisted all attempts to call him Wiedemann; he turned it into the rather charming "Penini." This was presently short- ened to Pen, and to all his friends he remained Pen Browning for life, calling himself more formally Robert Barrett Browning. The financial strain on his parents Mr. Kenyon insisted on meeting by the gift of £100 a year.

Browning had told Elizabeth that "he didn't believe he had the least touch in him of paternal instinct"; but when Pen was only nine days' old he was writing ecstatically to the Barrett sisters of his size, his strength, his astonishing quantity of hair. "I have just got three little tufts cut off,—for you and Miss Tripsack [Trepsack], and my own Mother . . . he follows lights and noises with his little great eyes and even hands—and when I make a chirrup to him with my lips, fairly takes hold of my nose!—All indubitable signs of his being what Mr. Disraeli calls the 'Coming Man.' "[1]

But the waiting and watching had been an immense strain, and hardly had Browning begun to recover from it in the joy of parenthood when the news came from England of his mother's death. The shock was too great—death treading thus on the heels of life. The bond between mother and son had been a close one. Browning had told Elizabeth of his own great physical resemblance to his mother (though this is hardly borne out by Alfred Domett's description of her head—so square that it always made him think of a tea caddy). Domett noted Browning's affectionate and courteous manner, revealing his deep affection; he felt how intensely united a family they were. "There was something peculiarly thrilling," Elizabeth wrote, "to a nature like his in the discord between the joy and the grief, in the thought that we were rejoicing here while his mother was dying." For a while he could hardly bear to look at his own child; his joy seemed almost literally turned into grief. He put aside comfort at first "passionately," she told Mrs. Jameson. "Now it begins to rise into sight again."[2]

Elizabeth, who loved her hard and unloving father so persistently, could understand and deeply sympathize. She wrote to her sister of the love so full in her husband's nature, of the sadness of his exile. For long his sleep was broken, his sadness almost constant. And he wept to an extent mysterious to our generation. He always did cry easily: when listening to great music or watching tragedy, when hearing his wife's poetry read, when reading his own (and the audience cried with him), even when visiting the room where Petrarch died. A far more prolonged grief was witnessed by those who passed him blindly weeping in the London streets months after his wife's death. The intense vitality which had resurrected Elizabeth was now pouring for the first time in his life into the realization of death. And after all we are judging as from another world in a century so different. The athletes of Homer wept, and at Trafalgar Nelson and Hardy kissed each other good-by not without tears.

Fortunately, as the hot weather approached, Florence became no

place for Elizabeth or the baby. Husband and wife went in advance of
the nursery party to find a good place for the summer. Lerici, Elizabeth
tells us, "seemed good for Robert," but she was relieved to find it too
expensive; the scene of Shelley's drowning recalled too keenly her own
personal tragedy.

Shelley being for Mrs. Miller the King Charles's head which cannot be kept out, she will have none of this. Ignoring Elizabeth's view
that Lerici suited Browning, she knows that the associations there were
"intolerable" to him. He had left "no written record" on a first visit to
Italy of "what *must have been* [italics mine] psychologically its capital
experience"; nor had he told anyone that what he "followed . . . looked
for" in the streets of Pisa were "the footsteps" of this poet of "old
conflicts, old betrayals": yet these things too she knows. It is not merely
the lack of evidence I find strange; it is the counterevidence of Elizabeth's words, *and* of Browning's Essay on Shelley [see Chapter XV,
p. 3]. Its writing would have been intrinsically impossible for a man in
the mental state Mrs. Miller depicts.

One fact, highly dramatized, betrays the dreamlike texture of the
whole. A "small, weightless object carefully packed and labeled" appears in Sotheby's Catalogue of a sale of Browning's effects; and Mrs.
Miller's book ends with the words, "It was a flower plucked from
Shelley's grave."

So it was. But it might as easily have been the laurel leaf from Byron's
garden or the ivy from his grave, picked half a century apart. It might
have been the plaster mask of Keats; Edmund Kean's green purse given
to Browning by Forster, or the lock of Milton's hair the gift of Leigh
Hunt—or supremely Elizabeth's (of which he had felt unworthy) "so
much of you—all precious that you are—as may be given in a lock of
your hair—I will live and die with it." Browning, though his thought
reached into the age of Existentialism, remained sentimentally a Victorian. A reviewer wrote lately that, rummaging in the *Times* office, he
found a thickly black-edged envelope. In it were two locks of Disraeli's
hair. [Presented by Queen Victoria?] The tribal customs of a past age
can only puzzle a later generation.

Robert and Elizabeth were surprised to discover in the reputedly worldly and anglicized Bagni di Lucca a glorious and almost inaccessible retreat. Three villages together constituted Lucca, and in a house above the highest of the three the Brownings made their temporary home. They spent two later summers there.

The black and white of a chessboard. Browning would use this simile in "Bishop Blougram's Apology" for the faith and unfaith in a man's soul; Elizabeth would use it of her husband's moods. Both of them tended to extremes—Elizabeth having, as she said, "a sad heart and a merry mind," Browning living habitually on the white squares of life's board, yet when on the black intensely aware of their blackness.

This was probably the first time Elizabeth had had to be the support to Robert instead of Robert to her. Fortunately her sympathy with his feelings was unfailing. For even after their arrival at Lucca he was writing to Sarianna as though, since his mother's death, he cared little for life. Years later, after their father died, Browning noted that his sister's mourning had in it no bitterness, for she had been a perfect daughter. Most of us suffer as he did with the longing to remake an unchangeable past.

Elizabeth wrote twice to her father-in-law and Sarianna, begging them to come and make their home with her and Robert; the refusal must have been something of a relief.

Two happy letters to Mrs. Jameson on August 11 and 13 show both parents thrilled over Penini's first tooth, and record Robert's remark: "Well, I never thought I could care so much for a child." And to Mrs. Martin she writes that Robert is as bad as she is "watching every movement of the baby."[3]

The letters had become more cheerful, beauty and time were doing their work of healing. And Browning was meditating on the poem— the two poems—which grew out of his joy and his suffering: "Christmas-Eve" and "Easter-Day."

"The beauty of the scenery and walks," writes Elizabeth, "is something past description; and Robert and I enjoy it to the uttermost only wishing we could draw to us all those whom we love. . . . Think of his twice snatching me up and carrying me up a long steep—long enough and steep enough to incur the risk of breaking a vessel in the chest or heart. I was so frightened that fatigue would have been nothing at all to it, and quite seriously angry."

On a longer expedition Elizabeth rode a donkey "along the dry beds of exhausted torrents, the loose rocks crumbling around us. At the top you look round on a great world of innumerable mountains, the faint sea beyond them. . . . Wasn't it daring of us to take Baby?" Perhaps more daring of Robert to take Ba on a ten-hour expedition.

Browning wrote to Leigh Hunt from Bagni di Lucca in October, 1857: "I never suspected the existence of those 'Sonnets from the Portuguese' till three years after they were written; they were shown to me at this very place eight years ago." He it was who "thought of the subterfuge of a name."[4]

Many years later (in 1864) he looked back again, seeing the same vivid picture, and in a letter to Julia Wedgwood he wrote:

> Yes, that was a strange, heavy crown, that wreath of Sonnets, put on me one morning unawares, three years after it had been twined—all this delay because I happened early to say something against putting one's loves into verse; then again I said something else on the other side, one evening at Lucca—and the next morning she said hesitatingly: "Do you know I once wrote some poems about *you*"—and then—"There they are, if you care to see them"—and there was the little Book I have here—with the last Sonnet dated two days before our marriage. How I see the gesture, and hear the tones—and, for the matter of that, see the window at which I was standing, with the tall mimosa in front, and little church-court to the right.
> . . . The publishing was through me—in the interests of the poet, I chose they should be added to the other works, not minding the undue glory to me, if the fact should become transparent. . . . The Portuguese—purposely an ambiguous title—was that Caterina who left Camoens the riband from her hair.

"A strange heavy crown" it must certainly have been, to face the publication of poems expressing that intensity, not of love so much—

for that they both expressed in their lives always and he was not backward at expressing it in poetry—but of an admiration, a setting of herself
so far beneath him, against which he had always fiercely striven. He
never forgot for a moment that the world was very very far from sharing
her estimate, and it must have taken a great deal of love for his wife, a
great deal of concern for her fame, to make him willing to publish such
lines as

> Thou, bethink thee art
> A guest for queens to social pageantries,
> With gages from a hundred brighter eyes
> Than tears even can make mine, to play thy part
> Of chief musician. What hast *thou* to do
> With looking from the lattice-lights at me,
> A poor, tired, wandering singer, singing through
> The dark, and leaning up a cypress tree?
> The chrism is on thine head,—on mine the dew,—
> And Death must dig the level where these agree.

I fancy had they not both been profoundly convinced that his
future fame was certain, these sonnets would have gone unpublished.
Certainly neither guessed how very very far in the future it would be,
that she would not even live to see it. And Browning, who steadily
maintained that his wife *was* the greater poet, is said to have declared
he dared not keep for himself alone the finest sonnets since Shakespeare.
Such a judgment, if he did indeed pronounce it, does more credit to
Browning's heart than to his head. But this need hardly surprise us.
From Bagni he was writing to Mrs. Jameson of his wife's "entirely
angel nature, as divine a heart as God ever made; I know more of her
every day; I who thought I knew something of her five years ago."
Elizabeth wrote to the same friend of his improvement in health and
spirits and how "Robert and I go out and lose ourselves in the woods
and mountains, and sit by the waterfalls on the starry and moonlit
nights. . . . We are both enjoying this great sea of mountains and our
way of life here."

Soon there were hopes of another baby and on December 21, Elizabeth writes of having avoided a miscarriage. "We ought to groan

elegiacally, or at least 'make the best of it' philosophically, when we talk of a possible second baby thirteen months after the first, instead of which we are just *pleased* like stupid people. Our English friends will hold up their hands in compassion I am sure."

The "disappointment and vexation" of a miscarriage were taken "philosophically," "Wiedemann does for us very well. . . . Robert and I contend who shall not cross him in any of his wishes—we are each of us dreadfully afraid of being the unpopular person . . . his royalty fails to corrupt him: he is full of love . . . huggings and kisses till Flush says 'something too much of this', and walks away from an excess of demonstration which he considers in bad taste."

Thus to Mrs. Martin. And to Mrs. Jameson she speaks of looking in amazement at this tiny living, thinking being "much as a savage does at a ticking watch—can it be alive. . . . Robert has much my feeling and we are never tired of examining him."[5] Apparently the first disappointment after Pen had no serious effect on Elizabeth's health. But, after yet another miscarriage in July (of 1850), Browning wrote to Mr. Kenyon that the doctor said "she had lost above a hundred ounces of blood within the twenty-four hours," and that "not one in five thousand women would suffer to the same extent. . . ." He had received Kenyon's letter "after sitting all night by the little patient white face, that could smile so much more easily than speak." She certainly had all the courage in the world, for before the end of September came another, her last, and worst, miscarriage. Whether she could survive was in doubt. She was "on ice for three days, . . . Robert and Wilson both up all night," for six weeks she could not walk across the floor. "Nobody (in the body) ever looked more ghastly than I did." But they went into the hills near Siena, and she made so swift a recovery that we soon find her visiting churches and boasting of having "walked to the top of San Miniato."

In these months of life and death and danger Browning had written and published two of his greatest poems, inspired certainly in part by intensity of emotion after the birth of his son, the death of his mother, the mortal danger of his wife.

13 Christmas-Eve and Easter-Day

> *Christ's place indeed is with the poets.*
> OSCAR WILDE

CHRISTMAS-EVE

A WORLD of thought and emotion is in the background of these poems, both spoken in the first person, both "poetry of experience."[1] In "Christmas Eve" the narrator shelters from the rain in the porch of a chapel as the sermon is beginning. The poem opens vividly with a description of repulsion by and revulsion from a chapel at once like and unlike the Clayton-Ready-Irons experiences of Browning's boyhood.

> They eyed me much as some wild beast
> That congregation still arriving . . .
> In came the flock: the fat weary woman,
> Panting and bewildered, down-clapping
> Her umbrella with a mighty report,
> Grounded it by me, wry and flapping,
> A wreck of whalebones . . .

Followed her the

> Little old-faced peaking sister-turned-mother
> Of the sickly babe she tried to smother

> Somehow up, with its spotted face,
> From the cold, on her breast, the one warm place . . .

Wincing at the door with "the gruff/Hinge's invariable scold/ Making my very blood run cold," he looked and listened: "humbly knew himself improper,/But could not shrink up small enough," as

> . . . the dingy satins
> Of a female something, past me flitted,
> With lips as much too white, as a streak
> Lay far too red on each hollow cheek;
> And it seemed the very door-hinge pitied
> All that was left of a woman once,
> Holding at least its tongue for the nonce.
> . . . from each that entered,
> I got the same interrogation—
> "What, you the alien, you have ventured
> "To take with us, the elect, your station?
> "A carer for none of it, a Gallio!"—
> Thus, plain as print, I read the glance
> At a common prey, in each countenance.

Thus must the boy Browning have felt, for all his bravado, when publicly rebuked by the Reverend Clayton. Today he retorts:

> But still, despite the pretty perfection
> To which you carry your trick of exclusiveness,
> And, taking God's word under wise protection,
> Correct its tendency to diffusiveness,
> And bid one reach it over hot plough-shares,—
> Still, as I say, though you've found salvation,
> If I should choose to cry, as now, "Shares!"
> See if the best of you bars me my ration!
> I prefer if you please, for my expounder
> Of the laws of the feast, the feast's own Founder . . ."

His old exasperation is back at the narrowness, the bigotry, which no love for his mother could exorcise. He had set the scene very differently from his boyhood's chapels: the creaking doors, the poverty-stricken flock, the outcasts of society, but here were the same spiritual experiences, the same mental processes to be observed—and observing them he was, with a good deal of contempt:

> These people have really felt, no doubt,
> A something, the motion they style the Call of them;
> And this is their method of bringing about,
> By a mechanism of words and tones
> (So many texts in so many groans)
> A sort of reviving and reproducing,
> More or less perfectly, (who can tell?)
> The mood itself, which strengthens by using . . .

Just so a tune in the head will set itself to the thump-thump and shriek-shriek of the train and repeat itself all through the journey, while to an unmusical neighbor the thumping is just thumping, the engine's noise is just noise: "Finding no dormant musical sprout/In him, as in me, to be jolted out."

The sermon for Browning is mere unmeaning sound, and he asks:

> After how many modes, this Christmas-Eve,
> Does the self-same, weary thing take place?
> The same endeavour to make you believe,
> And with much the same effect, no more:
> Each method abundantly convincing,
> As I say, to those convinced before,
> But scarce to be swallowed without wincing
> By the not-as-yet-convinced . . .

More and more impatient: "I very soon had enough of it./The hot smell and the human noises . . ./That placid flock, that pastor vociferant."

In the course of the poem will come two further experiences of a religious assembly—High Mass at St. Peter's, depicted with an intensity no Catholic poet has ever approached, and a Liberal Protestant lecture at Göttingen, conveying with equal vividness the opposite extreme of a rather pallid religion. These three are for Browning clearly the key modes of Christianity. At the end he will feel that the chapel, by far the least attractive in his description, is what God wants for him.

Coming out of the Chapel he turns to nature, through which: "my faith sprang first! . . ./—In youth I looked to these very skies,/And probing their immensities,/I found God there . . ."

Passing beyond the first lesson of God's power he finds love too, discovers:

> That he who endlessly was teaching,
> Above my spirit's utmost reaching,
> What love can do in the leaf or stone,
> (So that to master this alone,
> This done in the stone or leaf for me,
> I must go on learning endlessly) . . .

—learning the why of man's brief day on the "stupid" earth, which

> Suffers no change, but passive adds
>   Its myriad years to myriads,
> Though I, he gave it to, decay,
>   Seeing death come and choose about me,
> And my dearest ones depart without me . . .

The realization of eternity, of the vision of God face to face (and in Him of all we have loved), is met by the first immense experience of this poem. A moon rainbow was forming, typical surely of the white light which Browning felt he so often broke up into its prismatic hues:

> It rose, distinctly at the base
>   With its seven proper colours chorded,
> Which still, in the rising, were compressed,
> Until at last they coalesced,
>   And supreme the spectral creature lorded
> In a triumph of whitest white,—
> Above which intervened the night.

The white light is Anima's vision, prepared for often by anguish, leaving after it exhaustion and bewilderment. That he is imaging a tre-

mendous spiritual experience no student of the poem can doubt. He said
later that the one thing he had *seen* was the lunar rainbow. But in the
poem, beneath the white moon: "Another rainbow rose, a mightier, . . .
Rapture dying along its verge./Oh, whose foot shall I see emerge?" It is
a vision of Christ. But at first rejoicing and longing, like St. Peter, to
build "service-tabernacles three" where "I may worship," he realizes that
the figure is turned away from him, that he had perhaps lost Christ
through despising (as he so heartily had) the uncouth worshipers in
the chapel. Catching at His garment's hem he cries:

> "But not so Lord! It cannot be
> That thou, indeed, art leaving me—
> Me, that have despised thy friends! . . .
> I thought it best that thou, the spirit,
>   Be worshipped in spirit and in truth,
> And in beauty, as even we require it—
>   Not in the forms burlesque, uncouth,
> I left but now . . ."

Still clinging to Christ's robe, he is swept across the world from the
little English chapel to St. Peter's Square in Rome with its fountains:
"growing up eternally/Each to a musical watertree." Before him the
building

> With arms wide open to embrace
> The entry of the human race . . .
> The dark is rent, mine eye is free
> To pierce the crust of the outer wall,
> And I view inside, and all there, all,
> As the swarming hollow of a hive,
> The whole Basilica alive!
> Men in the chancel, body and nave,
> Men on the pillars' architrave,
> Men on the statues, men on the tombs,
> With popes and kings in their porphyry wombs,
> All famishing in expectation
> Of the main-altar's consummation. . . .
> Earth breaks up, time drops away,

In flows heaven, with its new day
Of endless life, when He who trod,
Very man and very God,
This earth in weakness, shame and pain,
Dying the death whose signs remain
Up yonder on the accursed tree,—
Shall come again, no more to be
Of captivity the thrall,
But the one God, All in all,
King of kings, Lord of lords,
As His servant John received the words,
"I died, and live for evermore!"

Yet I was left outside the door.

This line opens a fresh stanza. Browning feels that the Church he has seen at a worship he so magnificently describes has

Departed from the founder's base:
He will not bid me enter too,
But rather sit, as now I do,
Awaiting his return outside. . . .
I see the errors; but above
The scope of error, see the love—

The vision passes and Animus takes over, sometimes, I cannot help feeling "leaving its bright accomplice all aghast." It was almost impossible that Browning's conscious mind could have approved the Mass through which had come to him vision and inspiration. But it was a pity that reaction should carry him into talking of "raree shows" and "posturings and petticoatings." He could not accept intellectually a system to which he had not in fact applied his intellect.

But he had realized that love of men is called for by Christ's love, and: "Cautious this time how I suffer to slip/The chance of joining in fellowship/With any that call themselves his friends," he finds himself in the lecture hall at Göttingen University where a "hawk-nosed, high-cheek-boned Professor . . . three parts sublime to one grotesque," is lecturing, coughing (and spitting). "With a wan pure look, well-nigh celestial," this "sallow virgin-minded studious/Martyr to mild enthusiasm" is discussing "the Myth of Christ," of what value and "whence . . . derivable . . . (since plainly no such life was liveable)." He asks:

> Whether 'twere best opine Christ was,
> Or never was at all, or whether
> He was and was not, both together—
> It matters little for the name,
> So the idea be left the same.

Unlike the motley gathering in the chapel, his audience is "not a bad assembly neither,/Ranged decent and symmetrical/On benches . . ." We can almost see them with mildly admiring looks as he patronizes apostle and evangelist:

>   . . . understanding
>   How the ineptitude of the time,
> And the penman's prejudice, expanding
>   Fact into fable fit for the clime,
> Had, by slow and secure degrees, translated it
>   Into this myth, this Individuum,
> Which when reason had strained and abated it
>   Of foreign matter, left, for residuum,
> A Man! . . .

"The vesture still within my hand"—that vesture which the Gospel tells us brought healing—Browning felt

> I could interpret its command.
> This time he would not bid me enter
> The exhausted air-bell of the Critic.
> Truth's atmosphere may grow mephitic
> When Papist struggles with Dissenter, . . .
>   Each, that thus sets the pure air seething,
>   May poison it for healthy breathing—
> But the Critic leaves no air to poison;
> Pumps out with ruthless ingenuity

> Atom by atom, and leaves you—vacuity . . .
> (If mere morality, bereft
> Of the God in Christ, be all that's left.)

Had Christ demanded of his followers:

> "Believe in good,
> In justice, truth, now understood
> For the first time?"—or, "Believe in me,
> Who lived and died, yet essentially
> Am Lord of Life?"

Yet the question remains—*how* accept, how acknowledge, how worship? He does not feel inclined to go on with ". . . further tracking and trying and testing./" 'This tolerance is a genial mood,' " until the time and place " 'Where I may see saint, savage, sage/Fuse their respective creeds in one/Before the general Father's throne.' "

God "by God's own ways occult,/May—doth, I will believe—bring back/All wanderers to a single track."

But that track is not yet laid. Meanwhile, although:

> I cannot bid
> The world admit he stooped to heal
> My soul, as if in a thunder-peal
> Where one heard noise, and one saw flame,
> I only knew he named my name.

Can the poet rest in a "genial mood" of tolerance for all religions? No he must, as modern usage has it, be committed, and this commitment he believes best met in a worship "Where earthly aids being cast behind,/His All in All appears serene/With the thinnest human veil between."

He finds himself back in the chapel "bolt upright/On my bench as if I had never left it." There he realizes that treasure can as well be carried in an earthen as in a golden vessel:

> But the main thing is, does it hold good measure?
> Heaven soon sets right all other matters!—
> Ask, else, these ruins of humanity,

> This flesh worn out to rags and tatters,
>   This soul at struggle with insanity,
>   Who thence take comfort . . .

Only once in these experiences had Browning been swept off his feet, and that was by the Mass in St. Peters. Intensely critical of both chapel and lecture hall he was sheerly exalted by the silver trumpets, the worshiping crowd, the sense of a Presence. Now he reacts, hoping that the Pope may forgo "today's buffoonery," while for the professor he prays: "May Christ do for him what no mere man shall,/And stand confessed as the God of salvation!"

And the poem ends with the poet prepared to sing "The last five verses of the third section/Of the seventeenth hymn of Whitfield's Collection,/To conclude with the doxology."

EASTER-DAY

"Christmas-Eve" concerned different ways of approaching God through Christ. This poem is tackling a different problem—the difficulty of believing at all:

>   . . . could you joint
>   This flexile finite life once tight
>   Into the fixed and infinite,
>   You, safe inside, would spurn what's out . . .

But life is not thus: it *is* finite, as yet unfixed, scrappy, profoundly imperfect, and to the man who longs for a world "perfect and entire," a world "quite above faith," the poet answers:

>   No. The creation travails, groans—
>   Contrive your music from its moans . . .

Perhaps one reason why Browning's fundamental ideas are so furiously debated is that so far as he can be spoken of as belonging to a category, it is one highly suspect by extremists at both ends. He was fully and richly a Christian humanist, and while some Christians suspect humanism, even more humanists deny the possibility of the union. This he understood—in both doubts he all-but shared with an immense energy of imagination. It is not surprising that this poem begins: "How very hard it is to be/A Christian!"

This is the profounder and more difficult theme of "Easter-Day." Elizabeth felt she must reassure others—and perhaps herself—that Browning had *not* become an ascetic: It was (he said) one side of the question. This remark should be borne in mind by the critics who affirm that, in "Easter-Day" anyhow, Browning cannot be speaking as himself. Never is Browning more himself than when arguing with himself—and this argument is on two levels.

Intellectually it is hard to be a Christian because of the very nature of faith. "Blessed are they," Christ says, "who have *not* seen but have believed." "Faith," says the Epistle to the Hebrews, "is the substance of things hoped for, the evidence of things not seen." As Browning had reminded Elizabeth, to believe is not as easy as to breathe, "but there is no reward prepared for the feat of breathing and a great one for that of believing." Writing now of "how very hard it is to be/A Christian!— hard for you and me"—he goes on to treat the problem at a second level. The world around us not only challenges the Christian intellectually; the immense attractions of this world challenge him morally—and the one challenge reinforces at every step the power of the other. Browning already realized that he was in a post-Christian world, and he is haunted in this poem by the thought of the ease with which the martyrs died when Christ was still alive for them.

The carrying out of life's aims is never easy, but the Christian's aim is higher and is constantly obscured by fits of cold doubt: "You must mix some uncertainty/With faith, if you would have faith be." And, on behalf of the soul most shaken by doubt, he exclaims against the fallible judgments of men.

> . . . shall we award
> Less honour to the hull which, dogged
> By storms, a mere wreck, waterlogged,

> Masts by the board, her bulwarks gone
> And stanchions going, yet bears on,—
> Than to mere life-boats, built to save,
> And triumph o'er the breaking wave?

There seems from all evidence to exist a kind of pattern in human psychology after a bereavement. At first the lost wife, mother, friend, is vividly present: in prayers, in dreams, in daily life. Then comes the ache of emptiness when this realization of immortality—or as some think simply this psychological effect of grief and memory—becomes dimmed. Gradually the joy of life clamors to be felt; the sense of loss remains, but less poignantly; the vision of meeting again in a future life grows dimmer. And this can easily bring with it almost a wish to forget, to be able once more to enjoy daily delights intensely, fully.

And there is struggle in the mind alike and the senses: Shall we at the end: ". . . start up, at last awake/From life, that insane dream we take/For waking. . . ." Or will life indeed be followed by judgment— and if so, how defend what we made of it?

> . . . I resolved to say,
> "So was I framed by thee, such way
> I put to use thy senses here!
> It was so beautiful, so near,
> Thy world,—what could I then but choose
> My part there? . . .
>   Is it for this mood
> That Thou, whose earth delights so well,
> Hast made its complement a hell?"

In this mood, a mood known to every Christian who has found joy in life and in the world, he hears the words: " 'Life is done,/Time ends, Eternity's begun,/And thou art judged for evermore.' "

But what is the judgment? Precisely to stay forever in the world he has chosen—

> "This world,
> This finite life, thou hast preferred,
> In disbelief of God's plain word,

> To heaven and to infinity. . . .
>   Thou art shut
> Out of the heaven of spirit; glut
> Thy sense upon the world: 'tis thine
> For ever—take it!"
>   "How? Is mine
> The world?" (I cried, while my soul broke
> Out in a transport.) "Hast thou spoke
>   Plainly in that? Earth's exquisite
>   Treasures of wonder and delight,
>   For me?" . . .
> "All partial beauty was a pledge
> Of beauty in its plenitude:
> But since the pledge sufficed thy mood,
> Retain it!"

But "the eye is not filled with seeing, nor the ear with hearing." Painters try to abstract the one face

> With its one look, from throngs they saw.
> And that perfection in their soul,
> These only hinted at? The whole
> They were but parts of? . . .
> What visions will his right hand's sway
> Still turn to forms, as still they burst
> Upon him? How will he quench thirst,
> Titanically infantine,
> Laid at the breast of the Divine?

Music, in Browning's eyes the highest of the arts, he tries—and poetry. But none of the gleams "made visible in verse," the hints and intuitions which " 'pull the more into the less/Making the finite comprehend/Infinity,' " none of this is enough for the spirit of man: " 'else were permanent/Heaven on the earth its gleams were meant/To sting with hunger for full light.' "

Again he asks—in this poem as in the last—dream or vision? What, as he looks back, might have been only a "strange Northern Light," had seemed, like the moon rainbow, the setting for a great personal revela-

tion: Across the sky: "Sudden there went,/Like horror and astonishment,/A fierce vindictive scribble of red/Quick flame . . ."

"Christmas-Day" had shown Christ as Saviour. But when this gift of
the world was chosen "He stood there. Like the smoke/Pillared o'er
Sodom, when day broke,—/I saw Him."

The gift did not bring its anticipated fullness of delight, and
whether one believes or not in the supernatural, Browning is here driving home a fact of common human experience. An almost boundlessly
rich woman, with power of choice to go, do, have, anything and everything she wanted, once made me see her mere effort of choice as the
agony it had become. At that very time letters from blitzed England
spoke of joy in waking alive to the song of birds or the sight of flowers.
Class barriers were broken down, petty feuds healed, and human love
was constantly manifested in sacrifice.

It is not only the "spirit's hunger . . . unsated not unsatable" for
beauty, truth, the fullest use of senses and intellect, that has failed: eyes
suddenly opened he cries: " 'I pray,—/Leave to love only!' " It was the
problem of the boy Browning—and now of the man suffering from the
loss of a mother, loved indeed but selfishly, by one overabsorbed in the
discovery of the world. Now has come the unsought discovery of love—
not human only but divine.

> "Love is the best? 'Tis somewhat late!
> And all thou dost enumerate
> Of power and beauty in the world,
> The mightiness of love was curled
> Inextricably round about,
> Love lay within it and without,
> To clasp thee—but in vain! Thy soul
> Still shrunk from Him who made the whole,
> Still set deliberate aside
> His love! . . ."

These two poems are Browning's first clear intimation of belief, not
merely in a general idea of incarnation but specifically in that of the Son
of God. Could man " 'who was so fit instead/To hate, . . . invent that
scheme/Of perfect love?' " In the cloud-wrapped judge he had dis-

cerned "pity mixed/With the fulfillment of decree." That mysterious
fulfillment—the gift made eternal of the world deliberately chosen.
Now he is crying out for the old frustrations of a life reaching beyond
itself: " '. . . leave me not tied/To this despair, this corpse-like bride! . . .
Be all the earth a wilderness!/Only let me go on, go on,/Still hoping
ever and anon/To reach one eve the Better Land.' "
And mercy prevails over judgment:

> I knew Him through the dread disguise
> As the whole God within His eyes
> Embraced me.
> > When I lived again,
> The day was breaking—the grey plain
> I rose from, silvered thick with dew.
> Was this a vision? False or true?

For the rest of his life the dread will remain—dread of too much
ease, too smooth a path:

> "happy that I can
> Be crossed and thwarted as a man,
> Not left in God's contempt apart, . . .
>
> And think, "How dreadful to be grudged
> No ease henceforth as one that's judged.
> Condemned to earth for ever, shut
> From heaven!"
> > But Easter-Day breaks! But
> Christ rises! Mercy every way
> Is infinite,—and who can say?

Almost more than with any other does one feel the intolerableness
of the heckling that Browning alive or dead has been forced to endure
over this poem. His critics are demanding a John Stuart Mill to give
them logic instead of poetry, and it is hardly surprising that he should
have refused to acknowledge his identity with a man (or men) absorbed in vision (or dream) where Anima was working at a level deep
even for that ever-deep and mysterious source of inspiration.

As reported by Sharp, *Christmas-Eve and Easter-Day* was, according to one eminent cleric, "the most Christian poem of the century"; to another "the heterodox self-sophistication of a free-thinker."

Elizabeth said that her husband's grief for his mother's loss was assuaged by the realization that her God was his God, her Saviour his Saviour—and to some degree one understands, after reading these poems, the mockery such a claim has called forth.

Psychology is a modern science. Had it been developed earlier many of the worst evils of the more-or-less Christian centuries would have been avoided. Browning was ahead of his age when he recognized what his contemporary, the scientist Pasteur, also saw when he claimed to have the faith of a Breton peasant—and hoped one day to have that of a Breton peasant's wife. This does not mean (any more than does Newman's saying that all men have a reason, though not all men can give a reason) that he despised the mind's processes. Still less does it mean what Browning in his later years sometimes appeared to say—that love can be a substitute for mind.

What it does mean is—and this is surely what Browning held when he wrote *Christmas-Eve and Easter-Day*—that the approach to God, the apprehension of Him as Creator and Redeemer, is not the act of *one* faculty, heart or mind, but of a total human person. His mother was more than unlikely to understand what he himself could only imperfectly express; there could never have been between them the meeting of minds so richly present with Elizabeth; but as *persons* they loved and understood each other. And as persons God understood them both, even if in their worship they spoke different languages. If Catholic and Protestant had realized this fact of human nature, half the world's persecutions might have been avoided, though it would not, I suppose, have inhibited the persecutors who see God only as a mythical enemy to human progress.

14 Two Checkered Years

> *We called the chess-board white,*
> *—we call it black.*
>
> "BISHOP BLOUGRAM'S APOLOGY"

CHRISTMAS-EVE AND EASTER-DAY was poorly enough received. The publishers had timed it for the Easter of 1850 and two hundred copies were sold immediately. After this the sales slackened and as late as 1864 his publisher's account shows copies of this first edition still on hand. Of the reviewers De Vane says, "Whether they praised or blamed they generally misunderstood." This was almost invariably Browning's fate: "he has recklessly impaired," wrote the *Athenaeum* in an otherwise favorable review, "the dignity of his purpose by the vehicle chosen for its development." He was too Christian for the unbeliever, too flippant for the commonly solemn believer, too new for contemporary fashion.

But Joseph Milsand in the *Revue des deux Mondes* wrote with enthusiasm and understanding of Browning's religious philosophy, and with this French Protestant a warm friendship began when the Brownings went to Paris in 1851.

The years between marriage and the publication of *Men and Women* were full and rich, but Duckworth in his *Browning: Background and Conflict* notes the curious irony that the man who in his old age was said to have "dinnered himself away" had written in 1846: "I am convinced that general society depresses my spirit more than any other cause." It was Browning not Elizabeth who in their first months in Italy shunned the English-speaking society that tended to seek them out. Gradually they learned to select, but after two years of marriage Elizabeth told Arabel she had not been able to persuade Robert to dine out once. She writes, however, to Henrietta: "Last week five evenings out of the seven, we had somebody here . . . people fall in for coffee and talk."

"Here" was Casa Guidi; and in Florence, in Bagni di Lucca, in Rome, in Siena were friends who "looked in," friends to whose villas or apartments husband, wife, and presently child went together, or else Browning walked over by himself. Elizabeth grew so much stronger that she was able to walk with her husband many hours at a time. Among their friends were the American sculptor, William Wetmore Story, with his wife and children, who joined them at Lucca one year and had a neighboring villa at Siena another. Then there was "young Lytton" (later Lord Lytton)—son of the famous Edward Bulwer—who himself wrote under the penname of Owen Meredith.[1] On the Brownings' second visit to Lucca he occupied their spare room. "He lost nothing from the test of house intimacy with either of us—gained in fact much. Full of all sorts of good and nobleness he really is," wrote Elizabeth; and Lytton on his side was deeply grateful to her for her liberality in offering "to receive me and *my pipe*," and wrote to Browning: "It has been a great Era in my life to have met and known you and I often ask myself with shame if I am really worthy to seek your friendship."

It was Browning's only fault, Story noted, that he did not smoke— but Tennyson was wedded to the habit and when he could not find a particular tobacco in Florence "he was so disquieted . . . that he turned back to England and never went to Rome." Alfred Tennyson the Brownings much liked; and Frederick his brother, a lesser poet, became a great friend. Frederick spoke of Browning as "a man of infinite learning, jest and bonhomie and moreover a man of sterling heart that reverbs no hollowness."

The summer of 1850 was spent at Siena. Henry James, writing the biography of Story, sought in "the cluster of Siennese villas" an answer to "unanswerable questions" about "Robert Browning and Walter Savage Landor, and other spirits of the general scene . . . on the high terraces, meant for soft evenings and in the cool bare echoing rooms where shutters were pulled open for me to violet views." He felt as he gazed and dreamed a pang "not so much of accepted loss as of resented exclusion." There they stand still those old cool houses "on their communicating slopes, behind their overclambered walls and their winding accommodating lanes; there they stand in the gladness of their gardens . . . and in that wondrous mountain ring . . ."

No one better than James can help one to recreate those Italian days as the friends wandered leisurely through the lanes, drank tea on the terraces, or picnicked in the woods.

In 1851 the Brownings decided they must go to England. The journey went well. "The only sort of excitement," Elizabeth told her sisters, "that can be said to agree with me is the excitement of travelling." She could "bear more than many strong women."

From Venice she wrote to Arabel of "the fantastic beauty of the buildings, the mysterious silence of the waters, St. Mark's piazza by gaslight, with its great populace swept up and down as if by the breath of music, the moon on the lagunes and the gondolas passing in and out of the shadows with their little twinkling lamps."[1] Penini was chiefly pleased with what he called "the holy pigeons" in the piazza—and here as in Florence the mingling of classes thrilled Elizabeth: "I do love Christ's equality, the beating of heart to heart, the response of hand to hand."

The climate did not suit Browning, but did he write there "A Toccata of Galuppi?" Anyhow they stayed a month, went on by Milan, the Lakes and Paris, meeting, in Paris, Tennyson—just made Poet Laureate. He had left England, Elizabeth reported, "because you English have hunted him half to death. He says you are the greatest nation in the world and the most vulgar—and he hopes to have a little peace and liberty away from you." At Milan, Elizabeth climbed to the top of the Cathedral, an amazing sign of her new vitality, but to Arabel she wrote from Paris "the dreadful joy of seeing you again requires a little strength."

Both husband and wife had been at once longing for and dreading the return. Browning felt unable to face the home where his mother's absence would become too aching a void. Elizabeth longed yet hardly dared to hope for reconciliation with her father. The atmosphere is reflected in her abundant letters; Henrietta came to London to see her; George, at last reconciled, came around often to their lodgings and became "mine untle" to Pen; Arabel she saw constantly. And with the courage of despair, in almost daily secret visits to Wimpole Street, she even took the risk of meeting her father.

Finally, she tells Mrs. Martin, "I could not leave England without trying the possibility of his seeing me once, of his consenting to kiss my child once. So I wrote, and Robert wrote. . . . In reply he had a very violent and unsparing letter, with all the letters I had written to Papa through these five years *sent back unopened, the seals unbroken.* . . . He said he regretted to have been forced to keep them by him until now, through his ignorance of where he should send them. So there's the end. I cannot, of course, write again. God takes it all into His own hands, and I wait."

Meanwhile they had been received with real enthusiasm by many friends old and new; word pictures abound in contemporary memoirs, but mostly of Elizabeth. Browning is recorded as "talking loudly and with vivacity," her silence is variously interpreted: that she had not much chance of speaking, that she could speak only seriously or on serious matters. She had, said Sara Coleridge, "a weak plaintive voice," but there was "something very impressive in her dark eyes and brow."

Tennyson offered them his house and so did Browning's old friend Arnould. Fanny Kemble called and left tickets for her Shakespeare reading; Barry Cornwall (Mr. Procter) called daily "till business swept him out of town."

"Mr. Forster of the 'Examiner' gave us a magnificent dinner at Thames Ditton in sight of the swans; and we breakfast on Saturday with Mr. Rogers. . . . I can't tell you what else we have done or not done. It's a great dazzling heap of things new and strange. . . . Such kindness on all sides."

Thus Elizabeth chronicles to her old friend, Mrs. Martin. But "the sort of life is not perhaps the best for me and the sort of climate is really the worst."

They spent an evening with Carlyle, who, according to Henry James's father, showed his affection for Browning in the only way he ever showed it to his friends—by a condescending pity: "Poor John Mill," he would say, "Poor little Browning." But all the same he did frequently speak with warm admiration both of and to Browning.

To a friend visiting Italy he had written on February 16, 1851: "If at Florence you know the Poet Browning (one of the bravest and most gifted of English souls now living) I will send my affectionate remembrance to him." These words Browning annotated in 1885: "Written to a friend of his, who showed it to E.B.B., who characteristically would preserve what I ought to destroy." On their side, both Brownings venerated the old lion—"one of the great sights in England" said Elizabeth; and Browning wrote to him of "my five years' hunger for the sight of you and Mrs. Carlyle."

Above all—even above Carlyle—was for Elizabeth the reunion with "good joyous Kenyon" as her husband dubbed this dear friend and cousin.

Despite his initial shrinking Browning was far more completely happy than his wife. "I do believe," she wrote, "he would have been capable of never leaving England again, had such an arrangement been practical for us." He had as yet no torn feelings about the family that was left him: it was, said Elizabeth, "pure joy to him with his family and friends."

But an English winter was too perilous and before the end of September they left for the continent, accompanied by Carlyle.

In the volume entitled *Last Words of Thomas Carlyle* we find this: "Excursion (futile enough) to Paris" described at some length, curiously illustrating the then problems of foreign travel. Advice must be sought as to "passports, routes, conditions"—and such advice was so confusing that Carlyle welcomed the information that the Brownings too were going to Paris. He "walked to their place—had during that day and the next consultations with these fellow pilgrims," and postponed his own journey a day "for the sake of company who knew the way to travel. Such rumours, such surmises; the air was thick with suppositions, guesses, cautions. . . . The Brownings and their experience and friendly qualities were worth waiting for. Fare to Paris 22/-, wonderful. Thither and back 'by return ticket' £1.12—such had been the effect in prices of this 'Glass Palace' and the crowds attracted to it . . . and so away we went, Browning talking very loud and with vivacity, I silent rather, tending towards many thoughts."

Noting the "torpor of seasickness" as "a sorry phase of humanity," he goes on to describe how Browning, despite suffering from it, struggled with porters and customs men for their luggage, "brought it in all safe about half past ten and we could address ourselves to desired repose." Next morning, again, it was Browning who "did everything; I sat out of doors on some logs at my ease and smoked," and on arrival at Paris "the brave Browning fought for us, leaving me to sit beside the women. . . . I walked out to smoke . . . cigar ended I went in again. Browning still fighting (in the invisible distance). . . . Our luggage visible at last . . . Browning visible with report of a hackney coach; we think it is now over; rash souls, there is yet an endless uproar among the porters . . . even Browning has at last grown heated." And to Elizabeth he said, "Ah it's a triumph for these fellows to have a poet to do just their will and pleasure—that's the way in this world—The earth-born order about the heaven-born and think it's only as it should be."

Securing a cab for himself, French money and the key of his trunk from Browning, Carlyle at last got off to the hotel where he was to be the guest of the Ashburtons. He states, with an exclamatory note, that it was the most expensive in Paris, costing £45 for the week's stay of the Ashburtons, their two servants and himself. But he slept badly, disapproved strongly of the French and their theater ("their canine libertinage and soulless grinning over all that is beautiful and pious in human relations were profoundly saddening to me"). "I withdraw to the Brownings before seven. Great welcome there and tea in quiet. B. gives me (being cunningly led to it) copious account of the late 'revolutions' in Florence—such a fantastic piece of Drury Lane 'revolution' as I have seldom heard of." Next day: "Decide to vanish to Browning," whom he also misses sorely on the return journey but is comforted, after all the "passport showing; crowded botheration; steamer overflowing," by the "admirable silence, method and velocity" at London Bridge.

Carlyle wrote warmly from London: "Adieu dear Browning; commend me to the gentle excellent Lady and remember me now and then." They wanted him to come back, but he had had enough of Paris. Browning pleaded: ". . . won't you reconsider the matter . . . we here have had all the good fortune in your journey with us, and visits to us; the weather is admirable . . . the perfection of fresh warm clearness and we get all that to ourselves too." Beginning to write on Shelley, he has some of Carlyle's thoughts in mind: "I shall always hope—for a great incentive—to write my best *directly to you* some day."[2]

Meanwhile he set to work on this very important essay and Elizabeth told Arabel that he had "taken to his new room with green curtains, and sits there half in sun and half in shade 'doing' his Shelley to his heart's content . . . 'I feel in *such* good spirits' he says."

Did Browning know, when he wrote this essay, about Shelley's desertion of his wife, Harriet Westbrook? W. G. Kingsland states in *Robert Browning, Some Personal Reminiscences* that Browning told him he had only learned the facts later—and to Shelley's biographer, Dowden, Browning wrote of learning them about 1858. W. M. Rossetti's memory was of having been told—also by Browning—that he saw Harriet's letters when he was writing. But it was a good deal later, as De Vane notes, that he began to be seriously shaken about Shelley.

Looking at the internal evidence of the essay—if Hookham the bookseller did show Browning the letters at that time, it would be he who added the mitigating circumstances, related there, of Shelley's excitement approximating almost to madness, of the laudanum bottle, of his hallucinations visual and oral. All this Browning mentions, and he says also that Shelley would not wish his own name cleared at the cost of another's, which at least suggests that Browning had been told, too, how Harriet, poor woman, had first left Shelley. She had hoped confidently that he would follow her, but the fact by itself suggests at least a question mark. Surely the blackest blot on Shelley's character came later—his proposal that the three—Mary Godwin, he and Har-

riet—should live together, and the borrowing of money from his wife
when he returned with his mistress to England. Hearing about these,
rather than reading the letters, could be the point at which Browning
finally gave up the idol of his adolescence, whose influence had faded
by his twentieth year but whose poetry he still ranged with that of
Keats. With a total realization Browning could hardly have been "in
such good spirits" as he sat in sun and shade " 'doing' his Shelley."

The story of Harriet was not, of course, the whole of Shelley; there
was his immense generosity to Godwin, the fantastic father of his second
wife, who combined cadging with reproaches, and accepted money with
a grandiloquent assumption of high-mindedness. There was his indignant rage at the oppression of Ireland; his response to any human
need, even by self-sacrifice, where it did not impinge upon his sexual
desires. There was in him a true compassion for the needy only too rare
in the age of complacency and the class of sufficiency to which he belonged, and this appealed to the Browning who had written in *Sordello*
of the "sad dishevelled shape" borne by mankind in his own vision. At
moments one seems to hear in this essay some broken notes from what
might have been a marvelous dramatic monologue.

Browning in his essay sees Shelley already emerging from the
atheism of his youth on the way to a full Christian faith. This has been
smiled at as akin to Cardinal Wiseman's belief that Browning might
himself end up a Catholic. Neither idea is intrinsically absurd. To
Herford it appeared that Christian thought in some respects has "ranged
itself with Shelley," so that what he might have adopted "would have
been sufficiently unlike that which he assailed." Yet, too, he sees that
for Browning "the essence of Christianity lay at this time in something
not very remote from what he revered as the essence of Shelleyism—a
corollary as it were implicit in his thought."

Dowden in his smaller *Life of Shelley* goes further, seeing an immense change between the hostility and defiance of his boyhood at the
sight of York Minster and the days when, Dante in hand, he would sit
"a docile rebel . . . in the fragrant gloom" of Milan Cathedral. Dante
and the other medieval poets had become Shelley's companions. He
read Ariosto at Lucca, he translated scenes from the *Magico Prodigioso*

of Calderon, regretting that the "grey veil" of his own words should fall over those "perfect and glowing forms." Dowden notes, with the same interest as did Browning, if not an immediate approach to Christianity at least that "his imaginative delight" was "so little troubled by the ardours of the great Catholic poet," while Edmund Blunden has pointed out an almost personal devotion to Christ shown in *Prometheus:*

> Remit the anguish of that lighted stare;
> Close those wan lips; let that thorn-wounded brow
> Stream not with blood: it mingles with thy tears!

Christ's true followers are described as:

> The wise, the mild, the lofty and the just,
> Whom thy slaves hate for being like to thee,
> Some hunted by foul lies from their heart's home, . . .
> Some linked to corpses in unwholesome cells.

This is much like an attack on official Christians in defense of the Christian ideal. Perhaps Browning was not so absurd after all.

When the Brownings left London for Paris that autumn they were shortly followed by his father and sister. To Browning his father told a story of being persecuted by a neighboring widow, Mrs. Von Müller, and of his doubts concerning her moral character. Browning, with characteristic impetuosity and with the trustfulness he always felt toward those he loved, acted as foolishly as well might be; the one thing to do (he felt) was to bring the matter to an end forthwith. His father, he wrote to Mrs. Von Müller, had informed him of the manner in which she had annoyed him and of the persecution he had undergone for some time. But Mr. Browning senior had also written her a letter in which he spoke of "breaking off the match" on account of her "misconduct" from the time she was a girl: and (he asked) was the certainty of her first husband's death established when she married Von Müller? Browning knew nothing of this or other letters, but he must soon have learned that Mrs. Von Müller was bringing an action for breach of promise against his father.

Paris had brought relief to Elizabeth's cough, and both poets were busy enough. Browning is said to have written three poems in three days: *Love among the Ruins,* greeting the New Year on January 1, 1852; on January 2, *Women and Roses;* and on the third *Childe Roland.* In old age he told a friend that *Childe Roland* had taken two days to write. The amount of ink spilled in trying to find roots from which that poem grew is truly fantastic. Years later Mr. Nettleship of The Browning Society, after asking Browning three times about the poem's meaning and being told each time that it was just a kind of dream, managed to write eighteen pages expounding it. Browning laughed heartily and said no doubt it was all there, though he himself did not know it. "A quite obvious and naturally supernatural *dream,*" says Saintsbury, "one has dreamt things like it but inferior."

Legitimate as it is to examine the writings of a poet to discover meanings hidden from himself and even to search his subconscious, it has been decidedly overdone in Browning's case. I hardly dare to suggest that Browning's intense anxiety over his father's situation had some bearing on *Childe Roland.* Great writing, poetry especially, arises from intensity of feeling—and the feeling may be of all sorts. More than plain grief do prolonged anxiety and uncertainty, dogging the imagination, bring nightmares persisting into the day.

One can imagine husband and wife puzzling over what *had* really passed between old Browning and Mrs. Von Müller that could give ground for an action. Whatever the issue the publicity would be a hideous thing.

Both Brownings had an exaggerated fear of any invasion of their private lives—lives which through circumstances had become all too public. The appearance of Miss Mitford's Memoirs this winter shattered Elizabeth, for they told the story of that grief of which never to any human but her husband could she speak—the drowning of Bro. "I am morbid, I know," she wrote to Mrs. Jameson, "I can't bear some words even from Robert." And to George: "I felt inclined to go off to Egypt and burrow in the sand somewhere—She might as well have cut off my fingers as a proof of friendship."

In Paris they met and liked Dumas, but a great disappointment for Elizabeth was the failure to establish a friendship with George Sand.

Their introduction to her had come from Mazzini via Carlyle, who described her as the "Highpriestess of Anarchy." She was, he said, living now outside Paris "within sound of the 'Church Bell' she has lately *christened* at her Curé's request. After all I participate in your liking for the melody that runs thro' that strange 'beautiful incontinent' soul,—a *Modern* Magdalen, with the 'seven devils' mostly still in her." But in his journal he had earlier written (1840): "In the world there are few sadder, sicklier phenomena for me than George Sand and the response she meets with." And he described her circle as "a new Phallus worship, with Sue, Balzac and company for its prophets and Madame Sand for a virgin."

Browning had no liking for any of it and Elizabeth describes him as "a little proud" about making advances: "he wouldn't have our letters mixed up with the love letters of the actresses, or perhaps given to the 'premier comique' to read aloud in the green room." Also the weather was frightful. "But I represented to him that one might as well lose one's life as one's peace of mind for ever, and if I lost seeing her I should with difficulty get over it."

So Robert wrapped his wife up and got her into a closed carriage. It had been very good and kind of him "to let me go at all . . . She [George Sand] seems to live in the abomination of desolation— . . . crowds of ill-bred men who adore her *à genoux bas,* betwixt a puff of smoke and an ejection of saliva. . . . A noble woman under the mud be certain."

Browning was by no means certain—especially with a wife prepared to "adore" in this atmosphere of smoke and spitting—which she had abominated at Florence in the person of Father Prout. But he was generous and Elizabeth says, "We both tried hard to please her . . . only we always felt we couldn't penetrate—it was all vain." Robert had seen George Sand seven times, she writes later, but " 'can't get on with her,' he declares—'the ice breaks—and then there's a new frost.' "

Had he, one wonders, discussed the redoubtable lady with Milsand, who did not like her at all, and who spent the evening with the

Brownings at least once a week? "Robert and I really *love* him—there's no other word for it," Elizabeth wrote to Arabel. "I would let him marry *you*." Other friendships were made this year—with Lady Elgin, with whom Elizabeth was at one about "spiritualism, mesmerism, clairvoyance, visions and the like"; with Mr. Carré, a minister from Jersey "of the Newman St. Connexion," whose cures "in the name of Christ" she had no difficulty in believing but who thought evil spirits came through séances and hoped she would keep her heart pure from them.

Robert, she remarks in one letter, "was quite vexed that I wouldn't stay the Communion at the Church—he does dislike going out in that way." They did not, however, go to Carré's but to the French Independent Church; and she, at least, could not agree with Carré's sacramental views, thinking it "a clear scriptural doctrine that the 'priesthood' is absorbed into Christ's life and dignity." She could not "accept as small 'retail' popes such men as Mr. Owen and Mr. Carré."

Hoping that Arabel does not disapprove of the scamps they know and the table rapping ("nothing scarcely is too high or too low for me"), Elizabeth goes on to her dismay at having discovered "the profoundest infidelity" in the intellectual world. Mrs. Jameson had told her that in England nobody believes. "As to Germany you know how they tear the scriptures to pieces, with teeth and nails. The French socialists *use* Jesus Christ and deny him in the same sentence. To them he is crucified between Robespierre and Marat."

Perhaps the spiritualism which seems more and more to surround her, in Italy, England, France, above all among her American friends, but in which at this date she still called herself only a "potential believer," was for many a substitute for the Christianity they had lost.

Husband and wife were both hardly recovered from an attack of grippe when, in May, Browning's cousin James Silverthorne died, and he decided to go to England for the funeral. Elizabeth looked so pale and distraught that he gave up the idea. And she certainly tried to persuade herself that it was in Robert's own interests that she should keep him from the journey and the misery of a funeral at the scene of his mother's grave. One sees her building up her case as she writes, and a tirade follows against fixing "on such a subject" as funeral ceremonies: "in no paroxysm of anguish could I identify or appear to identify the dust there and the soul there."

Robert and Elizabeth were back in London when the case was brought against Mr. Browning. They were not present in court but read next morning the long report in *The Times*.[3]

Held before Lord Campbell and a special jury it is sad enough, even for an outsider, as a picture of the folly that could be reached by a man who had been for so many years a devoted husband. And at that date the fact that he must have begun this courtship so shortly after his wife's death would appear especially horrifying. What must it have meant for his son to read letters beginning: "My dearest, dearest, dearest, dearest, dearest, much-loved Minny"—and to realize that his father's own counsel could do no better than ask for a mitigation of sentence in consideration of the fact that his client was "a poor old dotard in love"? It was alleged, too, that the engagement with Mrs. Von Müller had been broken by the older Browning only "under the influence of his son."

This is the view taken by Cyrus Mason, who declares that his uncle really did want to marry the widow and that she, too, was attached to him. If so, why had he run away? Unfortunately, *The Times* report does not give the fifty long letters read in court, which in point of style and intelligence were favorably commented on by Lord Campbell. But it does give the evidence of Mrs. Von Müller's son-in-law, Samuel Sutor, which adds to the puzzle. Mr. Browning had evidently returned to London *after* his son had written to Mrs. Von Müller; for Mr. Sutor, who had seen the letter, says, "I asked as he was not then under the influence of his son, whether it was his intention to carry out his original views with Mrs. Von Müller. His reply was 'What do you mean?— Marry Mrs. Von Müller?—Certainly not.' I then said I had no other course to pursue than to send him a letter from a solicitor."

One unmentioned element in this story is the influence of Sarianna on both father and son. What had she said to her father? Few daughters desire a stepmother and Sarianna had been devoted to her mother. Her view of the case would have been presented both energetically and plausibly to Robert and Elizabeth. The impression given by the existing evidence is of a perplexed and vacillating man, of scales on which the weights changed constantly, of a man moreover whose intellect was far stronger when turned on books and ideas than on matters of practical life. Missing his wife, he would perhaps have liked more than a daughter! Yet he had clearly very real doubts concerning the woman who attracted him. The evidence that remains is too slight for any certain conclusion to be drawn from it. I am not writing a novel and real life is full of open questions.

It is almost impossible to exaggerate the agony suffered by Robert Browning and Elizabeth, as they imagined *The Times* report spread out in front of Mr. Barrett on the Wimpole Street breakfast table—or being read by Mrs. Jameson and Miss Mitford, by Carlyle and by their "dear Mr. Kenyon." Inside the Browning family Cyrus tells us that poor Reuben found on his desk at Rothschild's Bank next morning ladies' gloves and other tokens showing that there, too, the report had not gone unnoticed.

Browning had not, his wife said, "apprehended the real character of the letters . . . felt it to the heart of his heart and could scarcely raise his head after the blow of that dreadful newspaper." But to his father he went, "loved and pitied him." Damages had been set at £800 and the mystery is not lightened when we see Mr. Browning deciding to escape the alternatives of payment or debtors' prison by migrating to Paris. His son went over to install him there and then handled in England the business of disposing of the house his father had recently acquired. The old man, separated from home, friends, books, became ill and depressed, and his son grew more and more careworn. Even the kindness of friends, and the bitter-sweet of stolen visits to Arabel, could not make this a happy time for Elizabeth. As for Pen, since Wilson had gone home to her family both summers, he feared that his mother, too, would leave him and was convinced that a "mitaine" haunted Wimpole Street.

Miss Mitford and Elizabeth had corresponded over the *Memoirs,* Elizabeth apologizing for her own oversensitiveness and recognizing the "affectionateness and tender consideration" with which Miss Mitford had received her distressed remonstrances. Theirs was a very old friendship and an intimate correspondence went on for the rest of their lives.

But meeting this summer was a problem: while Wilson was away, Penini could not be left and, with all the people to be seen in London, Browning was deeply engaged. "He will like to see *you*," wrote Elizabeth, "and besides, he would as soon trust me to travel to Reading alone as I trust Penini to be alone here. I believe he thinks I should drop off my head and leave it under the seat of the rail-carriage if he didn't take care of it." So both were to go, but Wilson's overprolonged visit to her family prevented this half-dreaded, half-hoped-for meeting.

Browning did visit his old friend W. J. Fox—reconciled with his wife after Eliza Flower's death in 1846. Sarah's death had followed her sister's two years later. It could hardly have been a visit to lighten Browning's heavy thoughts in that painful year.

A more cheerful side is seen in the christening of Tennyson's son Hallam. Elizabeth could not go but, as Browning held the baby and tossed it in his arms, Tennyson remarked, "Ah, that is as good as a glass of champagne to him." And to Kenyon, Browning wrote later from Florence: "I felt all those spark-like hours in London struck out of the black element I was beset with, all the brighter for it." They met Charles Kingsley, too, that summer, "original and earnest," said Elizabeth, "and full of a genial and almost tender kindliness." They lunched with the Ruskins and were introduced by Mrs. Carlyle to Mazzini. "Oh such a fuss the Brownings made over Mazzini this day," wrote Mrs. Carlyle. "My private opinion of Browning, is, in spite of Mr. C's favour for him, that he is 'nothing' or very little more, 'but a fluff of feathers!' *She* is *true* and *good,* and a most *womanly* creature."

Mrs. Andrew Crosse gives at least a suggestion of why Mrs. Carlyle had taken so strong a dislike to Browning, when she describes him holding her kettle in his hands absorbed in conversation. "Can't you put it down?" said Mrs. Carlyle—and Browning did—on her new carpet where it left an indelible mark.

"See how fine he has grown," said his hostess bitterly. "He does not any longer know what to do with a kettle."

"Ye should have been more specific," said Carlyle.

Mrs. Crosse herself writes more warmly of the husband than of the wife. Elizabeth had a "distinctly hard-featured, non-sympathetical

aspect," her lower jaw betrayed the "strength of obstinacy." Her talk was
that of a reader: "the habit of conversing in a one-sided way with the
best books which is vastly different from conversing with the best men."
She felt, too, that while Browning's humanity was never at fault, "her
womanly nature leads her to hate the sinner and to scold him over-
much."

Later, after a tea party at Forster's, Mrs. Carlyle seemed dubious
even about Elizabeth. "I like Browning less and less; and even *she*
does not grow on me." But to Elizabeth, Jane Welsh Carlyle appeared
"full of thought and feeling and character," and at that date Mazzini
was one of her heroes "with his pale spiritual face and intense eyes. He
made me melancholy with his vain dreams and perilous assumptions
and set me wondering on what turf of Italy he would lie at last with a
bullet through that noble heart of his. Oh, it must come to this, be sure.
He does not understand, he does not see while the simplest of us can
see and understand." Later his failure to understand caused many
deaths, and his early admirers would grow embittered as Mazzini from
his English exile sent others to their fate in Italy.

When Mrs. Carlyle called upon Elizabeth, she brought with her
an American friend, Mrs. Twisleton, to whom Elizabeth confided at
a later meeting that her disposition was so anxious she was always building "dungeons in the air." This time on leaving London she felt, she
told Arabel, as though her soul had been dragged through a hedge
and had "left some torn shreds of itself on the thorns."

Paris, too, had its cares, but "Our old friends the Corkrans here,"
she wrote, "have out of love to us, quite adopted Mr. Browning as the
grandfather of their children, and Mrs. Corkran professes to have quite
fallen in love with his simplicity and other qualities." This would make
it easier to depart as they ought before it grew too cold. And "Do you
know, Arabel," wrote Elizabeth, "I was quite touched and sorry to leave
poor Mr. Browning and Sarianna in Paris. His simplicity and affectionateness drew me a good deal . . . He can't understand any of it . . .
struggles against facts and necessities . . . said dolefully that 'he knew
it had been a trouble to me.' '*Of course it has*,' said Robert, '*What did*

you imagine?' " Whereon Elizabeth felt obliged to assure him, "I wasn't troubled at all and rather liked it upon the whole."

Her pen flows on, not only when settled, at home, more or less, in this city or that, but on the journeys. The little desk with fitted inkstand would serve in the least hospitable of hotels or even in the diligence. Elizabeth always wrote on her knee.

"Oh Arabel," came a letter from Genoa on November 5 (for so astonishingly late had the fine weather tempted them to stay on in Paris), "I have repented, Robert has repented, everybody has repented taking the Mont Cenis route." The cold had been bitter, they were three nights without taking off their clothes. Pen alone, "a gypsy child," she felt, "had enjoyed everything."

And then in answer to her sister's curiosity—"Oh Arabel—'have we quarrelled?' 'How often have we quarrelled?' We are famous for quarrelling, are we not? That is because we love one another too much to be contented with temporising—It seems foolish to talk of such things—but for a man to love a woman after six years as he loves me, could only be possible to a man of very uncommon nature such as his—I cannot tell you what his devotion and tenderness are to me at every hour . . ."[4]

15 An Anglo-American Circle

We were all bachelors together.

ELIZABETH BARRETT BROWNING

IT IS not surprising after two such years to find Elizabeth rejoicing at being "home again" at Casa Guidi. At first it seemed to Browning quiet almost to deadliness, but soon the circle of friends[1] were around them once more and both were absorbed in their work, the main interruptions being caused by Elizabeth's uncertain health.

After one bad attack she writes to Henrietta: "Poor darling Robert . . . his nights have been diversified by keeping up the fire, boiling the coffee, and listening to the horrible cough which made sleep out of the question for either of us. Nothing could exceed his tender patience."

Browning's hopes, so often dashed, had begun to revive. To Milsand he wrote in February, 1853. "I have not left the house one evening since our return. I am writing—a first step to popularity for me—lyrics with more music and painting than before." To Forster, in June, he speaks of "a number of poems of all sorts and sizes and styles and subjects . . . the fruits of the years since I last turned the winch of the wine press. . . . I hope to be listened to, this time, and I am glad I have been made to wait this not very long while."[2]

Interesting that the time seemed now not very long. I think Browning always lived fully *in* the happiness or unhappiness of the hour. To William Allingham, he wrote in July: "We have been in Florence quietly in the old place after the old way, some eight months—gone like one!"

William Allingham was a minor poet, an Anglo-Irishman employed in Her Majesty's Customs, full of a passionate admiration for great literature, forming friendships with Leigh Hunt, Carlyle, both Brownings and above all Tennyson. There is an interesting ambivalence in his attitude to Browning, reflected in the *Letters* and *Diary*. Browning was, he told Leigh Hunt, "the Turner of poetry," but "more of an Italian than an Englishman which I think is a pity." And to Arthur Hughes he wrote: "The only quality Browning wants, to be perfect, is a little stupidity." But he had found *Sordello* "a piece of rich confusion, confusing one most confoundedly,"—and in later entries in the *Diary* grave doubts are expressed of "a want of solid basis . . . yet I always end by striking my breast in penitential mood and crying out 'O rich mind! wonderful Poet! strange great man.' "

Browning's letter to Allingham of July 3, 1853, tells something of the months that have gone so fast:

> The weather was milder than ever in winter, wetter than common in spring, and is now hotter than uncommon this great summertime; and what with rain and heat the greenness is such greenness, the color such color!—but you can't see them—tho' you have a right, if ever man had. I wish you the sight of a million fire-flies—lizards, as your love may desire, and a scorpion or two for the truth's sake—(they get under the windowsill of the room here). Then, plate-fulls of the fruit of that Japanese Pear which is a flower-tree in England and here a producer of great yellow knobs half plum, half apple, and the brilliantest Japan besides. But the best will be when we go (I take your arm in spirit you observe) to a villa up in the hill country next week . . . 'Tis in Giotto's country, the Mugello.[3]

"The heat has come in like a tiger with a spring," wrote Elizabeth to Arabel about this time. It was a happy letter, for Robert had been remarking that "we two being married just seven years I looked exactly seven years younger than when we married." Penini had been telling her that if she didn't eat more she would be a little baby when he was a great man and he would have to carry her. Pen, she admitted, got his own way with her, but Robert was strictly obeyed; there must be in him "a potentiality of wrath" for "he spoils the child as much as I do."

They had a new servant, Ferdinando Romagnoli (who, she hoped, would "make Wilson comfortable"), having just got rid of one who both smelled and looked terrible. "We have practised a hair's breadth of Christianity in keeping this man so long," said Elizabeth. They gave him a present as well as the month's wages and he was very grateful.

To Lucca they went—and there were the Storys and Lytton, with whom an amazing expedition was undertaken. Elizabeth wrote to George:

> The distance is six miles off, but the ground being absolutely perpendicular, the guides forced to walk at every animal's head to prevent a general precipitation, you can scarcely calculate the amount of necessary fatigue. Said I to Mr. Lytton as we approached home— "I am dying, how are you?" "A quarter of an hour ago," he answered, "I thought I should have to give it up, altogether, but now I am rather better." Think what the fatigue must have been to bring such an answer from a young man one & twenty who had ridden the whole way. Certainly he is very delicate. For a week afterwards I could not stir from the house but I never suffer permanently when the weather is so exquisite.

In Henry James's biography of Story we are told of less strenuous pleasures, of his taking tea with the Brownings and staying till almost midnight; of going "backward and forward," writes Elizabeth, "to tea-drinking and gossiping at one another's houses," while "our husbands hold the reins." And Story describes the picnic which inspired Browning's *"By the Fireside"*:

> The day was glorious, and after climbing an hour we arrived at a little old church. . . . The grand limestone mountains spring sharply up, with deep patches of purple shade and little grey towns perched here and there on the lower spines. Under the trees here

we spent nearly an hour, and then took our donkeys and horses again, and, after an hour and a half, passing over wild and grand scenery, with mountain-streams dripping and tumbling, and now and then over beds of red-veined jasper, we rounded a height bold and rugged as the Alps and saw before us the soft green velvety dome of Prato Fiorito, adorable name, covered with its short golden grass. Here we lay for half an hour and talked and gazed. . . .

A few days later

The whole day in the same woods with the Brownings. We went at ten o'clock carrying our provisions. Browning and I walked to the spot, and there, spreading shawls under the great chestnuts, we read and talked the live-long day, the Lima at our feet, babbling on, clear and brown, over the stones, and the distant rock-ribbed peaks taking the changes of the hours. In the afternoon we took a long walk through the grove and found wondrous *fungi*, some red as coral.

Story was a poet after his fashion, though some accused him of trying to set his feet in the too-big prints of his friend. Here he has set the scene in prose for Browning's poetry, for every detail of those rides, the rose-flesh mushrooms, the gray church, the heart of the woodland, Browning wove into the love story still so fresh and new that he could dream of a wondrous ending:

> My own confirm me! If I tread
> This path back, is it not in pride
> To think how little I dreamed it led
> To an age so blest that, by its side,
> Youth seems the waste instead? . . .
>
> But who could have expected this
>   When we two grew together first
> Just for the obvious human bliss,
>   To satisfy life's daily thirst
> With a thing men seldom miss?

Americans increasingly became the Brownings' friends, or, arriving in Europe as admirers, visited and described them. George Stillman Hillard in *Six Months in Italy* writes of Browning as "simple, natural, playful," Mrs. Browning all genius and sensibility. "Her tremulous voice," he wrote, "often flutters over her words like the flame of a dying candle over the wick. I have never seen a human frame which seemed so nearly a transparent veil for a celestial and immortal spirit."

Nathaniel Hawthorne in his *Italian Notebook* describes her as "a pale small person scarcely embodied at all," as elfin rather than earthly but "sweetly disposed towards the human race." To almost all these more casual acquaintance she appeared of far more importance than the husband, whom Lockhart approved of as "not at all like a damned literary man." Trollope, while he had never seen Browning "rough or uncourteous to the most exasperating fool," noted a "lurking smile" that made the utterers of platitudes and illogicalities a trifle uncomfortable.

Robert Lytton, at this time British attaché in Florence, cherished a romantic attachment to both husband and wife, whom he called in moments of special intensity "My king and my queen": "If all who know you feel as I do, they must ever seem drawn to lean on you and draw life and warmth from your great-hearted presence." At a reception given by him on the terrace at his Bellosguardo Villa were English, and American friends, and one Italian, the historian, Pasquale Villari: "We were all bachelors together," writes Elizabeth. She and Lytton were united in looking for "a new revelation and evangel . . . here are all the symptoms that preceded the Christian era and then as now the world seemed used up." Lytton's father would thirty years later be a founding member of the Society for Psychical Research and already was writing to his son of manifestations—one supposedly by Byron. It was "what some great Poet, gone mad, might write from Bedlam, preserving in his mental chaos all the mechanism of the art."

The absence of Italians from their circle is a little surprising. Margaret (Fuller) Ossoli, Jessie (White) Mario, and Mary (Thornton) Tassinari were Italian by marriage only; their husbands are barely mentioned. The Brownings had met Mazzini in London, admired but later repudiated him; Massimo d'Azeglio visited them in Rome, Gordigiano painted Elizabeth, and the poet Dall Ongaro translated her poetry. But only Pasquale Villari really belonged to the Florentine Circle—and his wife, Linda White, was English.

This Anglo-American group, whether believing or unbelieving, were constantly playing with spiritualism, and at this time Browning himself possibly thought of it almost as a game. He could count on his own power (as Elizabeth complained) of ruining a too successful séance by his laughter. Later he asked George to destroy all Elizabeth had written on the subject; but husband and wife never read each other's letters and I doubt if he yet guessed how overexcited hers were becoming—especially when she first met William Burnet Kinney, United States representative at Turin. Mr. Kinney was going through a process of conversion and told Elizabeth of "accounts from America of the most extraordinary character." Robert himself, while rebuking Elizabeth for credulity, confessed (she told Arabel) that "half his nature was taking my part and that therefore he had to strive against himself and me—which vexed him all the more."

Young Lytton meanwhile, probing for the "new evangel," was fascinated by another Florentine resident, Seymour Kirkup, from whom I found a letter at Balliol reminding Browning of his own unusual psychic powers. While Browning at this time denied any personal experiences, he many years later told a curious story of an Italian nobleman, brought one day to the Casa Guidi, who boasted of clairvoyant powers. Asking for some personal belonging of Robert's, he was given a pair of sleeve links, and exclaimed: "Something about these cries out 'murder!'" The links were taken from the dead body of a great uncle of the poet's who had been murdered long ago on his estate in Saint Kitts. Kirkup would certainly have refused to accept Browning's explanation that, while no one in Florence knew about the sleeve links, the shrewd Italian was guided by "the involuntary help of my own eyes and face."

Kirkup lived on in Florence till 1880 but already in 1853 he was an elder in their community. He had by his experiences been converted from materialism to belief in a spiritual world, but Elizabeth wrote to Henrietta: "to my mind, the man was somewhat hasty, after having heard in vain the mystical knockings at all the doors and windows of the universe his whole life long to come round suddenly through a rap on the door by means of a clairvoyante." And to Lytton she spoke of the futility of the supposed revelations—but also of the importance of continued experiment. She could not leave the subject alone, and Lytton was excitedly drawing her on.

"There is a real *poem*," she wrote a little later, "being lived between Mr. Kirkup and the 'spirits' so called. . . . And such a tragic face the old man has, with his bleak white beard. Even Robert is touched." According to Hawthorne, report called Kirkup a necromancer, talking with dead kings and emperors, talking even with Dante. His former medium's daughter (reputedly also his) he adopted, and through her would talk to her dead mother and other spirits. But however touched by the old man, whatever Browning's own potential, he would have no truck with spirits, and he used to recount with gusto how he caught Kirkup's medium cheating him.

Elizabeth's keen conviction of a surrounding world, from which signals reach us through those specially endowed to receive them, had been sharpened by the experience of her last meeting with Margaret Fuller, who had dined with them in the spring of 1850 the night before sailing for the States. She gave Pen a book inscribed "in memory" of her own small son who was going, too; she seemed full of fears and forebodings. And the ship sank. Just as Elizabeth had lost her brother did she lose a friend, not yet intimate but one to whom she was attracted by a strong sympathy.

But Lytton had been critical. Margaret Fuller was "only a petticoated pedant after all, with now and then blind notions of a restless heart tumbling and beating uneasily beneath a heap of books and dry dust of erudition." How right she had been to marry "that good-natured, adoring uncultivated count. . . . I was more interested in Madame Ossoli than in Margaret Fuller."[3]

Women at that date expected criticism when struggling for a life of freedom and full intellectual development, but no one sympathized more keenly than Elizabeth with intellectual—or sexual—rebellion. The lack of intellectual training for women, the domination by husbands, the lack of sympathy for the "fallen woman," stirred her to rage. She was irritated by the excitement over Florence Nightingale, for such work as nursing had always been admittedly feminine.[4] She does not appear to have recognized the vastness of that great woman's organizing powers, of the creation of a new world in hospitals, barracks, even homes. Elizabeth could not imagine why the quiet and conventional Jane Austen was so immensely admired, while Browning disliked the extravagant humor in Martin Chuzzlwit. He did not, it is true, mention Sairy Gamp or Betsey Prig, it is the American scenes he detests—but Picksniff too: there was perhaps a lack of complete humor in his make-up despite the plausible claim made by Herford that he was the Dickens and the Balzac of poetry in the creation of so wide a variety of men and women.

Compared with Jane Austen's the experience of both husband and wife was wide, compared with Dickens', it was narrow. These were only passing criticisms, but there seems a tendency to look out for the extraordinary; I can imagine Browning today studying with zest men who turn into women, women who turn into men, homosexuality and perversions. There was a fund of sanity in him, but there was something that had responded to the darker side of Wanley's *Wonders of the Little World*. As to Elizabeth, she knew, she told Arabel, too much of books in proportion to life. The life in a Jane Austen novel appeared so narrow: *Aurora Leigh* shows her in greater sympathy with Charlotte Brontë.

Elizabeth's health, the dawnings of what later became her fanatical excitement over spiritualism—and Pen. While he was still almost a baby, Browning had objected to his being so dressed that visitors mistook him for a girl, to his being taken to parties beyond his proper bedtime, to the spoiling, the lack of discipline with which this overexcitable and invalid mother treated her overexcitable only child. One friend had begged her seriously not to make "an idol" of him. She embroidered fantastic jackets for him, let his golden curls grow long, decorated his hat with an immense feather. She tells her sisters something of this, and that she means to have her way. Pen, she says, is as yet a "sort of neutral creature." If put into boy's clothes, he would look like "a small angel

travestied." But while Pen was so young, did it much matter? And
Browning certainly spoiled them both. There was so much leeway of
tenderness to be made up for her, her health and happiness were always
his first consideration.

These were clouds, but very light and small on a horizon glowing
with hope, while she was writing *Aurora Leigh* and he *Men and
Women* amid "the old magnificent mountains and chestnut woods and
great moonlights," as they lingered on at Lucca while the Storys preceded them to Rome. Browning wrote on October 7, 1853: "This poor
place has given up the ghost now, and we really want to get away." He
had heard "more about the fever at Rome than I care to infect this
paper with." In emulation of Story's pencil—"so happy at bridge-sides
and bits of rock and water"—he, too, is making sketches "that may
bring back this last happy time when the darker days arrive, as they
will, I suppose."

This letter was sadly prophetic, for the Roman fever struck their
friends. The Storys' small boy sickened first—and died. The Brownings
took the little girl into their apartment. But she, too, had got the fever.
On December 21, Elizabeth wrote to Mrs. Jameson:

> Ah dearest friend! You have heard how our first step into Rome
> was a fall, not into a catacomb but a fresh grave, . . . I doubt whether
> I shall get over it, and whether I ever shall feel that this is Rome.
> The first day at the bed's head of that convulsed and dying child;
> and the next two, three, four weeks in great anxiety about his little
> sister, who was all but given up. . . . It was not only sympathy. I
> was selfishly and intensely frightened for my own treasures . . .

Rome was certainly unhealthy, with constant recurrences of fever.
Months later Lytton wrote in great agitation: "I pray God you are both
well; if so, make haste and come out of that doomed city."

Edith Story has described how Thackeray visited her sickroom and
read her *The Rose and the Ring* (not yet published). Her door was
guarded by "the steadfast tramp of Pen Browning who was acting as
sentinel outside my door to prevent 'other horrid maladies' from coming
in." Pen also reproved Anne Thackeray for making too much noise.

Edith had several setbacks in Rome, so when she was a little better, the Storys decided to move to Naples. But at Velletri, their first stop, she had a bad relapse, was "in a state of all but insensibility." Story sent an urgent message, begging Browning to come and be with them at the end. Elizabeth dreaded his going and Pen gave vent to "the most piteous screams and sobs." Elizabeth hardly slept that night and did not know, she said, when she had had "such a concussion of nerves."

The next afternoon Browning returned all smiles with news that the child was much better. Elizabeth in a letter to Arabel showed a surprising lack of sympathy. She blamed Story for not facing up to the situation "in all manliness and fortitude," especially as he had with him at Velletri a wife, two servants, three physicians and "full pecuniary resources."

Certainly Browning had his problems, but they both seem to have enjoyed much of that winter in Rome. In an undated letter to Mrs. Story, Elizabeth writes of listening to the Miserere in the Sistine Chapel "very overcoming in its ejaculatory pathos. Then we have made various Campagna excursions with Mrs. Sartoris and Mrs. Kemble, dined in bosky villas and pinewood forests, and done the proper honour to your glorious opal mountains in the distance." In another letter to Arabel she speaks of Browning having been at fourteen, and she at "some five or six," of these excursions, one of which gave us "Two in the Campagna" (C. Day Lewis told me that of all Browning's lyrics he would choose this as the most perfect.)

Elizabeth wrote to Miss Mitford: "The talk was almost too brilliant for the sentiment of the scenery, but it harmonized entirely with the mayonnaise and champagne!" The party wandered off in various directions, but says Browning: "We sat down on the grass, to stray / In spirit better through the land, / This morn of Rome and May . . ."

Rome was socially a more worldly city than Florence, and more abounding in important English visitors. "If anyone wants small talk," wrote Elizabeth, "by handfuls of glittering dust swept out of salons, there's Mr. Thackeray besides."

"I think Mrs. Browning," wrote Anne Thackeray enthusiastically, "is the greatest woman I ever knew in my life." Browning she described

as "a dark short man, slightly but nervously built with a frank open
face, long hair streaked with grey and a large mouth which he opens
widely when he speaks, white teeth, a dark beard and a loud voice with
a slight lisp, and the best and kindest heart in the world."

But to Thackeray, Elizabeth was not attracted. "As to the society,"
she wrote to Arabel, "it rains lords and ladies for the especial benefit of
Mr. Thackeray perhaps." And to Henrietta (December 30, 1853):
"Mr. Thackeray . . . 'can't write in the morning without his good dinner
and two parties overnight.' From such a soil spring the Vanity Fairs!
He is an amusing man-mountain enough and very courteous to us—but
I never should get on with him much, I think—he is not sympathetical
to me." Nor to Lytton, who, transferred in 1854 to Paris, wrote often
to his "dearest ones." He had met Dickens and was "impressed by a
something powerful and electrical about him of vigorous intelligence
and goodness," but Thackeray, though "very kind and civil to me," he
could not like "very cordially."

In Rome the visitor in the mid-fifties seemed less aware of the
Risorgimento than anywhere in north Italy. Perhaps this was in part
because Rome cried aloud her own past at every step—the Forum and
the Colosseum, the ruins and the monuments, the very stones unheeded
or built into shrines and churches, themselves speaking of a second
civilization with years counted in many hundreds. And the Campagna

> . . . with its endless fleece
> Of feathery grasses everywhere!
> Silence and passion, joy and peace,
> An everlasting wash of air—
> Rome's ghost since her decease. . . .

> Such life here, through such length of hours,
> Such miracles performed in play,
> Such primal, naked forms of flowers,
> Such letting nature have her way
> While Heaven looks from its towers!

Again, leafing through *Men and Women*, one becomes aware of the variety of thought stirring in Browning's mind; of the power of the prismatic rays into which the white light he sought was more commonly broken. "Holy Cross Day," introduced by an extract from a Bishop's secretary of 1600 concerning a compulsory yearly sermon to the Jews of Rome, has a laconic note: "The present Pope abolished this bad business," which serves to remind us how long an evil period in the Church's history prolonged itself, to remind us of *how* evil it was.

> "God spoke, and gave us the word to keep,
> Bade never fold the hands nor sleep
> 'Mid a faithless world,—at watch and ward,
> Till Christ at the end relieve our guard.
> By His servant Moses the watch was set:
> Though near upon cock-crow we keep it yet. . . .
>
> "Thou! if thou wast He, who at mid-watch came,
> By the starlight, naming a dubious name!
> And if too heavy with sleep—too rash,
> With fear—O Thou, if that martyr-gash
> Fell on thee coming to take thine own,
> And we gave the Cross, when we owed the Throne—
>
> "Thou art the Judge. We are bruised thus.
> But the Judgment over, join sides with us!
> Thine too is the cause! and not more thine
> Than ours, is the work of these dogs and swine,
> Whose life laughs through and spits at their creed!
> Who maintain Thee in word and defy Thee in deed! . . .
>
> "We withstood Christ then? Be mindful how
> At least we withstand Barabbas now!
> Was our outrage sore? But the worst we spared,
> To have called these—Christians, had we dared!
> Let defiance to them pay mistrust, of Thee,
> And Rome make amends for Calvary!"

They had meant to go to England the summer of 1854, and in May left Rome for Florence. "Such nights we have between starlight and firefly-light, and the nightingales singing," wrote Elizabeth to Miss Mitford in June, herself longing to stay in Casa Guidi, but "constrained by duty and love" to go northward to their two families. But in July she writes: "Our reason for not going to England has not been from caprice, but a cross in money matters. A ship was to have brought us in something, and brought us in nothing instead, with a discount; . . . unable even to 'fly to the mountains' as a refuge from the summer heat. . . . That we should be able to sit quietly still at Florence and eat our bread and maccaroni is the utmost of our possibilities this summer."

"A comfort," she wrote to Sarianna, "is that Robert is considered here to be looking better than he ever was known to look." In a fit of depression, however, he had shaved off "his whole beard, whiskers and all," so horrifying Elizabeth that she demanded, under pain of all being at an end between them, that he grow it again "directly." But the beard "grew *white,* which was the just punishment of the gods."

Meanwhile he was trying to raise the necessary funds for their journey by letting Casa Guidi for a year, "which if the thing happens, will give us a lift." It has been said that another reason for the delay was that *Aurora Leigh* was not completed, and certainly the whole matter of manuscripts is something so changed by the invention of the typewriter that we have again to stir imagination to realize a different world. Everything not only written but *copied* by hand. Elizabeth at one point describes her husband as dictating his own completed manuscript for four hours daily "to an amanuensis." Only when a copy existed could the manuscript be trusted to an uncertain post. Sarianna copied for them both; Elizabeth and their friend Isa Blagden copied for Browning —and there was no such thing as taking a carbon. When they did go to London the following year, *Aurora Leigh* was still not finished, but Browning was able to hand *Men and Women* to his publisher.

London and Paris, Pisa and Florence, Siena, Le Havre, Lucca and Rome, weeks spent in leisurely travel from one to another Italian town, how incredibly changed a life for the woman who had spent years in a single room. But for Browning the change was even greater, for he had assumed a huge responsibility while Elizabeth remained the cherished, cared-for woman she had always been. Browning must now not only run his own life but hers, too. Both had in different ways been spoiled; both had been surrounded by a family, now almost totally lost. And if ever a life reminded two humans that we have not here a lasting city, it was this one of constant change—a "tent life" as Elizabeth once called it.

But with all the moves, the Brownings recognized a home at Casa Guidi. Florence was too hot in midsummer, too cold at midwinter for full comfort, but the Casa was the place they had furnished; it held their books and pictures; it was the best place for writing; it was the place where Penini had been born and which he loved. To picture their lives it is well to visit Rome and Siena, it is essential to muse awhile in the Casa Guidi, formerly known as Palazzo Guidi, the Brownings having chosen to change a mere palace into a home.

The street on which the living rooms look out is surprisingly narrow. The Church of San Felice seems oppressively close. There was just room, Elizabeth said, for two people to walk along the "terrace" abreast, and this is proof positive that Browning had kept his early slimness and that she did not wear a crinoline! I should call it a balcony rather than a terrace. The outlook on the court is pleasant, especially if shrubs and flowers are growing there, but the court is not large. The windows being at the end of exceptionally long rooms make the rear curiously dark even under a Florentine sky.

Miss Borchardt, secretary of the Linguistic Society of Florence, has put loving care into as full a restoration as may be of the rooms on this side which are rented by the Society, and imagination can easily replace the long table and upright chairs needed for their meetings with the rather splendid, rather heavy desks, sofas, armchairs, and book cases of the Browning era; can clothe the walls with the tapestries (bought for a few hundred lire), seen many years later by Anne Thackeray in Browning's London home. "Mythologies and metaphors and gardens and browsing flocks; the gods in Olympus and looking down upon a golden age . . . a messenger comes flying from the clouds.

We see far away blue hills and the towers of an ancient city; and is not that a distant gibbet depicted with a figure hanging to it just outside the city wall?" Browning's large desk is at Baylor University, and most of the furniture was photographed from the sketch made after Elizabeth's death. The long dining and drawing room, Elizabeth's equally long bedroom and tiny study, the kitchen with an odd little room above it, accessible only by a rope ladder in the days when it was the bedroom of Ferdinando, their second and permanent Italian manservant—all are on the San Felice side of the house. Looking on the Via Maggio and the Pitti Palace is Browning's room.

One wonders whether he at least did not crave at times for wider spaces, for he had not come from imprisonment in a London bedroom but from an open-air life, a large garden, a lot of walking and riding. He still walked constantly, sometimes with Elizabeth, sometimes alone, observing the streets and markets and churches, watching and overhearing the men and women.

A vivid picture is painted of the years 1854 to '57 in the *Letters and Memories* of a young American sculptor, Harriet (or Hatty) Hosmer, whom the Brownings had come to know on their first visit to Rome. At that date the Englishman, Gibson, regarded as a sculptor of genius, had taken this brilliant girl as a pupil; presently she would have her own studio with workmen under her; her works would sell for as much as £1,000; she would be "taken up" on a big scale by the English aristocracy. Kate Field, who would end up owning her own newspaper in Washington, wrote enviously of her a few years later: "Lady Ashburton got down on her knees to Hatty Hosmer the other day, and gave her a magnificent ring, a ruby heart surrounded with diamonds. Why she went on her knees is a mystery. Is not Hatty lucky? She is fortunate in everything." But Elizabeth relating the same story in a letter to Isa (probably of May 1860) attributes the gift (and posture) to Lady Marian Alford.

In 1854, at the outset of her career, very popular in the American and English circle in Rome, Hatty horrified the Italians by walking and even riding about quite alone. Gibson's letters to her begin "Dearest" or "My Little Hat" and are signed "your slave." Fanny Kemble writes: "My very dear little Capellina," both Brownings "Dearest Hatty." Elizabeth writes of Hatty as "the young American sculptress, who is a great pet of mine and Robert's and who emancipates the eccentric life of a perfectly emancipated woman by the perfect purity of hers. . . . She lives here all alone (at twenty-two); dines and breakfasts at the cafés precisely as a young man would; works at 6 o'clock in the morning till night, as a great artist must."

Harriet lived in Rome, but in a letter from Florence, Elizabeth writes of her in "a house of emancipated women." Miss Hayes was there, the translator of George Sand, who " 'dresses like a man down to the waist' (so the accusation runs). Certainly there's the waistcoat which I like—and the collar, neckcloth, and jacket made with a sort of wagtail behind, which I don't like. . . . They are both coming to us tonight, with Miss Blagden who occupies the apartment under theirs."

Isa Blagden was English and a novelist, never very famous and today forgotten except as the close friend of both Brownings. "A dozen or more good and dear women," Lytton wrote, "must have gone to the making of that one little body." With Miss Blagden stayed later the Irish feminist and reformer, Frances Power Cobbe, who observed how Isa and Browning "wrangled playfully." Miss Cobbe found him "always full of spirits, full of interest in everything from politics to hedge-flowers, cordial and utterly unaffected . . . a ripple of laughter round the sofa where he used to seat himself, generally beside some lady." Mid enthusiastic talk he "would push nearer and nearer till she frequently rose to avoid falling off."

The Brownings' acquaintance with Frances Cobbe began later than their friendship with the Storys, Lytton, and Frederick Tennyson; and one sees again both in an allusion to Elizabeth's pain-worn face and in the remarks about Robert's "wrangling" with Isa, the appearance of the light clouds looking in the earlier fifties no bigger than a man's hand. For in those bright days Elizabeth had reached the peak of her improved health, and spiritualism, the main subject of the wrangling, had only just begun to absorb her attention. They were a gay group of friends especially when Hatty joined them. Much of the summer of 1854 she passed with Isa, walking down to the Brownings' for break-

fast, playing with Pen, studying under Browning's guidance, breath-
lessly admiring Elizabeth. After her departure came letters from both
husband and wife. Says Browning:

> Writing to you, dearest Hatty, is almost like breaking a spell
> and driving you away, or at least putting in evidence for the first
> time that you are really gone, out of sight, out of hearing, out of
> reach. You won't, then, come in any more of a morning, or after-
> noon, in the old way? I can tell you, and you will believe it, I think,
> that often and often Ba and I have seen you, on the queer chair at
> the little end of the table, on the sofa, and in all old places of yours.
> You are dear and good to speak to us, as you do, and to feel, as you
> say, for us. Come back to us, at any distance of time, and you'll see
> whether we love you less, *more* it won't do to promise. Meantime
> both of us wish you well, with our whole heart.

Elizabeth sends messages from Pen and misses sorely "the third
coffee cup" at their breakfast table, while Browning asks, "What of the
Greek now, pupil of mine. . . . We see next to nobody, but make up a
rare fire and get on with our work. . . . Yet we had rather be idle and
have you."

In the Roman winter Harriet writes: "How often did I climb the
cold, cheerless, stone stairway which led to their modest apartment on
the third floor of 42 Bocca di Leone. Nothing cold or cheerless, however, when their door was gained."

On a later visit to Florence, again staying with Isa, Hatty would
sometimes have Browning's company in her pre-breakfast walk to the
Casa Guidi. Expressing a wish one morning to ride in the caretta of
Girolomo, their purveyor of vegetables, she received a ready assent from
him. "*Andra andra*," he said of his donkey, and it proved only too true.
First the footboard slipped from beneath their feet, next the seat slid
perilously backward, while the vegetables shot out on either side of
the cart. Determinedly the donkey galloped—not to the Casa Guidi but
to the home of Girolomo, halting so abruptly at the gate that they were
almost thrown to the ground, while Mrs. Girolomo voiced sympathy.
And worst of all the donkey would budge no more: "I did not say," re-

marked Girolomo, "that he would *come,* only that he would *go.*" Disheveled and famished they made their way home on foot, where Browning demanded breakfast before he would tell the tale.

This he did dramatically, reproducing, with the help of the Casa Guidi furniture, a rope and a few boards, the caretta and its donkey. Stocking it with vegetables from the kitchen he mounted on his improvised seat and re-enacted the morning's catastrophe. Hatty writes:

> Browning, who was a capital actor and possessed the keenest sense of the ridiculous, was inimitable in his role, pouring forth in Greek, Latin and the vernacular a torrent of threats, entreaties, and exhortations, addressed indiscriminately to the donkey, to Girolomo, and to San Antonio, while the clattering feet of the donkey, produced by an ingenious device indicating gradually accelerated speed, heightened the general effect and formed a running accompaniment to the recitative. A fine touch of realism was introduced by the vegetables, which, at stated intervals, but with utter disregard of Mrs. Browning's safety, were hurled about the room. No detail was lacking which could render illusion perfect, the catastrophe being reached in the sudden centrifugal impetus caused by the abrupt halt at the vineyard gate.
>
> "Nothing does Ba so much good as a good laugh," said Mr. Browning, gazing with satisfaction at her helpless condition and at her face glistening with tears, "and I will set this down as the laugh of her life."

Turning from Hatty to the memories of Mrs. Hugh Fraser, an English diplomatist's wife, is startling indeed. She comes on the scene a little later, when Elizabeth was obsessed by the question of Italian liberty. Pen (called "Penry" by Mrs. Fraser) "was constantly with us" in "a little company of children." She describes him as "beautifully dressed," but rather spoiled and inclined to be bossy with the other children. On Browning she is lyrical: ". . . his face was a noble one, clear and pale . . . his voice I remember well. It was deep and joyous as the wind when it sang through our cypresses."

But meeting Elizabeth was "an awesome experience," coming from

the blazing sun "into a great dark room. . . . Everything was intense—
the heat, the enthusiasm, the darkness, and I tried hard to get keyed
up. . . . The poetess was everything I did not like . . . great cavernous
eyes . . . big bushes of black ringlets . . . her face was hollow and ghastly
pale . . . why should that nice happy Mr. Browning have such a dis-
mally mournful lady for his wife . . . lacking in humour and terribly
sentimental?"

Mrs. Kinney, wife of William Burnet Kinney, visiting Casa Guidi
in 1854, thought it strange that Browning "never will allow that she
is ill, but now he must see it and feel it. . . ." An article in the *New
York Home Journal* had described Elizabeth as "a crooked, dried-up
old woman, with a horrible mouth." Mrs. Kinney rushed to her defense, writing of her "beauty of spirit," but not denying that "her frame
is shattered by disease." Browning was furious. " 'I see well enough yet'
as Benedick says—'without spectacles, and yet see nothing of the
matter.' " She should, he claimed, have described his wife as "beautiful
in person"—and he never forgave her well-meant intervention.

Mrs. Kinney's horror at hearing both Brownings proclaim George
Sand "a great woman" reflects perfectly the Victorian outlook which
they so frequently outraged, for they admitted that she had a series of
lovers. Lust, Elizabeth said, was no worse than intemperance or glut-
tony. George Sand's mind was "godlike," and she was kind and charitable. But, said Mrs. Kinney, "lascivious," with her unlawful loves.

"Love," exclaimed husband and wife together; "she never loved
anyone but herself."

Mrs. Kinney admired Mrs. Browning, but was critical of him.
Browning "labors in all he writes—not to *polish*, but to roughen it." He
was too "impulsive, often abusive in speaking of others and unsparing
in his ridicule and contempt of many whom the world calls poets," but
"she is good, never speaks ill of anyone and is kind and gentle, conciliat-
ing with all."

Mrs. Kinney was not alone in her view. The only opinion on record
that Elizabeth was critical, Robert kind, came from Mrs. Crosse. There
was as noted the lurking smile with which Browning could make the
fool feel himself just that. At Pisa an English couple had been spread-

ing unkind gossip about Elizabeth: she gave herself airs, had been too proud to return their call. Browning visited them and talked blandly of gossip he had heard, repeating their own words to them as of unnamed malicious folk while he watched them writhe. His language could be as violent in abuse as in enthusiasm, though most of the extreme instances recorded belong to his later life. But there certainly was in him "a potentiality of wrath." To the end of his life a friend noted how his face would blanch at a mention of Home, the medium or, sadly enough, of Harriet Hosmer, for this was one of the tiny handful among Browning's friendships which did not last.

Hatty Hosmer loved both Brownings, thinking Elizabeth "the most perfect human being I have ever known." A beautiful small sculpture of hers is their clasped hands, which perhaps suggested to the poet the lines in "James Lee's Wife":

> "As like as a Hand to another Hand!"
>   Whoever said that foolish thing,
> Could not have studied to understand
>   The counsels of God in fashioning
> Out of the infinite love of his heart,
>   This Hand . . .

Hatty thought Elizabeth's face "plain of feature," but redeemed by "wonderful dark eyes, large and loving and luminous as stars." But in the "large full lipped mouth" she thought there might be found "the key to some of Mrs. Browning's less delicate verse"—an allusion to the startling Victorian view which discovered coarseness in Elizabeth's attempts to bring social evils into the sight of those who should be working to cure them.

If the "later years," in which Harriet Hosmer's biographer tells us she was writing, mean that period in which she and Browning had quarreled, her description of him is not ungenerous:

> Years have passed, and photography now reveals to us a face of great intellectual power, but also the face of the comfortable man of the world, tinged, perhaps, with a certain sense of success, but in the days of which I write, he dwelt apart from the every-day world;

he stood, I think, on a higher plane, fulfilling in every sense the ideal we have formed of a poet. The broad forehead, the black and slightly waving hair, the keen and clear gray eyes, the fresh complexion of faintest olive hue, and very slight, as yet, the delicate frame. There were the genial, cheery voice, the unfailing joyous spirits of youth, the unique conversational gifts, witty, grave and gay by turns, with, over all, a manner as charming as any verse he ever penned. Accustomed as we now are to the halo which surrounds their names, it is difficult to associate their present popularity and fame with the *poco curante* mood in which they were then regarded. They lived a life of seclusion, unappreciated, unobserved. It is not too much to say, that outside a purely literary coterie, and their modest circle of personal friends few had heard their names. But what cared those great spirits for the outer world? They lived in a world of their own, happiest when alone therein.

16 Men and Women

Even now, as I am speaking ... there glides through the room the pageant of his persons ... men and women that live.

OSCAR WILDE

"ROBERT'S poems are magnificent," wrote Elizabeth to Henrietta in April, 1855, "and will raise him higher than he stands. We are up early working, working. Penini's lessons I never neglect—then I write.—Then dinner—then I criticise Robert's MSS. Altogether I have scarcely breath for reading. . . . Everybody admires at me for looking so well. How can I ever hope to be pitied, I who am always dying and it makes no difference?"

Browning had written to his publishers in 1853: "I shall give you something saleable one of these days—see if I don't," and his hopes for *Men and Women* ran high. For it contained his richest expression of the twofold ideal unfolded in prose in his essay on Shelley. Never have the objective and subjective poet, as he described them in this essay, been more fully fused than in himself. Milsand had already noted this, and there are flashes of likeness between what he wrote of Browning and what Browning wrote of Shelley; as we read the essay, our tendency is to forget Shelley and concentrate, as did Carlyle, on its author. Carlyle thought little of Shelley, "an extremely weak creature, and lamentable, much more than admirable. Weak in genius, weak in character . . . a poor thin, spasmodic, hectic, shrill and pallid being . . . something void, and Hades-like in the whole inner world of him. . . . In a word, it is not with Shelley but with Shelley's Commentator that I take up my quarters at all: and to this latter I will say with emphasis, Give us some more of *your* writing, my friend." He found in Browning "the authentic sound of a *human* voice" amid the "cackle" of the universe. "I honour and respect the weighty estimate you have formed of the Poetic Art; and I admire very much the grave expressiveness of style (a *little* too elaborate here and there), and the dignified tone."

Hastily withdrawn because the letters it was to introduce proved to be spurious, this essay should indeed be reprinted as an introduction to Browning's collected poems.

The "inexhaustible variety of existence," the "soul's delight in its own extended sphere of vision," "an irresistible sympathy with men" compelling him to offer them his "own provision of knowledge and beauty"—all this, in what Browning called the "objective" poet, sets him "on labour as other men are set on rest."

The "subjective" poet, gifted also "with the fuller perception of nature and man, is impelled to embody the theme he perceives, not so much with reference to the many below as to the one above him, the supreme Intelligence which apprehends all things in their absolute truth. Not what man sees, but what God sees—the Ideas of Plato, seeds of creation lying burningly in the Divine Hand—it is toward these that he struggles."

He is "rather a seer" therefore than a "fashioner"; yet "it is with this world, as starting point and basis alike, that we shall always have to concern ourselves: the world is not to be learned and thrown aside, but reverted to and relearned. The spiritual comprehension may be infinitely subtilised, but the raw material it operates upon must remain."

The two faculties of the objective poet and the subjective might issue from the same man "in successive perfect works," but "mere running in of the one faculty upon the other, is of course, the ordinary circumstance." In *Pauline*, in *Paracelsus*, in *Sordello* and *Pippa*, in the *Dramatic Romances and Lyrics*, in *Christmas Eve and Easter Day*, Browning had shown powers both subjective and objective, but the world around remained unresponsive, deaf, and blind. No wonder that he felt it was "the bestowment of life upon a labour, hard, slow and not sure." But "the misapprehensiveness of his age is exactly what a poet is sent to remedy; and the interval between his operation and the generally perceptible effect of it, is no greater, less indeed, than in many other departments of the great human effort. The 'E pur si muove' of the astronomer was as bitter a word as any uttered before or since by a poet over his rejected living work, in that depth of conviction which is so like despair."

Carlyle, more perceptive perhaps despite his growls than many a smoother critic, had realized the danger of a profound discouragement: "I liked the Essay extremely well indeed"; he wrote "a solid, well-wrought, massive, manful bit of discourse; and interesting to me over and above, as the first bit of *prose* I had ever seen from you;—I hope only the first of very many." Thus his letter began, for here was Browning writing in prose as he had advised. But verse or prose—"Seriously, dear Browning, you must at last gird up your loins again; and give us a right stroke of work . . . in whatever form your own *Daimon* bids. Only see that *he* does bid it; and then go on with your best speed."

Browning had obeyed his mentor by writing the best work of the best ten years of his life. I should like to adjure anyone reading this book to lay it down at this point, take up Browning's *Poetical Works* and reread *Men and Women*—every one of that marvelous and all-inclusive collection. In the Murray or Macmillan editions it is a little troublesome to find them all because of the various places where Browning (inadvisedly) has distributed them, but most are in *Dramatic Lyrics* and there is a date guide at the book's end. Even knowing them well already (some by heart) I found this rereading of the utmost value to a deeper understanding of Browning—and of the Shelley Essay which probably preceded most of these poems.

First for one's imagination come the incredible riches scattered by the objective poet: Lippo Lippi seeing

> The value and significance of flesh, . . .
> The beauty and the wonder and the power,
> The shapes of things, their colours, lights and shades,
> Changes, surprises— . . .
> > This world's no blot for us,

> Nor blank; it means intensely, and means good;
>   To find its meaning is my meat and drink.

Lippo is surely Browning on canvas, striking out new ways of seeing and saying, doubted by his Prior as Browning was by his world. Anything odder than comparing him to Andrea del Sarto, the "faultless painter," I can hardly conceive. Browning's art was crammed with faults, roughnesses, elisions, obscurities. Andrea says, "All is silver grey / Placid and perfect with my art." And he sighs longingly for his wife to do what Elizabeth was doing ceaselessly for Browning. Had she, says Andrea, "but brought a mind! / Some women do so. Had the mouth there urged / God and the glory! Never care for gain."[1]

Turn from the smooth-running lines of these two poems to "Master Hugues of Saxe-Gotha," an imaginary composer, to observe Browning in riotous high spirits expressed triumphantly by the meter and by what Chesterton has called a "frantic" astronomical image:

> Hallo, you sacristan, show us a light there!
>   Down it dips, gone like a rocket.
> What, you want, do you, to come unawares,
> Sweeping the Church up for first morning-prayers,
> And find a poor devil has ended his cares
>   At the foot of your rotten-runged rat-riddled stairs?
>   Do I carry the moon in my pocket?

Next go to the change in meter, meaning, imaginative power of that astonishing poem: "A Toccata of Galuppi." One longs to quote it all—the glimpse of Venice through the masks and balls and lovemaking ("Then more kisses!"—"Did *I* stop them, / When a million seemed so few?") Back to the plaintive music "sigh on sigh" which

Told them something? Those suspensions, those solutions—"Must we die?"
Those commiserating sevenths—"Life might last! we can but try!"

And then in the final verse the poet with all his vital energy turns upon the musician, who yet has imposed his own mood of gloom:

"Dust and ashes!" So you creak it, and I want the heart to scold.
Dear dead women, with such hair, too—what's become of all the gold
Used to hang and brush their bosoms? I feel chilly and grown old.

Even Carlyle did not fully understand, as none of Browning's critics of this period did at all, the fierce strain of poetic creation, the long period of gestation preceding it. We know of Browning's brain-and-liver fever, reducing him to a "shadow of a shade" around the time of the publication of *Pippa Passes;* of several other attacks of illness, during one of which he wrote "Artemus Prologuizes" (note the nightmare quality of that poem), and a great deal more not subsequently recorded; of another when he felt impelled to recite all the poems of Donne, of yet another which preceded the writing of *Paracelsus.* As we look at the years in Italy when he often appeared idle, something may indeed be attributed to a despondency following apparent failure, but far more to the fact that production of the highest quality must be spaced widely and irregularly, must grow in the mind as plant or baby from seed, before it can in its maturity be set down on paper:

> He stood and watched the cobbler at his trade,
> The man who slices lemons into drink,
> The coffee-roaster's brazier . . .
> He took such cognizance of men and things,
> If any beat a horse, you felt he saw;
> If any cursed a woman, he took note;
> Yet stared at nobody . . .

In most of these poems we see the "running-in" of subjective and objective; one can certainly imagine Browning "digging in his own soul" and himself speaking to God in much of what he wrote, but in his greatest poetry the two elements are most fully fused. "He would not," says Herford, "trumpet forth truth in his own person . . . he let it struggle up through the baffling density, or glimmer through the conflicting persuasions of alien minds, and break out in cries of angry wonder or involuntary recognition."

Two results are especially noteworthy: Browning's people are never lay figures, and to make them live he recreates not alone the thoughts which they utter, but the scenery, the circumstances, their fellowmen. Turn from his painters and musicians to the Arab physician Karshish, to the Greek poet Cleon, and with each you find a different world as well as a different man; human longings and divine responses are there always, but the settings are vividly various. Yet, too, for anyone who thinks that Browning's faith was just something imposed on him by, or caught from, his mother and wife, it must be baffling to find the different minds going by such different roads and all seeing God on their road and at its end. I began to reread *Men and Women* with just the human pictures in view, and I ended by wondering whether any poet has lived who named God more frequently—from a defense of painting "Adam's wife" naked as He created her, right up the scale to David singing of Incarnation and Redemption, or the "corregidor," who in his ceaseless pacing of the streets, his "cognizance of men and things" had been

> Thro' a whole campaign of the world's life and death,
> Doing the King's work all the dim day long,
> In his old coat and up to knees in mud,
> Smoked like a herring, dining on a crust,—
> And now the day was won relieved at once! . . .
>   Bless us all the while
> How sprucely we are dressed out, you and I!
> A second, and the angels alter that.

Elizabeth and he writing together did not always show each other what they wrote, and it is fascinating to find in *Aurora Leigh* the lines: "Earth's crammed with heaven / And every common bush afire with God." For thenabouts Browning was writing in "Transcendentalism"

> He with a "look you!" vents a brace of rhymes,
> And in there breaks the sudden rose herself,
> Over us, under, round us every side,
> Nay, in and out the tables and the chairs
> And musty volumes, . . .
> Buries us with a glory, young once more,
> Pouring heaven into this shut house of life.

Browning saw mud as well as stars; indeed, the stars shone in the mud at times and pseudo-stars fell as if from the sky. Beauty surrounded him in those years. One must return to Italy to become fully aware of the two poets as they lived, especially of the Browning of *Men and Women*. In the noise of the modern city it is hard to see him half dreaming at a street corner, aware still of stalls and barrows, vendors and buyers:

> River and bridge and street and square,
>   Lay mine, as much at my beck and call,
> Through the live translucent bath of air,
>   As the sights in a magic crystal ball.

The very markets are beset today by the motorist, the pedestrian's life not worth an hour's purchase. Even inside the churches the crowds seethe hour by hour, sight-seeing, with their guides telling them what to see. In a great church where Michael Angelo's last Pieta has found its home or where the walls are covered with frescoes, the apse with mosaics, the windows glowing with glass, you trip over their feet and are deafened by their voices. But learn which are the quiet hours—and in Rome in San Prassede, his "Church of peace"; or Santa Maria Maggiore with its marvelous vista of pillars; in the black and white Cathedral of Siena; in the Florentine churches, most of all familiar to him, you can still picture Browning drinking in beauty, observing absurdity, studying men and women of today, of the Renaissance, of the Middle Ages, of time and of eternity.

> On the arch where olives overhead
>   Print the blue sky with twig and leaf,
> (That sharp-curled leaf which they never shed)
>   Twixt the aloes, I used to lean in chief,
> And mark through the winter afternoons,
>   By a gift God grants me now and then,
> In the mild decline of those suns like moons,
>   Who walked in Florence, besides her men.

And out in the countryside, forsaking the be-motored high roads, wandering through hilly wooded bypaths you can still, as in "By the Fireside," find the quiet he lived in:

> But at afternoon or almost eve
>   'Tis better; then the silence grows

> To that degree, you half believe
>> It must get rid of what it knows,
> Its bosom does so heave.

Returning to the men and women, it is obvious enough that they are mostly, with considerable emphasis, men *and* women—sex apparent as a source of profound joy and grief, of conflict ending in peace or never ending, of the most agonizing problems in the human predicament. What is Browning telling us about sex in these poems and from what throne—or what prison—is he speaking? This last question would have appeared an absurd one till quite lately, yet Dowden wrote many years ago of a pitfall which the biographer should beware: a failure to realize that the fulness of his own happiness sharpened the poet's insight into the causes which may wreck the relations between men and women. One of these, already spoken of, is the "world's coarse thumb / and finger." In "Respectability" and "The Statue and the Bust," as again later in "Youth and Art," hesitation, delay, arise from worldly fears—whether of lack of money or loss of name. And here it is obvious enough that Browning speaks of a battle which ended in victory for Elizabeth and himself.

But there is another victory to be won as the years pass: victory over the problem of a real, a profound difference between the sexes, rendering them, as has been said, almost in essence incompatible. I fancy that in all men and women of genius this becomes less prominent, most such women having more of the male in them than their sisters, most such men having more in them of the woman than their fellows. Anyhow Browning could see exquisitely from the woman's viewpoint: read again "A Woman's Last Word," the ending in peace of a difficult giving:

> —Must a little weep, Love,
>> (Foolish me!)
> And so fall asleep, Love,
>> Loved by thee.

The tendency to give—a profound generosity flowing from love— he sees as stronger in woman than in man. But the first longing is stronger in man, the initial resistance in woman. In "A Serenade at the Villa" Browning depicts the lover serenading his mistress:

> Oh, how dark your villa was,
>> Windows fast and obdurate!
> How the garden grudged me grass
>> Where I stood—the iron gate
> Ground its teeth to let me pass!

And again in "Love in a Life" and "Life in a Love" "While the one eludes, must the other pursue," "So the chase takes up one's life, that's all."

But when he has won his prize it is man that tires soonest, and this is depicted above all in the exquisite lyric "In a Year" where the woman ponders how the very things, the looks, the gestures, which once awakened love now bear a part in killing it:

> Dear, the pang is brief,
>> Do thy part,
> Have thy pleasure! How perplexed
>> Grows belief!
> Well, this cold clay clod
>> Was man's heart:
> Crumble it, and what comes next?
>> Is it God?

A few of the lyrics concern sex but not marriage. "A Light Woman," snatched by a man to save his friend, a woman he does not want for himself and in the taking has lost the friend: ". . . a pear late basking over a wall; / Just a touch to try and off it came," but now

> With no mind to eat it, that's the worst!
>> Were it thrown in the road, would the case assist?
> 'Twas quenching a dozen blue-flies thirst
>> When I gave its stalk a twist.

"A Pretty Woman" was Mrs. Jameson's niece Gerardine, and the poem shows that Browning who had rather violently repudiated the idea that any man could wish to marry so mindless a girl had ended with an appreciation of "just a flower":

> Then how grace a rose? I know a way!
>   Leave it, rather.
>   Must you gather?
> Smell, kiss, wear it—at last, throw away!

Andrea del Sarto had married a woman as light as the one, as mindless as the other of these two, and Browning shows by contrast the woman he had won, to whom the best lyrics in the book are dedicated "Love Among the Ruins," "My Star," "One Word More" and most notably "By the Fireside." Yet he writes, too, of the problems and dangers surrounding the happiest of marriages. One of these is rather specially fascinating for a reason also connected with biography, and casts light on an important element in Browning's character. He shows in "Mesmerism" his very real fear of one element in spiritualism in which he firmly believed—the power of the soul to reach, to affect, to dominate other souls, in ways invisible, incomprehensible. Elizabeth had urged many years back the wonderful cure of her friend, Miss Martineau, as an argument in favor of mesmerism, but to Browning it was clear that the soul was owned by God alone, that no man must attempt to pass outside the human framework set by his Creator.

This awareness of human limitation becomes vivid in both "The Guardian Angel" and "Two in the Campagna." It is not before man or woman that Browning is bowing down in the Church at Fano: While asking the angel as God's minister to help that aching head of his "which too much thought expands" (and his wife "my angel" had, as he later wrote to Julia Wedgwood, "with her two little hands" once charmed away such distress and sent him into a peaceful sleep), the poem is a cry from the limited to the limitless, from the created to the Creator.

In like manner "Two in the Campagna" is very far from being a confession that the love, so triumphant in poems written around the same time "By the Fireside" and "One Word More," was in fact beginning to fail.[2] *The* problem of life Browning held was to pull the infinite into the finite—to fill time with eternity. His doctrine of the infinite moment is precisely the recognition that only for moments can this be done; here on earth at least "the good moment goes." But it goes to return again. It was there in the Campagna, it was there overwhelmingly by the ruined chapel in the mountains of "By the Fireside"; it was there in "One Word More" as the moon rose over Florence and he, leaving the world of men behind him could

> Cross a step or two of dubious twilight,
> Come out on the other side, the novel
> Silent silver lights and darks undreamed of,
> Where I hush and bless myself with silence.

But in the Campagna he has realized human limitations:

> Infinite passion, and the pain
> Of finite hearts that yearn.

An intending student of Browning should surely begin with this and the two earlier similar collections *Dramatic Lyrics* of 1842 and *Dramatic Romances and Lyrics* of 1845. With these also we are vexed by his tiresome habit of rearranging, but the order in which they were written, though interesting, does not greatly matter for their understanding. Of his *Dramatic Romances and Lyrics* he spoke in 1845 as "this dancing ring of men and women hand in hand"—and all three contain some of his famous dramatic monologues.

This form does not, of course, belong to Browning alone, but no one else has I think used it so powerfully. "In England," says Ezra Pound, "Browning refreshed the form of monologue or dramatic monologue or 'Persona,' the ancestry of which goes back at least to Ovid's *Heroides* which are imaginary letters in verse, and to Theocritus, and is thence lost in antiquity."[3] A glance at Theocritus (in translation) does not suggest that he gave much to Browning, and while Sappho's letter is good fun, Browning is infinitely more entertaining and profound than is Ovid. But when trying to write plays, he confessed that his problem was caring far more for character than for action; his plots would lag while his characters talked.

To Oscar Wilde it seemed that Browning was "the most supreme writer of fiction . . . from the point of view of a creator of character he ranks next to him who made Hamlet." Giving us a living procession of Browning's characters, Wilde comments, "His sense of dramatic situations is unrivaled." Wilde does not, as T. S. Eliot does, contrast the characters in the plays, who are impossible to remember, with the speakers of the monologues, who are impossible to forget. But it is Wilde who makes in advance the best comment on Eliot's judgment when he says: "Browning might have given us a Hamlet, who would have realised his mission by thought. . . . He made the soul the protagonist of life's tragedy and looked on action as the one undramatic element of a play."[4] And this is partly because the monologue is *not* the same thing as a soliloquy; it is self-revelation made in a sort of dialogue.

Robert Langbaum who has drawn out this distinction brilliantly in his *Poetry of Experience* suggests a comparison with Pope's *Eloisa to Abelard,* or we might recall Hamlet's "To be or not to be," for in a soliloquy the speaker is arguing with himself, is resolving, maybe changing his outlook, his intended action. In a monologue there is no change of viewpoint; the speaker is justifying himself, explaining himself, showing off to a gallery of one or more. And this is where the element of dialogue comes in; surely we can see and hear not only Blougram but Gigadibs, not only the Bishop but the "nephews" he is talking to, we can see the men to whom Karshish and Cleon were writing, the passer-by who flashed his light into Lippi's face, Andrea's wife listening not to her husband but for the cousin's whistle. Robert Langbaum rightly says that the "Soliloquy of the Spanish Cloister" should in fact be called a monologue; in his self-justification the speaker has given us the first taste of something more deeply penetrated in Guido in *The Ring and the Book*—an evil man hating a good and simple one just because of his goodness, and all unconsciously revealing that goodness and simplicity.

The dramatic monologue Langbaum sees as a form, little understood at Browning's date, especially suited to ours: ". . . it imitates not life, but a particular perspective towards life, somebody's experience of it." And it is the more true in that it imitates the structure of our own experience in which illuminations burn at the centre with certainty and then shade off into ambiguity and doubt. Abt Vogler's instant of doubt makes the ecstatic instant believable by providing it with a recognizable setting. . . . Far from weakening our confidence in the vision, the incompatibility throws us back upon the more intense instant as the primary certainty; while the judgment that proceeds from the less intense instant appears as a problematical speculation.[5]

Edwin Muir, gives us two other useful hints about a poet, "second," he claims, "only to Shakespeare and Chaucer" in his rich variety. Browning's contemporary world was shocked by his "love for the curious" and "for the violently ordinary," which "brought unexpected material into his poetry, and along with it, to deal with it, a vast new vocabulary." For Browning cared immensely for activity. "He could not," says Muir, "have seen with composure Tennyson's man come and till the field and lie beneath. He would have concentrated on the tilling of the field with an agricultural passion." He had a technical interest in all human activity. "When he wrote of painters, or priests, or lovers, or imposters, he wrote with a professional appreciation of the importance of their modes." Love being for him "the highest activity . . . he devoted his most intense imaginative consideration to it."

Another element, often disputed, seems to Muir undeniable by a reader of his lyrics—the sheer music, "tentative and casual music in which the thought seems to be experimentally finding its proper expression: almost a hand-to-mouth music." Everything in Browning's work is, Muir feels, "an enquiry beginning with a Perhaps and converging circuitously upon one of the cardinal truths in which he believed." Hence "this free, faintly interrogative, street music," of which "he was a master. . . . He used it with consummate ease and variety."[6]

Look then for people, look for music in *Men and Women*; you will find both.

17 Conviction
So Like Despair

Because the seeming solitary man
Speaking to God may have an audience too . . .

THE RING AND THE BOOK

BY MAY of 1855 Elizabeth had written more than seven thousand
lines of the endless *Aurora Leigh*, Browning was still adding to *Men
and Women,* and that summer found them in London seeing the same
old friends and many new ones. "Tomorrow," she wrote to Henrietta,
"we breakfast with Mr. Kenyon to meet half America and a quarter
of London." She told George: "In America he [Browning] is a power."
Had the United States agreed to international copyright—or had
Browning had there an admirer to do for him what Emerson did for
Carlyle—the Brownings would have been wealthy. Alone among the
great English writers at that time, Carlyle received for years more money
from his American than from his English publishers. Before *The French
Revolution* had brought him anything in England he had received £400
from the States. In the cause of England's prophet America's prophet
proved himself a good man of business, too. As it was, an occasional
publisher would pay the Brownings a little for sheets in advance (this
happened with *Aurora Leigh*), but wide pirating went on to the end
of their lives. Elizabeth wrote to Mrs. Jameson in an undated letter of
July or August:

The best news I can send you is that Robert has printed the first half volume . . . the work looks better than ever in print. . . . He has read these proofs to Mr. Fox (of Oldham), who gives an opinion that the poems are at the top of art in their kind. . . . Let me see what London news I have to tell you. We spent an evening with Mr. Ruskin, who was gracious and generous. . . . Robert took our young friend Leighton to see him afterwards, and was as kindly received. We met Carlyle at Mr. Forster's, and found him in great force, particularly in the damnatory clauses.

Elizabeth then had read *Men and Women* in manuscript. She says so often that they did not show each other what they were writing that this has been accepted too literally. She sometimes copied for him, he sometimes read unpublished poems aloud to her, and even to some of the Florentine circle; she had read a good deal of *Dramatis Personae,* published only after her death. When and how did she show her work to Robert? He had read the first six books of *Aurora Leigh* by March, 1856, months before publication; when he talks to their publisher of "looking after commas" for her this may refer either to manuscript or proof.

They were too busy, between proofs and the completing of *Aurora,* and too poor besides, to accept multitudinous invitations to country houses—from Sir Edward Lytton, the Custs, the Martins, the Alfred Tennysons and many others. The Barrett family had been shot away instantly by Papa—this time to Eastbourne, and there the Brownings hoped to follow them, since it would be hardly out of their way to Paris where the winter must be spent.

With all his generosity Mr. Kenyon sometimes forgot to send his yearly gift on the appointed date. Elizabeth writes "we are at the end of our purse and can't travel any more, not even to Taunton, where poor Henrietta, who is hindered from coming to me by a like pecuniary straitness, begs so hard that we should go." It was difficult even to "return visits to the hour, and hold engagements to the minute, when one has neither carriage nor legs, nor time at one's disposal. . . ." Yet "people may live very cheaply and very happily if they are happy otherwise." Another member of the Barrett family had been added to the disinherited. "Alfred is just married at the Paris Embassy to Lizzie Barrett . . . the third exile from Wimpole Street, the course of true love running remarkably rough in our house."

There were the Procters to be seen (Barry Cornwall his pen name was); his sharp-tongued wife, a little like Jane Carlyle, faithfully visited by Browning all through his later life; and the daughter Adelaide Anne, minor poet reputed to outsell Tennyson, with a face, said Elizabeth, "worth a drove of beauties." She is best known today by "The Lost Chord."

Of Tennyson's latest volume report declared: "The sale is great, *nearly five thousand copies already.*" The italics are Elizabeth's. And no doubt both husband and wife had high hopes of something similar for *Men and Women*—infinitely superior surely to *Maud* and appealing to far more various tastes. On one historic occasion a group had the opportunity to compare both poems and poets, while Dante Gabriel Rossetti made surreptitious sketches of them and William Michael Rossetti sat listening and taking notes. It was the second day the Laureate had spent with the Brownings. Elizabeth wrote to Mrs. Martin, he "dined with us, smoked with us, opened his heart to us (and the second bottle of port), and ended by reading *Maud* through from end to end and going away at half past two in the morning."

"Oh Hatty," wrote Browning to Harriet Hosmer, "why were you not here in London first, and you should have heard Alfred Tennyson read 'Maud' to us, and Mrs. Sartoris sing, and Ruskin and Carlyle talk, our three best remembrances."[1] Elizabeth thought Tennyson's reading "like articulated music." *Maud* was his favorite; my own parents often listened to it. Did he say to Elizabeth as he sometimes did to my mother, "Give me your hand that some electricity may pass from you to me?" And then he would perhaps forget the hand he held and wave it ardently in time with the music of his reading! As he finished he would say, "No one knows what *Maud* is till they hear me read it." Elizabeth talks of his "unexampled *naïveté!* Think of his stopping in *Maud* every now and then—'There's a wonderful touch! That's very tender. How beautiful that is!' Yes, and it *was* wonderful, tender, beautiful, and he read exquisitely in a voice like an organ, rather music than speech."

Browning gave them "Fra Lippo Lippi," and it is interesting to compare Elizabeth's rapture over Tennyson with the judgment of Henry James who, not present that night, had later opportunities to listen to both poets. Tennyson was often called "the Bard," and bardic Henry James found him. It should have been, he felt, a "prodigious occasion . . . I pinched myself for the determination of my identity and hung on the reader's deep-voiced chant for the credibility of his: I asked myself in fine why, . . . I failed to swoon away under the heaviest pressure I had doubtless ever known the romantic situation bring to bear." The great man remained the Bard, but "The character was just a rigid idiosyncracy."

James felt Browning to be not at all a bard but totally a poet. He read

> with all the exhibition of point and authority, the expressive particularisation, so to speak, that I had missed on the part of the Laureate; an observation through which the author of *Men and Women* appeared, in spite of the beauty and force of his demonstration, as little as possible, a Bard. He particularised if ever a man did, was heterogeneous and profane, composed of pieces and patches that betrayed some creak of joints, and addicted to the excursions from which these were brought home; so that he had to *prove* himself a poet, almost against all presumptions, and with all the assurance and all the character he could use. Was not this last in especial, the character, so close to the surface, with which Browning fairly bristled, what was most to come out in his personal delivery of the fruit of his genius? It came out almost to harshness; but the result was that what he read showed extraordinary life. During that audition at Aldworth the question seemed on the contrary not of life at all. . . ."[2]

Would James have felt the same at this date? Tennyson was the Laureate, the great success; Browning so much the failure that in discussions prior to Tennyson's appointment several names had been mentioned, including his wife's, but his own never. At the peak of his fame, the absurd Home, the spiritualist, could never have thought up such an explanation as he gave of Browning's uneasiness when "spirit hands" at a séance hovered around his wife's head and finally placed a wreath of flowers on it. Browning, said he, had been observed to place himself in the way in the obvious hope that the crown would rest on his own head. Home gave in *Incidents In My Life* a highly colored account of the incident. Browning briefly remarked that he had later seen Home and "relieved" himself. He was to do so yet more fully in "Mr. Sludge, the Medium."

Betty Miller gives in "The Séance at Ealing" (Cornhill magazine, January, 1957) a vivid description of the evening,[3] quoting at some length the letter Browning wrote immediately after it. Unwilling to embarrass his hosts he did not, as Home later claimed, rise from his seat; but he did look under the table and around it and was, he admitted, unable to account for some of the phenomena. That there had somehow been cheating Browning was convinced, but Home refused his request for another séance and in later years Browning convinced himself that he had spotted the tricks in this one. (Pen said that his father often told him so.) As Chesterton did not fail to see, the idea of Browning running round the room in the hope of spirit hands placing a wreath on his own head adds to the scene a pleasing touch of low comedy.

But for Browning, as he watched his wife's face, there could be no comedy—it was for him the first scene in a near-tragedy. For some years the group of friends had experimented, some in fun, some seriously, at table-turning and calling up spirits, real or imaginary. But now he was witnessing something deadly serious as Elizabeth submitted to the forces of a preternatural world at the hands of the first skilled practitioner she had encountered. Had he been as certain as he tried at times to believe he was, that it was *all* mere cheating, he would have feared it far less. Now he was seriously alarmed.

A friendship with Ruskin had sprung up on the Browning's last stay in London when they visited Denmark Hill and saw the Turner collection which Elizabeth found "divine." Ruskin wrote: "You are the only husband and wife whom I write single letters to this way, but I never think of you two separately—never of one without the other: I like getting those nice double letters too—a bit of white and brown like a black-cock's breast."

The muscular Christian, Charles Kingsley, bracketed the two men together as objects of his dislike:

> Leave to Robert Browning
> Beggars, fleas and vines;
> Leave to mournful Ruskin
> Popish Appenines . . .

Although Ruskin had praised with such enthusiasm the Bishop ordering his tomb, it was Elizabeth's poetry he loved best. "I am going to bind your poems in a golden binding and give them to my class of working men—as the purest and most exalting poetry in our language," he wrote in March, 1855. And a month later, trying to revive the medieval art of illumination, he had rejected a canto of Dante's in favor of Elizabeth's "Catarina to Camoens" with which his best workman was to create "one of the most glorious little burning books that ever had leaf turned by white finger . . . with deep blue and purple and golden embroidery."

"My husband is very much pleased," Elizabeth replied, "and particularly that you selected 'Catarina' which is his favorite among my poems for some personal fanciful reasons besides the rest."

Ruskin wanted her, however, to outlaw the "long compounded Greek words"—especially "nympholeptic," "When you have succeeded in all your designs upon the English language, I might perhaps most graphically describe it as

> Tesseric, pentic, hectic, hiptic,
> Maeno-daemonic, and dyspeptic,
> Hippid-ic, Pippid-ic, East-wind-nipped-ic,
> Stiffened like Styptic, doubled in dyptych,
> Possi-kephaly-chereseccliptic

The last line by the way (he concluded) really is a triumph of expression."

At the height of his fame as an art critic, self-chosen spokesman for the Pre-Raphaelite Brotherhood, Ruskin would have seemed the very person to welcome a novelty in the world of poetry as great as was Turner in that of art, and not dissimilar in what he claimed for the painter—that he tried to depict reality "irrespective of any conventional rules," as did artists before Raphael and not since. Like Browning, Ruskin was a devotee of Carlyle; and all three shared the experience of talking to the deaf world of their age. "Every day," Ruskin had written in *Modern Painters,* "convinces me more and more that no warnings can preserve from misunderstanding those who have no desire to understand."

Yet some of the pre-Raphaelites felt an element of this lack of desire in Ruskin's attitude to their poet. Rossetti read Browning's poetry aloud to him "in a rich voice." But he wrote to William Allingham:

> Ruskin on reading *Men and Women* (and with it some of the other works he didn't know before) declared them rebelliously to be a mass of conundrums, and compelled me to sit down before him and lay siege for one whole night; the result of which was that he sent me next morning a bulky letter to be forwarded to B. in which I trust he told him he was the greatest man since Shakespeare.

An immensely intelligent wife proofreading, friends like the Rossetti brothers, Fox, and Milsand, who thought Browning's poems "superhuman," created a warming atmosphere. In Paris the glow continued, with Milsand's information that about half the book was being translated for the *Revue des deux Mondes* and a letter from his publishers telling him of initial sales good enough to clear expenses. High spirits and the joy of being in Paris carried both husband and wife through the trial of finding themselves in rooms of which the only asset was yellow satin furniture, the apartment having been chosen by a zealous friend who described the satin as "worthy" of two poets. Penini had to sleep on the floor in his parents' room, and trunks remained unpacked till they could move two weeks later.

The rooms had been taken, Browning wrote to Hatty Hosmer, "against our will and protestation." It was "—an apartment with no bottom (for carriages were under it), no top (for the roof tiles were over it), no back (for there was an end to the house with the end of our room)" yet it was gaily he added that after two months' misery "we carried our dead and wounded to this pleasant house," 3 Rue de Grenelle. Here Anne Thackeray soon found them out. "A little warm, shabby apartment," she writes, "with a good fire always burning, and a big sofa, where she sat. . . . Mr. Browning would come in and talk. Pen was a little boy with long curls, and some of the grand gentlemen from Mrs. Sartoris' used to come in and sit by the fire."

Despite the exhausting effort of mounting "*au cinquième*," Elizabeth as well as Robert visited the Corkrans. Their small daughter Henriette, told to expect two poets, pictured them excitedly as dressed in togas and crowned with laurel leaves. Her disillusionment was boundless. Elizabeth, small, pale, and panting after the climb, gave no signs of genius; her husband dressed in brown with his loud voice and commonplace speech suggested a successful businessman; he devoured plum cake most unpoetically. But he gave great solace to little Henriette by dismissing as rubbish the ghostly visitants in whom her mother believed as firmly as did Elizabeth. Robert Browning, she felt, was far less like a poet than his gentle absent-minded father, but he would make short work of a ghost. Henceforward night frights were to be banished; she would repeat to herself, "Mr. Browning, who is a great man, says it is all nonsense."

The first cheerful information about sales was followed by a long silence. But then his publisher, Edward Chapman, seems never to have written a letter he could possibly avoid writing, so Browning was not unduly disquieted. More worrying were a few reviews that he had seen. On December 17, he wrote to Chapman:

> I was anxious to know . . . if the book continues to do well, and how well; the notices will come, I suppose next month. Meanwhile don't take to heart the zoological utterances I have stopped my ears against at Galignani's of late. 'Whoo-oo-oo-oo' mouths the big monkey—'Whee-ee-ee-ee' squeaks the little monkey and such a dig with the end of my umbrella as I should give the brutes if I couldn't

keep my temper and consider how they miss their nuts and ginger-bread!⁴

Could the *Quarterly* have been the "big monkey" which had asked of an earlier poem, "Why must it be *Pippa Passes* and not *Polly Passes*"; which felt that Browning ought like Tennyson to "make his own country the background of his poems. . . . The mode of thought, without being anti-English, constantly bears an indescribable savour of the continent."

And was the "little monkey" *The Christian Remembrancer,* which felt that a poet should preach sound morals and that "The Statue and the Bust" showed it as better to commit adultery than to hesitate, delay, give up; that "Fra Lippo Lippi" invited readers to sympathize with "that licentious monk-artist . . . apologising with unctuous minuteness for his shameless course of life." Browning's pictures of love "are coarse passion; his idea of beauty sensual."

The animal noises continuing, Browning wrote to William Alling-ham of "leaning over the rail of the literary pond" where "Goosey *Fraser* and Gander *Blackwood*" were cackling.⁵ However, more than counterbalancing these reviews, came warm praise from Carlyle, who wrote of his delight over a first glimpse of the book and his eagerness to read it through—"That old 'Corregidor' is a diamond"—and of how on a Christmas visit the best entertainment offered him had been read-ings aloud of *Men and Women,* given by Lady Ashburton, whose "melodious clear voice" was listened to with "rapt attention."

A letter from Leigh Hunt showed him of the same mind as Carlyle and the Rossettis. Browning answered: "you put a flower in my breast which I hardly dare look at, much less finger."

But what of the wider public? Browning wrote again to Chapman on January 17, 1856, reproaching the man,

> who has left me these two months without a word about the well or ill doing of my poems. Now do, do pray, dear Chapman, let us have the Christmas account to put a little life and heart into the end of this bleak month. I have read heaps of critiques at Galignani's, mostly stupid and spiteful, self-contradicting and contradictory of

each other. What effect such "rot" would have on me, in the case of the book being somebody else's, I know exactly, but how it works with the reading public, you must tell me if I am ever to know.

It may well have been this time a dislike of sending bad news that slowed Edward Chapman in writing, for *Men and Women* had stopped selling after the first spurt— a spurt representing probably the whole group of ardent Browningites who had hurried to buy on publication.

The Brownings left Paris for London at the end of June carrying with them *Aurora Leigh,* and a few days later Browning noted: "Read this book, this divine book, Wednesday night, July 9th '56." But both husband and wife felt a profound anxiety about its reception by the English critics and the English public. For not only did the poem tell the story of a raped girl left with an unwanted baby, but it laid open, too, a running sore in English life which society had decided to ignore. It was impossible that Elizabeth's sister Arabel who "overworks herself in London with schools and refuges and societies" could remain ignorant of London's underworld of pimps and prostitutes. And the Elizabeth Barrett who had written "The Cry of the Children" felt it a plain duty to speak out on this subject too. "If a woman ignores these wrongs," she wrote to her friend Mrs. Martin, "then may women as a sex continue to suffer them; there is no help for any of us—let us be dumb and die. I have spoken therefore, and in speaking have used plain words—words which look like blots . . . words which, if blurred or softened, would imperil perhaps the force and righteousness of the moral influence."

It is comic today to read these words and note what would have been thought a blot.

Elizabeth's husband had assured her that she "couldn't be coarse if she tried," but after all *he* had been called so in unmeasured terms— and she was a woman, that "gentler" and "weaker" sex who should go through life unaware of any but pleasant things, whose lives like her own poems, should be bound "in a golden binding with deep blue, purple and golden embroidery."

There was nothing they could do now but wait, and with all the swiftness of printers' work at that date they would be back in Florence long before publication.

Mr. Kenyon was in the Isle of Wight and he lent the Brownings his house in Devonshire Place, but this year there was not to be so much of London life, and the visit was overshadowed by a deep personal anxiety about Mr. Kenyon, as well as by the nervous fears for *Aurora's* fate. It was to be, little as they guessed it, Elizabeth's last visit to England.

They spent in the Isle of Wight "a happy sorrowful two weeks" with Arabel—who had again been hastily dismissed from London by her father as soon as he heard of the Brownings' arrival. The brothers, too, were at Ventnor and made a great fuss over Pen who "doubling his small fist" had threatened a boy of twelve: "I will show you that *I'm a boy*"—"great applause from the uncles," comments Elizabeth. Thence to Cowes to Mr. Kenyon and back via Taunton to see Henrietta—also, incredible as it would have seemed, for the last time.

Mr. Kenyon was plainly "very ill . . . Now and then he desires aloud to pass away and be at rest."

Elizabeth had dedicated *Aurora Leigh* to him and his death on December 3, 1856, cast a shadow over the poem's immense success, a success the degree of which astonished Elizabeth: "that golden-hearted Robert is in ecstacies," she wrote to Sarianna," far more than if it all related to a book of his own."

Kenyon left them £11,000, the larger part to Robert, and this (after a year of waiting for probate) relieved forever the habitual financial pressure. But Elizabeth, telling Mrs. Jameson of his death, wrote of the "sad, sad Christmas. . . . He has been in much what my father might have been, and now the place is empty twice over."

For Browning especially the legacy meant a great lightening of life's burdens. Elizabeth was amused by his detailed account book and the little heap of instantly paid bills. "You can't imagine," she wrote to Arabel, "how he lets his imagination buffett and torment him in the small uncertainties of life. . . . He says that he is anxious for *me* and not for *him*—but of what consequence is it whom one is anxious for, when the anxiety is perfectly unnecessary?"

With his present anxieties Elizabeth's sympathy was warmer, for

Robert's poetry was a great matter not a small one. Nor was she indifferent to the reviews of her own book, especially where they touched the question of her character. Now in Florence was repeated the previous year's experience in Paris—Browning haunting the Reading Room to bring back news of reviews, the post office to collect letters. Some few periodicals stigmatized *Aurora Leigh* as coarse. Its heroine, *The Tablet* wrote, was "a brazen-faced woman," and the reviewer compared the story to a romance by a French pornographic writer. "The world," wrote Arthur Clough, "rather cries Fye on *Aurora Leigh*— which however has ardent admirers." One friend told Elizabeth that " 'The mamas of England' in a body refuse to let their daughters read it. Still the daughters emancipate themselves and *do*."

This was one explanation of the sales, for that first edition was gone in a fortnight and the second a few months later. But there were other reasons, too. Nearly all the important papers and reviewers hailed it, even Mr. Aytoun in *Blackwood* "from the camp of the enemy (artistically and socially)." And, too, "Think of quite decent women taking the part of the book in a sort of *effervescence* which I hear of with astonishment. In fact, there has been an enormous amount of extravagance talked and written on the subject, and I *know it,* oh, I know it."

Typical of this extravagance was a letter from Robert Lytton full of enthusiasm both for *Men and Women* and *Aurora Leigh*. Writing to Browning he speaks first of being "overwhelmed" by a "power and beauty . . . which surpasses even my most ardent hopes . . . limits are not to be anticipated to the progression of which your genius is capable. The last will be best with you. . . . I am haunted by all I have read: new sensations of beauty, new thoughts of power from immeasurable depths. . . ." But, alas for his critical judgment, he goes on to pronounce *Aurora Leigh* "the solitary epic of the age," perhaps not inferior to Milton and Dante, possibly even superior "by just so much as this age is superior to theirs . . . this age of complicated sorrows and scattered knowledge." He marvels how Elizabeth from her "little fireside sofa" has "so silently acquired" such insight.

If Elizabeth was the woman I think her, she must have ground her teeth to find her "epic" put so high as to devaluate the otherwise true appreciation of her husband's undervalued masterpieces.

But Browning himself when writing of "this divine book," was not surely as wide of reality as in his exaggerated language about the *Sonnets from the Portuguese. Aurora Leigh* has in it some really great poetry and a great deal of acute observation. The absurd way in which the slum girl is made to talk as though she came from Cambridge, the plot, half copied (unconsciously) from *Jane Eyre,* the whole miserable Ninth Book cannot quite quench the excitement of passages where one feels the truth of Elizabeth's letter to Sarianna, acknowledging her debt to the greater mind companioning hers, yet urging too that she has kept her own profoundly personal outlook. *Aurora Leigh* though not the giant epic that so many proclaimed it, is well worth one or two readings.

Among the circle of friends in Florence, Frances Cobbe is representative in confessing that she did not dream Browning was as great a poet as Elizabeth.

> The utter unselfishness and generosity wherewith he gloried in his wife's fame—bringing us up constantly good reviews of her poems and eagerly recounting how many editions had been called for—perhaps helped to blind us stupid that we were! to his own claims. Never certainly did the proverb about the *irritabile genus* of Poets ever prove less true.

She wrote this many years later in her autobiography and added that in his days of fame Browning remained equally unassuming. Of Elizabeth she saw little. "But I am glad I looked into the splendid eyes which *lived* like coals in her pain-worn face."

But this year of 1856, as all hope of success for *Men and Women* vanished and he threw himself ardently into his wife's triumph, a note of bitterness is heard, chiefly about the idiot reviews "blackguardism from the 'Press,' all like those night-men who are always emptying their cart at my door . . . leave me to rub their noses in their own filth some fine day." In this same letter to Chapman (of December 3, 1856) he says that there is "such a thing to fear in these parts as a letter miscarrying."

But "If not, it's a shame of you, black and burning" not to have been at the trouble to send a line on how *Aurora Leigh* is going. He should not wait "for further notice from us (*Us*—I am the church-organ-bellows-blower that talked about *our* playing, but you know what I do in the looking after commas and dots to i's)."

POSTSCRIPT

> Hobbs hints blue—straight he turtle eats:
> > Nobbs prints blue—claret crowns his cup:
> Nokes outdares Stokes in azure feats,
> > Both gorge. Who fished the murex up?
> What porridge had John Keats?
> > > "Popularity"

Through this checkered story of hope, doubt, despair runs the thread of two correspondences, one with Ruskin, the other with Carlyle, which deepen the puzzle of the failure of *Men and Women*. For both men appeared to realize the greatness which had so struck Ruskin in the early dramatic monologue of a Renaissance bishop. He had too analyzed in *Modern Painters* a problem that was his and Browning's alike.

> The worst of it is this kind of concentrated writing needs so much *solution* before the reader can fully see the good of it, that people's patience fails them and they give up the thing as insoluble, though truly it ought to be to the current of common thought like Saladin's talisman, dipped in clear water, not soluble altogether, but making the element medicinal.

But now with warm admiration he mingled a great deal of half-humorous attack on the obscurity of Browning's new volume, picking out especially "Popularity." This poem was later selected by Chesterton as a prime example of Browning's obscurity, resulting from a mixture of insane haste and the assumption that all the world shared his own multitudinous bits of recondite knowledge. He was, for instance, pained at Ruskin questioning his use of "orris" for "iris." "Why don't you ask the next perfumer for a packet of *orris*-root? Don't (sic) everybody know 'tis a corruption of *iris*-root?" In the same way he felt that everybody must know about the murex (translated in modern editions in a footnote to the poem as a mollusk from which the Tyrian purple dye was obtained). Ruskin, said Browning, was asking of poetry the explicitness and detail needed in a business contract. "Why you look at my little song as if it were Hobbs' or Nobbs' lease of his house or testament of his devisings, wherein, I grant you, not a 'then and there', 'to him and to his heirs', 'to have and to hold' would be superfluous.' "

Browning had found Ruskin's long letter (perhaps the one written after Rossetti's night siege) "over-liberal of praise here and there, kindly and sympathetic everywhere . . . the whole letter precious indeed." He had delayed in replying—his letter is dated from Paris, December 10 '55—because "the strife of lodging hunting" had been "too sore . . . south-aspects, warm bedrooms and the like." But now, set free to think, he pours out his own philosophy of poetry and combats Ruskin's desire for what has been well called "reading for runners."

> For the deepnesses you think you discern,—may they be more than mere blacknesses! For the hopes you entertain of what may come of subsequent readings,—all success to them! For your bewilderment more especially noted—how shall I help *that*? We don't read poetry the same way, by the same law; it is too clear. I cannot begin writing poetry till my imaginary reader has conceded licences to me which you demur at altogether. I *know* that I don't make out my conception by my language; all poetry being a putting the infinite within the finite. You would have me paint it all plain out, which can't be; but by various artifices I try to make shift with touches and bits of outlines which *succeed* if they bear the conception from me to you. You ought, I think, to keep pace with the thought tripping from ledge to ledge of my 'glaciers,' as you call them; not stand poking your alpenstock into the holes, and demonstrating that no foot could have stood there;—suppose it sprang over there? In *prose* you may

criticise so—because that is the absolute representation of portions of truth, what chronicling is to history—but in asking for more *ultimates* you must accept less *mediates,* nor expect that a Druid stone-circle will be traced for you with as few breaks to the eye as the North Crescent and South Crescent that go together so cleverly in many a suburb.[6]

Elizabeth had earlier stressed to Ruskin her disbelief in his view that poems could and should be written with the thought of general, instant comprehension. Now Browning asks, "Do you think poetry was ever generally understood—or can be?"

Later in the letter he answers his own question.

No they, [poems] act upon a very few, who react upon the rest: as Goldsmith says, "some lords, my acquaintance, that settle the nation are pleased to be kind."

Don't let me lose *my* lord by seeming self-sufficiency or petulance: I look on my own shortcomings too sorrowfully, try to remedy them too earnestly: but I shall never change my point of sight.

Ruskin had spoken of writing about Browning's poetry and he would be proud "to be recognized by you as you propose." But he begs Ruskin to

try and know me before you make up your mind—I aim widely and want more than a glance to take in all I endeavour at, hit or miss. With your letter came one from Carlyle—I hide his gold words as if I had stolen them, as I partly have,—but he looks to what suits his own sight, in what I show. So God makes him, you and me.

Ruskin's reply to this letter has disappeared, but another long one from Browning on February 1, 1856, discusses both his answer and *Modern Painters,* Vol. III, sent with it. This letter, too, Browning had received with delight "with its kindness and care about me." He finds in Ruskin's writing

an arrangement of rockets of various sorts and sizes which I see you stoop over and put the fusee to—some explode, some *catch* at the

rim and one is certain of them,—and if some few hang fire, seemingly—they may no less go off of themselves when one least expects
it. . . . I witness to a great and noble lighting-up on the whole.[7]

Surely no bad description this of much of Browning himself! But
the most important element in the letter is the double confession, that in
the course of *Sordello* he had in certain passages spoken "in my own
person—not dramatically," and "knowing what my faith was and im-
measurably deeplier is" he would copy these out for Ruskin. All these
passages refer to that awareness of "Divine being or operation," which
Ruskin in his book had declared to be lacking in modern English poetry.

It is astonishing, leafing through *Sordello* in search of these passages,
to note how wide of the mark would have been one's guess. Not eternity
and time, not "the soul's absoluteness," not "This Human clear, as that
Divine concealed," not man, but nature

> The hermit bee
> Twirled so, and filed all day—The mansion's fit
> God counselled for—As easy guess the word
> That passed betwixt them, and became the third
> To (*God and*) the small, soft, unfrightened bee, as tax
> Him with one fault.

(*Alberic Romano was*)

> tied to a wild horse and trailed
> To death through rance and bramble-bush
> I take God's part and testify."

The insets are Browning's, and his testimony is to the nature whose
beauty and peace go on:

> Rustles the lizard and the cushats chirre
> Above the ravage.

But the final passage he chose was human—the

> child barefoot and rosy . . .
> Up and up goes he, singing all the while

> Some unintelligible words to beat
> The lark, God's poet, swooning at his feet.

By August of that year (1856) Ruskin was apologizing to Browning: "I was so ashamed of the way I had mangled that poem of yours that I dared not look you even by letter in the face." But by now he is sick of everything "except breakfast" and in no state "to attempt writing a letter to a poet. I don't see any use in poetry. I recollect you have written something nice about figs somewhere . . . after all there may be some sense in the kind of people who make railroads. . . . They say you are writing more poetry. I daresay I shall be very glad of this—someday— but I don't care just now." He has only enough animation left to wish the Brownings well "and to be sure that I am always affectionately Yours."[8]

Carlyle's real and profound belief in Browning, Browning's trust and belief in Carlyle brought forth yet another letter which one would give a great deal to be able to read. An irritating element in these correspondences is that we have Browning to Ruskin, Carlyle to Browning, but mostly suggestive indications only of the letters in between. Clearly this missing one from Browning was a real outpouring of soul to the man who was perhaps his chief ideal. How early Browning's letter was written we do not know, but in April, 1856 Carlyle is apologizing for his own delay in acknowledging a gift of *Men and Women* which came with it. He had read it "all, many of the Pieces again and again . . . able I was and am to give you *Euge!* Far beyond what I reckon you desire. . . . But you asked with so much loyalty, 'What shall I do to be saved, and gain the top of this sore upward course?'" He has long hesitated, having at length "renounced altogether the high thought of 'advising,'" having learned how "advice never fits the case; the case is not known to any Adviser, but only to the Advisee."

However, he will try—and what he had to say must have been heart-warming indeed of the

> excellent opulence of intellect in these two rhymed volumes: in-
> tellect in the big ingot shape and down to the smallest coin;—I shall

look far I believe to find such a pair of *eyes* as I see busy there in-
specting human life this long while. The keenest just insight into
men and things—and all that goes along with really good *insight*:
a fresh, valiant manful character, equipped with rugged humour,
with just love, just contempt, well carried and bestowed; in fine a
most extraordinary power of expression; such I must call it, whether
it be "expressive" *enough* or not. Rhythm there is too, endless
poetic fancy, symbolic *help* to express; and if not melody always or
often (for that would mean finish and perfection) there is what the
Germans call *Takt,* fine *dancing,* if to the music only of drums.[9]

Carlyle "in a private way" admits to himself "that here apparently is
the finest poetic genius, finest possibility of such, we have got vouch-
safed to us in this generation;" one which had "*grown,* in all ways since
I saw it last." It must *not* be lost in "the process of elaboration."

Such immense praise yet contained in it the seeds of the one criticism with which he felt he ought to be "equally honest. My friend it is
what they call 'unintelligibility!' That is a fact: you are dreadfully
difficult to understand." He is saying this in all sympathy; the cure is
not "easy, or the sin a mere perversity." He has himself had the same
struggle of "a man with very much to say," trying to say it in a world of
"the sordid, the prosaic, inane and unworthy. I see you pitching big
crags into the dirty, bottomless morass, trying to *found* your marble
work,—Oh it is a tragic condition withal!—But yet you *must* mend it
and alter." He will no longer forbid verse if Browning finds it "handier";
a man can be unintelligible in prose, too. One day Browning shall hear
his ideas of what poetry really is—meanwhile "Well, the sum of my
ideas is: if you took up some one *great* subject, and tasked all your
powers upon it for a long while, vowing to Heaven that you *would* be
plain to mean capacities, then—!—But I have done, *done.* Good be
with you always dear Browning; and high victory to sore fight!"

Author and publisher would contrive today to make known with
what excitement the foremost men of letters were admiring even when
they disagreed with Browning. Ruskin's opinion of a genius that had
caught the very heart of the Renaissance would have been printed on

the jacket of *Men and Women*. Leigh Hunt with a smile and Carlyle with a growl would agree to let their words be used in advertisements. But at that date books had no jackets. The art of advertisement was hardly born, and Browning would have felt it in the worst possible taste to send on private letters to his publishers. He did write to Chapman: "The half dozen people who know and could impose their opinions on the whole sty of grumblers say nothing to *them* (I don't wonder) and speak so low in my own ear that it's lost to all intents and purposes . . ."

Why did not these friends, Carlyle especially, shout from the housetops instead of speaking "privately" to Browning and to themselves? He lost much, I fancy, in those years through his absence abroad, but most of all through his wife's fantastic popularity and a lazy, indifferent publisher quite content that he should simply "look after commas and dots to i's" in that best seller *Aurora Leigh*.

18 Friends,
Family, and Frustration

Only one said, "I think the gesture strives
Against some obstacle we cannot see."

PRINCE HOHENSTIEL-SCHWANGAU

MR. BARRETT had characteristically refused to supply Kenyon's executors with Henrietta's address. She was to get a small legacy. But none of his strange acts, large or small, totally destroyed his hold on Elizabeth's affection. Relatives and friends had tried to bring about a reconciliation, but while saying he forgave his daughters, he declared that they had disgraced the family and to the last he refused to see them. Both had, of course, been cut out of his will.

In April, 1857, he died and Elizabeth wrote to Mrs. Jameson in July of "great bitterness which is natural. And some recoil against myself, more perhaps than is quite rational." She was beginning to recover and to "keep from vexing my poor husband who has been a good deal tried in all these things."

Imagination readily offers a picture of how much tried: to see his sick wife rending herself over the parent from whom she had with such difficulty been rescued; to hear her confess to a "sudden desolation" when all hope of a reconcilation—a hope she had deemed dead these many years—was again and finally extinguished.

Browning wrote to Hatty Hosmer a month after his father-in-law's death that Elizabeth had seen no one except Isa[1] and had not left the house: "She shall, if I have to carry her, before the week is out," he promised—and he did, indeed, bring his wife back to life, even if to a life less full than he had poured into her in Wimpole Street. We can hear an echo of the Love Letters: ". . . may you be better, less depressed. . . . Now *walk,* move . . . *anima mia dolce.*"

Her heavy thoughts were not lightened by any of the family support commonly induced by a shared bereavement. Elizabeth's brothers had for years traveled freely—to Jamaica, to various countries in Europe, but never to Italy. She had always had to seek out these men who, perhaps out of fear of their father, had never come to her. Even now they did not stir; but Arabel, at last set free, she confidently expected, and wrote begging for a long visit. She was deeply disappointed to hear that Arabel had sold the Wimpole Street house only to buy a smaller one in Delamere Terrace. Her social work absorbed her, and her sister's pressure only hurt her feelings.

The countersuggestion was made that Elizabeth should go to England, now that the barrier to their free and full intercourse had disappeared. But her repugnance for England was certainly increasing as her strength diminished and the sisters were growing apart in many ways. It must have been a severe shock for Elizabeth to hear that Henrietta thought Browning's "Karshish" blasphemous. And Arabel was perhaps closer to the narrow Christianity of the chapels where Browning had suffered in boyhood, was more remote from the spiritual and intellectual world in which husband and wife were now living.

Elizabeth had to reassure both sisters that Pen would not become a Romanist; she allowed him to go into the churches, but Romanism was not catching like measles. Henrietta's husband urged Elizabeth to be definite as to what denomination she belonged to; Arabel was really afraid she was drifting toward Rome. "I who do not care," Elizabeth commented, "for Councils of the Church or any human authority, only for the scriptures and for experience, do not feel myself in danger."

There were in her eyes dangers far more serious than vagueness about the form of Christianity to be selected. She was, indeed, prejudiced against "Romanism," but in a letter to Mrs. Jameson she expressed herself with strange force against a deeper danger: "Tell me, is not the

Inquisitionist's burning of bodies to save souls really tender mercy by the side of the intolerance of those materialists, who for the mere aggrandisement of their barren doctrines will torture souls. . . . A fanatical religion is pitiable—but a fanatical infidel is hateful and horrible."[2]

To all definitely ranged in the ranks of this or that belief or unbelief the Brownings appear to have presented a puzzle. Their views were strong, yet their liberalism insisted that opposite views should be frankly expressed and listened to. Elizabeth could write more freely to Henrietta than to her dear Arabel about the problems which staying at Delamere Terrace would present for herself, for Robert, and for their hostess:

> There would be *gêne* on both sides. The irregularities of our house are scandalous—not immoral, observe, but scandalous. From morning till night people are running out and in—all sorts of people; and when we are in London we can't help it. There are men who come and talk—talk, some of them did last summer, till one in the morning—and the freest sort of philosophy is talked. Robert would be in agonies of annoyance, even if Arabel could bear it. Fancy Mr. Stratton elbowed on the staircase by Mr. So-and-So whose "aim in life" is to "subvert Christianity"!![3]

So to Lucca they went again that year, and here Browning's already frequent vigils were increased by the sudden illness of young Lytton, staying at the hotel nearby, with Isa Blagden, who insisted on nursing him herself. Browning wrote to Sarianna: "Through sentimentality and economy combined, Isa would have no nurse (an imbecile arrangement), and all has been done by her with me to help. I have sat up four nights out of the last five, and sometimes been there nearly all day besides. Imagine what a pleasant holiday we all have!"

Browning was devoted to Isa and put up with it all for her sake. She was fifteen years older than Lytton, but was probably in love with him, while he appeared deeply devoted to her. Lytton, however, was devoted to many women. Elizabeth wrote when early in 1859 they heard of his engagement: "Is it good for him indeed, Isa?—and is it not bad for HER indeed?—Pray be humane you who are magnanimous."

The Brownings never felt quite the same to him again. A little later

Elizabeth wrote: "Was ever a sinner who coquetted so with his sins? Poor Lytton. Strong enough for neither vice or virtue."

But that was in the future. Meanwhile, Lytton made a rapid recovery. The holiday began to look rosier and Browning told his sister of bathing "in the river, a rapid little mountain stream every morning at 6½ . . . The strength of all sorts therefrom accruing is wonderful . . . by the bye in this new book of Ruskin's, the drawing book, he says *Aurora Leigh* is the finest poem written in any language this century."

Wilson, married now to Ferdinando, seemed about to produce a baby and was returned to Florence for the better handling of the event. Whereupon Pen became ill—the same gastric fever as Lytton's, short but sharp. He sat up in bed looking like a wraith, but told his mother that their new maid "tells *novelle* quite finely! Stories of the devil and how he rides on a golden saddle and with a silver bridle. Per Bacco!"

Decidedly it was not one of the Browning's best summers, but about one incident he wrote with much pleasure to Leigh Hunt. He had discovered in the house of a Mrs. Sisted, known as Queen of the Baths, the original of "that divine little poem" of Shelley's "The Indian Serenade." Much interlined, "the characters are all but illegible. . . ." Browning had with a good magnifying glass "rescued three or four variations" which he encloses: "Are not all these better readings. . . . Then I give them you as you gave us Milton's hair."[4]

In March, 1858, Elizabeth writes cheerfully from the Casa Guidi. Robert had taken up homeopathy. He had been having "such violent attacks of headache that he talked of congestion on the brain," she told Arabel. But now "Not only is the liver quite relieved, but the irritability of his nervous system is calmed down to a degree which I should never have expected from any physical remedy." His appetite was better, his face showed the improvement, he had given up wine and was "the stronger and more cheerful for all his sacrifices."

That spring Home was expected in Florence and husband and wife had struck a bargain—he promising not to kill the medium in the street if she would promise not to go to a séance. At the last minute, however "Robert throws his arms round me, calls me 'Darling' and says that I shall do 'anything I like': but I won't be tempted out of our conventions, seeing that in spite of *nux vomica* Robert is still Robert."

They spent this summer at Le Havre, a place of few attractions. Sea bathing was advised for Elizabeth, Etretat proved impossible, and they needed a house where they could accommodate Arabel and a brother or two besides Sarianna and Mr. Browning. Milsand came for ten days and these were by far the best ten days for Browning. But both husband and wife felt the ugliness of the place, and both missed the sort of life led at Lucca or Siena in the villas and lanes and on the hills; above all they missed the Italian skies.

Browning wrote to Isa of Pen "minnowizing away among the Tritons," of his sister's enjoyment, and of the "fresh looks and rude health" of his father. "Best of all, Ba's improvement in health is incontestable and rapid." Yet he envied Isa up above Florence "where you so pleasantly perch. I shall never see anything so dear to me elsewhere."

A second letter laments the dull days, so filled in "doing the hospitable" that he has written no poetry. "I began pretty zealously—but it's of no use now: nor will the world very greatly care . . ."

Elizabeth, too, was missing the Casa Guidi. "Poor ghost of a Ba," she wrote to Fanny Haworth, "dislodged ghost. I long for my dear lower life in Florence and feel coldly the upper world here," despite "warm comfort and joy in holding my dearest Arabel's hand."

Two friends, shared by husband and wife, were very much alike in their circumstances, very different in character: Fanny Haworth and Isa Blagden. Both rather solitary, both with a small income, Isa was independent, managed to earn such luxuries as she wanted by her pen, and gave in her friendships at least as much as she received. Fanny was, Elizabeth felt, greatly to be pitied. Browning had hinted, years earlier, that she could do far better than she did as a writer. Elizabeth felt that her social ambitions had destroyed higher ones, and also that a fatal indecision blocked her from happiness. "Poor Fanny, she will stay in England and long for Florence."

Isa had many friends sharing the Bellosguardo villa's amenities and expenses. Fanny, after much vacillation, formed an alliance with one rich friend, bringing her ease and luxury. Elizabeth was much amused by this and other "female marriages," as she calls them with no faintest implication of what might today be suggested by such a term. She and Fanny corresponded regularly; and Browning reckoned Fanny as so much among his wife's "dear ones" that she had the right to a special letter about Elizabeth's death.

Of unknown and reputedly Eurasian descent, Isa had won a unique position for herself by force of character and by her unfailing kindness. "An eager little lady," said Henry James; "universally beloved," said T. A. Trollope; a "bright delicate, electric woman," Browning called her; and to Kate Field she was "Our Lady of Bellosguardo." The Brownings lent her the Casa Guidi when they were in Rome, and entreated her to think of their books and belongings as her own. Browning wrote to her constantly, telling her of every improvement in Elizabeth's health, to "set your own dear quick-beating heart at ease." To her he later expressed his rage over the unfairness in England to *Poems before Congress*, repeating the publisher's jest that he hopes "the apartments in the Castle of St. Angelo [Rome's Tower of London!] are comfortable." As with Ruskin both husband and wife write, and Browning, parodying "emphatic opera singers," ends one letter "T'abbracio, ti striiiiiiiingo." He tells her he has been "a fool" to let Elizabeth catch cold, depicts Landor's behavior, sends every bit of gossip he can gather.

One long letter is devoted to a careful and encouraging criticism of Isa's writing; in another he admits his own many weak points, but also insists on his love of justice which should come before charity. Later he would refuse with characteristic crudity to subscribe to a fund for Mrs. Jameson's sisters; they had "sucked her dry" all her life, and now she is gone. "I don't feel inclined to offer the least squeeze from my nipples." With Isa Blagden, Browning is always in his shirt sleeves.

How one wonders did Barretts and Brownings mix at such close quarters? It was certainly in Paris that Elizabeth enjoyed Arabel most before the return to Italy.

William Allingham, who delighted in getting the friends he admired to talk of one another, records in his diary Tennyson's assenting to his description of Browning as "a vivid man," adding, "How he did flourish about when he was here." Now in Paris, calling on Thackeray at the Hotel Bristol, Allingham mentioned he had just been seeing Browning.

"Browning was here this morning," Thackeray said. "What spirits he has—almost too much for me in my weak state. He almost blew me out of bed!"
"A wonderful fellow, indeed!"
"Yes, and he doesn't drink wine."
"He's already screwed up to concert pitch."
"Far above it. But I can't manage his poetry. What do you say?" (I spoke highly of it).
"Well, you see, I want poetry to be musical, to run sweetly."
"So do I"—
"Then that *does for* your friend B.!"
I spoke of Browning's other qualities as so splendid as to make him, as it were, a law in himself. But Thackeray only smiled and declined further discussion.
"He has a good belief, in himself, at all events. I suppose he doesn't care whether people praise him or not."
"I think he does, very much."
"O does he? Then I'll say something about him in a number."[5]

Le Havre to Paris, Paris to Florence, Florence to Rome, Rome to Florence, Florence to Siena—the strain must have been considerable on the "unpractical" poet responsible for all practical arrangements, and for the care of a delicate woman, a child, and a household. For they always took maid and usually man, engaging furnished rooms, sometimes the same as in a previous year, sometimes looked for from a nearby hotel. The yellow-satin-furniture suite had conveyed its lesson: of their friends only the Storys could be trusted to discover anything suitable.

Many of the journeys were not without adventure. This year coming to France they had slept on the deck with nothing between them and the boards, to avoid a cabin packed with seasick passengers. Returning after a rather painful crossing of the Alps (Elizabeth, Browning wrote to Allingham, had had no food but a crust of bread for fourteen hours), they took ship from Genoa to Leghorn and in a *burrasca* "reeled about the sea in our little old Neapolitan boat." The journey took so long that they were given up for lost. Entering the Casa Guidi, Elizabeth met a friend who "stared at me aghast, as at a ghost of an old inhabitant of the house haunting the ancient place . . . Robert and I are delighted to feel here in a divine abstraction from civilized life."

But this "abstraction" would as usual be short lived. Only a month later, some American friends, Mr. and Mrs. Eckley, offered the Brownings their carriage for the journey to Rome. Insisting on paying for the hire of horses, they gratefully accepted the carriage. But of leaving Florence so quickly Pen remarked, "I must say it's the only *stupid* thing I ever did know you and Papa to do." On the journey two ox-drivers, hired to drag them up a mountain, had a furious row and one went for the other with his knife. "Robert rushed in between them and was thrown down," while Pen shrieked and Elizabeth "did the next best and fainted or all but fainted." They had already nearly gone over a precipice and another family had on that same road been robbed by bandits. But the knife had only torn Browning's coat, so they came off pretty well.

Sarianna was the main safety valve for Elizabeth's rage over the neglect of her husband by the English public.

Because of her own success, she wrote:

> I complain more about Robert, only he does not hear me complain. To *you* I may say that the blindness, deafness, and stupidity of the English public to Robert are amazing . . . while in America he's a power, a writer, a poet. . . . "Browning readings" here in Boston, "Browning evenings" there. . . . "It's worth *eating much dirt*" said an Englishman of high family and character here, "to get to Lady ———'s soirée." Americans will eat dirt to get to *us*. There's the difference . . . physicians, dentists, who serve me and refuse their fees . . . friends who give up their carriages and make other practical sacrifices are *not English*—no. . . .

This same neglectful public was ready enough to lionize Browning socially, as an asset in himself and not merely as the husband of the famous "poetess."

Elizabeth had gradually grown more social during the years when she had to persuade her husband that too much solitude was a mistake. It may be that he feared his own appetite for society which, once yielded to, would become enormous. And he was enormously popular, despite his tendency to bring out an intended compliment dangerously in reverse, saying to Mrs. Story, "I had a delightful evening at your house. *I never spoke to you once*"; and to a young artist discouraged over his work, "But, my dear fellow, if you were satisfied you would be so very easily satisfied."

Elizabeth advised him to avoid compliments and stick to politics, but she wrote to Sarianna "the women admire him everywhere too much for decency." And in Rome, "the most dissipated of places (to which Paris is grave and quiet)," Elizabeth describes her husband as scarcely knowing "if he stands on his feet or his head. . . . Dissipations decidedly agree with Robert there's no denying that, though he's terribly hypocritical, and prefers an evening with me at home, which has grown to be a kind of dissipation also."

The social life of Rome still whirled around them, Elizabeth as well as Robert being caught up in it—the occasional picnic, the frequent drive. Late nights away from her own fireside she avoided. But "We have soirées I assure you," she wrote to Arabel, "of as many as can be packed in our room—I pour out the tea in a corner, and Ferdinando carries it round on a tray." The Storys came and the Eckleys; Motley, the historian; Leighton, the painter; Odo Russell, the Cartwrights, Marshalls, Brackens.

This was in the Bocca di Leone, but it is hard to tell today either there or in the Via del Tritone how much of the present layout was included in their apartment. The Via del Tritone house is now offices, entirely remodeled, and the people there had never heard the name of Browning. But at 43 Bocca di Leone the poets were still a *"bel ricordo"* for their successors in the house that harbored them when Italy was in the making. A plaque on the wall declares immortal the songs in which they had prophetically announced her new destinies.

Put up on the centenary of Browning's birth by the Roman Municipality, it quoted in translation an overquoted verse:
Aprendo il mio cuore vi trovareste inciso Italia.

> Open my heart and you will see
> Graved inside of it, "Italy."

They had here ten rooms of varying sizes, none of them very big, but the sitting room was adequate to accommodate themselves and at least thirteen named guests. It was used early in 1859 for a smaller, more intimate affair.

"We have had a wedding here," writes Elizabeth to Arabel, "and Robert has 'given away' the bride, who is no other than Miss Fox." (This was the Eliza known as Tottie, who described the youthful Browning playing the piano on his birthday while the church bells pealed a greeting.) "Mr. Fox," Elizabeth went on, "had written from England to entreat Robert to take his place at the ceremony." And then they had bride and bridegroom and bride's cousin to dinner with "champagne and everything in order." But alas it did not end there, for Elizabeth felt obliged to agree that Tottie should paint her picture, sadly lamenting as the sittings proceeded that she "began by looking young and coarse like a milkmaid . . . and will end by being old and coarse like a cook."

Elizabeth had, by 1858, reached the peak of her success, but her health was becoming more and more precarious. After one of their broken nights she wrote to Sarianna: "If it had not been that I feared much to hurt him in having him so disturbed and worried, it would have been a very subtle luxury to me, this being ill and feeling myself dear. Do not set me down as too selfish."

But gradually the allusions to her health became less cheerful: "forgive my poor brittle body," she writes to Fanny Haworth, "which shakes and breaks." And to Mrs. Martin "The weight of the whole year . . . seems to have stamped out of me the vital fluid."

They had perhaps been presuming too much on the restored health of so many years—crossing the Alps in November, spending the night on the boards of an open deck, traveling in a cockleshell of a boat. She speaks in her letters of the greatly increased comfort when, thanks to the Kenyon legacy, they need no longer choose the cheapest modes of travel. But after Le Havre the axis of their lives became Florence, Rome, Siena. At Siena, in 1859, the Storys with Edith and two small boys were in a neighboring villa, Isa Blagden in a tiny cabin of a dwelling, and Walter Savage Landor with the Storys until Browning could find a room for him nearby. For he had adopted the old lion, now in his eighties, after his family had either turned him out or had been finally repudiated by him. "I believe," he wrote to Isa in August, 1859, "I am to have the poor dear old man permanently 'added to my portion' as the Methodists phrase it. *You* do the sister-of-charity business generally —and I am bound to act my best on 'Mr. Browning's First and Only Appearance in that Character, at particular Request,'—I hope I may add 'The Performance being exclusively for the Benefit of a distinguished Member of the Company.'"

He began by arranging for Landor's permanent residence, found rooms in Florence and had them decorated "very superiorly," bought furniture and rescued the old man's belongings from his family. Mme. Ferdinando Romagnoli, still spoken of as Wilson, undertook the charge of him and he was gradually being tamed, until only very occasionally would he dash the plate onto the floor if his dinner displeased him, or if she brought it a few minutes late. At Siena in the summer, Browning listened to him patiently, read aloud to him his own poetry, and coaxed the old lion into roaring softly.

Landor, though writing some elegant poetry, had won his chief fame by his *Imaginary Conversations*. "All the culture of the encyclopedists," says Ezra Pound, "reduced to manageable size and full of human life ventilated, given a human body, not merely indexed." Pound selects in *The ABC of Reading* some of Landor's poems which he justly calls "cantabile," and claims that Landor was "so far ahead of his British times that the country couldn't contain him."

But in fact it was not Landor's writing or ideas which drove him from his country, but his misfortunes, quarrels, and vendettas. He was often abominably treated, but he did not make it easy for anyone to treat him well. He wrote of himself: "I strove with none for none was worth my strife." Strange words from a man who had fled abroad to escape an action for slander brought by a clergyman's wife who was, he had hinted, a Lesbian.

Even had they been kind, which they clearly were not, Landor was the last man to endure patiently a life of dependence on his son and his son's wife.

Browning not only loved Landor, but was grateful to him for the poem which compared him to Chaucer on the roads of England—and then in Italy:

> But warmer climes
> Give brighter plumage, stronger wing; the breeze
> Of Alpine heights thou playest with, borne on
> Beyond Sorrento and Amalfi, where
> The Siren waits thee, singing song for song.

There were, too, in Landor qualities of generosity and affection for his friends, brought out in the rather idealized portrait drawn by Dickens. William Rossetti, staying with the Storys, recognized him as Boythorne in *Bleak House*. "He wore a large loose cap around which various flies were weaving their disquieting dance." Though "mildly composed" he said, "in a tone of resolved conviction, 'I have considered the matter, and I find that, of the many vile nuisances existing on the face of the earth, flies are the most strictly intolerable.' "

Elizabeth had no great liking for Landor. He was a burden on "dear darling Robert," who amused her by talking of " 'his gentleness and sweetness. . . .' Of self-restraint he has not a grain, and of suspiciousness many grains." Then, too, he hated Louis Napoleon. "Mrs. Browning," Edith Story recalled, "would be stirred past endurance by these assaults on her hero . . . and would raise her treble voice even to a shrill pitch in protest, until Mr. Browning would come into the fray as mediator."

All three Hawthornes write about the Brownings, who had been introduced to them in 1856 by Monckton Milnes, later Lord Houghton. Milnes's breakfast parties are his chief claim to fame. Carlyle used to say, Froude tells us, "that if Christ came again on earth Milnes would ask him to breakfast and the clubs would all be talking of the 'good things' that Christ had said."

Hawthorne thought Browning "simple and agreeable in manner, gently impulsive—talking as if his heart were uppermost." He was delighted to be told that of all his works *The Blythedale Romance* was Browning's favorite. "I hope I showed as much pleasure at his praise as he did at mine,—for I was glad to see how pleasantly it moved him." Although the two families never became intimate, it was to Browning that Una Hawthorne turned, after her mother's death, for help in deciphering the manuscript of *Septimus*.

Pen dances delightfully in and out of the letters and memoirs of the period. Mrs. Hawthorne meeting him in the passage felt he "looked like a waif of poetry, lovelier still in the bright light of the drawing room." At tea, passing the cakes, he was "graceful as Ganymede."

English visitors and all later biographers dwell on the golden curls and girlish dress, although this was not so startling in the Italy of those years as it seems universally today. In England at the age of six Pen had offered to fight a lad of twelve to show him that he too was a boy. But in Italy, Mrs. Hugh Fraser describes him as "well dressed" and he believed his new jacket had attracted the attention of the Queen of Naples. "I am," he claimed, "one of the sights of Rome!"

He was reading Dumas at nine, playing Beethoven at ten, and "has not given up drawing neither," wrote Elizabeth to Ruskin. But one Christmas, when his presents are recorded just before his ninth birthday, he received (by request) "a sword to dazzle the eyes," a box of tools and a carpenter's bench, and *Robinson Crusoe*. A little later, when told the story of St. John, he decided that the fate of the Apostle on Patmos was just like Robinson Crusoe.

He had been having lessons—Latin and mathematics—from a young Abbé with, said Elizabeth, a secret sympathy for the Risorgimento who came with them from Rome to Siena. Edith Story became his second pupil and Pen worked better, his mother said, not to be disgraced before her. She was many years his senior and he had a great affection for her. Landor spoke of Abelard and Heloise—Pen, not the Abbé, being Abelard.

His father gave him a handsome pony and brought it back to Rome with a groom to take charge of it. "I am supposed to be the spoiler," commented Elizabeth. They had to find some riding companions for Pen. "I object to Hatty Hosmer who has been thrown thirty times," his mother said. Wearing a crimson blouse, Pen was presented to various small Italian princes with whom he talked of ponies and played at leapfrog.

But better than princes or ponies were the Italian *contadini* whose sheep he helped to herd, whose cows he chased, whose games he learned, whose grapes he picked, "driving in the grape-carts (exactly of the shape of the Greek chariots), with the grapes heaped up round him . . . galloping thro' the lanes on his pony the colour of his curls." He read aloud the Venetian poet, Dall Ongaro, to the applauding grape-gatherers in the evening and "ate so many grapes he could eat nothing else whatever."

"*Sono Italiano,*" Pen would say, and in his journal his mother read: "This is the happiest day of my hole (*sic*) life, for now dearest Vittorio Emanuele is really *nostro re.*"

Getting near eleven, he resolved, he told his mother, to have no toys for Christmas; he would have "a microscope instead and study nature." She sent him to choose presents for some other children and he came back disconsolate. "I know it's foolish of me, Mama, but the shop looked so beautiful and everybody buying . . . and the *passionate* love of the old things came back to me, and I couldn't be *energetic* about the microscope any more." He wanted a toy gun instead. "After all, you see Mama, I am *not* a man yet."[6]

An engaging mixture of boy and child, speaking brokenly four languages, tenderhearted, talented, full of enterprise, but with no natural quality of perseverence and thoroughly spoiled through the best years for learning it, he emerges nonetheless as an entrancing little creature whom one would have spoiled with the rest of them—his parents and Wilson, Ferdinando and the Italian *contadini*—and even the French soldiers. He encountered a regiment on the Pincio, "made friends with ever so many captains," marched in their ranks, talked to some musical ones about Chopin and Stephen Heller, and with all about politics. "He had never been so happy in his life," but it was, indeed, a very happy life altogether. He did not see the shadows darkening. But Elizabeth wrote to Mrs. Martin in December, 1860, "For the first time I have had pain in looking into his face lately—which you will understand."

19 The Pope, Napoleon, and the Rest

"Come with me and deliver Italy!"

PRINCE HOHENSTIEL-SCHWANGAU

THE BROWNINGS had shown their faith in the country's future by investing most of their money in Italy. Arabel, in 1859, wrote inquiring how their "Tuscan funds" were affected by the war. "I said to Robert," Elizabeth answered, " 'Really I never thought of our money till this moment.' 'But I did' he returned. We are neither of us uneasy." Much more interesting to her was the fact of being visited by "Massimo d'Azeglio . . . one of the very noblest men in Italy," who had told them, "It is '48 over again with matured actors."

But a little later she was admitting that the money had depreciated "for the moment." It would be foolish to sell out, "our interests are here just as our hearts are in this cause."

And in another letter deploring the "infamous *lies* of The Times— I say *lies* . . . Arabel . . . I don't say mistakes," she says. "I used to have literal physical palpitations over the newspapers—tears in my eyes, sobs in my throat." Her pain *about England* shows her she is more of a patriot than she had thought.

It is not really surprising that *The Times* was at that date regarded abroad as the voice of England, considering how seriously its reports and articles were taken by the leading statesmen of both parties. Palmerston, the Whig premier, wrote to the editor in 1858, suggesting "less

personal asperity of tone" about Napoleon III, Elizabeth's idol, and in
March 1859 pressed home the danger of exasperating the Emperor until
"French means of aggression and English means of Defence are more
nearly equalized . . ." The Orsini plot to murder the Emperor had been
hatched by political refugees in England, and the bomb unsuccessfully
thrown was made in Birmingham! Like most Englishmen, *The Times*
Editor was friendly to Italy but both he and his correspondent in Paris
detested Napoleon and, although condemning the attempted assasina-
tion, hoped that the British government would make no concessions
"immediately after the offensive demonstrations which have been made
in France."

Elizabeth's "patriotism" was not of the same brand as that of *The
Times; Poems before Congress* published early in 1860 would identify
her in British eyes with the "offensive" demonstrators of Paris.

The funds were an excellent excuse for not going to England either
in '59 or '60. They would, wrote Elizabeth, certainly recover, it was only
a question of waiting. The Brownings were, besides, contributing as
much as they could afford to the war effort, and they did not want to
leave Italy at this exciting time. Elizabeth's intimates may have breathed
a sigh of relief, so violently abusive of England had her letters become.
On this subject as on spiritualism, there was a growing imbalance which
in calmer moments she recognized. "Just now," she wrote in March
1859, "I am scarcely of sane mind about Italy. It even puts down the
spirit subject. I pass through cold stages of anxiety and white heats of
rage."

And in July or August '59 to Sarianna "This is to certify that I am
alive after all, yes and getting stronger. Though the sense left to me is
of a peculiar frailty of being; no very marked opinion upon my hold of
life . . ."

In her more fevered states she seems curiously to match the Italian
scene which obsessed her. To the cool observer, however sympathetic,
there is about it all an atmosphere of grand opera: how fitted for the
stage are the declamations of Mazzini, his melancholy face, his unchang-
ing black, the continuing cloak-and-dagger conspiracies, the abortive
risings he inspired which were making him abhorrent to those who had

once ardently admired him. Working underground from England he did not understand the changes in Italy—on the one hand the growing strength of Piedmont, on the other the danger of premature risings. For each revolt was put down by Austria with attendant cruelties and made the solid work harder of building towards a free and united Italy.

Asked by Isa Blagden to help a fund for the Mazzinian Revolutionaries, Browning wrote "every sort of conceivable horror, shootings, burnings and murderings—and all absolutely to no good—to the victims' country, nor to Italy generally: and now that the failure is complete—*subscribe,* shall I?"

The words "cloak and dagger" conjure up the scene of de Rossi's assassination—a scene of grand opera if ever there was one—the young men hiding the murderer with their cloaks and shouting, as it might be singing, "Abasso Rossi, Morte a Rossi." And the scarlet blouse and white horse of Garibaldi; the single gun which could not be fired, but which was ceremoniously dragged along in the Sicilian invasion and, as a "property" of the invincible Garibaldi, struck terror into the opposing forces. Everything about Garibaldi is a little larger than life, but not at all too large for song and stage.

The Pope was back in Rome, and on matters domestic and material was proceeding with reforms. He had disbanded the army hurriedly recruited in 1848, Roman taxes were light and the national debt disappeared. The government was paternal, but the number of lay functionaries much increased. The Pope had been well received in Rome, although elsewhere—and especially in England, now crowded with exiles—his fantastic popularity had disappeared. He was spoken of now with contempt and loathing.

The French ambassador, Rayneval, had written in 1856 to his country's Foreign Minister, praising all that had been done in the line of hospitals, prisons, charitable establishments, expansion of trade, building of houses—and this with a taxation less than half that paid by Frenchmen. He concluded: "the pontifical administration bears the marks of wisdom, reason and progress." It was not what his government wished to hear and he lost his job shortly thereafter. For Napoleon had already begun the rather devious game he was to play between Rome and Turin, and an attack on papal administration was a necessary preliminary.

The renewal of the Italian struggle in 1858 is more familiar to most of us than the "dress rehearsal" of ten years earlier. Cavour had worked steadily, not for the federation wanted by Gioberti and the Pope, but for a united Italy ruled by the King of Piedmont. He had committed Piedmont to supplying a small army, drawn from Sardinia, on the side of France and England in the Crimea. Thus Piedmont could put the Italian case at the peace table.

As tortuous in his own way as Napoleon, though more single-minded, he conferred with the Emperor secretly at Plombières; and at the opening of the Piedmont Parliament in 1859 Victor Emmanuel spoke of the *"grido di dolore"* reaching him from all parts of Italy. The Neapolitan ambassador turned pale, those from neutral countries, England, Prussia, Russia—and France—were deeply impressed. It is said that Napoleon had suggested these words to Cavour, and he had already paved the way by his own attitude when the Italian political refugee, Orsini, had attempted to assassinate him a few months earlier. The bomb killed eight people in the crowd, but Napoleon expressed sympathy for a misguided patriot driven to violence.

Cavour now set himself skillfully to irritate Austria that that country might appear the aggressor, and an Austrian demand for the disarmament of Sardinia, followed by a curt refusal, produced the desired declaration of war. France joined her army to that of Piedmont and they won in June the victory of Magenta, entered Milan in triumph and won the double battle of Solferino and San Martino.

And then Napoleon ceased to be the generous ally, and met the Emperor of Austria at Villafranca to arrange terms of peace.

Perhaps one reason which makes it so difficult to understand Browning's *Prince Hohenstiel-Schwangau Saviour of Society* is that it is almost impossible to understand Napoleon III. Earlier the Brownings had been in Paris during the Emperor's *coup d'état* when Mrs. Browning declared that after all he marched by the will of the people. Browning was at least doubtful then, but when he began to write about him soon after

Villafranca, he was more doubtful still. When he wrote (or completed) the poem after Sedan, "It is," he wrote to Isa Blagden, "just what I imagine the man might, if he pleased, say for himself."

Whether he *would*—or even could—ever have said it is another question; and doubtless his own moods would vary between self-condemnation and self-defense:

> The universal vote we have: its urn
> We also have where votes drop, fingered o'er
> By the universal Prefect.

Was not that, to be honest, the state of things with most votes when an Emperor had to be considered? A tyrant in France, Napoleon expended all his liberal feelings on Poland and Italy. Cardinal Antonelli had replied sarcastically to one of his demands for reform in the Papal States by asking whether there was so much liberty in France that they wanted to export their surplus. In the private meeting at Plombières, Napoleon had demanded the annexation to France of Savoy and Nice, in return for his services in establishing the Kingdom of North Italy; but Cavour resented bitterly the full price now demanded for a half-done job. At Villafranca, Austria gave up Lombardy, but kept Venice. Tuscany, Parma, Modena and the Roman legations were added to the Northern Kingdom (by plebiscite) in the following year and France could in a sense claim that this was her work. She also claimed that Nice and Savoy were in fact French in composition, but the plebiscite there was held only *after,* and in confirmation of, the annexation. The "universal Prefect" was already a Frenchman!

Napoleon said that he had feared a Mazzinian revolution all over Italy, and certainly Mazzini in the background can never be forgotten. And the Italian populace had on the whole failed to volunteer for his army, while the Pope had been rapturously received on a tour of his States not long before. The Austrians were renowned for the cruelty with which they suppressed revolts; better wait and see, was probably the instinct of most Italians. Writing to congratulate Elizabeth on her lack of pariotism—"we and Prussia chiefly, shall be punished hereafter"—Ruskin lamented the Italian weakness. "It is not life. It is only galvanism—or at least the first staggering motion of a man blind and bound for half his life." As for the payment, it is likely that Browning has caught the varying moods of the Emperor—and his hand on the national pulse of France:

> Come with me and deliver Italy!
> Smite hip and thigh until the oppressor leave
> Free from the Adriatic to the Alps
> The oppressed one! . . .
>   "All for nought—
> Not even, say, some patch of province splice
> O'er the frontier? Some snug honorarium-fee
> Shut into glove and pocketed apace?"
> (Questions Sagacity) "in deference
> To the natural susceptibility
> Of folks at home, unwitting of that pitch
> You soar to . . .
>   . . . but prompt
> To recognize the cession of Savoy
> And Nice as marketable value!"

In the poem Napoleon repudiates this prompting of Sagacity: Let her prompt Metternich, not him; but in brute fact he followed it. "So Italy was free"; and France had made a first-rate bargain.

Italy Napoleon saw as a Federation, a United States of Italy, with the Pope as Chairman of the Board, his spiritual authority unquestioned —a free Church in a free State. Pius hesitated: one wonders what Cavour would have done if he had accepted. For the extremists in the Piedmont Parliament were against giving the Pope any position at all in the new Italy. They wanted the Papal States—the Romagna, Umbria and the Marches—with no question of indemnity for the Pope. And in the Romagna, Cavour was already closing convents.

The Pope's mind was made up when he realized that Napoleon assumed that the Romagna already belonged to Piedmont. He was first to lose a state and then to accept only limited powers over those that remained. He refused—on the strange principle we have noticed. Christ's robe was being torn "which remained whole even on the hill of Calvary," and he must share Christ's sufferings rather than be a party to this desecration.

The Sardinians, not satisfied with the Romagna, determined to invade Umbria and the Marches, while Cavour, not declaring war on Naples, was secretly supporting Garibaldi in his "Crusade of The Thousand"—for this was the tiny army with which he set out to conquer, or liberate, Sicily. "Try to navigate," wrote Cavour to Admiral Persano, "between Garibaldi and the Neapolitan cruisers. I hope you understand me."

More volunteers joined Garibaldi including some of the Sicilian peasants, who ran away at the first noise of guns but presently became useful soldiers. Naples was well and truly hated in the island. Palermo fell, the whole of Sicily was conquered and Garibaldi, without pausing, returned swifty to the mainland, entered Naples, and defeated the Neapolitan armies at the battle of Volturno. With no personal ambitions, he sought only to offer his conquest to Victor Emmanuel as "a new and brilliant jewel" for his crown. He himself would return to his goats and rocks on the island of Caprera.[1]

Meanwhile the Piedmont regular army were advancing against volunteer forces responding from many countries to the Pope's appeal for defenders of the States of the Church: young Irishmen came, sons of most of the French legitimists, Belgians and Poles—all with as great a sense of dedication as Garibaldi's Thousand. Less well led, too briefly welded into an army, they won the admiration of their foes when, greatly outnumbered, they were defeated at the battle of Castelfidardo. Umbria and the Marches were now added to the crown of Piedmont.

Napoleon had gone on a cruise and was inaccessible for the fortnight of this strange swift war. His armies did nothing except keep the Piedmontese from entering Rome and insist they depart from the narrow territory known as the Patrimony of St. Peter.

"So well I was," wrote Elizabeth, "with all the advantages of Rome in me, looking so well, that I was tired of hearing people say so . . . it was the blow on the *heart* about the peace, after all that excitement and exaltation . . . and then the sudden stroke and fall, and the impotent rage against all the nations of the earth— . . . Robert has been perfect to me. For more than a fortnight he gave up all his nights' rest to me, and even now he teaches Pen." And again, "my poor Robert who nursed me like an angel, prevented from sleeping for full three weeks."

And about the same time to Isa Blagden: "I dreamed lately that I followed a mystic woman . . . in white, with a white mask, on her head the likeness of a crown. I knew she was Italy. . . . All through my illness political dreams have repeated themselves, in inscrutable articles of peace and eternal provisional governments." And to Mr. Chorley: "I have been living and dying for Italy."

This was the woman who, discussing her own country, felt that "patriotism in the narrow sense is a virtue which will wear out, sooner or later, everywhere. Jew and Greek must drop their antagonisms; and if Christianity is ever to develop it will not respect frontiers." It was Robert, not she, who had been "frantic" about the horrors of the Crimean war. She "never, at worst, thought that the great tragedy of the world was going on *there* . . . there are more chronic cruelties and deeper wrongs."

Maybe, but one can only agree with the diagnosis of Henry James: "Mrs. Browning's correspondence," he says, "flushes and turns pale" as her letters "reflect her passion, her feverish obsession, with extraordinary vivacity and eloquence; but it is impossible not to feel, as we read, that to 'care,' in the common phrase, as she is caring is to entertain one's convictions as a malady and a doom. . . ." She had lost, James felt, that "saving and sacred sense of proportion," which great poets and geniuses keep "even in emotion and passion, even in pleading a cause and calling on the gods . . . we absolutely feel the beautiful mind and the high gift discredited by their engrossment."

James has a curious half sentence in this analysis "while the pulses of her companion much more clearly throb," which must refer to Browning and is certainly true of him. On this matter of a free and united Italy he was far from the opposition to his wife that marked his attitude on spiritualism. On only one point did he disagree—her curious estimate of Napoleon III. He annoyed her by the remark, "It was a great action; but he has taken eighteenpence for it, which is a pity." And although she admitted that it was "indelicate" to station

French soldiers in Savoy, to oversee the so-called free vote as to whether this people desired to belong to France, she still assumed that it would *be* a free vote. Henry James was in Switzerland at "the hour in which the French Emperor was to be paid by Victor Emmanuel the price of the liberation of Lombardy," and he recalled the "passionate protests" of the terrified Swiss as the power of "enormous and triumphant France ... to absorb great mouthfuls was being so strikingly exhibited."[2] But Elizabeth was writing: "The wailing in England for the Swiss and Savoyards, while other nationalities are to be trodden underfoot without intervention except what's called *aggression,* is highly irritating to me."

Very different from James's were the reactions of another American, Kate Field, who shared Elizabeth's views and had attached herself to the Brownings two years earlier in Rome. "You are very ambitious," Browning said to her approvingly; and, indeed, both husband and wife immensely appreciated the enterprising young Americans, Margaret Fuller, Hatty Hosmer, Kate Field, who defied convention and risked penury to do good work and win renown. Kate Field sacrificed a fortune by refusing to obey the rich uncle whose heir she was to be if she returned to the States and abandoned some of her social and political views. She wrote for various periodicals and was at this time poorly paid enough. Later she became an immensely successful journalist, running for five years a newspaper entitled *Kate Field's Washington.* And by an extraordinary turn of fate the fortune she had lost was made up for by shares given her by the Bell Telephone Company in gratitude for her skill and grace in demonstrating this marvelous new invention to Queen Victoria! The shares grew to the value of some two hundred thousand dollars, worth today well over a million.

Kate's position in the expatriate world of Italy was certainly not diminished by her radiant good looks. Her auburn hair is described and her blue eyes, which she matched on occasion with dress and hair ribbons. At a party where she showed the quality of her voice, the celebrated actress, Charlotte Cushman, was amazed, urged her to get first-class lessons, and with Isa Blagden welcomed Kate into their group of emancipated women. In the summer of 1860 she was in Florence and relieved both Brownings by sharing the ever-present burden of

Landor. Meeting him at Isa's house, she so entranced him that he told Elizabeth she was "the most charming young lady he had ever seen," "and you know, dear Kate," said Elizabeth, "he has seen a great many."

He offered to teach her Latin. She went daily for her lesson, spoke of him as "chivalry incarnate" and discerned "something of heaven about him." One evening, again at Isa's, as Kate kissed both her hostess and Elizabeth, Landor asked her, "Do you mean to stop there?" Getting a kiss himself he declared it the happiest day of his life. "Had I been sixty years younger you would not have kissed me." Not content with complimenting her in Latin phrase, he wrote a poem about the kiss—

> . . . given me in the sight of more
> Than ever saw me kissed before. . . .
> She came across nor greatly feared
> The horrid break of wintry beard.

At each of his own sallies Landor would "laugh immoderatley." The phrase recurs in the descriptions and one can fancy Elizabeth's relief that the old man should have a worshiping young girl to—yes, positively, to enjoy it![3]

Kate's letters home and letters to her from the Brownings bring again the sense of youth and gaiety at the Casa Guidi so vivid in Harriet Hosmer's memories. But there are two differences. Curiously enough it is the sculptor not the journalist who remembers the style of both Brownings' speech, thus bringing the past to life; but too one feels her past with them six years ago had more life in it. When Elizabeth's *Poems before Congress* were published, a letter from Browning congratulates Kate on being almost alone in understanding that greatly maligned volume. It is an angry and a sad one. The high spirits of the early fifties were chiefly his, they could still break out and did, but Elizabeth's physical ill health and mental misery could not but affect the atmosphere.

Something was happening with the Brownings, especially with Elizabeth, that so often happens as time draws on and acquaintance and admirers multiply. Many, many years later Browning wrote to Mrs. Fitzgerald, likening carelessness about health "to a foolish dancing one's heart over a precipice—and the only hard words my wife ever got from me were just on that account,—when she would run risks, be forgetful of taking meals, allow herself to be talked half-dead by inconsiderate visitors." There had been an occasion when two women were "each determined to sit the other out"—and one does not doubt Browning when he asserts "I used to grow brutal when her poor face began to show suffering."

Kate Field was not of such; she had sensitivity as well as gaiety, a sensitivity responding to what she felt as a "magnetic flood of love and poetry that was constantly passing between husband and wife."

Why, it has been asked, if Browning agreed with Elizabeth on the Italian situation, did he leave her alone to write about it?—and Mrs. Miller asks passionately why he did not speak out against the Emperor— long ago, in Paris, when Elizabeth and Pen were cheering his progress, after the bloody crushing of a popular insurrection. It was, one gathers, an act of treachery to Shelley's memory. Why, indeed, did not this admirer of his die on the barricades?

It is interesting that in fact Browning had in his essay on Shelley answered the question before it could be asked. Shelley's idealism had in youth led him to endeavor "to realise as he went on idealising; every wrong had simultaneously its remedy." And thus he committed himself to "expedients" often misconceived. But "gradually he was raised above the contemplation of spots and the attempt at effacing them, to the great abstract light and through the discrepancy of the creation, to the sufficiency of the First Cause. Gradually he was learning that the best way of removing abuses was to stand fast by truth."

Browning saw his own vocation also as the poet's; there were scores of fields where the social and political reformer must work, but all of them are relative. The poet is a man sent by God. His function is akin to that of the prophet: reading men and nature, proclaiming what he sees, he speaks for the speechless. As Robert Langbaum has pointed out, when Browning gets inside a man in a dramatic monologue, he unlocks the truth—not "by interpreting the facts according to some theory but by restoring to the facts their life, the beating hearts and high-blooded ticking brains of two centuries since." It is not insignificant that, just as he did not consider "Bishop Blougram's Apology" an attack but an Apologia, he was abused and praised later for blackening *and* for whitewashing Napoleon III in *Prince Hohenstiel-Schwangau.*

He was discovering "the most vital form" of the new period in the poetry that he was inaugurating. And like Eliot and Joyce, the former of whom owed him so great a debt, he was working to "dig below the ruins of official tradition to discover in myth an underground tradition, an inescapable because inherently psychological pattern into which to fit the chaotic present."[4]

Was Browning to abandon this effort, never more perfectly achieved than in *Men and Women,* in order to write what in an hour of constantly changing fortunes would be perhaps inappropriate a week after it was written? He was not, as to a large degree his wife was, a poet of the hour. It is fascinating to discover from her letters that he did try, that they had planned to write and to publish jointly. "When I showed him my ode on Napoleon he observed that I was gentle to England in comparison to what he had been, but after Villafranca (the Palmerston Ministry having come in) he destroyed his poem and left me alone, and I determined to stand alone. *What Robert had written no longer suited the moment.*" (Italics mine)

On the major issue of Italy's freedom they agreed totally; about Napoleon, no. It has been suggested that an earlier version of *Prince Hohenstiel-Schwangau* was the poem then "destroyed." This does not seem likely, for in his memory it existed then only as a prose sketch of an idea, "blown out" many years later, and in the light of later events, into a dramatic monologue.

Would it have been worth wounding Elizabeth at this juncture by diminishing the man, in her eyes a "sublime deliverer" lifted "to the level of pure song"? Was there any point in proving or disproving to the public that (in her vivid words) the Pope was "hard to manage even for the Emperor. It is hard to cut up a feather bed into sandwiches with the finest Damascus blade"? Was there much point even in defending England against her unmeasured attacks and trying to show her that the whole situation was more complex than she conceived?

Another factor which must always be remembered is Browning's

generous and wholehearted admiration for his wife's work. Often and
often he repeated that she, not he, was the poet. And although time has
proved him wrong, he was not quite as wrong as changing fashion has
for many years decreed. It would, indeed, be absurd to place her beside
him, but she was a true poet even if now dated. *Poems before Congress*
has in it fine lines which to those living through Italy's great hour must
have seemed even finer. For too many years each fortunate nation

> Beside her has dared to stand,
> And flout her with pity and scorn,
> Saying she is at rest,
>   She is fair, she is dead,
> And, leaving room in her stead
> To Us who are later born,
>   This is certainly best!

Elizabeth's own scorn for England found perhaps unfair but certainly effective expression:

> For where's our blessed "status quo,"
>   Our holy treaties, where,—
> Our rights to sell a race, or buy,
> Protect and pillage, occupy
>   And civilize despair?

"It's extraordinary," said Odo Russell (British representative in
Rome) to Browning, "the sensation your wife's book has made. Every
paper I see has something about it."

Comparing their relative standing at that date, Browning may well
have been wise to leave speech to his wife in the defense of Italy. When
his poem appeared to him outdated, "The poetical devil in me," said
Elizabeth, "burnt on for an utterance."

Browning's daimon was a different one. His surviving letters of
this period are fewer, their contents so much less rich, than hers, that
we are only too apt to view these years through Elizabeth's eyes and to
exaggerate, as Browning himself did later, the length of a pause in
which he was taking breath after *Men and Women* and was beginning
to write *Dramatis Personae.*

20 Mr. Sludge
and Mrs. Eckley

This trade of mine—I don't know, can't be sure
But there was something in it, tricks and all!

"MR. SLUDGE, THE MEDIUM"

HOW FAR Elizabeth had in her best days succeeded in freeing herself from the use of morphine it is hard to tell. Certainly she had cut it
down, and Browning had written exultingly to her sisters of her courage
in giving it up totally during the months before Pen's birth. "Where
is one among a thousand 'strongmen' that would have thrown himself on
the mercy of an angel, as she did on mine, quite another kind of being?"

In later years, rumors that she had returned to the drug must have
got abroad. Julia Ward Howe, furious at hearing that the Brownings
did not think much of her own verse, published two rhymed attacks in
her next volume. The first began:

> I hear you do not praise me, Barrett Browning, God inspired
> Nor you Robert with your manhood and your angels interlyred.

In curious contradiction to the phrase "God inspired" was the second
poem in which she repudiates for herself an inspiration now described
as of a very different kind:

> I shrink before the nameless draught
> That helps to such unearthly things,

> And if a drug could lift so high,
> I would not trust its treacherous wings.

Browning wrote to Isa Blagden that "Mrs. Story seemed to think we must be writhing under such awful blows." But he had called on Mrs. Crawford "in order to show her how much I despised her sister Mrs. Howe."

Maybe he did, but to despise its author did not mean to be indifferent to the publication of what had troubled himself so deeply. Elizabeth wrote quite calmly to Mrs. Eckley: "As to the verses, there is nothing in them which has displeased me ever so little, except just the allusion to the nameless drug . . . which is called a 'nameless drug', dear, and not morphine. . . . Also the imputation is perfectly true so far, that life is necessary to writing, and that I should not be alive except for the help of my morphine."

The "red hood of poppies," the "amreeta draught," which she had earlier called it, suggest a modern enthusiast talking about L.S.D. And despite the fits of depression, the reliance on the morphine, and the increasing physical weakness, all the friends Elizabeth did see testify to her lively interest in them and their affairs and her entire absence of bitterness.

The Eckley family continued to seek out the Brownings with a zeal that became embarrassing. They would arrange their times in Rome, their moves to Florence at the same dates, they were constantly offering the use of their carriages and horses. Browning liked David Eckley with whom he walked or rode in the early morning; and the son, another David, played with Pen. Sophia or Sophie Eckley attached herself fanatically to Elizabeth. She gave her so many presents that Elizabeth returned one, writing, "There's excess dear and extremity— and the beautiful cameo was meant to grow on your own marble throat."

The letters between them began in 1857 and pass rapidly into "Dearest Mrs. Eckley" and thence to "Dearest Sophie." In Rome they were carried by hand and written (often in pale pencil with no date) while the messenger waited.

Sophie's intensity of admiration Elizabeth repudiated: ". . . if indeed you could see the face of my soul . . . you see me high and I am
low—light and I am dark—it isn't a phrase of humility—God sees how
true it is." But gradually she began to return the rather feverish affection and admiration, writing of Sophie to Fanny Haworth: "Yes isn't
she a poetical, pure, lovely creature? She covers the earth with her own
white garments and walks clean-footed over dirty places."

The chief attraction was certainly Sophia Eckley's claim that she
walked with the spirits of the dead. She kept trying to persuade Elizabeth that she, too, had had experiences, but Elizabeth with all her cravings refused to become self-deceived. "You tell me," she wrote, "you are
sure of my having had communication with spirits belonging to me.
How can you possibly be sure, if I am not sure? There has been no
testimony worth a straw to me—though I kept my mind open and
ready." Yet she would like, she said, to wander through chestnut woods
"making the third with that strange spirit." It was, I suppose, a union
in the spirits that made Elizabeth so strangely call Sophie her dear
sister. She was practicing automatic writing with Fanny Haworth, too;
and she went on hoping. "A paper and pencil shall be near [she tells
Sophie] that 'they' (if they are gracious) may complete their gracious-
ness." One letter speaks of "our séance"; another says "I have the disks
ready."

With Browning, however intensely he disliked it, the subject was
out in the open, but presumably it was in reference to Sophie's husband
that Elizabeth assured her friend that Robert was "safe . . . not a word
shall be said . . . be calm."

Did Elizabeth fancy perhaps that her dead brother might be the
strange spirit that walked with Mrs. Eckley, or even—now that death
had erased the memories of his cruelty—her strange father? (The
thought of a spiritual Moulton Barrett, in a toga perhaps or clad in
light, seems highly implausible.)

Robert might be "safe," but the subject was again more serious than
when they had played with it at Florence. He had written to Isa from
Le Havre: "Do you still sit round a table and see who will turn it least
apparently? And you have patience still to hear the French spirits speak

thro' a young Lady, while the Flemish spirits stick in her throat? How mournful and old-fashioned it all sounds to me."

Spiritualism, madly the fashion in England, was even more so in the United States. Ruskin tells Elizabeth "that he does not laugh at the subject, neither does he believe." The author of *Uncle Tom's Cabin* claimed to have had manifestations, and her letters were comforting to Elizabeth whose own passionate interest was woven of many strands. Any possibility of enlarged knowledge fascinated her, and she had written to Mrs. Jameson years earlier: "I shall never have rest till I know what is to be known" and expecting from spiritualism "the breaking up of some of the deepest and dumbest mysteries of our double Being."

She had no faintest need for reassurance of immortality for herself; but others might achieve it through a greater exploration of the world of spirits. With all her denials to Mrs. Eckley of any contact during their experiments together, she wrote to Henrietta of one experience she did believe herself to have had—a manifestation of Dr. Channing, the Unitarian. "I asked him if he thought differently or the same of the Lord Jesus Christ. The answer was 'God was manifest in the flesh.' " In the spiritual world the realization of immortality had "overwhelmed" him even more than its beauty—immortality and the thinness of the veil *"between that life and this life."* Asked for a message of reassurance he quoted: *"Be of good cheer, your sins are forgiven you"*; asked had he seen the face of God he said, *"No, no, no, Child."*

It is all Elizabeth's own Credo, which seems an obvious explanation of some part of this approach to the world of spirits. But increasingly Elizabeth deemed it a religious science. Results, she held, were trivial only because "We don't bring serious souls and concentrated attention and holy aspirations to the spirits." But also "Death does not teach all things." There are foolish as well as wise spirits; there are spirits who "personate falsely," there may be mediums who cheat, but the power is "a physical faculty." Home is "quite an electric fire."

Her letters do, indeed, "flush and turn pale," not over Italian unity alone but also over this second burning topic, and unfortunately on both subjects Elizabeth seemed driven by a feverish need to convict if

she could not convince her correspondents. Browning may have been
wise to talk politics rather than pay compliments, but he "lectured" his
wife, she admits, when she railed in conversation with Odo Russell
against what she called the "ignominy" of England. The word recurs
in letters to all her English friends, and it is unlikely that they responded graciously (Harriet Martineau "set me down with her air of
serene superiority"). To others, Mrs. Jameson, for instance, the spiritualism appeared even more foolish than the politics. After a long letter to
her on the sins of England and the wrongs of Italy, Elizabeth received
the news of Mrs. Jameson's death, and every death was a fresh incentive for spiritualist investigations. Robert's heart, she declared, had
softened so that he allowed her to get the *Spiritual Magazine* from England. Telling Fanny Haworth of this she begs her to "get to see the
'hands' and the 'bodies' and the 'celestial garments,'" which a mutual
friend had "the privilege of being familiar with. *Touch* the hands."

When the *Spiritual Magazine* attacked *Poems before Congress*,
Robert confessed to a little malicious pleasure, but in fact he was getting
very little pleasure and a great deal of pain during those months. He
had got rid of Home, but now at his wife's side, day by day, driving with
her, sitting by her was another medium, in closest intimacy. Probably
at first he had only thought of Sophie Eckley as a rather silly little
woman and was horrified as the picture gradually unfolded.

Looking back, he claimed: "I cried 'poison' at first sniff—and suffered more, from maintaining it, than from any incident in my whole
life." This he wrote in 1863, having just received from Story the news
that Mrs. Eckley was trying to divorce his friend "poor dear, good,
simple David." "I do not believe one syllable of it," he said of her
charges. "You know that those inventions about spirits etc. were not at
all more prodigious than the daily-sprouting toadstools of that dung-hill
of a soul."[1]

How much was this hindsight, stimulated by the thought of his
friend's suffering and the memory of his wife's? For Elizabeth certainly
did suffer acutely when—how we do not know—she found she had
been deceived. To Fanny Haworth she now wrote of Sophie Eckley: "I
don't think she knows what truth is, and why it should be cared for. In

order to conciliate me she says she has given up her mediumship!! 'Because mediums are always suspected.'" And to Isa Blagden: "I feel inclined to grind my teeth and stamp. She sticks dear, like treacle . . . once I praised the sweetness—now I feel very sick at the adhesiveness . . . if she said she hated me how much easier I should feel."[2]

But it was of little use to get rid of an alleged medium while the all-absorbing topic remained. Browning must have been thinking of, even if not writing, *Mr. Sludge, the Medium,* while he suffered most over his wife's absorption in a difficult, dangerous quest from which he saw no happy issue. The poem expressed what he as well as she believed—that there was "something in it." But coming whence, leading whither? That question they answered differently. Sludge boldly claims:

> As for religion—why, I served it, sir!
> I'll stick to that! With my *phenomena*
> I laid the atheist sprawling on his back,
> Propped up St. Paul, or, at least, Swendenborg! . . .
>   Why, of old,
> Great men spent years and years in writing books
> To prove we've souls, and hardly proved it then.

Sludge admits to wide cheating and warms to a keen enjoyment in telling how he cheated, and above all how he was encouraged to cheat by those wanting to be gulled: "If such as came for wool, sir, went home shorn,/Where is the wrong I did them? 'Twas their choice." Yet as the poem goes on he tells, too, of things that no cheating can explain:

> I have presentiments; my dreams come true:
> I fancy a friend stands whistling all in white
> Blithe as a boblink, and he's dead I learn.
> I take dislike to a dog my favorite long,
> And sell him; he goes mad next week and snaps. . . .
> Why, which of those who say they disbelieve,
> Your clever people, but has dreamed his dream,
> Caught his coincidence, stumbled on his fact
> He can't explain, (he'll tell you smilingly)
> Which he's too much of a philosopher

To count as supernatural, indeed,
So calls a puzzle and problem, proud of it.

Today few people would question the existence of extrasensory
perception, however explained or even if admitted inexplicable. Sludge
has discovered in his own strange fashion a spiritual world surrounding
and permeating this one, has even discovered (in a very Browning
style!) the Creator of both:

We find great things are made of little things,
And little things go lessening till at last
Comes God behind them. Talk of mountains now?—
We talk of mould that heaps the mountain, mites
That throng the mould, and God that makes the mites.
The Name comes close behind a stomach-cyst,
The simplest of creations, just a sac
That's mouth, heart, legs and belly at once, yet lives
And feels, and could do neither, we conclude,
If simplified still further one degree:
The small becomes the dreadful and immense!

To believe this need not make the world of spirit fully understand-
able, still less subject to human manipulation: "I've told my lie,/And
seen truth follow, marvels none of mine;/All was not cheating, sir, I'm
positive!"

This poem is perhaps the most fascinating example of Browning's
power of speaking as, and for, the man most totally repugnant to him.
His sympathy with Sludge grows as he goes on, and the chief villain
becomes Hiram H. Horsefall, in whom we can perhaps detect Mrs.
Eckley. As Sludge says:

Who finds a picture, digs a medal up,
Hits on a first edition,—he henceforth
Gives it his name, grows notable: how much more
Who ferrets out a "medium"?

The desire to be cheated makes it bit by bit impossible for the
medium to refrain from cheating. It is well known that extrasensory
perception comes and goes, but the medium must always show himself

in possession of it to content his exploiter. He longs to say, "I saw no ghost at all./Inform your friends I made . . . well fools of them,/And found you ready-made."

The "owner" of the medium has a vested interest in convincing his friends. Horsefall pays Sludge liberally to go away and leave them in ignorance that they have been cheated. And what of a rich woman who could both employ mediums and pretend to powers of her own? The Eckleys of this world are worse than the Sludges, but if Browning had written a dramatic monologue in her person, he would, I fancy, have made a case even for Mrs. Eckley.

But he saw one figure in the drama studiously ignored by the other actors, compared with whose absence that of Hamlet would be insignificant. He wrote: "no trick too gross—absurdities are referred to as 'low spirits;' falsehoods to 'personating spirits'—and the one terrible apparent spirit, the Father of Lies, has it all his own way."[3]

21 The Last Months Together

The life in me abolished the death of things,
Deep calling unto deep . . .

THE RING AND THE BOOK

A YEAR or so spent on an effort to popularize *Sordello* ended in its remaining pretty much as it was. But by the spring of 1860 Elizabeth could write to an anxious Sarianna: "Robert deserves no reproaches, for he has been writing a good deal this winter—working at a long poem which I have not seen a line of, and producing short lyrics which I *have* seen and may declare worthy of him." There were other creative activities which she had to defend to his sister. "Robert waits for an inclination," she wrote, and this was true of the entire Italian period. He took up drawing, showing remarkable results in a couple of weeks. And then, turning to modeling, he began to work several hours a day in his friend Story's studio. Interestingly his wife, who had a far juster conception than the public of their relative quality, adds, "For me, if I have attained anything of force or freedom by living near the oak, the better for me. But I hope you don't think that I mimic him or lose my individuality."

"*Mr. Sludge, the Medium*" has often been suggested as the "long poem,"—and certainly, if this was written in Elizabeth's lifetime, it seems improbable that Browning would have shown it to her. But two letters, one to William Allingham and another to Mrs. Jameson, suggest a different answer. She wrote to Allingham from Rome in May, 1860: "Robert is writing, not political *poems,* but *a poem* in books, a line of which I have not seen—and also certain exquisite lyrics which I have seen. Neither he nor I have been idle this winter; nor mean to be idle this summer." The description "a poem in books" she gave also to Mrs. Jameson, and it can apply to nothing in *Dramatis Personae* except "James Lee's Wife." But part of this had been printed years earlier in the *Monthly Repository* for May, 1836, and Elizabeth must surely have seen it. It is all rather puzzling, and one is reminded of passing remarks of Browning's suggesting that he wrote a good deal of poetry which never saw the light. To Domett he had spoken in his youth of much writing and destroying. And what became of the "drawers full" of lyrics he mentioned to Archbishop Benson?

Improbable perhaps, but is it inconceivable that this poem "in books" was a first draft of something, destroyed then, begun again years later? For Elizabeth nowhere mentions what we learn from *The Ring and the Book,* that it was in 1860 he found on a stall in the marketplace of Florence the old yellow book he was to make so famous.

"That memorable day" he looked for the first time at the sordid detective story which he would lift into greatness, and it was on the terrace of the Casa Guidi that he first began to map out the countryside that had been its theater:

> . . . when hearts beat hard,
> And brains, high-blooded, ticked two centuries since,
> Give it me back! The thing's restorative
> I' the touch and sight.

Presently he would lay it aside for many months; the actual writing of the poem as we have it began only in 1864, but I think we must see his excitement over it, his periodic brooding over it, as underlying much of the time remaining of Browning's Italian life, after that day of the purchase, that walk home, reading as he walked:

> Still read I on, from written title page
> To written index, on, through street and street,
> At the Strozzi, at the Pillar, at the Bridge;

Till, by the time I stood at home again
In Casa Guidi by Felice Church,
Under the doorway where the black begins
With the first stone-slab of the staircase cold,
I had mastered the contents, knew the whole truth.

It was in Florence, too, that he began the metal work on the raw gold which would become a ring: "I fused my live soul and that inert stuff,/Before attempting smithcraft."

On that terrace where he and Elizabeth so often walked, walks shortening now as she grew weaker, he paced dreaming and looking out:

A bow-shot to the street's end, north away
Out of the Roman gate to the Roman road
By the river, till I felt the Appennine.
And there would lie Arezzo, the man's town,
The woman's trap and cage and torture-place,
Also the stage where the priest played his part. . . .
Till Rome itself, the ghastly goal, I reached.
Why, all the while,—how could it otherwise?—
The life in me abolished the death of things,
Deep calling unto deep . . .

Probably he talked little of the Book. Elizabeth did not want even to read it. Of her husband she says "reading hurts him. As long as I have known him he has not been able to read long at a time." *The* Book did not take long to master, but Browning read it eight times before he began to write. This winter he was already investigating the story in Rome and in Arezzo, and although his memory was in later years notoriously inaccurate, there must have been some basis for the story he told Lehmann of his placing twelve pebbles on the parapet to represent "the twelve chapters into which the poem is divided."

Meanwhile there was the modeling, rumors of which had excited Ruskin. "I think it possible," he wrote in December, 1859, "you may find a quite new form of expression of yourself in that direction." After all Rossetti was both poet and painter, Ruskin himself had tried to be both, and rumor soon had it that Browning was revealing a marked talent. "And so," Ruskin wrote in the following year, "Robert has made Cytherea in clay. I've been trying to draw her, so hard, but couldn't. It's very odd we (there's conceit for you) should take the same fancy together." And Elizabeth wrote to Sarianna early in '61: "It is wonderfully done, say the learned. He says all his happiness lies in clay now."

It was Robert's happiness, indeed, that most concerned her. "An active occupation," she told his sister,

> is salvation to him with his irritable nerves, saves him from ruminating bitter cud, and from the process which I call beating his dear head against the wall till it is bruised. . . . The modelling combines body-work and soul work, and the more tired he has been . . . the more he has exulted and been happy. . . . He has the material for a volume and will work at it this summer he says. . . . Oh the brain stratifies and matures creatively, even in the pauses of the pen.
>
> At the same time his treatment in England affects him naturally —and for my part I set it down as an infamy of the public. . . .

With all her hatred of papal rule, her belief in every rumor of the bad behavior of the Swiss Guards, her longing to see the Pope thrown out of the city, Elizabeth went in Rome only to Catholic churches where her prayers went up with the music. She found it all "beautiful and holy." She never had any idea of becoming a Catholic and in Florence they went "the regular proper way to the Swiss Church." But in the prayer and music in Rome, she said, "was the communion of saints."

Death had been crowding around them. Early in 1860 Mrs. Jameson had died quite unexpectedly, "a blot more on the world for me," wrote Elizabeth; but far worse was the blow of Henrietta's illness. She, the strongest of the three sisters, was stricken with cancer and Elizabeth could hardly bear not to rush to her, but knew that "I should just have increased the sum of evil." In another letter she writes almost bitterly of her destiny always "to be entirely useless to the people I should like to help" even "my own darling sister." She tended to suffer always from self-reproach, feeling now that she might have managed to go to England from Le Havre, had perhaps given in too much to her own physical weakness, yet realizing that she grew weaker all the time.

Henrietta died that autumn and Elizabeth wrote to Fanny Haworth: "It is a great privilege to be able to talk and cry; but *I cannot* you know."

Browning had taken every precaution that he should hear the news first and break it to his wife. By her wish he did not show her the poignant letter from Henrietta's husband, but she was haunted by the thought of the three tiny children and of never again seeing her sister on earth.

She had a comforting letter from Harriet Beecher Stowe, who shared her Christian faith and was also convinced of receiving messages from her own dead son. And Robert, Elizabeth writes, had been "most kind and tender" in her grief and had kept people away from her, but anyhow "gloomy lionesses with wounded paws don't draw the public, I thank God."

She believed in the communion of saints and intercessory prayer "not papistically nor with the vulgar purgatorial idea." "She is only in the next room—though for me I cannot see or hear her—others might." She is praying, "Help thou my unbelief. He is sufficient for this insufficiency." But this letter to Arabel goes on in a very shaky hand: "It seems . . . as if the blood of my heart *must* be left in stains on the stones of the road."

That Browning was right in fearing spiritualist "manifestations" for his wife's nerves—and perhaps even for her mental balance there can be no doubt. But whether he was right or wrong in his attribution of these things to the "Father of lies," there is no trace anywhere of their having dimmed Elizabeth's faith. Fanny Haworth had asked what if Christ be taken for a medium? "If," Elizabeth replies, "He walked on the sea as a medium, if virtue went out of Him as a mesmeriser, He also spoke the words which never man spoke, was born for us, and died for us, and rose from the dead as the Lord God our Saviour. But the whole theory of spiritualism, all the phenomena, are strikingly *confirmatory* of revelation . . ."

The forms in which the Christian faith were clad seemed to her outworn. Not Catholic theologians only, but Luther, too, "was a schoolman of the most scholastic sect; most offensive, most absurd." We must cast off these " 'old cerements' to the uttermost. We are entering on a Reformation far more interior than Luther's." And a part of that Reformation was, in her eyes, a getting closer to the spirits of the dead.

Well aware of her own growing weakness, she felt an increasing realization of life's brevity. "You catch the wind of the wheels in your face, it seems, as you get nearer the end," she writes to Mrs. Martin. And "How the spiritual world gets thronged to us with familiar faces, till at last, perhaps, the world here will seem the vague and strange world, even while we remain." And again: "Do not think that I think *any bond is broken,* or that anything is lost. We have been fed on the hill-side, and now there are twelve baskets of fragments remaining."

Elizabeth's fluctuations in both health and spirits made it difficult for Browning to realize that she was in fact growing weaker. She was as she said herself "always dying and it makes no difference." After her father's death and again after Henrietta's she went far down, only to pick up in sea air or in the peace and beauty of Siena. After every victory of the Sardinian army she exulted, a setback threw her into despair, and to a quite unusual degree her feelings affected her bodily. The flushing and turning pale, as noted by James, is constantly visible in her letters, but especially in the unpublished ones. "Nobody knows," she had written fifteen years before to Mrs. Martin, "what it is to have so much vital *will* in one and such a deathly impotence all around it"— and "I have naturally a melancholy heart and a merry mind . . . one mocks at the other."

Even if England proved impossible, they planned in 1861 to see Sarianna and the "dear Nonno," and Elizabeth felt confident that Arabel and perhaps her brothers would join them. She wrote to George in April: "Just now it is enough for me to gather together my courage for the journey to France—which seems to me very, very far. I feel more fit for going to Heaven sometimes." She had seen in Rome the English consul in whose arms Keats had died, revolting against death: "In ten years," he cried, "I should be a great poet." Elizabeth wrote: "There would be no answer to such 'divine despairs,' if it were not in the facts in which I deeply believe, that life and work, yes, the sort of work suitable to the artist-nature are continued on the outside of this crust of mortal manhood, and that the man will be permitted to completed himself, if not *here, there*."

But nothing ever could go right with Elizabeth's family. Arabel suggested joining some friends of her own to the party in Paris, and one sees the family problem as perhaps never before in Elizabeth's letter to Arabel: "When we are all brought together and rubbed against one another (as it makes my blood run cold to think of) there will be a gritting and grinding from which strangers are better excluded." Yet although not wanting strangers, she craves for her sister; *couldn't* Arabel anyhow come to Italy? "I am made of brown paper and tear at a touch."

To Fanny Haworth she was writing: "The future in this shifting world, what is it? . . . I have a stout pen and till its last blot it will write . . . but if you laid a hand on this heart, you would feel how it stops and staggers and fails."

The passionate interest in Italy kept pace with the personal griefs and the spiritualist speculations. The first new and enlarged parliament met at Turin at the beginning of this year; and the problems were vast in which Victor Emmanuel needed Cavour's statesmanship, and even his rather tortuous diplomacy. Could any Italian city remain indefinitely the capital of an Italy with another state, even a tiny one, cutting it in the midst and a ruler who was there through the support of French bayonets? Could the turbulent people of Naples and Sicily work with a democratic constitution? "I will have no state of siege," Cavour said. "Anybody can govern with a state of siege."

Men of Piedmont used to say, "We have a government, a chamber, a constitution—and the name for it all is Cavour." In the illness that came upon him he was heard to murmur again and again, "No siege." He wanted his king to rule free men.

He hoped for two things: the application of democratic principles throughout Italy and the advent of a younger Pope who would consent to compromise, or rather to accept the principle of a free Church in a free state. Pius was old, he would soon die.

But it was Cavour who died, and his death seems to have been Elizabeth's own deathblow. Her husband, supported by medical opinion, had decided that she was too weak for the journey to France, and in a letter to Sarianna, written from Florence, she laments the decision and tells her of the new and more than personal blow she had just received: "I can scarcely command voice or hand to name *Cavour*. That great soul, which meditated and made Italy, has gone to the Diviner Country. If tears or blood could have saved him to us, he should have had mine."

This letter was posted on June 7. And on June 13 she wrote to Mrs. Story: "I have felt beaten and bruised ever since . . . there's a crêpe on the flag, and the joy is as flowers on graves."

On June 29, Elizabeth died after an illness so brief and so like her customary attacks as hardly to have aroused alarm. Browning had thought her stronger and better and had on the twenty-third rejoiced that they had not been "pleasantly travelling" when the frightening attack came on. "We went immediately to Florence," writes William Story, who with his wife so dearly loved both Brownings. Looking around the desolate familiar room, they read from her portfolio an unfinished letter, "for her dear Italy were her last aspirations. The death of Cavour had greatly affected her . . . perhaps . . . broke her down." The cycle was complete as Browning said, looking around the room: "here we came fifteen years ago, here Pen was born. . . . She used to walk up and down this verandah in the summer evenings. . . . We saw from these windows the return of the Austrians. . . ." They had, he felt looking back over the years, "been all the time walking over a torrent on a straw."

It was well he had these two to help him, and Isa Blagden, who always spoke of that July as her "apocalyptic" month. She gave the only comfort a friend can give by listening to the high poetic utterance alternating with a simply human cry of desolation in which Browning poured out his grief. I suppose it was the poet in both the Brownings that made them so singularly expressive, while both so often said that they could not speak.

But for the first few days Browning was stunned, only writing to his sister and father, a few broken words: "My own Sis; Papa—you know what this means—it is all over—I cannot say more—All unexpected, unintelligible, but with no pain, no knowledge of what was to be. . . .

Don't come, nor send, nor be anxious. I have Peny to live for and attend
to with her in him. I could not break this to you—I will write again."

Four days later he could write to George Barrett, and then to Fanny
Haworth, and to Forster.

George he asked to forgive him if there was any pain he could have
spared him in the telling, "though I am too stupid to tell how;" Elizabeth had been prostrated by Cavour's death, had partially recovered
and then caught cold; "the usual attack," she had said, "no worse"; and
when the doctor (a stranger) was grave, she had dismissed his fears:
"It's only the experience I've had in plenty—they don't understand."

It was not the first time Browning had sat up night after night
watching and waiting while his wife passed through some alarming
crisis of her mysterious illness, but his letter to George Barrett shows him
in that agony of self-questioning which comes always after a calamity.
He had felt so strongly an instinct of impending disaster as to watch
each night, while Elizabeth supposed he "slept on a sofa." The best
doctor in the district had stayed till morning at the beginning of the
attack, had indeed been alarmed, fearing an abscess of the lung, but had
left saying, "She is certainly better this evening." She had "washed her
face and combed her hair without the least assistance," eaten the jelly
offered her and "drunk a glass of lemonade, not a quarter of an hour
before the end."

All this he tells George, only "to be relieved of your just reproach"
had he kept silence in conscious realization of the danger he unreason-
ingly felt, "for I could explain away every ill symptom."

"She rose every day," he wrote to Forster, "sat in the drawing-room
till evening, and so we talked. . . ." They made plans for the future: "we
both of us conceived a sudden dislike for this poor Casa Guidi we had
been happy in so long. . . . Pen surmised something from the talk—he
went to bid her goodnight: 'Are you really better?' '*Much* better.' He
asked twice more and was twice so answered. . . . Then I sat there all
night. She slept a while with heavy troubled breathing and woke oppressed. At times she would wander a very little in her mind, through
the slightly increased doses of morphine acting on the weakness of her
body. I would say 'Do you know me'—'know *you*' (And then what I

can't write) 'And you know where you are?'—'Why—not quite!' 'And you *feel?*' 'Comfortable—much better.' Only once she said 'Our lives are held by God.' "

Each letter has its own special touches, though there is much of repetition. "At four o'clock," he told Fanny Haworth, "there were symptoms that alarmed me." He sent for the doctor and called the Italian maid, Annunciata. "She smiled as I proposed to bathe her feet 'Well, you *are* making an exaggerated case of it.' Then came what my heart will keep till I see her and longer—the most perfect expression of her love to me within my whole knowledge of her—always smilingly, happily, and with a face like a girl's—and in a few minutes she died in my arms, her head against my cheek. These incidents so sustain me that I tell them to her beloved ones as their right."

Annunciata had first seen the change and cried out, "The blessed soul has passed away."

"She went like God's child into His presence," Browning told Forster, "with no more apprehension or difficulty than *that!* Dr. Wilson came presently—it was daylight. He says he expected nothing so sudden . . . there could have been no help; there was no pain."

Notes

Notes

INTRODUCTION

1 The quotations from Henry James are taken from "Browning in Westminster Abbey" (*The Speaker*, January 4, 1891).

2 I have no doubt that in the vast mass of Browning literature instances can be found of some such wild statements. I am discussing serious criticism, but even this seems all too often to separate poet and thinker and to be seeking weaknesses instead of admiring power and beauty. An interesting book, *The Browning Critics*, has been edited recently by Professors Litzinger and Knickerbocker. In it some of the best criticism in dispraise and in praise of Browning has been collected—the praise being so selected and arranged as to follow and reply to the dispraise.

CHAPTER 1 *The Browning Family*

1 In every known generation of the Browning family the eldest son was called Robert. Confusion seems best avoided by calling the poet alone by the name he made famous, calling his father Mr. Browning, and identifying grandfather and great-grandfather as such on their rare appearances.

2 There is probably an allusion to Cyrus Mason's rather spiteful account of the Browning family in Mrs. Orr's biography of the poet. She feels it important to deny an "assertion" that any relative except his father had given the youthful Browning financial help. Mrs. Orr knew both the poet and his sister intimately. Browning for many years visited her twice a week. She had fuller access to the personal papers remaining in the family than any subsequent biographer. The Mason manuscript is at Baylor University.

3 Both Mrs. Miller and I learned all that can be learned about the Barrett and Tittle backgrounds from Jeannette Marks' book, *The Family of the Barrett*. Miss Marks talked with the grandson of Alfred Barrett (one of Elizabeth's younger brothers), still resident in Jamaica, and investigated both there and at St. Kitts all the available records.

CHAPTER 2 *The Boy Browning*

1 This poem, "Development," was written in Browning's old age and appears in *Asolando*.

2 Browning describes this episode to Richard Hengist Horne, writing from Florence in December, 1848. See *Letters of Robert Browning*.

CHAPTER 3 *Pauline*

1   The assertion, frequently made today, that Browning ran away from
competition at school and university
could not, I fancy, have been uttered within his living memory. For
(1) there is no evidence whatever
to support it; (2) it is so intrinsically
unlikely. The boy and young man
who knew Latin, Greek, and French
as well as he did (to say nothing of
English), and who possessed the
immense power of mind displayed
in *Pauline,* would hardly have
encountered fellow students with
whom he would have feared competition; (3) it is "out of character"
(as Macready said when he refused
to act a part). This I can only hope
to show in the course of my two volumes.

2   There is some conflict of opinion
between William Sharp (author
also of minor poetry under the name
of Fiona Macleod) and Mrs. Orr in
the accounts of Browning's boyhood. Sharp's biography came first,
appearing in 1890, Mrs. Orr's in
1891. She is indignant over the allusion to gypsies and tramps, declaring that at no time would
Browning have indulged in "low life
pleasures."

3   That Browning thought he had
unveiled the time of his darkness is
seen in the curious introductory passage from Cornelius Agrippa, with
its unwarranted hope that "a great
many people" would read the poem.
But "some will be dull in thought
and slow minded," others

actually hostile and unfavorable to my
way of thought . . . not Apollo or all the
Muses or an angel from heaven could
clear me of their execration. I advise such
people not to read what I have written, to
give no mind to it, to forget it: it is nox-
ious, poisonous: the mouth of Hell is in
this book, spewing forth rocks which
might smash their heads if they are not
careful.

But those of you who come to the reading in all fairness, if you display as much
soundness of judgment as bees in gathering honey, may read without fear. I think
you will gain some small profit and much
pleasure. . . . If I on any matter have
spoken too freely, make allowance for my
youth: I was barely grown-up when I
composed the work. . . .

Cornelius Agrippa, an occult
philosopher of the sixteenth century, was also a magician reputed
to be able to cause an evil spirit to
enter and apparently resuscitate a
corpse. Himself companioned by a
devil in the shape of a black dog he
dismissed it on his deathbed crying,
"Begone evil beast, you have utterly
destroyed me."

4   Richard Garnett's *Life of W. J.
Fox* tells the story of Fox's ministry,
his journalism, his marriage and his
love for Eliza Flower. A charming
description of the Flower-Fox household is given by Mrs. Miller in
Robert Browning: A Portrait.

5   Caroline Fox had no connection
with W. J. Fox. A young Quaker
from the country, she describes in
Memories of Old Friends visiting
London, meeting Mill, hearing Carlyle lecture.

6   The copy of *Pauline* annotated by
Mill, with Browning's answers, is in
the Victoria and Albert Museum,
London.

Further books illustrating this
period of Browning's life are *Carlyle's Life in London,* edited by J. A.
Froude; *Necessary Evil: The Life
of Jane Welsh Carlyle* by Laurence
and Elizabeth Hanson; Harriet Martineau's *Autobiography;* and *John
Stuart Mill* by Michael St. John
Packe.

CHAPTER 4 *Paracelsus*

1 Autograph letters. University of Texas.

2 Edmund Gosse in *Personalia* is illuminating on his conversation with the aged Browning about this period of his youth.

    I cannot discover how Browning knew Benkhausen. He destroyed his early letters to his family, so we depend for the account of the Russian journey on the memory of his sister, Sarianna, whom Professor Hall Griffin saw frequently while he was writing about her brother. The vivid descriptions are borne out by Browning's poem, "Ivan Ivanovitch." Mrs. Bronson has told us about Browning and Prince Gagarin ("Browning in Venice," *Cornhill*, 1902).

3 Comte Amédée de Ripert-Monclar, to whom *Paracelsus* was dedicated, had become known to Browning through his half-uncle, William Shergold Browning, of Rothschild's bank in Paris. The count was a sort of unofficial representative of the French Royalists to the exiles in England. A number of Browning's letters to him have recently been discovered, but it is highly tantalizing that until they have been edited and published, a sight of them has been refused me.

4 From "An Epistle Containing the Strange Medical Experience of Karshish, the Arab Physician."

5 *Robert Browning and Julia Wedgwood, A Broken Friendship as Revealed by Their Letters* is chiefly valuable for Browning's later life, but contains also, like Gosse's *Personalia*, some of his own memories of youth.

6 In *Browning: Background and Conflict*, a very useful study of the poet's thought and critical reactions.

7 Mrs. Orr gives the letter to Fox in full. It is dated April 16, 1835.

CHAPTER 5 *Browning and Macready*

1 Autograph letter. Wellesley College collection.

2 It has seemed best in the tangled story of Browning's plays to let Macready have his say as fully as possible. His fascinating 800-page journal is contemporary—and I have used other contemporary records rather than relying on Browning's memory, which in old age was notoriously inaccurate.

    Of the quality of Browning's plays there are obviously two opinions—and also of the degree of their failure. For a more favorable one than I have given of either I suggest that the reader examine the plays, and read also the Griffin-Minchin biography (recently reissued in a new edition) particularly in relation to *Strafford*. It was called in the *Constitutional* (probably by Douglas Jerrold) a "noble tragedy," but after four days' success there followed a chapter of accidents: Vandenhoff, acting Pym, was offered an engagement in the States and withdrew with no notice. Instead of a replacement (were there no understudies in those days?) another play *Walter Tyrrel* was put on—a "scarecrow tragedy," with forest scenes, blue fire, moonlight effects—was vehemently applauded, and followed by a series of benefits chosen by the actors, only one of whom chose *Strafford*. This was its end— and the critics in the main had condemned it. But one hardly realizes from the Journal all the elements against which legitimate theater had to contend: live lions on the stage, a coach and six horses, a Burmese chariot drawn by Burmese bulls, followed by elephants, ostriches, circus riders on their horses—besides the exciting blue fire that had cut short Browning's play. Circus, pantomime, and drama were all crowded onto the early Victorian stage and badly needed sorting out.

3 Arnould's letter to Domett is printed in *Robert Browning and Alfred Domett* (p. 64).

4 This letter is in *New Letters of Robert Browning*.

CHAPTER 6 *Sordello into Suspense*

1 Ezra Pound in *The A. B. C. of Reading* selects Browning and Landor among the handful of poets he deals with. But more emphatically does he stress Chaucer (to whom Landor likened Browning), and the poet Sordello. "I see every reason," he says, "for studying Provençal verse." And "There was a period when the English lyric quality, the juncture of note and melody was very high. But to gauge that height, knowledge of Provence is extremely useful."

This, as well as the modern emphasis on Browning's own revelations in *Sordello* of his views on the poet's art, should always be borne in mind.

2 Undated in *New Letters of Robert Browning*, p. 18.

Carlyle is one of the most important figures in Browning's life and will reappear in Volume II. See especially *Letters to John Stuart Mill, John Sterling and Robert Browning*, and "Correspondence between Thomas Carlyle and Robert Browning," *Cornhill* magazine, May, 1915.

3 Autograph letter. University of Texas.

4 Mrs. Bridell-Fox wrote two sketches of her youthful memories: "Robert Browning," in *Argosy* magazine, February, 1890, and "Memories," in *The Girls' Own Paper*, July 19, 1890.

5 Moncure Daniel Conway was an American who succeeded Fox as minister at South Place. He fought for abolition in his own country despite his heritage of land and slaves in the South. He went gradually from a liberal Christianity, through Unitarianism, into free thought, and wrote an Autobiography from which the quotation is taken and in which he records Browning's expressions of faith, interpreting them as furious efforts to maintain an impossible position.

6 For Browning's feelings of perplexity and discouragement during this period see *Robert Browning and Alfred Domett*, from which the quotations are taken.

7 Told vividly in Garnett's *Life of Fox*.

CHAPTER 7 *Elizabeth Barrett*

1 The unpublished letters quoted in this chapter are in the Berg Collection—and also a copy of that rare volume: *Elizabeth Barrett Browning, Poems and Stories, with an Inedited Autobiography*.

2 Elizabeth's anguish is interpreted by Mrs. Miller as a haunting knowledge that she had wished for her brother's death: there was "a hidden rivalry buried so deep that she was ready to deny its existence"; the slain "familiar" was Bro.

Any imaginary horror is, of course, possible in a dream, especially if opium-induced. The psalmist speaks for all humans of "the terror of the night . . . the pestilence that stalks in the darkness." And that terror may well be of the dark world inside the self. But it is the torment, *not* the revelation, of a person. Elizabeth had loved her brother supremely; she had offered what money she had to facilitate his marriage, but she felt that her near-idolatry, keeping him at her side, had caused his death. Is Mrs. Miller's sinister interpretation of a nightmare necessary to account for her abiding grief?

3 See *Elizabeth Barrett to Miss Mitford,* edited by Betty Miller.

CHAPTER 8 *Robert and Elizabeth*

1 Santayana's "Poetry of Barbarism" can be found in his *Essays in Literary Criticism.* But the essence of his treatment of Browning is included in *Robert Browning: A Collection of Critical Essays* edited by Philip Drew, London 1966. Edwin Muir's essay is in the same book. Hoxie Fairchild's remarks are taken from his *Religious Trends in English Poetry.*

2 From Kenyon Typescript (British Museum), a copy of all the letters contained in Kenyon's *Letters of Elizabeth Barrett Browning—and* some letters and passages that he eventually decided not to print.

3 *The Letters of Robert Browning and Elizabeth Barrett Browning 1845–1846* were published in 1898. Robert Barrett Browning (Pen) their only son, thought "the correspondence should be given in its entirety." The book is almost unedited, has been reprinted several times, and is now very rare. I have used the pocket edition of 1913.

4 Leslie Stephen's remark is taken from *Studies of a Biographer* in

which he has many penetrating things to say of Browning.

5 See "New Light on the Brownings" by Edward Snyder and Frederick Palmer (*Quarterly Review* 1937).

6 Kenyon Typescript.

CHAPTER 9 *One Winter and Then ...*

1 Autograph letter. Wellesley College Library.

2 See *Letters of Elizabeth Barrett to B. R. Haydon.* Elizabeth Barrett was a sensitive as well as a brilliant letter writer; she never failed to sympathize with her correspondents. Although in these letters she tried to cure Haydon of his attitude of mistrust and suspicion, she also gave him some reason to hope that her admiration for his writing might overcome her objections to his attitudes—that she might really edit his book.

3 After writing this I realized that I must have unconsciously borrowed from Chesterton whose use of the same line from *Clive* I had forgotten.

CHAPTER 10 *Married in Italy*

1 Mrs. Jameson's letters are in The Pierpont Morgan Library, New York, but a great part of them have been printed in "From Paris to Pisa with the Brownings," *New Colophon,* 1950.

2 The daily life of the two poets in Italy is immensely documented, chiefly by Elizabeth. Only a small proportion of Robert's *Collected Letters, New Letters,* and *Dearest Isa* cover the years before his wife's death—besides those published in other people's writings, *e.g.,* Wil-

liam Allingham and Harriet Hosmer, or scattered unpublished in libraries. Moreover Elizabeth was as much his superior in prose as he was hers in poetry. The letters to Arabel in the Berg Collection, the canceled letters and passages in the Kenyon typescript, usefully and more intimately supplement the many volumes of her collected letters (for which see the Bibliography) She gives an immensely vivid picture. The great mass of surviving Browning letters belong to the years after his wife's death.

CHAPTER 11   *Italian Background*

For notes on this see Chapter 19.

CHAPTER 12
Life, Death and Danger

1 Browning's comments are quoted from a book entitled *From Robert and Elizabeth Browning: A Further Selection of the Barrett-Browning Family Correspondence.* Introduction and Notes by William Rose Benet. The book is of small importance and may be regarded as a supplement to *Letters to Her Sister* which with the Kenyon Collection (published and unpublished) are the chief sources for this chapter.
2 Kenyon Typescript.
3 Kenyon Typescript.
4 The first edition of *Sonnets from the Portuguese* appeared in 1850. But in 1894 Edmund Gosse spoke of a small private edition printed at Reading in 1847 and edited by Miss Mitford. Gosse said that Browning had "made a statement *to a friend,*" telling with vivid detail how Elizabeth had first shown him the sonnets at Pisa! Wise, the fa-

mous bibliographer, making this private edition known, spoke of Browning having told the story to *Gosse.* This sheer invention by Wise has led to endless discussion—the conclusion usually reached being that of an astonishing failure in Browning's memory or a hardly less surprising confusion on the part of Gosse.

Finally the Reading edition of *Sonnets from the Portuguese* itself came into question among a growing collection of modern first editions. Hall Griffin pays warm acknowledgement to Wise, De Vane calls his the "standard" bibligraphy of Browning's work "in spite of the inclusion of forgeries." Wise (with Nicoll) compiled the admirable *Literary Anecdotes of the Nineteenth Century.* To him we owe the great Ashley Collection at the British Museum. Yet, when doubt was cast on pamphlets in Wise's list claimed as first editions of Ruskin, Tennyson, Morris, Swinburne, both Brownings, etc., it seemed to John Carter and Graham Pollard important to investigate. Their findings are related in *An Enquiry into the Nature of Certain Nineteenth Century Pamphlets* (published in London and New York 1934).

The two most obvious lines were an examination of the paper and the type—and this alone was, as concerned the *Sonnets,* sufficiently convincing. Neither paper nor type were of a kind used before 1860. No history of any of these pamphlets could be traced back behind 1890. They were *too* clean, *too* unmarked, and uninscribed. Shocked at first by Wise's carelessness in not making such inquiries as "commonsense, let alone bibliographical duty, plainly demanded," they became more shocked by the fact that Wise had "engaged his full powers as bibliographer and authoritative collector in the establishing of his finds."

It looked increasingly as though all these forgeries came from the same hand. But with the Reading edition of *Sonnets from the Portuguese* a climax was reached: "we can," they said, "trace no alternative source than Wise for any copies of this forgery."

The great bibliographer was himself responsible for the forgeries.

5 The three above quotations are from the Kenyon Typescript.

CHAPTER 13
Christmas-Eve and Easter-Day

These poems, at the peak of Browning's religious thought, have been surprisingly little analyzed. Using different terms he and Newman a century ahead of their age are thinking along the same lines, are approaching the supreme Reality in the same fashion, not by a process of verbal ratiocination but by an act of the whole being. A discussion of any modification in his position belongs to my second volume.

J. Hillis Miller in *The Disappearance of God* gives a brilliant sketch of the universality of Browning's poetry and a comment on the contrast between his approach and that of other Victorians. "Only in Browning," he says, "of the writers studied here, are there hints and anticipations of that recovery of immanence which was to be the inner drama of twentieth century literature . . . being and value lie in *this* world, in what is immediate, tangible, present to man in earth, sun, sea, in the stars in their courses, and in what Yeats was to call 'the

foul rag and bone shop of the heart.' " Yet fascinatingly, when "Anima" is surely at work, Miller can only see Browning "stretched on the rack of a fading transcendentalism" reaching "a precarious unity only by the most extravagant stratagems of the spirit." But Browning's is the Christian God, at once immanent and transcendent.

While the force of *Christmas-Eve and Easter-Day* can be conveyed only by a great deal of quotation, it is quite peculiarly difficult to quote. Besides an amount of punctuation that would today be unusual, Browning puts in quotation marks thoughts belonging to *the time of the Experiences* and, in " Easter Day," one side of the long arguments which I believe to be the expression of two elements in himself. Also in quotation marks are the words spoken by the supernatural voice. To a lesser degree this problem of quotation recurs elsewhere in Browning's poetry.

2 See Chapter VI for a discussion of the conception of Anima and Animus. The theme has been developed by Henri Bremond, Paul Claudel, and E. I. Watkin.

CHAPTER 14   *Two Checkered Years*

1 See *Letters of Owen Meredith to Robert and Elizabeth Browning.*

2 Browning and Carlyle are apt to speak constantly of and to one another—probably both felt and enjoyed what Carlyle called the "curious difference" between his own gloom and Browning's cheerfulness. He gives a delightful picture in the volume published as *Last Words of Thomas Carlyle* (which covers this visit to Paris), and the corrspond-

ence between them was collected in an article by Alexander Carlyle in *The Cornhill* for May, 1915. Other letters are in the volumes *Letters to John Stuart Mill, John Sterling and Robert Browning* and in *New Letters of Thomas Carlyle*.

3 *The Times* of July 2, 1852 reporting COURT OF QUEEN'S BENCH Thursday, July 1 (Sittings at Nisi Prius at Guildhall, before Lord Campbell and a Special Jury, Von Müller v. Browning).

4 Apart from the unpublished letters to Arabel these two years are best reflected in *The Letters of Elizabeth Barrett Browning*, edited by Frederic G. Kenyon from which most of the quotations in this chapter are taken.

CHAPTER 15
An Anglo-American Circle

1 This entertaining group of friends and the atmosphere in which they lived can be caught in many books of the period—available in libraries even if, sadly, so often out of print. Perhaps first comes Henry James' *William Wetmore Story*; but the gossiping of Anne Thackeray Ritchie in *Records of Tennyson, Ruskin and Browning*, the *Letters to William Allingham* and Allingham's *Diary*, the memories of all three Hawthornes, Harriet Hosmer *Letters and Memories*, and *Letters from Owen Meredith to Robert and Elizabeth Browning*—all these make delightful reading. Above all, of course, are the collected *Letters of Elizabeth Barrett Browning*, and her letters to her sister Henrietta. (See bibliography for full titles.) A more recent book is *Browning to his American Friends*, edited with an

excellent introduction by Gertrude Reese Hudson. This book, however, belongs in great part to my second volume.

2 The letter to Milsand is quoted in the Griffin-Minchin biography, that to Forster is in *New Letters of Robert Browning*.

3 *Letters from Owen Meredith.*

4 *Letters of Elizabeth Barrett Browning*. A strange letter to Mrs. Jameson of February 24, 1855, calling such work as nursing a "retrograde" step in the question of women's rights.

CHAPTER 16   *Men and Women*

1 One or two critics, however, see Browning as Andrea—*kept from the fulfilment of his genius* by his *too*-religious wife, as earlier by his mother. I suppose the basic disagreement lies between their view and that of those who hold with Rossetti, Carlyle, Swinburne, André Gide, Ezra Pound, Robert Lowell, and others of their quality, that his was a genius richly fulfilled, ranking him as Landor claimed close to Chaucer.

2 This is Mrs. Miller's view of the poem. In his very interesting book *Amphibian* H. C. Duffin analyses in a long Appendix his reasons for calling her *Robert Browning: A Portrait* a "perverse book . . . it sets out to debunk, to denigrate and manipulates material to that end . . . chooses facts and omits others . . . a number of minute but significant distortions."

An unpublished letter of this period in the Kenyon typescript, quoted by Mrs. Miller, is one of Mr. Duffin's pieces of supporting evidence. Writing to Fanny Haworth, Elizabeth sympathises with a friend whose marriage has gone wrong: "Tell me if your friend recovers her dreams again. I can conceive of a strong attachment recovering from the shock of unexpected points of difference, and of two souls growing together after all." This Mrs. Miller calls "significant" in relation to Elizabeth's own feelings. But she does not quote the sentence with which the letter ends "You are right. There is poetry in my life—the ideal overflowed into life when I least hoped for it. But there is always poetry in life—is there not?—where there is love."

3 See *The A. B. C. of Readng.*

4 Oscar Wilde in *"The Critic as Artist."*

But Yeats comments: "Browning says that he could not write a successful play because interested not in character in action but in action in character."

Yeats himself needed "in lyric or in dramatic poetry, in some sense character in action; a pause in the midst of action perhaps, but action always its end and theme." (Quoted from *Essays and Introductions*, Clarendon Press, 1965, p. 530.)

5 See *The Poetry of Experience.*

6 See *Robert Browning: a Collection of Critical Essays.*

CHAPTER 17 *Conviction So Like Despair*

1 All letters to Harriet Hosmer are taken from her book *Letters and Memories.*

2 Henry James *The Middle Years*, pp. 104–6.

3 Browning described with some disgust how Home, a rather large young man, behaved with his host and hostess like a fond child "kissing

them abundantly." Mrs. Miller sees his disgust as arising from the caricature this presented of his own attitude to his parents. She sees a similar resemblance in the medium's cheating and the poet's "confidence trick." There is no evidence that Browning's behavior to his parents—even as a child—was other than that of any Victorian son. Kissing, says his cousin, was infrequent with him. Mrs. Miller's misreading of *Pauline* explains the theory that Browning himself is speaking through the mouth of Mr. Studge the Medium and that a sense of "the loss of his own integrity" is visible in his revulsion from Home.

4 The letters to Edward Chapman are in *New Letters of Robert Browning.*

5 *Letters to William Allingham.* It is a pity that these, the Ruskin and Hosmer letters are in no Browning collection.

6 In W. G. Collingwood, *Life and Work of Ruskin.*

7 Printed for private circulation by Baylor University. One hesitates to recommend for further reading Ruskin's Works in thirty-six volumes! But the volumes are admirably indexed and delightful to browse in. An excellent biography is *Ruskin the Great Victorian*, by Derrick Leon.

8 Unpublished letter. Baylor University.

9 In *Letters of Thomas Carlyle to John Stuart Mill, John Sterling and Robert Browning.*

CHAPTER 18 *Friends, Family and Frustration*

1 The most illuminating reading for this chapter is *Dearest Isa*, a collection of Browning's letters to Isabella

Blagden. Only thirty-nine out of the hundred and fifty-four letters belong to the period before Elizabeth's death, but they are of prime importance through their detailing of Browning's day-to-day life with its cares and anxieties from 1857 to 1861. Both husband and wife wrote constantly to Isa, and the quotations in this chapter are taken from *Dearest Isa.*

2   Kenyon Typescript, August 10, 1858.

3   *Letters to Her Sister,* August 15, 1857.

4   *Letters of Robert Browning,* October 6, 1857.

5   Diary of William Allingham. Thackeray was then editor of the *Cornhill Magazine.*

6   Kenyon Typescript. Letter to Mrs. Martin, December 29, 1859.

CHAPTER 19
The Pope, Napoleon, and the Rest

1   Considerations of space have obliged me to deal too briefly with the whole Italian background—above all with the fascinating figures of the leading characters. Hales's *Pio Nono,* Albert Guérard's *Napoleon III,* Trevelyan's *Garibaldi and the Thousand* are all fascinating reading. Although there are more recent books, Trevelyan's three still remain the most vivid record of the period. *The Leopard* by Lampedusa, although dealing with a later generation helps to explain the very real problem of an Italy historically and

ethnically so various as to have made Napoleon III as well as Pio Nono desire a federation of states rather than a unity dominated by a single one. These books also help us to a further understanding of why Browning was reluctant to set down anything approximating to a newspaper day-to-day commentary. My second volume will contain a further treatment of *Prince Hohenstiel-Schwangau.*

2   Henry James, *William Wetmore Story* and *Autobiography.*

3   See Lilian Whiting, *Kate Field: A Record,* and J. Forster, *Walter Savage Landor.* Also, for Landor's now underrated poetry, see Ezra Pound, *The A. B. C. of Reading.*

4   The quotation is from *The Poetry of Experience.* Note also the two recent volumes of essays collected by Doctors Litzinger and Knickerbocker and by Philip Drew (see Bibliography).

CHAPTER 20
Mr. Sludge and Mrs. Eckley

1   See *Browning and His American Friends* for his feelings about Mrs. Eckley expressed in his letters to William Wetmore Story.

2   Kenyon Typescript, May 10, 1860.

3   This letter of Browning's is not in any of his collected volumes. It was written to Miss de Gaudrion and is quoted in *The Family of the Barrett.* On the main subject of this chapter see Katharine Porter's *Spiritualism in the Browning Circle.*

Selective Bibliography

Selective Bibliography

THE Broughton-Northup-Pearson Browning Bibliography, with its supplement, lists under "Biography and Criticism" close to five thousand items, of which I do not claim to have read a quarter. Of those I have looked at some are entirely worthless, others more valuable than I had anticipated. There is, too, an indispensable minimum of reading about the world which surrounded Robert and Elizabeth Browning and the men and women who influenced them.

I have listed here, helpfully, I hope, for the student, a selection of books and articles covering the first half of Robert Browning's long life. There will be another bibliography for Vol. II.

WORKS OF ROBERT BROWNING

Essay on Chatterton. Edited by Donald Smalley. Harvard University Press, 1948.
An Essay on Percy Bysshe Shelley. Published for the Shelley Society by Reeves and Turner, 1888.
The Poetical Works of Robert Browning. John Murray, 1951. (First definitive edition Smith, Elder, 1896.)

BIOGRAPHIES

Browning, Elizabeth Barrett, Hitherto Unpublished Poems and Stories with an *Inedited Autobiography*. Boston, Bibliophile Society, 1914.
Burdett, Osbert, *The Brownings*. Constable, 1928.
Chesterton, G. K., *Robert Browning*. English Men of Letter Series, Macmillan, 1903.
Dowden, Edward, *The Life of Robert Browning*. Everyman's Library, J. M. Dent, 1904.

Griffin, W. Hall, and Minchin, H. C., *The Life of Robert Browning. With Notices of His Writings, His Family, and His Friends* (revised edition). Archon Books, 1966.

Hewlett, Dorothy, *Elizabeth Barrett Browning: A Life*. Knopf, 1952.

Hovelaque, Henri Léon, *La Jeunesse de Robert Browning*. Paris, Les Presses Modernes, 1932.

Miller, Betty, *Robert Browning: A Portrait*. John Murray, 1952.

Orr, Mrs. Sutherland, *Life and Letters of Robert Browning* (1891). New edition, revised and in part rewritten by Frederic G. Kenyon. John Murray, 1908.

Sharp, William, *Life of Robert Browning*. Walter Scott, 1890.

Taplin, Gardner B., *The Life of Elizabeth Barrett Browning*. John Murray, 1957.

Whiting, Lilian, *The Brownings: Their Life and Art*. Little Brown, 1911.

LETTERS

The Letters of Robert Browning and Elizabeth Barrett Barrett. Smith, Elder, 1899.

Robert Browning and Alfred Domett. Edited by Frederic A. Kenyon. Smith, Elder, 1906.

Letters of Robert Browning. Collected by Thomas J. Wise. Edited with an Introduction and Notes by Thurman L. Hood. Yale University Press, 1933.

Robert Browning and Julia Wedgwood. A Broken Friendship as Revealed in Their Letters. Edited by Richard Curle. John Murray and Jonathan Cape, 1937.

New Letters of Robert Browning. Edited with Introduction and Notes by William Clyde de Vane and Kenneth Leslie Knickerbocker. John Murray, 1951.

Dearest Isa: Robert Browning's Letters to Isabella Blagden. Edited by Edward C. McAleer. University of Texas Press, 1951.

Browning to His American Friends: Letters Between the Brownings, the Storys, and James Russell Lowell (1841–1890). Barnes and Noble, 1965.

Learned Lady: Letters from Robert Browning to Mrs. Thomas Fitzgerald 1876–1889. Edited by Edward C. McAleer. Harvard University Press, 1966.

From Robert and Elizabeth Browning: A Further Selection of the Barrett-Browning Family Correspondence. Introduction and Notes by William Rose Benét. John Murray, 1936.

Letters of the Brownings to George Barrett. Edited by Paul Landis. University of Illinois Press, 1958.

Letters of Elizabeth Barrett Browning Addressed to Richard Hengist Horne. With Comments on Contemporaries. Edited by S. R. Townshend Mayer. Richard Bentley, 1877.

The Letters of Elizabeth Barrett Browning. Edited with biographical additions by Frederic G. Kenyon. Smith, Elder, 1898.

Elizabeth Barrett Browning: Letters to Her Sister, 1846–1859. Edited by Leonard Huxley. John Murray, 1929.

Letters from Elizabeth Barrett to B. R. Haydon. Edited by Martha Hale Shackford. Oxford University Press, 1939.

Elizabeth Barrett to Miss Mitford. Edited by Betty Miller. Yale University Press, 1954.

GENERAL

(a) Books.

Adams, Sarah Flower, *Vivia Perpetua.* With a Memoir of the Author by E. Bridell Fox. Privately printed, 1893.

Allingham, Helen, and Williams, E. B. editors. *Letters to William Allingham.* Longmans, 1911.

Allingham, William, *A Diary.* Edited by H. Allingham and D. Radford. Macmillan, 1907.

Bates, Gerardine (Mrs. R. MacPherson), *Memoirs of the Life of Anna Jameson by Her Niece.* Boston, Roberts Brothers, 1878.

CARLYLE, THOMAS
  Last Words of ——, Longman's, 1892.
  Letters of —— *to John Stuart Mill, John Sterling and Robert Browning.* Edited by Alexander Carlyle. Stokes, 1923.
  New Letters of ——. Edited by Alexander Carlyle. John Lane, 1904.
  Reminiscences of ——. Edited by J. A. Froude. London, 1887.

Carr, J. Comyns, *Some Eminent Victorians.* Duckworth, 1908.

Carter, John, and Pollard, Graham. *An Enquiry into the Nature of Certain Nineteenth-Century Pamphlets.* Scribner's, 1934.

Clarke, Helen Archibald, *Browning's Italy: A Study of Italian Life and Art in Browning.* Baker Taylor Co., 1907.

Chesterton, G. K., *A Handful of Authors.* Sheed and Ward, 1953.

Clough, Arthur Hugh, *Correspondence of* ——. Edited by F. L. Mulhausen. Oxford, 1957.

Cobbe, Frances Power, *Life of* ——. Houghton Mifflin, 1894.

Collingwood, W. G., *Life and Works of Ruskin.* Methuen, 1893.

Conway, Moncure Daniel, *Autobiography, Memoirs, and Experiences.* Cassell, 1904.

Corkran, Henriette, *Celebrities and I.* Hutchinson, 1905.

Crosse, Cornelia, *Red-Letter Days of My Life*. Richard Bentley, 1892.

De Vane, William Clyde, *A Browning Handbook*. Second Edition. Appleton-Century-Croft, 1955.

——, *Browning's Parleyings: The Autobiography of a Mind*. Yale University Press, 1927.

Dowden, Edward, *The Life of Percy Bysshe Shelley*. Revised Edition, Kegan, Paul, 1896.

Drew, Philip (Edited). *Robert Browning: A Collection of Essays*. Methuen, 1966.

Duckworth, F. K. G., *Browning—Background and Conflict*. Ernest Benn, 1931.

Duffin, Henry Charles, *Amphibian: A Reconsideration of Browning*. Bowes & Bowes, 1956.

Duffy, Sir Charles Gavan, *Conversations with Carlyle*. Low, 1892.

Elwin, Malcolm, *Walter Savage Landor*. Macmillan, 1841.

Fairchild, Hoxie Neale, *Religious Trends in English Poetry, Volume IV*, Columbia University Press, 1957.

Fox, Caroline, *Memories of Old Friends*. Smith, Elder, 1882.

Fraser, Mrs. Hugh, *A Diplomat's Wife in Many Lands*. Dodd, Mead, 1913.

Froude, James Anthony, *Thomas Carlyle: Story of His Life in London 1834–1881*. Longmans, 1919.

Garnett, Richard, *The Life of W. J. Fox*. John Lane, 1910.

Gosse, Edmund, *Robert Browning: Personalia*. Fisher Unwin, 1890.

Guérard, Albert, *Napoleon III*. Howard University Press, 1943.

Hales, E. E. Y., *Pio Nono*. P. J. Kenedy, 1954.

Hanson, Lawrence and Elizabeth, *Necessary Evil: The Life of Jane Welsh Carlyle*. Macmillan, 1952.

Hare, Augustus, *The Story of My Life*. G. Allen, 1896.

Hawthorne, Julian, *Shapes That Pass*. Houghton, Mifflin, 1928.

Hawthorne, Nathaniel, *French and Italian Notebooks*. Strahan, 1871.

——, *Passages from English Notebooks*. Fields, Osgood, 1870.

Holloway, John, *The Victorian Sage*. Macmillan, 1953.

Home, Daniel Dunglas, *Incidents in My Life*. Longmans, 1871.

Horne, R. H., *A New Spirit of the Age*. Smith, Elder, 1844.

Hosmer, Harriet, *Letters and Memories*. Edited by Cornelia Carr. Moffat, Yard, 1912.

James, Henry, *Essays in London and Elsewhere*. Harper, 1893.

——, *The Private Life and Other Tales*. Harper, 1893.

——, *William Wetmore Story and His Friends*. Blackwood, 1903.

——, *Italian Hours*. Heinemann, 1909.

——, *The Middle Years*. Scribner's, 1917.

——, *Autobiography*. Scribner's, 1917.

Jones, Sir Henry, *Browning as a Philosopher and Religious Teacher*. Macmillan, 1891.

Kenyon, F. G., *Robert Browning and Alfred Domett*. Smith, Elder, 1906.

King, Roma, Jr., *The Bow and the Lyre: The Art of Robert Browning*. University of Michigan Press, 1957.

Knight, W. A., *Retrospects*. Smith, Elder, 1904.

Langbaum, Robert, *The Poetry of Experience*. Chatto and Windus, 1957.

Leon, Derrick, *Ruskin the Great Victorian*. Routledge and Kegan Paul, 1949.

Litzinger, Boyd, and Knickerbocker, K. L., *The Browning Critics*. University of Kentucky Press, 1965.

Lounsbury, T. R., *The Early Literary Career of Robert Browning*. Scribner's, 1911.

Lubbock, Percy, *Elizabeth Barrett Browning in Her Letters*. Smith, Elder, 1906.

Macpherson, Mrs. R. *See* Bates.

Macready, William Charles, *Diaries 1833–1851*. Edited by William Toynbee. Chapman and Hall, 1912.

Marks, Jeannette, *The Family of the Barretts: A Colonial Romance*. Macmillan, 1938.

Marriott, J. A. R., *The Makers of Modern Italy: Mazzini, Cavour, Garibaldi*. Clarendon, 1895.

Matthiessen, F. O., *The James Family*. Knopf, 1947.

Meredith, Owen (Lytton, E. Robert Bulwer), *Letters to Robert and Elizabeth Browning*. Edited by Aurelia B. Harlan and J. Lee Harlan, Jr. Baylor Browning Interests, 1936.

Mill, John Stuart, *Autobiography*. Columbia University Press, 1924.

Miller, J. Hillis, *The Disappearance of God*. Harvard University Press, 1963.

Minchin, H. C., *Walter Savage Landor: Last Days, Letters and Conversations*. Methuen, 1934.

Nicoll, Sir William Robertson, and Wise, Thomas, *Literary Anecdotes of the Nineteenth Century, Vol. I*. Dodd Mead, 1896.

Orr, Mrs. Sutherland, *A Handbook to the Works of Robert Browning*. Bell, 1885.

Packe, Michael St. John, *The Life of John Stuart Mill*. Secker and Warburg, 1954.

Pastor, Ludwig von, *History of the Popes. Volume XXXII*. J. Hodges, 1940.

Pearson, Hesketh, *Dickens, His Character, Comedy and Career*. Harper, 1949.

Porter, Katharine H., *Spiritualism in the Browning Circle*. University of Kansas Press, 1958.

Pottle, F. A., *Shelley and Browning: A Myth and Some Facts*. Pembroke Press, 1923.

Pound, Ezra, *The A.B.C. of Reading*. New Directions, 1960.

Quarles, Francis, *Emblemes Divine and Moral*. T. Tegg, 1845.

Ray, Gordon N., *Thackeray: The Age of Wisdom*. Oxford University Press, 1908.

Renton, R., *John Forster and His Friendships*. Chapman and Hall, 1912.

Ritchie, Anne Thackeray, *Records of Tennyson, Ruskin and Browning*. Harper, 1892.

————, *From Friend to Friend*. Murray, 1919.

Rossetti, William Michael, *Some Reminiscences*. Scribner's, 1906.

————, *Rossetti Papers, 1862–70*. Sands, 1903.

————, *Pre-Raphaelite Diaries and Letters*. Hurst & Blackett, 1900.

Rudman, H. W., *Italian Nationalism and English Letters: The Risorgimento and Victorian Men of Letters*. Columbia University Press, 1940.

Saintsbury, G., *Corrected Impressions*. Dodd Mead, 1895.

————, *History of English Prosody, Vol. III*. Macmillan, 1906.

Santayana, George, *The Poetry of Barbarism*. Scribner's, 1900.

Sotheby's Catalogue, "The Browning Collections," 1913.

Steegmuller, Francis, *The Two Lives of James Jackson Jarves*. Yale University Press, 1951.

Super, R. H., *Walter Savage Landor: A Biography*. New York University Press, 1954.

Symons, Arthur, *An Introduction to the Study of Browning*. Revised edition. J. M. Dent, 1906.

Trevelyan, George Macaulay, *Garibaldi and the Thousand*. Longmans, 1948.

————, *Garibaldi and the Making of Italy*. Longmans, 1948.

Untermeyer, Louis, *Makers of the Modern World*. Simon and Schuster, 1955.

Wanley, Nathaniel, *The Wonders of the Little World*. T. Basset, 1678.

Whiting, Lilian, *Kate Field: A Record*. Little Brown, 1899.

Whitla, William, *The Central Truth: The Incarnation in Browning's Poetry*. Toronto, 1953.

Wilde, Oscar, "The Critic as Artist" in *The Writings of Oscar Wilde*. New Lamb Publishing Company, 1909.

Woodham-Smith, Cecil, *Florence Nightingale*. McGraw-Hill, 1951.

Woolf, Virginia, *Flush: A Biography*. Harcourt, Brace, 1933.

Woolner, Amy (editor), *Thomas Woolner, His Life in Letters*. Chapman & Hall, 1917.

(b) *Articles.*

————, "Robert Browning at College," *New York Times*, December 31, 1960.

Baddely, Sir Vincent, "The Ancestry of Robert Browning," *Genealogists' Magazine*, March, 1938.

Boyce, G. K., "From Paris to Pisa with the Brownings." *New Colophon,* 1950.

Carlyle, Alexander, "Correspondence between Thomas Carlyle and Robert Browning," *Cornhill,* May, 1915.

Fairchild, Hoxie Neale, "Browning the Simple-Hearted Casuist," *University of Toronto Quarterly,* April, 1949.

Field, Kate, "Elizabeth Barrett Browning," *Atlantic,* September 1861.

Fox, E. Bridell, "Robert Browning," *Argosy,* 1890.

———, "Memories," *Girls' Own Annual,* 1890.

Furnivall, F. J., "Browning's Footman Ancestor," *Academy,* April 12, 1902.

Gosse, Edmund, "Edmund Gosse on Browning," *The Critic,* March 14, 1896.

Hudson, Gertrude Reese, *Robert Browning and His Son.* Publications of Modern Language Association, 1946.

Huxley, Leonard, "A Visitor to the Brownings at Casa Guidi from material supplied by O. S. Holt," *Cornhill,* January, 1924.

James, Henry, "Browning in Westminster Abbey," *Speaker,* January 4, 1891.

Kinney, Mrs. Elizabeth C. L., "A Day with the Brownings at Pratolino," *Scribner's Monthly,* December, 1870.

———, Italian Reminiscences, edited by Laura Stedman and G. J. Gould "With the Brownings at Florence," *Neal's Monthly,* January, 1913.

Miller, Betty, "The Child of Casa Guidi," *Cornhill,* Spring, 1949.

———, "This Happy Evening," *Twentieth Century,* CLIV, 1953.

———, "The Seance at Ealing," *Cornhill,* CLXIX, 1957.

Snyder, Edward, and Palmer, Frederick, "*New Light on the Brownings,*" *Quarterly Review,* July, 1957.

Stephen, Leslie, "Browning's Casuistry," *National Review,* December, 1962.

Index

About the Author

Maisie Ward was born in the Isle of Wight while Queen Victoria still spent part of each year there. Through her father, Wilfrid Ward, editor of the *Dublin Review* and biographer of Newman, she began a personal contact with the leading writers of the day which, as co-founder with her husband of the publishing house of Sheed and Ward, she has maintained. On her mother's side she is descended from John Winthrop, the very Puritan governor of the Massachusetts Bay Colony. Her own books have been mainly biographies, notably of her grandfather's friend (and enemy) Newman, and of her own friend Chesterton. She feels closer to Browning than to either.